武峰带你实战翻译

24篇真题通关

CATTI 英语三级笔译

含 2016—2021年真题与详解
 2015年真题与详解电子版

编著 ◎ 武峰

编者 ◎ 吴心月 张沈彤

北京理工大学出版社
BEIJING INSTITUTE OF TECHNOLOGY PRESS

版权专有　侵权必究

图书在版编目（CIP）数据

武峰带你实战翻译：24篇真题通关CATTI英语三级笔译/武峰编著．— 北京：北京理工大学出版社，2021.4（2022.8重印）

ISBN 978 – 7 – 5682 – 9794 – 3

Ⅰ.①武… Ⅱ.①武… Ⅲ.①英语 – 翻译 – 资格考试 – 习题集 Ⅳ.① H315.9 – 44

中国版本图书馆 CIP 数据核字（2021）第 078965 号

出版发行 / 北京理工大学出版社有限责任公司	
社　　址 / 北京市海淀区中关村南大街5号	
邮　　编 / 100081	
电　　话 /（010）68914775（总编室）	
（010）82562903（教材售后服务热线）	
（010）68944723（其他图书服务热线）	
网　　址 / http://www.bitpress.com.cn	
经　　销 / 全国各地新华书店	
印　　刷 / 三河市良远印务有限公司	
开　　本 / 787毫米 × 1092毫米　1/16	
印　　张 / 22	责任编辑 / 时京京
字　　数 / 549千字	文案编辑 / 时京京
版　　次 / 2021年4月第1版　2022年8月第2次印刷	责任校对 / 刘亚男
定　　价 / 85.80元	责任印制 / 李志强

图书出现印装质量问题，请拨打售后服务热线，本社负责调换

前　言

如何利用二十四篇真题通关CATTI英语三级笔译？

中华人民共和国人力资源和社会保障部翻译专业资格（水平）考试（CATTI）是从2003年开考的，我于2004年在北京新东方学校开始讲授这门课。近二十年来，我一直从事这门考试的教学与研究，虽然不敢说是这方面的教学专家，但是对于复习考试积累了一定的经验。

我一直都想写一本这方面的辅导用书，但遗憾的是，这些年一直从事教学与翻译工作，特别忙。直到2020年，北京时代云图图书有限责任公司与我联系，我们双方都对出版此书表现出了极大的兴趣，所以才有了现在这本书。

那么，我先来简单地说一下CATTI英语三级笔译（以下称为三笔）的考试情况：

三笔考试分为实务和综合两门课，综合相对来说比较简单，都是客观性命题，但是实务相对来说较难，主要考查学生的英汉互译能力，包括一篇800字左右的英译汉和一篇400字左右的汉译英，考试题材一般来说都是非文学翻译。除了早年曾经出现过文学翻译考题，近十年来考试的所有题目都是非文学题材。

英译汉主要选材于英美国家的刊物或某些新闻报道。文理科内容都可能出现，主题从科技到文化，从环保到社会焦点问题，文章的总体难度和大学英语六级阅读差不多，但是由于翻译和英语阅读考试有着天壤之别，所以不能从英语本身的难度来衡量翻译的难度。

汉译英主要选材于《政府工作报告》和政府白皮书等文件，以及和国家、社会相关的一些报道。涵盖了政治、经济、文化、社会、农业、教育等主题，文章的总体翻译难度较大，考生一般在这部分丢分较多，所以在复习时一定要注意提高汉译英的能力。

这主要包括两大方面：第一，考生需要长期大量积累各种词汇，不能总想着在考试时查字典（CATTI笔译考试可以带字典，推荐陆谷孙的《英汉大词典》和惠宇的《新世纪汉英大词典》），因为时间可能来不及；第二，考生也需要掌握汉译英的核心方法，把这些方法具体地运用在实践中，从而通过考试。

接下来，我想和大家谈谈，这本书将如何帮助大家通过考试。

首先，这是一本带解析的真题题集，既然是真题题集，便要求大家在看答案、看解析之前先把真题做一遍。当然，有人会说，我从来都没有学过翻译，对翻译的方法技巧等没有任何积累。我个人的建议是，可以看看我那本经典的《十二天突破英汉翻译》，因为那本书是介绍翻译方法和技巧的。

但我还想说的是，仅仅掌握方法和技巧，不去实践，不去大量练习，方法和技巧永远都是"我的"，你根本就不会运用方法和技巧来做题，所以这本书的意义可能就更大了。

为什么这么说呢？因为这本书把过去六年的考试真题，也就是十二篇英译汉和十二篇汉译英做了单词方面的解析。需要提醒广大考生一点：英译汉的单词解析需要掌握"熟词僻义"，特别是在例句中出现了不常见的意思时，我们一定要认真记忆，熟记熟背；汉译英的单词解析则更加重要，因为在大量的非文学翻译材料中有许许多多的常见短语和固定用法，这些短语和固定用法的翻译不能自己"编"，而是要在平时的学习中大量积累。

在单词部分之后，我们对每一句话都进行了详细的解析，英译汉部分还包括断句，汉译英部分还包括动词定位，因为这两点是英汉互译技巧中的核心。在句型解析中，我们对每一个句子中出现的翻译现象进行了解释，也解释了该现象是如何运用在英汉互译中的，这部分是本书的精华之一。

在解析完句型之后，本书提供了英汉互译的参考译文，这些参考译文有些是官方的译文，有些是出自我们之手，提供参考译文只是给大家一个参考的标准，并不是说这是唯一的译文或是完美的译法，因为这样的译文是不存在的。

所以也请"杠精们"远离这本书，不要急着张嘴就说"我觉得我会翻译得更好一些，比这些参考译文更好"，因为我写这本书的目的就是给大家提供一个解题的思路，帮助大家提高翻译能力，最终通过翻译考试。这不是一个翻译比赛，所以我们所有的考生没有必要认为"一定要考满分，一定要写出质量最高的译文"，因为考试就是考试，我们从功利的角度来说，无非是通过考试，拿到证书，然后再进一步学习。

参考译文之后，本书给大家总结了每一句的考点，也就是把这一句话中所出现的翻译方法和技巧给大家分析一下，而且哪怕下一句又出现了相同的考点，我们也会反复总结这些翻译方法和技巧，为什么要这么做呢？看上去很浪费笔墨，但是学习是一个反复加强记忆的过程。我当了二十年的老师，我总以为我讲一遍大家就能够学会，就能够记住，原本也以为"十二天真的能突破英汉翻译"，后来才发现这完全是不科学的，我可以在十二天之内把方法都教给你，但是具体如何运用，还是需要你好好练习这二十四篇真题。

介绍完本书的格局之后，我相信大家应该知道我们的良苦用心了，也应该知道如何去使用这样一本书，考生在复习的过程中，我个人认为，首先，需要掌握一定的翻译技巧和方法，有一定的词汇量；其次，跟着我们这本书，先自己做题，然后再看解析，我相信这样更加清晰一些；最后，每次CATTI考试之前，我们工作室都会推出考前的笔译冲刺课程，大家也可以报名，因为自己看书可能比较枯燥，来听听我们的讲解，有什么问题我们可以交流互动，也可以现场解决，以上就是我个人推荐的三笔复习路径。

虽然这个考试的难度相对来说比较大，但是经过这些年的经验积累，我们相信这本书和我们所提供的课程能够帮助大家最终通过考试。

写这本教学辅导用书是我多年以来的心愿，不敢说我是这个圈子中教龄最长的老师，也不敢说我是这个圈子中教这门考试最好的老师，因为我们的前辈有千千万，他们都是大师，我们的后辈也在不断地成长，在不断地超越我们，所以我们只能说是尽自己的全力做一点小小的贡献。

最后，在这里向大家表示感谢，特别感谢吴心月老师对本书英译汉词汇部分做出的贡献，感谢张沈彤老师对本书汉译英词汇部分做出的贡献，当然也要感谢北京时代云图图书有限责任公司和北京理工大学出版社的编辑老师们对这本书做出的贡献。

最后的最后，还是要感谢广大考生这些年来对武哥工作室的图书、网络课、面授课、文创产品，等等的大力支持，如果没有你们，我们的工作室也不会发展壮大到今天这般规模。

希望这本书给大家带来的是知识，是考试技巧，是翻译方法和经验总结，是最后通过考试的好消息，也希望大家通过考试后给我们报喜。

当然，一本辅导用书不可能没有瑕疵，希望广大考生和读者能不吝赐教，也希望能和大家一起探讨。若想联系我们，有以下几个渠道：

微博：BrotherFive　　公众号：Brotherfive 教翻译　　我是翻译家网站：www.tobetranslator.com

Brotherfive

目 录

第一章　2021年实务真题解析与方法技巧

第一节　2021年上半年三级笔译英译汉 001

第二节　2021年上半年三级笔译汉译英 011

第三节　2021年下半年三级笔译英译汉 024

第四节　2021年下半年三级笔译汉译英 043

第二章　2020年实务真题解析与方法技巧

第一节　2020年下半年三级笔译英译汉（A卷）......................................056

第二节　2020年下半年三级笔译汉译英（A卷）......................................071

第三节　2020年下半年三级笔译英译汉（B卷）......................................079

第四节　2020年下半年三级笔译汉译英（B卷）......................................095

第三章　2019年实务真题解析与方法技巧

第一节　2019年上半年三级笔译英译汉 105

第二节　2019年上半年三级笔译汉译英 125

第三节　2019年下半年三级笔译英译汉 135

第四节　2019年下半年三级笔译汉译英 151

第四章　2018年实务真题解析与方法技巧

第一节　2018年上半年三级笔译英译汉 163

第二节　2018年上半年三级笔译汉译英 181

第三节　2018年下半年三级笔译英译汉 190

第四节　2018年下半年三级笔译汉译英 207

第五章　2017年实务真题解析与方法技巧

第一节　2017年上半年三级笔译英译汉 216

第二节　2017年上半年三级笔译汉译英 234

第三节　2017年下半年三级笔译英译汉 245

第四节　2017年下半年三级笔译汉译英 263

第六章　2016年实务真题解析与方法技巧

第一节　2016年上半年三级笔译英译汉 273

第二节　2016年上半年三级笔译汉译英 299

第三节　2016年下半年三级笔译英译汉 313

第四节　2016年下半年三级笔译汉译英 334

第一章 2021年实务真题解析与方法技巧

第一节 2021年上半年三级笔译英译汉

Our lives are way more complex than those which allow us to stick to a monotonous restrictive diet.

Food psychologist Ridhi Golechha said, "If all of us could follow diets, we'd all have reached our goals. Real-life stresses such as lockdown anxiety, relationship conflicts, workload, financial stresses, exasperating parenting, teenager drama, and so much more directly impact how we feel and by virtue, what we eat. If, on paper, diets were so easy to follow, then we'd all be part of that tiny ten percent of people in the world (athletes, models, or actresses) — who are permanently fit."

We all know of those rough days when all we want is to drown our faces in a tub of ice cream or reach out for that melting chocolate cake. "Emotional eating is nothing but eating our emotions. We're all human with emotions and hunger. By that definition, all of us are emotional eaters, we turn to food when we're overwhelmed with anger, sadness, frustration, or any other significant emotions," explained Ridhi.

There's a reason why the butterfly comes back to suck sweet nectar from the flowers, in turn pollinating the rest of the garden. Humans, much like animals, birds, and insects, are hardwired for pleasure. But here's the catch: we humans are afraid of pleasure. If they eat a little slice of cheesy Pizza, they are afraid that they'll be overwhelmed with pleasure, lose control, and end up with finishing the whole Pizza. We fear this would result in a failed diet, weight gain, and massive guilty, so we avoid it altogether. But, it doesn't work.

When did the emotional eating become worrisome? Here are some easy tips for you to start: First, don't skip meals. Starving often confuses your biological hunger drives and makes you more vulnerable to eat your emotions. Second, understand the difference between actual physical hunger versus emotional hunger. Third, make a list of the top three emotions you feel weekly and start finding different ways to cope with them. Fourth, talk to an expert. It's better not to ignore your emotional eating since it can later cause health issues like bloating, gas, acidity, constipation, etc. Fifth, go for a walk or do something completely different that will take away your urge by distracting you momentarily.

Emotional eating is a message that reveals a deeper problem. Understanding yourself and the way you eat via Mind-Body Nutrition can address the root causes and enable you to live a life that is beyond food obsessions and the fear of failing your diets.

2021年上半年CATTI全国考试正常举行，这次考试又回到了我们熟悉的外刊主题，文章选自2020年11月印度 *Midday* 的一篇文章，文章主题为 Emotional Eating，总体难度不大，篇幅也非常符合考试的特点，总体符合CATTI英语三级笔译考试的要求和规律。

1 Our lives are way more complex than those which allow us to stick to a monotonous restrictive diet.

第一步 词汇解析

❶ monotonous，形容词，表示"单调的、单调乏味的"，比如：The monotonous dialogue made the film a complete flop.（单调的对白使这部电影一败涂地。）

❷ restrictive，形容词，表示"限制性的、约束的"，比如：If her marriage becomes too restrictive, she will break out and seek new horizons.（如果她的婚姻对她约束太多，她会挣脱出来去寻找新的天地。）

第二步 注意断句

Our lives are way more complex /than /those /which allow us to stick to a monotonous restrictive diet.

第三步 句型解析

❶ 第一段中，Our lives are way more complex 是主系表结构，than 引导了比较状语，those 是比较对象，which 引导了定语从句，从句较长，所以采用后置译法更好。

第四步 翻译来了

我们的生活方式比让我们坚持单一且节制的饮食方式更复杂一些。

本句出现了英文定语从句的译法。一般来说，定语从句按照"短前长后"的译法处理，较短的定语从句可以前置，较长的定语从句可以后置，这一切都取决于句子的通顺，并没有绝对的前置和后置译法。

2 Food psychologist Ridhi Golechha said, "If all of us could follow diets, we'd all have reached our goals. Real-life stresses such as lockdown anxiety, relationship conflicts, workload, financial stresses, exasperating parenting, teenager drama, and so much more directly impact how we feel and by virtue, what we eat. If, on paper, diets were so easy to follow, then we'd all be part of that tiny ten percent of people in the world (athletes, models, or actresses) — who are permanently fit."

第一步 词汇解析

❶ psychologist，名词，表示"心理学家、心理学研究者"，比如：Last night a top criminal psychologist cast doubt on the theory.（昨天晚上，一位顶级犯罪心理学家对该理论产生了怀疑。）

② **lockdown**，名词，表示"活动（或行动）限制"，比如：Prisoners have been placed on lockdown to prevent further violence at the jail.（已对囚犯实行活动限制，以免狱中再出现暴力行为。）

③ **workload**，名词，表示"工作量、工作负担"，比如：The sudden cancellation of Mr. Blair's trip was due to his heavy workload.（布莱尔先生突然取消行程是因为他工作繁重。）

④ **exasperating**，形容词，表示"使人恼怒的、惹人生气的"，比如：It is really exasperating that he has not turned up when the train is about to leave.（火车快开了，他还不来，实在急人。）

⑤ **parenting**，名词，表示"抚养、养育子女"，比如：Parenting is not fully valued by society.（养儿育女没有得到社会的充分重视。）

⑥ **on paper**，副词词组，表示"理论上"，比如：These figures may look good on paper but are cold comfort to the islanders themselves.（这些数字理论上看来可能不错，不过对岛民们起不到安慰的作用。）

⑦ **athlete**，名词，表示"运动员"，比如：Athletes need a good sense of balance.（运动员要有良好的平衡感。）

⑧ **permanently**，副词，表示"永久地、永远"，比如：The stroke left his right side permanently damaged.（中风使他的右半身永久受损。）

第二步 注意断句

Food psychologist Ridhi Golechha said, /"If all of us could follow diets, /we'd all have reached our goals. / Real-life stresses /such as lockdown anxiety, /relationship conflicts, /workload, /financial stresses, /exasperating parenting, /teenager drama, /and so much more /directly impact /how we feel /and by virtue, /what we eat. /If, /on paper, /diets were so easy to follow, /then we'd all be part of that tiny ten percent of people in the world (athletes, models, or actresses) — /who are permanently fit."

第三步 句型解析

① Food psychologist Ridhi Golechha said 是本句的主语和谓语，后面接直接引语，翻译时仍需要将逗号和双引号保留。Ridhi Golechha（里迪·格莱查），人名，这里采用的是音译法，注意名和姓之间要加·，英文的人名不确定如何翻译时，可以使用音译法，然后把英文人名抄下来，放在括号里，这样保险一些。

② 直接引语的第一句中，If all of us could follow diets 是条件状语从句，为主谓宾结构，we'd all have reached our goals 是主句，也是主谓宾结构。

③ 直接引语的第二句中，Real-life stresses such as lockdown anxiety, relationship conflicts, workload, financial stresses, exasperating parenting, teenager drama, and so much more directly impact 是本句的主语和谓语，stresses 和后面 such as 形成总分关系，翻译时注意总分关系的处理，虽然说中文是先分后总，英文是先总后分，但是"分"的内容太长也可以直接按照原始语序翻译。翻译不要拘泥于方法！！！

④ 直接引语的第二句中，how we feel 是第一个宾语从句，how 可以处理为"方式"，不要翻译为"怎么"，and 是并列连词，by virtue 是插入语，what we eat 是第二个宾语从句，what 可以处理为"饮食"，这里是代词指明要点的译法。

⑤ 直接引语的第三句中，If 引导条件状语从句，on paper 是插入语，表示"从理论上来说"，diets were so easy to follow 是主系表结构，then we'd all be part of that tiny ten percent of people in the world (athletes, models, or actresses) 是本句的主句，也是主系表结构，句中的括号依旧保留，后面的破折号也可以保留；who 引导定语从句，从句与先行词被破折号隔开，所以采用后置译法较好，代词指明要点，who 指的是前面这些人，are permanently fit 是系表结构。

第四步 翻译来了

食物心理学家里迪·格莱查（Ridhi Golechha）说："要是我们所有人都能够坚持节食，那么，我们的目标早就实现了。来自现实生活的压力，如活动受限带来的焦虑、感情上的矛盾、工作量大、经济压力、育儿烦恼、青春期问题等，都直接影响到我们的感受，并且由此影响到我们的饮食。从理论上来说，如果节食很容易做到的话，那么，我们都会成为世界上少数的一成人（运动员、模特或女演员）——这些人会永远保持苗条。"

本句考点总结

第一，本句考查了英文直接引语的译法，最简单的译法就是保留冒号和双引号，说话人的位置和说话的内容都保持不变。即说话人在什么位置，就放在什么位置翻译，当然，说话人放在句首也是可以接受的。

第二，中英文的总分关系，中文一般是先分后总，而英文则是先总后分，比如中文会说"我喜欢吃香蕉、苹果、梨子等水果"，但是英文的表达是 I like fruits such as bananas, apples and pears. 注意总分关系是如何在两种语言中体现出来的。

第三，关于英文代词的译法。英文中需要翻译的代词主要指第三人称 he，she，it，they 及其相应宾格和指示代词 this 和 that。这些单词在翻译时一定要注意，主要采用"不抽象、不具体"的译法。不能翻译成具体的人或物，但是也不能翻译为"他""她""它""他们""这个""那个"，要注意取中间的译法。

第四，本句出现了英文定语从句的译法。一般来说，定语从句按照"短前长后"的译法处理，较短的定语从句可以前置，较长的定语从句可以后置，这一切都取决于句子的通顺，并没有绝对的前置和后置译法。

3

We all know of those rough days when all we want is to drown our faces in a tub of ice cream or reach out for that melting chocolate cake. "Emotional eating is nothing but eating our emotions. We're all human with emotions and hunger. By that definition, all of us are emotional eaters, we turn to food when we're overwhelmed with anger, sadness, frustration, or any other significant emotions," explained Ridhi.

第一步 词汇解析

① drown，动词，表示"浸透、淹没、浸泡"，比如：We were drowning in data but starved of information.（我们淹没在大量的数据中却找不到有用的信息。）

② tub，名词，表示"盆、桶"，比如：There were tubs of flowers on the balcony.（阳台上有一盆盆的花。）

③ nothing but，副词词组，表示"只不过、仅仅"，比如：The whole story is nothing but a pack of lies.（整个叙述只不过是一派谎言。）

④ definition，名词，表示"定义、释义"，比如：Can you give a more precise definition of the word?（你能给这个词下个更确切的定义吗？）

⑤ overwhelm，动词，表示"（感情或感觉）充溢、难以禁受、压倒、击败"，比如：I was overwhelmed by the sheer quantity of information available.（已有的信息量大得令我不知所措。）

第二步 注意断句

We all know of those rough days /when all we want is to drown our faces in a tub of ice cream /or reach out for that melting chocolate cake. /"Emotional eating is nothing but eating our emotions. /We're all human with emotions and hunger. /By that definition, /all of us are emotional eaters, /we turn to food /when we're overwhelmed with anger, /sadness, /frustration, /or any other significant emotions," /explained Ridhi.

第三步 句型解析

❶ 第一句中，We all know of those rough days 是主谓宾结构，谓语 know of 在这里表示"经历过""有过"的意思，when 引导定语从句，修饰 rough days，all we want 是定语从句的主语，we want 也是定语从句，从句较短，可以采用前置译法，when 是引导词，可以模糊处理，采用不翻译的方法，is to drown 是 when 定语从句的谓语，our faces in a tub of ice cream 是该句的宾语和状语，or 是连接词，reach out for 是该句的另一个谓语，that melting chocolate cake 是该句的另一个宾语。

❷ 第二句 Emotional eating is nothing but eating our emotions 是直接引语的第一句，是主系表结构，nothing but 这里表示"只不过""仅仅"。

❸ 第三句 We're all human with emotions and hunger 是直接引语的第二句，是主系表结构，其中 with 引导的介词短语作定语，定语较短，可以采用前置译法。

❹ 以上两句按照逻辑关系可以合译，当然不合译也可以。

❺ 第四句 By that definition, all of us are emotional eaters, we turn to food when we're overwhelmed with anger, sadness, frustration, or any other significant emotions 是直接引语的第三句，By that definition 是句首的状语，all of us are emotional eaters 是主系表结构，we turn to food 是另一句的主句，这句和上一句之间应该有连词，但是该句是口语化表达，所以语法不必非常严格，when we're overwhelmed with anger, sadness, frustration, or any other significant emotions 是 when 引导的时间或是条件状语从句，其中 be overwhelmed with 表示"受到……冲击""受到……支配"等意思。

❻ 段末的 explained Ridhi 是动词和说话人的结构，这里可以翻译为说话人和动词的结构。

第四步 翻译来了

我们都有过艰难的岁月，只想把头埋进冰激凌桶里大吃或伸手去拿软心巧克力蛋糕。"情绪化饮食就是在吃我们的情绪，我们都是有情绪的人，也是会饿的人。按照此定义，我们都是情绪化的饮食者。我们被愤怒、悲伤、沮丧或其他重大情绪冲击时，我们就会想到吃。"里迪解释说。

> 🧑‍🏫 **本句考点总结**
>
> 第一，本句出现了英文定语从句的译法。一般来说，定语从句按照"短前长后"的译法处理，较短的定语从句可以前置，较长的定语从句可以后置，这一切都取决于句子的通顺，并没有绝对的前置和后置译法。

> 第二，本句考查了英文直接引语的译法，最简单的译法就是保留冒号和双引号，说话人的位置和说话的内容都保持不变。即说话人在什么位置，就放在什么位置翻译，当然，说话人放在句首也是可以接受的。

4 There's a reason why the butterfly comes back to suck sweet nectar from the flowers, in turn pollinating the rest of the garden. Humans, much like animals, birds, and insects, are hardwired for pleasure. But here's the catch: we humans are afraid of pleasure. If they eat a little slice of cheesy Pizza, they are afraid that they'll be overwhelmed with pleasure, lose control, and end up with finishing the whole Pizza. We fear this would result in a failed diet, weight gain, and massive guilty, so we avoid it altogether. But, it doesn't work.

第一步 词汇解析

① suck，动词，表示"吮吸、吸"，比如：Greenfly can literally suck a plant dry.（蚜虫的确能把一株植物吸干。）

② nectar，名词，表示"花蜜"，比如：Flowers are often fertilized by bees as they gather nectar.（花常在蜜蜂采蜜时被授粉。）

③ pollinate，动词，表示"授粉、传粉"，比如：Many of the indigenous insects are needed to pollinate the local plants.（需要很多种本土昆虫给当地植物授粉。）

④ hardwired，形容词，表示"基本的、固有的、无法改变的"，比如：Perception is not something that is hardwired into the brain.（感知并不是大脑固有的东西。）

⑤ end up with，动词词组，表示"以……结束"，比如：The weakest students can end up with a negative score.（最差的学生可能会以负分收场。）

⑥ massive，形容词，表示"大量的、巨大的"，比如：The government found itself confronted by massive opposition.（政府发现自己遭到强烈的反对。）

第二步 注意断句

There's a reason /why the butterfly comes back /to suck sweet nectar from the flowers, /in turn pollinating the rest of the garden. /Humans, /much like animals, /birds, /and insects, /are hardwired for pleasure. /But /here's the catch: /we humans are afraid of pleasure. /If they eat a little slice of cheesy Pizza, /they are afraid /that they'll be overwhelmed with pleasure, /lose control, /and end up with finishing the whole Pizza. /We fear /this would result in a failed diet, /weight gain, /and massive guilty, /so we avoid it altogether. /But, /it doesn't work.

第三步 句型解析

① 第一句中，There's a reason why 表示"是……的原因"；why 引导的定语从句中，the butterfly comes back 是主谓结构，to suck sweet nectar from the flowers 是不定式作目的状语，in turn pollinating the rest of the garden 是非谓语结构作伴随状语，直接翻译即可。本句翻译时不要处理为"……是有原因的"，因为句子前半部分过长，可以处理为"……，这是有原因的"，这样更加通顺。

❷ 第二句中，Humans 是主语，much like animals, birds, and insects 是插入语，用来解释说明 Humans，也可以理解为状语，多说一句：怎么理解也不影响你的翻译，are hardwired for pleasure 是系表结构。

❸ 第三句中，But 是转折连词，here's the catch 中的 catch 表示"圈套""陷阱"等，这里和上下文联系，处理为"不一样的地方"更合适，后面的冒号依旧保留，we humans are afraid of pleasure 是主谓宾结构，直接翻译即可。

❹ 第四句中，If 引导了条件状语从句，they eat a little slice of cheesy Pizza 是主谓宾结构，they are afraid 是主句中的主谓结构，that 引导了宾语从句，they'll be overwhelmed with pleasure, lose control, and end up with finishing the whole Pizza 是主语后面接三个谓语的结构。

❺ 第五句中，We fear 是主谓结构，this would result in a failed diet, weight gain, and massive guilty 是宾语从句，this 作为主语翻译为"这么做"，翻译为"这"不是特别通顺；a failed diet, weight gain, and massive guilty 是三个宾语，可以直接翻译，但是将偏正短语翻译为主谓结构更好；so 是并列连词，we avoid it altogether 是主谓宾结构，这里的 it 是代词，翻译为"它"不合适，所以整句处理为"所以我们干脆什么都不做"。

❻ 第六句中，But 是转折连词，it doesn't work 表示"不管用"，本句和上一句联系紧密，所以合译较为合适。

第四步 翻译来了

蝴蝶回来吸食花朵的花蜜，并在此过程中向花园其他花朵授粉，这是有原因的。人类和飞禽走兽、昆虫一样，生来就会享乐。但有个不一样的地方：我们人类害怕享乐。要是吃了一小片奶酪比萨，就怕会让快乐冲昏头脑，从而失去控制，最后把整个比萨都全吃完。我们担心这么做的话，节食会失败，体重会增加，产生深深的负罪感，所以我们干脆什么都不做，但是，这并不管用。

本句考点总结

第一，本句出现了英文定语从句的译法。一般来说，定语从句按照"短前长后"的译法处理，较短的定语从句可以前置，较长的定语从句可以后置，这一切都取决于句子的通顺，并没有绝对的前置和后置译法。

第二，本句中使用了"偏正结构变主谓结构"的译法，这是什么意思呢？也就是说偏正结构 gleaming eyes（炯炯有神的眼睛）可以翻译为主谓结构 Eyes are gleaming.（眼睛炯炯有神。）这种译法是为了让句子更加通顺，当然有时候也可以用"主谓结构变偏正结构"的译法。"主谓变偏正"或"偏正变主谓"在英汉互译当中都可能出现，须灵活使用。

第三，关于英文代词的译法。英文中需要翻译的代词主要指第三人称 he, she, it, they 及其相应宾格和指示代词 this 和 that。这些单词在翻译时一定要注意，主要采用"不抽象、不具体"的译法。不能翻译成具体的人或物，但是也不能翻译为"他""她""它""他们""这个""那个"，要注意取中间的译法。

5 When did the emotional eating become worrisome? Here are some easy tips for you to start: First, don't skip meals. Starving often confuses your biological hunger drives and makes you more vulnerable to eat your emotions. Second, understand the difference between actual physical hunger versus emotional hunger. Third, make a list of the top three emotions you feel weekly and start finding different ways to cope with them. Fourth, talk to an expert. It's better not to ignore your emotional eating since it can later cause health issues like bloating, gas, acidity, constipation, etc. Fifth, go for a walk or do something completely different that will take away your urge by distracting you momentarily.

第一步 词汇解析

① worrisome，形容词，表示"令人担心的、使人担忧的"，比如：His injury is worrisome.（他的伤情令人担忧。）

② skip，动词，表示"不做（应做的事等）、不参加、跳过（正常的步骤等）"，比如：I often skip breakfast altogether.（我常常干脆不吃早饭。）

③ drive，名词，表示"（人的）强烈欲望、本能需求"，比如：sex drives（性欲）。

④ vulnerable，形容词，表示"（身体上或感情上）脆弱的、易受……伤害的"，比如：People with high blood pressure are especially vulnerable to diabetes.（有高血压的人尤其易患糖尿病。）

⑤ versus，介词，表示"与……相对、与……相比"，比如：Only 18.8% of the class of 1982 had some kind of diploma four years after high school, versus 45% of the class of 1972.（1982 年那一届只有 18.8% 的学生在中学毕业四年后获得了某种文凭，而 1972 年那一届的这一比例是 45%。）

⑥ bloating，名词，表示"（身体或身体部位的）肿胀、膨胀"，比如：abdominal bloating and pain（腹部肿胀和疼痛）。

⑦ acidity，名词，表示"酸度、酸性、胃酸过多"，比如：Add honey to counterbalance the acidity.（加点蜂蜜来调和酸味。）

⑧ constipation，名词，表示"便秘"，比如：Try to make sure your bowel motions are regular and that you avoid any constipation.（尽量保证大便规律，避免便秘。）

⑨ urge，名词，表示"冲动、强烈的欲望"，比如：I have often talked about why we want to be mothers, but none of us can describe the urge exactly.（我经常谈到我们为什么想做母亲，但没有一个人能准确地描述这种冲动。）

⑩ momentarily，副词，表示"短促地、片刻地"，比如：He was momentarily dazzled by the strong sunlight.（强烈的阳光使他一时睁不开眼。）

第二步 注意断句

When did the emotional eating become worrisome? /Here are some easy tips for you to start: /First, /don't skip meals. /Starving often confuses your biological hunger drives /and makes you more vulnerable to eat your emotions. /Second, /understand the difference /between actual physical hunger versus emotional hunger. /Third, /make a list of the top three emotions /you feel weekly /and start finding different ways to cope with them. /Fourth, /talk to an expert. /It's better not to ignore your emotional eating /since it can later cause health issues /like bloating, /gas, /acidity, /constipation, /etc. /Fifth, /go for a walk /or do something completely different /that will take away your urge /by distracting you momentarily.

第三步 句型解析

① 第一句 When did the emotional eating become worrisome 是 When 引导的疑问句，句式较为简单，可以直接翻译。

② 第二句中，Here are some easy tips for you to start 是主系表结构的倒装，表达较为口语化，不要翻译得太生硬。

③ 第三句中，First 是数词状语，翻译为"第一""第一点"等都可以，don't skip meals 是祈使句，注意 skip 不要翻译为"跳过"，翻译为"不吃"更好，可以看看译文是怎么处理的，翻译要讲究通顺和舒适，而不是生硬地一个字对一个字。

④ 第四句中，Starving often confuses your biological hunger drives 是主谓宾结构，and 是并列连词，makes you more vulnerable to eat your emotions 是第二组谓语、宾语和宾语补足语的结构，其中 eat 翻译为"吃"就太不合适了，翻译为"让你情绪化饮食"更好一些。

⑤ 第五句中，Second 是数词状语，understand the difference 是祈使句，between actual physical hunger versus emotional hunger 是 between... versus 引导的后置定语。

⑥ 第六句中，Third 是数词状语，make a list of the top three emotions you feel weekly 是祈使句，其中 you feel weekly 是定语从句，从句较短，可以采用前置译法，and 是并列连词，start finding different ways to cope with them 是另一个祈使句。

⑦ 第七句中，Fourth 是数词状语，talk to an expert 是祈使句，可以直接翻译。

⑧ 第八句是 It's better 后接不定式 not to do 的结构，not to ignore your emotional eating 是真正的主语，It 是形式主语，这里也可以理解为事实与评论之间的关系，但是为了让句子通顺，It's better 可以翻译为"最好是"，since 引导原因状语从句，it can later cause health issues like bloating, gas, acidity, constipation, etc. 是主谓宾结构，like 引导了定语，这里是典型的总分关系，翻译的时候注意句子各个成分之间的顺序关系。

⑨ 第九句中，Fifth 是数词状语，go for a walk or do something completely different 是由 or 连接的两个祈使句，that 引导定语从句，从句较长，可以采用后置译法，will take away your urge 是谓语和宾语的结构，by distracting you momentarily 是方式状语，这个状语翻译时可以前置。

第四步 翻译来了

情绪化饮食什么时候开始变得让人担忧了呢？这里为你提供了一些简单的技巧来避免这种饮食习惯：首先，好好吃饭。饥饿经常让你的生理性饥饿冲动很"迷惑"，让你更容易情绪化饮食。第二，理解真实的饥饿和情绪化饥饿之间的区别。第三，每周列出你最常感受到的三种情绪，然后开始寻找不同的方法来应对这些情绪。第四，与专家交流。最好不要忽视你的情绪化进食，因为接下来，它会引发如腹胀、胀气、胃反酸、便秘等健康问题。第五，去散散步或做点其他完全不同的事情，这样能暂时分散你的注意力，从而带走你情绪化饮食的冲动。

本句考点总结

第一，本句出现了英文定语从句的译法。一般来说，定语从句按照"短前长后"的译法处理，较短的定语从句可以前置，较长的定语从句可以后置，这一切都取决于句子的通顺，并没有绝对的前置和后置译法。

> 第二，本句出现了事实（Facts）和评论（Comments）的译法。中文一般先事实，后评论，而英文则是一般先评论，后事实。比如：It is important for her to go abroad. 翻译为"对于她来说，出国是很重要的"。英文中 It is important 是评论，for her to go abroad 是事实。从中英文的对比来看，可以知道中英文语序分别是怎么安排的。
>
> 第三，中英文的总分关系，中文一般是先分后总，而英文则是先总后分，比如中文会说"我喜欢吃香蕉、苹果、梨子等水果"，但是英文的表达是 I like fruits such as bananas, apples and pears. 注意总分关系是如何在两种语言中体现出来的。

6

Emotional eating is a message that reveals a deeper problem. Understanding yourself and the way you eat via Mind-Body Nutrition can address the root causes and enable you to live a life that is beyond food obsessions and the fear of failing your diets.

第一步 词汇解析

❶ reveal，动词，表示"揭示、显示、透露"，比如：The report was a device used to hide rather than reveal problems.（这份报告不是为揭露问题，而是为掩盖问题而耍的花招。）

❷ address，动词，表示"设法解决"，比如：We must address ourselves to the problem of traffic pollution.（我们必须设法解决交通污染问题。）

❸ enable，动词，表示"使可能、使能够"，比如：Insulin enables the body to use and store sugar.（胰岛素使人体能够利用和贮存糖分。）

❹ obsession，名词，表示"痴迷、着魔"，比如：This untutored mathematician had an obsession with numbers.（这位非科班出身的数学家对数字特别痴迷。）

第二步 注意断句

Emotional eating is a message /that reveals a deeper problem. /Understanding yourself /and the way you eat /via Mind-Body Nutrition can address the root causes /and enable you to live a life /that is beyond food obsessions /and the fear of failing your diets.

第三步 句型解析

❶ 第一句中，Emotional eating is a message 是主系表结构，that 引导定语从句，reveals a deeper problem 是较短的定语从句，可以采用前置译法。

❷ 第二句中，Understanding yourself and the way you eat via Mind-Body Nutrition 是主语，主语中 Understanding yourself and the way you eat 是核心成分，via Mind-Body Nutrition 是状语，这个状语用来修饰前面的动名词短语，所以放在句首翻译更加合适，Mind-Body Nutrition 是一个网站的名称，可以用双引号，考试的时候如果你不知道这个背景，其实直接翻译就可以，不用考虑这些问题。

❸ 第二句的第一组谓语和宾语是 can address the root causes，and 是并列连词，enable you to live a life 是第二组谓语、宾语和宾语补足语，that 引导了较长的定语从句，可以采用后置译法，is beyond food obsessions and the fear of failing your diets 是系表结构，这里的 beyond 表示"超越某事"，food obsessions and the fear of failing your diets 是两组并列的名词短语。the fear of failing your diets 中的 fear 是典型的抽象名词，有动词词根，可以翻译为动词"害怕""恐惧"等。

第四步 翻译来了

情绪化进食传递了一个揭示更加深层次问题的讯息。通过"身心营养"来了解你自己以及饮食的方式能从根源上解决问题，让你过上一种舒心的生活，这种生活是不再对食物痴迷，也不会害怕节食失败的。

> **本句考点总结**
>
> 第一，本句出现了英文定语从句的译法。一般来说，定语从句按照"短前长后"的译法处理，较短的定语从句可以前置，较长的定语从句可以后置，这一切都取决于句子的通顺，并没有绝对的前置和后置译法。
>
> 第二，本句当中考查了"抽象名词"的译法。抽象名词一般位于冠词之后，又在介词之前，以"the + 抽象名词 + of"的形式居多。一般来说，抽象名词有两种译法。第一种，若抽象名词有动词词根，则翻译为动词，比如 the suggestion of mine，翻译为"我建议"，而不是"我的建议"；第二种，若抽象名词没有动词词根，可以增动词翻译，比如 the spirit of our nation，翻译为"我们民族所具有的精神"，而不是"我们民族的精神"。

这篇文章是典型的外刊文章，总体难度不大，大家在翻译时需要掌握翻译时间和对关键词的理解，比如 emotional eating 翻译为"情绪化饮食"比较好，翻译为"有情绪的吃饭"则不是很恰当。还要注意很多口语化的句子，翻译出来也要有口语化的感觉，而不是字对字地翻译，这种生硬的翻译在考试中一般很难得到高分。学会写中文，学会说中文，这两句话对学翻译的同学来说特别重要！

第二节 2021年上半年三级笔译汉译英

2020年11月中国开始了第七次人口普查。人口普查将为开启全面建设社会主义现代化国家新征程提供科学准确的统计信息支持。

人口普查是推动经济高质量发展的内在需求。当前，我国经济正处于转变发展方式、优化经济结构转换增长动力的攻关期。

及时查清人口数量、结构和分布这一基本国情，摸清人力资源结构信息，才能够更加准确地把握需求结构、城乡结构、区域结构、产业结构等状况，为推动经济高质量发展，建设现代化经济体系提供有力的支持。

人口普查，是完善人口发展战略和政策体系，促进人口长期均衡发展的迫切需要。自 2010 年第六次全国人口普查以来，我国人口发展的内在动力和外部条件发生了显著改变。人口总规模增长减缓，劳动年龄人口波动下降，老龄化程度不断加深。

　　全面查清我国人口数量、结构、分布、城乡住房等方面的最新情况，了解人口增长、劳动力供给、流动人口变化情况，摸清老年人口规模，为制定和完善未来收入、消费、教育、就业、养老、医疗、社会保障等政策措施提供基础，也为教育和医疗机构布局、儿童和老人服务设施建设、工商业服务网点分布、城乡道路建设等提供依据。

　　人口普查工作从方案制定、物资准备、试点、人员培训、入户登记到数据处理等一切工作都离不开人，队伍建设非常重要。能否组织好人口普查队伍，能否做好普查人员的选调，直接影响到普查的工作质量和数据质量。

　　2021 年上半年 CATTI 三级笔译考试的汉译英部分考查了有关第七次全国人口普查的内容。大部分内容来源于国务院新闻办公室关于人口普查的报告，文体比较正式，而且涉及较多当前热点词汇，专业名词较多，这些词汇也是在各类翻译考试中常见的词汇，希望大家多多背诵和记忆。

1　2020 年 11 月中国开始了第七次人口普查。人口普查将为开启全面建设社会主义现代化国家新征程提供科学准确的统计信息支持。

第一步　词汇解析

❶ 开始，begin to conduct，动词词组。这里的"开始"指的就是"开始进行"，begin 可以理解为弱势动词，conduct 可以理解为强势动词，翻译时运用了"谓语动词的过渡"译法。

组织并实施，conduct，动词，比如：I decided to conduct an experiment.（我决定做一项实验。）

❷ （全国）人口普查，national census，名词词组，比如：Data of national census 1990 was served as standard population to calculate standardized mortality rate.（以 1990 年全国人口普查数据作为标准人口，计算标化死亡率。）

❸ 全面建设社会主义现代化国家新征程，the new journey to the building of China's socialist modernization in all respects，名词词组。

全面，in all respects，介词词组，比如：This essay is admirable in all respects.（这篇文章在各方面都很值得欣赏。）"全面"还可以翻译为 overall/comprehensive/in an all-round way 等。

建设，the building of，名词词组，比如：The building of the new bridge will go ahead as planned.（新桥的修建将按计划进行。）

社会主义现代化国家，China's socialist modernization，名词词组。这里的"国家"指的就是"中国"，所以直接翻译为 China，也就是"中国的社会主义现代化建设"。

❹ 科学准确的统计信息，scientific and accurate statistical data，名词词组。

准确的，accurate，形容词，比如：Accurate records must be kept at all times.（任何时候都必须保存准确的记录。）

统计信息，statistical data，名词词组，比如：The statistical data showed there was a storm soon.（统计信息表明很快就有一次风暴。）statistical 作为多音节单词，一要注意读音，二要注意拼写时不要丢字母。

第二步 动词定位

2020年11月中国开始了第七次人口普查。人口普查将为开启全面建设社会主义现代化国家新征程提供科学准确的统计信息支持。

第三步 句型解析

❶ 第一句中，"2020年11月"是时间状语，可以用一般过去时，"中国"是本句的主语，"开始了"是谓语，"第七次人口普查"是宾语，译文这里使用了 began to conduct 的译法，是典型的汉译英的"谓语动词的过渡"，其实这么翻译完全没有必要，用简明的方式直接翻译为 began its seventh national census 即可。

❷ 第二句中，"人口普查"是本句主语，"将提供"是谓语，表示将来发生的事，所以使用一般将来时，"科学准确的统计信息"是宾语，实际上本句末尾的"支持"是动词，是二谓语形式，表示目的，即"来支持"，后面接名词宾语"新征程"to "开启全面建设社会主义现代化国家"。

第四步 翻译来了

China began to conduct its seventh national census in November 2020. The census will provide scientific and accurate statistical data to support the new journey to the building of China's socialist modernization in all respects.

本句考点总结

第一，句中出现了谓语动词过渡的译法，这是英汉互译当中非常难的知识点。中文是动态性语言，常用动词，用强势动词，英文是静态性语言，常用名词，用弱势动词，这点要牢记在心。比如 I give you my support. 不要翻译为"我给你我的支持"，直接翻译为"我支持你"即可，give 是弱势动词，support 是强势动词，因为中英文的差异，只要翻译强势动词，不须翻译弱势动词。这点常常在英译汉当中使用，汉译英中用得比较少！

第二，关于谓语动词的层次性。汉译英的核心问题是厘清句子当中多个动词之间的关系，我们要学会在多个动词当中找到最核心的动词，翻译为核心谓语（也称为一谓语）；找到其次核心的动词，翻译为分词、从句或是其他状语或定语的形式（也称为二谓语）；再找到不重要的动词，翻译为介词（也称为三谓语）；最后最不重要的动词，可以不译（也称为四谓语）。这些动词在句子当中如何划分层次，需要大家在长期不断的实践中摸索，而且每个句子的翻译也不是固定的。有些句子当中的"一谓语"（核心谓语），在别的译本当中可能就是"二谓语"或者是"三谓语"。只要句子整体结构正确，逻辑清晰，那这就是一个好的译本。

人口普查是推动经济高质量发展的内在需求。当前，我国经济正处于转变发展方式，优化经济结构转换增长动力的攻关期。

第一步 词汇解析

❶ 推动经济高质量发展，enhance the high-caliber economic development，动词词组。"推动经济高质量发展"翻译为英语词组，语序为"推动高质量的经济发展"。英语中，越靠近核心名词的修饰语越重要，越能代表核心名词的性质。

推动，enhance，动词，比如：This is an opportunity to enhance the reputation of the company.（这是提高公司声誉的机会。）"推动"还可以翻译为 push forward/promote/propel 等词。

质量，caliber，名词，比如：The caliber of teaching was very high.（教学质量非常高。）calibre 为英式拼写，caliber 为美式拼写。考试时，无论是英式拼写还是美式拼写，保持一致即可，翻译为 high quality 也是完全可以的。

❷ 内在需求，domestic need，名词词组，比如：This would cool domestic demand without the need for a big rise in interest rates.（这将在不需要大幅上调利率的情况下，给国内需求降温。）

❸ 见证，witness，动词，比如：Recent years have witnessed a growing social mobility.（近年来人们的社会流动性越来越大。）句中使用 witness/see 作为谓语动词时，主语一般为时间或地点。

❹ 转变（经济）发展方式，change modes of the economic development，动词词组。

方式，mode，名词，比如：a mode of behavior（行为模式）。mode 还有"（情感或行为的）状态、状况"的意思，比如：to be in holiday mode（处于节日的气氛中）。

❺ 优化经济结构，the optimization of the economic structure，名词词组。

优化，optimization，名词，比如：Performance optimization is an art.（性能优化是一种艺术。）optimization 来源于动词 optimize，表示"使优化"，比如：The new systems have been optimized for running Microsoft Windows.（新系统已经被优化，以便运行微软视窗系统。）

❻ 转换增长动力，the shift of the growth engine，名词词组。

engine 的词义来源于"发动机、引擎"，在这里是"动力"的意思。

shift 作为名词，还可表示"轮班"，比如：working in shifts（轮班工作）。

❼ 攻关期，tough period，名词词组，比如：It's going to be a very tough period.（这将是一段非常困难的时期。）这里的"攻关期"指的就是"集中力量研究、攻克某一课题或项目的时期"，也就是"较为艰难的时期"。

第二步 动词定位

人口普查<u>是</u><u>推动</u>经济高质量发展的内在需求。当前，我国经济<u>正处于</u><u>转变</u>发展方式，<u>优化</u>经济结构<u>转换</u>增长动力的攻关期。

第三步 句型解析

❶ 第一句中，"人口普查"是主语，前一句已经出现相同的名词，所以这里可以用其他名词或代词替代，谓语是"是"，译文处理为 come from，翻译为 be 动词也是可以的，宾语是"内在需求"，这里"推动经济高质量发展的"是定语，用来修饰"内在需求"，总体较为简单，可以直接翻译。

❷ 第二句中，"当前"是时间状语，"我国经济"是主语，"正处于"是核心谓语，"攻关期"是宾语，"转变发展方式，优化经济结构转换增长动力的"是三个定语，注意第二个定语和第三个定语之间中文没有用逗号，翻译时需要用 and 连接。注意译文的处理方式，译文将本句的主语换成了"我国"，将"经济"分别放在了后面的各个宾语中，这样的处理很机智，考试中实在想不到也无所谓，直接翻译即可。

第四步 翻译来了

The project comes from the domestic need to enhance the high-caliber economic development. At present, our country is witnessing the tough period of changing modes of the economic development, the optimization of the economic structure and the shift of the growth engine.

及时查清人口数量、结构和分布这一基本国情，摸清人力资源结构信息，才能够更加准确地把握需求结构、城乡结构、区域结构、产业结构等状况，为推动经济高质量发展，建设现代化经济体系提供有力的支持。

第一步 词汇解析

❶ 查清，need to be enumerated，动词词组，比如：These users need to be fully identified and enumerated.（需要完全识别并查清这些用户。）
列举、枚举，enumerate，动词，比如：I enumerate the work that will have to be done.（我将必要要做的工作一一列举出来。）

❷ 结构，composition，名词，比如：Television has transformed the size and social composition of the audience at great sporting occasions.（电视改变了大型体育赛事观众的数量及其社会构成。）
【同义词辨析】
composition：指不同部分或人的构成、组合方式；
framework：指构成某个体系或社会基础的信仰、观点、准则；
fabric：指社会、机构等的基本结构。

❸ 分布，distribution，名词，比如：The map shows the distribution of this species across the world.（地图上标明了这一物种在全世界的分布情况。）distribution 在商业领域还可表示"商品的运销和经销"。

❹ （人口的）基本国情，population fundamentals，名词词组。
基本规律、根本法则，fundamental，名词，比如：the fundamentals of modern physics（现代物理学的基本原理）。

❺ 人力资源结构，the constituents of human resources，名词词组。
成分、构成要素，constituent，名词，比如：Caffeine is the active constituent of drinks such as tea and coffee.（咖啡因是茶和咖啡这类饮品的活性成分。）

❻ 需求结构、城乡结构、区域结构、产业结构，the structure of demands, of urban and rural areas, of different regions, and of different industries，名词词组。这里采用了分配的方法，"结构"出现了多次，英文避免重复，只翻译一次，翻译为 structure。
城乡地区，urban and rural areas，名词词组，比如：The survey was carried out in both urban and rural areas.（该调查在城市和乡村地区都开展了。）

❼ 为……提供有力的支持，lend powerful support to，动词词组。
给予、提供（帮助、支持等），lend，动词，比如：I was more than happy to lend my support to such a good cause.（我非常乐意给这样美好的事业提供援助。）
常见用法：lend a hand，动词词组，表示"帮助"，比如：I went over to see if I could lend a hand.（我过去看我能不能帮上忙。）

❽ 推动经济高质量发展，drive forward the high-quality economic growth，动词词组。
"高质量"在上文中，翻译为 high-caliber，在这里翻译为 high-quality，要注意多样化的用词。

❾ 建设现代化经济体系，build up the economic modernization，动词词组。
现代化，modernization，名词，比如：All attempts at modernization were stamped on by senior officials.

（旨在实现现代化的努力统统受到高级官员的压制。）modernize 强调制度、方法等的现代化。

第二步 动词定位

及时<u>查清</u>人口数量、结构和分布这一基本国情，<u>摸清</u>人力资源结构信息，才能够更加准确地<u>把握</u>需求结构、城乡结构、区域结构、产业结构等状况，为<u>推动</u>经济高质量发展，<u>建设</u>现代化经济体系<u>提供</u>有力的支持。

第三步 句型解析

① 本句较长，所以在翻译时首先要想到动词分堆的问题，也就是我们常说的哪些动词放在一起翻译成一个新句子。本句共有六个动词，五个句子，所以在句子中部进行分堆是比较合适的。

② 第一句和第二句都以动词开头，所以放在一起翻译，可以增主语或是用被动语态的结构，译文中使用了被动语态。第一句中，"人口数量、结构和分布这一基本国情"是主语，这里又存在总分结构问题，"基本国情"是总，"人口数量、结构和分布"是分，中文先分后总，英文先总后分，本句核心动词是"查清"，使用被动语态，翻译为 be enumerated；第二句中，"人力资源结构信息"是主语，核心谓语是"摸清"，使用被动语态，翻译为 be understood。

③ 第三、四、五句也以动词开头，这里可以增主语"我们"，谓语是"才能够更加准确地把握"，宾语是"需求结构、城乡结构、区域结构、产业结构等状况"。后面两句不是并列结构，这里要理解句与句之间的关系，其实后面第四、五句是一个句子，句子的核心谓语是"提供"，宾语是"有力的支持"，"为推动经济高质量发展，建设现代化经济体系"是状语结构，也就是 provide/lend support to "推动 + 建设"。

若是再仔细分析这句话中两组核心谓语"把握"和"提供"之间的关系就不难发现，这还是两个动词形成的句子，可以考虑使用"并列、伴随、下沉"的结构。译文使用了非限定性定语从句，这是完全可以的，也是合适的。

译文在处理时还"炫技"了，本句在句首增加了 Only by doing so 这样的结构，这样一来句子的核心谓语还要进行部分倒装，我们在考试时完全没有必要这么做。

第四步 翻译来了

So, its population fundamentals, such as the number, composition and distribution, need to be enumerated, and information on the constituents of human resources must be clearly understood. Only by doing so can we correctly find out the structure of demands, of urban and rural areas, of different regions, and of different industries, and other conditions, which will lend powerful support to drive forward the high-quality economic growth and build up the economic modernization.

本句考点总结

第一，关于"动词分堆"的问题。中文里常常出现多个短句聚集的句型，我们一方面需要去考虑这些动词之间的关系，哪一个是最重要的，哪一个是其次重要的，哪一个又是最不重要的，这个过程称为分析"谓语动词的层次性"。除此之外，句子当中出现了大量的动词时，或者说大量的分句时，我们不可能将这些分句整体翻译为一个长句，那么，我们就需要考虑哪些动词放在一起翻译，这样的过程称为"动词分堆"。比如，一个句子当中有五个动词形成的五个分句，我们一般会考虑前三个动词翻译为一句，后两个动词翻译为一句，但是如何进行"分堆"要根据上下文的语境来判断，绝对不能形而上学，望文生义。

第二，中英文的总分关系，中文一般是先分后总，而英文则是先总后分，比如中文会说"我喜欢吃香蕉、苹果、梨子等水果"，但是英文的表达是 I like fruits such as bananas, apples and pears. 注意总分关系是如何在两种语言中体现出来的。

第三，汉译英句子中并列、伴随、下沉的结构。中文常常会出现多个句子聚集的情况，那么我们在翻译时需要考虑将这些句子进行"分堆"，但是"分堆"之后，一个句子中也可能会出现两个动词或两组动词，那么有两个动词或两组动词的句子我们该如何进行翻译呢？比如："我坐在那里看书"，这里有两个动词，一个是"坐"，一个是"看"，我们翻译时便会有三种方法：

第一种并列（两个动词并列的译法，使用并列连词连接，两个动词之间不一定是"并列"关系）：I sat there and read a book.

第二种伴随（将第二个动词翻译为二谓语，分词、从句、状语等都可以）：I sat there reading a book.

第三种下沉（将第一个动词翻译为二谓语，分词、从句、状语等都可以）：Siting there, I read a book.

需要说明的是，并列、伴随和下沉只是动词的形式问题，不代表动词之间的逻辑关系，用这三种形式翻译两个动词或两组动词都是可以的，大家可以根据句子上下文的关系来判断使用。

人口普查，是完善人口发展战略和政策体系，促进人口长期均衡发展的迫切需要。自 2010 年第六次全国人口普查以来，我国人口发展的内在动力和外部条件发生了显著改变。人口总规模增长减缓，劳动年龄人口波动下降，老龄化程度不断加深。

第一步 词汇解析

❶ 人口发展战略，the strategy of the population development，名词词组。
战略，strategy，名词，比如：the government's economic strategy（政府的经济策略）。

❷ 政策体系，policy framework，名词词组。
（体系的）结构、机制，framework，名词，比如：We need to establish a legal framework for the protection of the environment.（我们需要建立一个法律体系来保护环境。）framework 还可表示"（作为判断、决定等基础的）信仰、观点、准则"。

❸ 人口长期均衡发展，a long-term balanced population development，名词词组。
长期的，long-term，形容词，比如：a long-term investment（长线投资）。long-term 属于复合形容词，由形容词和名词构成。
均衡的，balanced，形容词，比如：a balanced diet（均衡的饮食）。

❹ 迫切需要，an urgent need，名词词组，比如：There is an urgent need for food and water.（有着对食品和水的迫切需要。）
特别需要、迫切要求，need，名词，比如：She felt the need to talk to someone.（她特别想和人聊聊。）

❺ 人口发展，populace progression，名词词组。

民众，populace，名词，比如：He had the support of large sections of the local populace.（他受到当地大部分百姓的拥护。）

❻ 内在动力，interior dynamics，名词词组。
内部的，interior，形容词，比如：The interior walls were painted green.（内墙被漆成了绿色。）
动力，dynamic，名词，比如：The dynamic of the market demands constant change and adjustment.（市场的动力要求有不断的变化和调整。）dynamics 作为复数型名词时，表示"变革动力"，比如：What is needed is insight into the dynamics of the social system.（所需要的就是对社会制度变革动力的洞悉。）

❼ 外部条件，exterior condition，名词词组，比如：the results of the interaction of interior and exterior conditions（内外条件共同作用的结果）。interior 和 exterior 是一对反义词。

❽ 人口总规模增长减缓，the slowing down of the overall population size growth，名词词组。

❾ 劳动年龄人口波动下降（趋势），a downward trend with fluctuation of the overall workforce age，名词词组。
下降趋势，a downward trend，名词词组，比如：The prices of consumer goods witnessed a downward trend.（消费品的价格呈现出下降趋势。）
波动，fluctuation，名词，比如：The erratic fluctuation of market prices is in consequence of unstable economy.（经济波动致使市场物价忽起忽落。）fluctuation 的动词形式为 fluctuate，同义词为 vary。
劳动力，workforce，名词，比如：a country where half the workforce is unemployed（一个半数劳动力失业的国家）。所以"劳动年龄人口"翻译为 the overall workforce age。

❿ 老龄化程度不断加深，the deepening of the aging society，名词词组。
老龄化社会，the aging society，名词词组，比如：The aging society has become a general phenomenon.（老龄化社会渐渐成为普遍现象。）

第二步 动词定位

人口普查，是完善人口发展战略和政策体系，促进人口长期均衡发展的迫切需要。自 2010 年第六次全国人口普查以来，我国人口发展的内在动力和外部条件发生了显著改变。人口总规模增长减缓，劳动年龄人口波动下降，老龄化程度不断加深。

第三步 句型解析

❶ 第一句中，"人口普查"是本句的主语，这里可以使用代词或其他名词进行替代，"是"是核心谓语，"迫切需要"是宾语，"完善人口发展战略和政策体系，促进人口长期均衡发展"是定语，宾语是 urgent need，所以后面接不定式作定语。"完善人口发展战略和政策体系"翻译为 improve the strategy of the population development and policy framework；"促进人口长期均衡发展"翻译为 promote a long-term balanced population development。

❷ 第二句中，"自 2010 年第六次全国人口普查以来"是典型的时间状语，这里由 Since 引导，所以后面的主句应当使用现在完成时，"我国人口发展的内在动力和外部条件"是主语，"发生了"是谓语，"显著改变"是宾语。这么分析正确吗？这样翻译的话主语过长，导致整个句子非常不平衡，所以这句应当使用 there be 句型，大家也可以把这个固定的句型用法记下来，"……发生了显著改变"翻译为 There be significant changes in...，这也是口译考试常用的一个句型，后面的 in 接"我国人口发展的内在动力和外部条件"。

❸ 第三句是三个单独的句子，全部是主谓结构，一眼看上去，"人口总规模增长"是主语，"减缓"是谓语，"劳动年龄人口波动"是主语，"下降"是谓语，"老龄化程度"是主语，"不断加深"是谓语，其实完全不对，因为这是口译的结构，再看看这句和上一句之间的关系，仔细体会体会。
前文说"内在动力和外部条件发生了显著改变"，后面三句刚好解释是如何"改变"的，所以合译

是不是更好呢？后面三个句子看上去是句子，但是处理为主谓结构的偏正译法是不是更好呢？也就是译为"减缓增长的人口总规模，劳动年龄人口波动下降的趋势，不断加深的老龄化程度"，再用 namely 与前一句话连接是不是非常完美呢？

第四步 翻译来了

The census is an urgent need to improve the strategy of the population development and policy framework and promote a long-term balanced population development. Since the sixth national census in 2010, there have been significant changes in the interior dynamics and exterior conditions on our country's populace progression, namely the slowing down of the overall population size growth, a downward trend with fluctuation of the overall workforce age, and the deepening of the aging society.

本句考点总结

第一，本句中使用了"主谓结构变偏正结构"的译法，这是什么意思呢？也就是说主谓结构 Eyes are gleaming.（眼睛炯炯有神。）可以翻译为偏正结构 gleaming eyes（炯炯有神的眼睛），这种译法是为了让句子更加通顺，当然有时候也可以用"偏正结构变主谓结构"的译法。"主谓变偏正"或"偏正变主谓"在英汉互译当中都可能出现，须灵活使用。

第二，在翻译中，无论是英译汉，还是汉译英，我们常常将长句断成短句，然后一句一句翻译，短的句子由于上下文的联系，也可以放在一起翻译。非文学翻译中分译与合译出现得比较少，但是在文学翻译中出现得特别多，特别要读懂上下文内在的关系。分译与合译没有固定的翻译规则，而且每个译者的尺度也是不同的，重要的前提就是句意正确和句意通顺。

5

全面查清我国人口数量、结构、分布、城乡住房等方面的最新情况，了解人口增长、劳动力供给、流动人口变化情况，摸清老年人口规模，为制定和完善未来收入、消费、教育、就业、养老、医疗、社会保障等政策措施提供基础，也为教育和医疗机构布局、儿童和老人服务设施建设、工商业服务网点分布、城乡道路建设等提供依据。

第一步 词汇解析

❶ 全面查清，need to be comprehensively probed，动词词组。
全面，comprehensively，副词，比如：They were comprehensively beaten in the final.（他们在决赛中一败涂地。）
调查，probe，动词，比如：The more they probed into his background, the more inflamed their suspicions would become.（他们越深入调查他的背景，对他的怀疑就会越强烈。）probe 用在医学领域中，表示"用探针探查"。

❷ 人口数量，the demographic number，名词词组。

人口结构的、人口统计的，demographic，形容词，比如：The demographic trend is towards an older population.（人口结构的变化呈现老龄化的趋势。）

③ 结构，makeup，名词，比如：The ideological makeup of the unions is now radically different from what it had been.（这些协会的意识形态构成如今与过去大相径庭。）本文中多次出现"结构"，分别翻译为不同的单词：constituent/composition/structure/makeup，体现了英语用词的多样性。

④ 劳动力供给，labor supply，名词词组，比如：The issues of labor supply include quantity, quality and location of supply, etc.（劳动供给的问题包括劳动供给数量、劳动供给质量和劳动供给地点等。）

labor 作为不可数名词，表示"劳动力"，尤指体力劳动者。若使用复数形式 labors，则表示"任务、工作"。

⑤ 流动人口变化情况，changes in the floating population，名词词组。

流动的、浮动的，floating，形容词，比如：a floating population（流动人口）。金融领域的术语"浮动汇率"，翻译为 floating exchange rates。

⑥ 老年人口规模，the population of senior citizens，名词词组。

老年人，senior citizens，名词词组，比如：services for senior citizens（为老年人提供的服务）。老年人还可以翻译为 the elderly/elder people 等。

⑦ 为……提供基础，lay a solid foundation for，动词词组，比如：It is my belief that the meeting today will lay a solid foundation for our future communication and liaison.（我相信，今天的会议将为今后我们之间的沟通和联系奠定扎实的基础。）

常见短语：shake the foundations of something，动词词组，表示"从根本上动摇"，比如：This issue has shaken the foundations of French politics.（这个问题从根本上动摇了法国的政治。）

⑧ 制定，formulate，动词，比如：to formulate a policy/theory/plan/proposal（制定政策、创立理论、构想计划、准备建议）。formulate 的派生词为 formulation/formulator。

⑨ 完善，improve，动词，比如：The bricks were bedded in sand to improve drainage.（沙里埋入砖块，以完善排水系统。）improve 常搭配介词 on/upon，表示"做出比……更好的成绩"，比如：We have certainly improved on last year's figures.（我们的业绩的确超过了去年的数字。）

⑩ 养老，pension system，名词词组，比如：The pension system in the country's rural areas is especially worrying.（该国农村地区的养老金体制尤为令人担忧。）这里的"养老"更大程度上指的是"养老金制度"。

⑪ 医疗，health care，名词词组，比如：the costs of health care for the elderly（老年人的医疗费用）。health care 包含两个方面：一是 prevention of illness and injuries，二是 treatment of illness and injuries。

⑫ 社会保障，social welfare，名词词组，比如：We will improve the urban and rural social welfare system.（我们会完善城乡社会保障体系。）

⑬ 政策措施，policies and practices，名词词组，比如：policies and practices of human resources（人力资源政策措施）。

惯例、常规，practice，名词，比如：a review of pay and working practices（对薪金和工作实践的回顾）。

⑭ 教育和医疗机构布局，arrange education and medical institutions，动词词组。

安排、筹备，arrange，动词，比如：The party was arranged quickly.（聚会很快就安排好了。）

机构，institution，名词，比如：financial institutions（金融机构）。

【同义词辨析】

institution：多指社会机构、社会团体；

institute：多指学术研究机构、高等学府。

⑮ 儿童和老人服务设施建设，build children and seniors facilities，动词词组。

老年人，senior，名词，比如：Tickets at the gate are $10, $7 for seniors (age 55 and up).［门票价格为 $10，老年人（55 岁及以上）为 $7。］

⑯ 工商业服务网点分布，locate commercial service depots，动词词组。
仓库、库房，depot，名词，比如：food depots（食物储藏室）。
文化小常识：
网点指的是商业、服务业等行业设置在各处的基层单位，比如：销售网点或固定维修网点。

第二步 动词定位

全面查清我国人口数量、结构、分布、城乡住房等方面的最新情况，了解人口增长、劳动力供给、流动人口变化情况，摸清老年人口规模，为制定和完善未来收入、消费、教育、就业、养老、医疗、社会保障等政策措施提供基础，也为教育和医疗机构布局、儿童和老人服务设施建设、工商业服务网点分布、城乡道路建设等提供依据。

第三步 句型解析

❶ 本句较长，所以在翻译时首先要想到动词分堆的问题，也就是我们常说的哪些动词放在一起翻译成一个新句子。本句共有七个动词，五个句子，所以在句子中部进行分堆是比较合适的，而且本句和第三段特别相似，可以用相似的方法来处理，也可以用不同的方法来处理。

❷ 译文将第一句单独翻译，动词位于句首可以使用增主语或是变成被动语态的方式来翻译。主语是"我国人口数量、结构、分布、城乡住房等方面的最新情况"，这里也是典型的总分结构，所以先翻译"最新情况"，再翻译"我国人口数量、结构、分布、城乡住房等方面"；谓语是"全面查清"，翻译为 need to be comprehensively probed。

❸ 第二句和第三句都不是很长，所以可以合译，处理为两个被动语态，但是两个动词"了解"和"摸清"意思相近，所以可以处理为一个核心动词 must be understood，而"人口增长、劳动力供给、流动人口变化情况"和"老年人口规模"则是主语，主语中还有两组范畴词"情况"和"规模"，可以不用翻译。

❹ 第四句缺少主语，主语其实是前面的三个句子，这里可以用"以上这些"来替代，翻译为 these data，谓语是"提供"，宾语是"基础"，状语是"为制定和完善未来收入、消费、教育、就业、养老、医疗、社会保障等政策措施"。本句主要考查名词词组，句中的"政策措施"，译文将其处理为 policies and practices，也可以看成范畴词，不翻译。

❺ 第五句也缺少主语，可以增主语，主语也是 these data，但是这里可以处理为代词 they，谓语是"提供"，宾语是"依据"，状语是"为教育和医疗机构布局、儿童和老人服务设施建设、工商业服务网点分布、城乡道路建设等"，后面四个状语看上去都是主谓结构，但是其实可以处理为动宾结构。
"教育和医疗机构布局、儿童和老人服务设施建设、工商业服务网点分布、城乡道路建设"分别处理为"布局教育和医疗机构、建设儿童和老人服务设施、分布工商业服务网点和建设城乡道路"，这样处理为动宾结构后，整个句子非常工整。当然，考试时你要真的想不到，直接翻译也是可行的。

第四步 翻译来了

Such recent developments as the demographic number, makeup, distribution, urban and rural housing, etc. need to be comprehensively probed. Population growth, labor supply, and changes in the floating population, and the population of senior citizens must be understood. These data will lay a foundation for formulating and improving the policies and practices for future income, spending, education, employment, pension system, health care, social welfare, etc. They also provide the bases for arranging education and medical institutions, building children and seniors facilities, locating commercial service depots, and constructing urban and rural roads, etc.

> **本句考点总结**
>
> 　　第一，关于"动词分堆"的问题。中文里常常出现多个短句聚集的句型，我们一方面需要去考虑这些动词之间的关系，哪一个是最重要的，哪一个是其次重要的，哪一个又是最不重要的，这个过程称为分析"谓语动词的层次性"。除此之外，句子当中出现了大量的动词时，或者说大量的分句时，我们不可能将这些分句整体翻译为一个长句，那么，我们就需要考虑哪些动词放在一起翻译，这样的过程称为"动词分堆"。比如，一个句子当中有五个动词形成的五个分句，我们一般会考虑前三个动词翻译为一句，后两个动词翻译为一句，但是如何进行"分堆"要根据上下文的语境来判断，绝对不能形而上学，望文生义。
>
> 　　第二，中英文的总分关系，中文一般是先分后总，而英文则是先总后分，比如中文会说"我喜欢吃香蕉、苹果、梨子等水果"，但是英文的表达是 I like fruits such as bananas, apples and pears. 注意总分关系是如何在两种语言中体现出来的。
>
> 　　第三，本句考查了英汉互译增减词的问题，一般来说英译汉增词，汉译英减词，常见增词的种类有：一、增加对象词（范围词），这是由上文缺少句子的某个部分造成的；二、增加范畴词，这是较难的一部分，常见的范畴词有"水平、方式、方法、问题、情况、途径和方面"，但是不仅仅有这些，还有其他很多；三、增加评论性词，这些常常出现在文学翻译中；四、增加动词，会在动词的"分配译法"中说明这点。

6

人口普查工作从方案制定、物资准备、试点、人员培训、入户登记到数据处理等一切工作都离不开人，队伍建设非常重要。能否组织好人口普查队伍，能否做好普查人员的选调，直接影响到普查的工作质量和数据质量。

第一步 词汇解析

① 方案制定，plan formulation，名词词组，比如：This is my winter vacation plan formulation.（这是我制订的寒假计划。）

② 物资准备，material preparation，名词词组，比如：It should be planned from construction technology, material preparation and labor organization.（应从施工技术、物资准备和劳动力组织方面进行筹划运作。）

③ 试点，pilot，动词，比如：Teachers are piloting a literature-based reading program.（老师们正在试开一门以文学为基础的阅读课程。）pilot 作为动词，表示"试点"时，特指试行计划或方案。

④ 人员培训，personnel training，名词词组，比如：Training mode determines the direction and quality of personnel training.（培训模式决定人员培训的方向和质量。）
personnel 作为复数型名词，表示"人员"；作为不可数名词，表示"人事部门"。

⑤ 入户登记，on-site registration，名词词组，比如：Visitors must present their name card for on-site registration.（现场登记时必须出示名片以资识别。）这里的"入户登记"指的就是"深入每一户家庭，现场登记"。
登记、注册，registration，名词，比如：the registration of students for a course（学生的选课登记）。

⑥ 数据处理，data processing，名词词组，比如：The company makes data-processing systems.（这个公司研发数据处理系统。）

加工、处理，process，动词，比如：facilities to process the data, and the right to publish the results（处理数据的设备和公布结果的权利）。

process 常见词组：in the process of，表示"在……过程中"，比如：The administration is in the process of drawing up a peace plan.（该政府正在起草一项和平计划。）

❼ 离不开……，be inseparable from，动词词组，比如：He firmly believes liberty is inseparable from social justice.（他坚信自由与社会正义是不可分开的。）inseparable 由三部分构成：in（否定前缀）+separate（分开）+ able（形容词词尾）。

❽ 队伍建设，team building，名词词组，比如：Team building, motivation, and performance feature widely in modern business-speak.（队伍建设、激励和绩效充斥在现代商业语言中。）

❾ 选调，select，动词，比如：All our hotels have been carefully selected for the excellent value they provide.（我们住的旅馆都是精心挑选的，最为合算。）

文化小常识：

选调是指选拔抽调。《新华月报》1951 年第 1 期："各单位于选调学员时，须认识工农干部对于文化的迫切需要和国家建设的长远利益，按照规定选送，不得敷衍充数。"

❿ 工作质量，work performance，名词词组，比如：One's educational background is not directly relevant to his work performance.（一个人的教育背景和他的工作表现没有直接的关联。）

业绩、工作情况，performance，名词，比如：He criticized the recent poor performance of the company.（他批评公司近期业绩不佳。）

⓫ 数据质量，data quality，名词词组，比如：This article discusses causes of poor data quality.（本文讨论造成数据质量差的原因。）

第二步 动词定位

人口普查工作从方案制定、物资准备、试点、人员培训、入户登记到数据处理等一切工作都离不开人，队伍建设非常重要。能否组织好人口普查队伍，能否做好普查人员的选调，直接影响到普查的工作质量和数据质量。

第三步 句型解析

❶ 第一句中，"人口普查工作"是主语，翻译为 the census work，谓语是"离不开"，翻译为 be inseparable from，"人"是宾语，后面的同位语"从方案制定、物资准备、试点、人员培训、入户登记到数据处理等一切工作"可以处理为 from... to...，这里的"等一切工作"可以看作范畴词，可以不译，也可以翻译。后面的"队伍建设非常重要"要考虑两句之间的关系，显然两句是因果关系，所以用 so 连接非常恰当。

❷ 第二句中，"能否组织好人口普查队伍，能否做好普查人员的选调"是本句的主语，考生看到"能否"最先想到的是 whether... or...，这样整个句子就处理为主语从句，但是译文处理为 the ability to "组织和选调人口普查队伍"，这样也是非常聪明的。本句的谓语是"直接影响到"，"普查的工作质量和数据质量"是宾语。注意宾语出现了两次"质量"，只翻译一次就可以。

第四步 翻译来了

The census work is inseparable from people, from plan formulation, material preparation, piloting, personnel training, on-site registration to data processing, so team building is very important. The ability to properly organize, select and utilize a census team will directly affect the work performance and data quality of the census.

本句考查了英汉互译增减词的问题，一般来说英译汉增词，汉译英减词，常见增词的种类有：一、增加对象词（范围词），这是由上文缺少句子的某个部分造成的；二、增加范畴词，这是较难的一部分，常见的范畴词有"水平、方式、方法、问题、情况、途径和方面"，但是不仅仅有这些，还有其他很多；三、增加评论性词，这些常常出现在文学翻译中；四、增加动词，会在动词的"分配译法"中说明这点。

这篇文章是典型的政府工作报告类型的文章，总体难度不大，主要的问题在词汇，句子结构尽量用并列结构，但是也要特别关注无主语句的结构。一般来说，无主语句使用增加主语（需要结合上下文）或被动语态的译法最好。而且从句型的角度来说，政工类报告往往是多个小句子构成大句子，因此也要搞清分句之间的关系，判断如何进行动词分堆。

第三节　2021 年下半年三级笔译英译汉

原文（请先通读全文）

Two domestic airlines already limit your ability to lean back in economy class. Even if the airline doesn't make the decision for you, it's the polite thing to do. And, most important, it's the right thing to do.

"Seat reclining is one of the most irritating, inconvenient, self-indulgent habits," says Simon Sapper, an organizational consultant and frequent traveler based in London. "Period."

But click around the internet for a while, and you'll find that this debate is far from settled. Many of the blogosphere's "experts" believe it's their God-given right to recline. Ironically, the loudest seat recliners don't even fly in economy class.

So, as a public service, let's settle this argument now. Reclining your airline seat is unacceptable because we're officially out of space. It's rude — and it's wrong.

There's no space to recline. Airlines are trying to squeeze more passengers on a plane to make more money. Before airline deregulation, many economy class seats had a generous 36 inches of "pitch," a rough measure of legroom. Today, some seats have as little as 28 inches.

"I feel most folks would rather sacrifice the 2 inches of reclining backward not to have someone sitting in their lap for the distance of a flight," says Mary Camillo, a travel advisor from Middletown, New Jersey. "Airlines should instill on passengers what parents have been trying to instill in their children for years. That is, if you do not have enough to share with everyone, then wait until you do."

Also, airlines should immediately stop using the phrase "Sit back, relax, and enjoy the flight." That's an invitation to lean back all the way. But it's a cruel joke. On two airlines — Delta and Spirit — you can't fully recline. On other airlines, you'll invade another passenger's personal space, which might lead to an unfriendly confrontation.

You can do a lot of things on a plane. For example, you can tell your life story to your seatmate. You can eat a Limburger cheese and Bermuda onion sandwich. You can press the flight attendant call button repeatedly. But all are probably bad ideas.

"Seat recline is a moral issue," says Jennifer Aspinwall, a frequent air traveler who writes the World On A Whim blog. "What do you do if the person in front of you reclines all the way? What if you turn around to discover that a 6-foot-4 passenger seated behind you? Do you eat your meal in your lap while the tray table cuts into your stomach or do recline as well and crush the legs of the person behind you?"

Airlines should lock their economy seats from reclining — permanently.

So if there's no room to recline your airplane seat, and it's wrong, why do so many airlines still allow it? Because if they didn't, it would be an admission that they no longer care about your comfort. Airlines are stacking you into a plane like cargo — no two ways about it.

"I wish all airlines would eliminate the recline function," says Larry Hickerson, a retired Air Force inspector and million-miler from Peoria, Arizona. "Since airlines went to ridiculously tight pitches, recline sets up an untenable situation."

Right now, about half the people reading this column probably want to name their firstborn after me. The other half want to kill me. And the airline folks? They're laughing.

The airline industry loves the seat reclining argument because it divides us. And while we're arguing about 2 inches of personal space, they're busy collecting more money from passengers and slowly — ever so slowly — removing even more room. This debate is the perfect distraction.

Whether you think reclining your airline seat is wrong or not, let's agree on one thing: Greedy airlines got us to this point. Fighting over the scraps of space won't fix it. If we ever needed thoughtful government regulation, maybe it is now.

How to deal with a seat recliner?

Reclining an airline seat is still allowed on most domestic flights. Here's how to deal with someone who leans into your airspace.

Ask them to lean forward. Timing and tone are important here. The moment someone leans back, gently tap the person on the shoulder and politely ask them if it would be possible not to recline their seat. Be. Extra. Nice.

Get a flight attendant involved. Some leaners are clever and wait for you to go to the restroom before leaning. Then they feign sleep, which makes you reluctant to bother them. Oldest trick in the book. You can always ask a flight attendant for help.

Move airplane seats. If you see another open seat in your class of service, feel free to move, as long as the seat belt sign isn't illuminated. You might also want to ask a flight attendant for permission. As a reminder, the seats in front of the exit row don't recline. So usually, an exit row seat means you'll keep your legroom. And maybe, your sanity.

2021年下半年CATTI全国考试如期举行，但是有些地区由于疫情并未举行考试，这几年疫情导致某些地区一直没有举行考试，请大家报考时也要注意相关政策。*本篇文章节选自2019年11月8日在《今日美国》上刊登的一篇关于旅游建议的报道，题目为 Do you have the right to recline your airline airplane seat? No, and here's why，文章的本质还是和我们熟悉的外刊是一样的，总体难度不大，但是篇幅有所增加，要求*

大家在相同时间内提高速度。注意：考虑到上下文的联系，所以对原文全文进行了解析，但考试真题并没有这么长！

Two domestic airlines already limit your ability to lean back in economy class. Even if the airline doesn't make the decision for you, it's the polite thing to do. And, most important, it's the right thing to do.

"Seat reclining is one of the most irritating, inconvenient, self-indulgent habits," says Simon Sapper, an organizational consultant and frequent traveler based in London. "Period."

第一步 词汇解析

❶ domestic，形容词，表示"国内的"，比如：This argument is only too blatantly an alibi for domestic repression. （这一辩解完全是在为国内的镇压活动开脱。）

❷ lean back，动词词组，表示"向后靠、向后倾斜"，比如：Lean back in a hot bath and forget all the cares of the day. （舒舒服服地躺着泡个热水澡，忘掉白天的一切烦恼。）

❸ economy class，名词词组，表示"（飞机上的）经济舱位"，比如：Several businessmen had to slum it in economy class. （几个商人只好将就着坐在经济舱里。）

❹ recline，动词，表示"（使座椅靠背）向后倾"，比如：Air France first-class seats recline almost like beds. （法国航空公司头等舱的坐椅可以调低成几乎像床一样。）

❺ irritating，形容词，表示"恼人的、使人生气的"，比如：They also have the irritating habit of interrupting. （他们还有打岔的烦人习惯。）

❻ self-indulgent，形容词，表示"放纵自己的、任性的"，比如：To buy flowers for myself seems wildly self-indulgent. （为自己买花似乎太放纵自己了。）

❼ consultant，名词，表示"顾问"，比如：She earns more since she repackaged herself as a business consultant. （自从把自己重新包装成商业顾问以来，她的收入增加了。）

❽ period，副词，表示"到此为止"，比如：The answer is no, period! （答复是不，不再说了！）

第二步 注意断句

Two domestic airlines already limit your ability to lean back in economy class. /Even if the airline doesn't make the decision for you, /it's the polite thing to do. /And, /most important, /it's the right thing /to do.

"Seat reclining is one of the most irritating, /inconvenient, /self-indulgent habits," /says Simon Sapper, /an organizational consultant and frequent traveler based in London. /"Period."

第三步 句型解析

❶ 第一段第一句中，Two domestic airlines already limit your ability 是主谓宾结构，to lean back in economy class 是不定式作定语，用来修饰前面的 ability，可以采用前置译法，若认为通顺，也可以采用后置译法。

❷ 第一段第二句中，Even if the airline doesn't make the decision for you 是让步状语从句，it's the polite thing to do 是主句，句式结构比较简单，但是翻译时还是要口语化一些，不要字对字翻译。

❸ 第一段第三句中，And 是并列连词，most important 是插入语，it's the right thing to do 是主系表结构，

这里的 it 是代词（也是后面的不定式 to do 的形式主语），可以指明要点，翻译为"你不要将座椅靠背向后倾"。

❹ 第二段是典型的"话 + 人 + 定（同）+ 话"结构，翻译时句子结构可以不变。外刊必考的内容之一就是直接引语，一定要保留原始的标点，再进行翻译。

❺ 直接引语中，Seat reclining is one of the most irritating, inconvenient, self-indulgent habits 是主系表结构，可以直接翻译，says Simon Sapper 是动词和说话人，后面接同位语 an organizational consultant and frequent traveler based in London。同位语可以用主谓译法或是并列译法，后面的直接引语 Period 是常见的口语表达，理解为"到这里即可"。

第四步　翻译来了

两家美国国内航空公司已经限制了你在经济舱将座椅靠背向后倾的能力。即使航空公司没有为你做出这样的决定，但是出于礼貌，你也不该这么做。最重要的是，你不要将座椅靠背向后倾，这么做是对的。

"座椅的靠背向后倾是最烦人、最不方便，且最放纵的一种习惯，"总部在伦敦的一个组织的顾问且经常旅行的西蒙·萨珀（Simon Sapper）说，"这种行为必须立即停止"。

本句考点总结

第一，关于英文代词的译法。英文中需要翻译的代词主要指第三人称 he, she, it, they 及其相应宾格和指示代词 this 和 that。这些单词在翻译时一定要注意，主要采用"不抽象、不具体"的译法。不能翻译成具体的人或物，但是也不能翻译为"他""她""它""他们""这个""那个"，要注意取中间的译法。

第二，本句考查了英文直接引语的译法，最简单的译法就是保留冒号和双引号，说话人的位置和说话的内容都保持不变。即说话人在什么位置，就放在什么位置翻译，说话人放在句首也是可以接受的。

第三，英文人名的翻译，这里采用的是音译法，注意名和姓之间要加·，英文的人名不确定如何翻译时，可以使用音译法，然后把英文人名抄下来，放在括号里，这样保险一些。

第四，本句考查了英文同位语的译法。同位语是两个前后相互说明的名词或名词短语，比如 Beijing, the capital of China，有两种译法。第一种是"并列译法"，翻译为"中国的首都北京"，第二种是"主谓译法"，翻译为"北京是中国的首都"。具体用哪一种，可以根据句子具体情况而定，有时两种都是可以使用的。

2 But click around the internet for a while, and you'll find that this debate is far from settled. Many of the blogosphere's "experts" believe it's their God-given right to recline. Ironically, the loudest seat recliners don't even fly in economy class.
So, as a public service, let's settle this argument now. Reclining your airline seat is unacceptable because we're officially out of space. It's rude — and it's wrong.

第一步 词汇解析

❶ far from，副词词组，表示"远没有、根本不、远远不"，比如：Research on the matter is far from conclusive. （对这一问题的研究还远远没有定论。）

❷ blogosphere，名词，表示"博客圈、博客世界"，比如：Consequently, even as the blogosphere continues to expand, only a few blogs are likely to emerge as focal points. （结果，尽管博客圈继续扩大，但仅有少数的博客有可能脱颖而出，成为关注的焦点。）

❸ ironically，副词，表示"具有讽刺意味地、讽刺的是"，比如：Ironically, for a man who hated war, he would have made a superb war cameraman. （具有讽刺意味的是，他这个痛恨战争的人曾有可能成为一个优秀的战地摄影师。）

❹ settle，动词，表示"解决（分歧、纠纷等）"，比如：It's time you settled your differences with your father. （现在你该解决同你父亲之间的分歧了。）

❺ officially，副词，表示"正式地、官方地"，比如：He officially announced his retirement from first-class cricket yesterday. （他昨天正式宣布退出甲级板球赛。）

第二步 注意断句

But /click around the internet for a while, /and you'll find /that this debate is far from settled. /Many of the blogosphere's "experts" believe /it's their God-given right to recline. /Ironically, /the loudest seat recliners don't even fly in economy class.

So, /as a public service, /let's settle this argument now. /Reclining your airline seat is unacceptable /because we're officially out of space. /It's rude — /and it's wrong.

第三步 句型解析

❶ 第一段第一句中，But 是并列连词，表示转折，click around the internet for a while 是祈使句，and 是并列连词，you'll find 是主谓结构，后面的 that 接宾语从句，this debate is far from settled 是主系表结构，也可以认为是被动语态。其实语法成分不重要，重要的是你要知道 settle 的意思。

❷ 第一段第二句中，Many of the blogosphere's "experts" believe 是主谓结构，后面接宾语从句 it's their God-given right to recline，这里的 God-given 理解为"上帝赋予的"，是形容词。

❸ 第一段第三句中，Ironically 是副词，可以单独成句，翻译为"具有讽刺意味的是"，the loudest seat recliners don't even fly in economy class 是主谓状结构，这句最难理解的是 the loudest seat recliners，不是指"座椅靠背向后倾斜最大声的人"，而应理解为"为这件事发声最大的人"。

❹ 第二段第一句中，So 是并列连词，表示结果，as a public service 是插入语，let's settle this argument now 是祈使句，句式结构较为简单，可以直接翻译。

❺ 第二段第二句中，Reclining your airline seat is unacceptable 是主系表结构。because 引导原因状语从句，we're officially out of space 也是主系表结构，句式结构较为简单，可以直接翻译。后一句较短，可以合译，It's rude — and it's wrong 是两个主系表结构，这里的破折号可以保留，也可以不保留；it 是代词，可以翻译为"这种做法"。

第四步 翻译来了

但是，如果你在互联网上搜索一下，那么，你会发现关于座椅靠背倾斜的争论还远远没有得到解决。许多博客圈的"专家"认为,座椅靠背倾斜是上帝赐予人们的权利。具有讽刺意味的是,关于这件事发声最大的乘客甚至并不在经济舱。

所以,作为一项公共服务,让我们现在来解决这个争论吧。把你的座位向后倾斜是不可接受的,因为我们要郑重地告诉大家,飞机座位舱已经没有空间了,所以,这种做法是粗鲁的,也是错误的。

本句考点总结

关于英文代词的译法。英文中需要翻译的代词主要指第三人称 he,she,it,they 及其相应宾格和指示代词 this 和 that。这些单词在翻译时一定要注意,主要采用"不抽象、不具体"的译法。不能翻译成具体的人或物,但是也不能翻译为"他""她""它""他们""这个""那个",要注意取中间的译法。

3

There's no space to recline. Airlines are trying to squeeze more passengers on a plane to make more money. Before airline deregulation, many economy class seats had a generous 36 inches of "pitch", a rough measure of legroom. Today, some seats have as little as 28 inches.

第一步 词汇解析

❶ squeeze,动词,表示"挤入、塞入",比如:There'll be enough room if we all squeeze up a little.(大家稍微挤一挤,地方就够了。)

❷ deregulation,名词,表示"放松管制、解除管制",比如:Prices have gone up 61 percent since deregulation.(价格自解除管制以来已经上涨 61%。)

❸ rough,形容词,表示"粗略的、大致的",比如:We were only able to make a rough estimate of how much fuel would be required.(我们只能对所需燃料作一个粗略的估计。)

❹ measure,名词,表示"判断、尺度、标准",比如:A clearly quantifiable measure of quality is not necessary.(没有必要对质量进行明确的定量测量。)

第二步 注意断句

There's no space to recline. /Airlines are trying to squeeze more passengers on a plane /to make more money. /Before airline deregulation, /many economy class seats had a generous 36 inches of "pitch", /a rough measure of legroom. /Today, /some seats have as little as 28 inches.

第三步 句型解析

❶ 第一句中,There's no space to recline 是 there be 句型,表示"没有向后倾斜的空间了"。

❷ 第二句中,Airlines are trying to squeeze more passengers on a plane 是主谓宾结构,后面的不定式 to make

❸ 第三句中，Before airline deregulation 是时间状语，主句中 many economy class seats had a generous 36 inches of "pitch" 是主谓宾结构，后面的 a rough measure of legroom 是同位语。这里要考虑 generous, 36 inches of "pitch" 和 a rough measure of legroom 之间的语言该如何组织，看看译文吧！是不是很有启发的意义呢？

❹ 第四句和第三句在句意上有一定的连接，可以合译，如果你认为不合译也通顺，当然也可以。Today 是时间状语，表示"如今"，some seats have as little as 28 inches 是主谓宾结构。

第四步　翻译来了

座椅靠背没有向后倾斜的空间了。航空公司正试图将飞机座舱腾出更多的空间来搭载乘客，这样可以赚更多的钱。在航空公司放松管制之前，许多经济舱座位都有 36 英寸的"间距"，粗略地算一下，这样的伸腿空间相当宽敞，但是，如今，一些座位只有 28 英寸的间距。

本句考点总结

本句考查了英文同位语的译法。同位语是两个前后相互说明的名词或名词短语，比如 Beijing, the capital of China，有两种译法，第一种是"并列译法"，翻译为"中国的首都北京"，第二种是"主谓译法"，翻译为"北京是中国的首都"。具体用哪一种，可以根据句子具体情况而定，有时两种都是可以使用的。

"I feel most folks would rather sacrifice the 2 inches of reclining backward not to have someone sitting in their lap for the distance of a flight," says Mary Camillo, a travel advisor from Middletown, New Jersey. "Airlines should instill on passengers what parents have been trying to instill in their children for years. That is, if you do not have enough to share with everyone, then wait until you do."

第一步　词汇解析

❶ sacrifice，动词，表示"牺牲"，比如：The designers have sacrificed speed for fuel economy.（设计者为节省燃料牺牲了速度。）

❷ lap，名词，表示"（人坐着时的）大腿部"，比如：There's only one seat so you'll have to sit on my lap.（只有一个座位，你只好坐在我腿上了。）

❸ New Jersey，地名，表示"新泽西州"，比如：New Jersey swept Detroit last season.（在上个赛季，新泽西队全胜底特律队。）

❹ instill，动词，表示"灌输、浸染"，比如：She instilled in the children the virtues of hard work, and making the best of what you have.（她慢慢给孩子们灌输勤奋工作的品德，教导他们充分利用现有的条件。）

第二步 注意断句

"I feel /most folks would rather sacrifice the 2 inches of reclining backward /not to have someone sitting in their lap /for the distance of a flight," /says Mary Camillo, /a travel advisor from Middletown, /New Jersey. /"Airlines should instill on passengers /what parents have been trying to instill in their children for years. /That is, /if you do not have enough to share with everyone, /then wait /until you do."

第三步 句型解析

❶ 本段是典型的"话＋人＋定（同）＋话"结构，翻译时句子结构可以不变。外刊必考的内容之一就是直接引语，一定要保留原始的标点，再进行翻译。

❷ 直接引语的第一句中，I feel 是主谓结构，后面是宾语从句，most folks would rather sacrifice the 2 inches of reclining backward not to have someone sitting in their lap 是主谓宾结构，这句是典型的 would rather do not to do 的结构，表示"宁愿做某事，也不会做某事"，for the distance of a flight 是状语，表示"在整个旅程之中"。

❸ says Mary Camillo 是动词和说话人，后面的同位语 a travel advisor from Middletown, New Jersey 可以采用主谓译法或并列译法。

❹ 直接引语的第二句中，Airlines should instill on passengers 是主谓状结构，what parents have been trying to instill in their children for years 实际上是宾语从句，只是宾语过长，所以才放在了句末，该从句是主谓宾状结构。

❺ 直接引语第三句的 That is 在口语中表示"那就是"，if you do not have enough to share with everyone 是 if 引导的条件状语从句，then wait 是主句，until you do 是时间状语从句。本句和上一句关系紧密，可以合译，也可以不合译。

第四步 翻译来了

"我觉得，大多数人都宁愿牺牲掉向后仰的两英寸，也不愿意让人在整个飞行途中坐在他们的腿上，"新泽西州米德尔敦的旅行顾问玛丽·卡米罗（Mary Camillo）说，"航空公司应该向乘客灌输父母多年来一直试图灌输给孩子的观念，那就是，如果你没有足够的东西可以和所有人分享，那就等到你拥有了足够的东西再分享吧。"

🧑 本句考点总结

第一，本句考查了英文直接引语的译法，最简单的译法就是保留冒号和双引号，说话人的位置和说话的内容都保持不变。即说话人在什么位置，就放在什么位置翻译，当然，说话人放在句首也是可以接受的。

第二，本句考查了英文同位语的译法。同位语是两个前后相互说明的名词或名词短语，比如 Beijing, the capital of China，有两种译法，第一种是"并列译法"，翻译为"中国的首都北京"，第二种是"主谓译法"，翻译为"北京是中国的首都"。具体用哪一种，可以根据句子具体情况而定，有时两种都是可以使用的。

第三，英文人名的翻译，这里采用的是音译法，注意名和姓之间要加·，英文的人名不确定如何翻译时，可以使用音译法，然后把英文人名抄下来，放在括号里，这样保险一些。

5

> Also, airlines should immediately stop using the phrase "Sit back, relax, and enjoy the flight." That's an invitation to lean back all the way. But it's a cruel joke. On two airlines — Delta and Spirit — you can't fully recline. On other airlines, you'll invade another passenger's personal space, which might lead to an unfriendly confrontation.

第一步 词汇解析

① phrase，名词，表示"短语、习语"，比如：The Italian phrase can be rendered as "I did my best."（这个意大利语的短语可以译为"我尽力了"。）

② Delta，专有名词，表示"达美航空"。

文化小常识：

达美航空公司（Delta Air Lines, Inc.）是一家总部位于美国佐治亚州亚特兰大的航空公司。

③ Spirit，专有名词，表示"精神航空"。

④ invade，动词，表示"侵犯、侵扰"，比如：Do the press have the right to invade her privacy in this way?（新闻界有权以这种方式侵犯她的隐私吗？）

⑤ confrontation，名词，表示"对抗、对峙、冲突"，比如：The issue has caused great tension between the two countries and could lead to a military confrontation.（这个问题使得两国关系非常紧张，可能会导致军事对抗。）

第二步 注意断句

Also, /airlines should immediately stop using the phrase /"Sit back, /relax, /and enjoy the flight." /That's an invitation to lean back all the way. /But it's a cruel joke. /On two airlines — /Delta and Spirit — /you can't fully recline. /On other airlines, /you'll invade another passenger's personal space, /which might lead to an unfriendly confrontation.

第三步 句型解析

① 第一句中，Also 是句首的副词作状语，airlines should immediately stop using the phrase 是主谓宾结构，双引号里的 Sit back, relax, and enjoy the flight 实际上是对前面 phrase 的解释，相当于同位语，用并列译法更好一些。

② 第二句 That's an invitation 是主系表结构，to lean back all the way 是不定式作定语，修饰 invitation，这里注意对 invitation 的理解，翻译为"邀请"不是非常通顺，翻译为"让某人做某事"更好。

③ 第三句较短，可以和上一句合译，But 是并列连词，表示转折；it's a cruel joke 是主系表结构，这里要注意 cruel 的含义，如果翻译为"残酷"，最好加上双引号，这样更好理解。

④ 第四句中，On two airlines 是状语，后面的破折号可以保留，也可以用译文中的同位语译法，Delta and Spirit 在翻译后可以保留英文，英文放在括号内，you can't fully recline 是主谓结构。

⑤ 第五句中，On other airlines 是状语，you'll invade another passenger's personal space 是主谓宾结构，句式结构较为简单，可以直接翻译。后面是非限定性定语从句，which 是关系代词，可以翻译为"这""这种行为"等，might lead to an unfriendly confrontation 是谓语和宾语的结构。

第四步 翻译来了

航空公司也应立即停止使用"坐好,放松,享受飞行"这样的话,这实际上是让乘客一直将座椅靠背往后倾斜,但这确实是一个"残酷"的玩笑。在达美航空(Delta)和精神航空(Spirit)这两家航空公司的飞机上,你不能完全倾斜座椅靠背。在其他航空公司的飞机上,你这么做则会侵犯到其他乘客的私人空间,这可能会引起一些不友好的冲突。

本句考点总结

第一,本句考查了英文同位语的译法。同位语是两个前后相互说明的名词或名词短语,比如 Beijing, the capital of China,有两种译法,第一种是"并列译法",翻译为"中国的首都北京",第二种是"主谓译法",翻译为"北京是中国的首都"。具体用哪一种,可以根据句子具体情况而定,有时两种都是可以使用的。

第二,英文人名的翻译,这里采用的是音译法,注意名和姓之间要加·,英文的人名不确定如何翻译时,可以使用音译法,然后把英文人名抄下来,放在括号里,这样保险一些。

6

You can do a lot of things on a plane. For example, you can tell your life story to your seatmate. You can eat a Limburger cheese and Bermuda onion sandwich. You can press the flight attendant call button repeatedly. But all are probably bad ideas.

"Seat recline is a moral issue," says Jennifer Aspinwall, a frequent air traveler who writes the World On A Whim blog. "What do you do if the person in front of you reclines all the way? What if you turn around to discover that a 6-foot-4 passenger seated behind you? Do you eat your meal in your lap while the tray table cuts into your stomach or do recline as well and crush the legs of the person behind you?"

第一步 词汇解析

❶ Limburger,专有名词,地名,表示"林堡"。
  文化小常识:
    林堡是位于比利时列日省部苇德尔河河谷的一座城市。
❷ Bermuda,专有名词,地名,表示"百慕大、百慕大群岛"。
  文化小常识:
    百慕大三角(Bermuda Triangle)地处北美佛罗里达半岛东南部,具体是指由英属百慕大群岛、美国的迈阿密和波多黎各的圣胡安三点连线形成的一个西大西洋三角地带,每边长约 2 000 千米。
❸ flight attendant,名词词组,表示"(客机的)乘务员、空乘人员",比如:Now that she's a flight attendant, foreign travel has lost its glamour for her.(她现在是空中乘务员了,去国外旅行对她已失去吸引力。)
❹ tray,名词,表示"盘、托盘",比如:He brought her breakfast in bed on a tray.(他把早餐用托盘给她送到床上。)

⑤ crush，动词，表示"压坏、压伤"，比如：Several people were crushed to death in the accident.（好几个人在事故中被压死了。）

第二步 注意断句

You can do a lot of things on a plane. /For example, /you can tell your life story to your seatmate. /You can eat a Limburger cheese and Bermuda onion sandwich. /You can press the flight attendant call button repeatedly. /But all are probably bad ideas.

"Seat recline is a moral issue," /says Jennifer Aspinwall, /a frequent air traveler /who writes the World On A Whim blog. /"What do you do /if the person in front of you reclines all the way? /What if you turn around to discover /that a 6-foot-4 passenger seated behind you? /Do you eat your meal in your lap /while the tray table cuts into your stomach /or do recline as well /and crush the legs of the person behind you?"

第三步 句型解析

① 第一段第一句 You can do a lot of things on a plane 是主谓宾状结构，句式结构较为简单，可以直接翻译。

② 第一段第二句中，For example 是状语，you can tell your life story to your seatmate 是主谓宾状结构，句式结构较为简单，可以直接翻译。

③ 第一段第三句 You can eat a Limburger cheese and Bermuda onion sandwich 是主谓宾结构，句式结构较为简单，可以直接翻译。

④ 第一段第四句 You can press the flight attendant call button repeatedly 是主谓宾状结构，句式结构较为简单，可以直接翻译。

⑤ 第一段第五句中，But 是并列连词，表示转折，all are probably bad ideas 是主系表结构，句式结构较为简单，可以直接翻译。

⑥ 第二段是典型的"话+人+定（同）+话"结构，翻译时句子结构可以不变。外刊必考的内容之一就是直接引语，一定要保留原始的标点，再进行翻译。

⑦ 直接引语第一句 Seat recline is a moral issue 是主系表结构，句式结构较为简单，可以直接翻译。says Jennifer Aspinwall 是动词和说话人，保留在原位进行翻译，a frequent air traveler who writes the World On A Whim blog 是说话人的同位语，包含定语从句，可以使用主谓译法或并列译法。

⑧ 直接引语的第二句中，What do you do 是主句，if the person in front of you reclines all the way 是 if 引导的条件状语从句。

⑨ 直接引语的第三句 What if you turn around to discover that a 6-foot-4 passenger seated behind you 是 What if 引导的一个使用了虚拟语气的句子，也是较为口语化的表达。you turn around 是主语和谓语，to discover 是不定式作结果状语，后面接的是宾语从句。

⑩ 直接引语的第四句中，Do you eat your meal in your lap 是主句，是一般疑问句，表示"你是不是把饭放在大腿上吃呢？"while the tray table cuts into your stomach 是时间状语从句，or 是选择连词，do recline as well 是第二个疑问句，其完整结构是 do you recline as well，后面的 and 是并列连词，crush the legs of the person behind you 是谓语和宾语。

第四步 翻译来了

你可以在飞机上做很多事，比如，你可以向邻座朋友讲述你的人生故事。你可以吃林堡芝士和百慕大洋葱三明治。你还可以重复按按钮呼叫空乘人员，但这样做好像都不太好。

"座椅靠背向后倾斜是一个道德问题，"詹妮弗·阿斯品沃尔（Jennifer Aspinwall）说，她是一位经常乘飞机旅行的人，她在其博客《突发奇想的世界》中写道："如果你前面的人一直向后斜躺着，你会怎么做？如果你转身发现一位身高 6 英尺 4 英寸的乘客坐在你后面怎么办？你是把饭放在自己的大腿上吃，而餐盘直接杵到你的胃部呢，还是向后躺着，压伤你身后人的双腿呢？"

> **本句考点总结**
>
> 第一，本句考查了英文直接引语的译法，最简单的译法就是保留冒号和双引号，说话人的位置和说话的内容都保持不变。即说话人在什么位置，就放在什么位置翻译，当然，说话人放在句首也是可以接受的。
>
> 第二，本句出现了英文定语从句的译法。一般来说，定语从句按照"短前长后"的译法处理，较短的定语从句可以前置，较长的定语从句可以后置，这一切都取决于句子的通顺，并没有绝对的前置和后置译法。

7

Airlines should lock their economy seats from reclining — permanently.
So if there's no room to recline your airplane seat, and it's wrong, why do so many airlines still allow it? Because if they didn't, it would be an admission that they no longer care about your comfort. Airlines are stacking you into a plane like cargo — no two ways about it.

第一步 词汇解析

① lock，动词，表示"锁、锁上、锁住"，比如：Would you be so kind as to lock the door when you leave？（请您出来时把门锁上好吗？）

② admission，名词，表示"承认"，比如：The company's silence on the subject has been taken as an admission of guilt.（在外界看来，公司在这个问题上保持沉默便是承认有罪。）

③ care about，动词词组，表示"关心、在意"，比如：They were tuned in to their own needs and didn't care about the feelings of other people.（他们只顾自己的需求，不在乎别人的感受。）

④ stack，动词，表示"使成叠（或成摞、成堆）地放在……、使码放在……"，比如：They were busy stacking the shelves with goods.（他们正忙着把货物摆上架呢。）

⑤ cargo，名词，表示"（船或飞机装载的）货物"，比如：The cargo was due to be unloaded in Singapore three days later.（货物定于三天后在新加坡卸载。）

第二步 注意断句

Airlines should lock their economy seats /from reclining — /permanently.

So /if there's no room to recline your airplane seat, /and it's wrong, /why do so many airlines still allow it? / Because if they didn't, /it would be an admission /that they no longer care about your comfort. /Airlines are stacking you into a plane like cargo — /no two ways about it.

第三步 句型解析

① 第一段中，Airlines should lock their economy seats from reclining 是主谓宾状结构，后面的破折号可以保留，这里的 permanently 起到对前面的句子加强语气的作用。

② 第二段第一句中，So 是并列连词，表示结果；if there's no room to recline your airplane seat 是 if 引导的条件状语从句，and 是并列连词，it's wrong 是条件状语从句的第二个分句；why do so many airlines still allow it 是 why 引导的疑问句，句式结构较为简单，可以直接翻译。

③ 第二段第二句中，Because 表示"原因"，if they didn't 是条件状语从句，这里的 they 指代的是"航空公司"，但是可以翻译为"他们"，因为前文出现过多次"航空公司"。it would be an admission 是主系表结构，这里的 it 实际上是形式主语，真正的主语是 that 引导的从句，而且本句中的 admission 是典型的抽象名词，有动词词根，可以翻译为动词"承认"，they no longer care about your comfort 是主谓宾结构。

④ 第二段第三句中，Airlines are stacking you into a plane like cargo 是主谓宾状的结构，破折号可以保留，后面的短语 no two ways about it 的意思是"确实是这样的"，译文根据上下文翻译为"这一点是毫无疑问的"，这样更加合适一些。

第四步 翻译来了

航空公司就应该永久性地锁住经济舱座椅靠背后倾的按钮。

那么，如果飞机上没有空间让你的座位向后倾斜，而且这样做是错误的话，那为什么还有那么多航空公司允许这样做呢？因为如果他们不允许这么做，那就等于承认他们不再关心你的舒适感了。但是现在航空公司确实把你像货物一样堆放在飞机上——这一点是毫无疑问的。

> **本句考点总结**
>
> 本句当中考查了"抽象名词"的译法。抽象名词一般处于冠词之后，又在介词之前，以"the + 抽象名词 + of"的形式居多，一般来说，抽象名词有两种译法。第一种，若抽象名词有动词词根，则翻译为动词，比如 the suggesting of mine，翻译为"我建议"，而不是"我的建议"；第二种，若抽象名词没有动词词根，可以增动词翻译，比如 the spirit of our nation，翻译为"我们民族所具有的精神"，而不是"我们民族的精神"。

"I wish all airlines would eliminate the recline function," says Larry Hickerson, a retired Air Force inspector and million-miler from Peoria, Arizona. "Since airlines went to ridiculously tight pitches, recline sets up an untenable situation."

Right now, about half the people reading this column probably want to name their firstborn after me. The other half want to kill me. And the airline folks? They're laughing.

第一步 词汇解析

① eliminate，动词，表示"消除、剔除、根除"，比如：You could never eliminate risk, but preparation and training could attenuate it.（风险不可能完全被消除，但可以通过防范和培训来降低。）

② Air Force，名词词组，表示"空军"，比如：An Air Force spokesman said the rescue operation was a race against time.（一名空军发言人说这次营救行动是在和时间赛跑。）

③ inspector，名词，表示"检查员、视察员、巡视员"，比如：After an inspection, the inspectors must publish a report.（在视察之后，视察者必须发表一份报告。）

④ Arizona，专有名词，地名，表示"亚利桑那州"，比如：Seventeen thousand Indians live in Arizona on a reservation.（1.7万印第安人生活在亚利桑那州的保留地。）

⑤ untenable，形容词，表示"难以捍卫的、站不住脚的、不堪一击的"，比如：This argument is untenable from an intellectual, moral and practical standpoint.（从智识、道德和现实的角度来看，这一论点是站不住脚的。）

⑥ column，名词，表示"专栏、栏目"，比如：She used the newspaper column as a platform for her feminist views.（她以这个报纸专栏为讲坛，宣传她的女权主义观点。）

⑦ firstborn，形容词，表示"头生的（子女）、初生的、第一胎生的"，比如：firstborn children（头胎孩子）。

第二步 注意断句

"I wish /all airlines would eliminate the recline function," /says Larry Hickerson, /a retired Air Force inspector and million-miler from Peoria, /Arizona. /"Since airlines went to ridiculously tight pitches, /recline sets up an untenable situation."

Right now, /about half the people reading this column probably want to name their firstborn after me. /The other half want to kill me. /And the airline folks? /They're laughing.

第三步 句型解析

① 第一段是典型的"话 + 人 + 定（同）+ 话"结构，翻译时句子结构可以不变。外刊必考的内容之一就是直接引语，一定要保留原始的标点，再进行翻译。

② 直接引语的第一句中，I wish 是主谓结构，后面接宾语从句 all airlines would eliminate the recline function，宾语从句也是主谓宾结构，句式结构较为简单，可以直接翻译。

③ says Larry Hickerson 是动词和说话人，a retired Air Force inspector and million-miler from Peoria, Arizona 是同位语，可以用主谓译法或并列译法。

④ 直接引语的第二句中，Since 引导了原因状语从句，airlines went to ridiculously tight pitches 是主谓宾结构，这里注意 ridiculously 的含义，实际上在这里它是一个程度副词，而不是表示"古怪地"；recline sets up an untenable situation 是主句，是主谓宾结构，这里也要注意 untenable 的意思，表示"让人尴尬、让人两难的"。

⑤ 第二段第一句中，Right now 是时间状语，about half the people reading this column 是主语，其中 reading this column 是分词结构，其位于名词后，相当于定语从句，从句较短，可以采用前置译法，probably want to name their firstborn after me 是谓语、宾语和状语。

⑥ 第二段第二句 The other half want to kill me 是主谓宾结构。

⑦ 第二段第三句 And the airline folks 是一个省略结构，直接翻译为"航空公司的人呢？"。最后一句 They're laughing 是主谓结构。

第四步 翻译来了

"我希望所有航空公司都能取消座椅向后倾斜功能,"来自亚利桑那州皮奥里亚的退休空军巡视员、百万英里飞行记录保持者拉里·希克森(Larry Hickerson)说,"既然飞机座舱内的间距极为紧张,那么,座椅后倾的功能会让大家很难堪。"

现在,大约有一半读此专栏的人可能想用我的名字给他们第一个出生的孩子命名,而另一半却想杀了我。航空公司的人呢?他们正在笑呢。

本句考点总结

第一,本句考查了英文直接引语的译法,最简单的译法就是保留冒号和双引号,说话人的位置和说话的内容都保持不变。即说话人在什么位置,就放在什么位置翻译,当然,说话人放在句首也是可以接受的。

第二,英文人名的翻译,这里采用的是音译法,注意名和姓之间要加·,英文的人名不确定如何翻译时,可以使用音译法,然后把英文人名抄下来,放在括号里,这样保险一些。

第三,本句考查了英文同位语的译法。同位语是两个前后相互说明的名词或名词短语,比如 Beijing, the capital of China,有两种译法,第一种是"并列译法",翻译为"中国的首都北京",第二种是"主谓译法",翻译为"北京是中国的首都"。具体用哪一种,可以根据句子具体情况而定,有时两种都是可以使用的。

第四,本句出现了分词或是分词短语位于名词后的译法。一般来说,分词或是分词短语位于名词后相当于定语或定语从句,定语按照"短前长后"的译法来进行翻译。

9

The airline industry loves the seat reclining argument because it divides us. And while we're arguing about 2 inches of personal space, they're busy collecting more money from passengers and slowly — ever so slowly — removing even more room. This debate is the perfect distraction.

Whether you think reclining your airline seat is wrong or not, let's agree on one thing: Greedy airlines got us to this point. Fighting over the scraps of space won't fix it. If we ever needed thoughtful government regulation, maybe it is now.

第一步 词汇解析

1. remove,动词,表示"去除、去掉",比如:The news removed any doubts about the company's future. (这个消息消除了一切有关公司未来的疑虑。)
2. distraction,名词,表示"分散注意力",比如:Total concentration is required with no distractions. (要全神贯注,不能有丝毫分神。)
3. greedy,形容词,表示"贪婪的、贪心的",比如:Genesis recorded a song which took a swipe at greedy property developers who bought up and demolished people's homes. (吉妮西丝录制了一首歌来抨击那些买下并毁坏人们家园的贪婪的房地产开发商。)

④ scrap，名词，表示"丝毫、一丁点"，比如：There's not a scrap of evidence to support his claim.（没有丝毫证据支持他的说法。）

⑤ thoughtful，形容词，表示"体贴的；思考的"，比如：Nancy, who had been thoughtful for some time, suddenly spoke.（南希沉思了一会儿，突然开口说话了。）

⑥ regulation，名词，表示"章程、规章制度、规则、法规"，比如：The new regulations will be of benefit to everyone concerned.（新规章将使所有有关人员受益。）

第二步 注意断句

The airline industry loves the seat reclining argument /because it divides us. /And while we're arguing about 2 inches of personal space, /they're busy collecting more money from passengers /and slowly — ever so slowly — removing even more room. /This debate is the perfect distraction.

Whether you think /reclining your airline seat is wrong or not, /let's agree on one thing: /Greedy airlines got us to this point. /Fighting over the scraps of space won't fix it. /If we ever needed thoughtful government regulation, / maybe it is now.

第三步 句型解析

① 第一段第一句中，The airline industry loves the seat reclining argument 是主句，是主谓宾结构，because 引导原因状语从句，it divides us 是主谓宾结构。

② 第一段第二句中，And 是并列连词，while 引导时间状语从句，we're arguing about 2 inches of personal space 是主谓宾结构；they're busy collecting more money from passengers 是主句，是主谓宾状结构，句式结构较为简单；and 是并列连词，slowly — ever so slowly — 是状语，这里的破折号可以保留；removing even more room 和前面的 collecting... 是并列结构。

③ 第一段第三句 This debate is the perfect distraction 是主系表结构。

④ 第二段第一句中，Whether 引导了状语从句，you think 是主谓结构，后面接宾语从句，reclining your airline seat is wrong or not 是主系表结构；let's agree on one thing 是祈使句，后面的冒号可以保留，冒号之后的句子 Greedy airlines got us to this point 是主谓宾状结构。

⑤ 第二段第二句中，Fighting over the scraps of space 是主语，won't fix it 是谓语和宾语，这里的 it 指的是"座椅向后倾斜"这件事。

⑥ 第二段第三句中，If 引导了条件状语从句，we ever needed thoughtful government regulation 是主谓宾结构，maybe it is now 是主句。这句话要特别注意从句的翻译，翻译为"如果我们需要贴心的政府监管的话"并不是特别合适，这里可以把"贴心"加上双引号，让大家更容易理解。

第四步 翻译来了

航空业喜欢这种关于座椅向后倾斜的争论，因为这能让我们产生分歧。我们在争论两英寸的个人空间时，他们正忙着从乘客那里赚更多的钱，并慢慢地——而且是非常缓慢地——夺走更多的空间，因为这场辩论完全分散了人们的注意力。

不管你认为把座椅向后倾斜是对还是错，我们可以在一点上达成共识：是贪婪的航空公司让我们走到了这一步。争夺狭小的座舱空间解决不了问题。如果我们需要"贴心"的政府监管的话，也许现在正是个好时机。

> How to deal with a seat recliner?
> Reclining an airline seat is still allowed on most domestic flights. Here's how to deal with someone who leans into your airspace.
> Ask them to lean forward. Timing and tone are important here. The moment someone leans back, gently tap the person on the shoulder and politely ask them if it would be possible not to recline their seat. Be. Extra. Nice.

第一步 词汇解析

❶ lean，动词，表示"倾斜、倚靠"，比如：Can I lean my bike against the wall?（我能把自行车靠在这墙上吗？）
❷ tone，名词，表示"语气、口气、腔调、口吻"，比如：His voice took on a more serious tone.（他说话的语气变得严肃起来。）
❸ tap，动词，表示"轻敲、轻拍"，比如：I tapped her on her shoulder.（我轻轻地拍了拍她的肩膀。）

第二步 注意断句

How to deal with a seat recliner?
Reclining an airline seat is still allowed on most domestic flights. /Here's how to deal with someone /who leans into your airspace.
Ask them to lean forward. /Timing and tone are important here. /The moment someone leans back, /gently tap the person on the shoulder /and politely ask them /if it would be possible not to recline their seat. /Be. Extra. Nice.

第三步 句型解析

❶ 第一段是 How 引导的不定式结构，这里的谓语 deal with 理解为"应对、对付"。
❷ 第二段第一句 Reclining an airline seat is still allowed on most domestic flights 使用了被动语态，可以用各种译法来处理，译文使用了"有'被'不用'被'"的译法，并且把后面的地点状语置于句首。
❸ 第二段第二句 Here's how to deal with someone who leans into your airspace 是倒装结构，原本的结构应该是 How to deal with someone who leans into your airspace is here，本句中还出现了 who 引导的定语从句，从句较短，可以采用前置译法。
❹ 第三段第一句 Ask them to lean forward 是祈使句，句式结构较为简单，可以直接翻译。
❺ 第三段第二句 Timing and tone are important here 是主系表结构，句式结构较为简单，可以直接翻译。
❻ 第三段第三句中，The moment 引导了时间状语从句，someone leans back 是主谓结构；主句是两个并列的祈使句，第一句 gently tap the person on the shoulder 后接 and，第二句是 politely ask them；if 引导宾语从句，it would be possible not to recline their seat 是 it 作形式主语的句型，not to recline their seat 才是真正的主语，所以翻译时注意语序，若按原本的语序翻译是通顺的，也可以直接翻译。
❼ 第三段第四句 Be. Extra. Nice. 是最有意思的。这部分每个单词的首字母是大写，后面都有句号，这是一种表示强调的方法，那么翻译成中文我们该怎么办呢？看看译文是怎么处理的哦！

第四步 翻译来了

那么，如何应对这些座椅向后倾斜的人呢？
大多数国内航班仍然允许椅背后倾。下面告诉你如何应对座椅后倾靠近你座舱的人。

首先，让他们身体前倾。提醒的时机和说话的语气在这里很重要。当有人靠在椅背上时，轻轻地拍一下那个人的肩膀，有礼貌地问他们是否可以不把座位向后倾斜。记住：要格外地友好！！！

> **本句考点总结**
>
> 第一，本句出现了被动语态的译法。被动语态是英文常见的一种形式，而在中文里常常少用"被"或者不用"被"。那么我们一般有什么样的译法呢？第一种是被动变主动，第二种是寻找替代词（比如："让……给""为……所"等结构），第三种是在科技文献中用"可以"来替代"被"，第四种是有"被"不用"被"。以上四种怎么用，那就看句子怎么通顺怎么翻译了啊！
>
> 第二，本句出现了英文定语从句的译法。一般来说，定语从句按照"短前长后"的译法处理，较短的定语从句可以前置，较长的定语从句可以后置，这一切都取决于句子的通顺，并没有绝对的前置和后置译法。

11

Get a flight attendant involved. Some leaners are clever and wait for you to go to the restroom before leaning. Then they feign sleep, which makes you reluctant to bother them. Oldest trick in the book. You can always ask a flight attendant for help.

Move airplane seats. If you see another open seat in your class of service, feel free to move, as long as the seat belt sign isn't illuminated. You might also want to ask a flight attendant for permission. As a reminder, the seats in front of the exit row don't recline. So usually, an exit row seat means you'll keep your legroom. And maybe, your sanity.

第一步 词汇解析

❶ feign，动词，表示"假装、装作、佯装"，比如：One morning, I didn't want to go to school, and decided to feign illness.（有天早晨我不想上学，于是决定装病。）

❷ reluctant，形容词，表示"不情愿的、勉强的"，比如：She was reluctant to admit she was wrong.（她不愿承认自己有错。）

❸ bother，动词，表示"打扰"，比如：Sorry to bother you, but there's a call for you on line two.（很抱歉打扰你一下，二号线有你的电话。）

❹ trick，名词，表示"诡计、花招"，比如：The kids are always playing tricks on their teacher.（孩子们经常耍些花招戏弄老师。）

❺ seat belt，名词词组，表示"（汽车或飞机上的）安全带"，比如：Children must use an approved child restraint or adult seat belt.（儿童必须使用经过认可的儿童安全带或成人座椅安全带。）

❻ illuminate，动词，表示"照明、照亮、照射"，比如：No streetlights illuminated the street.（这条街上没有照明的路灯。）

❼ permission，名词，表示"准许、许可、批准"，比如：You are not to leave your station without permission.

（未经允许，不得离开岗位。）

⑧ reminder，名词，表示"提醒、提示"，比如：These findings are a reminder that low pay is the other side of the coin of falling unemployment.（这些研究结果提醒人们，失业率下降的另一面是低薪。）

⑨ exit row，名词词组，表示"紧急出口"，比如：Can I sit in an exit row?（我可以坐紧急出口的那排座位吗？）

⑩ sanity，名词，表示"明智、理智、通情达理"，比如：His behavior was so strange that I began to doubt his sanity.（他行为怪异，我有点怀疑他是否神智正常。）

第二步 注意断句

Get a flight attendant involved. /Some leaners are clever /and wait for you to go to the restroom /before leaning. /Then they feign sleep, /which makes you reluctant to bother them. /Oldest trick in the book. /You can always ask a flight attendant for help.

Move airplane seats. /If you see another open seat /in your class of service, /feel free to move, /as long as the seat belt sign isn't illuminated. /You might also want to ask a flight attendant for permission. /As a reminder, /the seats in front of the exit row don't recline. /So usually, /an exit row seat means /you'll keep your legroom. /And maybe, /your sanity.

第三步 句型解析

① 第一段第一句 Get a flight attendant involved 是祈使句，这里的 get sb. involved 表示"让某人涉入"，但是这么翻译非常不通顺，翻译为"找某人帮忙"更好。

② 第一段第二句中，Some leaners are clever 是主系表结构，and 是并列连词，wait for you to go to the restroom 是谓宾状结构，before leaning 是时间状语。

③ 第一段第三句中，Then they feign sleep 是主谓宾结构，后面是 which 引导的非限定性定语从句，这里的 which 理解为"以上这件事"。

④ 第一段第四句不能算是句子，准确地说，这是省略句，其完整结构是 It is the oldest trick in the book，所以翻译时需要将主谓补全。

⑤ 第一段第五句 You can always ask a flight attendant for help 是主谓宾宾结构，这里要注意 ask sb. for help 结构。

⑥ 第二段第一句 Move airplane seats 是祈使句，可以直接翻译。

⑦ 第二段第二句中，If 引导了条件状语从句，you see another open seat 是主谓宾结构，in your class of service 是地点状语；feel free to move 是祈使句作主句；as long as 引导条件状语从句，the seat belt sign isn't illuminated 中的 illuminated 不要理解为"被点亮的"，理解为"亮了"即可。

⑧ 第二段第三句 You might also want to ask a flight attendant for permission 是主谓宾宾结构，注意这里的 ask sb. for permission 表示"征得某人的同意 / 允许"。

⑨ 第二段第四句中，As a reminder 是句首的状语，the seats in front of the exit row don't recline 是主谓结构。

⑩ 第二段第五句中，So usually 分别是连词和副词，an exit row seat means 是主谓结构，后面接宾语从句 you'll keep your legroom。后面一句 And maybe, your sanity 是省略句，完整结构是 And maybe, you'll keep your sanity。这句比较难理解，什么是"保持你的理智呢"，坐过飞机的小伙伴一定知道，紧急出口那里很危险，万一有突发状况，是需要配合空乘人员逃难的，所以"你要保持理智"，明白了吗？

第四步 翻译来了

其次，可以找一位空乘人员帮忙。有些将座椅向后倾斜的人很聪明，他们会等你去洗手间后再调整座位,然后他们假装睡觉,这就让你不愿打扰他们。这是老掉牙的伎俩,但是,你可以随时向空乘人员寻求帮助。

最后,你可以调换飞机座椅。如果在你的座舱看到另一个空座位,只要安全带指示灯没有亮起就可以随意移动。当然,你可能还需要征得空乘人员的同意。提醒一下,紧急出口处的座位不能倾斜。所以通常情况下,坐紧急出口处的座位就意味着你可以拥有宽敞的腿部摆放空间,也许,你还得保持理智。

> **本句考点总结**
>
> 本句出现了英文定语从句的译法。一般来说,定语从句按照"短前长后"的译法处理,较短的定语从句可以前置,较长的定语从句可以后置,这一切都取决于句子的通顺,并没有绝对的前置和后置译法。

这篇文章是典型的外刊文章,总体难度是这几年考试中相对来说较小的,但是如果大家没有坐飞机的经历,那么这个问题就不容易理解,所以这时了解文章的背景知识就显得尤为重要了。本文所出现的短句较多,注意句与句之间的合译,总体来说翻译方法使用得并不是特别明显,但是文章长,一定要控制翻译的时间,这样才能完美通过考试。

第四节 2021年下半年三级笔译汉译英

原文(请先通读全文)

当前,新冠疫情仍在全球蔓延,世界经济依然面临衰退风险。我们将坚持团结互助,与各国携手最终战胜新冠疫情。当前,疫苗是抵御疫情的关键。中国反对"疫苗民族主义",疫苗应成为全球公共产品。

中国迄今已向全球160多个国家和国际组织提供了抗疫物资援助,正在以不同方式向100多个国家和国际组织提供急需的疫苗,为全球疫情防控提供了强大助力。

接下来,中国将继续充分发挥自身优势,维护全球抗疫物资供应链稳定,将继续积极开展人道主义援助,向有需要的国家提供支持,将继续坚定秉持疫苗公共产品的"第一属性",让更多发展中国家用得起、用得上安全可靠的疫苗。

我们将坚持开放合作,与各国携手推动世界经济复苏。我们已顺利开启"十四五"规划,加快建设更高水平开放型经济新体制。

一个全面迈向高质量发展的中国,将更充分发掘自身超大市场潜力,为各国带来新的发展机遇。而一个持续扩大对外开放的中国,将进一步深化与各国互利合作,为世界经济复苏注入更多动力。

全人类是一个整体,生命与健康,生存与发展,是各国人民都应享有的平等权利。中国,将继续高举人类命运共同体旗帜,坚持共商共建共享原则,积极践行真正的多边主义,捍卫以《联合国宪章》为基础的国际秩序，持续完善全球治理体系，建设人类卫生健康共同体，与各国一道维护世界和平稳定，弥合人类发展鸿沟，共同开创更加美好的未来。

2021年下半年CATTI三级笔译考试汉译英部分的文章的主题和新冠疫情相关，出自王毅在外交部湖北全球特别推介活动上的致辞，参考译文来自外交部翻译室。这个题材在现在各类型的考试中都非常重要，所以希望大家把这类文章中的重点词汇全部记忆和背诵下来，这样在考试时就省去了查词典的烦恼。本文符合政工类文章的特点，句式不难，只要单词和词组的翻译基本不出错，那么整篇文章的翻译也就没有什么问题了！

当前，新冠疫情仍在全球蔓延，世界经济依然面临衰退风险。我们将坚持团结互助，与各国携手最终战胜新冠疫情。当前，疫苗是抵御疫情的关键。中国反对"疫苗民族主义"，疫苗应成为全球公共产品。

第一步 词汇解析

① 新冠疫情，COVID-19/coronavirus，专有名词。"新冠疫情"目前有多种译法，无论哪一种，写对即可。

② 蔓延，rage，动词，比如：Forest fires were raging out of control.（森林大火迅速蔓延，失去了控制。）rage表示"蔓延"时，常指疾病或火焰等；表示"猛烈地继续、激烈进行"时，常指暴风雨、战斗、争论等。

③ 面临，grapple with，动词词组，比如：The new government has yet to grapple with the problem of air pollution.（新政府尚未解决空气污染问题。）grapple与人搭配，表示"扭打、搏斗"，比如：They managed to grapple him to the ground.（他们终于把他摔倒在地。）

④ 衰退风险，the risk of a recession，名词词组，比如：And if house prices continue to fall, the risk of a recession will grow.（并且如果房价继续下跌，经济下滑的危险将会加大。）
经济衰退、经济萎缩，recession，名词，比如：The economy is in deep recession.（经济正处于严重的衰退之中。）

⑤ 坚持，uphold，动词，比如：In our international engagement, we will uphold principles, promote justice and practice equality.（在国际交往中，我们将坚持原则、伸张正义、践行平等。）
uphold的过去式和过去分词都是upheld。

⑥ 团结互助，solidarity and mutual assistance，名词词组。
团结，solidarity，名词，比如：community solidarity（社会团结）。
互助，mutual assistance，名词词组，比如：We should strengthen mutual assistance and deepen strategic cooperation.（我们要守望相助，深化战略合作。）

⑦ 战胜，prevail over，动词词组，比如：Justice will prevail over tyranny.（正义必将战胜暴虐。）
prevail常见词组：
1）与in连用，表示"盛行、流行"。
2）与on连用，表示"劝说"。

⑧ 疫苗，vaccine，名词，比如：There is no vaccine against HIV infection.（现在还没有预防艾滋病病毒传染的疫苗。）vaccine在计算机领域还可表示"杀毒软件"。

⑨ 是……的关键，hold the key，动词词组，比如：It may hold the key to our survival.（这可能是我们生存的关键。）
⑩ "疫苗民族主义"，"vaccine nationalism"，名词词组。
民族主义，nationalism，名词，比如：I think we'd better leave the subject of nationalism.（我想我们最好不要再谈论民族主义这个话题了。）
词汇小常识：
-ism 是英文中常见的后缀，其常见意思之一是"……主义""风格、语言上的特点""……学"。
⑪ 全球公共产品，a global public good，名词词组，比如：Reserve currency status is a global public good.（储备货币是一种全球公共商品。）

第二步 动词定位

当前，新冠疫情仍在全球蔓延，世界经济依然面临衰退风险。我们将坚持团结互助，与各国携手最终战胜新冠疫情。当前，疫苗是抵御疫情的关键。中国反对"疫苗民族主义"，疫苗应成为全球公共产品。

第三步 句型解析

❶ 第一句中，"当前"是时间状语，"新冠疫情"是本句的主语，"仍在全球蔓延"是谓语和地点状语，这里译文的时态用一般现在时或现在进行时都可以。译文中句首使用了 As we speak 是因为上下文，考试时可以不用这个结构。"世界经济"是主语，"面临"是谓语，"衰退风险"是宾语，这里译文的时态用一般现在时或现在进行时，这两句之间可以用 and 连接，表示并列。译文中的核心谓语"蔓延"翻译为 rage，"面临"翻译为 grapple with，个人认为比较难，考试时翻译得简单一点就好！
❷ 第二句中，"我们"是主语，"将坚持"是典型的一般将来时，"团结互助"是宾语，表示"团结和互助"；"携手"是谓语，"与各国"是状语，"最终战胜"是目的状语，"新冠疫情"是不定式中动词的宾语。这两个分句之间可以使用 and 或类似 as 这样的词连接。
❸ 第三句中，"当前"是时间状语，"疫苗"是主语，"是"是核心谓语，"抵御疫情的关键"是宾语，句式较为简单，可以直接翻译。
❹ 第四句中，"中国"是主语，"反对"是谓语，"疫苗民族主义"是宾语，这里的双引号在译文中依旧保留；第二个分句中，"疫苗"是主语，"应成为"是谓语，"全球公共产品"是宾语，注意句与句之间的连接，使用连词 and 连接较为恰当。

第四步 翻译来了

As we speak, COVID-19 is still raging in the world and the world economy is still grappling with the risk of a recession. We will uphold solidarity and mutual assistance as we work with other countries to prevail over the coronavirus. Vaccines hold the key in the battle against COVID-19. China opposes "vaccine nationalism" and believes that vaccines must be made a global public good.

本句考点总结

中英文的巨大差异在于中文是意合式语言，英文是形合式语言。中文的句子之间不用连词连接，而英文的句子之间必须使用连词，所以，我们在做汉译英时，要去体会和理解每个逗号前后句子之间的关系，到底是并列、转折、让步、因果、条件，还是别的什么关系，然后选择合适的连词进行连接，形成一个英文句子。始终要牢记一点：英文的两个句子之间必须要有连词连接。

中国迄今已向全球 160 多个国家和国际组织提供了抗疫物资援助，正在以不同方式向 100 多个国家和国际组织提供急需的疫苗，为全球疫情防控提供了强大助力。

第一步 词汇解析

❶ 提供……抗疫物资援助，donate supplies to，动词词组。
捐赠，donate，动词，比如：He frequently donates large sums to charity.（他经常向慈善机构大笔捐款。）
补给品，supply，名词，比如：What happens when food and petrol supplies run low?（食物和汽油这些补给品减少时会发生什么呢？）

❷ 以不同方式，by various means，介词词组，比如：In the urban area, people can kill time at night by various means.（在市区，人们可以以各种方式消磨晚间时光。）
方法、手段，means，名词，比如：The move is a means to fight crime.（这个行动是打击犯罪的一种手段。）

❸ 急需的，in urgent need，介词词组，比如：The earthquake victims are in urgent need of medical supplies.（地震灾民迫切需要医疗品。）
需要，in need，介词词组，比如：The building was in need of repair.（这座大楼需要维修了。）

❹ 为……提供了强大助力，give a strong boost to，动词词组。
帮助、激励，boost，名词，比如：Winning the competition was a wonderful boost for her morale.（赢得了那场比赛使她士气大振。）

❺ 全球疫情防控，the global COVID response，名词词组。这里的"疫情防控"指的就是"应对新冠肺炎"。

第二步 动词定位

中国迄今已向全球 160 多个国家和国际组织提供了抗疫物资援助，正在以不同方式向 100 多个国家和国际组织提供急需的疫苗，为全球疫情防控提供了强大助力。

第三步 句型解析

❶ 本句的主语是"中国"，"迄今"是时间状语，翻译为 so far 完全可以，要用现在完成时也是可以的；"已向全球 160 多个国家和国际组织"是双宾语中的间接宾语，"提供了"是核心动词，"抗疫物资援助"是直接宾语，核心动词在翻译时选择了 donate 这个动词。

❷ 第二个分句中，"正在"是现在进行时态的标志，这个分句与前一个分句之间可以用并列连词 and 连接；"以不同方式"是典型的方式状语，"向 100 多个国家和国际组织"是双宾语中的间接宾语，"提供"是核心动词，译文使用了 provide，"急需的疫苗"是直接宾语。第三个分句可以用伴随结构进行翻译，"为全球疫情防控"是状语，"提供了"是核心动词，译文使用了 give，"强大助力"是宾语。

第四步 翻译来了

We have donated supplies to over 160 countries and international organizations and are providing, by various means, vaccines to over 100 countries and international organizations in urgent need, thus giving a strong boost to the global COVID response.

> **本句考点总结**
>
> 第一，中英文的巨大差异在于中文是意合式语言，英文是形合式语言。中文的句子之间不用连词连接，而英文的句子之间必须使用连词，所以，我们在做汉译英时，要去体会和理解每个逗号前后句子之间的关系，到底是并列、转折、让步、因果、条件，还是别的什么关系，然后选择合适的连词进行连接，形成一个英文句子。始终要牢记一点：英文的两个句子之间必须要有连词连接。
>
> 第二，汉译英句子中并列、伴随、下沉的结构。中文常常会出现多个句子聚集的情况，那么我们在翻译时需要考虑将这些句子进行"分堆"，但是"分堆"之后，一个句子中也可能会出现两个动词或两组动词，那么有两个动词或两组动词的句子我们该如何进行翻译呢？比如："我坐在那里看书"，这里有两个动词，一个是"坐"，一个是"看"，我们翻译时便会有三种方法：
>
> 第一种并列（两个动词并列的译法，使用并列连词连接，两个动词之间不一定是"并列"关系）：I sat there and read a book.
>
> 第二种伴随（将第二个动词翻译为二谓语，分词、从句、状语等都可以）：I sat there reading a book.
>
> 第三种下沉（将第一个动词翻译为二谓语，分词、从句、状语等都可以）：Sitting there, I read a book.
>
> 需要说明的是，并列、伴随和下沉只是动词的形式问题，不代表动词之间的逻辑关系，用这三种形式翻译两个动词或两组动词都是可以的，大家可以根据句子上下文的关系来判断使用。

3 接下来，中国将继续充分发挥自身优势，维护全球抗疫物资供应链稳定，将继续积极开展人道主义援助，向有需要的国家提供支持，将继续坚定秉持疫苗公共产品的"第一属性"，让更多发展中国家用得起、用得上安全可靠的疫苗。

第一步 词汇解析

❶ 充分发挥自身优势，fully harness its strengths，动词词组。

利用，harness，动词，比如：We must harness the skill and creativity of our workforce.（我们必须尽量发挥全体职工的技能和创造力。）harness 强调利用或控制以产生能量。

优势、优点，strength，名词，常用复数形式，比如：The ability to keep calm is one of her many strengths.（能够保持冷静是她的多项长处之一。）

❷ 供应链，supply chain，名词词组，比如：Global supply chains have shown weak links.（全球供应链已显示出薄弱环节。）

❸ 人道主义援助，humanitarian assistance，名词词组，比如：We will be providing both civilian and military disaster relief and humanitarian assistance.（我们将调动军事和民间力量，提供救灾及人道援助。）

人道主义的，humanitarian，形容词，比如：humanitarian issues（人道主义问题）。

帮助、援助，assistance，名词，比如：She offered me practical assistance with my research.（她给我的研究提供了实实在在的援助。）

文化小常识：

人道主义援助是基于人道主义而对受助者作出物资上或物流上的支援，主要目的是拯救生命，舒缓不幸状况，以及维护人类尊严。

④ 坚定秉持……，stay committed to，动词词组，比如：The EU will stay committed to its integration process.（欧盟将继续致力于推进一体化建设。）"坚定秉持……"还可翻译为 be committed to。

⑤ "第一属性"，above anything else，介词词组，比如：His hard life taught him to value his family above anything else.（他艰苦的生活教他将珍视自己的家庭放在第一位。）这里的"第一属性"指的就是"比其他任何事情都重要"。

⑥ 用得起、用得上，can be affordable and accessible to，动词词组。这里的"用得起、用得上"指的就是"可以负担得起，也可以接触到……"。

支付得起的，affordable，形容词，比如：the availability of affordable housing（支付得起的房产的供应）。
（物品）易于接近的，accessible，形容词，比如：The center is easily accessible to the general public.（该中心对于广大公众来讲很便利。）

⑦ 安全可靠的，safe and effective，形容词词组，比如：The data confirm that this product is safe and effective.（数据证实此产品安全可靠。）

第二步　动词定位

接下来，中国将继续充分发挥自身优势，维护全球抗疫物资供应链稳定，将继续积极开展人道主义援助，向有需要的国家提供支持，将继续坚定秉持疫苗公共产品的"第一属性"，让更多发展中国家用得起、用得上安全可靠的疫苗。

第三步　句型解析

① 第一个分句中，"接下来"是时间状语，可以翻译，也可以不翻译，后面的"继续"可以表示相同含义；"中国"是主语，"将继续充分发挥"是核心谓语，译文使用了 continue to fully harness，宾语是"自身优势"，后面的动词"维护"则是二谓语，也是目的状语；"全球抗疫物资供应链"是动词的宾语，"稳定"是宾语补足语。

② 第二个分句中，"将继续积极开展"是核心谓语，本句缺少主语，因此译文中增加"我们"或"中国"；"人道主义援助"是宾语，后面的"提供支持"是并列的核心谓语，"向有需要的国家"是状语。注意这两句中的两个动词采用了并列译法，前一句中的两个动词采用了伴随译法。

③ 第三个分句中，"将继续坚定秉持"是核心谓语，本句也缺少主语，因此译文中增加"我们"或"中国"；"疫苗公共产品的'第一属性'"是宾语；后面的句子值得琢磨，前面的"继续坚定秉持"导致了"更多发展中国家用得起、用得上安全可靠的疫苗"，所以两句之间的逻辑关系是因果关系，译文使用的 so that 非常合适。译文将"安全可靠的疫苗"作为主语，can be affordable and accessible to 作为核心谓语，"更多发展中国家"作为宾语。

④ 注意三句之间的关系，在翻译时前两个句子之间使用了分号，第二句和第三句之间使用了分号和 and 的结构，这就是中英文之间意合和形合的差异。

第四步　翻译来了

China will continue to fully harness its strengths to keep the global supply chains for COVID supplies stable; China will continue to provide humanitarian assistance and support countries in need; and China will stay committed to making COVID vaccines a public good above anything else so that safe and effective vaccines can be affordable and accessible to more developing countries.

> **本句考点总结**
>
> 　　第一，汉译英句子中并列、伴随、下沉的结构。中文常常会出现多个句子聚集的情况，那么我们在翻译时需要考虑将这些句子进行"分堆"，但是"分堆"之后，一个句子中也可能会出现两个动词或两组动词，那么有两个动词或两组动词的句子我们该如何进行翻译呢？比如："我坐在那里看书"，这里有两个动词，一个是"坐"，一个是"看"，我们翻译时便会有三种方法：
> 　　第一种并列（两个动词并列的译法，使用并列连词连接，两个动词之间不一定是"并列"关系）：I sat there and read a book.
> 　　第二种伴随（将第二个动词翻译为二谓语，分词、从句、状语等都可以）：I sat there reading a book.
> 　　第三种下沉（将第一个动词翻译为二谓语，分词、从句、状语等都可以）：Siting there, I read a book.
> 　　需要说明的是，并列、伴随和下沉只是动词的形式问题，不代表动词之间的逻辑关系，用这三种形式翻译两个动词或两组动词都是可以的，大家可以根据句子上下文的关系来判断使用。
> 　　第二，中英文的巨大差异在于中文是意合式语言，英文是形合式语言。中文的句子之间不用连词连接，而英文的句子之间必须使用连词，所以，我们在做汉译英时，要去体会和理解每个逗号前后句子之间的关系，到底是并列、转折、让步、因果、条件，还是别的什么关系，然后选择合适的连词进行连接，形成一个英文句子。始终要牢记一点：英文的两个句子之间必须要有连词连接。

4 我们将坚持开放合作，与各国携手推动世界经济复苏。我们已顺利开启"十四五"规划，加快建设更高水平开放型经济新体制。

第一步　词汇解析

❶ 开放合作，openness and cooperation，名词词组。
　开放，openness，名词，比如：Yet this is a government which proclaims that it is all in favor of openness.（而这是一个宣称全力支持开放的政府。）书写的时候，需要注意 openness 由 open 和 ness 名词后缀构成，所以中间需要写两个 n。

❷ 世界经济复苏，world economic recovery，名词词组，比如：sluggish world economic recovery（世界经济复苏低迷）。
　recover 常见词组：recover from，表示"从……中恢复、痊愈"。

❸ 顺利开启，make a good start，动词词组。

❹ （实施）"十四五"规划，implement the 14th Five-Year Plan，动词词组。
　文化小常识：
　　2020 年 7 月 30 日，中共中央政治局召开会议，决定 2020 年 10 月在北京召开中国共产党第十九届中央委员会第五次全体会议，研究关于制定国民经济和社会发展第十四个五年规划。

执行、实施，implement，动词，比如：The government promised to implement a new system to control financial loan institutions.（政府许诺要实施新的制度来控制金融贷款机构。）

"十四五"规划，the 14th Five-Year Plan，专有名词。

❺ 更高水平开放型经济新体制，new systems for a higher-standard open economy，名词词组。

第二步 动词定位

我们将<u>坚持</u>开放合作，与各国<u>携手推动</u>世界经济复苏。我们已顺利<u>开启</u>"十四五"规划，加快<u>建设</u>更高水平开放型经济新体制。

第三步 句型解析

❶ 本句中，"我们"是主语，"将坚持"是谓语，"开放合作"是宾语；第二个分句中，"与各国"是状语，"携手"是核心谓语，"推动"是二谓语，也是目的状语，"世界经济复苏"是动词的宾语。

❷ 第二句中，"我们"是主语，"已顺利开启"是谓语，"'十四五'规划"是宾语；第二个分句中，核心谓语是"加快建设"，其中"加快"是状语，翻译为 at a fast pace，"更高水平开放型经济新体制"是宾语。

❸ 特别强调，第一句中的两个动词是核心动词和二谓语的关系，第二句中的两个动词是并列关系。大家要特别注意一句话中两个动词之间的关系。

第四步 翻译来了

We will uphold openness and cooperation as we work with other countries to promote world economic recovery. We have made a good start in implementing the 14th Five-Year Plan, and are developing new systems for a higher-standard open economy at a faster pace.

本句考点总结

汉译英句子中并列、伴随、下沉的结构。中文常常会出现多个句子聚集的情况，那么我们在翻译时需要考虑将这些句子进行"分堆"，但是"分堆"之后，一个句子中也可能会出现两个动词或两组动词，那么有两个动词或两组动词的句子我们该如何进行翻译呢？比如："我坐在那里看书"，这里有两个动词，一个是"坐"，一个是"看"，我们翻译时便会有三种方法：

第一种并列（两个动词并列的译法，使用并列连词连接，两个动词之间不一定是"并列"关系）：I sat there and read a book.

第二种伴随（将第二个动词翻译为二谓语，分词、从句、状语等都可以）：I sat there reading a book.

第三种下沉（将第一个动词翻译为二谓语，分词、从句、状语等都可以）：Sitting there, I read a book.

需要说明的是，并列、伴随和下沉只是动词的形式问题，不代表动词之间的逻辑关系，用这三种形式翻译两个动词或两组动词都是可以的，大家可以根据句子上下文的关系来判断使用。

5

一个全面迈向高质量发展的中国，将更充分发掘自身超大市场潜力，为各国带来新的发展机遇。而一个持续扩大对外开放的中国，将进一步深化与各国互利合作，为世界经济复苏注入更多动力。

第一步 词汇解析

① 迈向，pursue，动词，比如：He will pursue a trade policy that protects American workers.（他将努力实行保护美国工人的贸易政策。）"迈向"还可以翻译为 seek/aspire 等词。

② 充分发掘自身超大市场潜力，further unleash the potential of its huge market，动词词组。
释放，unleash，动词，比如：The announcement unleashed a storm of protest from the public.（公告引发了一场公众的抗议风暴。）
潜力、潜质，potential，名词，比如：All children should be encouraged to realize their full potential.（应当鼓励所有的儿童充分发挥他们的潜能。）potential 的常见词性之一为形容词。

③ 互利合作，mutually beneficial cooperation，名词词组。
有利的、有裨益的，beneficial，形容词，比如：A good diet is beneficial to health.（良好的饮食有益于健康。）同义词为 advantageous/favorable。

④ 为……注入更多动力，inject more impetus to，动词词组。
注入、增添，inject，动词，比如：She kept trying to inject a little fun into their relationship.（她一直设法给他们的关系增添一点情趣。）inject 常用来表示"注射药物或液体"，比如：Chemicals are injected into the fruit to reduce decay.（水果注入了化学品以防腐坏。）
动力，impetus，名词，比如：His articles provided the main impetus for change.（他的那些文章是促进变革的主要推动力。）

第二步 动词定位

一个全面<u>迈向</u>高质量发展的中国，将更充分<u>发掘</u>自身超大市场潜力，为各国<u>带来</u>新的发展机遇。而一个持续<u>扩大</u>对外开放的中国，将进一步<u>深化</u>与各国互利合作，为世界经济复苏<u>注入</u>更多动力。

第三步 句型解析

① 第一句中，"一个全面迈向高质量发展的中国"是主语，主语中有定语，可以翻译为定语从句，也可以翻译为分词短语，译文处理为 a country pursuing high-quality development 非常合适。主句的主语为"中国"，谓语是"将更充分发掘"，这里是典型的一般将来时，"自身超大市场潜力"是宾语，动词"带来"是二谓语，也是目的状语，动词宾语为"新的发展机遇"，"为各国"是状语。

② 第二句和第一句相似，"而一个持续扩大对外开放的中国"是主语，主语中有定语，可以翻译为定语从句，也可以翻译为分词短语，译文处理为 a country in the process of further opening up。主句的主语为"中国"，谓语是"将进一步深化"，"与各国"是状语，"互利合作"是宾语，动词"注入"是二谓语，也是目的状语，动词的宾语是"更多动力"，"为世界经济复苏"是状语。

③ 本段的两句是相同的结构，都使用了分词短语作定语的译法，主语为"中国"，后接不定式作目的状语，请大家认真体会。

第四步 翻译来了

As a country pursuing high-quality development, China will further unleash the potential of its huge market to bring new development opportunities to all countries. As a country in the process of further opening up, China will deepen mutually beneficial cooperation with other countries to inject more impetus to world economic recovery.

本句考点总结

汉译英句子中并列、伴随、下沉的结构。中文常常会出现多个句子聚集的情况，那么我们在翻译时需要考虑将这些句子进行"分堆"，但是"分堆"之后，一个句子中也可能会出现两个动词或两组动词，那么有两个动词或两组动词的句子我们该如何进行翻译呢？比如："我坐在那里看书"，这里有两个动词，一个是"坐"，一个是"看"，我们翻译时便会有三种方法：

第一种并列（两个动词并列的译法，使用并列连词连接，两个动词之间不一定是"并列"关系）：I sat there and read a book.

第二种伴随（将第二个动词翻译为二谓语，分词、从句、状语等都可以）：I sat there reading a book.

第三种下沉（将第一个动词翻译为二谓语，分词、从句、状语等都可以）：Siting there, I read a book.

需要说明的是，并列、伴随和下沉只是动词的形式问题，不代表动词之间的逻辑关系，用这三种形式翻译两个动词或两组动词都是可以的，大家可以根据句子上下文的关系来判断使用。

---

6 全人类是一个整体，生命与健康，生存与发展，是各国人民都应享有的平等权利。中国，将继续高举人类命运共同体旗帜，坚持共商共建共享原则，积极践行真正的多边主义，捍卫以《联合国宪章》为基础的国际秩序，持续完善全球治理体系，建设人类卫生健康共同体，与各国一道维护世界和平稳定，弥合人类发展鸿沟，共同开创更加美好的未来。

第一步 词汇解析

❶ 全人类，humankind，名词，比如：the origin of humankind（人类的起源）。humankind 是人类的总称，是可代替 mankind 的中性词。

❷ 继续高举……旗帜，stay committed to the vision of，动词词组。这里的"高举……旗帜"指的就是"坚持……愿景"。

❸ 人类命运共同体，a community with a shared future for mankind，名词词组。

文化小常识：
人类命运共同体旨在追求本国利益时兼顾他国合理关系，在谋求本国发展中促进各国共同发展。人类只有一个地球，各国共处一个世界，要倡导"人类命运共同体"意识。

❹ 共商共建共享原则，the principles of extensive consultation, joint contribution and shared benefits，名词词组。这里的"共商"指的就是"共同探讨、深入协商"。这里的"共建"指的就是"一起为……做出贡献"。咨询、商讨，consultation，名词，比如：acting in consultation with all the departments involved（和所有有关部门磋商后行事）。

共享，shared benefits，名词词组，指的就是"共享利益"。

⑤ 多边主义，multilateralism，名词，比如：Modern multilateralism must be practical.（现代多边主义应当是切实可行的。）

词汇小常识：
　　multi 是英文常见的前缀，一般表示"多"。比如：multifunction（多功能）。

⑥ 捍卫，safeguard，动词，比如：to safeguard a person's interests（维护某人的利益）。safeguard 作为名词，表示"安全设施、保护措施"。

⑦ 《联合国宪章》，the UN Charter，专有名词，注意首字母大写。

文化小常识：
　　《联合国宪章》是联合国的基本大法，它既确立了联合国的宗旨、原则和组织机构设置，又规定了成员国的责任、权利和义务，以及处理国际关系、维护世界和平与安全的基本原则和方法。

⑧ 国际秩序，the international order，名词词组，比如：What are your predictions on the international order in 2025?（你对 2025 年的国际秩序有何预测？）

⑨ 全球治理体系，the global governance system，名词词组。
统治方式、管理方式，governance，名词，比如：He will meet with officials from several countries to discuss ways to promote good governance.（他将与诸国官员会面，讨论如何促进对国家的良性管理。）governance 既可指国家的管理方式，也可指公司或组织的管理方式。

⑩ 人类卫生健康共同体，a global community of health for all，名词词组。
这里的"人类"不一定要翻译为 human 等词，译文中翻译为 for all。

⑪ 弥合人类发展鸿沟，bridge the development gap，动词词组。
消除（隔阂、鸿沟），bridge，动词，比如：It is unlikely that the two sides will be able to bridge their differences.（双方不太可能会消除彼此间的分歧。）

⑫ 共同开创更加美好的未来，create a brighter future for all，动词词组。这里的"共同"同样翻译为 for all。

第二步 动词定位

　　全人类是一个整体，生命与健康，生存与发展，是各国人民都应享有的平等权利。中国，将继续高举人类命运共同体旗帜，坚持共商共建共享原则，积极践行真正的多边主义，捍卫以《联合国宪章》为基础的国际秩序，持续完善全球治理体系，建设人类卫生健康共同体，与各国一道维护世界和平稳定，弥合人类发展鸿沟，共同开创更加美好的未来。

第三步 句型解析

❶ 本段第一句中，"全人类"是主语，"是"是谓语，"一个整体"是宾语，译文这里处理为单独的句子，考试时可以和第二个分句合译为一句，句与句之间用 and 连接。

❷ 第一句中的第二个分句中，"生命与健康，生存与发展"是主语，"是"是谓语，"各国人民都应享有的平等权利"是宾语。这里要注意分析句式结构，该句并不是要表达"生命与健康，生存与发展，是……平等权利"，中文欲表达的含义是"生命权、健康权、生存权和发展权是各国人民都平等享有的"，而且这里还有隐藏的被动语态，应该是"被享有的"，所以核心谓语应当翻译为 be equally enjoyed。

❸ 本段第二句中，"中国"是主语，"将继续高举"是第一组谓语，"人类命运共同体旗帜"是第一组宾语，翻译为 will stay committed to the vision of building a community with a shared future for mankind。这里的"高举旗帜"也可以翻译为 uphold the great banner of。
"坚持"是第二组谓语，"共商共建共享原则"是第二组宾语，翻译为 follow the principles of extensive consultation, joint contribution and shared benefits。

"积极践行"是第三组谓语,"真正的多边主义"是第三组宾语,翻译为 uphold true multilateralism。

"捍卫"是第四组谓语,"以《联合国宪章》为基础的国际秩序"是第四组宾语,翻译为 safeguard the international order based on the UN Charter。

❹ 本句到这里可以"分堆"了,有人问,为什么呢?考虑到这个句子较长,所以我们不能将所有的分句放在一起翻译。那么如何分堆呢?简单来说,前面一堆四个动词,后面一堆五个动词。

第二堆的主语还是"中国",第一组谓语是"持续完善",第一组宾语是"全球治理体系",翻译为 continue to improve the global governance system。

"建设"是第二组谓语,"人类卫生健康共同体"是第二组宾语,翻译为 build a global community of health for all。

❺ 译文在这里又分堆了,我个人认为完全没有必要,分开翻译也是可以的,主语是"中国",谓语是"与……一道",宾语是"各国",翻译为 work with other countries。后面的"维护"是第一组二谓语,也是目的状语,动词的宾语是"世界和平稳定",翻译为 to maintain world peace and stability;

第二组二谓语是"弥合",也是目的状语,动词的宾语是"人类发展鸿沟",翻译为 bridge the development gap。

第三组二谓语是"开创",还是目的状语,动词的宾语是"更加美好的未来",注意第二组和第三组之间需要用连词 and 连接,翻译为 and create a brighter future for all。

第四步 翻译来了

Humankind is a global community. The rights to life, health, survival, and development must be equally enjoyed by people of all countries. China will stay committed to the vision of building a community with a shared future for mankind, follow the principles of extensive consultation, joint contribution and shared benefits, uphold true multilateralism, and safeguard the international order based on the UN Charter. China will continue to improve the global governance system and build a global community of health for all. China will work with other countries to maintain world peace and stability, bridge the development gap, and create a brighter future for all.

本句考点总结

第一,中英文的巨大差异在于中文是意合式语言,英文是形合式语言。中文的句子之间不用连词连接,而英文的句子之间必须使用连词,所以,我们在做汉译英时,要去体会和理解每个逗号前后句子之间的关系,到底是并列、转折、让步、因果、条件,还是别的什么关系,然后我们选择合适的连词进行连接,形成一个英文的句子。始终要牢记一点:英文的两个句子之间必须要有连词连接。

第二,本句出现了中文里隐藏被动语态的译法。被动语态是英文常见的一种形式,而在中文里常常少用"被"或者不用"被"。那么中文当中一般如何隐藏被动语态呢?第一种是被动变主动,第二种是寻找替代词(比如:"让……给""为……所"等结构),第三种是在科技文献中用"可以"来替代"被",第四种是有"被"不用"被",在中文里识别出来以上四种隐藏的被动语态不是一件容易的事,需要大家仔细认真地识别这种现象,在汉译英时体现出来。

第三,关于"动词分堆"的问题。中文里常常出现多个短句聚集的句型,我们一方面需要去考虑这些动词之间的关系,哪一个是最重要的,哪一个是其次重要的,哪一个又是最不重要的,

> 这个过程称为分析"谓语动词的层次性"。除此之外,句子当中出现了大量的动词时,或者说大量的分句时,我们不可能将这些分句整体翻译为一个长句,那么,我们就需要考虑哪些动词放在一起翻译,这样的过程称为"动词的分堆"。比如,一个句子当中有五个动词形成的五个分句,我们一般会考虑前三个动词翻译为一句,后两个动词翻译为一句,但是如何进行"分堆"要根据上下文的语境来判断,绝对不能形而上学,望文生义。

这篇文章是典型的政府工作报告类文章,而且其主题还是较为主流的新冠疫情问题,除了单词需要掌握以外,更加重要的是句与句之间的连接问题。大家不难发现,本篇文章没有什么高深的句与句之间的关系,译文基本都是处理为两个动词之间的关系,而且多用并列、伴随结构,少有下沉结构,所以考试时还是以简单的句式结构为主,不要用太难的表达!不要炫技!不要用复杂的结构!!!

第二章 2020 年实务真题解析与方法技巧

第一节 2020 年下半年三级笔译英译汉（A 卷）

原文（请先通读全文）

At 51, Cathy McDonnell wanted to put her Oxford physics degree and former experience crunching data to better use. She had worked part-time in a school for several years while her three children were young, but she wanted to get back into the corporate world.

Several applications later, she was getting nowhere. Then a friend told her about "returnships", a form of later-life work experience that some companies are experimenting with to help older people — mainly women — return to work, often after breaks to care for families.

Cathy eventually secured a place on an 11-week "Career Returners" programme, open to men and women, which included being buddied with a 20-year-old male student. He helped to acquaint her with new technology, such as using an iPhone and accessing the company's virtual private network from her laptop so she could work from home but still access internal files.

"On the assessment day, I thought they must have been looking at my project management skills. But they weren't looking at us for specific roles. They were just thinking, 'These women have a lot to offer, let's see what they can do.' That was refreshing."

A clutch of companies in the UK and the US have spotted an opportunity in hiring female returnees, who can put to use again technical skills learnt earlier in their careers. They believe middle-aged women returning after a break make particularly good employees, because they bring a fresh perspective.

Women tend to combine high emotional intelligence with strong leadership and organisational skills. There is a "massive pool of highly skilled people who want to return to work," says the head of an engineering company. "Recruitment agencies typically view people who have had two years out as a risk, but we see them as a great opportunity."

In fact, by hiring female returnees, companies can access hard skills these women developed in their former high-level jobs — and for a discount. In return, employers coach older females back into working life.

Through her returnship, Cathy gained a full-time role as an operations data consultant. She still is earning less than she would like to. "But it's a foot in the door and the salary is up for review in six months," she says.

It is still overwhelmingly women who stay home to care for young families. UK government figures show that women account for around 90 per cent of people on extended career breaks for caring reasons.

A lack of older women working, particularly in highly skilled roles, is costing the UK economy £50 billion a year, according to a report. The report found that men over 50 took home nearly two-thirds of the total wages paid out to everyone in that age range in 2015.

It blamed the pay gap on the low-skilled, part-time roles older women often accept. Some 41 per cent of women in work in the UK do so part-time, as opposed to only 11 per cent of men.

A study last year by economists found "robust evidence of age discrimination in hiring against older women" in a range of white and blue-collar jobs. The data show that it is harder for older women to find jobs than it is for older men regardless of whether they have taken a break from working.

2020年上半年CATTI考试由于疫情没有举行，下半年11月份的考试如约而至，但是部分考生是在周六参加考试，部分考生是在周日参加考试，所以就有两套试卷，和往年两次考试共四套试卷是一样的。这次考试又回到了外刊的主题，文章选自于2017年英国《金融时报》(*Financial Times*)的一篇文章，我们非常熟悉的直接引语和间接引语回来了，我们非常熟悉的同位语现象也回来了。

> **1** At 51, Cathy McDonnell wanted to put her Oxford physics degree and former experience crunching data to better use. She had worked part-time in a school for several years while her three children were young, but she wanted to get back into the corporate world.

第一步 词汇解析

❶ Cathy McDonnell，凯茜·麦克唐纳，人名，这里采用的是音译法，注意名和姓之间要加"·"，翻译英文人名不确定时，可以使用音译法，然后把英文人名抄下来，放在括号里，这样保险一些。

❷ Oxford，专有名词，表示"牛津大学"。
文化小常识：
　　牛津大学（University of Oxford），简称"牛津"（Oxford），位于英国牛津，世界顶尖的公立研究型大学，采用书院联邦制。其与剑桥大学并称为牛剑，是罗素大学集团成员，被誉为"金三角名校"和"G5超级精英大学"。

❸ physics，名词，表示"物理学"，比如：It is possible to combine Computer Science with other subjects, for example Physics.（将计算机科学与其他学科，如物理学，结合起来是可能的。）

❹ crunch，动词，表示"（快速大量地）处理信息、数字捣弄"，例如：number crunching（数字运算）。

❺ corporate，形容词，表示"企业的"，比如：Many corporate methods have been adopted by American managers in imitation of Japanese practice.（美国的管理人员效仿日本人的做法，采用了很多经营公司的方法。）

第二步 注意断句

At 51, /Cathy McDonnell wanted to put her Oxford physics degree and former experience crunching data /to better use. /She had worked part-time /in a school /for several years /while her three children were young, /but /she wanted to get back into the corporate world.

第三步 句型解析

❶ 第一句中，At 51 是时间状语，Cathy McDonnell 是主语，和前面的 At 51 形成了同位语关系，"主谓译法"或"并列译法"都是可以的，wanted to put her Oxford physics degree and former experience crunching data 是谓语和宾语，to better use 是不定式作目的状语。

❷ 第二句中，She had worked part-time 是主谓状结构，in a school 是地点状语，for several years 是时间状语，while her three children were young 是 while 引导的时间状语从句，这里的 while 表示"当时"，but 是表示转折的连词，she wanted to get back into the corporate world 是主谓宾结构。

第四步 翻译来了

51 岁那一年，凯茜·麦克唐纳（Cathy McDonnell）想更好地利用自己牛津大学的物理学学位和以前处理数据的工作经验。她之前几年在一所学校做兼职，当时三个孩子还小，但是她现在想回到企业上班。

本句考点总结

本句考查了英文同位语的译法。同位语是两个前后相互说明的名词或名词短语，比如 Beijing, the capital of China，有两种译法。第一种是"并列译法"，翻译为"中国的首都北京"，第二种是"主谓译法"，翻译为"北京是中国的首都"。具体用哪一种，可以根据句子具体情况而定，有时两种都是可以使用的。

2

Several applications later, she was getting nowhere. Then a friend told her about "returnships", a form of later-life work experience that some companies are experimenting with to help older people — mainly women — return to work, often after breaks to care for families.

第一步 词汇解析

❶ application，名词，表示"申请"，比如：The application forms have now been simplified.（申请表格现已被简化了。）

❷ break，名词，表示"间断、暂停"，比如：Use these natural breaks to stop and do self-reflection.（利用这些正常的间歇期暂停一下，进行自我反省。）

❸ care for，动词词组，表示"照顾、关心"，比如：His natural mother was unable to care for him so he was raised by an aunt.（他的生母不能照顾他，所以他是姑姑抚养大的。）

第二步 注意断句

Several applications later, /she was getting nowhere. /Then /a friend told her about "returnships", /a form of later-life work experience /that some companies are experimenting with /to help older people — /mainly women — /return to work, /often after breaks to care for families.

第三步 句型解析

❶ 第一句中，Several applications later 是时间状语，主句 she was getting nowhere 是主谓状结构，时间状语直接翻译为"几封申请之后"句意不是非常完整，翻译为"她递交了几份工作申请之后"更好，主句直接翻译为"一无所获"。

❷ 第二句中，Then 是表示时间的状语，a friend told her about "returnships" 是主谓宾和状语结构，这里需要仔细理解 "returnships"，后面的 a form of later-life work experience 就解释了这个单词的含义，所以翻译为"返岗"更好，这里的同位语可以译为主谓结构，也可以译为并列结构，这个同位语中还有定语从句，所以采用后置译法更好。that 引导定语从句，some companies are experimenting with 是主谓结构，to 引导的不定式作目的状语，help older people 是谓宾结构，后面的破折号依旧保留，mainly women 放在原位翻译，return to work 是 help 的宾语补足语，often after breaks to care for families 也是状语结构，用于补充说明"他们不去工作的原因"，所以在翻译时需要增主语"他们"。

第四步 翻译来了

她递交了几份工作申请之后，一无所获。一个朋友随后告诉她关于"返岗"（returnship）的项目，这是在晚年就业的一种方式，目前一些公司正在试行这一项目，是为了帮助岁数大的人——主要是女性——重返工作岗位，通常她们由于照顾家庭而中断了工作。

本句考点总结

第一，本句考查了英文同位语的译法。同位语是两个前后相互说明的名词或名词短语，比如 Beijing, the capital of China，有两种译法。第一种是"并列译法"，翻译为"中国的首都北京"，第二种是"主谓译法"，翻译为"北京是中国的首都"。具体用哪一种，可以根据句子具体情况而定，有时两种都是可以使用的。

第二，本句出现了英文定语从句的译法。一般来说，定语从句按照"短前长后"的译法处理，较短的定语从句可以前置，较长的定语从句可以后置，这一切都取决于句子的通顺，并没有绝对的前置和后置译法。

---

3 Cathy eventually secured a place on an 11-week "Career Returners" programme, open to men and women, which included being buddied with a 20-year-old male student. He helped to acquaint her with new technology, such as using an iPhone and accessing the company's virtual private network from her laptop so she could work from home but still access internal files.

第一步 词汇解析

❶ secure，动词，表示"（尤指经过努力）获得、招致"，比如：He secured a place for himself at law school.（他在法学院取得了学籍。）

❷ buddy，动词，表示"交往、结交、交朋友、做好朋友"，比如：You and your neighbour might want to buddy up to make the trip more enjoyable.（你同你的邻居或许应该结伴旅游，热闹一点。）

❸ acquaint with，动词词组，表示"熟悉、使了解"，比如：You will first need to acquaint yourself with the filing system.（你首先需要熟悉文件归档方法。）

❹ virtual，形容词，表示"虚拟的"，比如：New technology has enabled development of an online "virtual library".（新技术已经使在线"虚拟图书馆"的发展成为可能。）

❺ access，动词，表示"访问、存取（计算机文件）、到达、进入、使用"，比如：You need a password to access the computer system.（使用这个计算机系统需要口令。）

第二步 注意断句

Cathy eventually secured a place /on an 11-week "Career Returners" programme, /open to men and women, / which included being buddied with a 20-year-old male student. /He helped to acquaint her with new technology, / such as using an iPhone /and accessing the company's virtual private network /from her laptop /so she could work from home /but still access internal files.

第三步 句型解析

❶ 第一句中，Cathy eventually secured a place 是主谓宾结构，on an 11-week "Career Returners" programme 是状语，open to men and women 是形容词短语作后置定语，因为有逗号隔开，所以相当于非限定性定语从句，翻译时可以后置。之后的 which 引导了一个非限定性定语从句，翻译时可以后置，included being buddied with a 20-year-old male student 是谓宾结构，表示"和一个 20 岁的男学生共同工作"。

❷ 第二句中，He helped to acquaint her with new technology 是主谓宾和状语结构，这里的代词是第二次出现，所以可以翻译为"他"。such as 是举例，using an iPhone 是动宾结构，and 是并列连词，accessing the company's virtual private network from her laptop 是动宾状结构，这里是总分关系，所以先翻译 such as 之后的内容，再翻译之前的总结内容。so 是表示结果的连词，she could work from home 是主谓状结构，but 是表示转折的并列连词，still access internal files 是谓语和宾语，这两句之间的关系是转折，表示"虽然在家工作，但是也可以看到公司的内部文件"。

第四步 翻译来了

凯茜最终进入了一个为期 11 周的"职业返岗人"（Career Returners）项目，这个项目面向所有男性和女性，包括与一名 20 岁的男学生共同工作。他帮助凯茜熟悉如使用苹果手机，从笔记本电脑进入公司的虚拟专用网络等新技术，这样一来，她虽然居家办公，但是也可以看到公司的内部文件。

> **本句考点总结**
>
> 第一，形容词短语位于名词后，作后置定语，相当于定语从句，从句较短，根据"短前长后"的译法翻译。
>
> 第二，非限定性定语从句是用逗号隔开的定语从句，这样的句子一般都要，后置译法，在翻译时需要翻译出关系代词 which、who 等词，指明这些词的指代关系，将这些代词翻译出来。
>
> 第三，中英文的总分关系，中文一般是先分后总，而英文则是先总后分，比如中文会说"我喜欢吃香蕉、苹果、梨子等水果"，但是英文的表达是 I like fruits such as bananas, apples and pears. 注意总分关系是如何在两种语言中体现出来的。

> "On the assessment day, I thought they must have been looking at my project management skills. But they weren't looking at us for specific roles. They were just thinking, 'These women have a lot to offer, let's see what they can do.' That was refreshing."

第一步 词汇解析

❶ assessment，名词，表示"评估、评定"，比如：There is little assessment of the damage to the natural environment.（几乎未对自然环境破坏程度做出评估。）

❷ specific，形容词，表示"特定的、特有的、独特的"，比如：The student is invited to test each item for himself by means of specific techniques.（邀请学生们采用特定的技术自己去测试每个项目。）

❸ refreshing，形容词，表示"令人耳目一新的、别具一格的"，比如：It made a refreshing change to be taken seriously for once.（总算有一次受到认真对待了，这变化真是令人耳目一新。）

第二步 注意断句

"On the assessment day, /I thought /they must have been looking at my project management skills. /But /they weren't looking at us /for specific roles. /They were just thinking, /'These women have a lot to offer, /let's see /what they can do.' /That was refreshing."

第三步 句型解析

❶ 本句是典型的直接引语，所以翻译时保留原来的标点，这一两年外刊考得没有以前多，2020 年只有一次考试，还是出现了这样的题目，我们的"快乐"又回来了！

❷ 第一句 On the assessment day 是时间状语，I thought 是主谓结构，后面是宾语从句，they must have been looking at my project management skills 是主谓宾结构，这里要特别注意时态 must have been，表示"（过去）肯定要做某事"，还要注意 look at 的含义，不能理解为"看"，而是"了解、考查、考核"的意思。第二句中的 But 是表示转折含义的并列连词，they weren't looking at us for specific roles 是主谓宾状结构，这句和上一句有一定的关系，所以可以用逗号合译。第三句 They were just thinking 是主谓结构，之后的单引号可以保留，These women have a lot to offer 是主谓宾宾补结构，这里的 offer 是"做事"的意思，let's see what they can do 是祈使句结构。That was refreshing 是评论性的句子，这里的 refreshing 表示"和以前不一样"，口语中翻译为"挺有意思的"比较好。

第四步 翻译来了

"在项目评估那天，我认为他们一定会考查我的项目管理技能，但是，他们并没有想让我们担任特定的职位。他们只是在想：'这些女性能做许多事情，让我们看看这些人能做什么工作。'这种情况还挺有意思的。"

> **本句考点总结**
>
> 在翻译中，无论是英译汉，还是汉译英，我们常常将长句断成短句，然后一句一句翻译，短的句子由于上下文的联系，也可以放在一起翻译。分译与合译在非文学翻译出现得比较少，但是在文学翻译中出现得特别多，特别要读懂上下文内在的关系。分译与合译没有固定的翻译要求，而且每个译者的尺度也是不同的，重要的前提就是句意正确和句意通顺。

5

A clutch of companies in the UK and the US have spotted an opportunity in hiring female returnees, who can put to use again technical skills learnt earlier in their careers. They believe middle-aged women returning after a break make particularly good employees, because they bring a fresh perspective.

第一步 词汇解析

① a clutch of，量词，表示"一群、一批"，比如：The party has attracted a clutch of young southern liberals.（聚会吸引了一群南部的年轻开明人士。）

② spot，动词，表示"看见、看出、注意到、发现"，比如：I finally spotted my friend in the crowd.（我终于在人群中看见了我的朋友。）

③ returnee，名词，表示"回归的人、归国的人"，比如：This policy doesn't specify what kind of returnee qualifies as high-level.（这项政策并没有清楚地表明什么是高水平的归国人员。）

④ perspective，名词，表示"态度、观点"，比如：His experience abroad provides a wider perspective on the problem.（他在国外的经历使他以更广阔的视角看待这个问题。）

第二步 注意断句

A clutch of companies /in the UK and the US /have spotted an opportunity /in hiring female returnees, /who can put to use again technical skills /learnt earlier in their careers. /They believe /middle-aged women /returning after a break /make particularly good employees, /because they bring a fresh perspective.

第三步 句型解析

① 第一句中，A clutch of companies 是主语，in the UK and the US 是地点状语，have spotted an opportunity 是谓语和宾语，in hiring female returnees 是状语，逗号后是 who 引导的非限定性定语从句，可以采用后置译法，can put to use again technical skills 是谓语和宾语结构，learnt earlier in their careers 是过去分词短语作定语，定语较短，采用前置译法。

② 第二句中，They believe 是主谓结构，这里的 They 是第二次出现，可以翻译为"他们"，后面接宾语从句，从句中 middle-aged women 是主语，returning after a break 是现在分词短语作定语，相当于定语从句，从句较短，采用前置译法，make particularly good employees 是谓宾结构，because 是原因状语引导词，they bring a fresh perspective 是主谓宾结构。

第四步 翻译来了

不少英美国家的公司在聘用返岗女性的过程中发现了机会，这些女性可以再次施展在之前工作中所学到的技术和技能。他们认为，中断一段时间之后再次工作的中年女性将会让她们成为特别好的员工，因为她们会带来全新的视角。

> **本句考点总结**
>
> 第一，非限定性定语从句是用逗号隔开的定语从句，这样的句子一般都要采用后置译法，在翻译时需要翻译出关系代词 which、who 等词，指明这些词的指代关系，将这些代词翻译出来。
>
> 第二，本句出现了分词或分词短语位于名词后的译法。一般来说，分词或分词短语位于名词后相当于定语或定语从句，定语按照"短前长后"的译法来进行翻译。

6 Women tend to combine high emotional intelligence with strong leadership and organisational skills. There is a "massive pool of highly skilled people who want to return to work," says the head of an engineering company. "Recruitment agencies typically view people who have had two years out as a risk, but we see them as a great opportunity."

第一步 词汇解析

① emotional intelligence，名词词组，表示"情商（人际交往和沟通技巧）"，比如：This is an age when we boast of our emotional intelligence and we claim to feel each other's pain. （这是一个我们都在夸耀自己的情商，声称能感受彼此伤痛的时代。）

② organisational，形容词，表示"组织的"，比如：Evelyn's excellent organisational skills were soon spotted by her employers. （伊夫琳出色的组织能力很快就被老板发现。）

③ massive，形容词，表示"巨大的"，比如：This could mean a massive furlough of government workers. （这可能意味着大量的政府工作人员要暂时下岗。）

④ a massive pool of，形容词词组，表示"大量的、许多的"，比如：a massive pool of cheap labour（大量廉价劳动力）。

⑤ recruitment，名词，表示"招聘"，比如：You've been in graduate recruitment for five years. （你已经从事毕业生招聘工作五年了。）

第二步 注意断句

Women tend to combine high emotional intelligence /with strong leadership and organisational skills. / There is a "massive pool of highly skilled people /who want to return to work," /says the head of an engineering company. / "Recruitment agencies typically view people /who have had two years out /as a risk, /but we see them as a great opportunity."

第三步 句型解析

① 第一句中，Women tend to combine high emotional intelligence 是主谓宾结构，with strong leadership and organisational skills 是状语，这里是典型的 combine...with... 的结构，表示"把……和……结合"。

② 第二句中，There is a "massive pool of highly skilled people who want to return to work" 是典型的 there be 句型，也是直接引语，其中还有 who 引导的定语从句，从句较短，可以用前置译法，当然也要根据句子的通顺来判断。says the head of an engineering company 是动词和说话人，可以放在原位翻译。

③ 第三句还是直接引语，Recruitment agencies typically view people 是主谓宾结构，后面接 who 引导的定语从句，定语从句中 have had two years out 是谓宾状结构，这里的 out 是"不上班、中断工作"的意思，as a risk 是状语。but 是表示转折的并列连词，we see them as a great opportunity 是主谓宾状结构，要注意代词 them，这里指代前文的"中断了两年工作的人"。

第四步 翻译来了

女性易把高情商和强大的领导力和组织技能结合在一起。"有大量的高技术人才想再次就业"，一家工程公司的负责人说，"人才招聘机构通常把中断工作两年的人视为一项风险，但是，我们却把他们当作一个契机。"

> **本句考点总结**
>
> 第一，本句出现了英文定语从句的译法。一般来说，定语从句按照"短前长后"的译法处理，较短的定语从句可以前置，较长的定语从句可以后置，这一切都取决于句子的通顺，并没有绝对的前置和后置译法。
>
> 第二，本句考查了英文直接引语的译法，最简单的译法就是保留冒号和双引号，说话人的位置和说话的内容都保持不变。即说话人在什么位置，就放在什么位置翻译，当然，说话人放在句首也是可以接受的。

7 In fact, by hiring female returnees, companies can access hard skills these women developed in their former high-level jobs — and for a discount. In return, employers coach older females back into working life.

第一步 词汇解析

① discount，名词，表示"折扣"，比如：Much of the discount is pocketed by retailers instead of being passed on to customers.（折扣的大部分进了零售商的腰包，而顾客没有得到实惠。）

② coach，动词，表示"训练、培养、指导、辅导"，比如：She has coached hundreds of young singers.（她培养了许许多多的青年歌手。）

第二步 注意断句

In fact, /by hiring female returnees, /companies can access hard skills /these women developed /

in their former high-level jobs — /and for a discount. /In return, /employers coach older females back /into working life.

第三步 句型解析

❶ 第一句中，In fact 是状语，表示"实际上"，by 引导方式状语，表示"通过"，后面接动宾短语 hiring female returnees, companies can access hard skills 是主句，是主谓宾结构，后面接定语从句，these women developed 是定语从句中的主谓结构，in their former high-level jobs 是状语，之后的破折号依旧保留，and for a discount 是状语，这里要注意 discount 的理解，这个单词原意是"打折、折扣"，本句中理解为"以比较低的成本"。

❷ 第二句中，In return 是状语，表示"作为回报"，employers coach older females back into working life 是主谓宾状结构，这里的 coach 表示"指导、训练"。

第四步 翻译来了

实际上，公司聘用这些返岗女性，可以用较低的成本来得到她们以前在高级岗位上所获得的硬技术。而作为回报，他们又指导这些年长的女性重返工作岗位。

本句考点总结

本句出现了英文定语从句的译法。一般来说，定语从句按照"短前长后"的译法处理，较短的定语从句可以前置，较长的定语从句可以后置，这一切都取决于句子的通顺，并没有绝对的前置和后置译法。

---

8 Through her returnship, Cathy gained a full-time role as an operations data consultant. She still is earning less than she would like to. "But it's a foot in the door and the salary is up for review in six months," she says.

第一步 词汇解析

❶ consultant，名词，表示"顾问"，比如：She earns more since she repackaged herself as a business consultant.（自从把自己重新包装成商业顾问以来，她的收入就增加了。）

❷ be up for，动词词组，表示"为……做好打算"，比如：A rare collection of china will be up for sale next month.（有一批珍贵的瓷器将于下月出售。）

❸ review，名词，表示"评审、审查、重新调整"，比如：The president ordered a review of US economic aid to Jordan.（总统下令对美国向约旦提供的经济援助进行审查。）

第二步 注意断句

Through her returnship, /Cathy gained a full-time role /as an operations data consultant. /She still is earning less /than she would like to. /"But it's a foot in the door /and the salary is up for review /in six months," / she says.

第三步 句型解析

❶ 第一句中，Through her returnship 是状语，不要翻译为"通过'返岗'"，直接翻译为"返岗后"更加简单易懂，Cathy gained a full-time role 是主句的主谓宾结构，as an operations data consultant 是状语。

❷ 第二句中，She still is earning less 是主谓状结构，than she would like to 是比较状语从句，句式简单，直接翻译。

❸ 第三句是直接引语，大家都很熟悉，But 是表示转折的并列连词，it's a foot in the door 是主系表状结构，也是常用的固定表达，表示"进入了这个行业"，and 是并列连词，the salary is up for review 是主系表结构，in six months 是时间状语，she says 是说话人和动词，放在原位或是句首都是可以的。

第四步 翻译来了

返岗后，凯西得到了一份运营数据顾问的全职工作。她现在挣的仍然比她想要的少。她说："但是至少已经入行了，工资会在半年后重新调整。"

本句考点总结

本句考查了英文直接引语的译法，最简单的译法就是保留冒号和双引号，说话人的位置和说话的内容都保持不变。即说话人在什么位置，就放在什么位置翻译，当然，说话人放在句首也是可以接受的。

---

9 It is still overwhelmingly women who stay home to care for young families. UK government figures show that women account for around 90 per cent of people on extended career breaks for caring reasons.

第一步 词汇解析

❶ overwhelmingly，副词，表示"（数量）巨大地、压倒性地"，比如：The House of Commons has overwhelmingly rejected calls to bring back the death penalty for murder.（下议院以压倒性的多数驳回了对谋杀罪恢复死刑判决的呼吁。）

❷ figure，名词，表示"数字、数据"，比如：The two sets of figures are not significantly different.（这两组数字没有明显的差别。）

❸ account for，动词词组，表示"（数量或比例上）占"，比如：Computers account for 5% of the country's commercial electricity consumption.（计算机占该国商业用电的5%。）

❹ extended，形容词，表示"延长了的、扩展了的"，比如：Obviously, any child who receives dedicated teaching over an extended period is likely to improve.（很明显，任何长期接受用心教育的孩子都有可能取得进步。）

第二步 注意断句

It is still overwhelmingly women /who stay home /to care for young families. /UK government figures show /

that women account for around 90 per cent of people /on extended career breaks /for caring reasons.

第三步 句型解析

❶ 第一句中，It is still overwhelmingly women 是主系表结构，后面接 who 引导的定语从句，to care for young families 是目的状语，本句是典型的强调结构，翻译时也要翻译出强调的感觉。

❷ 第二句中，UK government figures show 是主谓结构，后面接 that 引导的宾语从句，women account for around 90 per cent of people 是主谓宾结构，后面状语中的 on 表示"在……方面"，for caring reasons 表示"由于要照顾（孩子）"。

第四步 翻译来了

目前还有大量的女性在家带孩子。英国政府的数据显示，有 90% 左右的女性因为要照顾孩子还在延长中断工作的时间。

 本句考点总结

本句出现了英文定语从句的译法。一般来说，定语从句按照"短前长后"的译法处理，较短的定语从句可以前置，较长的定语从句可以后置，这一切都取决于句子的通顺，并没有绝对的前置和后置译法。

10 A lack of older women working, particularly in highly skilled roles, is costing the UK economy £50 billion a year, according to a report. The report found that men over 50 took home nearly two-thirds of the total wages paid out to everyone in that age range in 2015.

第一步 词汇解析

❶ billion，名词，表示"十亿"，比如：Worldwide sales reached 2.5 billion.（全球销售额达到了 25 亿。）
❷ pay out，动词词组，表示"支付、花费"，比如：The company pays out a large share of its profits in dividends.（该公司将很大一部分利润用作红利。）
❸ age range，名词词组，表示"年龄范围"，比如：The average age range is between 35 and 55.（平均年龄在 35 岁到 55 岁之间。）

第二步 注意断句

A lack of older women working, /particularly in highly skilled roles, /is costing the UK economy £50 billion a year, /according to a report. /The report found /that men over 50 took home nearly two-thirds of the total wages /paid out to everyone /in that age range /in 2015.

第三步 句型解析

① 第一句中，A lack of older women working 是主语，其中 lack 是典型的抽象名词，有动词词根，可以翻译为动词"缺少"，particularly in highly skilled roles 是状语，is costing the UK economy £50 billion a year 是谓宾补结构，according to a report 也是状语成分，这里表示某种观点，可以放在句首翻译。由于本句主语过长，可以单独成句，用本位词"这"替代主语，为了让句子更加通顺，这里增词"导致"，而且 cost 原本表示"花费"，本句中理解为"导致……损失"。

② 第二句中，The report found 是主谓结构，that 引导宾语从句，men over 50 是主语，表示"50岁以上的男性"，took home nearly two-thirds of the total wages 是谓语和宾语，实际上句子的结构是 took nearly two-thirds of the total wages home，但是中间的宾语过长，所以将状语 home 前置。paid out to everyone 是过去分词短语做定语，修饰 the total wages，从句较短，采用前置译法，in that age range 是状语，in 2015 也是状语。要特别注意这句话中宾语修饰词的排序以及数字的翻译，这里的数字是评论性词，所以要放在句末翻译，而不是放在句中翻译，这也是"事实与评论"之间的关系。

第四步 翻译来了

一份报告显示，缺乏年长的女性员工，特别是在高技术岗位上，这导致英国经济每年损失500亿英镑。这份报告还发现，2015年，50岁以上的男性工资总额约占发放给该年龄段所有人工资总额的三分之二。

本句考点总结

第一，本句当中考查了"抽象名词"的译法。抽象名词一般处于冠词之后，又在介词之前，以"the + 抽象名词 + of"的形式居多。一般来说，抽象名词有两种译法。第一种，若抽象名词有动词词根，则翻译为动词，比如 the suggestion of mine，翻译为"我建议"，而不是"我的建议"；第二种，若抽象名词没有动词词根，可以增动词翻译，比如 the spirit of our nation，翻译为"我们民族所具有的精神"，而不是"我们民族的精神"。

第二，英译汉时，若句子主语过长，那么可以单独成句，形成一个完整的主谓宾的句子，这样翻译是为了避免句子过于臃肿。当主语单独成句时，句子的谓语和宾语缺少主语，那么可以增加"这""这些""这一切""这样"等词作为句子的主语，这样的词称为"本位词"，被这些词所代替的部分称为"外位语"。

第三，本句出现了分词或分词短语位于名词后的译法。一般来说，分词或分词短语位于名词后相当于定语或定语从句，定语按照"短前长后"的译法来进行翻译。

第四，本句出现了事实(Facts)和评论(Comments)的译法。中文一般先事实，后评论，而英文一般先评论，后事实。比如：It is important for her to go abroad. 翻译为"对于她来说，出国是很重要的"。英文中 It is important 是评论，for her to go abroad 是事实，从中英文的对比来看，可以知道中英文语序分别是怎么安排的。

11. It blamed the pay gap on the low-skilled, part-time roles older women often accept. Some 41 per cent of women in work in the UK do so part-time, as opposed to only 11 per cent of men.

第一步 词汇解析

1. blame on，动词词组，表示"归咎于、把责任推给……"，比如：Police are blaming the accident on dangerous driving.（警方把事故原因归咎于危险驾驶。）
2. pay gap，名词词组，表示"收入差距"，比如：narrow the gender pay gap（缩小男女之间的收入差距）。
3. as opposed to，介词词组，表示"而、相对于"，比如：200 attended, as opposed to 300 the previous year.（出席的有 200 人，而前一年是 300 人。）

第二步 注意断句

It blamed the pay gap /on the low-skilled, /part-time roles /older women often accept. /Some 41 per cent of women in work /in the UK do so part-time, /as opposed to only 11 per cent of men.

第三步 句型解析

1. 第一句中，It 是主语，指上文中的"报告"，blamed the pay gap 是谓语和宾语，on the low-skilled, part-time roles 是状语，older women often accept 是省略引导词的定语从句，从句较短，采用前置译法。
2. 第二句中，Some 41 per cent of women in work in the UK 是主语，do so part-time 是谓语和宾语，as opposed to only 11 per cent of men 是状语，这里表示"和只有 11% 的男性所做的工作相比"。本句中的 so 表示"这样、如此"，替代了上文说的某种情况，其实也就是"女性从事低技能和兼职工作"。

第四步 翻译来了

该报告把收入差距归咎于年长的女性总是从事一些低技能和兼职工作。在英国，约有 41% 的女性从事兼职工作，相比较而言，只有 11% 的男性会这么做。

> **本句考点总结**
>
> 本句出现了英文定语从句的译法。一般来说，定语从句按照"短前长后"的译法处理，较短的定语从句可以前置，较长的定语从句可以后置，这一切都取决于句子的通顺，并没有绝对的前置和后置译法。

12. A study last year by economists found "robust evidence of age discrimination in hiring against older women" in a range of white and blue-collar jobs. The data show that it is harder for older women to find jobs than it is for older men regardless of whether they have taken a break from working.

第一步 词汇解析

① robust,形容词,表示"强劲的、富有活力的",比如:robust economic growth(强劲的经济增长)。
② age discrimination,名词词组,表示"年龄歧视",比如:Age Discrimination in Employment Act(反就业年龄歧视法案)。
③ blue-collar,形容词,表示"蓝领的",比如:By 1925, blue-collar workers in manufacturing industry became the largest occupational group.(到1925年,制造业的蓝领工人成了最大的职业群体。)
④ regardless of,介词词组,表示"不管、不顾、不理会",比如:The amount will be paid to everyone regardless of whether they have children or not.(不管有没有孩子,每个人都会得到相同的金额。)

第二步 注意断句

A study /last year /by economists found /"robust evidence of age discrimination in hiring against older women" /in a range of white and blue-collar jobs. /The data show /that it is harder for older women /to find jobs /than it is for older men /regardless of whether they have taken a break from working.

第三步 句型解析

① 第一句 A study last year by economists found 是主语和谓语,其中有 last year 和 by economists 两组状语,想一想怎么翻译呢!"robust evidence of age discrimination in hiring against older women" 是本句的宾语,in a range of white and blue-collar jobs 是状语,表示"在白领和蓝领这两个领域的招聘中,'针对雇佣年长女性的年龄歧视的明显证据'",这不通顺啊!那怎么办呢?可以采用偏正换主谓的译法,翻译为"在白领和蓝领这两个领域的招聘中,'有强有力的证据证明,在雇佣年长女性的年龄方面存在歧视'"。
② 第二句 The data show 是主谓结构,that 引导宾语从句,it is harder for older women to find jobs 是 it 作形式主语的句型,后面的不定式是真正的主语,than it is for older men 是比较状语从句。这句话还要注意 harder 的翻译,harder 是评论性词,所以要放在句末翻译,而不是放在句中翻译,这也是"事实与评论"之间的关系。regardless of 后面接了一个 whether 引导的状语从句 whether they have taken a break from working,其中的 they 指代"女性"。

第四步 翻译来了

去年,一项由经济学家所进行的研究发现,在白领和蓝领这两个行业中,"有强有力的证据证明,在雇佣年长女性方面存在年龄歧视"。有数据显示,不论年长的女性是否中断过工作,她们在找工作方面比年长的男性都要难。

本句考点总结

第一,本句中使用了"主谓结构变偏正结构"的译法,这是什么意思呢?也就是说主谓结构 Eyes are gleaming.(眼睛炯炯有神。)可以翻译为偏正结构 gleaming eyes(炯炯有神的眼睛),这种译法是为了让句子更加通顺,当然有时候也可以用"偏正结构变主谓结构"的译法。"主谓变偏正"或"偏正变主谓"在英汉互译当中都可能出现,须灵活使用。

第二,本句出现了事实(Facts)和评论(Comments)的译法。中文一般先事实,后评论,而英文一般先评论,后事实。比如:It is important for her to go abroad. 翻译为"对于她来说,出国是很重要的"。英文中 It is important 是评论,for her to go abroad 是事实,从中英文的对比来看,可以知道中英文语序分别是怎么安排的。

这篇文章是疫情之后第一次考试的英译汉，我也敢肯定这原本应该是 2020 年上半年的考题，文章探讨了年长女性返岗工作的一些情况，总体来说还是比较简单的，比机考时代之前的文章简单，而且也是典型的外刊材料。翻译时要注意各种翻译现象，让句子更加通顺，非文学翻译要注意"信"和"达"。

第二节 2020 年下半年三级笔译汉译英（A 卷）

现在，以互联网为代表的信息技术迅速发展，引领了社会生产新变革，创造了人类生活新空间，拓展了国家治理新领域。中国大力实施网络强国战略、国家信息化战略、国家大数据战略、"互联网+"行动计划。

中国大力发展电子商务，推动互联网和实体经济深度融合发展，改善资源配置。这些措施为推动创新发展、转变经济增长方式、调整经济结构发挥积极作用。

中国欢迎公平、开放、竞争的市场，在自身发展的同时，致力于推动全球数字经济发展。中国主张自由贸易，反对贸易壁垒和贸易保护主义。

我们希望建立开放、安全的数字经济环境，确保互联网为经济发展和创新服务。我们主张互联网接入应公平、普遍。中国愿加强同其他国家和地区在网络安全和信息技术方面的交流与合作。

我们应共同推进互联网技术的发展和创新，确保所有人都能平等分享数字红利，实现网络空间的可持续发展。

2020 年下半年 CATTI 考试的汉译英阐述了有关网络空间的合作问题。2017 年 3 月经由中央网络安全和信息化委员会批准，外交部和国家互联网信息办公室共同发布了《网络空间国际合作战略》，考试内容选择了其中的一些段落，本文的参考译文由外交部翻译室提供。

现在，以互联网为代表的信息技术迅速发展，引领了社会生产新变革，创造了人类生活新空间，拓展了国家治理新领域。中国大力实施网络强国战略、国家信息化战略、国家大数据战略、"互联网+"行动计划。

第一步 词汇解析

❶ 互联网，the Internet，名词，比如：The Internet has become part of everyday life.（互联网已成为日常生活的一部分。）我们常说的"互联网接入"翻译为 Internet access。

❷ 信息技术，information technology，名词词组，比如：Some groups of consumers are slow to pick up trends in the use of information technology.（有些顾客群对信息技术应用方面的潮流反应迟钝。）

071

❸ 迅速发展，the rapid advancement，名词词组。

❹ 引领，bring about，动词词组，比如：The only way they can bring about political change is by putting pressure on the country.（他们能引起政治变化的唯一办法就是向该国施加压力。）

❺ 拓展（了）新领域，create new space，动词词组。
拓展，create，动词，比如：We set business free to create more jobs.（我们让企业自由以创造更多的就业机会。）

❻ 治理，governance，名词，比如：a new set of rules of the governance of the community（管理社区的一套新规则）。同根词：government，名词，表示"政府"。

❼ 大力实施，vigorously implement，动词词组，比如：We will vigorously implement the strategy for intellectual property rights.（我们要大力实施知识产权战略。）
强有力地，vigorously，副词，比如：The party campaigned vigorously in the north of the country.（该党在本国北部展开了强有力的竞选运动。）
实施，implement，动词，比如：The government promised to implement a new system to control financial loan institutions.（政府许诺要实施新的制度来控制金融贷款机构。）同义词：carry out。

❽ 网络强国战略，the national strategies for cyber development，名词词组。
网络，cyber，形容词，比如：the cyber age（计算机网络时代）。cyber 为缩写，单词全拼为：cybernetics。cyber- 可作为前缀，用于构成各种形容词和名词，表示"计算机的、电脑的"。

❾ 国家信息化战略，the national strategies for IT application，名词词组，这类词组翻译较为固定，建议直接记忆。
应用，application，名词，比如：Students learned the practical application of the theory they had learned in the classroom.（学生们学会了课堂上所学理论的实际应用。）

❿ "互联网+"，"Internet Plus"，专有名词，这类词组翻译较为固定，建议直接记忆。

第二步 动词定位

现在，以互联网为代表的信息技术迅速**发展**，**引领**了社会生产新变革，**创造**了人类生活新空间，**拓展**了国家治理新领域。中国大力**实施**网络强国战略、国家信息化战略、国家大数据战略、"互联网+"行动计划。

第三步 句型解析

❶ 第一句中，"现在"是时间状语，"以互联网为代表的信息技术迅速发展"看上去是主谓结构，但是后面的三个动词"引领""创造"和"拓展"才是真正的核心谓语，所以这里的主谓结构需要处理为偏正短语，主语就变成"迅速发展 of 信息技术 + 以互联网为代表的（定语/定语从句）"。本句的三个动宾短语分别是"引领了社会生产新变革""创造了人类生活新空间"和"拓展了国家治理新领域"。总体来说，本句的难点在于主语的形式，一个句子确定了谓语才能确定主语。

❷ 第二句中，"中国"是主语，"大力实施"是核心谓语，"网络强国战略"是第一个宾语，"国家信息化战略"是第二个宾语，"国家大数据战略"是第三个宾语，"'互联网+'行动计划"是第四个宾语，注意第三个和第四个宾语之间用 and 连接。本句翻译需要注意两点：第一，"战略"出现三次，只需要翻译一次，可以认为是形容词分配的原则；第二，注意时态，第一句使用了现在完成时，第二句使用了现在进行时，翻译时也可以全部都用一般现在时。

第四步 翻译来了

Today, the rapid advancement of information technology represented by the Internet has brought about new ways of social production, created new space for people's life, and opened new horizons of state governance. China is vigorously implementing the national strategies for cyber development, IT application, big data and the "Internet Plus" action plan.

 本句考点总结

第一，本句中使用了"主谓结构变偏正结构"的译法，这是什么意思呢？也就是说主谓结构 Eyes are gleaming.（眼睛炯炯有神。）可以翻译为偏正结构 gleaming eyes（炯炯有神的眼睛），这种译法是为了让句子更加通顺，当然有时候也可以用"偏正结构变主谓结构"的译法。"主谓变偏正"或"偏正变主谓"在英汉互译当中都可能出现，须灵活使用。

第二，本句考查了形容词的"分配"译法和动词或名词的"分配"译法。形容词分配的译法是两个或多个形容词位于名词之前，"翻译公式"是 (A+B)*C=AC+BC，比如 international and strategic questions 翻译为"国际问题和战略问题"；动词或名词分配的译法是一个动词位于多个名词宾语之前，或者一个名词位于多个名词前，"翻译公式"是 A*(B+C)=AB+AC，比如 wear a hat and a scarf 翻译为"戴着帽子，系着围巾"。而汉译英时，以上这些方法全部要反过来使用。

2　中国大力发展电子商务，推动互联网和实体经济深度融合发展，改善资源配置。这些措施为推动创新发展、转变经济增长方式、调整经济结构发挥积极作用。

第一步　词汇解析

❶ 大力发展，work to encourage the development，动词词组。"大力发展"的翻译可以理解为"谓语动词的过渡"，work 为弱势动词，encourage 为强势动词。

❷ 电子商务，e-commerce，名词，比如：the anticipated explosion of e-commerce（预期中电子商务的激增）。e- 作为前缀，表示"电子的"，用于构成名词和动词。

❸ 实体经济，real economies，名词词组，比如：to allow more financial resources to be channeled into the real economies（让更多的金融活水流入实体经济）。

经济小常识：
　　实体经济包括物质的、精神的产品和服务的生产、流通等经济活动。包括农业、工业、交通、通信业、商业服务业、建筑业、文化产业等物质生产和服务部门。

❹ 深度融合，integration，名词，比如：They promote social integration and assimilation of minority ethnic groups into the culture.（他们提倡少数民族团体与该文化的社会融合及同化。）

❺ 改善，optimize，动词，比如：optimize the environment for investment（优化投资环境）。optim（最好）+ize→使最优化。"改善"还可以翻译为 improve/perfect。

❻ 资源配置，the allocation of resources，名词词组。

配置，allocation，名词，比如：A State Department spokeswoman said that the aid allocation for Pakistan was still under review.（国务院的一位女发言人说对巴基斯坦的援助配置仍在审核中。）allocation 常与 make 搭配，表示"进行分配"。

❼ 推动创新发展，drive innovation，动词词组。
推动，drive，动词，比如：The mill is driven by the water.（磨是由水驱动的。）

❽ 转变经济增长方式，transform growth model，动词词组。
转变，transform，动词，比如：Past scenes are transformed.（过去的景象已经改观。）

【同义词辨析】
transform：指人或物在形状、外观、形式、性质等方面发生的彻底变化，失去原状成为全新的东西；
convert：指进行全部或局部改变以适应新的功能或用途，指信仰或态度时，强调较激烈、大的改变；
alter：常指轻微的改变，强调基本上保持原物、原状的情况下所进行的部分改变。

❾ 调整经济结构，adjust economic structure，动词词组。
调整，adjust，动词，比如：To attract investors, Panama has adjusted its tax and labour laws.（为了吸引投资者，巴拿马已经调整了其税务及劳动法规。）

❿ 发挥积极作用，play an important role，动词词组，比如：They are playing an increasingly important role in safeguarding peace.（他们对保卫和平起着越来越重要的作用。）"发挥积极作用"也可以翻译为 play a positive role/play an active role。

第二步 动词定位

中国大力<u>发展</u>电子商务，<u>推动</u>互联网和实体经济深度融合发展，<u>改善</u>资源配置。这些措施为<u>推动</u>创新发展、<u>转变</u>经济增长方式、<u>调整</u>经济结构<u>发挥</u>积极作用。

第三步 句型解析

❶ 第一句中，"中国"是主语，由于上一句已经提到，所以这里可以用代词 It，"大力发展"是谓语，"电子商务"是宾语，"推动"是第二组谓语，"互联网和实体经济深度融合发展"是第二组宾语，注意这里的"融合发展"可以视"发展"为范畴词，所以只需要将"融合"翻译为 integration，"深度"可以翻译为 deeply，也可以不翻译，"改善"是第三组谓语，"资源配置"是第三组宾语。本句的"大力发展"和"改善"译者都使用了"谓语动词的过渡"，将副词翻译为动词，动词译为其他形式，特别是"改善"翻译为 endeavors to optimize，前面增加 endeavor，其实在考试中完全没有必要，直接翻译即可。

❷ 第二句中，主语是"这些措施"，实际上指的是上文的做法，可以认为是"本位词"，后面用 which 引导非限定性定语从句，"发挥积极作用"是核心谓语和宾语，翻译为 play an important role in，"为推动创新发展、转变经济增长方式、调整经济结构"是状语，同时也是三个动宾短语，注意第二个和第三个动宾短语之间需要用 and 连接。

第四步 翻译来了

It works to encourage the development of e-commerce, promotes integration of the digital and real economies and endeavors to optimize the allocation of resources, which will play an important role in driving innovation, transforming growth model and adjusting economic structure.

本句考点总结

第一，句中出现了谓语动词过渡的译法，这是英汉互译当中非常难的知识点。中文是动态性语态，常用动词，用强势动词，英文是静态性语言，常用名词，用弱势动词，这点要牢记在心。比如 I give you my support. 不要翻译为"我给你我的支持"，直接翻译为"我支持你"即可，give 是弱势动词，support 是强势动词，因为中英文的差异，只要翻译强势动词，不须翻译弱势动词。这点常常在英译汉当中使用，汉译英中用得比较少！

第二，本句考查了英汉互译增减词的问题，一般来说英译汉增词，汉译英减词，常见增词的种类有：一、增加对象词（范围词），这是由上文缺少句子的某个部分造成的；二、增加范畴词，这是较难的一部分，常见的范畴词有"水平、方式、方法、问题、情况、途径和方面"，但是不仅仅有这些，还有其他很多；三、增加评论性词，这些常常出现在文学翻译中；四、增加动词，会在动词的"分配译法"中说明这点。

第三，本位词与外位语的关系。中文里一般用"这""这些""这么""这一切""这样"等词来替代前面出现过的句子，那么，以上这些词被称为"本位词"，被替代的句子称为"外位语"。翻译的时候需要特别注意，前面被替代的句子正常翻译即可，而出现的"这""这些""这么""这一切""这样"等词不能翻译为 this, all, these 等词（这属于口译的译法），而要使用"逗号 + which"的非限定性定语从句的译法。反过来说，英译汉时如果出现了"逗号 + which"的非限定性定语从句的译法，且不知道 which 指代的是什么，那么将 which 翻译为"这""这些""这么""这一切""这样"岂不是更好？

3. 中国欢迎公平、开放、竞争的市场，在自身发展的同时，致力于推动全球数字经济发展。中国主张自由贸易，反对贸易壁垒和贸易保护主义。

第一步 词汇解析

 竞争的，competitive，形容词，比如：Japan is a highly competitive market system.（日本实行的是一个高度竞争的市场体制。）

❷ 致力于，commit，动词，比如：The council has committed large amounts of money to housing projects.（市政会在住宅项目上投入了大量资金。）commit to 表示"把……托付给、把……置于"；commit oneself 表示"使承担义务、使承诺"。

❸ 数字经济，a stronger digital economy，名词词组。句中"数字经济发展"的意思是"更强大的数字经济"。

数字（的），digital，形容词，比如：The signal will be converted into digital code.（信号将被转变成数字编码。）

❹ 自由贸易，free international trade，名词词组。句中"自由贸易"的意思是"国际间的自由贸易"。

❺ 贸易壁垒，trade barriers，名词词组，比如：The lowering of trade barriers has led to a free-for-all among exporters.（降低贸易壁垒导致出口商各自为政。）

❻ 贸易保护主义，trade protectionism，名词词组，比如：In the past year or so, countries have voiced opposition to trade protectionism.（一年多来，各国表达了反对贸易保护主义的立场。）

保护主义，protectionism，名词，比如：The aim of the current round of talks is to promote free trade and to avert the threat of increasing protectionism.（本轮会谈的目的是促进自由贸易，消除日益加剧的贸易保护主义的威胁。）-ism 表示"各种主义，宗教"，比如：empiricism（经验主义）、eclecticism（折中主义）。

第二步 动词定位

中国欢迎公平、开放、竞争的市场，在自身发展的同时，致力于推动全球数字经济发展。中国主张自由贸易，反对贸易壁垒和贸易保护主义。

第三步 句型解析

❶ 第一句第一分句中，"中国"是核心主语，"欢迎"是谓语，"公平、开放、竞争的市场"是宾语。"在自身发展的同时"是第二分句的时间状语，"致力于"是谓语动词，"推动全球数字经济发展"是宾语，本句在第一句和第二句之间可以增加并列连词 and，当然和译文一样分成两句翻译也是可以的。译文注意到了第二句的主语"中国"可以使用代词 it。

❷ 第二句中，"中国"是主语，可以用代词 It，"主张"是谓语，"自由贸易"是宾语，"反对"是第二个谓语，"贸易壁垒和贸易保护主义"是第二组宾语，句式结构简单，直接翻译即可。

第四步 翻译来了

China welcomes the fair, open and competitive market. While pursuing its own development, it commits to promoting a stronger digital economy globally. It supports free international trade and opposes trade barriers and trade protectionism.

我们希望建立开放、安全的数字经济环境，确保互联网为经济发展和创新服务。我们主张互联网接入应公平、普遍。中国愿加强同其他国家和地区在网络安全和信息技术方面的交流与合作。

第一步 词汇解析

❶ 数字经济，the digital economy，名词词组，比如：The power and ambition of the giants of the digital economy are astonishing.（数字经济巨头们的力量和雄心令人震惊。）

文化小常识：

数字经济，作为一个内涵比较宽泛的概念，凡是直接或间接利用数据来引导资源发挥作用，推动生产力发展的经济形态都可以纳入其范畴。

❷ 为……服务，serves，动词，单词原形为：serve，比如：I really do not think that an inquiry would serve any useful purpose.（我真的认为一次咨询不会起什么作用。）句中"为……服务"的意思是"起……作用"，而不是"为谁服务或效力"。

❸ 创新，innovation，名词，比如：We must promote originality, inspire creativity and encourage innovation.（我们必须提倡独创性，激发创造力，鼓励创新。）

❹ 主张，call for，动词词组，比如：The reaction to this is to call for proper security in all hospitals.（对此类状况的反应是要求所有医院都采取相应的安全措施。）call for 还表示"接某人"，比如：I'll call for you at seven o'clock.（我 7 点钟去接你。）

❺ 互联网接入应公平、普遍，fair and universal access to the Internet，名词词组。

❻ 加强交流与合作，seek enhanced cooperation and exchange，动词词组。句中"加强交流与合作"的意思是"愿寻求深层次的合作与交流"。

深层次的，enhanced，形容词。

❼ 网络安全，cyber security，名词词组，比如：Government should attach great importance to cyber security.（政府应该十分重视网络安全。）

【同义词辨析】

safety：强调意外造成，如疏忽、事故、环境、外界因素等；

security：强调有意的人为因素造成，如偷窃、间谍、抢劫、入侵等。

第二步 动词定位

我们希望建立开放、安全的数字经济环境，确保互联网为经济发展和创新服务。我们主张互联网接入应公平、普遍。中国愿加强同其他国家和地区在网络安全和信息技术方面的交流与合作。

第三步 句型解析

❶ 第一句中，"我们希望"是主谓结构，后面接宾语。"建立开放、安全的数字经济环境"是第一组动宾短语，可以用增主语或是被动语态的译法，译文处理成了一个名词短语，没有翻译"建立"，之后的"确保互联网为经济发展和创新服务"作目的状语，用 to 来连接。特别要注意宾语中的"经济发展和创新"，译文处理为 the economy and innovation，这里的"发展"可以理解为范畴词，但是翻译为 the development 也是可以的。

❷ 第二句中，"我们"是主语，"主张"是谓语，"互联网接入应公平、普遍"是宾语，这里需要注意宾语的结构，"互联网接入应公平、普遍"是主谓结构，翻译为宾语从句没有问题，也可以处理为主谓结构的偏正译法，变成偏正短语"公平和普遍的互联网接入"。

❸ 第三句中，"中国"是主语，"愿加强"是谓语，"交流与合作"是宾语，"同其他国家和地区"是地点状语，"在网络安全和信息技术方面的"是定语，翻译为英语则作状语，表示"在……方面"。译文把"愿加强"翻译为 wishes to seek the enhanced...，这是"谓语动词的过渡"，将强势动词翻译为 seek the enhanced...，其实在考试中直接翻译为 wish to enhance 也是可以的。

第四步 翻译来了

We hope an open and secure environment for the digital economy to ensure the Internet serves the economy and innovation. We call for fair and universal access to the Internet. China wishes to seek enhanced cooperation and exchange with other countries and regions on cyber security and information technology.

> ### 本句考点总结
>
> 第一，本句考查了英汉互译增减词的问题，一般来说英译汉增词，汉译英减词，常见增词的种类有：一、增加对象词（范围词），这是由上文缺少句子的某个部分造成的；二、增加范畴词，这是较难的一部分，常见的范畴词有"水平、方式、方法、问题、情况、途径和方面"，但是不仅仅有这些，还有其他很多；三、增加评论性词，这些常常出现在文学翻译中；四、增加动词，会在动词的"分配译法"中说明这点。
>
> 第二，本句中使用了"主谓结构变偏正结构"的译法，这是什么意思呢？也就是说主谓结构 Eyes are gleaming.（眼睛炯炯有神。）可以翻译为偏正结构 gleaming eyes（炯炯有神的眼睛），这种译法是为了让句子更加通顺，当然有时候也可以用"偏正结构变主谓结构"的译法。"主谓变偏正"或"偏正变主谓"在英汉互译当中都可能出现，须灵活使用。
>
> 第三，句中出现了谓语动词过渡的译法，这是英汉互译当中非常难的知识点。中文是动态性语态，常用动词，用强势动词，英文是静态性语言，常用名词，用弱势动词，这点要牢记在心。比如 I give you my support. 不要翻译为"我给你我的支持"，直接翻译为"我支持你"即可，give 是弱势动词，support 是强势动词，因为中英文的差异，只要翻译强势动词，不须翻译弱势动词。这点常常在英译汉当中使用，汉译英中用得比较少！

5 我们应共同推进互联网技术的发展和创新，确保所有人都能平等分享数字红利，实现网络空间的可持续发展。

第一步 词汇解析

① 发展，advancement，名词，比如：the advancement of science（科学的发展）。"发展"还可翻译为 promotion/progress/ongoing/headway。
② 平等分享，equal sharing，名词词组，比如：equal sharing by both parties（由双方平等分享）。
③ 数字红利，digital dividends，名词词组。
   红利，dividends，名词，单词原形为：dividend，比如：an individual's share of a dividend（个人分红份额）。
④ 网络空间，cyberspace，名词，比如：a report circulating in cyberspace（一则在网络空间里传播的报道）。
⑤ 可持续发展，sustainable development，名词词组，比如：The concept of sustainable development has been defined as profitable.（人们认为可持续发展的概念是有益的。）

第二步 动词定位

我们应共同<u>推进</u>互联网技术的发展和创新，<u>确保</u>所有人都能平等<u>分享</u>数字红利，<u>实现</u>网络空间的可持续发展。

第三步 句型解析

① 本句中的"我们"是主语，"共同推进"是谓语，"互联网技术的发展和创新"是宾语，宾语因为有"的"的结构，可以翻译为 of 结构，即 the advancement and innovation of Internet technology。

❷ 第二个动词"确保"和第三个动词"实现"与第一个动词在词义上有相近之处,所以可以根据"动词分配"的反向使用,只翻译一次,当然翻译为三个动词也没错。

❸ 第二个宾语"所有人都能平等分享数字红利"是主谓结构,要是处理为宾语,则是主谓结构的偏正译法,变成偏正短语"数字红利的平等分享 by 所有人"(译文没有出现"所有人",原因不得而知);第三个宾语是"网络空间的可持续发展",直接翻译即可。

第四步　翻译来了

We should enhance the advancement and innovation of Internet technology together, equal sharing of digital dividends and sustainable development of the cyberspace.

本句考点总结

第一,本句考查了形容词的"分配"译法和动词或名词的"分配"译法。形容词分配的译法是两个或多个形容词位于名词之前,"翻译公式"是 (A+B)*C=AC+BC,比如 international and strategic questions 翻译为"国际问题和战略问题";动词或名词分配的译法是一个动词位于多个名词宾语之前,或者一个名词位于多个名词前,"翻译公式"是 A*(B+C)=AB+AC,比如 wear a hat and a scarf 翻译为"戴着帽子,系着围巾"。而汉译英时,以上这些方法全部要反过来使用。

第二,本句中使用了"主谓结构变偏正结构"的译法,这是什么意思呢?也就是说主谓结构 Eyes are gleaming.(眼睛炯炯有神。)可以翻译为偏正结构 gleaming eyes(炯炯有神的眼睛),这种译法是为了让句子更加通顺,当然有时候也可以用"偏正结构变主谓结构"的译法。"主谓变偏正"或"偏正变主谓"在英汉互译当中都可能出现,须灵活使用。

这篇文章主要阐述了全球在网络空间上的合作,整篇文章句子结构工整,难度不大,以排比句式为主,翻译时尽量不要"炫技",核心问题还是单词和词组的翻译,当然一些较难的翻译现象,比如"谓语动词的过渡""增词与减词"等还是要注意的。

第三节　2020 年下半年三级笔译英译汉(B 卷)

原文(请先通读全文)

In December 2019, a cluster of pneumonia cases were found. Scientists believe that it was caused by a previously unknown virus — now named COVID-19.

Coronaviruses have the appearance of a crown. Crown in Latin is called "corona" and that's how these viruses got their name. There are different types of coronaviruses that cause respiratory and sometimes gastrointestinal of symptoms.

It's known that coronaviruses circulate in a range of animals. But the animals which transmit COVID-19 are not known yet. And the exact dynamics of how the virus is transmitted is yet to be determined.

From what is known so far, there can be a number of symptoms ranging from mild to severe. There can be fever and respiratory symptoms such as cough and shortness of breath.

In more severe cases, there's been pneumonia, kidney failure and death. There is currently no specific medication for the virus and treatment is supportive care. There is currently no vaccine to protect against the virus. Treatment and vaccines are in development.

Nevertheless, we are committed to combatting the COVID-19 epidemic. It's certainly troubling that so many people and countries have been affected, so quickly. Now that the virus has a foothold in so many countries, the threat of a pandemic has become very real. But it would be the first pandemic in history that could be controlled. The bottom line is: we are not at the mercy of this virus.

The great advantage we have is that the decisions we all make — as governments, businesses, communities, families and individuals — can influence the trajectory of the epidemic. We need to remember that with decisive, early action, we can slow down the virus and prevent infections. Among those who are infected, most will recover.

It's also important to remember that looking only at the total number of reported cases and the total number of countries doesn't tell the full story. This is an uneven epidemic at the global level. Different countries are in different scenarios, requiring a tailored response. It's not about containment or mitigation. It's about both.

All countries must take a comprehensive blended strategy for controlling their epidemics and pushing this deadly virus back. Countries that continue finding and testing cases and tracing their contacts not only protect their own people, they can also affect what happens in other countries and globally.

The WHO has consolidated its guidance for countries in four categories: those with no case; those with sporadic cases; those with clusters; and those with community transmission. For all countries, the aim is the same: stop transmission and prevent the spread of the virus.

For the first three categories, countries must focus on finding, testing, treating and isolating individual cases and following their contacts. In areas with community spread, testing every suspected case and tracing their contacts become more challenging. Action must be taken to prevent transmission at the community level to reduce the epidemic to manageable clusters.

2020年下半年CATTI考试的英译汉如我们所料地考到了新冠疫情的相关内容，多年以来，CATTI考试从来没有出过有关当前时事的文章，这是第一次，也是新的情况，所以大家一定要关注当前的时政大事。本篇文章源于世界卫生组织的宣传片和其总干事的一篇讲话，文章是拼接而成的。文章的词汇是这几年大家熟知的医学词汇，基本的翻译现象也比较多，请大家认真学习。

In December 2019, a cluster of pneumonia cases were found. Scientists believe that it was caused by a previously unknown virus — now named COVID-19.

第一步 词汇解析

❶ cluster，名词，表示"（人或物的）组、群、簇"，比如：A cluster of vultures crouched on the carcass of a dead buffalo. （一群秃鹫蹲伏在一具野牛的尸体上。）

❷ pneumonia，名词，表示"肺炎"，比如：Most people do not have to be hospitalized for asthma or pneumonia. （大多数哮喘或肺炎患者无须住院。）

❸ case，名词，表示"病例、病案"，比如：the case of a 57-year-old man who had suffered a stroke（一个患过中风的57岁男子的病例）。

❹ COVID-19，专有名词，表示"新型冠状病毒肺炎"。

医学小常识：

新型冠状病毒肺炎（Corona Virus Disease 2019，COVID-19），简称"新冠肺炎"，世界卫生组织命名为"2019冠状病毒肺炎"，是指2019新型冠状病毒感染导致的肺炎。

第二步 注意断句

In December 2019, /a cluster of pneumonia cases were found. /Scientists believe /that it was caused by a previously unknown virus — now named COVID-19.

第三步 句型解析

❶ 第一句中，In December 2019 是时间状语，a cluster of pneumonia cases were found 是主谓结构，是典型的被动语态，可以用"被动变主动"的译法，当然只要句子通顺，用其他译法也是可以的。

❷ 第二句中，Scientists believe 是主谓结构，后面接 that 引导的宾语从句，it was caused 是宾语从句的主谓，也是被动语态，可以用"有被不用被"的译法，当然只要句子通顺，用其他译法也是可以的，by 引导状语结构，表示"由"，a previously unknown virus — now named COVID-19 表示"以前未知的病毒——现在命名为'新冠病毒'"，这里的破折号可以保留，也可以省略，或直接用逗号。

第四步 翻译来了

2019年12月出现了多例肺炎病例。科学家们认为，这种肺炎是由一种以前未知的病毒引起的，现在命名为"2019新型冠状病毒肺炎"（COVID-19）。

本句考点总结

本句出现了被动语态的译法。被动语态是英文常见的一种形式，而在中文里常常少用"被"或者不用"被"。那么我们一般有什么样的译法呢？第一种是被动变主动，第二种是寻找替代词（比如："让……给""为……所"等结构），第三种是在科技文献中"可以"来替代"被"，第四种是有"被"不用"被"。以上四种怎么用，那就看句子怎么通顺怎么翻译了啊！

2

> Coronaviruses have the appearance of a crown. Crown in Latin is called "corona" and that's how these viruses got their name. There are different types of coronaviruses that cause respiratory and sometimes gastrointestinal of symptoms.

第一步 词汇解析

❶ coronavirus，名词，表示"冠状病毒"，比如：Mouse Hepatitis virus (MHV) is a common coronavirus of laboratory mice.（小鼠肝炎病毒（MHV）是一种动物冠状病毒。）

❷ crown，名词，表示"冠、王冠"，比如：The crown was set with precious jewels — diamonds, rubies and emeralds.（王冠上镶嵌着稀世珍宝——有钻石、红宝石、绿宝石。）

❸ Latin，名词，表示"拉丁语"，比如：Very few students learn Latin now.（现在学拉丁语的学生少得很。）

❹ corona，名词，表示"冠状物"，比如：Her hair is a burning corona, her eyes are white-hot flakes.（他的头发如燃烧的皇冠，他的眼中放射出白炽的火花。）

❺ respiratory，形容词，表示"呼吸的"，比如：These gases will seriously damage the patient's respiratory system.（这些毒气会严重损害患者的呼吸系统。）

❻ gastrointestinal，形容词，表示"胃肠的"，比如：gastrointestinal diseases（胃肠疾病）。

❼ symptom，名词，表示"症状"，比如：One prominent symptom of the disease is progressive loss of memory.（这种疾病的一个显著症状就是记忆逐渐丧失。）

第二步 注意断句

Coronaviruses have the appearance of a crown. /Crown in Latin is called "corona" /and that's how these viruses got their name. /There are different types of coronaviruses /that cause respiratory and sometimes gastrointestinal of symptoms.

第三步 句型解析

❶ 第一句中，Coronaviruses have the appearance of a crown 是主谓宾结构，这里的 appearance 表示"外观、外表"。

❷ 第二句中，Crown in Latin is called "corona" 是主谓结构，也是被动语态，可以用"有被不用被"的译法，这里的 "corona" 是典型的中间语言，这个知识点在三笔考试中出现的不多，大家只需要记得：用于解释的英语或者是其他语言可以不用翻译。and 是并列连词，that's how these viruses got their name 是主系和表语从句的结构。

❸ There are different types of coronaviruses 是 there be 结构，表示"有"，that 引导定语从句，从句中的 cause respiratory and sometimes gastrointestinal of symptoms 是谓宾结构。从句较短，可以采用前置译法，但是也可以根据句子的通顺程度选择使用前置译法还是后置译法。这里的 cause 后面跟了两组宾语，可以用"动词的分配"译法。

第四步 翻译来了

冠状病毒和皇冠长得很像，在拉丁语言中称为"corona"（冠状物），这类病毒也因此而得名。冠状病毒有不同的种类，会引起呼吸道的症状，有时也会引起胃肠道的症状。

本句考点总结

第一,本句出现了被动语态的译法。被动语态是英文常见的一种形式,而在中文里常常少用"被"或者不用"被"。那么我们一般有什么样的译法呢?第一种是被动变主动,第二种是寻找替代词(比如:"让……给""为……所"等结构),第三种是在科技文献中用"可以"来替代"被",第四种是有"被"不用"被"。以上四种怎么用,那就看句子怎么通顺怎么翻译了啊!

第二,本句出现了英文定语从句的译法。一般来说,定语从句按照"短前长后"的译法处理,较短的定语从句可以前置,较长的定语从句可以后置,这一切都取决于句子的通顺,并没有绝对的前置和后置译法。

第三,本句考查了形容词的"分配"译法和动词或名词的"分配"译法。形容词分配的译法是两个或多个形容词位于名词之前,"翻译公式"是 (A+B)*C=AC+BC,比如 international and strategic questions 翻译为"国际问题和战略问题";动词或名词分配的译法是一个动词位于多个名词宾语之前,或者一个名词位于多个名词前,"翻译公式"是 A*(B+C)=AB+AC,比如 wear a hat and a scarf 翻译为"戴着帽子,系着围巾"。

3

It's known that coronaviruses circulate in a range of animals. But the animals which transmit COVID-19 are not known yet. And the exact dynamics of how the virus is transmitted is yet to be determined.

第一步 词汇解析

① circulate,动词,表示"循环、流转、传播",比如:The cells of the body, especially those of the brain, can live only minutes without circulating blood.(如果血液不循环,肌体细胞,尤其是脑细胞,只能存活几分钟。)

② transmit,动词,表示"传播、传染",比如:There was no danger of transmitting the infection through operations.(不存在通过手术传播这种传染病的风险。)

③ exact,形容词,表示"精确的、准确的",比如:We need to know the exact time the incident occurred.(我们需要了解事情发生的确切时间。)

④ dynamic,名词,表示"(人或事物)相互作用、动态",比如:the dynamics of the social system(社会体制的动态)。

第二步 注意断句

It's known /that coronaviruses circulate in a range of animals. /But /the animals /which transmit COVID-19 are not known yet. /And the exact dynamics of how the virus is transmitted /is yet to be determined.

第三步 句型解析

① 第一句中,It's known 一般翻译为"人们认为"或"众所周知",that 引导主语从句,coronaviruses circulate in a range of animals 是主谓状结构，这里的 circulate 表示"循环、散播、传播"。

❷ 第二句中，But 是表示转折的并列连词，the animals 是主语，which transmit COVID-19 是定语从句，从句较短，采用前置译法，are not known yet 是谓语，也是被动语态，可以用"被动变主动"的译法。这句和上一句形成了对比，一个"知道"，一个"不知道"，可以合译。

❸ 第三句中，And 是并列连词，the exact dynamics of how the virus is transmitted 是主语，is yet to be determined 也是被动语态，可以用"有被不用被"的译法。

第四步 翻译来了

众所周知，新冠病毒是在动物界中传播的，但是，尚不知道有哪些动物传播这种病毒，并且病毒是如何传播的具体细节还有待确定。

> **本句考点总结**
>
> 第一，本句出现了被动语态的译法。被动语态是英文常见的一种形式，而在中文里常常少用"被"或者不用"被"。那么我们一般有什么样的译法呢？第一种是被动变主动，第二种是寻找替代词（比如："让……给""为……所"等结构），第三种是在科技文献中用"可以"来替代"被"，第四种是有"被"不用"被"。以上四种怎么用，那就看句子怎么通顺怎么翻译了啊！
>
> 第二，本句出现了英文定语从句的译法。一般来说，定语从句按照"短前长后"的译法处理，较短的定语从句可以前置，较长的定语从句可以后置，这一切都取决于句子的通顺，并没有绝对的前置和后置译法。
>
> 第三，在翻译中，无论是英译汉，还是汉译英，我们常常将长句断成短句，然后一句一句翻译，短的句子由于上下文的联系，也可以放在一起翻译。非文学翻译中分译与合译出现得比较少，但是在文学翻译中出现得特别多，特别要读懂上下文内在的关系。分译与合译没有固定的翻译规则，而且每个译者的尺度也是不同的，重要的前提就是句意正确和句意通顺。

4 From what is known so far, there can be a number of symptoms ranging from mild to severe. There can be fever and respiratory symptoms such as cough and shortness of breath.

第一步 词汇解析

❶ fever，名词，表示"发烧、发热"，比如：Symptoms of the disease include fever and weight loss.（这种疾病的症状包括发烧和体重减轻。）

❷ cough，名词，表示"咳嗽"，比如：I couldn't stop coughing.（我咳嗽不止。）

❸ shortness，名词，表示"不足、简短"，比如：Any exercise that causes undue shortness of breath should be stopped.（任何导致呼吸出现困难的锻炼都应停止。）

第二步 注意断句

From what is known so far, /there can be a number of symptoms /ranging from mild to severe. / There can be fever and respiratory symptoms /such as cough and shortness of breath.

第三步 句型解析

❶ 第一句中，From what is known so far 是状语，there can be a number of symptoms 是 there be 句型，ranging from mild to severe 是现在分词短语做定语，相当于定语从句，采用前置译法，表示"从轻到重的范围"，这里可以增范围词"新冠肺炎"，因为"出现了大量的……"这个句子单独翻译会比较唐突。

❷ 第二句中的 There can be fever and respiratory symptoms 也是 there be 句型，such as cough and shortness of breath 是 such as 引导的举例，可以考虑为总分关系，但是也要考虑句子的通顺程度。

❸ 第一句和第二句较短，而且两句之间有明显的联系，所以可以合译。

第四步 翻译来了

从目前所了解到的情况来看，新冠肺炎会有大量的重症和轻症，可能会出现发热和呼吸道的症状，比如咳嗽和气短。

> **本句考点总结**
>
> 第一，本句出现了分词或分词短语位于名词后的译法。一般来说，分词或分词短语位于名词后相当于定语或定语从句，定语按照"短前长后"的译法来进行翻译。
>
> 第二，在翻译中，无论是英译汉，还是汉译英，我们常常将长句断成短句，然后一句一句翻译，短的句子由于上下文的联系，也可以放在一起翻译。非文学翻译中分译与合译出现得比较少，但是在文学翻译中出现得特别多，特别要读懂上下文内在的关系。分译与合译没有固定的翻译规则，而且每个译者的尺度也是不同的，重要的前提就是句意正确和句意通顺。

5

In more severe cases, there's been pneumonia, kidney failure and death. There is currently no specific medication for the virus and treatment is supportive care. There is currently no vaccine to protect against the virus. Treatment and vaccines are in development.

第一步 词汇解析

❶ kidney failure，名词词组，表示"肾衰竭"，比如：He was being treated for kidney failure.（他因肾衰竭正在接受治疗。）

❷ specific，形容词，表示"特定的、（药）具有特效的"，比如：There are several specific problems to be dealt with.（有好几个特定问题要解决。）

❸ medication，名词，表示"药、药物"，比如：Are you currently taking any medication?（你在服用什么药吗？）

④ supportive，形容词，表示"支持的、鼓励的"，比如：The silent majority of supportive parents and teachers should make their views known.（表示支持的父母和老师是沉默的大多数，他们应该公开表达他们的观点。）

⑤ vaccine，名词，表示"疫苗"，比如：Researchers around the world are collaborating to develop a new vaccine.（世界各地的研究人员正在合作培育一种新的疫苗。）

第二步 注意断句

In more severe cases, /there's been pneumonia, /kidney failure and death. /There is currently no specific medication for the virus /and treatment is supportive care. /There is currently no vaccine to protect against the virus. /Treatment and vaccines are in development.

第三步 句型解析

① 第一句中，In more severe cases 是状语，there's been pneumonia, kidney failure and death 是典型的 there be 句型，表示"有"。

② 第二句中，There is currently no specific medication for the virus 也是 there be 句型，这里的 for 是介词，可以翻译为动词"治疗"，and 是并列连词，treatment is supportive care 是主系表结构，注意理解这里的 supportive care，医学上表示"支持疗法"。

③ 第三句 There is currently no vaccine to protect against the virus 还是 there be 句型，较为简单，直接翻译即可。

④ 第四句 Treatment and vaccines are in development 是主系表结构，in development 表示"正在研究中"。

⑤ 本句共有四个句子，有些句子之间有一定的联系，可以考虑合译。

第四步 翻译来了

某些更为严重的患者会出现肺炎、肾衰竭以及死亡。目前针对这种病毒没有特效药，只有支持疗法，也没有疫苗预防这种病毒，治疗方案和疫苗都在研究当中。

Nevertheless, we are committed to combatting the COVID-19 epidemic. It's certainly troubling that so many people and countries have been affected, so quickly. Now that the virus has a foothold in so many countries, the threat of a pandemic has become very real. But it would be the first pandemic in history that could be controlled. The bottom line is: we are not at the mercy of this virus.

第一步 词汇解析

① nevertheless，副词，表示"尽管如此、不过、然而"，比如：Most marriages fail after between five and nine years. Nevertheless, people continue to get married.（大部分婚姻在婚后第五年至第九年间失败，然而，人们仍会选择结婚。）

② epidemic，名词，表示"流行病"，比如：Hospitals were already fully extended because of the epidemic.（这场流行病已使各医院以最大负荷运转。）

❸ troubling，形容词，表示"令人不安的"，比如：There was something in the darker recesses of his unconscious that was troubling him.（在他潜意识的隐秘的深处有一些东西让他觉得不安。）

❹ foothold，名词，表示"据点、立足点"，比如：Businesses are investing millions of dollars to gain a foothold in this new market.（商家们正投资数百万美元以求在新市场中获得立足点。）

❺ pandemic，名词，表示"（全国或全球性）流行病、大流行病"，比如：One pandemic of Spanish flu took nearly 22 million lives worldwide.（西班牙流感的大爆发夺去了全球近 2 200 万人的生命。）

❻ bottom line，名词词组，表示"底线"，比如：The bottom line is that we have to make a decision today.（底线是：我们今天必须做出决定。）

❼ at the mercy of，介词词组，表示"完全由……支配、任由……摆布"，比如：Ordinary people are at the mercy of faceless bureaucrats.（普通人的命运任凭那些平庸刻板的官僚们摆布。）

第二步 注意断句

Nevertheless, /we are committed to combatting the COVID-19 epidemic. /It's certainly troubling /that so many people and countries have been affected, /so quickly. /Now that /the virus has a foothold in so many countries, /the threat of a pandemic has become very real. /But /it would be the first pandemic in history /that could be controlled. / The bottom line is: /we are not at the mercy of this virus.

第三步 句型解析

❶ 第一句中，Nevertheless 是转折连词，we are committed to combatting the COVID-19 epidemic 是主谓宾结构，直接翻译即可。

❷ 第二句中，It's certainly troubling 是主系表结构，It 是形式主语，真正的主语是后面 that 引导的主语从句，实际上 that 引导的从句是事实，而 certainly troubling 是评论，这点可以看出来吧？从句中 so many people and countries have been affected 是主谓结构，也是典型的被动语态，可以用"寻找替代词"的译法，so quickly 是状语，用于补充说明。

❸ 第三句中，Now that 作为引导词，表示"既然"，the virus has a foothold in so many countries 是主谓宾状结构，主句 the threat of a pandemic has become very real 是主系表结构，本句较为简单，可以直接翻译，这里的 threat 可以看作典型的抽象名词，增动词翻译更加通顺，考试时你也可以不增词。

❹ 第四句中，But 是表示转折的连词，it would be the first pandemic in history 是主系表结构，that 引导定语从句，从句较短，采用前置译法，从句 that could be controlled 又是被动语态，还是可以用"寻找替代词"的译法。

❺ 第五句中，The bottom line is 是主语和系动词，这里的冒号可以保留，表语从句 we are not at the mercy of this virus 是主系表结构，可以直接翻译。

第四步 翻译来了

尽管如此，我们也正在致力于对抗新冠肺炎疫情。这么多人，这么多国家都受到了影响，而且病毒传播速度如此之快，这一点是令人不安的。既然这种病毒已经在许多国家传播，那么疫情所产生的威胁是切实存在的。但是，这也会是历史上第一次可以受到控制的疫情。我们的底线是：我们不能受到病毒的控制。

本句考点总结

第一，本句出现了被动语态的译法。被动语态是英文常见的一种形式，而在中文里常常少用"被"或者不用"被"。那么我们一般有什么样的译法呢？第一种是被动变主动，第二种是寻找替代词（比如："让……给""为……所"等结构），第三种是在科技文献中用"可以"来替代"被"，第四种是有"被"不用"被"。以上四种怎么用，那就看句子怎么通顺怎么翻译了啊！

第二，本句出现了事实 (Facts) 和评论 (Comments) 的译法。中文一般先事实，后评论，而英文一般先评论，后事实。比如：It is important for her to go abroad. 翻译为"对于她来说，出国是很重要的"。英文中 It is important 是评论，for her to go abroad 是事实，从中英文的对比来看，可以知道中英文语序分别是怎么安排的。

第三，本句当中考查了"抽象名词"的译法。抽象名词一般处于冠词之后，又在介词之前，以"the + 抽象名词 + of"的形式居多。一般来说，抽象名词有两种译法。第一种，若抽象名词有动词词根，则翻译为动词，比如 the suggestion of mine，翻译为"我建议"，而不是"我的建议"；第二种，若抽象名词没有动词词根，可以增动词翻译，比如 the spirit of our nation，翻译为"我们民族所具有的精神"，而不是"我们民族的精神"。

第四，本句出现了英文定语从句的译法。一般来说，定语从句按照"短前长后"的译法处理，较短的定语从句可以前置，较长的定语从句可以后置，这一切都取决于句子的通顺，并没有绝对的前置和后置译法。

7

The great advantage we have is that the decisions we all make — as governments, businesses, communities, families and individuals — can influence the trajectory of the epidemic. We need to remember that with decisive, early action, we can slow down the virus and prevent infections. Among those who are infected, most will recover.

第一步 词汇解析

1. trajectory，名词，表示"发展轨迹、轨道、弹道、轨迹"，比如：My career seemed to be on a downward trajectory.（我的事业似乎在走下坡路。）
2. decisive，形容词，表示"坚决的、果断的、决断的"，比如：This is a time of decisive action and quick thinking.（这个时候应该果断行动，快速反应。）
3. infection，名词，表示"传染、感染"，比如：AIDS lowers the body's resistance to infection.（艾滋病降低了身体的抗感染能力。）

第二步 注意断句

The great advantage /we have is /that the decisions we all make — /as governments, /businesses, /communities, /families /and individuals — /can influence the trajectory of the epidemic. /We need to remember /that with decisive, /early action, /we can slow down the virus and prevent infections. /Among those who are infected, /most will recover.

第三步 句型解析

❶ 第一句中，The great advantage we have is 是主谓结构，we have 是定语从句，从句较短，采用前置译法，that 引导表语从句，the decisions we all make 是从句的主语，we all make 也是定语从句，从句较短，采用前置译法，之后的破折号可以保留，若为了通顺也可以省略，其中所有名词 as governments, businesses, communities, families and individuals 表示上文的 we（这些人或者机构），can influence the trajectory of the epidemic 是表语从句的谓语和宾语，其中 trajectory 可以认为是典型的抽象名词，无动词词根，可以增动词"发展"。

❷ 第二句中，We need to remember 是主谓结构，that 引导宾语从句，with decisive, early action 是 with 引导的方式状语，we can slow down the virus and prevent infections 是主谓宾结构，这里也有翻译的小知识点需要注意，你直接翻译为"降低病毒"肯定不对，增词"病毒传播的速度"才好。

❸ 第三句中，Among those who are infected 是介词短语和较短的定语从句，从句可以前置，most will recover 是主谓结构，这里的 most 表示"大多数人"，你要直接翻译为"在感染的人群中，大多数都会康复"其实也不通顺，可以看看译文怎么处理的哦！

第四步 翻译来了

　　我们拥有的最大的优势在于，我们所做出的决定，包括政府、企业、社区、家庭和个人所做出的决定都会影响疫情发展的态势。我们必须要记住，只有采取果断和尽早的行动，我们才能降低病毒传播的速度，并且预防感染。大多数感染的人都会康复的。

🧑‍🏫 本句考点总结

　　第一，本句当中考查了"抽象名词"的译法。抽象名词一般处于冠词之后，又在介词之前，以"the + 抽象名词 + of"的形式居多，一般来说，抽象名词有两种译法。第一种，若抽象名词有动词词根，则翻译为动词，比如 the suggestion of mine，翻译为"我建议"，而不是"我的建议"；第二种，若抽象名词没有动词词根，可以增动词翻译，比如 the spirit of our nation，翻译为"我们民族所具有的精神"，而不是"我们民族的精神"。

　　第二，本句出现了英文定语从句的译法。一般来说，定语从句按照"短前长后"的译法处理，较短的定语从句可以前置，较长的定语从句可以后置，这一切都取决于句子的通顺，并没有绝对的前置和后置译法。

　　第三，本句考查了英汉互译增减词的问题，一般来说英译汉增词，汉译英减词，常见增词的种类有：一、增加对象词（范围词），这是由上文缺少句子的某个部分造成的；二、增加范畴词，这是较难的一部分，常见的范畴词有"水平、方式、方法、问题、情况、途径和方面"，但是不仅仅有这些，还有其他很多；三、增加评论性词，这些常常出现在文学翻译中；四、增加动词，会在动词的"分配译法"中说明这点。

It's also important to remember that looking only at the total number of reported cases and the total number of countries doesn't tell the full story. This is an uneven epidemic at the global level. Different countries are in different scenarios, requiring a tailored response. It's not about containment or mitigation. It's about both.

第一步 词汇解析

① uneven，形容词，表示"无定型的、不规则的、无规律的"，比如：an uneven distribution of resources（资源的不均衡分配）。

② scenario，名词，表示"方案、情况、设想"，比如：Let me suggest a possible scenario.（我来设想一种可能出现的情况。）

③ tailored，形容词，表示"特制的、专门的"，比如：Special programmes of study are tailored to the needs of specific groups.（制订特殊课程，以满足特定群体的需要。）

④ containment，名词，表示"遏制、控制、抑制"，比如：Fire crews are hoping they can achieve full containment of the fire before the winds pick up.（消防队员希望趁着风还没有起来将火势完全控制住。）

⑤ mitigation，名词，表示"减轻、缓解"，比如：In mitigation, the defence lawyer said his client was seriously depressed at the time of the assault.（为了减轻罪行，辩护律师说他的当事人在袭击人的时候精神极度压抑。）

第二步 注意断句

It's also important /to remember /that looking only at the total number of reported cases and the total number of countries doesn't tell the full story. /This is an uneven epidemic at the global level. /Different countries are in different scenarios, /requiring a tailored response. /It's not about containment or mitigation. /It's about both.

第三步 句型解析

① 第一句中，It's also important 中的 It 是形式主语，后面的 to remember 是真正的主语，这里也是"事实与评论"的关系，that 引导宾语从句，looking only at the total number of reported cases and the total number of countries 是从句的主语，doesn't tell the full story 是从句的谓语和宾语，tell the full story 是固定用法，表示"看到事情的全貌"，本句表示"看清整个疫情的态势"。

② 第二句 This is an uneven epidemic at the global level 是主系表状结构，这里的 uneven 特别需要注意，翻译为"无规律的，分布不均衡的"。

③ 第三句中，Different countries are in different scenarios 是主系表结构，requiring a tailored response 是现在分词短语作伴随状语，不是定语从句，相当于谓语和宾语的结构，可以在 requiring 前增主语"不同的国家"。

④ 第四句 It's not about containment or mitigation 是主系表结构，这里的 It 指的是上文的 response，后一句较短，It's about both 也是主系表结构，因为句意有联系，所以可以合译。这里的 containment or mitigation 若翻译为"控制和减缓"，感觉读者不太能明白，增词"疫情"会使译文读起来更加通顺，这里属于典型的增对象词。

第四步 翻译来了

要记住，只看报告的病例数量和国家总数并不能看清整个疫情的态势，这一点同样重要。在全球层面来看，疫情的分布是没有规律的，不同的国家处于不同的境地，各个国家也需要专门的对应策略，这不仅关乎于控制或减缓疫情，而是两手都要抓。

🧑‍🏫 本句考点总结

第一，本句出现了事实 (Facts) 和评论 (Comments) 的译法。中文一般先事实，后评论，而英文一般先评论，后事实。比如：It is important for her to go abroad. 翻译为"对于她来说，出国是很重要的"。英文中 It is important 是评论，for her to go abroad 是事实，从中英文的对比来看，可以知道中英文语序分别是怎么安排的。

第二，本句出现了分词或分词短语位于名词后的译法，一般来说，分词或分词短语位于名词后相当于定语或定语从句，但是这也要具体问题具体分析，本句则是状语结构，这个知识点要注意。

第三，本句考查了英汉互译增减词的问题，一般来说英译汉增词，汉译英减词，常见增词的种类有：一、增加对象词（范围词），这是由上文缺少句子的某个部分造成的；二、增加范畴词，这是较难的一部分，常见的范畴词有"水平、方式、方法、问题、情况、途径和方面"，但是不仅仅有这些，还有其他很多；三、增加评论性词，这些常常出现在文学翻译中；四、增加动词，会在动词的"分配译法"中说明这点。

第四，在翻译中，无论是英译汉，还是汉译英，我们常常将长句断成短句，然后一句一句翻译，短的句子由于上下文的联系，也可以放在一起翻译。非文学翻译中分译与合译出现得比较少，但是在文学翻译中出现得特别多，特别要读懂上下文内在的关系。分译与合译没有固定的翻译规则，而且每个译者的尺度也是不同的，重要的前提就是句意正确和句意通顺。

 9

All countries must take a comprehensive blended strategy for controlling their epidemics and pushing this deadly virus back. Countries that continue finding and testing cases and tracing their contacts not only protect their own people, they can also affect what happens in other countries and globally.

第一步 词汇解析

❶ blended，形容词，表示"混杂的、混合的"，比如：blended fabric（混纺织物、混纺布）。

❷ deadly，形容词，表示"致命的、非常的"，比如：a deadly disease currently affecting dolphins（目前影响海豚的一种致命疾病）。

第二步 注意断句

All countries must take a comprehensive blended strategy for controlling their epidemics /and pushing this deadly virus back. /Countries /that continue finding and testing cases and tracing their contacts /not only protect their own people, /they can also affect /what happens in other countries and globally.

第三步 句型解析

① 第一句中，All countries must take a comprehensive blended strategy 是主谓宾结构，for 引导目的状语，controlling their epidemics and pushing this deadly virus back 是两个动宾短语，直接翻译即可。

② 第二句中，Countries 是主语，that 引导定语从句，that continue finding and testing cases and tracing their contacts 是定语从句，从句较长，可以采用后置译法，但是也要考虑到通顺的问题，not only protect their own people 是谓语和宾语结构。第二分句中，they 是主语，can also affect 是谓语，what happens in other countries and globally 是宾语从句，这里的 what 是代词，可以理解为"发生的一切"，也就是"疫情的形势"。

第四步 翻译来了

所有国家必须要采取综合多样的策略来控制疫情，对抗这种致命的病毒。坚持寻找病例，测试病例，追踪接触者的国家不仅可以保护自己的人民，而且也可以影响其他国家和全球的疫情。

> **本句考点总结**
>
> 第一，本句出现了英文定语从句的译法。一般来说，定语从句按照"短前长后"的译法处理，较短的定语从句可以前置，较长的定语从句可以后置，这一切都取决于句子的通顺，并没有绝对的前置和后置译法。
>
> 第二，本句考查了英汉互译增减词的问题，一般来说英译汉增词，汉译英减词，常见增词的种类有：一、增加对象词（范围词），这是由上文缺少句子的某个部分造成的；二、增加范畴词，这是较难的一部分，常见的范畴词有"水平、方式、方法、问题、情况、途径和方面"，但是不仅仅有这些，还有其他很多；三、增加评论性词，这些常常出现在文学翻译中；四、增加动词，会在动词的"分配译法"中说明这点。

The WHO has consolidated its guidance for countries in four categories: those with no case; those with sporadic cases; those with clusters; and those with community transmission. For all countries, the aim is the same: stop transmission and prevent the spread of the virus.

第一步 词汇解析

① consolidate，动词，表示"使加强、使巩固"，比如：With this new movie he has consolidated his position as the country's leading director.（他新执导的影片巩固了他作为全国最佳导演的地位。）

② guidance，名词，表示"指导"，比如：The government should give clear guidance on the content of religious

education.（政府应该给出明确的关于宗教教育内容的指导方针。）
③ sporadic，形容词，表示"间断发生的、零星的"，比如：The sound of sporadic shooting could still be heard.（仍能听见零星的枪声。）
④ transmission，名词，表示"传播、传染"，比如：Heterosexual contact is responsible for the bulk of HIV transmission.（艾滋病病毒大半是经异性性接触传播的。）

第二步 注意断句

The WHO has consolidated its guidance for countries in four categories: /those with no case; /those with sporadic cases; /those with clusters; /and those with community transmission. /For all countries, /the aim is the same: /stop transmission /and prevent the spread of the virus.

第三步 句型解析

① 第一句中，The WHO has consolidated its guidance for countries 是主谓宾结构，in four categories 是状语，后面的冒号可以保留，those with no case，those with sporadic cases，those with clusters 和 those with community transmission 是四种不同的情况，翻译时分号可以变成顿号。
② 第二句中，For all countries 是状语，the aim is the same 是主系表结构，后面的冒号可以保留，stop transmission and prevent the spread of the virus 是两个动宾短语，这两个动宾短语含义相似，可以只翻译一次。

第四步 翻译来了

世界卫生组织对于四类国家加强了防疫指导：没有病例的国家、病例散发的国家、病例聚集爆发的国家和存在社区传播的国家。对于所有国家来说，目标都是一样的：阻止病毒传播。

For the first three categories, countries must focus on finding, testing, treating and isolating individual cases and following their contacts. In areas with community spread, testing every suspected case and tracing their contacts become more challenging. Action must be taken to prevent transmission at the community level to reduce the epidemic to manageable clusters.

第一步 词汇解析

① isolate，动词，表示"（使）隔离、孤立"，比如：Patients with the disease should be isolated.（这种病的患者应予以隔离。）
② suspected case，名词词组，表示"疑似病例"，比如：There is one suspected case in the country.（该国出现了一起疑似病例。）
③ challenging，形容词，表示"具有挑战的"，比如：Mike found a challenging job as a computer programmer.（迈克找到了一份富有挑战性的工作——当电脑程序员。）
④ manageable，形容词，表示"可操纵的、可处理的"，比如：He will now try to cut down the task to a manageable size.（他现在要努力把任务的规模降至可控的范围。）

第二步 注意断句

For the first three categories, /countries must focus on finding, /testing, /treating /and isolating individual cases /and following their contacts. /In areas /with community spread, /testing every suspected case and tracing their contacts /become more challenging. /Action must be taken to prevent transmission /at the community level /to reduce the epidemic /to manageable clusters.

第三步 句型解析

❶ 第一句中，For the first three categories 是状语，countries must focus on finding, testing, treating and isolating individual cases 是主谓宾结构，and 是并列连词，following their contacts 是第二组谓语和宾语。

❷ 第二句中，In areas with community spreads 是地点状语，这里的 with 是介词，可以翻译为动词，表示"有、存在"，testing every suspected case and tracing their contacts 是主语，become more challenging 是系表结构，而且本句主语过长，可以单独成句，后面用本位词"这"进行替代。

❸ 第三句中，Action must be taken to prevent transmission 是主谓状结构，也是典型的被动语态，可以用"被动变主动"的译法。at the community level 是地点状语，to reduce the epidemic 是目的状语，to manageable clusters 是介词短语，这里的 to 表示"达到"。

第四步 翻译来了

对于前三类国家来说，重点要发现、检测、治疗、隔离单个病例，并跟踪其接触者。存在社区传播的地区，每一个疑似病例都需要检测，还要追踪其接触者，这变得很具有挑战性。必须采取行动阻止病毒在社区传播，要把疫情降低到可控的聚集范围。

本句考点总结

第一，关于"介改动"的译法。英文里的介词常常翻译为动词，比如 He went to Beijing by plane. 翻译为"他坐飞机去北京"，这里的 by 翻译为"坐"，这就是"介改动"的译法。

第二，英译汉时，若句子主语过长，那么可以单独成句，形成一个完整的主谓宾句子，这样翻译是为了避免句子过于臃肿。当主语单独成句时，句子的谓语和宾语缺少主语，那么可以增加"这""这些""这一切""这样"等词作为句子的主语，这样的词称为"本位词"，被这些词所代替的部分称为"外位语"。

第三，本句出现了被动语态的译法。被动语态是英文常见的一种形式，而在中文里常常少用"被"或者不用"被"。那么我们一般有什么样的译法呢？第一种是被动变主动，第二种是寻找替代词（比如："让……给""为……所"等结构），第三种是在科技文献中用"可以"来替代"被"，第四种是有"被"不用"被"。以上四种怎么用，那就看句子怎么通顺怎么翻译了啊！

这篇文章是这两年国际国内最热点的时事，所以文章中的单词和词组大家应该都非常熟悉，在翻译时，

速度应该要控制在两小时之内。文章里各种英译汉的现象都出现了,最重要的应该是"被动语态"的译法,因为科技文献的特点就是这个,所以请大家务必认真学习和训练这个知识点。

第四节 2020年下半年三级笔译汉译英(B卷)

水稻是世界上最主要的粮食作物之一,世界上一半以上人口(包括中国60%以上人口)都以稻米作为主食。中国是世界上最早种植水稻的国家,至今已有7 000年左右的历史,当前水稻产量占全国粮食作物产量近一半。

水稻作为主要的粮食,无论对中国还是对世界的重要性都是不言而喻的。中国在超级杂交水稻(super hybrid rice)生产方面成就突出,关键人物便是袁隆平,被誉为"中国杂交水稻之父"。

他的名字不仅在中国家喻户晓,在国际上也享有盛誉。袁隆平于上世纪60年代开始杂交水稻研究。他带领科研团队使中国杂交水稻一直领先于世界水平,不仅不断实现杂交水稻的高产量目标,而且在生产实践中不断推广应用,从实际上解决了中国人吃饭难的问题。

袁隆平还多次到美国、印度等国家传授技术,为30多个国家和地区的政府官员和科研工作者讲学,促进杂交水稻技术造福世界。

1987年11月3日,联合国教科文组织在巴黎总部向袁隆平颁发科学奖,认为他的科研成果是"第二次绿色革命"。2004年,袁隆平获得世界粮食奖(the World Food Prize),表彰他为人类提供营养丰富、数量充足的粮食所做出的突出贡献。

2020年下半年CATTI考试的另一篇汉译英是有关"杂交水稻之父"袁隆平先生的,这篇文章原本是刊登在《中国画报》英文版的一篇英文报道,但是考试却成了汉译英题目,这种情况在之前的CATTI考试中也出现过。原文也有部分删减,总体难度不是很大,但是要特别注意本文的一些时态问题。

水稻是世界上最主要的粮食作物之一,世界上一半以上人口(包括中国60%以上人口)都以稻米作为主食。中国是世界上最早种植水稻的国家,至今已有7 000年左右的历史,当前水稻产量占全国粮食作物产量近一半。

第一步 词汇解析

❶ 水稻,rice,名词,比如:grow rice(种水稻)。句中"水稻"的意思是"大米",所以可以翻译为rice。"种植稻米",翻译为cultivate rice。

❷ 最主要的粮食作物,most eaten staple foods,名词词组。句中"最主要的粮食作物"的意思是"吃得最

多的主食",也可以直接翻译为 an important cereal crop。

主食,staple foods,名词词组,比如:Retail prices of staple foods remain unchanged.（主食的零售价保持不变。）

food 表示"食品、伙食、养料"的统称时,是不可数名词,不加 -s;food 表示某种可吃的食物时,为可数名词。a food 指一种食物,foods 指多种食物,可加 -s。

❸ 人口,inhabitant,名词,比如:the inhabitants of Boise（博伊斯的居民）。

❹ 以……作为主食,feed,动词,比如:There's enough here to feed an army.（这儿的东西足以养活一支军队。）

❺ 最早种植水稻的国家,earliest rice planting country,名词词组。

种植,planting,动词,单词原形为:plant,比如:He says he plans to plant fruit trees and vegetables.（他说他计划栽种果树和蔬菜。）下文提到 plantation 一词,表示"大面积栽培植物"。

❻ 占,account for,动词词组,比如:Computers account for 5% of the country's commercial electricity consumption.（电脑占了这个国家商业用电的 5%。）"占"还可以翻译为 take up 等词或词组。

❼ 全国粮食作物产量,its total grain crop output,名词词组。

作物,crop,名词,比如:a subsistence crop（口粮作物）。

第二步 动词定位

水稻<u>是</u>世界上最主要的粮食作物之一,世界上一半以上人口（包括中国 60% 以上人口）都以稻米<u>作为</u>主食。中国<u>是</u>世界上最早<u>种植</u>水稻的国家,至今已<u>有</u> 7 000 年左右的历史,当前水稻产量<u>占</u>全国粮食作物产量近一半。

第三步 句型解析

❶ 第一句第一分句中,"水稻"是主语,"是"是第一个动词,"世界上最主要的粮食作物之一"是宾语。第二分句中,"世界上一半以上人口（包括中国 60% 以上人口）"是主语,"稻米"是宾语,"以……作为"是谓语,"主食"是状语,两句之间用并列连词 and 连接没有问题,但是你想想怎么才能把这两句话更自然、通顺地连接在一起呢?我们可以把第二分句的主语处理成"水稻",谓语动词是"养活了",宾语是"世界上一半以上人口（包括中国 60% 以上人口）",这不就完事了吗?这时一个句子有两个动词,又该如何处理呢?是不是"并列""伴随"或"下沉"的结构呢?译文处理为下沉结构,第一组谓语和宾语直接变成了同位语 one of the most eaten staple foods in the world。

❷ 第二句第一分句中,"中国"是主语,"是"是谓语,"世界上最早种植水稻的国家"是宾语,第二分句"至今已有 7 000 年左右的历史"也就是"中国种植水稻的历史有 7 000 年左右",其中"的历史"是典型的范畴词,可以减词,主谓宾非常清晰,两句可以使用共同的主语"中国"。第三分句"当前水稻产量"是主语,"产量"是典型的范畴词,可以减词,"占"是核心谓语,"全国粮食作物产量近一半"是宾语,句子之间可以用 and 连接。那么本句的第一分句和第二分句有两个动词,你该如何处理呢?是不是"并列""伴随"或"下沉"的结构呢?译文处理为下沉结构,第一组谓语和宾语直接变成了同位语 As the world's earliest rice planting country。

❸ 本句注意时态的问题,第一句因为没有明确的时间状语,可以用一般现在时,第二句提到了"已有 7 000 年左右",可以用现在完成时。

第四步 翻译来了

Rice, one of the most eaten staple foods in the world, feeds over half of the global inhabitants, including 60 percent of China's population. As the world's earliest rice planting country, China has practiced rice plantation for nearly 7,000 years, and today rice accounts for nearly 50 percent of its total grain crop output.

> **本句考点总结**
>
> 第一，汉译英句子中并列、伴随、下沉的结构。中文常常会出现多个句子聚集的情况，那么我们在翻译时需要考虑将这些句子进行"分堆"，但是"分堆"之后，一个句子中也可能会出现两个动词或两组动词，那么有两个动词或两组动词的句子我们该如何进行翻译呢？比如："我坐在那里看书"，这里有两个动词，一个是"坐"，一个是"看"，我们翻译时便会有三种方法：
>
> 第一种并列（两个动词并列的译法，使用并列连词连接，两个动词之间不一定是"并列"关系）：I sat there and read a book.
>
> 第二种伴随（将第二个动词翻译为二谓语，分词、从句、状语等都可以）：I sat there reading a book.
>
> 第三种下沉（将第一个动词翻译为二谓语，分词、从句、状语等都可以）：Siting there, I read a book.
>
> 需要说明的是，并列、伴随和下沉只是动词的形式问题，不代表动词之间的逻辑关系，用这三种形式翻译两个动词或两组动词都是可以的，大家可以根据句子上下文的关系来判断使用。
>
> 第二，本句考查了英汉互译增减词的问题，一般来说英译汉增词，汉译英减词，常见增词的种类有：一、增加对象词（范围词），这是由上文缺少句子的某个部分造成的；二、增加范畴词，这是较难的一部分，常见的范畴词有"水平、方式、方法、问题、情况、途径和方面"，但是不仅仅有这些，还有其他很多；三、增加评论性词，这些常常出现在文学翻译中；四、增加动词，会在动词的"分配译法"中说明这点。

2 水稻作为主要的粮食，无论对中国还是对世界的重要性都是不言而喻的。中国在超级杂交水稻（super hybrid rice）生产方面成就突出，关键人物便是袁隆平，被誉为"中国杂交水稻之父"。

第一步 词汇解析

❶ 主要的粮食，the "greatest force" in grain，名词词组。句中"主要的粮食"的意思是"粮食作物中的主力"，直接翻译也可以。

❷ 不言而喻的，important，形容词，比如：The most important thing in my life was my career.（我生活中最重要的部分是我的事业。）句中"不言而喻的"的意思是"不用说就可以明白，形容道理很浅显"。

与上文搭配，"……的重要性是不言而喻的"意思是"非常重要的"。

❸ 超级杂交水稻，super hybrid rice，名词词组。

农业小常识：

　　超级杂交水稻是农业农村部超级杂交水稻培育计划的成果，该计划于1996年提出，"杂交水稻之父"袁隆平主持培育计划。

❹ 在生产方面成就突出，successfully put into large-scale production，动词词组。句中"在生产方面成就突出"的意思是"成功投入大规模生产"。

大规模的，large-scale，形容词，比如：a large-scale military operation（一次大规模的军事行动）。

❺ 袁隆平，Yuan Longping，人名。人名音译即可，姓和名的首字母大写，姓和名要分开书写。

❻ 被誉为，dubbed，动词，单词原形为：dub，比如：Today's session has been widely dubbed as a "make or break" meeting.（今天的会议被大众称为"不成则散"的会议。）dub + 人名 + 称号，表示"授予……称号"。

❼ "中国杂交水稻之父"，"Father of Hybrid Rice in China"，专有名词，首字母大写，按照字面翻译即可，沿用原文符号。词组中"中国"是地点状语，翻译为 in China。

第二步 动词定位

　　水稻作为主要的粮食，无论对中国还是对世界的重要性都是不言而喻的。中国在超级杂交水稻 (super hybrid rice) 生产方面成就突出，关键人物便是袁隆平，被誉为"中国杂交水稻之父"。

第三步 句型解析

❶ 第一句中，"水稻"是主语，"作为"是谓语，"主要的粮食"是宾语，"无论对中国还是对世界"是状语，"的重要性都是不言而喻的"表示"是非常重要的"，这样一来本句有两个动词，一个是"作为"，另一个是"是"，两个动词的句子最简单，"并列""伴随""下沉"的结构随意使用。译文将主语处理为"'水稻'的作用"属于典型的增范畴词，较难。

❷ 第二句中，"中国"是主语，"在超级杂交水稻（super hybrid rice）生产方面"是状语，这里有两点需要说明：第一，"超级杂交水稻"后面的英文 super hybrid rice 是原文给出的，所以翻译时直接使用；第二，"生产方面"中的"方面"是典型的范畴词，可以不翻译。"成就突出"是谓语和宾语，本句也是"事实与评论"的关系，译文可以处理为"中国成功地大规模生产超级杂交水稻"。第二个分句是"关键人物便是袁隆平，被誉为'中国杂交水稻之父'"，其中两个动词，一个是"是"，一个是"被誉为"，其实这里可以形成第二个句子，而这两个动词之间肯定是"伴随结构"，后面用定语从句即可。但是译文的结构较难，第一分句翻译后使用 without the efforts of Yuan Longping 的结构，将句子处理为三谓语介词短语，再接伴随结构 dubbed，这个结构过于难，不建议大家使用。

第四步 翻译来了

　　The role of rice, the "greatest force" in grain, is important to China and the whole world. China was the first country to successfully put super hybrid rice into large-scale production, and that effort would not have succeeded without the efforts of Yuan Longping, dubbed the "Father of Hybrid Rice in China."

本句考点总结

第一，汉译英句子中并列、伴随、下沉的结构。中文常常会出现多个句子聚集的情况，那么我们在翻译时需要考虑将这些句子进行"分堆"，但是"分堆"之后，一个句子中也可能会出现两个动词或两组动词，那么有两个动词或两组动词的句子我们该如何进行翻译呢？比如："我坐在那里看书"，这里有两个动词，一个是"坐"，一个是"看"，我们翻译时便会有三种方法：

第一种并列（两个动词并列的译法，使用并列连词连接，两个动词之间不一定是"并列"关系）：I sat there and read a book.

第二种伴随（将第二个动词翻译为二谓语，分词、从句、状语等都可以）：I sat there reading a book.

第三种下沉（将第一个动词翻译为二谓语，分词、从句、状语等都可以）：Siting there, I read a book.

需要说明的是，并列、伴随和下沉只是动词的形式问题，不代表动词之间的逻辑关系，用这三种形式翻译两个动词或两组动词都是可以的，大家可以根据句子上下文的关系来判断使用。

第二，本句考查了英汉互译增减词的问题，一般来说英译汉增词，汉译英减词，常见增词的种类有：一、增加对象词（范围词），这是由上文缺少句子的某个部分造成的；二、增加范畴词，这是较难的一部分，常见的范畴词有"水平、方式、方法、问题、情况、途径和方面"，但是不仅仅有这些，还有其他很多；三、增加评论性词，这些常常出现在文学翻译中；四、增加动词，会在动词的"分配译法"中说明这点。

第三，本句出现了事实(Facts)和评论(Comments)的译法。中文一般先事实，后评论，而英文一般先评论，后事实。比如：It is important for her to go abroad. 翻译为"对于她来说，出国是很重要的"。英文中 It is important 是评论，for her to go abroad 是事实，从中英文的对比来看，可以知道中英文语序分别是怎么安排的。

第四，关于谓语动词的层次性。汉译英的核心问题是厘清句子当中多个动词之间的关系，我们要学会在多个动词当中找到最核心的动词，翻译为核心谓语（也称为一谓语）；找到其次核心的动词，翻译为分词、从句或是其他状语或定语的形式（也称为二谓语）；再找到不重要的动词，翻译为介词（也称为三谓语）；最后最不重要的动词，可以不译（也称为四谓语）。这些动词在句子当中如何划分层次，需要大家在长期不断的实践中摸索，而且每个句子的翻译也不是固定的。有些句子当中的"一谓语"（核心谓语），在别的译本当中可能就是"二谓语"或者是"三谓语"。只要句子整体结构正确，逻辑清晰，那这就是一个好的译本。

3 他的名字不仅在中国家喻户晓，在国际上也享有盛誉。袁隆平于上世纪 60 年代开始杂交水稻研究。他带领科研团队使中国杂交水稻一直领先于世界水平，不仅不断实现杂交水稻的高产量目标，而且在生产实践中不断推广应用，从实际上解决了中国人吃饭难的问题。

第一步 词汇解析

① 家喻户晓，a widely-known name，名词词组。句中"家喻户晓"的意思是"家家户户都知道"，形容人所共知。这里与主语的"名字"相结合，翻译为"众所周知的名字"。

众所周知的，widely-known，比如：It is widely-known that CFCs can damage the ozone layer.（众所周知氯氟烃会破坏臭氧层。）widely-known 属于复合形容词，由副词+过去分词构成，中间加连字符，比如：recently-built（刚建的）。

② 在国际上（也）享有盛誉，a globally influential figure，名词词组。句中"在国际上享有盛誉"的意思是"具有全球影响力的人物"。

figure 表示人，特指重要人物，比如：The movement is supported by key figures in the three main political parties.（这场运动由三个主要政党的重要人物支持。）

③ 上世纪 60 年代，1960s，时间状语。句中的"上世纪"指的是 20 世纪 60 年代，翻译为 1960s。

④ 实现高产量目标，produce high yields，动词词组。"实现目标"直接翻译为 achieve the target 也可以。

产量，yield，名词，比如：improving the yield of the crop（增加农作物的产量）。

⑤ 推广应用，wide application，名词词组，比如：the wide application of electronic computers in science and technology（电子计算机在科学技术方面广泛的应用）。

⑥ 解决了……的问题，succeed in doing sth.，动词词组，比如：We have already succeeded in working out ground rules with the Department of Defense.（我们已和国防部成功地制定出了基本原则。）

⑦ （解决）吃饭难，ensure stayed fed，动词词组。这里使用了 ensure + done 的结构，表示"确保……被做"。stay 表示"保持……的状态"。fed 为 feed 的过去分词。

第二步 动词定位

他的名字不仅在中国<u>家喻户晓</u>，在国际上也<u>享有盛誉</u>。袁隆平于上世纪 60 年代<u>开始</u>杂交水稻研究。他带领科研团队使中国杂交水稻一直<u>领先于</u>世界水平，不仅不断<u>实现</u>杂交水稻的高产量目标，而且在生产实践中不断<u>推广应用</u>，从实际上<u>解决了</u>中国人吃饭难的问题。

第三步 句型解析

① 第一句中，"他的名字"是主语，表示"他这个人"，并不是"名字"，"不仅在中国家喻户晓"表示"在中国很出名"，"在国际上也享有盛誉"表示"在国际上也很出名"，这里可以使用 not only...but also...。

② 第二句中，"袁隆平"是主语，第二次出现，翻译为 Yuan，这样的代称是完全可以的，"于上世纪 60 年代"是时间状语，"开始"是谓语，"杂交水稻研究"是宾语，注意使用一般过去时。

③ 第三句中，"他带领科研团队"是主谓宾结构，"使……处于"是谓语，"中国杂交水稻"是宾语，"一直领先于世界水平"是宾语补足语，这样的分析是对的吗？我们来重新分析：本句主语出现了句子，但是主语一般只能是词或短语，所以这里可以使用"主谓结构变偏正结构"的译法，也就是"他的科研团队"，将"带领的"处理为四谓语，不翻译，谓语是"领先于世界"，翻译为 led the world，宾语是"杂交水稻"。后面还有三个分句，第一个分句"不仅不断实现杂交水稻的高产量目标"是谓语和宾语，第二个分句"而且在生产实践中不断推广应用"是谓语，其中"在生产实践中"是状语，这两个分句可以用 not only...but also...。"从实际上解决了中国人吃饭难的问题"是谓语和宾语，最终形成分词的伴随结构，但是译文并不是这么处理的。译文的主语和我们分析的一致，后面三个动宾短语为了只用一组 not only...but also...，从而把第一个短语和第二个短语合译为"在广泛地运用后取得高产量"，第三个

短语翻译为"成功地让中国人有饭吃",这样翻译当然是可以的,但是句式结构过难,不建议大家这么翻译,考试的时候还是"守规矩"最重要。

第四步 翻译来了

He is not only a widely-known name in China, but also a globally influential figure. Yuan began hybrid rice research in the 1960s. His team led the world in the breeding techniques and development strategy, which not only produced high yields in wide application but also succeeded in ensuring China's population stayed fed.

> **本句考点总结**
>
> 第一,本句中使用了"主谓结构变偏正结构"的译法,这是什么意思呢?也就是说主谓结构 Eyes are gleaming.(眼睛炯炯有神。)可以翻译为偏正结构 gleaming eyes(炯炯有神的眼睛),这种译法是为了让句子更加通顺,当然有时候也可以用"偏正结构变主谓结构"的译法。"主谓变偏正"或"偏正变主谓"在英汉互译当中都可能出现,须灵活使用。
>
> 第二,关于谓语动词的层次性。汉译英的核心问题是厘清句子当中多个动词之间的关系问题,我们要学会在多个动词当中找到最核心的动词,翻译为核心谓语(也称为一谓语);找到其次核心的动词,翻译为分词、从句或是其他状语或定语的形式(也称为二谓语);再找到不重要的动词,翻译为介词(也称为三谓语);最后最不重要的动词,可以不译(也称为四谓语)。这些动词在句子当中如何划分层次,需要大家在长期不断的实践中摸索,而且每个句子的翻译也不是固定的。有些句子当中的"一谓语"(核心谓语),在别的译本当中可能就是"二谓语"或者是"三谓语"。只要句子整体结构正确,逻辑清晰,那这就是一个好的译本。

4 袁隆平还多次到美国、印度等国家传授技术,为 30 多个国家和地区的政府官员和科研工作者讲学,促进杂交水稻技术造福世界。

第一步 词汇解析

① 传授技术,share techniques,动词词组。句中"传授"的意思是"分享"。

② 国家和地区,countries and regions,名词词组,比如:A lot of countries and regions around the world have issued e-passports.(全球已有多个国家和地区签发了电子护照。)译文针对"国家和地区"增加了不同的地区,其中,Latin America 表示"拉丁美洲"。

③ 政府官员和科研工作者,counterpart,名词,比如:The Secretary of State and his Russian counterpart met to try to nail down the elusive accord.(美国国务卿与俄罗斯外交部长会晤,试图确定这项表述模糊的协议。)counterpart 的意思是"对应的人或物",原文中"政府官员和科研工作者"指的就是"袁隆平相对应的人士"。

④ 造福世界，deliver the benefits to the world，动词词组。
benefit，名词，比如：He will receive about $921,000 in retirement benefits.（他将获得大约九十二万一千美元的退休福利。）

第二步 动词定位

袁隆平还多次到美国、印度等国家传授技术，为 30 多个国家和地区的政府官员和科研工作者讲学，促进杂交水稻技术造福世界。

第三步 句型解析

① 本句第一分句中，"袁隆平"是主语，翻译为 Yuan，当然翻译为 He 也是可以的，"还多次到美国、印度等国家"是状语，这里的"到"表示"在"，"传授"是谓语，"技术"是宾语。
② 第二分句中，"30 多个国家和地区的政府官员和科研工作者"是宾语，"讲学"是谓语，这里注意将"政府官员和科研工作者"这个短语放在了"传授技术"的后面，"政府官员和科研工作者"就是 counterparts，所以在这里并没有翻译，当然你在考试时按照原本的句型翻译也是可以的。译文在"国家和地区"后面增了 in Asia, Africa, and Latin America，个人觉得完全没有必要。
③ 第三分句中，"促进"是谓语，"杂交水稻技术"是宾语，"造福世界"是宾语补足语。
④ 本句由三个动词构成，第一个动词和第二个动词是并列关系，第三个动词高度抽象，所以可以处理为目的状语，也就是二谓语。

第四步 翻译来了

Yuan shared his techniques with his counterparts in the United States and India and lectured in over 30 countries and regions in Asia, Africa, and Latin America to promote the skills of hybrid rice to deliver the benefits to the world.

> **本句考点总结**
>
> 关于谓语动词的层次性。汉译英的核心问题是厘清句子当中多个动词之间的关系问题，我们要学会在多个动词当中找到最核心的动词，翻译为核心谓语（也称为一谓语）；找到其次核心的动词，翻译为分词、从句或是其他状语或定语的形式（也称为二谓语）；再找到不重要的动词，翻译为介词（也称为三谓语）；最后最不重要的动词，可以不译（也称为四谓语）。这些动词在句子当中如何划分层次，需要大家在长期不断的实践中摸索，而且每个句子的翻译也不是固定的。有些句子当中的"一谓语"（核心谓语），在别的译本当中可能就是"二谓语"或者是"三谓语"。只要句子整体结构正确，逻辑清晰，那这就是一个好的译本。

 1987 年 11 月 3 日，联合国教科文组织在巴黎总部向袁隆平颁发科学奖，认为他的科研成果是"第二次绿色革命"。2004 年，袁隆平获得世界粮食奖（the World Food Prize），表彰他为人类提供营养丰富、数量充足的粮食所做出的突出贡献。

第一步 词汇解析

❶ 联合国教科文组织，UNESCO，专有名词，全称为 United Nations Educational Scientific and Cultural Organization。

文化小常识：

联合国教科文组织是联合国在国际教育、科学和文化领域成员最多的专门机构。该组织旨在通过教育、科学和文化促进各国合作，对世界和平和安全做出贡献。

❷ 总部，headquarter，名词，比如：The bank for which he worked had its headquarters in Paris.（他工作的这家银行总公司设在巴黎。）

❸ 颁发，grant，动词，比如：grant a scholarship to a student（授予一个学生奖学金）。

❹ 科学奖，the Science Prize of the year，专有名词，首字母大写。of the year 表示"当年的"，也就是授予当年（1987年）的科学奖。

文化小常识：

联合国教科文组织科学奖，用于奖励对发展这个组织成员国或地区做出杰出贡献的人或团体，特别是在科学技术研究和教育领域，或是在工程式和工业领域做出贡献的人或团体。

❺ 认为，cite，动词，比如：He cited the fall in unemployment as one of the government's successes.（他举出失业人数的下降作为政府的一项业绩。）

❻ 科研成果，scientific and technological achievements，名词词组，比如：Those exhibits present the most advanced scientific and technological achievements.（这些展览显示了先进的科研成果。）

❼ "第二次绿色革命"，"second green revolution"，专有名词，沿用原文符号即可。

文化小常识：

第二次绿色革命是指国际社会通过共同努力，运用以基因工程为核心的现代生物技术，培育既高产又富含营养的动植物新品种以及功能菌种。

❽ 世界粮食奖，the World Food Prize，专有名词，首字母大写。

文化小常识：

世界粮食奖，国际上在农业领域方面的最高荣誉，由诺贝尔和平奖获得者美国人诺曼·博洛格博士于1986年设立。

❾ 人类，mankind，名词，比如：the evolution of mankind（人类的进化）。

【同义词辨析】

man：指各时代的全体人类；mankind：集体名词，语体庄重，泛指过去、现在和未来的人类；

humanity：书面用词，集合名词，多用于文学作品。

❿ 营养丰富、数量充足的粮食，nutritious, sufficient food，名词词组。

有营养的，nutritious，形容词，比如：It is always important to choose enjoyable, nutritious foods.（选择好吃的、有营养的食品总是很重要的。）

足够的，sufficient，形容词，比如：Lighting levels should be sufficient for photography without flash.（照明程度对无闪光灯摄影应该足够了。）

⓫ 突出贡献，outstanding contribution，名词词组，比如：He made an outstanding contribution to science.（他对科学做出了卓越的贡献。）

第二步 动词定位

1987年11月3日，联合国教科文组织在巴黎总部向袁隆平颁发科学奖，认为他的科研成果是"第二次绿色革命"。2004年，袁隆平获得世界粮食奖（the World Food Prize），表彰他为人类提供营养丰富、数量充足的粮食所做出的突出贡献。

第三步 句型解析

① 第一句中,"1987 年 11 月 3 日"是时间状语,时间的翻译顺序一般是"月 + 日 + 年",当然"日 + 月 + 年"也是可以的。"联合国教科文组织"是主语,"在巴黎总部"是地点状语,"颁发"是谓语,"科学奖"是宾语,"袁隆平"也是宾语,本句使用一般过去时。"认为"是第二个谓语动词,后面接宾语从句,从句中"他的科研成果"是主语,"是"是谓语,"'第二次绿色革命'"是宾语。译文这里的处理和我们所说的基本一致,第一分句中的 granted 是一谓语,第二分句中的 citing 是二谓语,但是后面的宾语从句直接处理为状语结构 as,这也是动词变成介词译法的一种,这不也就是"三谓语"吗?

② 第二句中,"2004 年"是时间状语,"袁隆平"是主语,"获得"是谓语,"世界粮食奖(the World Food Prize)"是宾语,"表彰"看上去是动词,但这里表示了"获得奖项"的原因,可以处理成动词 take 后面接 for 作原因状语,这里也是动词变成介词,变成"三谓语"的经典表达。"突出贡献"是"表彰"的宾语,翻译为 outstanding contribution,"他为人类提供营养丰富、数量充足的粮食所做出的"是定语,也就是 contribution 后面跟的 to providing nutritious, sufficient food to the mankind,这个短语中有两个翻译的小知识点:第一,"所做出"是"贡献"的谓语,这里可以翻译为四谓语,直接省略不译;第二,"他为人类提供营养丰富、数量充足的粮食"看上去是个主谓宾结构,但是翻译为动宾状结构"提供营养丰富、数量充足的粮食 to 人类"更好,前面的"他"则和"贡献"合译。

第四步 翻译来了

On November 3, 1987, the UNESCO granted him the Science Prize of the year at its headquarters in Paris, citing his scientific and technological achievements as the "second green revolution". In 2004, Yuan Longping took the World Food Prize for his outstanding contribution to providing nutritious, sufficient food to the mankind.

本句考点总结

关于谓语动词的层次性。汉译英的核心问题是厘清句子当中多个动词之间的关系问题,我们要学会在多个动词当中找到最核心的动词,翻译为核心谓语(也称为一谓语);找到其次核心的动词,翻译为分词、从句或是其他状语或定语的形式(也称为二谓语);再找到不重要的动词,翻译为介词(也称为三谓语);最后最不重要的动词,可以不译(也称为四谓语)。这些动词在句子当中如何划分层次,需要大家在长期不断的实践中摸索,而且每个句子的翻译也不是固定的。有些句子当中的"一谓语"(核心谓语),在别的译本当中可能就是"二谓语"或者是"三谓语"。只要句子整体结构正确,逻辑清晰,那这就是一个好的译本。

译后总结

这篇文章主要介绍袁隆平对世界农业做出的贡献,其中特别要注意具体时间点上用不同的时态,而且本文也有较多的专有名词需要翻译。在文章句式结构方面,特别要注意如何处理每个句子中的动词问题,也就是大家熟悉的"谓语动词的层次性"的问题。

第三章 2019年实务真题解析与方法技巧

第一节 2019年上半年三级笔译英译汉

Both WHO's constitution and the declaration assert that health is a human right, not a privilege for those who can afford it. Over time, that right has made its way into both national and international law.

But importantly, the right to health is not simply a noble idea on a piece of paper. It has been a platform for major improvements in global health. Since 1948, life expectancy has increased by 25 years. Maternal and childhood mortality have plummeted.

Smallpox has been eradicated and polio is on the brink. We have turned the tide on the HIV/AIDS epidemic. Deaths from malaria have dropped dramatically. New vaccines have made once-feared diseases easily preventable. And there are many other causes for celebration.

But even as we continue to struggle with old threats, new ones have arisen. Climate change will have profound effects on health. Antimicrobial resistance has the potential to undo the gains of modern medicine.

Vaccine hesitancy is putting millions of young lives at risk. Noncommunicable diseases, including heart disease, stroke, cancer, diabetes, hypertension, lung diseases and mental illnesses have become the major killers of our time. And of course, we continue to face the ever-present threat of outbreaks and other health emergencies.

In the past 12 months, WHO has responded to 47 emergencies in 50 countries. We are currently responding to an outbreak of Ebola in the Democratic Republic of the Congo, very near the border with Uganda.

As of today, there have been 373 cases and 216 deaths since the outbreak started in August. So far, we have managed to prevent Ebola from spreading across the border, largely because we have much better tools with which to fight Ebola than at any time in history.

More than 32,000 people have been vaccinated, which is one of the reasons the outbreak has not spread further than it has. We also have ways to treat those infected. So far, 150 people have been treated with one of four drugs.

14 million travelers have been screened, there have been more than 190 safe and dignified burials, we have done door-to-door advocacy in almost 4,000 households and we have trained more than 500 community leaders. But this outbreak has been much more difficult to control, largely because of the security situation in eastern DRC.

Armed groups operating in the area conduct regular attacks on the city of Beni, the epicenter of the outbreak. And every time there is an attack, the virus gets an advantage. Vaccination and contact tracing are disrupted.

Health security and health systems are the two sides of the same coin. The best long-term investment in protecting and promoting the right to health is to invest in stronger health systems.

Because there is simply no other way to achieve universal health coverage and the Sustainable Development Goals than primary health care, with a focus on health promotion and disease prevention. But it will also require

WHO and the global health community to work in a much more integrated and coherent way.

That's why WHO and 10 other international health agencies have agreed to work together on a Global Action Plan for Healthy Lives and Well-Being. The plan has three strategic approaches: integrate, accelerate and account.

First, we have committed to integrate many of our processes to increase our collective efficiency. Second, we have committed to accelerate progress by identifying areas of work in which we can truly bend the curve and make more rapid progress towards the health-related SDGs — like research and development, data and sustainable financing.

And third, we have committed to keep each other accountable, both to the people we serve, and to the donors and partners who expect results from the resources they give us.

2019 年上半年的 CATTI 英译汉又是关于卫生健康的内容，主要介绍了 WHO（世界卫生组织）对卫生健康权利的阐述。这篇文章属于典型的非文学翻译，也是国际组织公文的典范，总体不是特别难。但是从 2019 年开始，CATTI 英语笔译考试出现了新情况，英译汉的段落比之前的年份多 150-200 字，所以大家要提高做题的速度。另外，2019 年上半年也是笔考时代的最后一次，从 2019 年下半年开始，CATTI 笔译考试全面进入机考时代。

Both WHO's constitution and the declaration assert that health is a human right, not a privilege for those who can afford it. Over time, that right has made its way into both national and international law.

第一步 词汇解析

❶ constitution，专有名词，表示《组织法》。
   文化小常识：
   世界卫生组织《组织法》是由国际组织在 1946 年 07 月 22 日于纽约签订的条约。

❷ declaration，专有名词，表示《世界人权宣言》。
   文化小常识：
   《世界人权宣言》是联合国的基本法之一。1948 年 12 月 10 日，联合国大会通过第 217A（Ⅲ）号决议并颁布《世界人权宣言》。这一具有历史意义的《宣言》颁布后，大会要求所有会员国广为宣传，并且"不分国家或领土的政治地位，主要在各级学校和其他教育机构加以传播、展示、阅读和阐述。"

❸ assert，动词，表示"明确肯定、断言"，比如：The scientist asserted that there is no water on the moon.（那位科学家断言月球上没有水。）

❹ privilege，名词，表示"特权、特殊待遇"，比如：Officials of all member states receive certain privileges and immunities.（各成员国的官员均享有某些特权和豁免权。）

❺ over time，介词词组，表示"随着时间的过去"，比如：The rocks have eroded away over time.（这些岩石随着时间的推移逐渐风化了。）

第二步 注意断句

Both WHO's constitution and the declaration assert /that health is a human right, /not a privilege for those /who can afford it. /Over time, /that right has made its way into both national and international law.

第三步 句型解析

❶ 第一句中，Both WHO's constitution and the declaration assert 是主谓结构，后面接 that 引导的宾语从句，宾语从句中的 health is a human right 是主系表结构，not a privilege 是第二组表语结构，for those 是状语，这里的 those 表示的是"某些人"，who 引导定语从句，从句较短，可以采用前置译法。本句中有两个要点，第一个是 constitution 在这里表示 WHO 的"《组织法》"，这点需要会翻译，不能翻译为"宪法"；第二个是 the declaration 在这里表示的是"《世界人权宣言》"，如果真不知道，可以翻译为"宣言"，问题不是很大。

❷ 第二句中，Over time 是时间状语，that right has made its way 是主谓宾结构，into both national and international law 是状语，这里考查了形容词的分配问题，要翻译为"各国法律和国际法"，而不是"国家和国际法"。

第四步 翻译来了

世界卫生组织《组织法》与《世界人权宣言》均强调健康是一项人权，而不是有经济实力者享有的特权。随着时间的推移，健康权已载入各国法律和国际法中。

本句考点总结

第一，本句出现了英文定语从句的译法。一般来说，定语从句按照"短前长后"的译法处理。较短的定语从句可以前置，较长的定语从句可以后置，这一切都取决于句子的通顺，并没有绝对的前置和后置译法。

第二，本句考查了形容词的"分配"译法和动词或名词的"分配"译法。形容词分配的译法是两个或多个形容词位于名词之前，"翻译公式"是 (A+B)*C=AC+BC，比如 international and strategic questions 翻译为"国际问题和战略问题"；动词或名词分配的译法是一个动词位于多个名词宾语之前，或者一个名词位于多个名词前，"翻译公式"是 A*(B+C)=AB+AC，比如 wear a hat and a scarf 翻译为"戴着帽子，系着围巾"。

---

2 But importantly, the right to health is not simply a noble idea on a piece of paper. It has been a platform for major improvements in global health. Since 1948, life expectancy has increased by 25 years. Maternal and childhood mortality have plummeted.

第一步 词汇解析

1. platform，名词，表示"平台"，比如：The demonstration provided a platform for a broad cross section of speakers.（示威集会为具有广泛代表性的人士提供了发表意见的平台。）

2. life expectancy，名词词组，表示"预期寿命"，比如：A number of social factors influence life expectancy.（诸多社会因素左右着人的预期寿命。）

   文化小常识：

   人口平均预期寿命是指假若当前的分年龄死亡率保持不变，同一时期出生的人预期能继续生存的平均年数。它以当前分年龄死亡率为基础计算，但实际上，死亡率是不断变化的。因此，平均预期寿命是一个假定的指标。

3. increase by，动词词组，表示"增长了"，比如：increase by 10%（增长了10%）。

4. maternal，形容词，表示"母亲的"，比如：Maternal age affects the baby's survival rate.（母亲的年龄影响婴儿的成活率。）

5. mortality，名词，表示"死亡率"，比如：Mortality from lung cancer is still increasing.（死于肺癌的人数仍在上升。）

6. plummet，动词，表示"暴跌、速降"，比如：In Tokyo share prices have plummeted for the sixth successive day.（东京股价已连续第六天猛跌。）

第二步 注意断句

But importantly, /the right to health is not simply a noble idea /on a piece of paper. /It has been a platform /for major improvements /in global health. /Since 1948, /life expectancy has increased by 25 years. /Maternal and childhood mortality have plummeted.

第三步 句型解析

1. 第一句中，But importantly 是转折连词和副词，the right to health is not simply a noble idea 是主系表结构，这里的 not simply 表示"不仅仅是"，on a piece of paper 是状语。

2. 第二句中，It 是主语，这里指的是前一句提到的"健康权"，has been a platform 是系表结构，for major improvements 是状语，in global health 也是状语，这里的 platform 需要仔细理解，表示"全球健康状况各项重大进步所展示的舞台"，下一句马上就解释了。这里的"状况"可以看作增范畴词，也可以不增；这里的"展示"也是增词，由于 platform 是抽象名词，无动词词根，所以增动词，也可以不增。

3. 第三句中，Since 1948 是时间状语，life expectancy has increased by 25 years 是主谓状结构，直接翻译即可。

4. 第四句中，Maternal and childhood mortality have plummeted 是主谓结构，第三句和第四句都是短句，而且内容有关联，可以合译。

第四步 翻译来了

但重要的是，健康权不仅仅是纸上空谈。健康权已经成为全球健康状况各项重大进步所展示的舞台。自1948年以来，人类预期寿命延长了25岁，产妇和儿童死亡率快速下跌。

> **本句考点总结**
>
> 第一，本句考查了英汉互译增减词的问题，一般来说英译汉增词，汉译英减词，常见增词的种类有：一、增加对象词（范围词），这是由上文缺少句子的某个部分造成的；二、增加范畴词，这是较难的一部分，常见的范畴词有"水平、方式、方法、问题、情况、途径和方面"，但是不仅仅有这些，还有很多其他的；三、增加评论性词，这些常常出现在文学翻译中；四、增加动词，会在动词的"分配译法"中说明这点。
>
> 第二，本句当中考查了"抽象名词"的译法。抽象名词一般处于冠词之后，又在介词之前，以"the＋抽象名词＋of"的形式居多。一般来说，抽象名词有两种译法。第一种，若抽象名词有动词词根，则翻译为动词，比如 the suggestion of mine，翻译为"我建议"，而不是"我的建议"；第二种，若抽象名词没有动词词根，可以增动词翻译，比如 the spirit of our nation，翻译为"我们民族所具有的精神"，而不是"我们民族的精神"。
>
> 第三，在翻译中，无论是英译汉，还是汉译英，我们常常将长句断成短句，然后一句一句翻译，短的句子由于上下文的联系，也可以放在一起翻译。非文学翻译中，分译与合译出现得比较少，一般按照正常句子翻译即可，但是在文学翻译中出现得特别多，特别要读懂上下文内在的关系。分译与合译没有固定的翻译规则，而且每个译者的尺度也是不同的，重要的前提就是句意正确和句意通顺。

3 Smallpox has been eradicated and polio is on the brink. We have turned the tide on the HIV/AIDS epidemic. Deaths from malaria have dropped dramatically. New vaccines have made once-feared diseases easily preventable. And there are many other causes for celebration.

第一步　词汇解析

① smallpox，名词，表示"天花、天花病毒"，比如：He gave money to the World Health Organization to help defeat smallpox.（他向世界卫生组织提供资金以帮助消灭天花。）

② eradicate，动词，表示"根除、消灭、杜绝"，比如：Polio has been virtually eradicated in Brazil.（在巴西，脊髓灰质炎实际上已经根除。）

③ polio，名词，表示"脊髓灰质炎、小儿麻痹症"，比如：The first authoritative study of polio was published in 1840.（关于小儿麻痹症的第一篇权威性研究报告发表于1840年。）

④ tide，名词，表示"潮流、趋势、动向"，比如：It takes courage to speak out against the tide of opinion.（跟舆论趋向唱反调需要勇气。）

⑤ epidemic，名词，表示"流行病"，比如：Hospitals were already fully extended because of the epidemic.（这场流行病已使各医院以最大负荷运转。）

⑥ malaria，名词，表示"疟疾"，比如：A new advance has been made in the control of malaria.（在控制疟疾方面已取得新的进展。）

⑦ dramatically，副词，表示"显著地、急剧地"，比如：His quality of life has improved dramatically since the operation.（手术后他的生活质量大大改善了。）

❽ vaccine，名词，表示"疫苗"，比如：There is no vaccine against HIV infection.（现在还没有预防艾滋病病毒传染的疫苗。）

第二步 注意断句

Smallpox has been eradicated /and polio is on the brink. /We have turned the tide /on the HIV/AIDS epidemic. /Deaths from malaria have dropped dramatically. /New vaccines have made once-feared diseases easily preventable. /And there are many other causes for celebration.

第三步 句型解析

❶ 第一句中，Smallpox has been eradicated 是主谓结构，也是典型的被动语态，可以使用"有被不用被"的译法，and 是并列连词，polio is on the brink 是主系表结构，也表示"要被消灭了"。

❷ 第二句中，We have turned the tide 是主谓宾结构，表示"改变了……趋势"，on the HIV/AIDS epidemic 是状语，表示"在……方面"，本句和上一句都是在阐述疾病的问题，其实用"疾病"做主语更好。

❸ 第三句中，Deaths from malaria 是主语，have dropped dramatically 是谓语和状语，前三句都是谈疾病被消灭，而且都是短句，所以可以合译。

❹ 第四句中，New vaccines 是主语，have made once-feared diseases 是谓语和宾语，easily preventable 是宾语补足语，用于解释说明宾语。

❺ 第五句中，And 是并列连词，there are many other causes for celebration 是 there be 句型，表示"有"，直接翻译是"有值得庆贺的理由"。第四句和第五句谈到了医学方面的进步，而且是短句，可以合译。

第四步 翻译来了

天花已经消灭了，脊髓灰质炎也已处在被消灭的边缘，艾滋病毒/艾滋病的势头得到扭转，疟疾致死的现象急剧减少。新疫苗让曾经令人恐惧的疾病变得易于预防，还有很多其他值得庆祝的理由。

本句考点总结

第一，本句出现了被动语态的译法。被动语态是英文常见的一种形式，而在中文里常常少用"被"或者不用"被"。那么我们一般有什么样的译法呢？第一种是被动变主动，第二种是寻找替代词（比如："让……给""为……所"等结构），第三种是在科技文献中用"可以"来替代"被"，第四种是有"被"不用"被"。以上四种怎么用，那就看句子怎么通顺怎么翻译了啊！

第二，在翻译中，无论是英译汉，还是汉译英，我们常常将长句断成短句，然后一句一句翻译，短的句子由于上下文的联系，也可以放在一起翻译。非文学翻译中，分译与合译出现得比较少，一般按照正常句子翻译即可，但是在文学翻译中出现得特别多，特别要读懂上下文内在的关系。分译与合译没有固定的翻译规则，而且每个译者的尺度也是不同的，重要的前提就是句意正确和句意通顺。

4 But even as we continue to struggle with old threats, new ones have arisen. Climate change will have profound effects on health. Antimicrobial resistance has the potential to undo the gains of modern medicine.

第一步 词汇解析

① arise，动词，表示"发生、产生"，比如：A new crisis has arisen.（新危机已经出现。）
② profound，形容词，表示"深切的、深远的"，比如：My father's death had a profound effect on us all. （父亲的去世深深地影响了我们全家。）
③ antimicrobial resistance，名词词组，表示"抗微生物药物的耐药性"。
④ undo，动词，表示"消除、取消、废止、破坏、毁掉"，比如：He undid most of the good work of the previous manager.（他把前任经理的大部分功绩都毁掉了。）

第二步 注意断句

But /even /as we continue to struggle with old threats, /new ones have arisen. /Climate change will have profound effects /on health. /Antimicrobial resistance has the potential /to undo the gains of modern medicine.

第三步 句型解析

① 第一句中，But 是表示转折的并列连词，even 是副词，表示"甚至"，译者处理为"就在……之时"，这里的"在……之时"是 as 引导的时间状语从句，we continue to struggle with old threats 是主谓状结构，主句 new ones have arisen 是主谓结构，较为简单，可以直接翻译。
② 第二句中，Climate change will have profound effects 是主谓宾结构，on health 是状语，表示"在健康方面"。
③ 第三句中，Antimicrobial resistance has the potential 是主谓宾结构，to 引导了不定式短语作结果状语，但要是翻译为"有潜力做某事"则非常不通顺，翻译为"有可能做某事"更好，undo the gains of modern medicine 是动宾短语，这里的 gains 是典型的抽象名词，无动词词根，可以增动词"取得"。

第四步 翻译来了

但是，就在我们继续对抗既有的健康威胁之时，新的健康威胁已经出现。气候变化会对健康产生深远影响。抗微生物药物的耐药性有可能让现代医学取得的成果荡然无存。

本句考点总结

本句当中考查了"抽象名词"的译法。抽象名词一般处于冠词之后，又在介词之前，以"the + 抽象名词 + of"的形式居多。一般来说，抽象名词有两种译法。第一种，若抽象名词有动词词根，则翻译为动词，比如 the suggestion of mine，翻译为"我建议"，而不是"我的建议"；第二种，若抽象名词没有动词词根，可以增动词翻译，比如 the spirit of our nation，翻译为"我们民族所具有的精神"，而不是"我们民族的精神"。

> Vaccine hesitancy is putting millions of young lives at risk. Noncommunicable diseases, including heart disease, stroke, cancer, diabetes, hypertension, lung diseases and mental illnesses have become the major killers of our time. And of course, we continue to face the ever-present threat of outbreaks and other health emergencies.

第一步 词汇解析

① hesitancy，名词，表示"犹豫"，比如：I noticed a certain hesitancy in his voice.（我注意到他的声音有点犹豫。）

② noncommunicable，形容词，表示"不会传染的"，比如：noncommunicable diseases（非传染性疾病）。

③ stroke，名词，表示"中风"，比如：He had a minor stroke in 1987, which left him partly paralysed.（他1987年曾患轻度中风，之后就半身不遂了。）

④ diabetes，名词，表示"糖尿病"，比如：People with high blood pressure are especially vulnerable to diabetes.（有高血压的人尤其容易患糖尿病。）

⑤ hypertension，名词，表示"高血压"，比如：He suffered from hypertension and accompanying heart problems.（他患有高血压和由此引起的心脏问题。）

⑥ emergency，名词，表示"突发事件、紧急情况"，比如：This door should only be used in an emergency.（这道门只能在紧急情况下使用。）

第二步 注意断句

Vaccine hesitancy is putting millions of young lives at risk. /Noncommunicable diseases, /including heart disease, /stroke, /cancer, /diabetes, /hypertension, /lung diseases and /mental illnesses have become the major killers of our time. /And of course, /we continue to face the ever-present threat /of outbreaks and other health emergencies.

第三步 句型解析

① 第一句中，Vaccine hesitancy is putting millions of young lives at risk 是主谓宾宾补的结构，这里要注意"疫苗犹豫"可以用双引号表示强调，当然不加也是可以的。

② 第二句中，Noncommunicable diseases, including heart disease, stroke, cancer, diabetes, hypertension, lung diseases and mental illnesses 是主语，要注意这里的翻译现象，中文一般来说先分后总，英文一般来说先总后分，所以翻译状语时，需要先翻译"各种疾病"，再翻译"等非传染性疾病"，have become the major killers of our time 是系表结构。

③ 第三句中，And 是并列连词，of course 是副词短语，可以放在原位翻译，we continue to face the ever-present threat of outbreaks and other health emergencies 是主谓宾结构，这里特别要注意 ever-present 这个形容词的翻译，若翻译为"我们还在面临着无时无刻不在的疫情暴发和其他突发卫生事件的威胁"，这样中心词"威胁"前的定语较长，因此，还不如将 ever-present 拿出来单独翻译，把它看作评论性词。

第四步 翻译来了

"疫苗犹豫"正危及数百万年轻人的生命。心脏病、中风、癌症、糖尿病、高血压、肺病和精神疾病等非传染性疾病已成为当今时代的头号杀手。当然，我们还面临着疫情暴发和其他突发卫生事件的威胁，这些威胁无时无刻不在。

> 🧑‍🏫 **本句考点总结**
>
> 　　第一，中英文的总分关系，中文一般是先分后总，而英文则是先总后分，比如中文会说"我喜欢吃香蕉、苹果、梨子等水果"，但是英文的表达是 I like fruits such as bananas, apples and pears. 注意总分关系是如何在两种语言中体现出来的。
>
> 　　第二，本句出现了事实（Facts）和评论（Comments）的译法。中文一般先事实，后评论，而英文则是一般先评论，后事实。比如：It is important for her to go abroad. 翻译为"对于她来说，出国是很重要的"。英文中 It is important 是评论，for her to go abroad 是事实。从中英文的对比来看，可以知道中英文语序分别是怎么安排的。

6 In the past 12 months, WHO has responded to 47 emergencies in 50 countries. We are currently responding to an outbreak of Ebola in the Democratic Republic of the Congo, very near the border with Uganda.

第一步　词汇解析

❶ Ebola，专有名词，表示"埃博拉"。
医学小常识：
　　埃博拉是一种十分罕见的病毒，1976年在苏丹南部和刚果（金）（旧称扎伊尔）的埃博拉河地区发现它的存在后，引起医学界的广泛关注和重视，"埃博拉"由此而得名。这是一个用来称呼一群属于纤维病毒科埃博拉病毒属下数种病毒的通用术语。

❷ Democratic Republic of the Congo，专有名词，表示"刚果民主共和国"。
文化小常识：
　　刚果民主共和国，简称刚果（金），位于非洲中部，东邻乌干达、卢旺达、布隆迪、坦桑尼亚，南接赞比亚、安哥拉，北连南苏丹和中非，西隔刚果河与刚果（布）相望。

❸ Uganda，专有名词，表示"乌干达"。
文化小常识：
　　乌干达共和国，简称乌干达。是位于非洲东部的国家，横跨赤道，东邻肯尼亚，南接坦桑尼亚和卢旺达，西接刚果（金），北连南苏丹。

第二步　注意断句

In the past 12 months, /WHO has responded to 47 emergencies /in 50 countries. /We are currently responding to an outbreak of Ebola /in the Democratic Republic of the Congo, /very near the border with Uganda.

第三步 句型解析

① 第一句中，In the past 12 months 是时间状语，WHO has responded to 47 emergencies 是主谓宾结构，in 50 countries 是地点状语。

② 第二句中，We are currently responding to an outbreak of Ebola 是主谓宾结构，in the Democratic Republic of the Congo 是地点状语，very near the border with Uganda 是前面地点状语的同位语，可以使用"并列译法"或是"主谓译法"。

第四步 翻译来了

在过去的 12 个月内，世卫组织应对了 50 个国家的 47 起突发事件。我们目前正在处理邻近乌干达边境的刚果民主共和国爆发的埃博拉疫情。

本句考点总结

本句考查了英文同位语的译法。同位语是两个前后相互说明的名词或名词短语，比如 Beijing, the capital of China，有两种译法。第一种是"并列译法"，翻译为"中国的首都北京"，第二种是"主谓译法"，翻译为"北京是中国的首都"。具体用哪一种，可以根据句子具体情况而定，有时两种都是可以使用的。

---

7 As of today, there have been 373 cases and 216 deaths since the outbreak started in August. So far, we have managed to prevent Ebola from spreading across the border, largely because we have much better tools with which to fight Ebola than at any time in history.

第一步 词汇解析

① as of，介词词组，表示"截至"，比如：In the event that available vacation is not used as of the end of the benefit year, employees may not carry unused time forward to the next benefit year.（如果截至当年年末，员工尚有假期未休完，员工不得将未使用的假期转到下一年度。）

as of 作为表达时间的词，通常有三种含义，需要结合上下文选择含义：（1）自……起；（2）在……时候；（3）截至……。

第二步 注意断句

As of today, /there have been 373 cases and 216 deaths /since the outbreak started /in August. /So far, /we have managed to prevent Ebola from spreading /across the border, /largely because we have much better tools /with which to fight Ebola than at any time /in history.

第三步 句型解析

① 第一句中，As of today 是时间状语，表示"迄今为止"，there have been 373 cases and 216 deaths 是 there be 句型，表示"有"，since 引导时间状语从句，the outbreak started in August 是主谓状的结构。

❷ 第二句中，So far 是时间状语，表示"到目前为止"，we have managed to prevent Ebola from spreading across the border 是主谓宾宾补的结构，这里的 prevent...from... 表示"阻止……做某事"。largely because 引导原因状语从句，we have much better tools 是主谓宾结构，这里的 tools 指的是"方法、手段"，翻译为"工具"不是特别好，with which 引导定语从句，从句中省略主语和谓语，to 引导的不定式短语作目的状语，fight Ebola than at any time in history 表示"在历史上比其他任何时候（有史以来）对抗埃博拉的"。这个定语从句较长，可以采用后置译法，但是译文却使用了前置译法，注意后置与前置还是以通顺为标准。

第四步 翻译来了

自八月暴发以来，迄今已有 373 例确诊病例和 216 例死亡病例。到目前为止，我们已成功阻止埃博拉病毒蔓延至边境外，这主要是因为我们采用了有史以来最好的几种手段对抗埃博拉病毒。

> **本句考点总结**
>
> 本句出现了英文定语从句的译法。一般来说，定语从句按照"短前长后"的译法处理。较短的定语从句可以前置，较长的定语从句可以后置，这一切都取决于句子的通顺，并没有绝对的前置和后置译法。

8 More than 32,000 people have been vaccinated, which is one of the reasons the outbreak has not spread further than it has. We also have ways to treat those infected. So far, 150 people have been treated with one of four drugs.

第一步 词汇解析

❶ vaccinate，动词，表示"给……接种疫苗"，比如：He thinks he can find a way to vaccinate the elephants from a safe distance.（他认为自己能找到一种从安全距离给大象接种疫苗的方法。）

❷ infect，动词，表示"传染、使感染"，比如：The infected cells then migrate to other areas of the body.（受感染的细胞接着转移到身体的其他部位。）

第二步 注意断句

More than 32,000 people have been vaccinated, /which is one of the reasons the outbreak has not spread further / than it has. /We also have ways to treat those infected. /So far, /150 people have been treated /with one of four drugs.

第三步 句型解析

❶ 第一句中，More than 32,000 people have been vaccinated 是主谓结构，也是典型的被动语态，这里可以

用"有被不用被"的译法，逗号后是 which 引导的非限定性定语从句，一般来说翻译非限定性定语从句都是采用后置译法，is one of the reasons 是系表结构，表示"是……的原因之一"。其实从句中的 the outbreak has not spread further 也是一个定语从句，由省略了的引导词 why 引导，这个定语从句较短，可以采用前置译法，than it has 是比较状语从句，表示"比原来应该有的"，这个句子和前面的"进一步扩散"在一定程度有相同的含义，所以可以只翻译一次，没有必要翻译成"这是疫情比原来应该有的、并没有进一步扩散的原因之一"。

❷ 第二句中，We also have ways to treat those infected 是主谓宾定结构，这里的不定式短语作定语，定语较短，可以采用前置译法。

❸ 第三句中，So far 是时间状语，150 people have been treated 是主谓结构，也是典型的被动语态，这里可以用"有被不用被"的译法，with one of four drugs 是 with 引导的状语。

第四步 翻译来了

已经有超过 3.2 万人接种了疫苗，这是疫情没有进一步扩散的原因之一。此外，我们也有治疗感染者的方法。到目前为止，已有 150 人接受了四种药物中的一种治疗。

本句考点总结

第一，本句出现了被动语态的译法。被动语态是英文常见的一种形式，而在中文里常常少用"被"或者不用"被"。那么我们一般有什么样的译法呢？第一种是被动变主动，第二种是寻找替代词（比如："让……给""为……所"等结构），第三种是在科技文献中用"可以"来替代"被"，第四种是有"被"不用"被"。以上四种怎么用，那就看句子怎么通顺怎么翻译了啊！

第二，非限定性定语从句是用逗号隔开的定语从句，这样的句子一般都要采用后置译法，在翻译时需要翻译出关系代词 which，who 等词，指明这些词的指代关系，将这些代词翻译出来。

第三，本句出现了英文定语从句的译法。一般来说，定语从句按照"短前长后"的译法处理。较短的定语从句可以前置，较长的定语从句可以后置，这一切都取决于句子的通顺，并没有绝对的前置和后置译法。

---

14 million travelers have been screened, there have been more than 190 safe and dignified burials, we have done door-to-door advocacy in almost 4,000 households and we have trained more than 500 community leaders. But this outbreak has been much more difficult to control, largely because of the security situation in eastern DRC.

第一步 词汇解析

❶ screen, 动词，表示"筛查、检查"，比如：Men over 55 should be regularly screened for prostate cancer. （55 岁以上的男性应定期做前列腺癌检查。）

② dignified，形容词，表示"庄重的、庄严的、有尊严的"，比如：They suggested that she make a dignified exit in the interest of the party.（他们建议她为了政党的利益体面地下台。）

③ burial，名词，表示"埋葬"，比如：Her body was sent home for burial.（她的尸骨已运回家乡安葬。）

④ advocacy，名词，表示"（对某思想、行动方针、信念的）拥护、支持、提倡、宣传"，比如：I support your advocacy of free trade.（我支持你自由贸易的主张。）

⑤ DRC，缩写，指上文中的 the Democratic Republic of the Congo（刚果民主共和国）。

第二步 注意断句

14 million travelers have been screened, /there have been more than 190 safe and dignified burials, /we have done door-to-door advocacy /in almost 4,000 households /and we have trained more than 500 community leaders. / But /this outbreak has been much more difficult to control, /largely because of the security situation /in eastern DRC.

第三步 句型解析

① 第一句的第一分句中，14 million travelers have been screened 是主谓结构，也是典型的被动语态，这里可以用"有被不用被"的译法；第二分句中，there have been more than 190 safe and dignified burials 是 there be 句型，表示"有"；第三分句中，we have done door-to-door advocacy 是主谓宾结构，这里的 advocacy 表示"宣传、倡导"的意思，in almost 4,000 households 是地点状语，可以翻译为"我们已经挨家挨户地宣传了近 4 000 户"，也可以按照译文那样翻译为"挨家挨户宣传近 4 000 户"。and 是并列连词，连接第四分句，we have trained more than 500 community leaders 是主谓宾结构，可以翻译为"我们已经培训了 500 多名社区领导"，也可以按照译文这样翻译为"500 多名社区领导接受了培训"，这样四个句子的主语都比较客观。

② 第二句中，But 是表示转折的并列连词，this outbreak has been much more difficult to control 是主系表结构，largely because of 引导原因状语，the security situation in eastern DRC 表示"刚果民主共和国东部的安全局势"。

第四步 翻译来了

1 400 万名游客经过筛查，已经有超过 190 人得到安全、体面地埋葬，挨家挨户宣传近 4 000 户，500 多名社区领导接受了培训。但此次疫情控制难度加大，这主要归咎于刚果民主共和国东部的安全局势。

> **本句考点总结**
>
> 本句出现了被动语态的译法。被动语态是英文常见的一种形式，而在中文里常常少用"被"或者不用"被"。那么我们一般有什么样的译法呢？第一种是被动变主动，第二种是寻找替代词（比如："让……给""为……所"等结构），第三种是在科技文献中用"可以"来替代"被"，第四种是有"被"不用"被"。以上四种怎么用，那就看句子怎么通顺怎么翻译了啊！

> Armed groups operating in the area conduct regular attacks on the city of Beni, the epicenter of the outbreak. And every time there is an attack, the virus gets an advantage. Vaccination and contact tracing are disrupted.

第一步 词汇解析

① armed，形容词，表示"携带武器的、持枪的、荷枪实弹的"，比如：Three armed groups were contending for power.（三个武装集团在争夺权力。）

② Beni，专有名词，表示"贝尼市"。

③ epicenter，名词，表示"疫情中心"，是由 epidemic + center 两个单词构成的，比如：the epicenter of COVID-19（新冠疫情的中心）。

④ tracing，名词，表示"踪迹、足迹、遗迹"，比如：The local church has traces of fifteenth-century frescoes.（当地教堂仍留有十五世纪壁画的遗迹。）

第二步 注意断句

Armed groups operating in the area conduct regular attacks /on the city of Beni, /the epicenter of the outbreak. /And every time /there is an attack, /the virus gets an advantage. /Vaccination and contact tracing are disrupted.

第三步 句型解析

① 第一句中，Armed groups operating in the area 是主语，conduct regular attacks 是谓语和宾语（这个结构的难点就是"谓语动词的过渡"，三级笔译中出现得比较少，二级笔译中比较多），on the city of Beni 是地点状语，the epicenter of the outbreak 和前面的地点状语形成同位语关系，可以用"主谓译法"或是"并列译法"。

② 第二句中，And 是并列连词，every time 是时间状语从句的引导词，there is an attack 是时间状语从句，the virus gets an advantage 是主句，若翻译为"每次有一次袭击，病毒就会有了一个机会"，这根本不是翻译！翻译为"每次袭击都为病毒创造了有利的条件"，这样不是更加通顺吗？

③ 第三句中，Vaccination and contact tracing are disrupted 是主谓结构，是典型的被动语态，因为这三个句子之间有本质上的联系，而且都是短句，所以可以合译，那么这个句子自然而然地就可以用"被动变主动"的译法。

第四步 翻译来了

该地区活动的武装分子频繁袭击疫情的中心贝尼市（Beni），而每次袭击都为病毒创造了有利的条件，从而中断了疫苗接种和接触者追踪工作。

> **本句考点总结**

第一，句中出现了谓语动词过渡的译法，这是英汉互译当中非常难的知识点。中文是动态性语言，常用动词，用强势动词；英文是静态性语言，常用名词，用弱势动词，这点要牢记在心。比如 I give you my support. 不要翻译为"我给你我的支持"，直接翻译为"我支持你"即可。give 是弱势动词，support 是强势动词，因为中英文的差异，只要翻译强势动词，不须翻译弱势动词。这点常常在英译汉当中使用，汉译英中用得比较少！

第二，本句考查了英文同位语的译法。同位语是两个前后相互说明的名词或名词短语，比如 Beijing, the capital of China，有两种译法。第一种是"并列译法"，翻译为"中国的首都北京"，第二种是"主谓译法"，翻译为"北京是中国的首都"。具体用哪一种，可以根据句子具体情况而定，有时两种都是可以使用的。

第三，本句出现了被动语态的译法。被动语态是英文常见的一种形式，而在中文里常常少用"被"或者不用"被"。那么我们一般有什么样的译法呢？第一种是被动变主动，第二种是寻找替代词（比如："让……给""为……所"等结构），第三种是在科技文献中用"可以"来替代"被"，第四种是有"被"不用"被"。以上四种怎么用，那就看句子怎么通顺怎么翻译了啊！

第四，在翻译中，无论是英译汉，还是汉译英，我们常常将长句断成短句，然后一句一句翻译，短的句子由于上下文的联系，也可以放在一起翻译。非文学翻译中，分译与合译出现得比较少，一般按照正常句子翻译即可，但是在文学翻译中出现得特别多，特别要读懂上下文内在的关系。分译与合译没有固定的翻译规则，而且每个译者的尺度也是不同的，重要的前提就是句意正确和句意通顺。

11 Health security and health systems are the two sides of the same coin. The best long-term investment in protecting and promoting the right to health is to invest in stronger health systems.

第一步 词汇解析

❶ two sides of the same coin，名词词组，表示"一个问题的两方面"，比如：The minister reportedly stressed that economic and political reforms were two sides of the same coin.（据报道，部长强调经济改革和政治改革是一个问题的两个方面。）

第二步 注意断句

Health security and health systems are the two sides of the same coin. /The best long-term investment /in protecting and promoting the right to health /is to invest in stronger health systems.

第三步 句型解析

❶ 第一句中，Health security and health systems are the two sides of the same coin 是主系表结构，这句话说

到了"卫生安全"和"卫生体系"两个方面,这里的 health 指的是"卫生、医疗",而不是"健康"。

❷ 第二句中,The best long-term investment in protecting and promoting the right to health 是主语,这里的 the right to health 指的是"人类健康的权利",the best long-term investment 是核心词,in protecting and promoting the right to health 是用来修饰这个中心词的,is 是系动词,to invest in stronger health systems 是表语,表示"投资更加强大的医疗卫生体系",这里的 health 也是"卫生、医疗"的意思。所以一词多义非常重要,一个单词在一个句子当中出现多次都有可能是不同的含义,一定要根据上下文来判断。

第四步 翻译来了

卫生安全和卫生体系是同一事物的两个方面。保护和促进健康权的最佳长期投资方式是投资更加强大的医疗卫生体系。

12

Because there is simply no other way to achieve universal health coverage and the Sustainable Development Goals than primary health care, with a focus on health promotion and disease prevention. But it will also require WHO and the global health community to work in a much more integrated and coherent way.

第一步 词汇解析

❶ universal health coverage,名词词组,表示"全民健康覆盖",比如:accelerate progress towards universal health coverage(加速迈向全民健康覆盖)。

❷ integrated,形容词,表示"各部分密切协调的、综合的",比如:an integrated transport system(综合运输体系)。

❸ coherent,形容词,表示"合乎逻辑的、有条理的、清楚易懂的",比如:The subjects of the curriculum form a coherent whole.(课程中的科目构成了一个连贯的整体。)

第二步 注意断句

Because there is simply no other way /to achieve universal health coverage and the Sustainable Development Goals /than primary health care, /with a focus on health promotion and disease prevention. /But /it will also require WHO and the global health community /to work /in a much more integrated and coherent way.

第三步 句型解析

❶ 第一句中,Because 引出的是上一句的原因,there is simply no other way 是 there be 句型,表示"根本没有其他的方法",to 引导目的状语,achieve universal health coverage and the Sustainable Development Goals 表示"实现全民健康覆盖与可持续发展目标"。(注意:这里的"可持续发展目标"是联合国提出的,所以首字母大写,翻译时,可以直接翻译,然后把英文全部抄写下来,加上括号,放在译文后。)than 引导比较状语,primary health care 和 with a focus on health promotion and disease prevention 是同位语关系,也可以说后者解释了前者,注意 focus 是典型的抽象名词,有动词词根,可以翻译为动词"重点关注",所以这个结构可以用"主谓译法"来翻译。以上这样的分析大家应该能够看懂吧,但是如果再仔细看就会发现一个经典的词组 no other...than...,表示"除了……、再也没有其他的……",翻译时应先翻译 than 之后的结构,因为这个句子是"废话",中文先说废话,再说主句,英文先说主句,再说

废话。

❷ 第二句中，But 是表示转折的并列连词，it 是主语，will also require WHO and the global health community 是谓语和宾语，to work 是宾语补足语，in a much more integrated and coherent way 是方式状语，直接翻译就是"这还要求世卫组织和全球卫生界以一种协调和连贯的方式来工作"，这么翻也不通顺，看看参考译文是怎么处理的。

第四步 翻译来了

基础的卫生医疗重点关注促进健康和预防疾病，而除了此法，根本没有其他方法可以实现全民健康覆盖与可持续发展目标（Sustainable Development Goals）。但这还需要世卫组织与全球卫生界更加协调一致地努力。

📖 本句考点总结

第一，本句考查了英文同位语的译法。同位语是两个前后相互说明的名词或名词短语，比如 Beijing, the capital of China，有两种译法。第一种是"并列译法"，翻译为"中国的首都北京"，第二种是"主谓译法"，翻译为"北京是中国的首都"。具体用哪一种，可以根据句子具体情况而定，有时两种都是可以使用的。

第二，本句当中考查了"抽象名词"的译法。抽象名词一般处于冠词之后，又在介词之前，以"the + 抽象名词 + of"的形式居多。一般来说，抽象名词有两种译法。第一种，若抽象名词有动词词根，则翻译为动词，比如 the suggestion of mine，翻译为"我建议"，而不是"我的建议"；第二种，若抽象名词没有动词词根，可以增动词翻译，比如 the spirit of our nation，翻译为"我们民族所具有的精神"，而不是"我们民族的精神"。

第三，本句考查了中英文语序的问题，一般来说，中文的语序是"主语+废话（定语、状语、补语、插入语，等等）+重要成分"，而英文的语序是"废话（定语、状语、补语、插入语，等等）+主语+重要成分+废话（定语、状语、补语、插入语，等等）"，翻译时需要注意调整语序。

---

13 That's why WHO and 10 other international health agencies have agreed to work together on a Global Action Plan for Healthy Lives and Well-Being. The plan has three strategic approaches: integrate, accelerate and account.

第一步 词汇解析

❶ approach，名词，表示"方式、方法"，比如：We need to take a different approach to the problem.（我们应该采用另一种方法来解决这一问题。）

❷ account，动词，表示"归咎于……"，比如：He has been asked to account for his conduct.（他被要求对他的行为负责。）

第二步 注意断句

That's why /WHO and 10 other international health agencies have agreed to work together /on a Global Action Plan for Healthy Lives and Well-Being. /The plan has three strategic approaches: /integrate, /accelerate and / account.

第三步 句型解析

① 第一句中，That's why 表示"所以"，WHO and 10 other international health agencies have agreed to work together 是主谓宾结构，on a Global Action Plan for Healthy Lives and Well-Being 是状语，其中的名词短语是固定用法，所以首字母大写，翻译时直译，然后把英文全部抄写下来，加上括号，放在译文后。

② 第二句中，The plan has three strategic approaches 是主谓宾结构，翻译时冒号依旧保留，后面是三个动词，说到了三个方法，所以翻译为动词肯定不对，这里需要增词，翻译为动宾结构，integrate 表示"整合流程"，accelerate 表示"加快进程"，account 表示"承担责任"。有人问，这里的增词是怎么看出来的？继续往下读文章就会发现 First, Second, third, 就明白是怎么回事了，所以翻译一定要根据上下文，而不是自己瞎编乱造！

第四步 翻译来了

所以，世卫组织与其他 10 个国际卫生机构同意共同推行"全球健康生活与福祉行动计划"（Global Action Plan for Healthy Lives and Well-Being）。这项计划有三大战略方法：整合流程、加快进程与承担责任。

> **本句考点总结**
>
> 本句考查了英汉互译增减词的问题，一般来说英译汉增词，汉译英减词，常见增词的种类有：一、增加对象词（范围词），这是由上文缺少句子的某个部分造成的；二、增加范畴词，这是较难的一部分，常见的范畴词有"水平、方式、方法、问题、情况、途径和方面"，但是不仅仅有这些，还有很多其他的；三、增加评论性词，这些常常出现在文学翻译中；四、增加动词，会在动词的"分配译法"中说明这点。

14

First, we have committed to integrate many of our processes to increase our collective efficiency. Second, we have committed to accelerate progress by identifying areas of work in which we can truly bend the curve and make more rapid progress towards the health-related SDGs — like research and development, data and sustainable financing.

第一步 词汇解析

① collective，形容词，表示"集体的"，比如：It was a collective decision.（这是集体的决定。）

❷ bend，动词，表示"把……弄弯"，比如：Mark the pipe where you want to bend it.（在管子上要弄弯的地方做个记号。）
❸ curve，名词，表示"曲线、弧线、曲面、弯曲"，比如：The driver lost control on a curve and the vehicle hit a tree.（司机在拐弯处失控，撞在了一棵树上。）
❹ SDGs，缩写，指上文中的 Sustainable Development Goals（可持续发展目标）。

第二步 注意断句

First, /we have committed to integrate many of our processes /to increase our collective efficiency. /Second, /we have committed to accelerate progress /by identifying areas of work /in which we can truly bend the curve /and make more rapid progress /towards the health-related SDGs — /like research and development, /data /and sustainable financing.

第三步 句型解析

❶ 第一句中，First 是副词，we have committed to integrate many of our processes 是主谓宾结构，不定式短语 to increase our collective efficiency 作目的状语，这里要注意 our 不翻译，因为前面已经出现了 we "我们"。
❷ 第二句中，Second 是副词，we have committed to accelerate progress 是主谓宾结构，by 引导方式状语，identifying areas of work 表示"确定工作领域"，in which 引导定语从句，从句较长，可以采用后置译法。定语从句中，we can truly bend the curve 是主谓宾结构，bend the curve 表示"扭转局势"，and 是并列连词，make more rapid progress 是第二组谓语和宾语。towards the health-related SDGs 是状语，表示"在与健康相关的可持续发展目标方面"。注意！这个状语是和主句的 progress 相关，不是从句的 progress，要是看错了，就很有可能会理解错！之后的破折号可以保留，译文使用的括号也是可以的，都是用来表示解释说明，like 用来举例，research and development, data and sustainable financing 表示"研发、数据和可持续融资"。

第四步 翻译来了

首先，我们已承诺整合诸多流程，提高集体效率；其次，我们已承诺在与健康相关的可持续发展目标（如研发、数据和可持续融资）方面加快进程，其方式是通过确定工作领域，在这些领域当中我们能够真正扭转局势并取得进步。

本句考点总结

第一，关于英文代词的译法。英文中需要翻译的代词主要指第三人称 he, she, it, they 及其相应宾格和指示代词 this 和 that。这些单词在翻译时一定要注意，主要采用"不抽象、不具体"的译法。不能翻译成具体的人或物，但是也不能翻译为"他""她""它""他们""这个""那个"，要注意取中间的译法。

第二，本句出现了英文定语从句的译法。一般来说，定语从句按照"短前长后"的译法处理。较短的定语从句可以前置，较长的定语从句可以后置，这一切都取决于句子的通顺，并没有绝对的前置和后置译法。

15. And third, we have committed to keep each other accountable, both to the people we serve, and to the donors and partners who expect results from the resources they give us.

第一步 词汇解析

1. accountable，形容词，表示"（对自己的决定、行为）负有责任的、有责任的"，比如：The major service industries should be accountable to their customers.（主要的服务行业应该对它们的顾客负责。）
2. donor，名词，表示"捐赠者"，比如：The donor prefers to remain anonymous.（捐赠者不希望被披露姓名。）

第二步 注意断句

And third, /we have committed to keep each other accountable, /both to the people /we serve, /and to the donors and partners /who expect results from the resources /they give us.

第三步 句型解析

1. 本句中，And third 是连词和副词，直接翻译即可，we have committed to keep each other accountable 是主谓宾宾补的结构，后面是 both...and... 的结构。
2. both to the people 是第一组"人"，we serve 是较短的定语从句，可以采用前置译法，and to the donors and partners 是第二组"人"，who 引导定语从句，expect results from the resources 是从句中的谓语、宾语和状语，they give us 又是一个定语从句，这里要搞清楚 they 和 us 的关系，they 指的是 the donors and partners，us 指的是作者，这个定语从句较短，也可以采用前置译法。所以 both...and... 内部的定语从句全部都可以前置，翻译为"不仅要对……负责，也要对……负责"，特别是第二部分，翻译为"也要对希望从他们给我们的资源中获得成效的捐赠者和合作者负责"，这根本就不是人话，看看参考译文是怎么处理的。

第四步 翻译来了

最后，我们已承诺人人承担责任，不仅要对所服务的对象负责，也要对出资出力、期待有所成效的捐赠者和合作者负责。

本句考点总结

第一，本句出现了英文定语从句的译法。一般来说，定语从句按照"短前长后"的译法处理。较短的定语从句可以前置，较长的定语从句可以后置，这一切都取决于句子的通顺，并没有绝对的前置和后置译法。

第二，关于英文代词的译法。英文中需要翻译的代词主要指第三人称 he, she, it, they 及其相应宾格和指示代词 this 和 that。这些单词在翻译时一定要注意，主要采用"不抽象、不具体"的译法。不能翻译成具体的人或物，但是也不能翻译为"他""她""它""他们""这个""那个"，要注意取中间的译法。

　　这篇文章探讨了关于国家卫生医疗体制与公民健康权的问题，文章虽然很长，但是难度不大，只有部分句子结构比较难理解，大部分句子结构还是非常清晰的，所有的翻译现象几乎都出现过了，所以，希望大家注意两点：一、在考试中要抓紧时间，提高翻译速度；二、要能够及时准确地发现所有翻译现象，并在译文中体现出来。

第二节　2019年上半年三级笔译汉译英

　　互联网在中国改革开放中的重要作用怎么说都不为过。从2000年开始，中国互联网应用的普及，到现在快20年的时间。尤其是在最后的这15年，互联网为保持高速发展起到了决定性的作用。

　　经济发展有两个东西是至关重要的：第一就是提高生产效率，提升产品质量，生产出更有创意的设计；第二就是保持渠道畅通，使工厂生产的东西以最快的速度、最低的成本送到消费者的手里。互联网在这两个环节都为中国的产业发展起到了决定性的作用。

　　互联网的发展在设计理念和设计人才方面极大地缩小了我们与国际先进的国家的差距。通过互联网，我们可以以更快的速度获取全球最先进的设计技术和理念。更重要的是通过互联网可以产生更多的效应。这就极大地加快了经济发展的速度。

　　在渠道的领域，互联网的效果更加明显，比如电商。老百姓通过互联网更容易表达他自己的意愿，更容易对我们现有的一些产品提出一些批评性的意见，而这些也都更好地推动企业的生产，推动政府职能的现代化。

　　首先，是城市人和农村人在获取信息和沟通信息上平等，大家都可以通过互联网实时看到中国的发展和中国城市的发展。互联网刺激百姓谋求美好生活的意愿，并且将意愿化为前行的强大动力。

 译前指导

　　2019年上半年的CATTI汉译英内容为互联网在中国发展中的作用，也是官方关于互联网对中国发展的影响的重要阐述，译文来自官方。本文属于典型的非文学翻译，单词相对不是很难，句式结构也比较工整，但文章的长度较前些年有所有增加。2019年下半年机考之后，英汉互译的篇幅普遍都加长了，所以大家还是要多多训练打字速度，提高翻译速度。

> **1** 互联网在中国改革开放中的重要作用怎么说都不为过。从2000年开始，中国互联网应用的普及，到现在快20年的时间。尤其是在最后的这15年，互联网为保持高速发展起到了决定性的作用。

第一步　词汇解析

❶ 互联网，the Internet，名词词组，比如：Distance is no problem on the Internet.（在互联网上，距离已不

成问题。）我们常说的"互联网接入"翻译为 Internet access。

❷ 改革开放，Reform and Opening-up，专有名词，比如：With the deepening of Reform and Opening-up, the economy of China has developed rapidly.（随着改革开放的深化，中国的经济有了迅猛的发展。）
"改革开放"的翻译较为多样化，比如：Reform and Open/Reform and Opening-up/ Reform and Open to the Outside World。政府白皮书中常提到的"坚持改革开放"，搭配动词 persist in/adhere to。

❸ 怎么说都不为过，cannot be overstated，动词词组，比如：The seriousness of the crime cannot be overstated.（这一罪行的严重性怎么说都不为过。）这一词组中，要注意 cannot 不能分开写，在正式文体或学术写作中，尽量不要出现缩写。
夸大，overstate，动词，比如：The authors no doubt overstated their case with a view to catching the public's attention.（作者们毫无疑问夸大了他们的案例以吸引公众的注意力。）

❹ ……的普及，popularity，名词，比如：the popularity of table tennis（乒乓球的普及）。popularity 常与 among/with 连用。popularity among，表示"在……中受欢迎"；popularity with，表示"受到……欢迎"。

❺ 20 年，two decades，名词词组，比如：Two decades ago, consumer spending accounted for 58% of Asia's GDP.（20 年前，消费者支出占亚洲 GDP 的 58%。）译文中表示所属关系，two decades 以字母 s 结尾，所以要写为 two decades'，而不能是 two decades's。

❻ 在最后的这 15 年，the last 15 years，名词词组，比如：We have campaigned against whaling for the last 15 years.（我们最近 15 年一直参加反对捕鲸的运动。）
"最后的"表示的就是"最近的"，翻译为 last，比如：Much has changed since my last visit.（自我上次来访后，变化很大。）

❼ 为……起到了决定性的作用，has played a decisive role in，动词词组，词组原形为：play a decisive role in，比如：Verbs play a decisive role in the Japanese sentences.（动词在日语句子中起着决定性的作用。）
决定性的，decisive，形容词，比如：his decisive victory in the presidential elections（他在这次总统选举中的决定性胜利）。

❽ 保持高速发展，sustaining rapid development of the country，动词词组，词组原形为：sustain rapid development of the country。本文说的是"保持国家的高速发展"，所以翻译的时候增词 the country。
保持，sustain，动词，比如：Recovery can't be sustained unless more jobs are created.（除非有更多的工作机会被创造出来，否则复苏无法保持下去。）
高速发展，rapid development，名词词组，比如：The rapid development of technology means that she is now far behind, and will need retraining.（科技的快速发展意味着她现在已经远远落后了，将需要再训练。）

第二步 动词定位

互联网在中国改革开放中的重要作用怎么说都不为过。从 2000 年开始，中国互联网应用的普及，到现在快 20 年的时间。尤其是在最后的这 15 年，互联网为保持高速发展起到了决定性的作用。

第三步 句型解析

❶ 本文讨论了互联网在中国发展中的作用，所以文章整体使用一般现在时态比较好。

❷ 第一句中，"互联网在中国改革开放中的重要作用"是主语，"怎么说都不为过"是谓语，这是比较常见的固定用法，翻译为 cannot be overstated。

❸ 第二句中，"从 2000 年开始"是时间状语，"中国互联网应用的普及"是主语，"到"实际上是谓语，也就是"走过了"的意思，"现在快 20 年的时间"也就是"近 20 年"，是宾语，以上这样的结构是最简单的，考试的时候当然是用最简单的结构。参考译文译得比较难，译文首先将"2000 年"处理为主

语，将谓语改为"标志、见证"，宾语成为"互联网在中国所经历的近二十年的普及（应用）"，这样一来，宾语中的定语又比较长，分别形成了前置的定语 nearly two decades' 和定语从句 the Internet has enjoyed in China。实话实说，这种句式结构确实漂亮，但是考生在考试当中很难想到。

❹ "尤其是在最后的这 15 年"是典型的时间状语，"互联网"是主语，"起到了决定性的作用"是谓语和宾语，"为保持高速发展"是状语，这里也需要强调"高速发展"指的是"中国的高速发展"或"国家的高速发展"，所以这里需要增对象词，让句子更加明确。

第四步 翻译来了

The importance of the Internet in China's Reform and Opening-up cannot be overstated. The year of 2000 marks the beginning of nearly two decades' popularity the Internet has enjoyed in China. Especially over the last 15 years, the Internet has played a decisive role in sustaining rapid development of the country.

本句考点总结

第一，关于汉译英时态的问题。一般来说，在外宣类文章当中，我们采用一般现在时态比较多。若有具体的时间状语，比如表示将来的，那么就用一般将来时，比如表示过去的，那么就用一般过去时。尽量少用非常"奇怪"和"少见"的时态，因为谓语动词的形式变化可能会出错。

第二，本句考查了英汉互译增减词的问题，一般来说英译汉增词，汉译英减词，常见增词的种类有：一、增加对象词（范围词），这是由上文缺少句子的某个部分造成的；二、增加范畴词，这是较难的一部分，常见的范畴词有"水平、方式、方法、问题、情况、途径和方面"，但是不仅仅有这些，还有很多其他的；三、增加评论性词，这些常常出现在文学翻译中；四、增加动词，会在动词的"分配译法"中说明这点。

经济发展有两个东西是至关重要的：第一就是提高生产效率，提升产品质量，生产出更有创意的设计；第二就是保持渠道畅通，使工厂生产的东西以最快的速度、最低的成本送到消费者的手里。互联网在这两个环节都为中国的产业发展起到了决定性的作用。

第一步 词汇解析

❶ 有，is enabled by，动词词组，使用了被动语态，单词原形为：enable，比如：enable passage of a bill（使议案得以通过）。这里的"有"翻译为 enable，意思是"这两个东西使经济得以发展"。

❷ 至关重要地，crucially，副词，比如：Chewing properly is crucially important.（正确地咀嚼是至关重要的。）

❸ 两个东西，two factors，名词词组，比如：The two factors are directly linked.（这两个因素直接联系在一起。）这里的"东西"指的就是"影响的因素"。

因素，factors，名词，单词原形为：factor，比如：Physical activity is an important factor in maintaining fitness.（体育活动是保持健康的一个重要因素。）

④ 提高生产效率，improve production efficiency，动词词组，比如：Optimize equipment to improve production efficiency.（优化设备，以提高生产效率。）

"提高"可以翻译为 raise/enhance/increase/boost 等。

效率，efficiency，名词，比如：There are many ways to increase agricultural efficiency in the poorer areas of the world.（有许多提高世界较贫困地区农业效能的方法。）

⑤ 提升产品质量，higher product quality，名词词组，这里翻译为"更高的产品质量"。

⑥ 更有创意的设计，more creative designs，名词词组，比如：come up with more creative and innovative designs（推出更有创意和更新颖的设计）。design 用复数 designs 时，常表示"企图、图谋、阴谋"，搭配介词 on/upon/against。

⑦ 保持渠道畅通，open channels，动词词组，比如：All channels of communication need to be kept open.（所有沟通渠道都得保持畅通无阻。）channels 常表示"官方渠道、正式程序"。

⑧ 最低的成本，the lowest cost，名词词组，比如：We're trying to get the best benefit for the lowest cost.（我们正努力用最低的成本创造最高的效益。）

⑨ 送到……手里，can be delivered to，动词词组，使用了被动语态，词组原形为：can deliver，比如：Next Monday is the soonest we can deliver.（我们交货最早要到下星期一。）deliver 还有一个常见用法，表示"发表"，比如：deliver a speech（发表演讲）。

⑩ 为……起到了作用，accounts for，动词词组，词组原形为：account for，比如：The poor weather may have accounted for the small crowd.（天气不好可能是人来得少的原因。）

account for 后面加数字，表示"（数量、比例上）占"，比如：Computers account for 5% of the country's commercial electricity consumption.（电脑占了这个国家商业用电的 5%。）

⑪ 产业发展，industrial development，名词词组，比如：Industrial development is being concentrated in the west of the country.（产业发展在国家的西部集中开展。）

⑫ 决定性（地），decisively，副词，比如：He clearly and decisively came down on the side of the president.（他明确而坚定地宣布支持总统一方。）

第二步 动词定位

经济发展<u>有</u>两个东西<u>是</u>至关重要的：第一就是<u>提高</u>生产效率，<u>提升</u>产品质量，<u>生产</u>出更有创意的设计；第二就是<u>保持</u>渠道畅通，使工厂生产的东西以最快的速度、最低的成本<u>送到</u>消费者的手里。互联网在这两个环节都为中国的产业发展<u>起到了</u>决定性的作用。

第三步 句型解析

① 第一句中，"经济发展有两个东西是至关重要的"简单理解可以翻译为 there be 句型，但是译文在这里炫技了，译者将这个结构理解为隐藏被动语态，使用了 be enabled by 这样的结构，大家可以学习使用，中文里的冒号依旧保留。

② 冒号之后，"第一"直接翻译为 first，"就是提高生产效率，提升产品质量，生产出更有创意的设计"是包含三个动词短语的句子，因为是动词开头，所以使用不定式更加合适，在第二个和第三个动词之间增加 and 表示并列关系，简单翻译即可，但是译文又炫技了，先将"提高生产效率"翻译为动词词组，后面接 with 独立主格结构，将"提升产品质量"理解为"更好的产品质量"，将"生产出更有创意的设计"理解为"更有创意的设计"。以上这样的变化其实是将中文的动态性语言变成英文的静态性语言，

个人觉得在三级笔译考试当中没有必要翻译得这么难，在二级笔译考试当中可以借鉴这些方法。

❸ "第二"直接翻译为 second，但要注意和前一句之间需要有 and 连接，"就是保持渠道畅通"，这是一个不定式结构，"使工厂生产的东西以最快的速度、最低的成本送到消费者的手里"和前面的"渠道"有什么关系呢？仔细分析会发现是"工厂生产的东西能通过这样的渠道（被）送达消费者的手里以（at）最快的速度和最低的成本。"以上这个句子的分析大家应该能够看得懂，这就是我们经常所说的"中文的英文语序"，所以在这里将第二个句子翻译为定语从句，用 through which 进行连接。

❹ 第二句中，"互联网"是主语，"在这两个环节"是状语，"都为中国的产业发展"也是状语，"起到了决定性的作用"是谓语和宾语，上文我们已经学习过 play a decisive role in 的结构了，参考译文为了让句子更加多样，则换了一个方式，翻译为 the Internet decisively accounts for China's industrial development，使用了 accounts for 这样一个短语，大家可以学习使用。

第四步 翻译来了

The economic development is enabled, crucially, by two factors: first, to improve production efficiency with higher product quality and more creative designs, and second, to open channels through which factory products can be delivered to customers at the fastest speed and the lowest cost. That is how the Internet decisively accounts for China's industrial development.

本句考点总结

第一，本句出现了中文里隐藏被动语态的译法。被动语态是英文常见的一种形式，而在中文里常常少用"被"或者不用"被"。那么中文当中一般如何隐藏被动语态呢？第一种是被动变主动，第二种是寻找替代词（比如："让……给""为……所"等结构），第三种是在科技文献中用"可以"来替代"被"，第四种是有"被"不用"被"。在中文里识别出来以上四种隐藏的被动语态不是一件容易的事，需要大家仔细认真地识别这种现象，在汉译英时体现出来。

第二，"中文的英文语序"不能称之为翻译方法，而是汉译英时的一个步骤。若中文句子不符合英文的语序，你需要把中文的句子变成英文的语序，然后往里面"插词"，这样翻译起来更加容易，所以大家要学着将较难的中文句子变成英文的语序，然后再进行翻译。

---

3 互联网的发展在设计理念和设计人才方面极大地缩小了我们与国际先进的国家的差距。通过互联网，我们可以以更快的速度获取全球最先进的设计技术和理念。更重要的是通过互联网可以产生更多的效应。这就极大地加快了经济发展的速度。

第一步 词汇解析

❶ 设计理念和设计人才，design concepts and talents，名词词组。这里采用了形容词的分配译法，"设计"一词出现了两次，英文为避免重复，只翻译一次，翻译为 design。

❷ 极大的，significantly/greatly，副词。

significantly，副词，比如：Profits have increased significantly over the past few years.（几年来，利润大幅度提高了。）

greatly，副词，比如：People would benefit greatly from a pollution-free vehicle.（人们将极大地受益于无污染汽车。）

❸ 缩小了差距，narrow our gap，动词词组，比如：make contribution to narrow our gap in area and culture（为缩小我们在地域、文化方面的差距做出贡献）。narrow 作动词时，常与 down 搭配，表示"缩小、压缩、缩减"。

❹ 国际先进的国家，advanced countries，名词词组，比如：Agricultural productivity remained low by comparison with advanced countries like the United States.（与美国等发达国家相比，农业生产率仍很低。）先进的，advanced，形容词，比如：advanced techniques（先进技术）。

❺ 以更快的速度获取，a faster access，名词词组。
获取，access，名词，还可作动词用，比如：You've illegally accessed and misused confidential security files.（你已经非法获取并盗用了机密文件。）access 表示"获取"时，尤指获取电脑信息。access 后常接介词 to，再加其他成分，比如：access to the President（见到总统）。

❻ 最先进的，state-of-the-art，形容词，比如：the production of state-of-the-art military equipment（最先进的军事装备的生产）。state-of-the-art 强调学科或技术等在当前或某一时期的最新水平。

❼ 设计技术，design techniques，名词词组，比如：new materials and design techniques（新材料和设计技术）。

❽ 产生更多的效应，bring about more effects，动词词组。
产生，bring about，动词词组，比如：The only way they can bring about political change is by putting pressure on the country.（他们能引起政治变化的唯一办法就是向该国施加压力。）

❾ 加快了……速度，speed up，动词词组，比如：I have already taken steps to speed up a solution to the problem.（我已经采取措施加快解决这个问题。）反义词：slow down。

第二步 动词定位

互联网的发展在设计理念和设计人才方面极大地<u>缩小了</u>我们与国际先进的国家的差距。<u>通过</u>互联网，我们可以以更快的速度<u>获取</u>全球最先进的设计技术和理念。更重要的是<u>通过</u>互联网可以<u>产生</u>更多的效应。这就极大地<u>加快了</u>经济发展的速度。

第三步 句型解析

❶ 第一句中，"互联网的发展"是主语，"在设计理念和设计人才方面"是状语，"方面"是典型的范畴词，可以不翻译，"极大地缩小了"是核心谓语，"我们与国际先进的国家的差距"是宾语，这个句子还是比较简单的，只需要注意把状语放在句首或句末。

❷ 第二句中，"通过互联网"是典型的状语，"我们"是主语，"以更快的速度"是方式状语，"获取"是核心谓语，"全球最先进的设计技术和理念"是宾语，这个句子也是比较简单的，译文在这里炫技了，使用了被动语态 we are offered...，可以学着使用。

❸ 第三句中，"更重要的是"翻译为 More importantly，"通过互联网"是状语，"可以产生更多的效应"是谓语和宾语，这里缺少主语，可以使用增主语或者"主动变被动"的译法，但是译文又炫技了，直接用"互联网"作主语，从而不翻译"通过互联网"这个词组，这样处理十分机智。

❹ 最后一句中，"这"是典型的本位词，所以可以使用非限定性定语从句的译法，和前一句合译，"就极大地加快了经济发展的速度"是定语从句当中的谓语和宾语。

第四步 翻译来了

The development of the Internet has significantly narrowed our gap with the advanced countries in design concepts and talents. We are offered a faster access to the world's state-of-the-art design techniques and concepts via the Internet. More importantly, it can bring about more effects, which has greatly sped up the economic development.

> **本句考点总结**
>
> 第一，本句考查了英汉互译增减词的问题，一般来说英译汉增词，汉译英减词，常见增词的种类有：一、增加对象词（范围词），这是由上文缺少句子的某个部分造成的；二、增加范畴词，这是较难的一部分，常见的范畴词有"水平、方式、方法、问题、情况、途径和方面"，但是不仅仅有这些，还有很多其他的；三、增加评论性词，这些常常出现在文学翻译中；四、增加动词，会在动词的"分配译法"中说明这点。
>
> 第二，本位词与外位语的关系。中文里一般用"这""这些""这么""这一切""这样"等词来替代前面出现过的句子，以上这些词被称为"本位词"，被替代的句子称为"外位语"。翻译的时候需要特别注意，前面被替代的句子正常翻译即可，而出现的"这""这些""这么""这一切""这样"等词不能翻译为 this、all、these 等词（这属于口译的译法），而要使用"逗号 + which"的非限定性定语从句的译法。反过来说，英译汉时如果出现了"逗号 + which"的非限定性定语从句，且不知道 which 指代的是什么，那么将 which 翻译为"这""这些""这么""这一切""这样"岂不是更好？

 在渠道的领域，互联网的效果更加明显，比如电商。老百姓通过互联网更容易表达他自己的意愿，更容易对我们现有的一些产品提出一些批评性的意见，而这些也都更好地推动企业的生产，推动政府职能的现代化。

第一步 词汇解析

① 渠道，channels，名词，常用复数，比如：The Americans recognize that the UN can be the channel for greater diplomatic activity.（美国人承认联合国是更重要的外交活动的渠道。）

② ……的效果更加明显，have an even more evident effect，动词词组，此处，even 与比较级连用，表示"更加"，比如：On television he made an even stronger impact as an interviewer.（他作为采访者在电视上造成了更大的影响。）

③ 电商，e-commerce，名词，比如：the anticipated explosion of e-commerce（预期中电子商务的激增）。"电商"的全称为"电子商务"，e- 前缀，表示"电子的"。

④ 老百姓，the ordinary people，名词词组，I strongly suspect that most ordinary people would agree with me.（我强烈地感觉，大多数老百姓会赞同我。）

⑤ 表达意愿，express will，动词词组。常见的动宾搭配，建议直接记忆。will 还有"遗嘱"的意思，比如：Attached to his will was a letter he had written to his wife just days before his death.（遗嘱中附带的是他

去世前几天写给妻子的一封信。)

⑥ 对……提出批评性的意见，share critical comments on，动词词组。
批评性的，critical，形容词，比如：His report is highly critical of the trial judge.（他的报道对承审法官是高度批判的。）反义词：uncritical。在阅读中，表明态度的词有 critical（批评的）；questioning（质疑的）；approving（满意的）；objective（客观的）。

⑦ 现有的产品，existing products，名词词组，比如：This is similar to our existing products or services.（这与我们现有的产品或服务相似。）

⑧ （更好地）推动，facilitate，动词，比如：The new airport will facilitate the development of tourism.（新机场将促进旅游业的发展。）"推动"还可以翻译为：promote/propel/motivate/push forward。

⑨ 企业，enterprises，名词，单词原形为：enterprise，比如：There are plenty of small industrial enterprises.（有很多小型的工业企业。）"企业"还可以翻译为：establishment/business/firm/corporation/company。
【同义词辨析】
company：多指生产或销售产品的公司、商号，也可指经办服务性项目的公司；
corporation：多指一个人拥有或多人联办的大公司，也指在其他地区或国家拥有分公司的公司；
firm：含义广泛，可指公司、商行或商号。规模可大可小，经营、管理的人员可多可少。

⑩ 政府职能，government functions，名词词组。
职责、职能，functions，名词，单词原形为：function，比如：perform a function（履行职责）。

⑪ 现代化，modernization，名词，比如：Successful agricultural reform is also a sine qua non of Mexico's modernization.（成功的农业改革也是墨西哥实现现代化的必要条件。）

第二步 动词定位

在渠道的领域，互联网的效果更加明显，比如电商。老百姓通过互联网更容易表达他自己的意愿，更容易对我们现有的一些产品提出一些批评性的意见，而这些也都更好地推动企业的生产，推动政府职能的现代化。

第三步 句型解析

❶ 第一句中，"在渠道的领域"是状语，这里的"领域"是典型的范畴词，可以不译，"互联网的效果"是主语，"更加明显"是谓语，但是这里的主语过长，可以取偏正短语中的偏作主语，即"互联网"是主语，"有了"是谓语，"明显的效果"是宾语，"比如电商"是状语，总体来看，这句比较简单，但是要注意换主语的问题。

❷ 第二句中，"老百姓"是主语，"通过互联网"是状语，"更容易"实际上是评论，"表达他自己的意愿"是事实，之后的分句中，"更容易"也是评论，"对我们现有的一些产品提出一些批评性的意见"也是事实，那么这个句子怎么处理呢？初中我们就学过 it's easy for somebody to do something，但是这毕竟是翻译考试，是不是要稍微难一点呢？译文这里将"通过互联网"作为主语，使用 It（因为前面已经多次提到了"互联网"）makes it easier for somebody to do something 的结构，这样是否能看懂呢？

❸ 本句的后半句出现了"而这些"，是典型的本位词，可以使用非限定性定语从句的译法，"都更好地推动"是谓语，"企业的生产"是宾语，"推动"是第二个谓语，"政府职能的现代化"是第二个宾语。

第四步 翻译来了

As for channels, the Internet has an even more evident effect, such as, on e-commerce. It has made it easier for the ordinary people to express their own will and share critical comments on some of our existing products, which will facilitate the production of enterprises and the modernization of government functions.

> **本句考点总结**
>
> 第一，本句考查了英汉互译增减词的问题，一般来说英译汉增词，汉译英减词，常见增词的种类有：一、增加对象词（范围词），这是由上文缺少句子的某个部分造成的；二、增加范畴词，这是较难的一部分，常见的范畴词有"水平、方式、方法、问题、情况、途径和方面"，但是不仅仅有这些，还有很多其他的；三、增加评论性词，这些常常出现在文学翻译中；四、增加动词，会在动词的"分配译法"中说明这点。
>
> 第二，本句出现了事实（Facts）和评论（Comments）的译法。中文一般先事实，后评论，而英文则是一般先评论，后事实。比如：It is important for her to go abroad. 翻译为"对于她来说，出国是很重要的"。英文中 It is important 是评论，for her to go abroad 是事实。从中英文的对比来看，可以知道中英文语序分别是怎么安排的。
>
> 第三，本位词与外位语的关系。中文里一般用"这""这些""这么""这一切""这样"等词来替代前面出现过的句子，以上这些词被称为"本位词"，被替代的句子称为"外位语"。翻译的时候需要特别注意，前面被替代的句子正常翻译即可，而出现的"这""这些""这么""这一切""这样"等词不能翻译为 this、all、these 等词（这属于口译的译法），而要使用"逗号 + which"的非限定性定语从句的译法。反过来说，英译汉时如果出现了"逗号 + which"的非限定性定语从句，且不知道 which 指代的是什么，那么将 which 翻译为"这""这些""这么""这一切""这样"岂不是更好？

5 首先，是城市人和农村人在获取信息和沟通信息上平等，大家都可以通过互联网实时看到中国的发展和中国城市的发展。互联网刺激百姓谋求美好生活的意愿，并且将意愿化为前行的强大动力。

第一步 词汇解析

① 城市人和农村人，people in urban and rural areas，名词词组，比如：We will focus on increasing the basic incomes of low-income people in both urban and rural areas.（我们将着力提高城乡低收入群众的基本收入。）这里采用了分配的方法，"人"出现了两次，英文为避免重复，只翻译一次，翻译为 people。

② 获取信息和沟通信息，accessing and communicating information，动词词组，词组原形为：access and communicate information。这里采用了分配的方法，"信息"出现了两次，英文为避免重复，只翻译一次，翻译为 information。

③ 实时，in real time，介词词组，比如：It is now possible to hold a video conference in real time on a mobile phone.（现在可能在移动电话上举行实时电视会议。）句中"实时"的意思是"某事进行的同时"。

④ 看到，witness，动词，比如：India has witnessed many political changes in recent years.（印度近些年已经见证了许多政治变革。）witness 的常见用法之一：无灵主语作主语，表示"历经了……的发展"。

⑤ 刺激，stimulate，动词，比如：America's priority is rightly to stimulate its economy.（美国的首要任务

133

自然是刺激经济。）同义词：motivate/evoke。同根词：stimulus，名词，表示"刺激物"；stimulant，名词，表示"兴奋剂"。

❻ 百姓，common people，名词词组，比如：Shakespeare's work was popular among the common people in his day.（莎士比亚的作品在他那个年代很受百姓的欢迎。）本句中的 common people 与上文出现的 the ordinary people 意思相同，可以进行同义替换。

❼ 谋求美好生活，seek a better life，动词词组，比如：It's only human to seek a better life.（谋求美好生活不过是人之常情。）

❽ 意愿，aspiration，名词，比如：the needs and aspirations of our pupils（我们学生的需求和志向）。aspiration 一般不可数，后常接介词 for/after/to。

【同义词辨析】
aspiration：表示"志向、渴望"，指某人要求达到某种崇高目标的决心和气魄；
ambition：表示"雄心、野心"；
pretension：表示"主张、抱负"。

❾ 将……化为，turn...into，动词词组，比如：The fighting is threatening to turn into full-scale war.（这次冲突可能要演变成全面战争。）

❿ 强大动力，a powerful driving，名词词组，比如：Good morality is a powerful driving force to education.（良好的道德品质是教书育人的强大动力。）"动力"还可以翻译为 motive force/driving force/impetus。

第二步 动词定位

首先，是城市人和农村人在获取信息和沟通信息上平等，大家都可以通过互联网实时看到中国的发展和中国城市的发展。互联网刺激百姓谋求美好生活的意愿，并且将意愿化为前行的强大动力。

第三步 句型解析

❶ 第一句中，"首先"翻译为 First，"城市人和农村人"是主语，"在获取信息和沟通信息上"是状语，"平等"表示"可以平等地做某事"，也就是 be equal in doing something，这是不是"事实与评论"的关系呢？第二分句中，"大家"是主语，"通过互联网"是状语，"实时看到"是谓语，"中国的发展和中国城市的发展"是宾语，简单翻译为并列结构即可，但是译文这里处理为非限定性定语从句，也就是二谓语伴随结构。这个句子中定语形容词的分配译法要学会使用哦！

❷ 第二句中，"互联网"是主语，"刺激"是谓语，"百姓"是宾语，"谋求美好生活的意愿"是宾语补足语，第二分句中，"并且"是并列连词，"将……化为……"是动词，"意愿"是宾语，"前行的强大动力"是宾语补足语，注意两个分句之间可以用并列连词 and 连接。

第四步 翻译来了

Firstly, people in urban and rural areas, by going online, are equal in accessing and communicating information, which allows all of them to witness the development of China and Chinese cities in real time. The Internet then stimulates the aspirations of common people to seek a better life, and turns their aspirations into a powerful driving force for development.

第一，本句出现了事实（Facts）和评论（Comments）的译法。中文一般先事实，后评论，而英文则是一般先评论，后事实。比如：It is important for her to go abroad. 翻译为"对于她来说，出国是很重要的"。 英文中 It is important 是评论，for her to go abroad 是事实。从中英文的对比来看，可以知道中英文语序分别是怎么安排的。

第二，本句考查了形容词的"分配"译法和动词或名词的"分配"译法。形容词分配的译法是两个或多个形容词位于名词之前，"翻译公式"是 (A+B)*C=AC+BC，比如 international and strategic questions 翻译为"国际问题和战略问题"；动词或名词分配的译法是一个动词位于多个名词宾语之前，或者一个名词位于多个名词前，"翻译公式"是 A*(B+C)=AB+AC，比如 wear a hat and a scarf 翻译为"戴着帽子，系着围巾"。而汉译英时，以上这些方法全部要反过来使用。

译后总结

这篇文章谈到了互联网对中国发展的巨大作用，整体句式结构比较工整，但是单词有一定难度，而且隐藏在文章中的一些翻译现象不太容易识别，比如句子中"事实与评论"的关系，需要换主语的问题等，考生需要在考试中快速、准确地把握这些翻译现象，这样才更容易通过考试。

第三节　2019年下半年三级笔译英译汉

In today's interconnected world, culture's power to transform societies is clear. Its diverse manifestations — from our cherished historic monuments and museums to traditional practices and contemporary art forms — enrich our everyday lives in countless ways.

Heritage constitutes a source of identity and cohesion for communities disrupted by bewildering change and economic instability. Creativity contributes to building open, inclusive and pluralistic societies. Both heritage and creativity lay the foundations for vibrant, innovative and prosperous knowledge societies.

Culture is who we are and what shapes our identity. No development can be sustainable without including culture. UNESCO ensures that the role of culture is recognized through a majority of the Sustainable Development Goals (SDGs), including those focusing on quality education, sustainable cities, the environment, economic growth, sustainable consumption and production patterns, peaceful and inclusive societies, gender equality and food security.

No development can be sustainable without a strong culture component. Indeed only a human-centered approach to development based on mutual respect and open dialogue among cultures can lead to lasting, inclusive and equitable results. Yet until recently, culture has been missing from the development strategy.

To ensure that culture takes its rightful place in development strategies and processes, UNESCO has adopted a three-pronged approach: it spearheads worldwide advocacy for culture and development, while engaging with the international community to set clear policies and legal frameworks and working on the ground to support governments and local stakeholders to safeguard heritage, strengthen creative industries and encourage cultural pluralism.

Today, creativity is emerging as one of the most promising avenues for changing how we see cities. Whether by revitalizing the local economy, rethinking transport or housing policies, reclaiming urban spaces, or opening up new horizons for young people, creativity is one of the driving forces behind urban policies and initiatives. Cities worldwide are focusing their attention on the cultural and creative industries as an inspiration for their future.

This vision is promoted by elected representatives and city policy-makers, who see it as a strategic lever for innovation when it comes to tackling contemporary urban issues, whether on an economic, social or environmental front.

More importantly, however, it is a vision shared by professionals and citizens, who are taking action in their own neighborhoods and communities to build more sustainable and more human cities.

This vision of creative urban governance is the driving force behind the UNESCO Creative Cities Programme and Network. Since its creation in 2004, the Network has established itself as a strategic platform for promoting and sharing this new approach to sustainable cities.

Through its standard-setting and operational actions, UNESCO has paved the way for demonstrating the essential role of creativity in urban sustainability, assisting national and local authorities and advocating this vision at an international level.

Culture and creativity play a key role in sustainable urban development. They contribute to diversifying the economy and generating jobs, but they also enhance the quality of life of citizens by participating to a city's social structure and cultural diversity.

2019年下半年的CATTI笔译考试进入机考时代，打字速度和翻译速度成了重点，而且很明显，考试文章的长度比以前长一些。本篇文章是关于文化在城市和国家发展中的作用，总体来看很符合非文学翻译的特点，而且所有的翻译现象都很好地体现了出来。

In today's interconnected world, culture's power to transform societies is clear. Its diverse manifestations — from our cherished historic monuments and museums to traditional practices and contemporary art forms — enrich our everyday lives in countless ways.

第一步 词汇解析

❶ interconnected，形容词，表示"（使）相互连接的、（使）互相联系的"，比如：Bad housing, debt and poverty are interconnected.（恶劣的住房条件、负债以及贫困是相互关联的。）

❷ manifestation，名词，表示"显示、表明、表示"，比如：New York is the ultimate manifestation of American values.（纽约是美国价值观的终极体现。）

❸ monument，名词，表示"历史遗迹"，比如：It's an old building, but that doesn't qualify it as an ancient monument.（这是一座老建筑，但不足以称为古迹。）

❹ contemporary，形容词，表示"当代的、现代的"，比如：Consumption rather than saving has become the central feature of contemporary societies.（现代社会的主要特征是消费而不是储蓄。）

❺ enrich，动词，表示"充实、使丰富"，比如：The study of science has enriched all our lives.（科学研究丰富了我们的整个生活。）

第二步 注意断句

In today's interconnected world, /culture's power to transform societies is clear. /Its diverse manifestations — /from our cherished historic monuments and museums /to traditional practices and contemporary art forms — /enrich our everyday lives /in countless ways.

第三步 句型解析

❶ 第一句中，In today's interconnected world 是地点状语，表示"在当今紧密联系的世界中"，culture's power to transform societies 是主语，表示"文化改变社会的力量"，但由于主语过长，所以单独成句，这里又是偏正短语，可以翻译为主谓结构，表示"文化是改变社会的力量"，后面的 is clear 是系表结构，缺少主语，增主语"这"，这是本位词和外位语的用法。

❷ 第二句中，Its diverse manifestations 是主语，表示"它多样的表现形式"，后面的破折号可以保留，破折号中间的内容是用来解释说明的，from our cherished historic monuments and museums to traditional practices and contemporary art forms 表示"从珍贵的历史古迹和博物馆，到传统习俗和当代的艺术形式"，enrich 是核心谓语，our everyday lives 是宾语，in countless ways 是状语。其实本句直接翻译即可，但是译文让主语单独成句，可能是考虑到破折号内的内容较长。在核心谓语 enrich 前增主语"这"，和上一句的方法一模一样。

第四步 翻译来了

在当今紧密联系的世界中，文化是改变社会的力量，这点显而易见。文化拥有多样的表现形式 —— 从珍贵的历史古迹和博物馆，到传统习俗和当代的艺术形式 —— 这些都极大地丰富了我们的日常生活。

本句考点总结

第一，本句中使用了"偏正结构变主谓结构"的译法，这是什么意思呢？也就是说偏正结构 gleaming eyes（炯炯有神的眼睛）可以翻译为主谓结构 Eyes are gleaming.（眼睛炯炯有神。）这种译法是为了让句子更加通顺，当然有时候也可以用"主谓结构变偏正结构"的译法。"主谓变偏正"或"偏正变主谓"在英汉互译当中都可能出现，须灵活使用。

第二，英译汉时，若句子主语过长，那么可以单独成句，形成一个完整的主谓宾句子，这样翻译是为了避免句子过于臃肿。当主语单独成句时，句子的谓语和宾语缺少主语，那么可以增加"这""这些""这一切""这样"等词作为句子的主语，这样的词称为"本位词"，被这些词所代替的部分称为"外位语"。

2

Heritage constitutes a source of identity and cohesion for communities disrupted by bewildering change and economic instability. Creativity contributes to building open, inclusive and pluralistic societies. Both heritage and creativity lay the foundations for vibrant, innovative and prosperous knowledge societies.

第一步 词汇解析

① heritage，名词，表示"遗产（指国家或社会长期形成的历史、传统和特色）"，比如：Manchester has a rich cultural, economic and sporting heritage.（曼彻斯特有丰富的文化、经济和体育遗产。）

② cohesion，名词，表示"凝聚性、内聚力"，比如：By 1990, it was clear that the cohesion of the armed forces was rapidly breaking down.（显然，到 1990 年时，武装部队的凝聚力正迅速瓦解。）

③ bewildering，形容词，表示"令人困惑的、令人不知所措的、让人晕头转向的"，比如：A glance along his bookshelves reveals a bewildering array of interests.（看一眼他的书架就知道他兴趣繁杂。）

④ inclusive，形容词，表示"包容的"，比如：The academy is far more inclusive now than it used to be.（该学会的包容性比过去强了很多。）

⑤ pluralistic，形容词，表示"多元性的、多元化的"，比如：Our objective is a free, open and pluralistic society.（我们的目标是建立一个自由、开放和多元化的社会。）

⑥ vibrant，形容词，表示"充满生机的、生气勃勃的"，比如：Tom felt himself being drawn towards her vibrant personality.（汤姆感觉自己被她充满朝气的个性所吸引。）

第二步 注意断句

Heritage constitutes a source of identity and cohesion /for communities disrupted /by bewildering change and economic instability. /Creativity contributes to building open, /inclusive /and pluralistic societies. /Both heritage and creativity lay the foundations /for vibrant, /innovative /and prosperous knowledge societies.

第三步 句型解析

① 第一句中，Heritage constitutes a source of identity and cohesion 是主谓宾结构，这里的 heritage 指的是"遗产"，因为和上一句有联系，所以增词翻译为"文化遗产"更好，本句的含义就是"文化遗产成了（构成了）认同感和凝聚力的一种渊源"。for communities 是状语，community 理解为"社会"，后面接过去分词短语，disrupted by bewildering change and economic instability 相当于定语从句，修饰 identity and cohesion for communities，定语较长，可以采用后置译法，这里的 disrupted 表示"打断、打乱"，连在一起表示"社会的认同感和凝聚力被复杂的变化和经济的不稳定打断了"。以上这个句子是本文较为难理解的一个地方，特别要注意语序问题，注意前因后果，首先是"社会的认同感和凝聚力被复杂的变化和经济的不稳定打断了"，然后才是"文化遗产却成了（构成了）认同感和凝聚力的一种渊源"，要弄清楚翻译的语序，这点特别重要。

② 第二句中，Creativity contributes to building open, inclusive and pluralistic societies 是典型的主谓宾结构，直接翻译即可，这里的 contributes to 表示"有助于做某事"。

③ 第三句中，Both heritage and creativity 是主语，lay the foundations 是谓语和宾语，for vibrant, innovative and prosperous knowledge societies 是状语，由于本句和上一句有一定的联系，特别是阐述了"文化遗产"和"创造力"之间的关系，所以可以合译。

第四步 翻译来了

复杂的社会变化和不稳定的经济形势造成了社会认同感和凝聚力的缺失，这时文化遗产却成了社会认同感和凝聚力的一种渊源。创造力对于建立一个开放包容的多元社会有很大帮助，而文化遗产和创造力都为建立具有活力的、创新性的和繁荣的知识型社会奠定了基础。

> **本句考点总结**
>
> 第一，本句出现了分词或分词短语位于名词后的译法。一般来说，分词或分词短语位于名词后相当于定语或定语从句，定语按照"短前长后"的译法来进行翻译。
>
> 第二，本句考查了中英文语序的问题，一般来说，中文的语序是"主语+废话（定语、状语、补语、插入语，等等）+重要成分"，而英文的语序是"废话（定语、状语、补语、插入语，等等）+主语+重要成分+废话（定语、状语、补语、插入语，等等）"，翻译时需要注意调整语序。

3 Culture is who we are and what shapes our identity. No development can be sustainable without including culture. UNESCO ensures that the role of culture is recognized through a majority of the Sustainable Development Goals (SDGs), including those focusing on quality education, sustainable cities, the environment, economic growth, sustainable consumption and production patterns, peaceful and inclusive societies, gender equality and food security.

第一步 词汇解析

❶ shape，动词，表示"塑造"，比如：shape student behavior（塑造学生行为）。

❷ identity，名词，表示"身份"，比如：The donor's identity is a close secret.（捐赠人的身份是一个严加保守的秘密。）

❸ UNESCO，专有名词（缩写），表示"联合国教科文组织"。
文化小常识：

联合国教育、科学及文化组织简称联合国教科文组织（United Nations Educational, Scientific and Cultural Organization，缩写为 UNESCO），于1946年11月16日正式成立，总部设在法国首都巴黎，现有195个成员，是联合国在国际教育、科学和文化领域成员最多的专门机构。该组织旨在通过教育、科学和文化促进各国合作，对世界和平和安全作出贡献，其主要机构包括大会、执行局和秘书处。

❹ Sustainable Development Goals (SDGs)，专有名词，表示"联合国可持续发展目标"。
文化小常识：

联合国可持续发展目标（Sustainable Development Goals，缩写为 SDGs），是联合国制定的17个全球发展目标，在2000–2015年千年发展目标（MDGs）到期之后继续指导2015-2030年的全球发展工作。2015年9月25日，联合国可持续发展峰会在纽约总部召开，联合国193个成员国在峰会上正式通过17个可持续发展目标。可持续发展目标旨在从2015年到2030年间以综合方式彻底解决社会、经济和环境三个维度的发展问题，转向可持续发展道路。

❺ gender，名词，表示"性别"，比如：Many factors are important, for example class, gender, age and ethnicity. （许多因素都很重要，如阶级、性别、年龄及民族。）

第二步 注意断句

Culture is who we are /and what shapes our identity. /No development can be sustainable /without including culture. /UNESCO ensures /that the role of culture is recognized /through a majority of the Sustainable Development Goals (SDGs), /including those focusing on quality education, /sustainable cities, /the environment, /economic growth, /sustainable consumption /and production patterns, /peaceful and inclusive societies, /gender equality /and food security.

第三步 句型解析

❶ 第一句中，Culture is 是主系结构，后面接两个表语从句，who we are 翻译为"我们是谁"不好，翻译为"我们的身份"更好，and 是并列连词，what shapes our identity 翻译为"什么塑造了我们的身份"不好，翻译为"塑造这一身份的因素"更好，这里主要还是代词的译法。

❷ 第二句中，No development can be sustainable 是主干，without including culture 是 without 引导的状语，双重否定句可以直接翻译，也可以翻译为肯定句，比如"唯有文化的支撑，发展才可能是可持续的"。

❸ 第三句中，UNESCO ensures 是主谓结构，that 引导宾语从句，the role of culture is recognized through a majority of the Sustainable Development Goals (SDGs) 是主谓状结构，这里也是典型的被动语态，可以用"寻找替代词"或"有被不用被"的译法。including 后面的内容都是举例，按照总分原则，这些成分应该放在句中翻译，但是状语过长，甚至比主句还长，还是放在原位翻译更好，读起来更加通顺。为了句子通顺，后面的这些举例可以适当增词，比如 sustainable cities 翻译为"可持续的城市发展"而不是"可持续的城市"，the environment 翻译为"环境问题"而不是"环境"等，增词只是为了句子通顺，有些是范畴词，有些是对象词，当然只要觉得句子通顺也可以不增。

第四步 翻译来了

文化表现出我们的身份，也是塑造这一身份的因素。唯有文化的支撑，发展才可能是可持续的。联合国教科文组织（UNESCO）确信，文化的重要作用在多数联合国可持续发展目标（SDGs）中已经得以体现，其主要关注：高质量教育、可持续的城市发展、环境问题、经济增长、可持续消费和生产模式、和平和包容的社会、性别平等以及粮食安全。

> **本句考点总结**
>
> 第一，关于英文代词的译法。英文中需要翻译的代词主要指第三人称 he, she, it, they 及其相应宾格和指示代词 this 和 that。这些单词在翻译时一定要注意，主要采用"不抽象、不具体"的译法。不能翻译成具体的人或物，但是也不能翻译为"他""她""它""他们""这个""那个"，要注意取中间的译法。

第二，本句出现了被动语态的译法。被动语态是英文常见的一种形式，而在中文里常常少用"被"或者不用"被"。那么我们一般有什么样的译法呢？第一种是被动变主动，第二种是寻找替代词（比如："让……给""为……所"等结构），第三种是在科技文献中用"可以"来替代"被"，第四种是有"被"不用"被"。以上四种怎么用，那就看句子怎么通顺怎么翻译了啊！

第三，本句考查了英汉互译增减词的问题，一般来说英译汉增词，汉译英减词，常见增词的种类有：一、增加对象词（范围词），这是由上文缺少句子的某个部分造成的；二、增加范畴词，这是较难的一部分，常见的范畴词有"水平、方式、方法、问题、情况、途径和方面"，但是不仅仅有这些，还有很多其他的；三、增加评论性词，这些常常出现在文学翻译中；四、增加动词，会在动词的"分配译法"中说明这点。

No development can be sustainable without a strong culture component. Indeed only a human-centered approach to development based on mutual respect and open dialogue among cultures can lead to lasting, inclusive and equitable results. Yet until recently, culture has been missing from the development strategy.

第一步　词汇解析

❶ component，名词，表示"组成部分、成分"，比如：Enriched uranium is a key component of a nuclear weapon.（浓缩铀是核武器的关键组成部分。）

❷ human-centered，形容词，表示"以人为本的"，比如：We adhere to human-centered corporate culture construction.（我们坚持以人为本的企业文化建设。）

❸ equitable，形容词，表示"平等的"，比如：We believe you can redistribute this money in a way that's equitable to take care of the poor of the inner city.（我们相信你能够重新分配这笔钱，以公平合理的方式照顾市中心的贫民。）

第二步　注意断句

No development can be sustainable /without a strong culture component. /Indeed /only a human-centered approach to development /based on mutual respect and open dialogue among cultures /can lead to lasting, /inclusive and /equitable results. /Yet /until recently, /culture has been missing from the development strategy.

第三步　句型解析

❶ 第一句中，No development can be sustainable 是主干，without a strong culture component 是 without 引导的状语，双重否定句可以直接翻译，也可以翻译为肯定句，比如"唯有强大的文化支撑，发展才是可持续的"。

❷ 第二句中，Indeed 是副词，表示"确实"，only a human-centered approach to development 是主语，based on mutual respect and open dialogue among cultures 是状语，修饰前面的 approach to development，虽然状

语很长，但前置翻译还是比较通顺的，can lead to lasting, inclusive and equitable results 是谓语和宾语。

❸ 第三句中，Yet 是表示转折的副词，until recently 是时间状语，culture has been missing from the development strategy 是主谓状结构，这里是典型的被动语态，可以用"有被不用被"的译法。另外，这里的 missing 表示"缺席、缺失"，要是翻译为"缺席"的话，可以增加双引号，表示一种比喻的含义。

第四步 翻译来了

唯有强大的文化支撑，发展才是可持续的。确实，只有基于不同文化之间的相互尊重和开放对话，以及以人为本的发展方式才能带来长期、包容和平等的发展成果。而直到现在，文化因素在发展战略中也一直"缺席"。

本句考点总结

本句出现了被动语态的译法。被动语态是英文常见的一种形式，而在中文里常常少用"被"或者不用"被"。那么我们一般有什么样的译法呢？第一种是被动变主动，第二种是寻找替代词（比如："让……给""为……所"等结构），第三种是在科技文献中用"可以"来替代"被"，第四种是有"被"不用"被"。以上四种怎么用，那就看句子怎么通顺怎么翻译了啊！

---

5 To ensure that culture takes its rightful place in development strategies and processes, UNESCO has adopted a three-pronged approach: it spearheads worldwide advocacy for culture and development, while engaging with the international community to set clear policies and legal frameworks and working on the ground to support governments and local stakeholders to safeguard heritage, strengthen creative industries and encourage cultural pluralism.

第一步 词汇解析

❶ rightful，形容词，表示"合适的、恰当的、应有的"，比如：The Baltics' own democratic traditions would help them to regain their rightful place in Europe.（波罗的海各国本身的民主传统将有助于其恢复在欧洲应有的地位。）

❷ three-pronged，形容词，表示"三个步骤的、三管齐下的"，比如：The bank has a three-pronged strategy for recovery.（银行有一套三管齐下的复苏战略。）

❸ spearhead，动词，表示"做……的先锋、带头做"，比如：He is spearheading a campaign for a new stadium in the town.（他正发起一项运动，呼吁在城里新建一座体育场。）

❹ advocacy，名词，表示"拥护、提倡、主张"，比如：I support your advocacy of free trade.（我支持你自由贸易的主张。）

❺ international community，名词词组，表示"国际社会"，比如：The United Nations has appealed for help from the international community.（联合国已经呼吁国际社会提供援助。）

⑥ stakeholder,名词,表示"利益相关者、股东",比如:in stakeholder theory perspective(从利益相关者理论来看)。

⑦ safeguard,动词,表示"保护、保障、捍卫",比如:The new card will safeguard the company against fraud.(新卡将保护公司免遭诈骗。)

⑧ pluralism,名词,表示"多元化、多元性",比如:cultural pluralism(文化的多元化)。

第二步 注意断句

To ensure /that culture takes its rightful place /in development strategies and processes, /UNESCO has adopted a three-pronged approach: /it spearheads worldwide advocacy for culture and development, /while engaging with the international community /to set clear policies and legal frameworks /and working on the ground /to support governments and local stakeholders /to safeguard heritage, /strengthen creative industries /and encourage cultural pluralism.

第三步 句型解析

① 本句中,句首是 To 引导不定式短语作目的状语,ensure 之后是 that 引导的宾语从句,culture takes its rightful place 是主谓宾结构,in development strategies and processes 是状语,这里要注意 development 翻译为"发展"后,作为形容词需要采用分配译法,翻译为"发展战略和发展进程"。

② UNESCO has adopted a three-pronged approach 是主干,也是主谓宾结构,后面的冒号依旧保留,it spearheads worldwide advocacy for culture and development 是 UNESCO 做的第一件事,特别注意 spearheads 的译法,翻译为"带头做某事"是完全可以的,但是译文将动词变为动宾短语,翻译为"发挥'领头羊'作用"也非常好,这里用到了词性转换的译法,另外把 advocacy 看作抽象名词,有动词词根,翻译为动词"倡导",这样整个句子就"活"了。

③ while 之后为了 it(UNESCO)做的第二件事,engaging with the international community 是动宾结构,其后是 to 引导的不定式短语作目的状语,set clear policies and legal frameworks 表示"同国际社会一道制定明确的政策和法律框架",and 是并列连词,后面的 working on the ground 和前面的 engaging with 是并列关系,所以是 UNESCO 做的第三件事,表示"落在实处做某事",后面是两个 to 引导的不定式短语作目的状语,其中 support governments and local stakeholders 是动宾关系,safeguard heritage, strengthen creative industries 和 encourage cultural pluralism 是三个并列的动宾短语。

④ 本句将三个方面的"举措"分别翻译为"首先""其次"和"最后",这是非常经典的,看出来是哪三个方面才是本句的要点。

第四步 翻译来了

联合国教科文组织为确保文化在发展战略和发展进程中有其应有的位置,已经采取了三个方面的举措:首先,发挥"领头羊"作用,在世界范围内倡导文化发展;其次,同国际社会一道制定明确的政策和法律框架;最后,切实支持政府和当地相关利益者保护文化遗产,加强创意产业,鼓励文化多元化。

本句考点总结

第一，本句考查了形容词的"分配"译法和动词或名词的"分配"译法。形容词分配的译法是两个或多个形容词位于名词之前，"翻译公式"是 (A+B)*C=AC+BC，比如 international and strategic questions 翻译为"国际问题和战略问题"；动词或名词分配的译法是一个动词位于多个名词宾语之前，或者一个名词位于多个名词前，"翻译公式"是 A*(B+C)=AB+AC，比如 wear a hat and a scarf 翻译为"戴着帽子，系着围巾"。

第二，本句考查了英汉互译关于"词性转换"的问题，这是个很宏观的考点。一般来说，为了让句子更加通顺，可以把任何一个词从一个词性转换成另一个词性，比如"高兴的"可以换为"高兴地"，这样纯属为了句子通顺，没有什么固定的套路。

第三，本句当中考查了"抽象名词"的译法。抽象名词一般处于冠词之后，又在介词之前，以"the + 抽象名词 + of"的形式居多。一般来说，抽象名词有两种译法。第一种，若抽象名词有动词词根，则翻译为动词，比如 the suggestion of mine，翻译为"我建议"，而不是"我的建议"；第二种，若抽象名词没有动词词根，可以增动词翻译，比如 the spirit of our nation，翻译为"我们民族所具有的精神"，而不是"我们民族的精神"。

Today, creativity is emerging as one of the most promising avenues for changing how we see cities. Whether by revitalizing the local economy, rethinking transport or housing policies, reclaiming urban spaces, or opening up new horizons for young people, creativity is one of the driving forces behind urban policies and initiatives. Cities worldwide are focusing their attention on the cultural and creative industries as an inspiration for their future.

第一步 词汇解析

① avenue，名词，表示"选择、途径、手段"，比如：We will explore every avenue until we find an answer.（我们要探索一切途径，直到找到答案为止。）

② revitalize，动词，表示"使新生、使复兴、使恢复活力（或健康）"，比如：Congress has tried dozens of approaches to revitalize decaying urban and rural areas.（国会已试行过数十种方法来重振正在走向衰败的城乡地区。）

③ reclaim，动词，表示"开拓（耕地或建筑用地）"，比如：The site for the airport will be reclaimed from the swamp.（这片湿地将会被开发来建机场。）

④ driving force，名词词组，表示"驱动力"，比如：Consumer spending was the driving force behind the economic growth in the summer.（顾客消费是夏季经济增长的强大推动力。）

⑤ inspiration，名词，表示"灵感"，比如：Dreams can be a rich source of inspiration for an artist.（梦境可以成为艺术家灵感的丰富源泉。）

第二步 注意断句

Today, /creativity is emerging as one of the most promising avenues /for changing /how we see cities. /Whether /by revitalizing the local economy, /rethinking transport or housing policies, /reclaiming urban spaces, /or opening up new horizons for young people, /creativity is one of the driving forces /behind urban policies and initiatives. /Cities worldwide are focusing their attention /on the cultural and creative industries /as an inspiration for their future.

第三步 句型解析

❶ 第一句中，Today 是时间状语，creativity is emerging 是主谓结构，as one of the most promising avenues 是状语，这里的 be emerging as 可以作为固定搭配来记忆，表示"成了……"，for 引导状语，表示"对于"，changing 后面跟宾语从句 how we see cities。

❷ 第二句中，Whether 和 or 引导了表示"无论……还是……"的一组状语，by 引导方式状语，revitalizing the local economy 表示"振兴本地经济"，rethinking transport or housing policies 表示"考虑重新制定交通或住房政策"，reclaiming urban spaces 表示"开拓城市空间"，or opening up new horizons for young people 表示"抑或是为年轻人开辟新天地"，creativity is one of the driving forces 是主干，为主系表结构，behind urban policies and initiatives 是状语，总体句式结构不难，可以直接翻译。

❸ 第三句中，Cities worldwide are focusing their attention 是主谓宾结构，on the cultural and creative industries 是状语，as an inspiration for their future 是方式状语，这里的 as 表示"作为"。

第四步 翻译来了

如今，创造力对于改变人们如何看待城市是最具前景的方法之一。无论是振兴本地经济，还是考虑重新制定交通或住房政策，开拓城市空间，抑或是为年轻人开辟新天地，创造力才是制定城市政策及倡议的一大推动力。世界范围内的各个城市都将重心放在文化创意产业上，为未来的发展提供灵感。

This vision is promoted by elected representatives and city policy-makers, who see it as a strategic lever for innovation when it comes to tackling contemporary urban issues, whether on an economic, social or environmental front.

第一步 词汇解析

❶ vision，名词，表示"想象、展望、愿景"，比如：I have a vision of a society that is free of exploitation and injustice.（我希望建立一个没有剥削和不公的社会。）

❷ elected representative，名词词组，表示"当选代表"，比如：the newly elected representative（新当选的代表）。

❸ policy-maker，名词，表示"（政治）政策制定者、决策人"，比如：top economic policy-makers（最高经济决策者们）。

❹ lever，名词，表示"杠杆"，比如：An elevator mechanic can work the machinery directly by turning this lever.（电梯修理工可以转动这根杠杆直接操作机器。）

❺ tackle，动词，表示"应付、处理、解决（难题或局面）"，比如：The government is determined to tackle inflation.（政府决心解决通货膨胀问题。）

第二步 注意断句

This vision is promoted /by elected representatives and city policy-makers, /who see it as a strategic lever for innovation /when it comes to tackling contemporary urban issues, /whether on an economic, /social /or environmental front.

第三步 句型解析

① 本句中，This vision is promoted 是主谓结构，而且也是典型的被动语态，可以用"寻找替代词"的译法来翻译，by elected representatives and city policy-makers 是状语，表示两类人，逗号后面是由 who 引导的非限定性定语从句，非限定性定语从句一般采用后置译法较好。

② 定语从句中，see it as a strategic lever for innovation 是谓宾状结构，要特别注意代词 it 的译法，可以用模糊翻译法翻译为"其"，when it comes to tackling contemporary urban issues 是 when it comes to doing 的结构，表示"谈到……时"，whether on an economic, social or environmental front 也是状语结构，表示"无论……还是……"。译文中将 strategic lever 翻译为"战略杠杆"，并且使用了双引号，表示强调和说明，考试时也可以不用。

第四步 翻译来了

这一愿景是由当选的代表和城市的决策者共同提出的，谈到解决经济、社会、环境等方面的当代城市问题时，这些人将其视为创新的"战略杠杆"。

> **本句考点总结**
>
> 第一，本句出现了被动语态的译法。被动语态是英文常见的一种形式，而在中文里常常少用"被"或者不用"被"。那么我们一般有什么样的译法呢？第一种是被动变主动，第二种是寻找替代词（比如："让……给""为……所"等结构），第三种是在科技文献中用"可以"来替代"被"，第四种是有"被"不用"被"。以上四种怎么用，那就看句子怎么通顺怎么翻译了啊！
>
> 第二，非限定性定语从句是用逗号隔开的定语从句，这样的句子一般都要采用后置译法，在翻译时需要翻译出关系代词 which，who 等词，指明这些词的指代关系，将这些代词翻译出来。
>
> 第三，关于英文代词的译法。英文中需要翻译的代词主要指第三人称 he, she, it, they 及其相应宾格和指示代词 this 和 that。这些单词在翻译时一定要注意，主要采用"不抽象、不具体"的译法。不能翻译成具体的人或物，但是也不能翻译为"他""她""它""他们""这个""那个"，要注意取中间的译法。

 More importantly, however, it is a vision shared by professionals and citizens, who are taking action in their own neighborhoods and communities to build more sustainable and more human cities.

第一步 词汇解析

❶ professional，名词，表示"专业人士"，比如：Always seek professional legal advice before entering into any agreement.（在签订任何协定之前一定要先征求法律专业人士的意见。）

第二步 注意断句

More importantly, /however, /it is a vision shared by professionals and citizens, /who are taking action in their own neighborhoods and communities /to build more sustainable and more human cities.

第三步 句型解析

❶ 句首的 More importantly 是状语，however 是转折副词，表示"然而"，是插入语，可以放在句首翻译。

❷ 主干 it is a vision 是主系表结构，shared by professionals and citizens 是过去分词短语位于名词后，相当于定语从句，从句较短，可以采用前置译法，逗号后面是由 who 引导的非限定性定语从句，非限定性定语从句一般采用后置译法较好。

❸ 定语从句中，are taking action in their own neighborhoods and communities 是谓宾状结构，不定式短语 to build more sustainable and more human cities 作目的状语。本句结构非常清晰，看清楚结构，弄明白单词，直接翻译即可。

第四步 翻译来了

然而，更加重要的是，这是专业人士和居民们的共同愿景，他们在自己的社区里采取行动，以建设更加可持续、更加人性化的城市。

本句考点总结

第一，本句出现了分词或分词短语位于名词后的译法。一般来说，分词或分词短语位于名词后相当于定语或定语从句，定语按照"短前长后"的译法来进行翻译。

第二，非限定性定语从句是用逗号隔开的定语从句，这样的句子一般都要采用后置译法，在翻译时需要翻译出关系代词 which，who 等词，指明这些词的指代关系，将这些代词翻译出来。

---

9 This vision of creative urban governance is the driving force behind the UNESCO Creative Cities Programme and Network. Since its creation in 2004, the Network has established itself as a strategic platform for promoting and sharing this new approach to sustainable cities.

第一步 词汇解析

❶ governance，名词，表示"治理、统治、管理"，比如：They believe that a fundamental change in the governance of Britain is the key to all other necessary changes.（他们认为从根本上改变英国的统治方式是促成其他所有必要变革的关键所在。）

❷ Creative Cities Programme and Network，专业名词，表示"全球创意城市网络"。
文化小常识：
全球创意城市网络，是联合国教科文组织于2004年推出的一个项目，旨在通过对成员城市促进当地文化发展的经验进行认可和交流，从而达到在全球化环境下倡导和维护文化多样性的目标。

第二步 注意断句

This vision of creative urban governance is the driving force /behind the UNESCO Creative Cities Programme and Network. /Since its creation in 2004, /the Network has established itself /as a strategic platform /for promoting and sharing this new approach to sustainable cities.

第三步 句型解析

❶ 第一句中，This vision of creative urban governance is the driving force 是主系表结构，behind the UNESCO Creative Cities Programme and Network 是状语，句式结构简单，直接翻译即可。

❷ 第二句中，Since 引导时间状语，其中 creation 是典型的抽象名词，有动词词根，可翻译为动词"提出"，翻译为"创造"不准确，the Network has established itself 是主谓宾结构，as a strategic platform 是状语，for 引导目的状语，表示"为了"，promoting and sharing this new approach to sustainable cities 是动宾结构。译文将 establish...as 理解为"成了"，这样更好，直译为"把……建设为"过于生硬，不是很好，而且译文将后面的目的状语 for doing 翻译为定语"的"的结构，这也是可以的，考试时翻译为状语或定语都可以。

第四步 翻译来了

创意性城市的治理愿景就是联合国教科文组织全球创意城市网络（UNESCO Creative Cities Programme and Network）背后的驱动力。自2004年提出以来，这一网络已经成了一个推广和分享城市可持续发展新理念的战略平台。

> **本句考点总结**
>
> 本句当中考查了"抽象名词"的译法。抽象名词一般处于冠词之后，又在介词之前，以"the + 抽象名词 + of"的形式居多。一般来说，抽象名词有两种译法。第一种，若抽象名词有动词词根，则翻译为动词，比如 the suggestion of mine，翻译为"我建议"，而不是"我的建议"；第二种，若抽象名词没有动词词根，可以增动词翻译，比如 the spirit of our nation，翻译为"我们民族所具有的精神"，而不是"我们民族的精神"。

Through its standard-setting and operational actions, UNESCO has paved the way for demonstrating the essential role of creativity in urban sustainability, assisting national and local authorities and advocating this vision at an international level.

第一步 词汇解析

❶ pave the way,表示"(为……)铺平道路,创造条件",比如:This decision paved the way for changes in employment rights for women.(这项决议为修改妇女就业权利创造了条件。)

❷ demonstrate,动词,表示"展示、演示、示范",比如:Her job involves demonstrating new educational software.(她的工作包括演示新的教学软件。)

第二步 注意断句

Through its standard-setting and operational actions, /UNESCO has paved the way for demonstrating the essential role of creativity /in urban sustainability, /assisting national and local authorities /and advocating this vision /at an international level.

第三步 句型解析

❶ 句首的 Through its standard-setting and operational actions 是状语,要特别注意这个状语的逻辑主语是什么,是主句的主语 UNESCO,那么这里的两个名词词组是不是可以看成是抽象名词呢?完全可以,翻译时可以增词"制定"。

❷ 主句中,UNESCO 是主语,has paved the way for 是谓语,demonstrating the essential role of creativity in urban sustainability 是第一组宾语和状语,assisting national and local authorities 是第二组宾语和状语,and 是并列连词,advocating this vision at an international level 是第三组宾语和状语,三个并列的宾语直接翻译即可,请务必注意状语的位置。

第四步 翻译来了

联合国教科文组织通过制定标准化和可实施的行动方案,为展现城市可持续发展的创造性作用,协助各个国家和地方政府,并在国际上倡导这一理念铺平了道路。

本句考点总结

本句当中考查了"抽象名词"的译法。抽象名词一般处于冠词之后,又在介词之前,以"the + 抽象名词 + of"的形式居多。一般来说,抽象名词有两种译法。第一种,若抽象名词有动词词根,则翻译为动词,比如 the suggestion of mine,翻译为"我建议",而不是"我的建议";第二种,若抽象名词没有动词词根,可以增词翻译,比如 the spirit of our nation,翻译为"我们民族所具有的精神",而不是"我们民族的精神"。

Culture and creativity play a key role in sustainable urban development. They contribute to diversifying the economy and generating jobs, but they also enhance the quality of life of citizens by participating to a city's social structure and cultural diversity.

第一步 词汇解析

❶ diversify，动词，表示"（使）多样化"，比如：The company's troubles started only when it diversified into new products.（当公司增加新产品时，麻烦才开始的。）

❷ generate，动词，表示"创造、产生、制作、造出"，比如：Brainstorming is a good way of generating ideas.（集思广益是出主意的好办法。）

第二步 注意断句

Culture and creativity play a key role /in sustainable urban development. /They contribute to diversifying the economy and generating jobs, /but they also enhance the quality of life of citizens /by participating to a city's social structure and cultural diversity.

第三步 句型解析

❶ 第一句中，Culture and creativity play a key role 是主谓宾结构，in sustainable urban development 是状语，play a key role in 表示"在……发挥重要作用"。

❷ 第二句第一分句中，They 是主语，因为是第二次提到，所以可以直接翻译为代词"他们"，contribute to 是谓语，表示"有助于"，diversifying the economy and generating jobs 是宾语，but 是表示转折含义的并列连词，they also enhance the quality of life of citizens 是第二分句的主谓宾结构，by 引导方式状语，participating to a city's social structure and cultural diversity 是动宾短语，这里表示"参与城市社会结构和文化多样性"，这么翻译肯定不好，动词分配两次，分别翻译为"改造城市社会结构"和"提高文化多样性"是比较好的。

第四步 翻译来了

文化创意在城市可持续发展中起到了重要的作用，它们不仅有助于实现经济多元化，创造就业，而且还可以通过改造城市社会结构，提高文化多样性，从而帮助提高居民们的生活质量。

本句考点总结

本句考查了形容词的"分配"译法和动词或名词的"分配"译法。形容词分配的译法是两个或多个形容词位于名词之前，"翻译公式"是 (A+B)*C=AC+BC，比如 international and strategic questions 翻译为"国际问题和战略问题"；动词或名词分配的译法是一个动词位于多个名词宾语之前，或者一个名词位于多个名词前，"翻译公式"是 A*(B+C)=AB+AC，比如 wear a hat and a scarf 翻译为"戴着帽子，系着围巾"。

译后总结

这篇文章属于典型的非文学翻译，是 UNESCO 对于城市和国家发展的一些阐述，文章总体难度不大，可能是第一次机考的原因，考试中心选择了相对容易的题目，但是翻译现象还是一一出现了。从现在起，请大家一定要多多关注打字速度和翻译速度这两个方面，这是未来翻译考试的要点。其实，翻译靠手写本身就不科学，现在从事翻译行业，谁还手写啊！

第四节 2019年下半年三级笔译汉译英

作为中国浙江省省会，杭州是中国历史文化名城。距今约5 300年的"良渚文化"遗址（位于杭州余杭区）是中华文明发祥地之一。

杭州素以美丽的山水著称。中国古代有句谚语，"上有天堂，下有苏杭"，表达了古往今来人们对于这座美丽城市的由衷喜爱。

位于杭州西南的西湖，以其秀丽的湖光山色和众多名胜古迹而成为闻名中外的旅游胜地。2011年被正式列入《世界遗产名录》。此外，气势浩荡的钱塘江大潮，每年吸引无数游客。

杭州拥有丰富的历史文化遗迹。南起杭州、北到北京的京杭大运河始建于1631年，全长约1 797公里，是世界上最长、最古老的人工水道。2014年6月22日，京杭大运河正式列入《世界遗产名录》。

在世界上，杭州颇具名声。早在13世纪，意大利著名旅行家马可·波罗赞叹杭州为"世界上最美丽之城"。

杭州曾被美国《纽约时报》评为"2011年全球最值得去的41个地方"之一，还被联合国环境规划署评为"国际花园城市"。

杭州还曾在中美建交的过程中扮演过重要角色。2015年1月，中国提出"旅游外交"政策。杭州作为著名旅游城市，又率先实践"旅游外交"。

2019年下半年的CATTI笔译汉译英材料是一段关于杭州概况的介绍，总体来看句式结构不难，主要还是考查一些名词短语的翻译，这些常见的名词短语一定要熟记熟练，不要想着等到考试的时候再查字典。实话实说，带字典是可取的，但是只要不会的词汇就查字典，考试时间明显是不够的！

作为中国浙江省省会，杭州是中国历史文化名城。距今约5 300年的"良渚文化"遗址（位于杭州余杭区）是中华文明发祥地之一。

第一步 词汇解析

❶ 浙江省，Zhejiang Province，地名，注意首字母大写，Zhejiang不能分开写。

❷ 省会，capital，名词，比如：a provincial capital（省会）。capital与范围不同的区域搭配，词义不同：与国家搭配，表示"首都"；与自治区搭配，表示"首府"；与省份搭配，表示"省会"。capital还表示"……之都"，比如：the capital of the wine trade（葡萄酒贸易之都）。

❸ 是，be known as，动词词组，比如：She is known as a great beauty.（她是一个众所周知的大美人。）这里"是"的意思是"以……闻名"，翻译为be动词也是完全可以的。

❹ 历史文化名城，a historical and cultural city，名词词组，比如：Changsha is a historical and cultural city with rich background.（长沙是一座底蕴丰富的历史文化名城。）

❺ 距今，trace back，动词词组，比如：His ancestors trace back to the 16th century.（他的祖先可上溯到16世纪。）

❻ "良渚文化"遗址，"The Liangzhu Archaeological Ruins"，专有名词，注意首字母大写。
考古遗址，archaeological ruins，名词词组，比如：It includes several popular tourist attractions and has several beaches and archaeological ruins.（这包含一些热门旅游景点、海滩和考古遗址。）

文化小常识：
　　良渚文化分布的中心地区在钱塘江流域和太湖流域，而遗址分布最密集的地区则在钱塘江流域的东北部和东部。该文化遗址最大的特色是出土的玉器。

❼ 位于，situate in，动词词组，常用被动语态 be situated in，比如：The hotel is beautifully situated in a quiet spot near the river.（旅馆环境优美，坐落在河边一个僻静的地方。）

❽ 余杭区，Yuhang District，地名，注意首字母大写，Yuhang 不能分开写。district 以行政、司法、教育目的划分，缩写为 dist.，district 的范围比 region 小。

❾ 中华文明发祥地，an important Chinese civilization cradle，名词词组。
发祥地，cradle，名词，"发祥地"原指帝王出生或创业的地方，现指某事物或某事业起源的地方，比如：Greece was the cradle of western civilization（希腊是西方文明的发祥地。）

第二步 动词定位

　　<u>作为</u>中国浙江省省会，杭州<u>是</u>中国历史文化名城。<u>距</u>今约 5 300 年的"良渚文化"遗址（位于杭州余杭区）<u>是</u>中华文明发祥地之一。

第三步 句型解析

❶ 第一句中，第一分句中的"作为"是动词，"中国浙江省省会"是宾语。第二分句中的"杭州"是核心主语，"是"是谓语，"中国历史文化名城"是宾语，本句有两个动词，一个是"作为"，一个是"是"，所以翻译时应该考虑到"并列""伴随""下沉"的结构，译文把"作为"处理为 As（下沉结构），核心动词"是"处理为 be known as。

❷ 第二句和第一句的结构非常相似，"距今"是第一个动词，"约 5 300 年的"是表示时间的定语，"'良渚文化'遗址"是本句的主语，后面括号和括号里的内容依旧保留，"位于杭州余杭区"是谓状结构，"是"是核心谓语，"中华文明发祥地之一"是宾语。整句可以用"'良渚文化'遗址"作主语，"距"作为下沉结构，翻译为 tracing back about 5, 300 years，核心谓语翻译为 is，宾语是 an important Chinese civilization cradle。这里还要注意地点的翻译，中文地点从大到小，英文则是从小到大，比如"杭州市余杭区"，英文要翻译为 Yuhang District, Hangzhou。

第四步 翻译来了

　　As the capital of Zhejiang Province in China, Hangzhou is known as a historical and cultural city. "The Liangzhu Archaeological Ruins" (situated in Yuhang District, Hangzhou), tracing back about 5, 300 years, is an important Chinese civilization cradle.

本句考点总结

　　本句考查了汉译英句子中并列、伴随、下沉的结构。中文常常会出现多个句子聚集的情况，那么我们在翻译时需要考虑将这些句子进行"分堆"，但是"分堆"之后，一个句子中也可能会出现两个动词或两组动词，那么有两个动词或两组动词的句子我们该如何进行翻译呢？

比如："我坐在那里看书"，这里有两个动词，一个是"坐"，一个是"看"，我们翻译时便会有三种方法：

第一种并列（两个动词并列的译法，使用并列连词连接，两个动词之间不一定是"并列"关系）：I sat there and read a book.

第二种伴随（将第二个动词翻译为二谓语，分词、从句、状语等都可以）：I sat there reading a book.

第三种下沉（将第一个动词翻译为二谓语，分词、从句、状语等都可以）：Sitting there, I read a book.

需要说明的是，并列、伴随和下沉只是动词的形式问题，不代表动词之间的逻辑关系，用这三种形式翻译两个动词或两组动词都是可以的，大家可以根据句子上下文的关系来判断使用。

2　杭州素以美丽的山水著称。中国古代有句谚语，"上有天堂，下有苏杭"，表达了古往今来人们对于这座美丽城市的由衷喜爱。

第一步　词汇解析

❶ 以……著称，be famous for，动词词组，比如：He is famous for his tough-minded professionalism.（他强悍的职业作风十分有名。）

❷ 美丽的山水，beautiful sceneries，名词词组，比如：Guilin is known for its beautiful sceneries.（桂林因风景优美而出名。）句中"山水"的意思是"景色"，翻译为 scenery。

【同义词辨析】

scene：指具体的、局部的或一时的景色，可以是自然形成的，也可以是人工造成的；

view：多指从远处或高处所见的景色；

sight：指旅游观光的风光，包括城市景色和自然风光景色，也指人造景物或奇特的景色；

scenery：指一个国家或某一地区的整体自然风景；

landscape：多指内陆的自然风光。

❸ 中国古代（有句）谚语，a Chinese saying，名词词组，比如：As a Chinese saying goes, "seeing is believing".（中国有句谚语"眼见为实"。）As a Chinese saying goes 这一用法在引用谚语时常加在谚语之前，希望大家熟悉这一句型，并学会运用。本句中的"古代"也可以翻译出来，翻译为 As an ancient Chinese saying goes。

谚语，saying，名词，比如：We also realize the truth of that old saying: Charity begins at home.（我们也明白那句老话很有道理：仁爱始于家庭。）

❹ "上有天堂，下有苏杭"，"Up above there is heaven; down below there are Suzhou and Hangzhou"，长句。本句采用相对直译的方法，考试的时候按照字面意思简单理解后再翻译即可。

文化小常识：

"上有天堂，下有苏杭"是我国民间流传的谚语，出自宋代范成大《吴郡志》，意在赞叹江南美景，可与天堂相媲美。

❺ 古往今来，through the ages，介词词组，比如：These customs have been handed down through the ages.

（这些风俗是世世代代传下来的。）"古往今来"意思是"从古到今"，泛指很长一段时间。这一成语也可以翻译为 from ancient times/from ancient to modern times。表示"长时期、许多年"时，age 常用复数，比如：The dust of ages was piled inches high over the books.（书籍上面多年积尘厚达数英寸。）

❻ 由衷喜爱，sincere love，名词词组。"由衷"意思是"衷心的、出自内心的、发自肺腑的"；也指"出自内心的情意和向别人指出内心的情感"。由衷的，sincere，形容词，比如：He's sincere in his views.（他的意见是诚恳的。）

第二步 动词定位

杭州素以美丽的山水<u>著称</u>。中国古代<u>有</u>句谚语，"上<u>有</u>天堂，下<u>有</u>苏杭"，<u>表达</u>了古往今来人们对于这座美丽城市的由衷喜爱。

第三步 句型解析

❶ 第一句中，"杭州"是主语，因为上文已经出现了 Hangzhou，所以这里可以用 The city 来替代，"美丽的山水"是宾语，"素以……著称"是核心动词，翻译为 is famous for。

❷ 第二句中，"中国古代有句谚语"是主谓宾结构，可以用 there be 句型，后面的"上有天堂，下有苏杭"是同位语，用来解释说明"谚语"。第二个动词"表达"，是二谓语，这里可以处理为定语从句或分词的伴随结构，译文处理为非限定性定语从句 which expresses，宾语是"人们由衷的喜爱"，"古往今来"是时间状语，"对于这座美丽城市"是状语。

❸ 注意这两句话可以合译，因为前面说到了杭州是以美景闻名，后面是形容杭州如何，简单合译用并列连词 and，复杂一点可以用表示结果的 so。

第四步 翻译来了

The city is famous for its beautiful sceneries in the world, so there is a Chinese saying, "Up above there is heaven; down below there are Suzhou and Hangzhou", which expresses the sincere love of people through the ages for the beautiful city.

本句考点总结

该句考查了汉译英句子中并列、伴随、下沉的结构。中文常常会出现多个句子聚集的情况，那么我们在翻译时需要考虑将这些句子进行"分堆"，但是"分堆"之后，一个句子中也可能会出现两个动词或两组动词，那么有两个动词或两组动词的句子我们该如何进行翻译呢？比如："我坐在那里看书"，这里有两个动词，一个是"坐"，一个是"看"，我们翻译时便会有三种方法：

第一种并列（两个动词并列的译法，使用并列连词连接，两个动词之间不一定是"并列"关系）：I sat there and read a book.

第二种伴随（将第二个动词翻译为二谓语，分词、从句、状语等都可以）：I sat there reading a book.

第三种下沉（将第一个动词翻译为二谓语，分词、从句、状语等都可以）：Sitting there, I read a book.

需要说明的是，并列、伴随和下沉只是动词的形式问题，不代表动词之间的逻辑关系，用这三种形式翻译两个动词或两组动词都是可以的，大家可以根据句子上下文的关系来判断使用。

位于杭州西南的西湖，以其秀丽的湖光山色和众多名胜古迹而成为闻名中外的旅游胜地。2011年被正式列入《世界遗产名录》。此外，气势浩荡的钱塘江大潮，每年吸引无数游客。

第一步 词汇解析

❶ 西湖，West Lake，地名，比如：Do you go to West Lake?（你去西湖了吗？）

❷ 秀丽的湖光山色，beautiful natural landscapes，名词词组，比如：China is one of the greatest countries in the world, with beautiful natural landscapes and friendly people.（中国是世界上最好的国家之一，自然风光美丽、人民热情友好。）

湖光山色，natural landscapes，名词词组，比如：The natural landscape of Tibet is worthwhile to visit.（西藏的自然景观很值得去参观。）

"湖光山色"的意思是"湖的风光，山的景色"，指有水有山，风景秀丽。

❸ 名胜古迹，historical sites，名词词组，比如：There are a variety of tourist attractions and historical sites in London.（伦敦有各种各样的旅游景点和名胜古迹。）

❹ 闻名中外的旅游胜地，a world-known tourist attraction，名词词组。"中外"的意思是"世界范围"，所以"闻名中外"翻译为world-known。

旅游胜地，tourist attraction，名词词组，比如：Buckingham Palace is a major tourist attraction.（白金汉宫是重要的旅游胜地。）

❺ 被（正式）列入，be included in，动词词组，比如：It was included in the UNESCO world heritage list in 1996.（它在1996年被列入联合国教科文组织世界遗产名录。）include 表示"列为……的一部分"时，常用被动语态，比如：be included as a candidate（列为候选人之一）。

❻ 《世界遗产名录》，the World Heritage List，专有名词。这类书名、电影名、电视剧名等，在机考打字时，需要首字母大写，使用斜体；在纸质答卷上，需要首字母大写，加双引号。

文化小常识：

《世界遗产名录》是于1976年世界遗产委员会成立时建立的。被世界遗产委员会列入《世界遗产名录》的地方，将成为世界级的名胜，可接受"世界遗产基金"提供的援助，还可由有关单位组织游客进行游览。

❼ 气势浩荡的，magnificent，形容词，比如：a magnificent country house in wooded grounds（林地中一座漂亮的村宅）。

❽ 钱塘江大潮，tidal bores of Tsien-tang，名词词组。涌潮，tidal bore，名词。钱塘江，Tsien-tang，专有名词，属于威妥玛式标音法，要是不会翻译，直接用汉语拼音 Qiantang River 也是可以的。

语言小常识：

威妥玛式标音法，在1958年中国推广汉语拼音方案前被广泛用于人名和地名注音，影响较大。1958年后，逐渐废止。中国大陆一些已成习用的专有名词依然使用这一方法，比如：I-ching（易经）和 Tai-chi（太极）。

❾ 吸引，attract，动词，比如：The Cardiff Bay project is attracting many visitors.（加的夫湾工程吸引着众多参观者。）"吸引"还可以翻译为 draw/appeal to 等词。

❿ 无数（的），countless，形容词，比如：She brought joy to countless people through her music.（她通过自己的音乐把快乐带给了无数人。）

第二步 动词定位

位于杭州西南的西湖,以其秀丽的湖光山色和众多名胜古迹而成为闻名中外的旅游胜地。2011 年被正式列入《世界遗产名录》。此外,气势浩荡的钱塘江大潮,每年吸引无数游客。

第三步 句型解析

❶ 第一句中,"位于杭州西南的"是定语,"西湖"是主语,"以其秀丽的湖光山色和众多名胜古迹"是原因状语,"成为"是核心动词,表示"是","闻名中外的旅游胜地"是表语,这里是系表结构,而且非常合适用一般现在时。译文在处理"位于"和"是"这两个动词的时候,使用了双动词的下沉译法,前一个动词翻译为 Located in,另一个动词翻译为核心动词 is。

❷ 第二句中,"2011 年"是时间状语,"被正式列入"是核心谓语,但是这里缺少主语,主语是"西湖",第二次提到用代词 it,《世界遗产名录》是宾语。

❸ 第三句中,"此外"是状语,"气势浩荡的钱塘江大潮"是主语,"每年"是时间状语,"吸引"是核心谓语,"无数游客"是宾语。

第四步 翻译来了

Located in the southwest of Hangzhou, West Lake is a world-known tourist attraction for its beautiful natural landscapes and many historical sites. In 2011, it was officially included in *the World Heritage List*. Besides, the magnificent tidal bores of Tsien-tang are attracting countless tourists every year.

本句考点总结

本句考查了汉译英句子中并列、伴随、下沉的结构。中文常常会出现多个句子聚集的情况,那么我们在翻译时需要考虑将这些句子进行"分堆",但是"分堆"之后,一个句子中也可能会出现两个动词或两组动词,那么有两个动词或两组动词的句子我们该如何进行翻译呢?比如:"我坐在那里看书",这里有两个动词,一个是"坐",一个是"看",我们翻译时便会有三种方法:

第一种并列(两个动词并列的译法,使用并列连词连接,两个动词之间不一定是"并列"关系):I sat there and read a book.

第二种伴随(将第二个动词翻译为二谓语,分词、从句、状语等都可以):I sat there reading a book.

第三种下沉(将第一个动词翻译为二谓语,分词、从句、状语等都可以):Sitting there, I read a book.

需要说明的是,并列、伴随和下沉只是动词的形式问题,不代表动词之间的逻辑关系,用这三种形式翻译两个动词或两组动词都是可以的,大家可以根据句子上下文的关系来判断使用。

---

4 杭州拥有丰富的历史文化遗迹。南起杭州、北到北京的京杭大运河始建于 1631 年,全长约 1 797 公里,是世界上最长、最古老的人工水道。2014 年 6 月 22 日,京杭大运河正式列入《世界遗产名录》。

第一步 词汇解析

❶ 拥有，boast，动词，比如：The houses will boast the latest energy-saving technology.（这些房屋将采用最新节能技术。）boast 一词本身暗含"丰富的"的意思，所以原文中的"丰富的"不需要翻译。

❷ 历史文化遗迹，historical and cultural sites，名词词组，比如：The Longmen Grottoes is one of the major historical and cultural sites under state protection in China.（龙门石窟是我国重点文物保护单位。）

❸ 京杭大运河，Beijing-Hangzhou Grand Canal，专有名词，注意首字母大写。
大运河，Grand Canal，专有名词，比如：The Grand Canal runs through his hometown.（大运河流经他的家乡。）

文化小常识：
京杭大运河始建于春秋时期，是世界上里程最长、工程最大的古代运河。"京杭"指的是"北京至杭州"，翻译为 Beijing-Hangzhou。

❹ 始建，found，动词，比如：The town was founded in 1610.（该城镇兴建于 1610 年。）

❺ 最古老的，with the oldest history，介词词组，比如：one of the subject matter works with the oldest history in Chinese auspicious pictures（中国吉祥图案中最古老的作品题材之一）。句中"最古老的"的意思是"历史悠久的"，所以翻译为 the oldest 也是可以的。

❻ 人工水道，artificial waterway，名词词组。
人工的、人造的，artificial，形容词，比如：The city is dotted with small lakes, natural and artificial.（这座城市满是天然和人造的小湖泊。）
水道、航道，waterway，名词，比如：There are more than 400 miles of waterways to explore in the area.（此地有 400 多英里的航道有待勘察。）

❼ （被）列入，was selected，被动语态，单词原形为：select，比如：Voters are selecting candidates for both U.S. Senate seats and for 52 congressional seats.（选民们正在选举美国参议院议席的候选人和 52 个众议院席位的候选人。）

第二步 动词定位

杭州<u>拥</u>有丰富的历史文化遗迹。南<u>起</u>杭州、北<u>到</u>北京的京杭大运河始<u>建</u>于 1631 年，全长约 1 797 公里，<u>是</u>世界上最长、最古老的人工水道。2014 年 6 月 22 日，京杭大运河正式<u>列入</u>《世界遗产名录》。

第三步 句型解析

❶ 第一句中，"杭州"是主语，"拥有"是谓语，"丰富的历史文化遗迹"是宾语，这也是典型的一般现在时。

❷ 第二句中，"南起杭州、北到北京的"是定语，这里的动词"起"和"到"都不要翻译，直接写成 Beijing-Hangzhou 即可，当然翻译为 from...to 也行，但是"京杭大运河"是专有名词，还是记一下吧。"始建于"是谓语，"1631 年"是状语，"（是）全长约 1 797 公里"是第二组谓语和宾语，但是可以处理为前面主语的定语，翻译为 The 1,797-km-long Beijing-Hangzhou Grand Canal，"是"是第三个动词，"世界上最长、最古老的人工水道"是宾语。仔细看会发现本句有三个动词分别为"建""是""是"，第二个"是"处理为定语或同位语，本句剩余两个动词"建""是"的双动词结构再不会翻译就说不过去了吧！

❸ 第三句中，"2014 年 6 月 22 日"是时间状语，"京杭大运河"是主语，因为是第二次提到，可以使用代词 it，"正式列入"是谓语，为隐藏的被动语态，应该是"被列入"，宾语是《世界遗产名录》。

第四步 翻译来了

Hangzhou boasts lots of historical and cultural sites. The 1,797-km-long Beijing-Hangzhou Grand

Canal, founded in 1631, is the longest artificial waterway with the oldest history in the world. On June 22, 2014, it was also officially selected into *the World Heritage List*.

 **本句考点总结**

　　第一，汉译英句子中并列、伴随、下沉的结构。中文常常会出现多个句子聚集的情况，那么我们在翻译时需要考虑将这些句子进行"分堆"，但是"分堆"之后，一个句子中也可能会出现两个动词或两组动词，那么有两个动词或两组动词的句子我们该如何进行翻译呢？比如："我坐在那里看书"，这里有两个动词，一个是"坐"，一个是"看"，我们翻译时便会有三种方法：

　　第一种并列（两个动词并列的译法，使用并列连词连接，两个动词之间不一定是"并列"关系）：I sat there and read a book.

　　第二种伴随（将第二个动词翻译为二谓语，分词、从句、状语等都可以）：I sat there reading a book.

　　第三种下沉（将第一个动词翻译为二谓语，分词、从句、状语等都可以）：Sitting there, I read a book.

　　需要说明的是，并列、伴随和下沉只是动词的形式问题，不代表动词之间的逻辑关系，用这三种形式翻译两个动词或两组动词都是可以的，大家可以根据句子上下文的关系来判断使用。

　　第二，本句出现了中文里隐藏被动语态的译法。被动语态是英文常见的一种形式，而在中文里常常少用"被"或者不用"被"。那么中文当中一般如何隐藏被动语态呢？第一种是被动变主动，第二种是寻找替代词（比如："让……给""为……所"等结构），第三种是在科技文献中用"可以"来替代"被"，第四种是有"被"不用"被"。在中文里识别出来以上四种隐藏的被动语态是一件不容易的事，需要大家仔细认真地识别这种现象，在汉译英时体现出来。

5

在世界上，杭州颇具名声。早在 13 世纪，意大利著名旅行家马可·波罗赞叹杭州为"世界上最美丽之城"。

第一步　词汇解析

 颇具名声，enjoys its high reputation，动词词组，词组原形为：enjoy one's high reputation，比如：enjoys high reputation among customers（在广大用户中颇具名声）。句中"颇具名声"的意思是"相当有名声"，形容名人或名物"名气很大"。

名声，reputation，名词，比如：Alice Munro has a reputation for being a very depressing writer.（艾丽斯·门罗有文风抑郁的名声。）

② 著名旅行家，a renowned traveler，名词词组。

著名的，renowned，形容词，比如：The area is renowned for its Romanesque churches.（这个地区以其罗马式教堂闻名。）

【同义词辨析】

famous：表示"有名的"，这是最常用的单词，通常用于褒义。与此相对，表示"臭名昭著的"用 infamous 或 notorious；

well-known：表示"为人所熟知的"，褒义和贬义都可用；
famed：表示"（获得了名声后）有名的"；
renowned：表示"（因具有某一特征、技艺等而）有名的"；
eminent/distinguished：表示"（因在某专业领域内杰出而）有名的"。

❸ 马可·波罗，Marco Polo，人名。注意这类约定俗成的人名要按照官方的译名来翻译，不建议自己编造。
文化小常识：
马可·波罗，意大利旅行家、商人，代表作品有《马可·波罗游记》。

❹ 赞叹，praise，动词，比如：The American president praised Turkey for its courage.（美国总统称赞了土耳其的勇气。）这个单词一般侧重公开赞叹或称赞，比如：The police officer was praised for his bravery.（这名警官因为英勇而受到表扬。）

第二步 动词定位

在世界上，杭州颇**具**名声。早在13世纪，意大利著名旅行家马可·波罗**赞叹**杭州为"世界上最美丽之城"。

第三步 句型解析

❶ 本句的"在世界上"是地点状语，"杭州"是主语，"颇具"是谓语，"名声"是宾语，本句要注意和上句的连接，中文是意合式语言，句子之间一般不用连词，但英文是形合式语言，句子之间用连词较多，所以译文使用了 Moreover 之类的词，还要注意"杭州"又出现了，需要使用 the city 或 it 这样的词替代。

❷ 第二句的"早在13世纪"是时间状语，注意谓语使用一般过去时，"意大利著名旅行家马可·波罗"是主语，这里有同位语现象，翻译为 Marco Polo, a renowned Italian traveler，注意英文先翻译姓名再翻译职称，"赞叹"是核心动词，"杭州"是宾语，这里可以用代词 it，"为'世界上最美丽之城'"是状语。译文在句末增词 in his notes，因为在当时历史条件下没有关于马可·波罗的影像资料，全都是文字记载，特别像《马可·波罗游记》，所以这样的增词是合理的，但在考试中真的想不到也没有关系！

第四步 翻译来了

Moreover, the city enjoys its high reputation around the globe. In the 13th century, Marco Polo, a renowned Italian traveler praised it as "the most beautiful city in the world" in his notes.

本句考点总结

第一，中英文的巨大差异在于中文是意合式语言，英文是形合式语言。中文的句子之间不用连词连接，而英文的句子之间必须使用连词，所以，我们在做汉译英时，要去体会和理解每个逗号前后句子之间的关系，到底是并列、转折、让步、因果、条件，还是别的什么关系，然后选择合适的连词进行连接，形成一个英文句子。始终要牢记一点：英文的两个句子之间必须要有连词连接。

第二，本句考查了英汉互译增减词的问题，一般来说英译汉增词，汉译英减词，常见增词的种类有：一、增加对象词（范围词），这是由上文缺少句子的某个部分造成的；二、增加范畴词，这是较难的一部分，常见的范畴词有"水平、方式、方法、问题、情况、途径和方面"，但是不仅仅有这些，还有其他很多；三、增加评论性词，这些常常出现在文学翻译中；四、增加动词，会在动词的"分配译法"中说明这点。

杭州曾被美国《纽约时报》评为"2011 年全球最值得去的 41 个地方"之一，还被联合国环境规划署评为"国际花园城市"。

第一步 词汇解析

① 被评为，be named as，动词词组，比如：He was named as the probable successor.（他被指定为可能的继承人。）"被评为"还可以翻译为 be rated as/be awarded 等词。

② 《纽约时报》，*The New York Times*，专有名词。这类书名、电影名、电视剧名等，在机考打字时，需要首字母大写，使用斜体；在纸质答卷上，需要首字母大写，加双引号。

文化小常识：
《纽约时报》是一份在美国纽约出版的日报，在全世界发行，有相当大的影响力，是美国高级报纸、严肃刊物的代表，长期以来拥有良好的公信力和权威性。

③ "2011 年全球最值得去的 41 个地方"，"the 41 Places to Go Globally in 2011"，名词词组，注意大写首字母。原文中使用双引号，译文中沿用原文符号即可，机考时注意中文为全角符号，英文为半角符号。而且，原文中的数字为阿拉伯数字，翻译时也使用阿拉伯数字。"2011 年"为时间状语，所以要加介词 in，因为不表示所属关系，所以不建议使用 of。

④ 联合国环境规划署，the United Nations Environment Programme，专有名词，注意首字母大写。

文化小常识：
联合国环境规划署中文简称"环境署"，是联合国系统内负责全球环境事务的牵头部门和权威机构。

⑤ "国际花园城市"，"International Garden City"，专有名词，注意首字母大写。这类不是十分复杂的名词词组按照字面意思直接翻译即可。

第二步 动词定位

杭州曾被美国《纽约时报》**评为**"2011 年全球最值得去的 41 个地方"之一，还被联合国环境规划署**评为**"国际花园城市"。

第三步 句型解析

① 本句的主语是"杭州"，注意"杭州"又出现了，需要使用 the city 或 it 这样的词替代。第一个谓语是"被评为"，状语是"美国的《纽约时报》"，这里的"美国"可以不翻译，因为在英语语境中写出的 *The New York Times*，大家都知道是美国的，这里属于减词。本句的宾语是"2011 年全球最值得去的 41 个地方"之一，这个词组虽然说有固定表达，但是考试时也可以自己编一个，比如 41 Best Places to Go in the World。

② 本句的第二个谓语是"被评为"，因为两个动词相同，所以可以只翻译一次，这里也是动词分配译法的反向使用；状语是"联合国环境规划署"，宾语是"'国际花园城市'"。

第四步 翻译来了

Hangzhou was not only named as one of "the 41 Places to Go Globally in 2011" by *The New York Times*, but also "International Garden City" by the United Nations Environment Programme.

> ### 本句考点总结
>
> 　　第一，本句考查了英汉互译增减词的问题，一般来说英译汉增词，汉译英减词，常见增词的种类有：一、增加对象词（范围词），这是由上文缺少句子的某个部分造成的；二、增加范畴词，这是较难的一部分，常见的范畴词有"水平、方式、方法、问题、情况、途径和方面"，但是不仅仅有这些，还有其他很多；三、增加评论性词，这些常常出现在文学翻译中；四、增加动词，会在动词的"分配译法"中说明这点。
>
> 　　第二，本句考查了形容词的"分配"译法和动词或名词的"分配"译法。形容词分配的译法是两个或多个形容词位于名词之前，"翻译公式"是 (A+B)*C=AC+BC，比如 international and strategic questions 翻译为"国际问题和战略问题"；动词或名词分配的译法是一个动词位于多个名词宾语之前，或者一个名词位于多个名词前，"翻译公式"是 A*(B+C)=AB+AC，比如 wear a hat and a scarf 翻译为"戴着帽子，系着围巾"。而汉译英时，以上这些方法全部要反过来使用。

7　杭州还曾在中美建交的过程中扮演过重要角色。2015年1月，中国提出"旅游外交"政策。杭州作为著名旅游城市，又率先实践"旅游外交"。

第一步　词汇解析

① 中美建交，the establishment of China-US full diplomatic relations，名词词组。"中美建交"指的是"全面建立中美外交关系"。

正式的，full，形容词，比如：a full member（正式成员）。

外交的，diplomatic，形容词，比如：The job requires diplomatic skills of a high order.（这项工作需要高超的外交技巧。）

【同义词辨析】

relation: 强调客观上的关系，不强调感情色彩；

relationship: 侧重强调感情色彩较重的关系。

② 扮演过重要角色，has played a significant part，动词词组，词组原形为：play a significant part。"扮演过重要角色"还可以翻译为 has played a key role。

③ 提出，propose，动词，比如：He has proposed a resolution limiting the role of U.S. troops.（他提出了一项限制美军作用的决议。）propose 表示"正式提出"。派生词：proposal，名词，表示"提案、建议"。考点：draft proposal，表示"草案"；legislative proposal，表示"立法提案"。

④ "旅游外交"政策，the policy of "Tourism Diplomacy"，名词词组，注意首字母大写。

文化小常识：

　　旅游外交指一个国家在旅游国际合作方面的活动，如参加国际旅游组织和会议，跟别的国家互设旅游办事处，进行旅游合作交流方面的谈判、签订条约和协定等。

⑤ 率先，take the lead in，动词词组，比如：Governments and enterprises should take the lead in bettering the environment.（政府和企业应该带头改善环境。）"率先"还可以翻译为 be the first to do something 等词。

❻ 实践，put into practice，动词词组，比如：The active fiscal policy has been put into practice for four years in our country.（我国已连续四年实施了积极的财政政策。）

第二步 动词定位

杭州还曾在中美<u>建交</u>的过程中<u>扮演</u>过重要角色。2015 年 1 月，中国<u>提出</u>"旅游外交"政策。杭州<u>作为</u>著名旅游城市，又率先<u>实践</u>"旅游外交"。

第三步 句型解析

❶ 第一句中，"杭州"是主语，注意"杭州"再次出现，需要使用 The city 或 It 这样的词替代。"还曾在中美建交的过程中"是状语，这里的"过程中"是典型的范畴词，可以不翻译。"扮演过"是核心谓语，"重要角色"是宾语，本句可以使用现在完成时或一般过去时。

❷ 第二句中，"2015 年 1 月"是时间状语，"中国"是主语，"提出"是核心谓语，"'旅游外交'政策"是宾语，这句较为简单，但要注意使用一般过去时。

❸ 第三句中，"杭州"是主语，"杭州"在本文最后一次出现，选择用全称 Hangzhou 是可以的，"作为著名旅游城市"虽然有动词，但是可以处理成 as 引导的状语，"又率先实践"是核心谓语，"'旅游外交'政策"是宾语。以上两句之间可以使用连词合译，当然考试时翻译为单独的句子也是可以的。

第四步 翻译来了

The city has played a significant part in the full establishment of China-US diplomatic relations. In January 2015, China proposed the policy of "Tourism Diplomacy" and Hangzhou, as a famous tourist city, took the lead again in putting the policy into practice.

本句考点总结

本句考查了英汉互译增减词的问题，一般来说英译汉增词，汉译英减词，常见增词的种类有：一、增加对象词（范围词），这是由上文缺少句子的某个部分造成的；二、增加范畴词，这是较难的一部分，常见的范畴词有"水平、方式、方法、问题、情况、途径和方面"，但是不仅仅有这些，还有其他很多；三、增加评论性词，这些常常出现在文学翻译中；四、增加动词，会在动词的"分配译法"中说明这点。

译后总结

这篇文章介绍了杭州的整体概况，也是机考时代的第一篇汉译英。让我们没有想到的是，这篇文章居然这么简单，大家在练习这篇文章的过程中，我觉得可以反复实践"动词分层的原理"和"双动词翻译的基本方法"，还要特别注意名词翻译的多样性，比如名词第一次翻译成名词，第二次翻译成半称，第三次翻译成代词，第四次省略不译等，最后还要注意的是，中文的同一词汇要用不同的英文单词来进行翻译，从而体现出词汇的多样性，比如本文中的"列为""扮演重要作用""著名的"等，所以在学习汉译英时，我们还是要大量储备词汇，不能反复使用一个单词翻译，这样才能在考试中获得高分。

第四章 2018年实务真题解析与方法技巧

第一节 2018年上半年三级笔译英译汉

Improved human well-being is one of the greatest triumphs of the modern era. The age of plenty has also led to an unexpected global health crisis: two billion people are either overweight or obese.

Developed countries have been especially susceptible to unhealthy weight gain. However, developing countries are now facing a similar crisis.

Obesity rates have peaked in high income countries but are accelerating elsewhere. The combined findings of the World Health Organization and the World Bank showed that in 2016 Asia was home to half the world's overweight children. One quarter were in Africa. Residents of developing nation cities are increasingly susceptible to obesity.

According to India's National Institute of Nutrition, over a quarter of urban-dwelling men and nearly half of women are overweight.

This crisis will test the political resolve of governments that have historically focused on ending hunger. These governments must understand that the factors making cities convenient and productive also make their residents prone to obesity.

Urbanites enjoy a variety of food. Additionally, international fast food chains are flourishing in developing countries. The health risks of such diets are compounded by the sedentary lifestyles of urban dwellers.

People's leisure time is also being occupied by television, movies, and video games in the growing number of households. The alarming implication of these trends is that developing countries may become sick before they get rich.

That sickness may, in turn, cripple health systems. The yearly health care costs in Southeast Asia of obesity-related complications like diabetes and cardiovascular disease are already as high as US $10 billion.

Such diseases are an added burden on countries already struggling to manage primary health care needs. Policies related to taxation, urban design, education and awareness and the promotion of localized food systems may help control obesity at a lower cost than eventual medical treatment for an increasingly overweight population.

Some governments have already experimented with direct interventions to control obesity, such as taxation on unhealthy foods and drinks. The US pioneered the soda tax movement. Thailand, Brunei, and Singapore have adopted similar measures. South Africa is likely to introduce a sugar tax beginning in April 2018.

The city of Berkeley in California recognizes that taxes alone are not enough to address obesity. Proceeds from the city's sugar tax are used to support child nutrition and community health programs. This underscores the importance of education and awareness.

There is also promise in initiatives. Urban design holds significant power to reshape lifestyle patterns and public health. Improving the attractiveness of public space can draw residents out of their cars and living rooms.

A recent study of urban neighborhoods in Shanghai and Hangzhou found that middle-income residents living in walkable neighborhoods enjoy better health than residents who lived in less walkable neighborhoods in urban China.

Finally, healthier lifestyles begin in grocery store aisles. Governments should encourage tighter connections between agricultural production systems, urban grocers and food vendors. Such initiatives can also help urban residents better understand the mechanics of food sourcing.

This raises awareness about the relationship between natural foods and healthy lifestyles. Combining controls on unhealthy foods with policies that incentivize healthy eating and active lifestyles can reduce obesity rates.

Improving public health is an important policy developing countries should take from both an economic and social point of view. To quote the recent Global Nutrition Report, reducing obesity will boost global development.

2018 年上半年的 CATTI 英译汉文章的主题为卫生健康，主要介绍了全世界各国居民饮食与健康之间的关系。这篇文章属于典型的非文学翻译，全篇几乎没有出现直接引语和间接引语的译法，和前几年的考试有所区别，其他翻译现象非常明显，请大家仔细识别。

Improved human well-being is one of the greatest triumphs of the modern era. The age of plenty has also led to an unexpected global health crisis: two billion people are either overweight or obese.

第一步 词汇解析

① triumph，名词，表示"巨大成功、重大成就、伟大胜利"，比如：The bridge is a triumph of modern engineering.（这座桥是现代工程的一大成就。）

② era，名词，表示"时代、年代"，比如：A new era was brought into being by the war.（那场战争催生了一个新的时代。）

③ lead to，动词词组，表示"导致"，比如：Many factors can lead to growth retardation in unborn babies.（许多因素可以导致胎儿发育迟缓。）

④ overweight，形容词，表示"超重的"，比如：People who are overweight run a risk of a heart attack or stroke.（超重的人有犯心脏病和中风的危险。）

⑤ obese，形容词，表示"过分肥胖的、臃肿的、虚胖的"，比如：Obese people tend to have higher blood pressure than lean people.（胖的人常常比瘦的人血压高。）

第二步 注意断句

Improved human well-being is one of the greatest triumphs /of the modern era. /The age of plenty has also led to an unexpected global health crisis: /two billion people are either overweight or obese.

第三步 句型解析

① 第一句中，Improved human well-being 是主语，is 是系动词，one of the greatest triumphs of the modern era 是表语，翻译时注意主语的译法，翻译为"改善的民生"不是很通顺，进行"偏正互换"更加通顺，翻译为"民生的改善"更好。

❷ 第二句中，The age of plenty 是主语，has also led to 是谓语，an unexpected global health crisis 是宾语，冒号依旧保留，two billion people are either overweight or obese 是主系表结构。

第四步 翻译来了

民生的改善是现代最伟大的成就之一。这样一个富足的年代也导致了预料之外的全球健康危机：有二十亿人要么超重，要么肥胖。

> **本句考点总结**
>
> 本句中使用了"偏正结构变主谓结构"的译法，这是什么意思呢？也就是说偏正结构 gleaming eyes（炯炯有神的眼睛）可以翻译为主谓结构 Eyes are gleaming.（眼睛炯炯有神。）这种译法是为了让句子更加通顺，当然有时候也可以用"主谓结构变偏正结构"的译法。"主谓变偏正"或"偏正变主谓"在英汉互译当中都可能出现，须灵活使用。

2 Developed countries have been especially susceptible to unhealthy weight gain. However, developing countries are now facing a similar crisis.

第一步 词汇解析

❶ susceptible，形容词，表示"易受影响（或伤害等）的、易患（病）的"，比如：Walking with weights makes the shoulders very susceptible to injury.（负重行走时肩膀很容易受伤。）

❷ gain，名词，表示"（尤指财富、重量的）增值、增加"，比如：Regular exercise helps prevent weight gain.（经常锻炼有助于防止体重增加。）

第二步 注意断句

Developed countries have been especially susceptible to unhealthy weight gain. /However, /developing countries are now facing a similar crisis.

第三步 句型解析

❶ 第一句 Developed countries have been especially susceptible to unhealthy weight gain 是主系表结构，但要注意翻译的问题，你要直接翻译为"发达国家的人尤其容易不健康的发胖"肯定会让别人无法理解，所以把 unhealthy 这个长的形容词拿出来单独翻译，译为小句子"从而引起了健康问题"，这其实也是文学的译法，希望大家能学习学习。

❷ 第二句中，However 是转折连词，developing countries are now facing a similar crisis 是主谓宾结构，而且是现在进行时态，使用"正"字更好。

第四步 翻译来了

发达国家的人尤其容易发胖，从而引起了健康问题。然而，发展中国家目前正面临着相似的危机。

Obesity rates have peaked in high income countries but are accelerating elsewhere. The combined findings of the World Health Organization and the World Bank showed that in 2016 Asia was home to half the world's overweight children. One quarter were in Africa. Residents of developing nation cities are increasingly susceptible to obesity.

第一步 词汇解析

① obesity，名词，表示"肥胖"，比如：Obesity can increase the risk of heart disease.（肥胖会增加患心脏病的危险。）

② peak，动词，表示"达到高峰、达到最高值"，比如：Oil production peaked in the early 1980s.（20 世纪 80 年代初期，石油产量达到了最高峰。）

③ accelerate，动词，表示"（使）加速、加快"，比如：The runners accelerated smoothly around the bend.（赛跑运动员在转弯处顺畅地加速。）

④ World Health Organization，专有名词，表示"世界卫生组织"。
文化小常识：
　　世界卫生组织（英文名称：World Health Organization，缩写 WHO，中文简称世卫组织）是联合国下属的一个专门机构，总部设置在瑞士日内瓦，只有主权国家才能加入，是国际上最大的政府间卫生组织。

⑤ World Bank，专有名词，表示"世界银行"。
经济小常识：
　　世界银行是世界银行集团的简称，国际复兴开发银行的通称；也是联合国的一个专门机构。世界银行成立于 1945 年，1946 年 6 月开始营业，由国际复兴开发银行、国际开发协会、国际金融公司、多边投资担保机构和国际投资争端解决中心五个成员机构组成。

第二步 注意断句

Obesity rates have peaked /in high income countries /but are accelerating elsewhere. /The combined findings of the World Health Organization and the World Bank showed /that /in 2016 /Asia was home to half the world's overweight children. /One quarter were in Africa. /Residents of developing nation cities are increasingly susceptible to obesity.

第三步 句型解析

① 第一句中，Obesity rates have peaked in high income countries 是主谓状结构，but 是表转折的连词，are accelerating elsewhere 是第二组谓状结构。

② 第二句中，The combined findings of the World Health Organization and the World Bank 是主语，showed 是

谓语，that 引导宾语从句，in 2016 是时间状语，Asia was home to half the world's overweight children 是主系表结构，特别要注意 was home to 的译法，这里使用了"无灵主语句"变"有灵主语句"的译法。
❸ 第三句 One quarter were in Africa 是主系表结构，这句和上一句关系紧密，可以合译。
❹ 第四句 Residents of developing nation cities are increasingly susceptible to obesity 是主系表结构，是现在进行时态，正常翻译即可。

第四步 翻译来了

肥胖率在高收入国家已经达到顶峰，但在其他国家也正在不断上升。世界卫生组织和世界银行的综合调查结果显示，2016 年，亚洲的肥胖儿童占世界肥胖儿童总数的一半，非洲则占了四分之一。发展中国家的城市居民越来越容易发胖。

本句考点总结

第一，本句考查了"有灵主语句"和"无灵主语句"的转换。一般来说，以有生命的物体作为主语的句子，称为"有灵主语句"，而以无生命的物体作为主语的句子，称为"无灵主语句"，中文常用有灵主语，而英文则常用无灵主语，注意两者之间的互换。但是这种互换是为了让句子更加通顺，不是每个句子都需要用这种方法翻译。

第二，在翻译中，无论是英译汉，还是汉译英，我们常常将长句断成短句，然后一句一句翻译，短的句子由于上下文的联系，也可以放在一起翻译。非文学翻译中，分译与合译出现得比较少，一般按照正常句子翻译即可，但是在文学翻译中出现得特别多，特别要读懂上下文内在的关系，分译与合译没有固定的翻译规则，而且每个译者的尺度也是不同的，重要的前提就是句意正确和句意通顺。

4 According to India's National Institute of Nutrition, over a quarter of urban-dwelling men and nearly half of women are overweight.

第一步 词汇解析

❶ India's National Institute of Nutrition，专有名词，表示"印度国立营养研究所"。
❷ dwell，动词，表示"居住"，比如：They are concerned for the fate of the forest and the Indians who dwell in it.（他们为这片森林及居住于其中的印第安人的命运而担心。）

第二步 注意断句

According to India's National Institute of Nutrition, /over a quarter of urban-dwelling men /and nearly half of women /are overweight.

第三步 句型解析

❶ 本句中的 According to India's National Institute of Nutrition 是状语结构，表示"根据印度国立营养研究

所（India's National Institute of Nutrition）的报告"，这里需要注意 India's National Institute of Nutrition 是专有名词，第一次提到，可以直接翻译，然后用括号把这个专有名词抄下来。

❷ over a quarter of urban-dwelling men and nearly half of women are overweight 是主系表结构。

第四步 翻译来了

根据印度国立营养研究所（India's National Institute of Nutrition）的报告，城镇人口中有超过四分之一的男性和将近一半的女性超重。

This crisis will test the political resolve of governments that have historically focused on ending hunger. These governments must understand that the factors making cities convenient and productive also make their residents prone to obesity.

第一步 词汇解析

❶ resolve，名词，表示"决心、决定"，比如：The difficulties in her way merely strengthened her resolve.（她所遇到的困难只是让她更加坚定。）

❷ prone to，动词词组，表示"易于遭受"，比如：As they shorten, cells become more prone to disease and death.（细胞变小后就会更容易感染疾病，也更容易死亡。）

第二步 注意断句

This crisis will test the political resolve of governments /that have historically focused on ending hunger. / These governments must understand /that the factors making cities convenient and productive also make their residents prone to obesity.

第三步 句型解析

❶ 第一句中，This crisis will test the political resolve of governments 是主谓宾结构，表示"这场危机将会考验各国政府的政治决心"，后面是 that 引导的定语从句 that have historically focused on ending hunger，从句较短，可以采用前置译法，这里采用后置译法也是比较通顺的。还要注意 historically 的译法，直接翻译为"历史上地"不是非常通顺，翻译为"曾经"更好一些。

❷ 第二句中，These governments must understand 是主谓结构，注意这里 These governments 翻译为"这些国家的政府"，直接翻译为"这些政府"也可以，但是增对象词"国家"更好一些，后面的 that 引导宾语从句。宾语从句中，the factors making cities convenient and productive 是主语，主语中有现在分词短语位于名词后，相当于定语从句，从句较短，可以采用前置译法，also make their residents prone to obesity 是谓宾宾补的结构，要注意 their 的译法，不要翻译为"他们的"，用代词的模糊翻译法，翻译为"其"更好一些。

第四步 翻译来了

这场危机将考验各国政府的政治决心，他们曾把工作重心放在如何消除饥饿上。这些国家的政府必须明白，让城市便捷、生产力提高的因素也会让其居民容易肥胖。

 本句考点总结

第一，本句出现了英文定语从句的译法。一般来说，定语从句按照"短前长后"的译法处理，较短的定语从句可以前置，较长的定语从句可以后置，这一切都取决于句子的通顺，并没有绝对的前置和后置译法。

第二，本句考查了英汉互译增减词的问题，一般来说英译汉增词，汉译英减词，常见增词的种类有：一、增加对象词（范围词），这是由上文缺少句子的某个部分造成的；二、增加范畴词，这是较难的一部分，常见的范畴词有"水平、方式、方法、问题、情况、途径和方面"，但是不仅仅有这些，还有很多其他的；三、增加评论性词，这些常常出现在文学翻译中；四、增加动词，会在动词的"分配译法"中说明这点。

第三，关于英文代词的译法。英文中需要翻译的代词主要指第三人称 he, she, it, they 及其相应宾格和指示代词 this 和 that。这些单词在翻译时一定要注意，主要采用"不抽象、不具体"的译法。不能翻译成具体的人或物，但是也不能翻译为"他""她""它""他们""这个""那个"，要注意取中间的译法。

6

Urbanites enjoy a variety of food. Additionally, international fast food chains are flourishing in developing countries. The health risks of such diets are compounded by the sedentary lifestyles of urban dwellers.

第一步 词汇解析

① urbanite，名词，表示"都市人、城市居民"，比如：the urbanite's recreation time（城市居民的休闲时间）。

② chain，名词，表示"连锁商店"，比如：a supermarket chain（连锁超市）。

③ flourish，动词，表示"繁荣、昌盛、兴旺、茁壮成长"，比如：Few businesses are flourishing in the present economic climate.（在目前的经济气候下，很少有企业兴旺发达。）

④ compound，动词，表示"使加重、使恶化"，比如：The problems were compounded by severe food shortages.（严重的食物短缺使问题进一步恶化。）

⑤ sedentary，形容词，表示"久坐不动的"，比如：Obesity and a sedentary lifestyle have been linked with an increased risk of heart disease.（肥胖和久坐不动的生活方式被认为会增加患心脏病的概率。）

⑥ dweller，名词，表示"居民、居住者"，比如：The number of city dwellers is growing.（城市居民的数量正在增长。）

第二步 注意断句

Urbanites enjoy a variety of food. /Additionally, /international fast food chains are flourishing / in developing countries. /The health risks of such diets are compounded /by the sedentary lifestyles of urban dwellers.

第三步 句型解析

① 第一句中，Urbanites enjoy a variety of food 是主谓宾结构，可以直接翻译。
② 第二句中，Additionally 是副词，表示"除此之外"，international fast food chains are flourishing in developing countries 是主谓状结构。这两句都是短句，而且句子之间也有联系，可以用逗号连接。
③ 第三句中，The health risks of such diets 是主语，are compounded by the sedentary lifestyles of urban dwellers 是典型的被动语态，这里需要理解 compound 的含义，表示"加剧"，句子中有 by 的结构，一般不用"被动变主动"的译法，但这里这么处理似乎更加通顺，若有更好的译法也是可以的。

第四步 翻译来了

都市人能享受各种各样的美食，除此之外，国际快餐连锁店也在发展中国家蓬勃发展。城市居民久坐不动的生活方式加剧了这种饮食习惯的健康风险。

本句考点总结

本句出现了被动语态的译法。被动语态是英文常见的一种形式，而在中文里常常少用"被"或者不用"被"。那么我们一般有什么样的译法呢？第一种是被动变主动，第二种是寻找替代词（比如："让……给""为……所"等结构），第三种是在科技文献中用"可以"来替代"被"，第四种是有"被"不用"被"。以上四种怎么用，那就看句子怎么通顺怎么翻译了啊！

7

People's leisure time is also being occupied by television, movies, and video games in the growing number of households. The alarming implication of these trends is that developing countries may become sick before they get rich.

第一步 词汇解析

① leisure，名词，表示"闲暇、空闲、休闲"，比如：It was hard to draw clear lines of demarcation between work and leisure.（在工作和闲暇之间很难划出明确的界限。）
② occupy，动词，表示"占用（空间、面积、时间等）"，比如：Administrative work occupies half of my time.（行政事务占用了我一半的时间。）
③ alarming，形容词，表示"令人忧虑的、让人担心的"，比如：The high rate of heart disease is alarming.（心脏病发病率之高令人担心。）
④ implication，名词，表示"可能的影响（或作用、结果）"，比如：They failed to consider the wider implications of their actions.（他们没有考虑到他们的行动会产生更广泛的影响。）

第二步 注意断句

People's leisure time is also being occupied /by television, /movies, /and video games /in the growing number of households. /The alarming implication of these trends is /that developing countries may become sick /before they get rich.

第三步 句型解析

❶ 第一句中，People's leisure time is also being occupied by television, movies, and video games in the growing number of households 是典型的被动语态，这里的 in the growing number of households 是地点状语，可以放在句首翻译，若放在句末通顺，也是可以的。People's leisure time is also being occupied by television, movies, and video games 这里的被动语态可以使用"寻找替代词"的译法，翻译为"让……给……"。

❷ 第二句中，The alarming implication of these trends is 是主系结构，后面的 that 引导表语从句，从句 developing countries may become sick 是主系表结构，before they get rich 是时间状语从句，这里翻译为"在他们变富之前就生病了"是完全可以的，但是译文使用了"未富先病"，实在是非常经典。而且在 The alarming implication of these trends 中，implication 是典型的抽象名词，可以进行增词翻译，翻译为"会引起令人担忧的后果"。

第四步 翻译来了

在越来越多的家庭中，人们的休闲时光也正在让电视、电影和电子游戏给占据。这些趋势会引起令人担忧的后果，即发展中国家的人们可能会未富先病。

本句考点总结

第一，本句出现了被动语态的译法。被动语态是英文常见的一种形式，而在中文里常常少用"被"或者不用"被"。那么我们一般有什么样的译法呢？第一种是被动变主动，第二种是寻找替代词（比如："让……给……""为……所"等结构），第三种是在科技文献中用"可以"来替代"被"，第四种是有"被"不用"被"。以上四种怎么用，那就看句子怎么通顺怎么翻译了啊！

第二，本句当中考查了"抽象名词"的译法。抽象名词一般处于冠词之后，又在介词之前，以"the＋抽象名词＋of"的形式居多。一般来说，抽象名词有两种译法。第一种，若抽象名词有动词词根，则翻译为动词，比如 the suggestion of mine，翻译为"我建议"，而不是"我的建议"；第二种，若抽象名词没有动词词根，可以增动词翻译，比如 the spirit of our nation，翻译为"我们民族所具有的精神"，而不是"我们民族的精神"。

---

8 That sickness may, in turn, cripple health systems. The yearly health care costs in Southeast Asia of obesity-related complications like diabetes and cardiovascular disease are already as high as US $10 billion.

第一步 词汇解析

❶ cripple，动词，表示"严重毁坏（或损害）"，比如：Let's try to cripple their communications.（我们试着破坏他们的通信设备吧。）

❷ health care，名词词组，表示"医疗（服务）"，比如：the costs of health care for the elderly（老年人的医疗费用）。

❸ complication,名词,表示"并发症",比如:Blindness is a common complication of diabetes.(失明是糖尿病常见的并发症。)

❹ diabetes,名词,表示"糖尿病",比如:People with high blood pressure are especially vulnerable to diabetes.(有高血压的人尤其容易患糖尿病。)

❺ cardiovascular,形容词,表示"心血管的",比如:Smoking places you at serious risk of cardiovascular and respiratory disease.(吸烟会大大增加罹患心血管和呼吸道疾病的风险。)

第二步 注意断句

That sickness may, /in turn, /cripple health systems. /The yearly health care costs /in Southeast Asia of obesity-related complications /like diabetes and cardiovascular disease /are already as high as US $10 billion.

第三步 句型解析

❶ 第一句中,That sickness 是主语,in turn 是插入语,表示"接下来",可以放在原位翻译,也可以放在句首翻译,cripple health systems 是谓语和宾语。

❷ The yearly health care costs in Southeast Asia of obesity-related complications like diabetes and cardiovascular disease 是主语,这个主语很有意思,需要分析一下,The yearly health care costs in Southeast Asia 表示"东南亚国家每年的医保费用",但是是关于什么病的医保费用呢?后面的 of 已经解释了,of obesity-related complications like diabetes and cardiovascular disease 又是总分结构,所以先翻译谁,后翻译谁,大家应该清楚了吧!这个主语的关键点是需要"拆分",你要是直译,这里的定语太长了,非常不合适,所以还是要一个点一个点翻译,比如"每年""东南亚国家"等。后面为系表结构 are already as high as US $10 billion,这里的 as...as 表示"多达"。

第四步 翻译来了

肥胖导致的疾病继而会破坏医疗体系。每年,在东南亚国家,用于治疗糖尿病、心血管疾病等与肥胖相关的并发症所花费的医保费用已高达 100 亿美元。

Such diseases are an added burden on countries already struggling to manage primary health care needs. Policies related to taxation, urban design, education and awareness and the promotion of localized food systems may help control obesity at a lower cost than eventual medical treatment for an increasingly overweight population.

第一步 词汇解析

❶ taxation,名词,表示"税、税收",比如:Employment and taxation are the issues of politics.(就业和征税是政治问题。)

❷ awareness,名词,表示"意识",比如:environmental awareness(环保意识)。

❸ eventual,形容词,表示"最后的、最终的",比如:His foolish behavior led to his eventual failure.(他的愚蠢行为导致了最终的失败。)

第二步 注意断句

Such diseases are an added burden on countries /already struggling /to manage primary health care needs. / Policies /related to taxation, /urban design, /education and awareness /and the promotion of localized food systems / may help control obesity /at a lower cost /than eventual medical treatment /for an increasingly overweight population.

第三步 句型解析

❶ 第一句中，Such diseases are an added burden on countries 是主系表状结构，翻译的时候需要注意，如果翻译为"这些疾病是国家一个增加的负担"，这就不太好，把 added burden 理解为动宾短语，翻译为"增加负担"更好，already struggling to manage primary health care needs 是现在分词短语作定语，定语较长，可以采用后置译法，也就是单独成句，为了让句子更加通顺，放在句首翻译也是可以的。

❷ 第二句中，Policies related to taxation, urban design, education and awareness and the promotion of localized food system 是主语，这里的主语较长，可以单独成句，Policies 是中心词，related to taxation, urban design, education and awareness and the promotion of localized food system 是过去分词短语作定语，定语较长，可以采用后置译法，翻译为"制定相关的……"。

但是这个定语也要注意：taxation（税收），urban design（城市设计），education and awareness（教育和意识）and the promotion of localized food system（本地化食品体系的推广）是四个并列的短语，但是第三个中的 awareness 需要增对象词"健康"，要不然大家摸不着头脑，不知道是什么"意识"，后面的 promotion 也是典型的抽象名词，有动词词根，可以翻译为动词"推广"，这样分析是不是清晰很多呢？

❸ 第二句的谓语和宾语是 may help control obesity，at a lower cost 是状语，than 引导比较状语，eventual medical treatment for an increasingly overweight population 是状语的主要内容，这里的 treatment 是典型的抽象名词，可以增动词"花费"，翻译为"相比于持续增长的超重人口最终所花费的治疗费用来说"。

第四步 翻译来了

对于已经在努力满足初级医保需求的国家来说，这些疾病无疑增加了负担。相比于持续增长的超重人口最终所花费的治疗费用来说，制定与税收、城市设计、教育和健康意识以及推广本地化食品体系相关的政策可能有助于以更低的成本控制肥胖。

📖 本句考点总结

第一，本句出现了分词或分词短语位于名词后的译法。一般来说，分词或分词短语位于名词后相当于定语或定语从句，定语按照"短前长后"的译法来进行翻译。

第二，英译汉时，若句子主语过长，那么可以单独成句，形成一个完整的主谓宾句子，这样翻译是为了避免句子过于臃肿。当主语单独成句时，句子的谓语和宾语缺少主语，那么可以增加"这""这些""这一切""这样"等词作为句子的主语，这样的词称为"本位词"，被这些词所代替的部分称为"外位语"。

第三，本句考查了英汉互译增减词的问题，一般来说英译汉增词，汉译英减词，常见增词的种类有：一、增加对象词（范围词），这是由上文缺少句子的某个部分造成的；二、增加范畴词，这是较难的一部分，常见的范畴词有"水平、方式、方法、问题、情况、途径和方面"，但是不仅仅有这些，还有很多其他的；三、增加评论性词，这些常常出现在文学翻译中；四、增加动词，会在动词的"分配译法"中说明这点。

第四，本句当中考查了"抽象名词"的译法。抽象名词一般处于冠词之后，又在介词之前，以"the+抽象名词+of"的形式居多。一般来说，抽象名词有两种译法。第一种，若抽象名词有动词词根，则翻译为动词，比如 the suggestion of mine，翻译为"我建议"，而不是"我的建议"；第二种，若抽象名词没有动词词根，可以增动词翻译，比如 the spirit of our nation，翻译为"我们民族所具有的精神"，而不是"我们民族的精神"。

10

Some governments have already experimented with direct interventions to control obesity, such as taxation on unhealthy foods and drinks. The US pioneered the soda tax movement. Thailand, Brunei, and Singapore have adopted similar measures. South Africa is likely to introduce a sugar tax beginning in April 2018.

第一步 词汇解析

① intervention，名词，表示"干涉、干预"，比如：He favoured a middle course between free enterprise and state intervention.（他更倾向于在自由经营与国家干预之间走一条中庸之道。）
② pioneer，动词，表示"开创、倡导"，比如：a new technique pioneered by surgeons in a London hospital（由伦敦一家医院的外科医生开发使用的新技术）。
③ Brunei，专有名词，表示"文莱"。
地理小常识：
文莱达鲁萨兰国，简称文莱（Brunei），位于东南亚的婆罗洲北岸，和马来西亚的砂拉越、沙巴合称北婆三邦，是一个君主专制国家。

第二步 注意断句

Some governments have already experimented /with direct interventions /to control obesity, /such as taxation on unhealthy foods and drinks. /The US pioneered the soda tax movement. /Thailand, /Brunei, /and Singapore have adopted similar measures. /South Africa is likely to introduce a sugar tax /beginning in April 2018.

第三步 句型解析

① 第一句中，Some governments have already experimented 是主谓结构，with direct interventions 是方式状语，这里表示"用……方式"，to control obesity 是目的状语，表示"为了……"，之后的 such as 表示举例，taxation on unhealthy foods and drinks 则是两个例子。
② 第二句中，The US pioneered the soda tax movement 是主谓宾结构，soda tax movement 表示"苏打税行动"，直接翻译就好，其实表示的是"对碳酸饮料进行收税"。
③ 第三句中，Thailand, Brunei, and Singapore have adopted similar measures 是主谓宾结构，较为简单，但要注意这句和上一句有关，而且都是短句，可以合译。
④ 第四句中，South Africa is likely to introduce a sugar tax 是主系表结构，beginning in April 2018 是后置定语，本句和上一句也有关系，可以合译，因为都是在举例。

> **第四步 翻译来了**

一些国家政府已经尝试通过直接干预来控制肥胖，例如，对非健康食品和饮料进行征税。美国率先开始收取苏打税的行动，泰国、文莱和新加坡也采取了类似的措施，南非可能会在 2018 年 4 月开始征收糖税。

 本句考点总结

在翻译中，无论是英译汉，还是汉译英，我们常常将长句断成短句，然后一句一句翻译，短的句子由于上下文的联系，也可以放在一起翻译。非文学翻译中，分译与合译出现得比较少，一般按照正常句子翻译即可，但是在文学翻译中出现得特别多，特别要读懂上下文内在的关系。分译与合译没有固定的翻译规则，而且每个译者的尺度也是不同的，重要的前提就是句意正确和句意通顺。

---

11 The city of Berkeley in California recognizes that taxes alone are not enough to address obesity. Proceeds from the city's sugar tax are used to support child nutrition and community health programs. This underscores the importance of education and awareness.

第一步 词汇解析

① Berkeley，专有名词，表示"伯克利"。
地理小常识：
伯克利市（City of Berkeley），简称伯克利（Berkeley），是美国加州旧金山湾区东岸丘陵地上的城市，隶属于阿拉米达县（Alameda County），是世界著名高等学府加州大学伯克利分校（UC Berkeley）所在地。

② address，动词，表示"设法解决、处理、对付"，比如：We must address ourselves to the problem of traffic pollution.（我们必须设法解决交通污染问题。）

③ proceeds，名词，表示"收益、收入、进款、所得收入"，比如：The proceeds of the concert will go to charity.（这次音乐会的收入将捐给慈善机构。）

④ nutrition，名词，表示"营养、滋养"，比如：Some of the diseases of middle age may be prevented by improving nutrition.（中年时期的一些疾病可以通过改善营养的方式来预防。）

⑤ underscore，动词，表示"强调、突出、强化"，比如：The Labor Department figures underscore the shaky state of the economic recovery.（劳工部的数据进一步印证了经济复苏状况的不稳定。）

第二步 注意断句

The city of Berkeley in California recognizes /that taxes alone are not enough /to address obesity. /Proceeds /from the city's sugar tax are used /to support child nutrition and community health programs. /This underscores the importance of education and awareness.

第三步 句型解析

❶ 第一句中，The city of Berkeley in California recognizes 是主谓结构，that 引导宾语从句，从句中的 taxes alone are not enough to address obesity 是含有 enough to do sth. 的系表结构，表示"足以做某事"。

❷ 第二句中，Proceeds from the city's sugar tax are used 是主谓结构，要注意这里被动语态的译法，可以使用"有被不用被"的译法，后面的不定式 to support child nutrition and community health programs 是目的状语。

❸ 第三句中，This underscores the importance of education and awareness 是主谓宾结构，要注意 this 指代的是上文的内容，所以这里可以合译，而且更加重要的是 awareness 的译法，这里直接翻译为"意识"可以，但是若增对象词"健康"则会更加通顺。

第四步 翻译来了

加利福尼亚的伯克利市则认识到，仅仅依靠税收还不足以解决肥胖问题。该市的糖类税收所得均用于支持儿童营养和社区健康计划，这凸显了教育和健康意识的重要性。

本句考点总结

第一，本句出现了被动语态的译法。被动语态是英文常见的一种形式，而在中文里常常少用"被"或者不用"被"。那么我们一般有什么样的译法呢？第一种是被动变主动，第二种是寻找替代词（比如："让……给""为……所"等结构），第三种是在科技文献中用"可以"来替代"被"，第四种是有"被"不用"被"。以上四种怎么用，那就看句子怎么通顺怎么翻译了啊！

第二，本句考查了英汉互译增减词的问题，一般来说英译汉增词，汉译英减词，常见增词的种类有：一、增加对象词（范围词），这是由上文缺少句子的某个部分造成的；二、增加范畴词，这是较难的一部分，常见的范畴词有"水平、方式、方法、问题、情况、途径和方面"，但是不仅仅有这些，还有很多其他的；三、增加评论性词，这些常常出现在文学翻译中；四、增加动词，会在动词的"分配译法"中说明这点。

12

There is also promise in initiatives. Urban design holds significant power to reshape lifestyle patterns and public health. Improving the attractiveness of public space can draw residents out of their cars and living rooms.

第一步 词汇解析

❶ initiative，名词，表示"倡议、新方案"，比如：a United Nations peace initiative（联合国的和平倡议）。

❷ reshape，动词，表示"重塑、改造、改组"，比如：The collapse of old certainties is reshaping the political parties.（陈规旧矩的崩塌正在重塑各个政党。）

第二步 注意断句

There is also promise /in initiatives. /Urban design holds significant power /to reshape lifestyle patterns and public health. /Improving the attractiveness of public space can draw residents out of their cars and living rooms.

第三步 句型解析

1. 第一句中，There is also promise in initiatives 是 there be 结构，表示"有"的含义，本句表示"倡议中也有希望的"，这里的"有"理解为"蕴含"更好一些。
2. 第二句中，Urban design holds significant power 是主谓宾结构，to reshape lifestyle patterns and public health 是不定式短语作目的状语，当然理解为定语也是可以的，这里只要明确意思，句式结构正确就可以。
3. 第三句中，Improving the attractiveness of public space 是本句的主语，这里的 attractiveness 可以理解为"吸引力"，意译为"美观度"更好，can draw residents out of their cars and living rooms 是谓宾状结构。

第四步 翻译来了

这些倡议是有希望的。城市设计是重塑生活方式和公共健康的重要力量。提升公共空间的美观度可以吸引居民离开自己的汽车和客厅。

13

A recent study of urban neighborhoods in Shanghai and Hangzhou found that middle-income residents living in walkable neighborhoods enjoy better health than residents who lived in less walkable neighborhoods in urban China.

第一步 词汇解析

1. walkable neighborhood，名词词组，表示"步行街区"，比如：live in a walkable neighborhood（住在一个适合步行的社区）。

第二步 注意断句

A recent study of urban neighborhoods /in Shanghai and Hangzhou found /that middle-income residents /living in walkable neighborhoods /enjoy better health /than residents /who lived in less walkable neighborhoods /in urban China.

第三步 句型解析

1. 本句中，A recent study of urban neighborhoods in Shanghai and Hangzhou found 是主语和谓语，后面 that 引导了宾语从句。middle-income residents 是宾语从句的主语，living in walkable neighborhoods 是现在分词短语作定语，相当于定语从句，从句较短，可以采用前置译法，enjoy better health 是谓语和宾语，than 引导了比较状语，residents 后是 who 引导的定语从句，从句较长，采用后置译法比较合适。
2. 但是，本句要注意宾语从句的译法，为什么这么说呢？因为其中包括了比较状语，是不是"事实与评论"之间的关系呢？是不是要先翻译 than 后面的内容，再翻译 better health 呢？这样一来，who 引导的定语从句是不是前置好一些呢？所以，定语到底前置还是后置，还是要看句子的通顺程度。

第四步 翻译来了

最近，上海和杭州城市社区的研究发现，在中国城市中，和居住在步行街区较少的社区居民相比，居住在步行街区多的中等收入居民要更为健康。

> **本句考点总结**
>
> 第一，本句出现了分词或分词短语位于名词后的译法。一般来说，分词或分词短语位于名词后相当于定语或定语从句，定语按照"短前长后"的译法来进行翻译。
>
> 第二，本句出现了英文定语从句的译法。一般来说，定语从句按照"短前长后"的译法处理。较短的定语从句可以前置，较长的定语从句可以后置，这一切都取决于句子的通顺，并没有绝对的前置和后置译法。
>
> 第三，本句出现了事实（Facts）和评论（Comments）的译法。中文一般先事实，后评论，而英文则是一般先评论，后事实。比如：It is important for her to go abroad. 翻译为"对于她来说，出国是很重要的"。英文中 It is important 是评论，for her to go abroad 是事实。从中英文的对比来看，可以知道中英文语序分别是怎么安排的。

14

Finally, healthier lifestyles begin in grocery store aisles. Governments should encourage tighter connections between agricultural production systems, urban grocers and food vendors. Such initiatives can also help urban residents better understand the mechanics of food sourcing.

第一步 词汇解析

① grocery store，名词词组，表示"食品杂货店"，比如：I worked stocking shelves in a grocery store.（我在一家杂货店工作，负责为货架上货。）

② aisle，名词，表示"走道、过道"，比如：The best seats are in the aisle and as far forward as possible.（最好的座位在过道处，越靠前越好。）

③ grocer，名词，表示"食物杂货商"，比如：The cook and the grocer haggled over the price of eggs.（厨师和杂货商为蛋价计较个没完。）

④ vendor，名词，表示"（某种产品的）销售公司"，比如：software vendors（软件销售商）。

⑤ mechanic，名词，表示"（过程、系统、动作等）运作方式、（具体的）方法、技巧"，比如：What are the mechanics of this new process?（这一新工序如何操作？）

第二步 注意断句

Finally, /healthier lifestyles begin /in grocery store aisles. /Governments should encourage tighter connections /between agricultural production systems, /urban grocers /and food vendors. /Such initiatives can also help urban residents better understand the mechanics of food sourcing.

第三步 句型解析

① 第一句中，Finally 是时间副词，healthier lifestyles begin in grocery store aisles 是主谓状结构，较为简单，

可以直接翻译。

❷ 第二句中，Governments should encourage tighter connections 是主谓宾结构，between agricultural production systems, urban grocers and food vendors 是 between...and... 引导的状语，这里要注意先翻译状语，再翻译谓语和宾语，然后翻译废话，最后翻译主句。

❸ 第三句中，Such initiatives can also help urban residents better understand the mechanics of food sourcing 是主谓宾宾补的结构，这里的 the mechanics of food sourcing 表示"食物采购机制"。

第四步 翻译来了

最后，健康的生活方式要从菜市场的货架通道开始。政府应鼓励农业生产系统、城市的菜场和食品供应商之间建立更加紧密的联系。这些倡议还可以帮助城市居民更好地了解食物采购机制。

> **本句考点总结**
>
> 本句考查了中英文语序的问题，一般来说，中文的语序是"主语＋废话（定语、状语、补语、插入语，等等）＋重要成分"，而英文的语序是"废话（定语、状语、补语、插入语，等等）＋主语＋重要成分＋废话（定语、状语、补语、插入语，等等）"，翻译时需要注意调整语序。

15

This raises awareness about the relationship between natural foods and healthy lifestyles. Combining controls on unhealthy foods with policies that incentivize healthy eating and active lifestyles can reduce obesity rates.

第一步 词汇解析

❶ incentivize，动词，表示"激励"，比如：incentivize further reform（激励进一步开放）。

第二步 注意断句

This raises awareness about the relationship /between natural foods and healthy lifestyles. /Combining controls on unhealthy foods /with policies /that incentivize healthy eating and active lifestyles /can reduce obesity rates.

第三步 句型解析

❶ 第一句中，This 是主语，这里指代的是上文所说的事情，可以直接翻译为"这"，raises awareness about the relationship 是谓宾状结构，between natural foods and healthy lifestyles 也是状语，所以需要状语先翻译，再翻译主要内容。特别提醒一点，awareness 和上文一样，最好也是增词，增"健康"较好。

❷ 第二句中，Combining controls on unhealthy foods with policies that incentivize healthy eating and active lifestyles 是本句的主语，主语中首先要看到 combine...with... 结构，这里表示"把……和……联系起来"，而且还要注意 policies 后面的从句，这里是 that 引导的定语从句，从句较短，可以采用前置译法。can reduce 是本句的谓语，obesity rates 是宾语，但是这里英文的主语过长，可以单独成句，后面用"这"来代替整个句子。

第四步 翻译来了

这提高了人们对天然食品和健康生活方式之间关系的认识。将控制不健康食品与鼓励健康饮食和积极生活方式的政策相结合，这会降低肥胖率。

本句考点总结

第一，本句考查了中英文语序的问题，一般来说，中文的语序是"主语+废话（定语、状语、补语、插入语，等等）+重要成分"，而英文的语序是"废话（定语、状语、补语、插入语，等等）+主语+重要成分+废话（定语、状语、补语、插入语，等等）"，翻译时需要注意调整语序。

第二，本句考查了英汉互译增减词的问题，一般来说英译汉增词，汉译英减词，常见增词的种类有：一、增加对象词（范围词），这是由上文缺少句子的某个部分造成的；二、增加范畴词，这是较难的一部分，常见的范畴词有"水平、方式、方法、问题、情况、途径和方面"，但是不仅仅有这些，还有很多其他的；三、增加评论性词，这些常常出现在文学翻译中；四、增加动词，会在动词的"分配译法"中说明这点。

第三，本句出现了英文定语从句的译法。一般来说，定语从句按照"短前长后"的译法处理。较短的定语从句可以前置，较长的定语从句可以后置，这一切都取决于句子的通顺，并没有绝对的前置和后置译法。

第四，英译汉时，若句子主语过长，那么可以单独成句，形成一个完整的主谓宾句子，这样翻译是为了避免句子过于臃肿。当主语单独成句时，句子的谓语和宾语缺少主语，那么可以增加"这""这些""这一切""这样"等词作为句子的主语，这样的词称为"本位词"，被这些词所代替的部分称为"外位语"。

Improving public health is an important policy developing countries should take from both an economic and social point of view. To quote the recent Global Nutrition Report, reducing obesity will boost global development.

第一步 词汇解析

❶ quote，动词，表示"引用、引述"，比如：He quoted a passage from the minister's speech.（他引用了部长的一段讲话。）

❷ Global Nutrition Report，专有名词，表示《全球营养报告》。

❸ boost，动词，表示"使增长、推动、改进"，比如：They're putting up new hotels in order to boost tourism in the area.（他们正在盖新旅馆以促进该地区的旅游业。）

第二步 注意断句

Improving public health is an important policy /developing countries should take /from both an economic and social point of view. /To quote the recent Global Nutrition Report, /reducing obesity will boost global development.

第三步 句型解析

❶ 第一句中，Improving public health is an important policy 是主系表结构，developing countries should take from both an economic and social point of view 是定语从句，从句省略了引导词 that，因为 that 指代先行词 an important policy，在句中作 take 的宾语，所以可以省略，后面的 from both an economic and social point of view 是状语，也可以认为是插入语，表示"从经济和社会角度"，这样分析完，整个句子就非常好理解了，这个定语从句可以前置，也可以后置，还是以通顺为主。

❷ 第二句中，To quote the recent Global Nutrition Report 表示"在此引用……"，reducing obesity will boost global development 是主谓宾结构。

第四步 翻译来了

改善公共卫生，是发展中国家应该从经济和社会角度考虑的一项重要政策。在此引用最新的《全球营养报告》，减少肥胖将推动全球发展。

> **本句考点总结**
>
> 本句出现了英文定语从句的译法。一般来说，定语从句按照"短前长后"的译法处理。较短的定语从句可以前置，较长的定语从句可以后置，这一切都取决于句子的通顺，并没有绝对的前置和后置译法。

译后总结

这篇文章探讨了关于肥胖和国家发展的问题，文章整体难度不大，少见地没有考查直接引语和间接引语。本文中一些关于国家发展的专业词汇需要掌握，并且对于常见的翻译现象，比如：定语从句的翻译、被动语态的翻译、代词的译法等还是要熟悉，而且要继续巩固，这样考试的时候才能熟练运用。

第二节 2018年上半年三级笔译汉译英

（请先通读全文）

煤炭是地球上储量最为丰富的能源，但反对使用煤炭的声浪日益高涨。煤炭巨大的碳排放量引起气候

变化，从而引起公众的担忧。

煤炭与其他能源相比，竞争力已经有所下降了。以美国为例，页岩气的出现造成部分出煤量因价格过高而被挤出市场。

美国去年煤炭需求接近 9.2 亿吨。由于天然气价格下跌，今年美国煤炭需求将减少 6 000 万到 8 000 万吨。数据显示，煤炭满足了全球大约 30% 的能源需求，提供 40% 以上的电力。

在人口第一和第二大国中国和印度，煤炭所满足的能源需求比例甚至达到 70% 左右。

中国的煤炭消费量在去年已经下滑，煤炭进口下降了 11%，这是十年来的首次下降。中国经济增速已经放缓，同时也做出极大努力削减煤炭使用以减少煤炭污染。

由于燃煤发电厂没有满负荷运行，再加上煤炭供应充足，造成国际煤炭价格压低。煤出口价格从去年的峰值下跌了约 60%。

2018 年上半年 CATTI 汉译英的主题是国际能源，主要介绍了目前全世界煤炭储量和煤炭使用的情况。这篇文章属于典型的非文学翻译，全篇要注意的是数字的翻译，文章总体篇幅不长，很符合三级笔译考试的套路，而且翻译现象非常多，请大家一定要注意理解和学习。

 煤炭是地球上储量最为丰富的能源，但反对使用煤炭的声浪日益高涨。煤炭巨大的碳排放量引起气候变化，从而引起公众的担忧。

第一步 词汇解析

① 储量，reserves，名词，常用复数，比如：proven oil reserves（已探明的石油藏量）。

② ……的声浪日益高涨，这里理解为"日益高涨的声浪"，surging voices，名词词组。
日益高涨的，surging，现在分词作定语，比如：Seagulls hover over the surging waves.（海鸥在惊涛骇浪上翱翔。）"日益高涨的"还可以翻译为 rising 或 growing。

③ 碳排放量，carbon emissions，名词词组，比如：impose a ceiling on carbon emissions（设定碳排放上限）。
散发物、发出物，emission，比如：automotive emissions of pollutants（机动车排出的污染物质）。

④ 气候变化，climate change，名词词组，比如：Climate change is still very much a subject for debate.（气候变化很大程度上仍是一个争论的话题。）

⑤ 引起，cause，动词，比如：The insecticide used on some weeds can cause health problems.（喷洒在野草上的杀虫剂会引发各种健康问题。）"引起"还可以翻译为 give rise to/arouse/lead to。

⑥ 担忧，concern，名词，比如：The group has expressed concern about reports of political violence in Africa.（该集团已对有关非洲政治暴力的报道表示担忧。）

第二步 动词定位

煤炭是地球上储量最为丰富的能源，但反对使用煤炭的声浪日益高涨。煤炭巨大的碳排放量引起气候变化，从而引起公众的担忧。

第三步 句型解析

❶ 第一句中,"煤炭"是主语,"是"是系动词,"地球上"是状语,"储量最为丰富的"是定语,这里可以翻译为定语,也可以处理为状语 with the most reserves,"能源"是表语。"但"是并列连词,表示转折,"反对使用煤炭的声浪日益高涨"看上去好像是主谓结构,但是再看看句型结构就会发现这是不对的,这里的"声浪"是事实,"日益高涨"是评论,所以这里中文的英文语序应当是"有了日益高涨的反对使用煤炭的声浪(声音)",所以用 there be 句型是不是更加简单呢?而且还要注意处理动词"反对"和"使用",既然使用了 there be 句型,那么动词"反对"可以变成介词 against,动词"使用"也可变成抽象名词短语 the use of,这样可以理解吗?看了这么多解析,其实汉译英不就是解决动词的问题吗?就是谓语动词的层次性!

❷ 第二句中,"煤炭巨大的碳排放量"是主语,表示"巨大的煤炭排放量",这两个定语的顺序需要注意,"引起"是谓语,"气候变化"是宾语,"从而引起"是第二个谓语,"公众的担忧"是第二个宾语。其实一个句子有两个动词是最好翻译的,想想"并列""伴随""下沉"该怎么选择呢?但是,仔细看看句子的意思会发现,第二个动词之前的"从而"表示了前后的关系,所以第二个动词翻译为"伴随"更好,所以第二个动词使用分词结构或者定语从句都可以,参考译文使用了分词 leading to 的结构。

❸ 本类非文学体裁的翻译多用一般现在时态,有具体时间状语时需要注意区别,过去时间用一般过去时,将来时间用一般将来时。

第四步 翻译来了

Coal is some kind of energy with the most reserves on the earth, but there have been surging voices against the use of coal. Huge carbon emissions cause climate change, leading to public concerns.

本句考点总结

第一,关于谓语动词的层次性。汉译英的核心问题是厘清句子当中多个动词之间的关系,我们要学会在多个动词当中找到最核心的动词,翻译为核心谓语(也称为一谓语);找到其次核心的动词,翻译为分词、从句、其他状语或定语的形式(也称为二谓语);再找到不重要的动词,翻译为介词(也称为三谓语);最后最不重要的动词,可以不译(也称为四谓语)。这些动词在句子当中如何划分层次,需要大家在长期不断的实践中摸索,而且每个句子的翻译也不是固定的。有些句子当中的"一谓语"(核心谓语),在别的译本当中可能就是"二谓语"或者是"三谓语"。只要句子整体结构正确,逻辑清晰,那这就是一个好的译本。

第二,本句出现了事实(Facts)和评论(Comments)的译法。中文一般先事实,后评论,而英文则是一般先评论,后事实。比如:It is important for her to go abroad. 翻译为"对于她来说,出国是很重要的"。 英文中 It is important 是评论,for her to go abroad 是事实。从中英文的对比来看,可以知道中英文语序分别是怎么安排的。

煤炭与其他能源相比,竞争力已经有所下降了。以美国为例,页岩气的出现造成部分出煤量因价格过高而被挤出市场。

第一步 词汇解析

① 与……相比，compare with，动词词组，比如：It's much easier compared with last time.（这与上次相比容易得多。）注意这一词组一般使用被动语态，很少出现 comparing with。

② 能源，power sources，名词词组，比如：a variety of alternative power sources（多种替代能源）。还可以翻译为 energy resources/energy/the sources of energy。

③ 竞争力，competitive，形容词，比如：Only those homes offered for sale at competitive prices will secure interest from serious purchasers.（只有那些以具有竞争力的价格出售的房子才能吸引真正购买者的兴趣。）

④ 页岩气，shale gas，名词词组，比如：The extraction of shale gas is controversial.（页岩气开采是存有争议的。）

⑤ 造成，result in，动词词组，比如：Such a war could result in the use of chemical and biological weapons.（这样一场战争可能导致使用生化武器。）

⑥ 出煤量，coal output，名词词组，比如：Our coal output has increased by three times.（我们的出煤量增长了三倍。）

⑦ ……被挤出，has been squeezed out of，动词词组，词组原形为：squeeze out，比如：Supermarkets are squeezing out small shops.（超市正挤垮小商店。）

第二步 动词定位

煤炭与其他能源相比，竞争力已经有所下降了。以美国为例，页岩气的出现造成部分出煤量因价格过高而被挤出市场。

第三步 句型解析

① 第一句中，"煤炭"是主语，"与其他能源相比"是状语，使用 Compared with 的结构非常合适，"竞争力"又是主语，"已经有所下降了"是谓语，这句的主语好像是"煤炭的竞争力"，实际上并不是！这句和上一句一模一样，还是"事实与评论"的关系，"煤炭的竞争力"是事实，"已经有所下降"是评论，那么这一句中文的英文语序是不是"煤炭有了有所下降的竞争力"呢？而且还是现在完成时态。

② 第二句中，"以美国为例"是举例，可以使用最简单的 for example，"页岩气的出现"是主语，参考译文使用了 the arrival of，非常经典，"造成"是核心谓语，译文使用了 result in，当然你用 cause 等词也可以。"部分出煤量因价格过高而被挤出市场"是宾语，而且是宾语从句，从句中的"部分出煤量"是主语，"而被挤出市场"是被动语态，动词使用 be squeezed out of，"因价格过高"是典型的原因状语，可以使用 due to、because of 等词，因为这些引导词都是引导词组的，所以这里的"价格过高"要处理为偏正短语"过高的价格"，当然若使用 because 等词，那么用主谓结构的句子即可。

第四步 翻译来了

Compared with other types of power sources, coal has become less competitive. In the US, for example, the arrival of shale gas results in the fact that some coal output has been squeezed out of the market due to its high price.

> **本句考点总结**
>
> 第一,本句出现了事实(Facts)和评论(Comments)的译法。中文一般先事实,后评论,而英文则是一般先评论,后事实。比如:It is important for her to go abroad. 翻译为"对于她来说,出国是很重要的"。英文中 It is important 是评论,for her to go abroad 是事实。从中英文的对比来看,可以知道中英文语序分别是怎么安排的。
>
> 第二,本句中使用了"偏正结构变主谓结构"的译法,这是什么意思呢?也就是说偏正结构 gleaming eyes(炯炯有神的眼睛)可以翻译为主谓结构 Eyes are gleaming.(眼睛炯炯有神。)这种译法是为了让句子更加通顺,当然有时候也可以用"主谓结构变偏正结构"的译法。"主谓变偏正"或"偏正变主谓"在英汉互译当中都可能出现,须灵活使用。

美国去年煤炭需求接近 9.2 亿吨。由于天然气价格下跌,今年美国煤炭需求将减少 6 000 万到 8 000 万吨。数据显示,煤炭满足了全球大约 30% 的能源需求,提供 40% 以上的电力。

第一步 词汇解析

❶ 接近,approach,动词,比如:Oil prices have approached their highest level for almost ten years.(石油价格几乎已达到近十年来的最高水平。)

❷ 吨,ton,名词,比如:Hundreds of tons of oil spilled into the ocean.(数百吨石油溢出流入大海。)常见的表示重量的单位还有:kilogram(千克)、gram(克)、milligram(毫克)等。

❸ 天然气,natural gas,名词词组,比如:More than half of all U.S. households are heated with natural gas.(超过半数的美国家庭用天然气供暖。)

❹ 数据,statistics,名词,比如:Official statistics show real wages declining by 24%.(官方统计数据表明,实际工资水平下降了 24%。)statistics 表示"统计资料"时,用作复数,表示"学科",也就是"统计学"时,用作单数。

❺ ……显示,according to,固定搭配,比如:The van raced away, according to police reports, and police gave chase.(警方的报告显示,这辆货车飞驰而去,警方进行了追赶。)

❻ 满足……,meet,动词,比如:meet the needs and demands of a new age(满足新时代的需要和要求)。

❼ 提供,generate,动词,比如:The company, New England Electric, burns coal to generate power.(新英格兰电力公司燃烧煤来发电。)generate 一词特指"产生电、热、光等"。

❽ 电力,power,名词,比如:The shortage of power dims the streets.(由于电力不足,街道昏暗。)"电力"也可以翻译为 electricity 或 electric power。

第二步 动词定位

美国去年煤炭需求接近 9.2 亿吨。由于天然气价格下跌,今年美国煤炭需求将减少 6 000 万到 8 000 万吨。数据显示,煤炭满足了全球大约 30% 的能源需求,提供 40% 以上的电力。

第三步 句型解析

❶ 第一句中，"美国去年煤炭需求"是主语，注意不要使用各种"奇怪"的短语结构，直接翻译为 US coal demand，简单一点比较好，时间状语"去年"可以放在句首，也可以放在句末，本句需要使用一般过去时态，谓语是"接近"，宾语是"9.2亿吨"，特别注意数字的写法，写成 920 million tons 非常合适，很少写成 920,000,000 tons。

❷ 第二句中，"由于天然气价格下跌"是原因状语，可以处理为 because 后面接从句的结构，主句中的"今年"是时间状语，"美国煤炭需求"是主语，"将减少"是谓语，"6 000万"是第一个状语，"到 8 000 万吨"是第二个状语，按照以上结构翻译即可，但是译文的译法的确非常难，首先将"天然气价格下跌"作为主语，"减少"是谓语，"美国煤炭需求"是宾语，"6 000万"是第一个状语，"8 000万吨"是第二个状语。以上这种译法非常难，其实完全没有必要，作为一个考生还是老老实实地简单翻译吧，考生的目的是通过考试，不要搞得那么难。

❸ 第三句中，"数据"是主语，"显示"是谓语，也可以翻译为 According to，将动词翻译为介词，这也是一种比较好的方法，"煤炭"是主语，"满足了"是谓语，"全球大约 30% 的能源需求"是宾语，"提供"是第二个谓语，"40% 以上的电力"是第二个宾语，但是要注意这里的"40% 以上的电力"指的是"全球的"，所以这里增一个对象词可能更加合适一点。

第四步 翻译来了

US coal demand approached 920 million tons last year. However, falls of natural gas price will decrease US coal demand by 60 to 80 million tons this year. According to statistics, coal meets about 30 percent of global energy needs and generates more than 40 percent of the world's power.

本句考点总结

本句考查了英汉互译增减词的问题，一般来说英译汉增词，汉译英减词，常见增词的种类有：一、增加对象词（范围词），这是由上文缺少句子的某个部分造成的；二、增加范畴词，这是较难的一部分，常见的范畴词有"水平、方式、方法、问题、情况、途径和方面"，但是不仅仅有这些，还有很多其他的；三、增加评论性词，这些常常出现在文学翻译中；四、增加动词，会在动词的"分配译法"中说明这点。

---

4 在人口第一和第二大国中国和印度，煤炭所满足的能源需求比例甚至达到 70% 左右。

第一步 词汇解析

❶ 人口第一和第二，这里可以理解为"人口众多的"，populous，形容词，比如：Indonesia is the fifth most populous country in the world.（印度尼西亚是世界上人口第五大国。）

❷ ……的比例，the percentage of/a high proportion of，名词词组。the percentage of，名词词组，比如：The percentage of girls in engineering has increased substantially.（工科女生的比例已经大大增长。）a high proportion of，名词词组，比如：A high proportion of the new arrivals are skilled professionals.（很大一部分新来的人们是技术熟练的专业人士。）第二个词组更加能表达出比例之高的含义。

❸ 达到，reach，动词，比如：Cutbacks in staff reached to the hundreds.（裁员达数百名。）这里"达到"还可以翻译为介词词组 up to。

第二步 动词定位

在人口第一和第二大国中国和印度，煤炭所满足的能源需求比例甚至达到 70% 左右。

第三步 句型解析

❶ "在人口第一和第二大国中国和印度"是本句的状语，这里看上去很简单，但是翻译时需要注意同位语的关系，这里的"人口第一和第二大国"和"中国和印度"是同位语，翻译时用逗号处理比较简单，In the (first and second) most populous countries in the world, China and India 中，把 first 和 second 用括号括起来，这是一种很好的办法。

❷ 主句中"煤炭所满足的能源需求比例"是主语，"能源需求比例"是主语的核心词，"煤炭所满足的"是定语，可以用定语从句，也可以用过去分词，谓语是"甚至达到"，宾语是"70% 左右"。

第四步 翻译来了

In the (first and second) most populous countries in the world, China and India, the percentage of energy needs met by coal even reaches to about 70 percent.

中国的煤炭消费量在去年已经下滑，煤炭进口下降了 11%，这是十年来的首次下降。中国经济增速已经放缓，同时也做出极大努力削减煤炭使用以减少煤炭污染。

第一步 词汇解析

❶ 消费量，consumption，名词，比如：the daily consumption of food（食物的日消耗量）。

❷ 下滑、下降，decline/fall，动词 / 名词。
decline，动词，比如：The number of staff has declined from 217,000 to 114,000.（员工人数已从 217 000 减少到 114 000。）
fall，名词，表示"下降"，比如：There was a sharp fall in the value of the dollar.（美元的价值有大幅下降。）
表示"下降"的单词或词组有很多，比如：descend/drop/decrease。

❸ 放缓，slow down，动词词组，比如：There is no cure for the disease, although drugs can slow down its rate of development.（这种病没法治，尽管药物可以延缓病情的发展。）

❹ 做出极大努力，make strenuous efforts to，动词词组。
劲头十足的，strenuous，形容词，比如：She made strenuous efforts to tame her anger.（她竭力压制心头怒火。）
努力做某事，make efforts to do something，动词词组，比如：He made efforts to save her.（他用尽全力去救她。）

第二步 动词定位

中国的煤炭消费量在去年已经下滑，煤炭进口下降了 11%，这是十年来的首次下降。中国经济增速已经放缓，同时也做出极大努力削减煤炭使用以减少煤炭污染。

第三步 句型解析

❶ 第一句的第一分句中，"中国的煤炭消费量"是主语，"在去年"是时间状语，"已经下滑"是谓语，第二分句中，"煤炭进口"是主语，"下降了"是谓语，"11%"是宾语，第三分句中，"这是十年来的首次下降"是主系表结构，但是这么翻译不太好，要考虑三个句子之间的关系，也要考虑动词之间的关系，第一分句是主句没问题，而且主谓也非常明确，第二分句和第一分句有关系，表示"煤炭进口量下降11%"，这里可以处理为第一分句的伴随状语，后面的"这是十年来的首次下降"是同位语结构，这样三个句子就联系在一起了。中文是意合式语言，句子之间不用连词，但是英文是形合式语言，句子之间需要用连词，这也是非常重要的知识。

❷ 第二句的第一分句中，"中国经济增速"是主语，"已经放缓"是谓语，第二分句中，"同时也做出……"是第二个谓语，但是仔细看看有没有问题呢？当然有问题了，因为这两句的主语不一致，要统一主语才好，第一分句和第二分句的主语都统一为"中国"，这样的话，第一分句则变成"中国放缓了经济增速"，第二分句则是"中国同时也做出极大努力削减煤炭使用以减少煤炭污染"，这样两个分句有两个动词，第一个是"放缓"，第二个是"做出"，两个动词应该如何解决呢？当然是"并列""伴随"或是"下沉"了。译文使用了"下沉"结构，将第一分句处理为状语结构，翻译为 With its economic growth having slowed down，主句则是 China is making strenuous efforts，为主谓宾结构，"削减"是二谓语，翻译为不定式短语作目的状语，"煤炭使用"是宾语，"以减少"又是一个不定式短语作目的状语，"煤炭污染"是宾语。

第四步 翻译来了

Coal consumption in China declined last year, with 11 percent decrease in imports, the first fall in a decade. With its economic growth having slowed down, China is making strenuous efforts to cut coal use as a way to reduce pollution.

> **本句考点总结**
>
> 第一，中英文的巨大差异在于中文是意合式语言，英文是形合式语言。中文的句子之间不用连词连接，而英文的句子之间必须使用连词。所以，我们在做汉译英时，要去体会和理解每个逗号前后句子之间的关系，到底是并列、转折、让步、因果、条件，还是别的什么关系，然后选择合适的连词进行连接，形成一个英文的句子。始终要牢记一点：英文的两个句子之间必须要有连词连接。
>
> 第二，汉译英句子中并列、伴随、下沉的结构。中文常常会出现多个句子聚集的情况，那么我们在翻译时需要考虑将这些句子进行"分堆"。但是"分堆"之后，一个句子中也可能会出现两个动词或两组动词，那么有两个动词或两组动词的句子我们该如何进行翻译呢？比如："我坐在那里看书"，这里有两个动词，一个是"坐"，一个是"看"，我们翻译时便会有三种方法：

第一种并列（两个动词并列的译法，使用并列连词连接，两个动词之间不一定是"并列"关系）：I sat there and read a book.

第二种伴随（将第二个动词翻译为二谓语，分词、从句、状语等都可以）：I sat there reading a book.

第三种下沉（将第一个动词翻译为二谓语，分词、从句、状语等都可以）：Sitting there, I read a book.

需要说明的是，并列、伴随和下沉只是动词的形式问题，不代表动词之间的逻辑关系，用这三种形式翻译两个动词或两组动词都是可以的，大家可以根据句子上下文的关系来判断使用。

第三，关于谓语动词的层次性。汉译英的核心问题是厘清句子当中多个动词之间的关系，我们要学会在多个动词当中找到最核心的动词，翻译为核心谓语（也称为一谓语）；找到其次核心的动词，翻译为分词、从句、其他状语或定语的形式（也称为二谓语）；再找到不重要的动词，翻译为介词（也称为三谓语）；最后最不重要的动词，可以不译（也称为四谓语）。这些动词在句子当中如何划分层次，需要大家在长期不断的实践中摸索，而且每个句子的翻译也不是固定的。有些句子当中的"一谓语"（核心谓语），在别的译本当中可能就是"二谓语"或者是"三谓语"。只要句子整体结构正确，逻辑清晰，那这就是一个好的译本。

6 由于燃煤发电厂没有满负荷运行，再加上煤炭供应充足，造成国际煤炭价格压低。煤出口价格从去年的峰值下跌了约60%。

第一步 词汇解析

❶ 燃煤发电厂，coal-fired power plants，名词词组，比如：About 50 coal-fired power plants are scheduled to begin operating in Europe.（在欧洲大约有50座燃煤发电厂将投入使用。）
用……作燃料的，-fired，与名词连用，比如：oil-fired central heating（烧油的中央供暖装置）。

❷ 满负荷，at one's full capacity，介词词组。
负载量，capacity，名词，比如：an aircraft with a bomb-carrying capacity of 1,000 pounds（一架炸弹装载量达1 000磅的飞机）。

❸ 供应充足，with adequate supply，介词词组，比如：provide you with adequate supply and professional technical support（为您提供充足的货源和专业的技术支持）。

❹ ……压低，push down，动词词组，比如：The government did everything it could to push down inflation.（政府已经竭尽全力遏制通货膨胀。）

❺ 峰值，peak，名词，比如：Membership was already near its peak.（会员人数已接近最高数值。）

第二步 动词定位

由于燃煤发电厂没有满负荷运行，再加上煤炭供应充足，造成国际煤炭价格压低。煤出口价格从去年的峰值下跌了约60%。

第三步 句型解析

1. 第一句中,"由于燃煤发电厂没有满负荷运行,再加上煤炭供应充足"是原因状语从句,这里的"由于"可以翻译为 As 或 Because 等词,从句中,"燃煤发电厂"是主语,"没有满负荷运行"是谓语,"再加上"实际上是伴随状语,这里用 with 非常合适,既然用 with,那后面就要接短语,这里"煤炭供应充足"实际上是主谓结构,要变成短语就要使用"主谓结构的偏正译法",翻译为 adequate coal supply。本句的最后一个分句"造成国际煤炭价格压低"是主句,所以"造成"不翻译,直接翻译"国际煤炭价格压低",也是主谓结构,非常简单,可以直接翻译。这句和上文的第四句非常相似,大家可以用"燃煤发电厂没有满负荷运行,再加上煤炭供应充足"作为主语,"造成"作为谓语,"国际煤炭价格压低"作为宾语,这样就可以把主句和从句合为一句。但是,我的劝告是:怎么简单,怎么翻译。

2. 第二句中,"煤出口价格"是主语,"从去年的峰值"是状语,"下跌了"是谓语,"约 60%"是宾语,注意这里有"从去年",所以本句需要用现在完成时态。

第四步 翻译来了

As coal-fired power plants don't run at their full capacity, with adequate coal supply, the global coal prices have pushed down. Export prices of coal have fallen by about 60 percent from last year's peak.

这篇文章介绍了当前全球煤炭市场及其在各国的情况,专业名词较多,但句子结构不是特别难,所以请大家多多积累词汇。对于常见的汉译英的方法,如动词的分堆问题、动词的分层问题、"事实与评论"等问题还是要烂熟于胸,加强真题的训练,才能在考试中取得好成绩。

第三节 2018 年下半年三级笔译英译汉

Traces of microplastics and hazardous chemicals found in majority of snow and ice samples taken earlier this year. Plastic and traces of hazardous chemicals have been found in Antarctica, one of the world's last great wildernesses, according to a new study.

Researchers spent three months taking water and snow samples from remote areas of the continent earlier this year. These have now been analysed and researchers have confirmed the majority contained "persistent hazardous chemicals" or microplastics.

The findings come amid growing concern about the extent of the plastic pollution crisis which scientists have warned risks "permanent contamination" of the planet. Earlier this week, the UN warned it is one of the world's biggest environmental threats and said although 60 countries were taking urgent action more needed to be done.

The new report by researchers at Greenpeace is part of global campaign to create the world's biggest ocean sanctuary in the seas around Antarctica to protect the fragile ecosystem from industrial fishing and climate change.

Frida Bengtsson, of Greenpeace's Protect the Antarctic campaign, said the findings proved that even the most remote areas of the planet were not immune from the impact of manmade pollution.

"We need action at source, to stop these pollutants ending up in the Antarctic in the first place, and we need an Antarctic ocean sanctuary to give space for penguins, whales and the entire ecosystem to recover from the pressures they're facing," she said.

Seven of the eight sea-surface water samples tested contained microplastics such as microfibres. Seven of the nine snow samples tested contained detectable concentrations of the persistent hazardous chemicals — polyfluorinated alkylated substances, or PFAS.

Researchers said the chemicals are widely used in many industrial processes and consumer products and have been linked to reproductive and developmental issues in wildlife. They said the snow samples gathered included freshly fallen snow, suggesting the hazardous chemicals had come from contaminated rain or snowfall.

Prof. Alex Rogers, a specialist in sustainable oceans at the Oxford Martin school, Oxford University, said the discovery of plastics and chemicals in Antarctica confirmed that manmade pollutants were now affecting ecosystems in every corner of the world.

And he warned the consequences of this pervasive contamination remained largely unknown. "The big question now is what are the actual consequences of finding this stuff here? Many of these chemicals are pretty nasty and as they move up the food chain, they may be having serious consequences for the health of wildlife, and ultimately humans. The effects of microplastics on marine life, likewise, are largely not understood," he said.

There is relatively little data on the extent of microplastics in Antarctic waters, and researchers said they hoped this new study would lead to a greater understanding of the global extent of plastic and chemical pollutants.

Bengtsson said: "Plastic has now been found in all corners of our oceans, from the Antarctic to the Arctic and at the deepest point of the ocean, the Mariana trench.

We need urgent action to reduce the flow of plastic into our seas and we need large-scale marine reserves — like a huge Antarctic ocean sanctuary which over 1.6m people are calling for — to protect marine life and our oceans for future generations."

2018年下半年的CATTI英译汉是有关南极洲环境污染的问题。文章整体难度不大，但是文章长度较之前有所增加。本篇文章是典型的外刊文章，又考查了直接引语和间接引语的翻译知识，在之前的文章中，我们已经详细地分析了这种句型的译法，在这篇文章的翻译中，我们要继续巩固，并且大家对这种科技文献的框架要进一步熟悉。

> **1** Traces of microplastics and hazardous chemicals found in majority of snow and ice samples taken earlier this year. Plastic and traces of hazardous chemicals have been found in Antarctica, one of the world's last great wildernesses, according to a new study.

第一步 词汇解析

 trace，名词，表示"痕迹、遗迹、踪迹"，比如：Police searched the area but found no trace of the escaped prisoners.（警方搜索了那一地区，但未发现越狱逃犯的任何踪迹。）

❷ hazardous，形容词，表示"危险的、有害的"，比如：They have no way to dispose of the hazardous waste they produce.（他们没有办法处理掉自己产生的有害废料。）

❸ chemical，名词，表示"化学制品、化学品"，比如：This chemical has a wide range of industrial uses.（这种化学制品在工业上用途广泛。）

❹ sample，名词，表示"样本、样品"，比如：The blood samples are sent to the laboratory for analysis.（血样要送往实验室进行分析。）

❺ Antarctica，专有名词，表示"南极洲"，比如：No minerals have yet been exploited in Antarctica.（南极洲的矿藏还未被开采。）

❻ wilderness，名词，表示"未开发的地区、荒无人烟的地区、荒野"，比如：This area has been christened "Britain's last wilderness".（这个地区被命名为"英国最后的荒野"。）

第二步 注意断句

Traces of microplastics and hazardous chemicals /found in majority of snow and ice samples taken earlier this year. /Plastic and traces of hazardous chemicals have been found /in Antarctica, /one of the world's last great wildernesses, /according to a new study.

第三步 句型解析

❶ 第一句中，Traces of microplastics and hazardous chemicals 是主语，found 是谓语，in majority of snow and ice samples taken earlier 是宾语，this year 是时间状语，本句要注意的是宾语的结构，宾语中的 taken earlier 是典型的过去分词短语作定语，定语较短，可以采用前置译法。而且在翻译本句时，若从主语开始翻译，翻译为"微塑料和有害化学物质的踪迹在今年早些时候采集的大部分冰雪样本中发现了"，这样不是特别通顺，若将宾语翻译为主语则更加通顺，译文为"今年早些时候采集的大部分冰雪样本中发现了微塑料和有害化学物质的踪迹"。

❷ 第二句中，Plastic and traces of hazardous chemicals have been found in Antarctica 是主谓状结构，而且是被动语态，可以使用被动语态的各种译法，只要句子通顺即可，译文使用了"被动变主动"的译法，one of the world's last great wildernesses 和前面的 Antarctica 形成了同位语关系，这种结构的翻译不算难吧！according to a new study 是状语，这种状语放在句首翻译更加通顺一些。

第四步 翻译来了

今年早些时候采集的大部分冰雪样本中发现了微塑料和有害化学物质的踪迹。一项新的研究表明，在南极洲发现了塑料和有害化学物质的踪迹，而南极洲是世界上最后的几片荒野之一。

本句考点总结

第一，本句出现了分词或分词短语位于名词后的译法。一般来说，分词或分词短语位于名词后相当于定语或定语从句，定语按照"短前长后"的译法来进行翻译。

第二，本句出现了被动语态的译法。被动语态是英文常见的一种形式，而在中文里常常少用"被"或者不用"被"。那么我们一般有什么样的译法呢？第一种是被动变主动，第二种是寻找替代词（比如："让……给""为……所"等结构），第三种是在科技文献中用"可以"来替代"被"，第四种是有"被"不用"被"。以上四种怎么用，那就看句子怎么通顺怎么翻译了啊！

第三，本句考查了英文同位语的译法。同位语是两个前后相互说明的名词或名词短语，比如 Beijing, the capital of China，有两种译法。第一种是"并列译法"，翻译为"中国的首都北京"，第二种是"主谓译法"，翻译为"北京是中国的首都"。具体用哪一种，可以根据句子具体情况而定，有时两种都是可以使用的。

2

Researchers spent three months taking water and snow samples from remote areas of the continent earlier this year. These have now been analysed and researchers have confirmed the majority contained "persistent hazardous chemicals" or microplastics.

第一步 词汇解析

1. continent，名词，表示"大陆、陆地"，比如：Ancient historians wrote of a lost continent beneath the ocean.（古代史学家写过一个有关沉没海底大陆的事迹。）
2. analyse，动词，表示"分析"，比如：We haven't had time to analyse those samples yet.（我们还没有时间分析那些样本。）
3. confirm，动词，表示"证实、证明"，比如：The results of the experiment confirmed our predictions.（实验结果证实了我们的预测。）
4. persistent，形容词，表示"连绵的、持续的、反复出现的"，比如：His cough grew more persistent until it never stopped.（他咳嗽持续的时间越来越长，直到咳个不停。）

第二步 注意断句

Researchers spent three months taking water and snow samples /from remote areas of the continent earlier /this year. These have now been analysed /and researchers have confirmed /the majority contained "persistent hazardous chemicals" or microplastics.

第三步 句型解析

1. 第一句中，Researchers spent three months taking water and snow samples 是主谓宾结构，这里使用了 spend time doing something 的结构，from remote areas of the continent earlier 是地点状语，this year 是时间状语，本句较为简单，可以直接翻译。
2. 第二句中，These have now been analysed 是主谓结构，而且是被动语态，可以使用被动语态的各种译法，只要句子通顺即可，译文使用了"被动变主动"的译法，这里的 these 指的是前文的 water and

snow samples，and 是并列连词，researchers have confirmed 是第二个并列句的主谓结构，后面接宾语从句 the majority contained "persistent hazardous chemicals" or microplastics，这个宾语从句是主谓宾结构。

第四步 翻译来了

今年早些时候，研究人员花了三个月的时间从这片大陆的偏远地区采集了水和雪的样本。目前已经对这些物质进行了分析，研究人员已证实，大部分都含有"持久性的危险化学物质"或微塑料。

本句考点总结

本句出现了被动语态的译法。被动语态是英文常见的一种形式，而在中文里常常少用"被"或者不用"被"。那么我们一般有什么样的译法呢？第一种是被动变主动，第二种是寻找替代词（比如："让……给""为……所"等结构），第三种是在科技文献中用"可以"来替代"被"，第四种是有"被"不用"被"。以上四种怎么用，那就看句子怎么通顺怎么翻译了啊！

3

The findings come amid growing concern about the extent of the plastic pollution crisis which scientists have warned risks "permanent contamination" of the planet. Earlier this week, the UN warned it is one of the world's biggest environmental threats and said although 60 countries were taking urgent action more needed to be done.

第一步 词汇解析

1. amid，介词，表示"在……过程中、在……中"，比如：He finished his speech amid tremendous applause.（他在雷鸣般的掌声中结束了演讲。）
2. extent，名词，表示"程度、限度"，比如：The extent of the damage could not have been foreseen.（损害的程度是无法预见到的。）
3. permanent，形容词，表示"永久的、永恒的"，比如：The government is ready to declare a permanent ceasefire.（政府已准备宣布永久的停火。）
4. contamination，名词，表示"污染"，比如：Some people are still suffering ill effects from the contamination of their water.（一些人仍在承受水质受污染的恶果。）
5. urgent，形容词，表示"紧急的、紧迫的、迫切的"，比如：The money could be better spent on more urgent cases.（这笔钱用于较紧迫的事情也许会更好。）

第二步 注意断句

The findings come /amid growing concern about the extent of the plastic pollution crisis /which scientists have warned risks "permanent contamination" of the planet. /Earlier this week, /the UN warned /it is one of the world's biggest environmental threats /and said /although 60 countries were taking urgent action /more needed to be done.

第三步 句型解析

❶ 第一句中，The findings come 是主谓结构，amid growing concern about the extent of the plastic pollution crisis 是状语，这里的 amid 表示"正值……之际"，特别注意状语的翻译，growing concern about the extent of the plastic pollution crisis 表示"不断增长的对塑料污染危机程度的担忧"，这么翻译和主语不太好连接，还不如直接把"的"的偏正结构翻译为主谓结构，增主语词"人们"，整个句子变成"人们对塑料污染危机的程度日益担忧之际"，这样更加通顺一些。which 引导定语从句，scientists have warned 是主谓结构，其实是定语从句的一个插入语，定语从句实际上缺主语 the plastic pollution crisis，risks 是谓语，"permanent contamination" of the planet 是宾语。本句定语从句较长，所以采用后置译法较好。

❷ 第二句中，Earlier this week 是时间状语，the UN warned 是主谓结构，it is one of the world's biggest environmental threats 是宾语从句，并且是主系表结构，注意这里代词 it 的指代，你可以不翻译，但是要知道指代的是前文的"塑料污染危机"，and 是并列连词，said 后面接了第二个宾语从句，宾语从句中的 although 60 countries were taking urgent action 是让步状语从句，more needed to be done 是主句，这里还有被动语态，注意使用不同的译法让句子更加通顺。还有一个小知识点：60 countries were taking urgent action 是主谓宾结构，表示"60 个国家正在采取迫切的行动"，但是后面好像少些什么，这里增对象词"这一污染"更好，当然不增也勉强通顺。

第四步 翻译来了

这一发现正值人们对塑料污染危机的程度日益担忧之际，科学家们警告说，塑料污染危机可能给地球带来"永久性污染"的风险。本周早些时候，联合国警告说，这是世界上最大的环境威胁之一，并且说，尽管有 60 个国家正在采取迫切的行动来制止这一污染，但是还需要更多的行动。

🧑‍🏫 本句考点总结

第一，本句中使用了"主谓结构变偏正结构"的译法，这是什么意思呢？也就是说主谓结构 Eyes are gleaming.（眼睛炯炯有神。）可以翻译为偏正结构 gleaming eyes（炯炯有神的眼睛），这种译法是为了让句子更加通顺，当然有时候也可以用"偏正结构变主谓结构"的译法。"主谓变偏正"或"偏正变主谓"在英汉互译当中都可能出现，须灵活使用。

第二，本句出现了英文定语从句的译法。一般来说，定语从句按照"短前长后"的译法处理。较短的定语从句可以前置，较长的定语从句可以后置，这一切都取决于句子的通顺，并没有绝对的前置和后置译法。

第三，本句出现了被动语态的译法。被动语态是英文常见的一种形式，而在中文里常常少用"被"或者不用"被"。那么我们一般有什么样的译法呢？第一种是被动变主动，第二种是寻找替代词（比如："让……给""为……所"等结构），第三种是在科技文献中用"可以"来替代"被"，第四种是有"被"不用"被"。以上四种怎么用，那就看句子怎么通顺怎么翻译了啊！

第四，本句考查了英汉互译增减词的问题，一般来说英译汉增词，汉译英减词，常见增词的种类有：一、增加对象词（范围词），这是由上文缺少句子的某个部分造成的；二、增加范畴词，这是较难的一部分，常见的范畴词有"水平、方式、方法、问题、情况、途径和方面"，但是不仅仅有这些，还有很多其他的；三、增加评论性词，这些常常出现在文学翻译中；四、增加动词，会在动词的"分配译法"中说明这点。

> The new report by researchers at Greenpeace is part of global campaign to create the world's biggest ocean sanctuary in the seas around Antarctica to protect the fragile ecosystem from industrial fishing and climate change.

第一步 词汇解析

① Greenpeace，专有名词，表示"绿色和平组织"。
   文化小常识：
   绿色和平组织简称绿色和平（Greenpeace），国际非政府组织。前身是 1971 年 9 月 15 日成立于加拿大的"不以举手表决委员会"，1979 年改为绿色和平组织，总部设在荷兰阿姆斯特丹。
② campaign，名词，表示"运动（为社会、商业或政治目的而进行的一系列有计划的活动）"，比如：It was this campaign that established the paper's reputation.（正是这场运动确立了这家报纸的声誉。）
③ sanctuary，名词，表示"鸟兽保护区、禁猎区、庇护"，比如：a bird/wildlife sanctuary（鸟类/野生动物保护区）。
④ fragile，形容词，表示"脆弱的、易碎的、易损的"，比如：Oil pollution could damage the fragile ecology of the coral reefs.（石油污染可能破坏珊瑚礁脆弱的生态环境。）

第二步 注意断句

The new report /by researchers at Greenpeace is part of global campaign /to create the world's biggest ocean sanctuary /in the seas /around Antarctica /to protect the fragile ecosystem /from industrial fishing and climate change.

第三步 句型解析

① 本句中，The new report by researchers at Greenpeace 是主语，is part of global campaign 是系表结构，后面的动词不定式短语作目的状语，create the world's biggest ocean sanctuary 是动宾结构，in the seas around Antarctica 是地点状语，注意这个地点状语和前一句有关，和后一句无关，之后的动词不定式短语也是目的状语，protect the fragile ecosystem from industrial fishing and climate change 是动宾结构，其中含有 protect...from... 的结构。
② 本句主要看清两个 to 引导的不定式结构，翻译时需要后置，而不能前置，翻译时译文处理为"目的是"和"以"，这种中文词汇也要学会使用。

第四步 翻译来了

绿色和平组织（Greenpeace）研究人员所发表的最新报告是全球保护行动的一部分，目的是在南极洲周围海域创建世界上最大的海洋保护区，以保护脆弱的生态系统免受捕捞业和气候变化的影响。

> Frida Bengtsson, of Greenpeace's Protect the Antarctic campaign, said the findings proved that even the most remote areas of the planet were not immune from the impact of manmade pollution.

第一步 词汇解析

❶ Frida Bengtsson，佛里达·本特森，人名，这里采用的是音译法，注意名和姓之间要加·，翻译英文人名不确定时，可以使用音译法，然后把英文人名抄下来，放在括号里，这样保险一些。

❷ immune，形容词，表示"有免疫力的、不受影响的"，比如：Our immune systems are killing billions of germs right now.（我们的免疫系统正在杀死数以十亿计的细菌。）

❸ manmade，形容词，表示"人造的"，比如：manmade environment（人造环境）。

第二步 注意断句

Frida Bengtsson, /of Greenpeace's Protect the Antarctic campaign, /said /the findings proved /that even the most remote areas of the planet were not immune from the impact of manmade pollution.

第三步 句型解析

❶ 本句中，Frida Bengtsson 和 of Greenpeace's Protect the Antarctic campaign 是同位语关系，这里的 of 表示"其中一员"，said 是本句的谓语，后面接宾语从句。

❷ the findings 是宾语从句的主语，proved 是谓语，that 引导了一个表语从句，even the most remote areas of the planet 是表语从句的主语，were not immune from the impact of manmade pollution 是系表状结构，其实这里也就是 be immune from 的结构，表示"无法免受……"。

第四步 翻译来了

"绿色和平组织保护南极运动"的佛里达·本特森（Frida Bengtsson）说，这些发现证明，即使是地球上最偏远的地区也无法免受人类污染的影响。

> ### 本句考点总结
>
> 本句考查了英文同位语的译法。同位语是两个前后相互说明的名词或名词短语，比如 Beijing, the capital of China，有两种译法。第一种是"并列译法"，翻译为"中国的首都北京"，第二种是"主谓译法"，翻译为"北京是中国的首都"。具体用哪一种，可以根据句子具体情况而定，有时两种都是可以使用的。

"We need action at source, to stop these pollutants ending up in the Antarctic in the first place, and we need an Antarctic ocean sanctuary to give space for penguins, whales and the entire ecosystem to recover from the pressures they're facing," she said.

第一步 词汇解析

❶ pollutant，名词，表示"污染物、污染物质"，比如：A steady stream of California traffic clogs the air with pollutants.（加利福尼亚川流不息的车流使空气中充斥着污染物。）

❷ in the first place，介词短语，表示"首先、起初、一开始"，比如：In the first place you are not old and in the second place you are a very attractive man.（首先你不老，其次你是个富有魅力的男人。）

❸ penguin，名词，表示"企鹅"，比如：There are all sorts of animals, including bears, pigs, kangaroos, and penguins.（有各种各样的动物，包括熊、猪、袋鼠和企鹅。）

❹ whale，名词，表示"鲸"，比如：Whales and dolphins are still being slaughtered for commercial gain.（人们仍然为了商业利益大肆捕杀鲸鱼和海豚。）

第二步 注意断句

"We need action /at source, /to stop these pollutants ending up /in the Antarctic /in the first place, /and we need an Antarctic ocean sanctuary /to give space for penguins, /whales /and the entire ecosystem /to recover from the pressures /they're facing," /she said.

第三步 句型解析

❶ 本句为直接引语，翻译时说话人和动作可以放在句首，也可以放在句末，所有标点依旧保留。

❷ 双引号内 We 是主语，need action 是谓语和宾语，at source 是状语，表示"从源头上"，to 引导目的状语，stop these pollutants ending up 是动宾状结构，in the Antarctic 是地点状语，in the first place 也是状语。and 是并列连词，we need an Antarctic ocean sanctuary 是主谓宾结构，to 引导目的状语，give space for penguins, whales 是动宾结构，and 又是并列连词，后面的名词 the entire ecosystem 和 penguins, whales 并列，to 又引导目的状语，from the pressures 是状语，they're facing 是定语从句，从句较短，可以采用前置译法，注意这里的 they 指代的是前面的 penguins, whales and the entire ecosystem，而且更加重要的是这里的 give space for 是"动词的分配"，需要翻译两次。

❸ she said 是直接引语的说话人和动词，直接翻译即可，可放在句首，也可放在句末。

第四步 翻译来了

她说："我们需要从源头上采取行动，首先阻止这些污染物进入南极，我们需要一个南极海洋保护区，为企鹅、鲸鱼提供空间，并且为整个生态系统提供空间，让它们从正面临的压力中恢复过来。"

本句考点总结

第一，本句考查了英文直接引语的译法，最简单的译法就是保留冒号和双引号，说话人的位置和说话的内容都保持不变。即说话人在什么位置，就放在什么位置翻译，当然，说话人放在句首也是可以接受的。

第二，本句出现了英文定语从句的译法。一般来说，定语从句按照"短前长后"的译法处理。较短的定语从句可以前置，较长的定语从句可以后置，这一切都取决于句子的通顺，并没有绝对的前置和后置译法。

第三，本句考查了形容词的"分配"译法和动词或名词的"分配"译法。形容词分配的译法是两个或多个形容词位于名词之前，"翻译公式"是 (A+B)*C=AC+BC，比如 international and strategic questions 翻译为"国际问题和战略问题"；动词或名词分配的译法是一个动词位于多个名词宾语之前，或者一个名词位于多个名词前，"翻译公式"是 A*(B+C)=AB+AC，比如 wear a hat and a scarf 翻译为"戴着帽子，系着围巾"。

Seven of the eight sea-surface water samples tested contained microplastics such as microfibres. Seven of the nine snow samples tested contained detectable concentrations of the persistent hazardous chemicals — polyfluorinated alkylated substances, or PFAS.

第一步 词汇解析

① microfibre，名词，表示"微纤维、超细纤维"，比如：Microfibre fabrics are both water resistant and windproof.（微纤维织物既防水又防风。）

② detectable，形容词，表示"可觉察的、可发现的、可查出的"，比如：The noise is barely detectable by the human ear.（这种噪音人的耳朵几乎是察觉不到的。）

③ concentration，名词，表示"浓度、含量"，比如：glucose concentrations in the blood（血液中的葡萄糖含量）。

④ polyfluorinated alkylated substances，专有名词，表示"聚氟化烷基化物质（PFAS）"。

第二步 注意断句

Seven of the eight sea-surface water samples tested contained microplastics /such as microfibres. /Seven of the nine snow samples tested contained detectable concentrations of the persistent hazardous chemicals — /polyfluorinated alkylated substances, /or PFAS.

第三步 句型解析

① 第一句中，Seven of the eight sea-surface water samples tested 是主语，这里只需要注意 tested 是过去分词位于名词后，相当于定语即可，contained 是谓语，microplastics 是宾语，such as microfibres 是举例，这里又是总分关系，中文先分后总，英文先总后分，翻译时注意语序。

② 第二句中，Seven of the nine snow samples tested 是主语，这里只需要注意 tested 是过去分词位于名词后，相当于定语即可，contained 是谓语，detectable concentrations of the persistent hazardous chemicals 是宾语，之后的破折号依旧保留，最难的是这个化学词组，万一不会翻译怎么办？我来教你，polyfluorinated alkylated substances 不就是 PFAS 吗？所以你翻译为 PFAS (polyfluorinated alkylated substances) 不就可以了吗？这样多简单。

第四步 翻译来了

在测试的八个海表水样本中，有七个含有像微纤维一样的微塑料。在测试的九个雪样本中，有七个样本含有可检测到的持久性有害化学物质——聚氟化烷基化物质 (PFAS)。

> **本句考点总结**
>
> 中英文的总分关系，中文一般是先分后总，而英文则是先总后分，比如中文会说"我喜欢吃香蕉、苹果、梨子等水果"，但是英文的表达是 I like fruits such as bananas, apples and pears. 注意总分关系是如何在两种语言中体现出来的。

> **8** Researchers said the chemicals are widely used in many industrial processes and consumer products and have been linked to reproductive and developmental issues in wildlife. They said the snow samples gathered included freshly fallen snow, suggesting the hazardous chemicals had come from contaminated rain or snowfall.

第一步 词汇解析

① reproductive，形容词，表示"生殖的、繁殖的"，比如：Not all doctors truly understand the reproductive cycle.（并非所有的医生都真正了解生殖周期。）

② developmental，形容词，表示"发育中的"，比如：developmental stage（发育阶段）。

③ snowfall，名词，表示"降雪"，比如：The total rain and snowfall amounted to 50mm.（降雨量和降雪量共达 50 毫米。）

第二步 注意断句

Researchers said /the chemicals are widely used /in many industrial processes and consumer products /and have been linked to reproductive and developmental issues /in wildlife. /They said /the snow samples gathered included freshly fallen snow, /suggesting the hazardous chemicals had come from contaminated rain or snowfall.

第三步 句型解析

① 第一句中，Researchers said 是主谓结构，后面接宾语从句，the chemicals are widely used 是宾语从句的主语和谓语，是典型的被动语态，用"可以"来替代"被"，in many industrial processes and consumer products 是状语，表示"在……方面"。and 是并列连词，have been linked to reproductive and developmental issues 是第二组谓语和宾语，这里的 be linked to 也是典型的被动语态，用什么方法翻译完全取决于通顺，in wildlife 是状语。

② 第二句中，They said 是主谓结构，后面接宾语从句，the snow samples gathered included freshly fallen snow 是主谓宾结构，这里只需要注意 gathered 是过去分词位于名词后，相当于定语即可，逗号之后的 suggesting 是伴随状语，suggesting 在这表示"表明"，而不是"建议"，the hazardous chemicals had come from contaminated rain or snowfall 是主谓宾结构。

第四步 翻译来了

研究人员表示，这些化学物质可广泛应用于工业过程和消费品中，并与野生动物的生殖和发育问题密切相关。他们说，收集到的雪样本中包括刚刚才下的雪，这表明，危险的化学物质来自受到污染的雨或降雪。

> **本句考点总结**
>
> 本句出现了被动语态的译法。被动语态是英文常见的一种形式，而在中文里常常少用"被"或者不用"被"。那么我们一般有什么样的译法呢？第一种是被动变主动，第二种是寻找替代词（比如："让……给""为……所"等结构），第三种是在科技文献中用"可以"来替代"被"，第四种是有"被"不用"被"。以上四种怎么用，那就看句子怎么通顺怎么翻译了啊！

9 Prof. Alex Rogers, a specialist in sustainable oceans at the Oxford Martin school, Oxford University, said the discovery of plastics and chemicals in Antarctica confirmed that manmade pollutants were now affecting ecosystems in every corner of the world.

第一步 词汇解析

❶ Prof. Alex Rogers，亚历克斯·罗杰斯教授，人名，这里采用的是音译法，注意名和姓之间要加·，翻译英文人名不确定时，可以使用音译法，然后把英文人名抄下来，放在括号里，这样保险一些。

❷ specialist，名词，表示"专家"，比如：My doctor referred me to a specialist.（我的医生让我去找一位专家诊治。）

❸ Oxford University，专有名词，表示"牛津大学"。

文化小常识：

　　牛津大学（University of Oxford），简称"牛津"（Oxford），位于英国牛津，世界顶尖的公立研究型大学，采用书院联邦制。其与剑桥大学并称为"牛剑"，是罗素大学集团成员，被誉为"金三角名校"和"G5超级精英大学"。

第二步 注意断句

　　Prof. Alex Rogers, /a specialist /in sustainable oceans /at the Oxford Martin school, /Oxford University, /said /the discovery of plastics and chemicals /in Antarctica confirmed /that manmade pollutants were now affecting ecosystems /in every corner of the world.

第三步 句型解析

❶ Prof. Alex Rogers 和 a specialist in sustainable oceans at the Oxford Martin school, Oxford University 是同位语关系，翻译时可以处理为并列结构或主谓结构，而且要注意地点状语的翻译，中文的地点从大到小，英文的地点从小到大。

❷ said 是本句的核心谓语，后面接宾语从句，the discovery of plastics and chemicals in Antarctica 是宾语从句的主语，其中 discovery 是典型的抽象名词，有动词词根，可以翻译为动词"发现"，confirmed 是谓语，后面接 that 引导的宾语从句，manmade pollutants were now affecting ecosystems 是主谓宾结构，in every corner of the world 是地点状语，这个宾语从句的主语过长，可以单独成句，主语可以用本位词"这"进行替代。

第四步 翻译来了

牛津大学牛津马丁学院可持续海洋专家亚历克斯·罗杰斯教授（Prof. Alex Rogers）表示，南极洲发现了塑料和化学物质，这证实了人类的污染物正在影响世界各地的生态系统。

> **本句考点总结**
>
> 第一，本句考查了英文同位语的译法。同位语是两个前后相互说明的名词或名词短语，比如 Beijing, the capital of China，有两种译法。第一种是"并列译法"，翻译为"中国的首都北京"，第二种是"主谓译法"，翻译为"北京是中国的首都"。具体用哪一种，可以根据句子具体情况而定，有时两种都是可以使用的。
>
> 第二，本句当中考查了"抽象名词"的译法。抽象名词一般处于冠词之后，又在介词之前，以"the + 抽象名词 + of"的形式居多。一般来说，抽象名词有两种译法。第一种，若抽象名词有动词词根，则翻译为动词，比如 the suggestion of mine，翻译为"我建议"，而不是"我的建议"；第二种，若抽象名词没有动词词根，可以增动词翻译，比如 the spirit of our nation，翻译为"我们民族所具有的精神"，而不是"我们民族的精神"。
>
> 第三，英译汉时，若句子主语过长，那么可以单独成句，形成一个完整的主谓宾句子，这样翻译是为了避免句子过于臃肿。当主语单独成句时，句子的谓语和宾语缺少主语，那么可以增加"这""这些""这一切""这样"等词作为句子的主语，这样的词称为"本位词"，被这些词所代替的部分称为"外位语"。

10 And he warned the consequences of this pervasive contamination remained largely unknown. "The big question now is what are the actual consequences of finding this stuff here? Many of these chemicals are pretty nasty and as they move up the food chain, they may be having serious consequences for the health of wildlife, and ultimately humans. The effects of microplastics on marine life, likewise, are largely not understood," he said.

第一步 词汇解析

❶ pervasive，形容词，表示"遍布的、充斥各处的、弥漫的"，比如：a pervasive smell of damp（四处弥漫的潮湿味儿）。

❷ stuff，名词，表示"东西、物品"，比如：I don't know how you can eat that stuff!（我不明白你怎么能吃那种东西！）

❸ nasty，形容词，表示"极差的、危险的、严重的"，比如：My little granddaughter caught her heel in the spokes of her bicycle — it was a very nasty wound.（我小孙女的脚跟夹到自行车的轮辐里了，伤得很严重。）

④ food chain，名词词组，表示"食物链"，比如：The whole food chain is affected by the overuse of chemicals in agriculture.（整个食物链因农业生产过程过多使用化学品而受到影响。）

⑤ ultimately，副词，表示"最后、最终"，比如：A poor diet will ultimately lead to illness.（糟糕的饮食终将导致疾病。）

⑥ marine，形容词，表示"海洋的"，比如：Pollution can harm marine life.（污染会危及海洋生物。）

⑦ likewise，副词，表示"同样地、类似地、也、还"，比如：Her second marriage was likewise unhappy.（她的第二次婚姻也不幸福。）

⑧ largely，副词，表示"在很大程度上、多半、主要地"，比如：The team's success was largely due to her efforts.（这个队的成功在很大程度上是她努力的结果。）

第二步 注意断句

And he warned /the consequences of this pervasive contamination remained largely unknown. /"The big question now is /what are the actual consequences of finding this stuff here? /Many of these chemicals are pretty nasty /and as they move up the food chain, /they may be having serious consequences /for the health of wildlife, / and ultimately humans. /The effects of microplastics on marine life, /likewise, /are largely not understood," /he said.

第三步 句型解析

① And 是并列连词，表示和上一句的连接，可以不用翻译。第一句中，he warned 是主谓结构，后面接宾语从句，the consequences of this pervasive contamination 是宾语从句的主语，remained largely unknown 是系表结构。其中，consequences 是典型的抽象名词，没有动词词根，可以增动词"产生"，当然若句子通顺，不增词也是可以的。

② 第二句又是直接引语，这样的套路我们应该已经非常熟悉了，保留原始标点是最好的。直接引语中，The big question now is 是主语和系动词，后面接表语从句，what are the actual consequences of finding this stuff here 是主系表结构的疑问句，这个句子翻译没有什么问题吧！其中，consequences 是典型的抽象名词，没有动词词根，可以增动词"产生"，当然若句子通顺，不增词也是可以的。第二句 Many of these chemicals are pretty nasty 是主系表结构，and 是并列连词，as 引导时间状语从句，这里的 they 指代了前文的 Many of these chemicals，第二次出现，可以翻译为"它们"，而后面主语中的 they 可以不翻译，may be having serious consequences 是谓语和宾语，for the health of wildlife 是状语，and 是并列连词，ultimately humans 是另一组状语。

③ 第三句中，The effects of microplastics on marine life 是主语，likewise 是插入语，表示观点，可以置于句首翻译，are largely not understood 是典型的被动语态，用什么方法翻译完全取决于通顺，这里的 effect 是典型的抽象名词，没有动词词根，可以增动词"造成"，这样句子更加通顺。he said 是说话人和动词，直接翻译即可，可以放在句首，也可以放在原位翻译。

第四步 翻译来了

他还警告说，这种无处不在的污染所产生的后果在很大程度上仍不为人知。他说："现在的主要问题是，在这里发现这些污染物实际产生的后果是什么呢？这些化学物质中有许多是非常有害的，它们沿着食物链向上移动时，可能会对野生动物的健康造成严重影响，最终危及人类。同样来说，微塑料对海洋生物造成的影响在很大程度上也是不为人知的。"

本句考点总结

第一，本句当中考查了"抽象名词"的译法。抽象名词一般处于冠词之后，又在介词之前，以"the + 抽象名词 + of"的形式居多。一般来说，抽象名词有两种译法。第一种，若抽象名词有动词词根，则翻译为动词，比如 the suggestion of mine，翻译为"我建议"，而不是"我的建议"；第二种，若抽象名词没有动词词根，可以增动词翻译，比如 the spirit of our nation，翻译为"我们民族所具有的精神"，而不是"我们民族的精神"。

第二，关于英文代词的译法。英文中需要翻译的代词主要指第三人称 he, she, it, they 及其相应宾格和指示代词 this 和 that。这些单词在翻译时一定要注意，主要采用"不抽象、不具体"的译法。不能翻译成具体的人或物，但是也不能翻译为"他""她""它""他们""这个""那个"，要注意取中间的译法。

第三，本句考查了英文同位语的译法。同位语是两个前后相互说明的名词或名词短语，比如 Beijing, the capital of China，有两种译法。第一种是"并列译法"，翻译为"中国的首都北京"，第二种是"主谓译法"，翻译为"北京是中国的首都"。具体用哪一种，可以根据句子具体情况而定，有时两种都是可以使用的。

第四，本句当中出现了插入语的成分，插入语不表示观点时，一般需要放在原位翻译，原始的标点符号保留；插入语表示观点时，可以放在句首翻译。

11

There is relatively little data on the extent of microplastics in Antarctic waters, and researchers said they hoped this new study would lead to a greater understanding of the global extent of plastic and chemical pollutants.

第一步 词汇解析

 water，名词，表示"水域、（某江、河、湖、海的）水域"，比如：The two countries are in dispute over the boundaries of their coastal waters.（两国在近海水域分界线上尚存分歧。）

第二步 注意断句

There is relatively little data /on the extent of microplastics /in Antarctic waters, /and researchers said /they hoped /this new study would lead to a greater understanding /of the global extent of plastic and chemical pollutants.

第三步 句型解析

❶ There is relatively little data 是 there be 句型，这里的 relatively little 表示"很少、几乎没有"，on 表示"在某方面"，这里可以将介词翻译为动词"表明"，the extent of microplastics in Antarctic waters 表示"南极水域微塑料的范围"。and 是并列连词，researchers said 是主谓结构，they hoped 是宾语从句的主谓结构，其后是省略了引导词 that 的宾语从句，this new study would lead to 是这个宾语从句的主谓结构，a greater understanding of the global extent of plastic and chemical pollutants 是宾语，宾语中 understanding 是典型的抽象名词，有动词词根，翻译为"了解"。

第四步 翻译来了

目前，还很少有数据表明南极水域微塑料的范围，研究人员表示，他们希望这项新研究能让人们更加深入地了解全球塑料和化学污染物的范围。

🧑‍🎓 本句考点总结

本句当中考查了"抽象名词"的译法。抽象名词一般处于冠词之后，又在介词之前，以"the + 抽象名词 + of"的形式居多。一般来说，抽象名词有两种译法。第一种，若抽象名词有动词词根，则翻译为动词，比如 the suggestion of mine，翻译为"我建议"，而不是"我的建议"；第二种，若抽象名词没有动词词根，可以增动词翻译，比如 the spirit of our nation，翻译为"我们民族所具有的精神"，而不是"我们民族的精神"。

---

12. Bengtsson said: "Plastic has now been found in all corners of our oceans, from the Antarctic to the Arctic and at the deepest point of the ocean, the Mariana trench."

第一步 词汇解析

❶ Arctic，专有名词，表示"北极、北极圈"，比如：Arctic explorers（北极探险者）。
❷ Mariana trench，专有名词，表示"马里亚纳海沟"。

地理小常识：

马里亚纳海最深处的地方达 6-11 千米，是已知的海洋最深处，这里水压高、完全黑暗、温度低、含氧量低，且食物资源匮乏，因此成为地球上环境最恶劣的区域之一。马里亚纳海沟是板块俯冲地带，海底地质运动非常活跃，海山火山岩的物质组成及成因等是海洋地质科学家感兴趣的问题。

第二步 注意断句

Bengtsson said: /"Plastic has now been found /in all corners of our oceans, /from the Antarctic to the Arctic / and at the deepest point of the ocean, /the Mariana trench."

第三步 句型解析

❶ 本句还是直接引语的结构，Bengtsson said 是主谓结构，直接引语中，Plastic has now been found 是主谓结构，是典型的被动语态，因为没有 by，而且后面都是地点，所以可以使用"被动变主动"的译法，in all corners of our oceans 是地点状语，from the Antarctic to the Arctic 是解释说明前面的"海洋中的各处"，and 是并列连词，at the deepest point of the ocean 是另一个地点状语，the Mariana trench 是前面词组的同位语，可以译为并列结构或主谓结构。

第四步 翻译来了

本特森（Bengtsson）说："从南极到北极，再到海洋最深处的马里亚纳海沟，在海洋的各个角落都发现了塑料。"

> ### 本句考点总结
>
> 　　第一，本句出现了被动语态的译法。被动语态是英文常见的一种形式，而在中文里常常少用"被"或者不用"被"。那么我们一般有什么样的译法呢？第一种是被动变主动，第二种是寻找替代词（比如："让……给""为……所"等结构），第三种是在科技文献中用"可以"来替代"被"，第四种是有"被"不用"被"。以上四种怎么用，那就看句子怎么通顺怎么翻译了啊！
>
> 　　第二，本句考查了英文同位语的译法。同位语是两个前后相互说明的名词或名词短语，比如 Beijing, the capital of China，有两种译法。第一种是"并列译法"，翻译为"中国的首都北京"，第二种是"主谓译法"，翻译为"北京是中国的首都"。具体用哪一种，可以根据句子具体情况而定，有时两种都是可以使用的。

13

"We need urgent action to reduce the flow of plastic into our seas and we need large-scale marine reserves — like a huge Antarctic ocean sanctuary which over 1.6m people are calling for — to protect marine life and our oceans for future generations."

第一步 词汇解析

① large-scale，形容词，表示"大规模的、大批的、大范围的"，比如：The United States is making preparations for a large-scale airlift of 1,200 American citizens.（美国正在为运送 1 200 名美国公民的大规模空运做准备。）

② reserve，名词，表示"（动植物）保护区、自然保护区"，比如：Marine biologists are calling for Cardigan Bay to be created a marine nature reserve to protect the dolphins.（海洋生物学家号召将卡迪根湾建成一个海洋自然保护区来保护海豚。）

③ call for，动词词组，表示"呼吁、要求"，比如：It's a situation that calls for a blend of delicacy and force.（这种情况下需要的是刚柔并济。）

第二步 注意断句

"We need urgent action /to reduce the flow of plastic /into our seas /and we need large-scale marine reserves — / like a huge Antarctic ocean sanctuary /which over 1.6m people are calling for — /to protect marine life and our oceans for future generations."

第三步 句型解析

① 本句中，We need urgent action 是主谓宾结构，to 引导不定式作目的状语，reduce the flow of plastic into our seas 是动宾结构，这里的 flow 是典型的抽象名词，有动词词根，翻译为"流入"。and 是并列连词，we need large-scale marine reserves 是主谓宾结构，之后的破折号依旧保留，like 表示举例，a huge Antarctic ocean sanctuary 是名词短语，后面 which 引导了定语从句，从句较短，可以采用前置译法，后面的破折

依旧保留，to 引导不定式作目的状语，protect marine life and our oceans for future generations 是动宾关系。

第四步 翻译来了

"我们需要采取紧急的行动，减少塑料流入海洋，我们需要建立大规模的海洋保护区——比如超过 160 万人正在呼吁建立的大型南极海洋保护区——目的是为子孙后代保护海洋生物和海洋。"

本句考点总结

第一，本句出现了英文定语从句的译法。一般来说，定语从句按照"短前长后"的译法处理。较短的定语从句可以前置，较长的定语从句可以后置，这一切都取决于句子的通顺，并没有绝对的前置和后置译法。

第二，本句当中考查了"抽象名词"的译法。抽象名词一般处于冠词之后，又在介词之前，以"the + 抽象名词 + of"的形式居多。一般来说，抽象名词有两种译法。第一种，若抽象名词有动词词根，则翻译为动词，比如 the suggestion of mine，翻译为"我建议"，而不是"我的建议"；第二种，若抽象名词没有动词词根，可以增动词翻译，比如 the spirit of our nation，翻译为"我们民族所具有的精神"，而不是"我们民族的精神"。

译后总结

这篇文章探讨了世界海洋污染问题以及应对的策略，也是典型的外刊文章。文章中也就这么几个常见的翻译现象：被动语态的翻译、定语从句的翻译、抽象名词的译法等，其实大家看完这本书就会发现，外刊的套路就是这些，也没有什么新鲜的知识了，所以要牢牢掌握这些方法。

第四节 2018 年下半年三级笔译汉译英

原文（请先通读全文）

河南是中华民族和文明的重要发源地。中国四大发明中，指南针，造纸技术和火药都发明于河南。

河南拥有厚重的文化历史，大量的历史文物，文物数量居全国首位。河南拥有大量的历史文物和文化遗迹，8 处国家级风景名胜、358 个国家重点文物保护单位、4 个世界级地质公园、11 个国家级自然保护区。

河南是中国重要的经济大省，2017 国内生产总值稳居中国第 5 位。2017 年河南生产总值 44 988 亿元，比上年增长 7.8%，人均生产总值 47 130 元，增长 7.4%。粮食种植面积达 10 135 千公顷，粮食产量 5 973.4 万吨，比上年增加 26.8 万吨。

全部工业增加值 18 807 亿元，增长 7.4%，社会消费品零售总额 19 666 亿元，增长 11.6%。全民居民消费价格比上年上涨 1.4%。

河南是"一带一路"的重要中心。河南已经与200多个国家和地区建立贸易联系。河南要以其更有吸引力的政策，更友好的营商环境，广迎四海宾客，实现更高层次的互利共赢。

2018年下半年的CATTI汉译英介绍了中国河南省的主要情况，这种题材在以前的考试中都没有出现过，当年在出现时引起了很大的反响，其实主要还是考生对数字翻译不是特别敏感，简单一句话：阿拉伯数字基本照抄下来就行，不需要做什么更改，其余的翻译现象还是比较老套。

1 河南是中华民族和文明的重要发源地。中国四大发明中，指南针，造纸技术和火药都发明于河南。

第一步 词汇解析

① 河南，Henan Province，地名，翻译时应补全，翻译为"河南省"。"河南"应用汉语拼音进行音译，首字母大写，写为一个单词Henan，后加省份Province，首字母大写，中国的其他省份也是相同的译法。

② 中华民族和文明，the Chinese nation and civilization，名词词组，这里表达的意思是"中华民族和（中华）文明"。

③ 发源地，birthplace，名词，比如：Athens, the birthplace of the ancient Olympics（雅典，古代奥林匹克运动的发祥地）。

④ 中国四大发明，ancient China's four great inventions，名词词组。四大发明起源于古代，所以翻译为ancient。四大发明，four great inventions，专有名词，比如：Do you know China's four great inventions?（你知道中国的四大发明吗？）

⑤ 指南针，compass，名词，比如：The compass needle was pointing north.（罗盘指针指向北方。）

⑥ 造纸技术，paper-making，名词，比如：Bark may be used as raw material for paper-making.（树皮可以做造纸的原料。）

⑦ 火药，gunpowder，名词，比如：The potentially lethal device was made from a length of hose packed with gunpowder, primers, and shrapnel.（这个能致命的装置是用一根装满火药、引信和弹片的软管做出来的。）四大发明之一的"活字印刷术"，翻译为typography。

第二步 动词定位

河南是中华民族和文明的重要发源地。中国四大发明中，指南针，造纸技术和火药都发明于河南。

第三步 句型解析

① 第一句中，"河南"是主语，"是"是谓语，"中华民族和文明的重要发源地"是宾语，宾语中有"的"，所以使用of结构，翻译为an important birthplace of the Chinese nation and civilization，因为本句是对于一般事实的陈述，所以翻译为一般现在时会好一些。

② 第二句中，"中国四大发明中"是状语，表示"在……其中"，用of结构翻译为定语会更好。"指南针，造纸技术和火药"是主语，"都发明于"是谓语，是典型的隐藏被动语态，表示"被发明"，"河南"是

地点状语，因为前文已经出现了 Henan Province，所以这里使用部分名词 the province 的译法。这里要注意的是有关总述和分述的问题，中文常常分述，英文常常总述，所以这里翻译为 Three of ancient China's four great inventions，和后面的三种东西形成同位语关系是非常合适的。

第四步　翻译来了

Henan Province is an important birthplace of the Chinese nation and civilization. Three of ancient China's four great inventions, the compass, the paper-making and the gunpowder were made in the province.

> **本句考点总结**
>
> 本句出现了中文里隐藏被动语态的译法。被动语态是英文常见的一种形式，而在中文里常常少用"被"或者不用"被"。那么中文当中一般如何隐藏被动语态呢？第一种是被动变主动，第二种是寻找替代词（比如："让……给""为……所"等结构），第三种是在科技文献中用"可以"来替代"被"，第四种是有"被"不用"被"。在中文里识别出来以上四种隐藏的被动语态不是一件容易的事，需要大家仔细认真地识别这种现象，在汉译英时体现出来。

2

河南拥有厚重的文化历史，大量的历史文物，文物数量居全国首位。河南拥有大量的历史文物和文化遗迹，8处国家级风景名胜、358个国家重点文物保护单位、4个世界级地质公园、11个国家级自然保护区。

第一步　词汇解析

① 拥有……，boast/be home to，动词/动词词组。
boast，动词，比如：The houses will boast the latest energy-saving technology.（这些房屋将采用最新的节能技术。）
be home to，动词词组，比如：Jamaica is home to over two million people.（牙买加是两百多万人的家乡。）

② 厚重的文化历史，a time-honored history and profound culture，名词词组。
历史悠久的，time-honored，形容词，比如：a time-honored practice（传统的习俗）。这一单词仅用于名词前，作定语，我们常说的"老字号"，可以翻译为 time-honored brand。

③ 历史文物，cultural relics，名词词组，比如：He enjoys collecting Chinese cultural relics.（他喜欢收藏中国文物。）
遗物，relic，名词，比如：a museum with relics of great explorers（收藏伟大探险家遗物的博物馆）。

④ ……数量，number，动词，比如：The firm's staff numbers 46 persons.（这家公司有职员46人。）

⑤ 文化遗迹，cultural heritage sites，名词词组，比如：World heritage sites and cultural relics in Sichuan Province is top-ranked nationwide.（四川省的世界遗产和文化遗存都位居全国前列。）
遗留物、传统，heritage，名词，比如：a rich heritage of folklore（丰富的民间文学）。

⑥ 国家级风景名胜，national places of interest，名词词组。
风景名胜，places of interest，名词词组，比如：The places of interest in China are too numerous to mention.

（中国的名胜古迹不胜枚举。）

❼ 国家重点文物保护单位，major historic and cultural sites under state protection，名词词组。

【同义词辨析】

historic：通常指历史上有名的、具有历史意义或历史价值的；

historical：通常指历史上的或历史的，侧重历史上出现过或与历史有关的。

在……的保护下，under the protection of，介词词组，比如：Many British wild animals are now under the protection of the Wildlife and Countryside Act.（英国的许多野生动物现在受到《野生生物及乡野法》的保护。）

❽ 世界级地质公园，global geological park，名词词组。

地质的，geological，形容词，比如：With geological maps, books, and atlases you can find out all the proven sites of precious minerals.（有了地质地图、书籍和地图册，你就可以找到所有已探明的珍贵矿藏的位置。）

❾ 国家级自然保护区，national nature reserves，名词词组。

自然保护区，nature reserves，名词词组，比如：set up new nature reserves for pandas（建立新的熊猫自然保护区）。

第二步 动词定位

河南拥有厚重的文化历史，大量的历史文物，文物数量居全国首位。河南拥有大量的历史文物和文化遗迹，8处国家级风景名胜、358个国家重点文物保护单位、4个世界级地质公园、11个国家级自然保护区。

第三步 句型解析

❶ 第一句中，"河南"是主语，"拥有"是谓语，"厚重的文化历史"是第一个宾语，"大量的历史文物"是第二个宾语，"文物数量"是第二个主语，"居"是谓语，"全国首位"是宾语，这么分析确实没有错，这么翻译也没有错，两个动词之间用and连接即可。但是如何让句子显得更加有层次感呢？那肯定是仔细理解两个句子之间的关系，第一个句子的动词是"拥有"，第二个句子的动词是"居"，但是第一个句子宾语中的"历史文物"和第二句中的"文物数量居全国首位"有一定关系吧？所以这里可以这样来理解："拥有"是第一个动词，但是翻译两次，第一次是在句首翻译成Boast，第二次是翻译成核心谓语be home to，后面的"居"翻译成伴随结构，这样整个句子成了"下沉+核心+伴随"的结构，是不是更加精妙呢？

❷ 第二句中，"河南"是主语，"拥有"是谓语，"大量的历史文物和文化遗迹，8处国家级风景名胜、358个国家重点文物保护单位、4个世界级地质公园、11个国家级自然保护区"都是宾语，其实这里考查了名词词组的译法，没有任何结构上的难点。但是大家要注意代词的小知识，本文多次出现"河南"，中文常用名词，而英文则要用各种方法来规避，比如第一次用全称，第二次用半称，第三次用代词，第四次直接用there be句型。

第四步 翻译来了

Boasting a time-honored history and profound culture, it is home to a great many of cultural heritage sites, ranking the first in China in terms of cultural relics. There are 8 national places of interest, 358 major historic and cultural sites under state protection, 4 global geological parks and 11 national nature reserves in Henan.

> **本句考点总结**
>
> 汉译英句子中并列、伴随、下沉的结构。中文常常会出现多个句子聚集的情况,那么我们在翻译时需要考虑将这些句子进行"分堆"。但是"分堆"之后,一个句子中也可能会出现两个动词或两组动词,那么有两个动词或两组动词的句子我们该如何进行翻译呢?比如:"我坐在那里看书",这里有两个动词,一个是"坐",一个是"看",我们翻译时便会有三种方法:
>
> 第一种并列(两个动词并列的译法,使用并列连词连接,两个动词之间不一定是"并列"关系):I sat there and read a book.
>
> 第二种伴随(将第二个动词翻译为二谓语,分词、从句、状语等都可以):I sat there reading a book.
>
> 第三种下沉(将第一个动词翻译为二谓语,分词、从句、状语等都可以):Sitting there, I read a book.
>
> 需要说明的是,并列、伴随和下沉只是动词的形式问题,不代表动词之间的逻辑关系,用这三种形式翻译两个动词或两组动词都是可以的,大家可以根据句子上下文的关系来判断使用。

3 河南是中国重要的经济大省,2017 国内生产总值稳居中国第 5 位。2017 年河南生产总值 44 988 亿元,比上年增长 7.8%,人均生产总值 47 130 元,增长 7.4%。粮食种植面积达 10 135 千公顷,粮食产量 5 973.4 万吨,比上年增加 26.8 万吨。

第一步 词汇解析

① 经济大省,major provincial economy,名词词组,意思是"主要的地方经济"。
省域经济、地方经济,provincial economy,名词词组,比如:Marine products contribute a significant share to the provincial economy.(水制品为地方经济做出了巨大贡献。)

② 国内生产总值,GDP,专有名词,全称为 Gross Domestic Product。
经济领域常用缩写:
消费物价指数,CPI,专有名词,全称为 Consumer Price Index;
国民生产总值,GNP,专有名词,全称为 Gross National Product。

③ 万亿,trillion,名词,比如:a 4 trillion dollar debt(一笔 4 万亿美元的债务)。

④ 上年,the previous year,名词词组,比如:CBS's ratings again showed huge improvement over the previous year.(哥伦比亚广播公司的收视率比过去一年又有了大幅提高。)"上年"的意思就是"去年",也就是前一年。我们常说的"前年",翻译为 the year before last。

⑤ 人均,per capita,形容词,比如:They have the world's largest per capita income.(他们有世界上最高的人均收入。)per,介词,表示"每",比如:per week(每周)、per month(每月)、per hour(每小时)。

⑥ 粮食种植面积,the sown area of grain,名词词组,比如:keep the sown area of grain stable(稳定粮食种植面积)。
种植面积,the sown area,名词词组,比如:the wheat sown area(小麦种植面积)。

⑦ 公顷,hectare,名词,比如:3 tons of soya beans per hectare(每公顷约 3 吨的大豆)。

⑧ 粮食产量，the total output of grain，名词词组，比如：The total output of grain in 2008 was 528.50 million tons.（2008年粮食总产量为52 850万吨。）

⑨ 比……，compared with，动词词组，词组原形为：compare with，比如：It's much easier compared with last time.（这与上次相比容易得多。）

⑩ 本句涉及大量如"上升"等描述趋势的词汇，这类词汇的表达较为灵活，既可以使用名词，也可以使用动词，但要注意区分介词to和by，to表示"……至"，by表示"……了"。

第二步 动词定位

河南**是**中国重要的经济大省，2017国内生产总值**稳居**中国第5位。2017年河南生产总值44 988亿元，比上年**增长**7.8%，人均生产总值47 130元，**增长**7.4%。粮食种植面积**达**10 135千公顷，粮食产量5 973.4万吨，比上年**增加**26.8万吨。

第三步 句型解析

❶ 第一句中，"河南"是主语，"是"是谓语，"中国重要的经济大省"是宾语，"2017国内生产总值"是主语，"稳居"是谓语，"中国第5位"是宾语，两个句子之间用and连接即可，还是比较简单的，但是如果分析一下这一句和下一句之间的关系，就会发现一些问题。

❷ 第二句中，"2017年河南生产总值"是主语，这里的谓语"达到/是"省略了，宾语是"44 988亿元"，"比上年增长7.8%"是状语，第二分句的主语是"人均生产总值"，这里的谓语"达到/是"省略了，宾语是"47 130元"，"增长7.4%"是状语，两句之间依旧是并列关系，可以用并列连词连接，但是再看看和上一句的关系，就会发现第一句的第一分句是总述，第二分句开始谈经济，第二句的第一分句谈的是GDP，第二分句谈的是人均GDP，应该怎么做呢？是不是先翻译第一句的第一分句，单独成句，第一句的第二分句和第二句的第一分句合译，第二句的第二分句单独成句呢？以上的解析能理解吗？当然按照前面的分析翻译也是可以的哦！这就是实务这门课考到60分和考到90分的区别！

❸ 第三句中，"粮食种植面积"是主语，"达"是谓语，"10 135千公顷"是宾语，第二分句中，"粮食产量"是主语，这里的谓语"达到/是"省略了，宾语是"5 973.4万吨"，"比上年增加26.8万吨"是状语。这里谈两个问题：第一，关于数字翻译的问题，阿拉伯数字照抄即可，比如2007年翻译为2007，但是有些大数字要注意，比如26.8万，翻译为268,000非常合适，千分位用逗号隔开，但是5 973.4万翻译为59,734,000则不是很合适，因为数字太长，显得不协调，翻译为59.734 million更加合适，即出现了百万以上的大数字时用"整数/小数 + million/billion/trillion"更好一些；第二，本句也是两个并列结构，但总是用并列译法也不是很好，结构有些枯燥，所以翻译第二分句时译者使用了同位语结构，直接用主语和宾语，省略了谓语，这样也是可以的，后面的状语"增长"，也翻译为同位语an increase of。

第四步 翻译来了

Henan is China's major provincial economy. Its GDP of 2017, fifth in China, was 4.4 988 trillion Yuan, up by 7.8% over the previous year. In terms of its GDP per capita, the figure was 47,130 Yuan, up by 7.4%. The sown area of grain covered 10.135 million hectares and the total output of grain 59.734 million tons, an increase of 268,000 tons compared with that of the previous year.

> **本句考点总结**
>
> 在翻译中，无论是英译汉，还是汉译英，我们常常将长句断成短句，然后一句一句翻译，短的句子由于上下文的联系，也可以放在一起翻译。非文学翻译中，分译与合译出现得比较少，一般按照正常句子翻译即可，但是在文学翻译中出现得特别多，特别要读懂上下文内在的关系。分译与合译没有固定的翻译规则，而且每个译者的尺度也是不同的，重要的前提就是句意正确和句意通顺。

  全部工业增加值 18 807 亿元，增长 7.4%，社会消费品零售总额 19 666 亿元，增长 11.6%。全民居民消费价格比上年上涨 1.4%。

第一步 词汇解析

❶ 工业增加值，the value added of the industrial sector，名词词组。工业部门，the industrial sector，名词词组，比如：Natural gas consumption increases in the industrial sector and the electric power sector.（工业和电力行业中，天然气消费将上升。）

经济小常识：
　　工业增加值是指工业企业在报告期内以货币形式表现的工业生产活动的最终成果。

❷ 社会消费品，consumer goods，名词词组，比如：The choice of consumer goods available in local shops is small.（本地商店中可供选择的社会消费品很少。）

❸ 零售总额，the total retail sales，名词词组，比如：That is just about a tenth of the total retail sales.（这大约是零售总额的十分之一。）

❹ 全民，all residents，名词词组，比如：Not all residents are in opposition to the offshore oil plans.（并非所有的居民都反对近海石油计划。）句中"全民"的意思是"所有居民"。

❺ 居民消费价格，the consumption prices，名词词组。

❻ 比上年……，on year-over-year basis，介词词组，比如：In America, consumer prices in January were up 4.3% on year-over-year basis.（今年一月，美国的消费价格同比上涨了 4.3%。）

经济小常识：
　　同比就是"比去年同期"，比如：今年 8 月比去年 8 月。
　　环比就是"比上个月"，今年 8 月比今年 7 月。
　　当然这里的单位不一定是月，可以是任何时间单位。

第二步 动词定位

　　全部工业增加值 18 807 亿元，<u>增长</u> 7.4%，社会消费品零售总额 19 666 亿元，<u>增长</u> 11.6%。全民居民消费价格比上年 <u>上涨</u> 1.4%。

第三步 句型解析

❶ 第一句中，"全部工业增加值"是主语，这里的谓语"达到/是"省略了，宾语是"18 807 亿元"，"增长

7.4%"是状语,第二分句"社会消费品零售总额"是主语,这里的谓语"达到/是"省略了,宾语是"19 666 亿元","增长 11.6%"是状语。两个句子之间可以是并列关系,使用 and 连接是合适的,当然和参考译文一样,使用分译的方法也可以。

❷ 第二句中,"全民居民消费价格"是主语,"比上年"是时间状语,"上涨"是谓语,"1.4%"是宾语,参考译文增加了"在河南""在 2017 年",这都是对象词或是表示范围的词,若看不出来也是可以不增的。

❸ 做一点小小的说明:文章中所有的"增加""下降",只要不带"到(to)",都是表示"了(by)",也就是说中文"增加"和"增加了"是一回事,这点务必要注意,特别是在口译考试中出现得特别多!

第四步 翻译来了

The total value added of the industrial sector was 1.8 807 trillion Yuan, up by 7.4% over the previous year. And the total retail sales of consumer goods reached 1.9 666 trillion Yuan, up by 11.6% over the previous year. The consumption prices of all residents in Henan in 2017 went up by 1.4% on year-over-year basis.

> **本句考点总结**
>
> 本句考查了英汉互译增减词的问题,一般来说英译汉增词,汉译英减词,常见增词的种类有:一、增加对象词(范围词),这是由上文缺少句子的某个部分造成的;二、增加范畴词,这是较难的一部分,常见的范畴词有"水平、方式、方法、问题、情况、途径和方面",但是不仅仅有这些,还有很多其他的;三、增加评论性词,这些常常出现在文学翻译中;四、增加动词,会在动词的"分配译法"中说明这点。

河南是"一带一路"的重要中心。河南已经与 200 多个国家和地区建立贸易联系。河南要以其更有吸引力的政策,更友好的营商环境,广迎四海宾客,实现更高层次的互利共赢。

第一步 词汇解析

❶ 重要中心,an important pivot,名词词组,比如:Human capital is an important pivot point of knowledge economy.(人力资本是知识经济最重要的支撑点。)中心点,pivot,名词,比如:West Africa was the pivot of the cocoa trade.(西非是可可豆贸易的中心。)

❷ "一带一路",the Belt and Road Initiative,专有名词,注意首字母大写。

文化小常识:

"一带一路"是"丝绸之路经济带"和"21 世纪海上丝绸之路"的简称。2013 年 9 月和 10 月中国国家主席习近平分别提出建设"新丝绸之路经济带"和"21 世纪海上丝绸之路"的合作倡议。

倡议,initiative,名词,比如:a United Nations peace initiative(联合国的和平倡议)。

❸ 与……建立联系，establish connections with，动词词组，比如：Clients can break the time and geographical limits to establish connections with enterprises.（客户不受地域限制与企业建立联系）。

❹ 更有吸引力的政策，more attractive policies，名词词组。有吸引力的，attractive，形容词，比如：goods attractive in price and quality（价廉物美的货物）。

❺ 更友好的营商环境，more friendly business environment，名词词组。
营商环境，business environment，名词词组，比如 international business environment（国际营商环境）。

❻ 广迎四海宾客，open wider to the outside，动词词组。这类具有中国特色的短语，建议采用直接解释的方法翻译，也就是"扩大对外开放"。

❼ 更高层次的，at higher level，介词词组，比如：This indicates that where equal spatial ability exists, women can perform at a higher level than men.（这表明，在空间能力平等的情况下，女性能比男性表现出更高的水平。）

❽ 互利共赢，mutual benefit and win-win cooperation，名词词组。"互利"和"共赢"的意思相似，只翻译一次也可以，翻译为 mutual benefit。

第二步 动词定位

河南是"一带一路"的重要中心。河南已经与 200 多个国家和地区建立贸易联系。河南要以其更有吸引力的政策，更友好的营商环境，广迎四海宾客，实现更高层次的互利共赢。

第三步 句型解析

❶ 第一句中，"河南"是主语，"是"是谓语，"'一带一路'的重要中心"是宾语，但是这句太短，可以和后面一句进行合译，并且两句的主语相同，可以用下沉结构，把这里的"是"翻译为 as 结构，那么这两句的核心谓语是"建立"，"贸易联系"是宾语，"与 200 多个国家和地区"是状语结构。总之这样的结构需要大家学会翻译，如何处理两个动词之间的关系是汉译英的核心问题之一。

❷ 第二句中，"河南"是主语，"要以其更有吸引力的政策，更友好的营商环境"是状语，这里的"以"可以处理为介词 With，核心谓语是"广迎"，"四海宾客"是宾语，解释一下就是"实现更大的对外开放"，第二个动词是"实现"，宾语是"更高层次的互利共赢"，这两个动词之间可以理解为并列关系，也可以理解为目的关系，还可以理解为伴随关系，参考译文理解成了伴随关系。

第四步 翻译来了

As an important pivot of the Belt and Road Initiative, Henan has established trade connections with over 200 countries and regions in the world. With more attractive policies and more friendly business environment, it will open wider to the outside, thus achieving mutual benefit and win-win cooperation at higher level.

译后总结

这篇文章介绍了河南省当前的一些情况和整体的发展形势，要注意两个动词的句子如何翻译，以及分译和合译的使用，特别要注意数字该如何翻译，这个知识点在后面几年的考试中出现得不是特别多，但是也不能掉以轻心，谁也不能保证未来的考试中不会出现。

第五章
2017年实务真题解析与方法技巧

第一节　2017年上半年三级笔译英译汉

All Luciano Faggiano wanted when he purchased the seemingly unremarkable building at 56 Via Ascanio Grandi, was to open a restaurant. The only problem was the toilet. Sewage kept backing up.

So Mr. Faggiano enlisted his two older sons to help him dig a trench and investigate. He predicted the job would take about a week.

"We found underground corridors and other rooms, so we kept digging," said Mr. Faggiano, 60. His search for a sewage pipe, which began in 2000, became one family's tale of discovery.

Lecce was once a critical crossroads in the Mediterranean. Severo Martini, a member of the City Council, said archaeological relics turn up on a regular basis — and can present a headache for urban planning.

A project to build a shopping mall had to be redesigned after the discovery of an ancient Roman temple beneath the site of a planned parking lot.

One week quickly passed, as father and sons discovered a tomb of the Messapians, who lived in the region centuries before the birth of Jesus. Soon, the family discovered a chamber used to store grain by the ancient Romans.

If this history only later became clear, what was immediately obvious was that finding the pipe would be a much bigger project than Mr. Faggiano had anticipated.

He did not initially tell his wife about the extent of the work. He tied a rope around the chest of his youngest son, Davide, then 12, and lowered him to dig in small, darkened openings. "I made sure to tell him not to tell his mama," he said.

His wife, soon became suspicious. "We had all these dirty clothes, every day," she said. "I didn't understand what was going on."

After watching the Faggiano men haul away debris in the back seat of the family car, neighbors also became suspicious and notified the authorities. Investigators arrived and shut down the excavations, warning Mr. Faggiano against operating an unapproved archaeological work site. Mr. Faggiano responded that he was just looking for a sewage pipe.

A year passed. Finally, Mr. Faggiano was allowed to resume his pursuit of the sewage pipe on condition that heritage officials observed the work. An underground treasure house emerged, as the family uncovered ancient vases, Roman devotional bottles, an ancient ring with Christian symbols, medieval artifacts, hidden frescoes and more.

Today, the building is Museum Faggiano, an independent archaeological museum authorized by the Lecce government.

Mr. Faggiano is now satisfied with his museum, but he has not forgotten about the restaurant. A few years into his excavation, he finally found his sewage pipe. It was, indeed, broken.

He has since bought another building and is again planning for a restaurant, assuming it does not need any renovations. "I still want it," he said of the restaurant. "I'm very stubborn."

2017 年上半年的 CATTI 英译汉也是外刊中的文章，主要讲述了意大利某城市一家人在挖掘下水道的时候发现了一片古代城池的废墟，后续围绕这个主题而展开的故事。这篇文章和我们之前做的英译汉非常相似，重点还是要掌握有关直接引语和间接引语的译法，各种翻译现象也很多，需要大家识别。

> **1** All Luciano Faggiano wanted when he purchased the seemingly unremarkable building at 56 Via Ascanio Grandi, was to open a restaurant. The only problem was the toilet. Sewage kept backing up.

第一步 词汇解析

① Luciano Faggiano，卢西亚诺·法加诺，人名，这里采用的是音译法，注意名和姓之间要加·，翻译英文人名不确定时，可以使用音译法，然后把英文人名抄下来，放在括号里，这样保险一些。

② seemingly，副词，表示"好似、看上去"，比如：A seemingly endless line of trucks waits in vain to load up.（看上去没有尽头的一排卡车徒劳地等着装货。）

③ unremarkable，形容词，表示"普通的、不值得注意的"，比如：a tall, lean man, with an unremarkable face（一个又高又瘦、长相普通的男子）。

④ sewage，名词，表示"（下水道的）污水、污物"，比如：treatment of raw sewage（原始污物的处理）。

⑤ back up，动词词组，表示"堵塞"，比如：The port was backed up.（港口拥塞了。）

第二步 注意断句

All Luciano Faggiano wanted /when he purchased the seemingly unremarkable building /at 56 Via Ascanio Grandi, /was to open a restaurant. /The only problem was the toilet. /Sewage kept backing up.

第三步 句型解析

① All Luciano Faggiano wanted 是第一句的主语，all 是主语核心词，Luciano Faggiano wanted 是定语从句，定语从句较短，可以采用前置译法。when he purchased the seemingly unremarkable building at 56 Via Ascanio Grandi 是 when 引导的时间状语从句，一定要分析清楚这个时间状语从句到底和哪个动词有关，这样翻译时才不会出错。when 引导的这个句子放在句中，把它拿到句首或者句末来分析，相对来说就比较简单了，你再看看这样的结构：When he purchased the seemingly unremarkable building at 56 Via Ascanio Grandi, all Luciano Faggiano wanted was to open a restaurant. 但是你在翻译的时候要注意从句当中代词 he 的译法，中文里哪个句子先出现，哪个句子当中是名词，也就是说这里的 he 需要翻译成卢西亚诺·法加诺（Luciano Faggiano），而不是"他"。而且还要注意这个时间状语从句中的地点状语 at,

先翻译地点状语再翻译"房子",这样会更加通顺一些;而且译文当中也"炫技"了,将较长的形容词短语 the seemingly unremarkable 拿出来单独翻译,译为"而这栋房子似乎不怎么起眼",这种译法实际上是我们所说的文学译法,但是在非文学当中也可以使用。本句的主句是 All Luciano Faggiano wanted was to open a restaurant,若翻译为"他想要的一切就是开一家饭店",再和从句相联系,这翻译腔也太严重了,参考译文把时间状语从句和主句进行了"融合",然后长的形容词和副词单独成句,放在句子末尾,这样的句式结构难道不是非常符合中文的表达习惯吗?

❷ 第二句 The only problem was the toilet 是主系表结构,第三句 Sewage kept backing up 是主谓宾结构,需要分析这两个短句之间的关系,第一句说的是"马桶的问题",第二句解释了"马桶有什么问题",所以两个短句应进行合译,这样整个句子的结构就非常明确了。

第四步 翻译来了

卢西亚诺·法加诺(Luciano Faggiano)当初买下了阿斯卡尼奥格兰迪街56号(56 Via Ascanio Grandi)这栋房子就是为了开家餐馆,而这栋房子似乎不怎么起眼。这地方只有一个问题,就是厕所里的马桶,因为下水道总是堵塞。

本句考点总结

第一,本句出现了英文定语从句的译法。一般来说,定语从句按照"短前长后"的译法处理,较短的定语从句可以前置,较长的定语从句可以后置,这一切都取决于句子的通顺,并没有绝对的前置和后置译法。

第二,关于英文代词的译法。英文中需要翻译的代词主要指第三人称 he,she,it,they 及其相应宾格和指示代词 this 和 that。这些单词在翻译时一定要注意,主要采用"不抽象、不具体"的译法。不能翻译成具体的人或物,但是也不能翻译为"他""她""它""他们""这个""那个",要注意取中间的译法。

第三,在翻译中,无论是英译汉,还是汉译英,我们常常将长句断成短句,然后一句一句翻译,短的句子由于上下文的联系,也可以放在一起翻译。非文学翻译中,分译与合译出现得比较少,一般按照正常句子翻译即可,但是在文学翻译中出现得特别多,特别要读懂上下文内在的关系,分译与合译没有固定的翻译规则,而且每个译者的尺度也是不同的,重要的前提就是句意正确和句意通顺。

2

So Mr. Faggiano enlisted his two older sons to help him dig a trench and investigate. He predicted the job would take about a week.

第一步 词汇解析

❶ enlist,动词,表示"招募、征募",比如:Many men were enlisted during the war.(战争时期许多男子应募入伍。)

❷ dig,动词,表示"挖掘",比如:I grabbed the spade and started digging.(我抓起铁锹开始挖了起来。)

❸ trench，名词，表示"沟渠"，比如：an irrigation trench（灌溉渠）。
❹ predict，动词，表示"预计"，比如：The weather scientists predicted a cold winter.（气象专家预计冬天会很冷。）

第二步 注意断句

So /Mr. Faggiano enlisted his two older sons to help him dig a trench and investigate. /He predicted the job would take about a week.

第三步 句型解析

❶ So 引导表示因果的并列句，翻译为"所以"。
❷ Mr. Faggiano enlisted his two older sons 是本句的主干，是主谓宾结构，这里的 enlist 翻译为"招来"比较好，to help him dig a trench and investigate 是 to 引导的不定式短语，为目的状语，也就是"来帮忙挖沟，调查一下这件事情"。
❸ 第二句中，He predicted 是主谓结构，后面接宾语从句，宾语从句 the job would take about a week 也是主谓宾结构，较为简单可以直接翻译。

第四步 翻译来了

因此，法加诺先生招来他的两个大儿子帮忙挖沟，查查是怎么回事。他预计，这项工作大概会花上一个星期。

"We found underground corridors and other rooms, so we kept digging," said Mr. Faggiano, 60. His search for a sewage pipe, which began in 2000, became one family's tale of discovery.

第一步 词汇解析

❶ corridor，名词，表示"走廊"，比如：There were doors on both sides of the corridor.（走廊的两侧都有门。）
❷ a sewage pipe，名词词组，表示"下水道"，比如：Bathroom had less of a sewage pipe smell.（浴室的管道有点儿污水味。）
❸ tale，名词，表示"（尤指包含惊险内容的）故事"，比如：He listened to my tale of woe.（他听了我悲伤的故事。）

第二步 注意断句

"We found underground corridors and other rooms, /so we kept digging," /said Mr. Faggiano, /60. /His search for a sewage pipe, /which began in 2000, /became one family's tale of discovery.

第三步 句型解析

❶ 第一句是典型的直接引语，所谓直接引语就是有双引号的句子，在翻译时需要保留双引号，说话人在什么位置，就放在什么位置翻译，尽量不要改变句子的结构，当然，说话人放在句首翻译也是一种常见的译法。

❷ 直接引语中，We found underground corridors and other rooms 是主谓宾结构，so 连接并列句，表示"所以"，we kept digging 是主谓宾结构，后面的 said Mr. Faggiano 是完全倒装结构，翻译时需要把人放在前面，把"说"放在后面，后面的数字 60 表示"年纪"，所以翻译为"60 岁的法加诺先生"即可。

❸ 第二句中，His search for a sewage pipe 是主语，但是要注意主语当中非常典型的现象，search 是典型的抽象名词，有动词词根，可以翻译为动词"寻找"，所以主语可以译为"他寻找下水道"，但是这么翻译就变成了主谓宾结构，所以在这里进行增词，翻译为"他寻找下水道这项工作"。逗号之后是非限定性定语从句 which began in 2000，这里可以使用后置译法，became 是主句的系动词，one family's tale of discovery 是主句的表语，可以把 discovery 认为是抽象名词，因为有动词词根，所以翻译为动词"去探索"，翻译为名词"探索的故事"也是可以的。记住一句非常重要的话：译文直译时若特别通顺，则直译，不要想着那些乱七八糟的方法，方法是用来解决问题的，不是增加麻烦的。

第四步 翻译来了

60 岁的法加诺先生说："我们发现了一些地下走廊和其他一些房间，所以我们就一直挖了下去。"法加诺这项寻找下水道的工作始于 2000 年，最后演变成了一个家庭探索的故事。

本句考点总结

第一，本句考查了英文直接引语的译法，最简单的译法就是保留冒号和双引号，说话人的位置和说话的内容都保持不变。即说话人在什么位置，就放在什么位置翻译，当然，说话人放在句首也是可以接受的。

第二，本句当中考查了"抽象名词"的译法。抽象名词一般处于冠词之后，又在介词之前，以"the + 抽象名词 + of"的形式居多。一般来说，抽象名词有两种译法。第一种，若抽象名词有动词词根，则翻译为动词，比如 the suggestion of mine，翻译为"我建议"，而不是"我的建议"；第二种，若抽象名词没有动词词根，可以增动词翻译，比如 the spirit of our nation，翻译为"我们民族所具有的精神"，而不是"我们民族的精神"。

第三，非限定性定语从句是用逗号隔开的定语从句，这样的句子一般都要采用后置译法，在翻译时需要翻译出关系代词 which，who 等词，指明这些词的指代关系，将这些代词翻译出来。

---

4 Lecce was once a critical crossroads in the Mediterranean. Severo Martini, a member of the City Council, said archaeological relics turn up on a regular basis — and can present a headache for urban planning.

第一步 词汇解析

❶ critical，形容词，表示"关键的、重要的"，比如：He says setting priorities is of critical importance.（他说确定轻重缓急至关重要。）

② Mediterranean，名词，地名，表示"地中海地区"，比如：one of the most dynamic and prosperous cities in the Mediterranean（地中海地区最具活力、最为繁荣的城市之一）。

地理小常识：

地中海是欧洲、非洲和亚洲大陆之间的一块海域，由北面的欧洲大陆、南面的非洲大陆和东面的亚洲大陆包围着，西面通过直布罗陀海峡与大西洋相连，是世界最大的陆间海。

③ member，名词，在这里表示"议员"，不是"成员"，比如：He was elected to Parliament as the Member for Leeds.（他被选入国会作为利兹市的议员。）

④ the City Council，名词词组，表示"市议会"，比如：The City Council has voted almost unanimously in favour.（市议会几乎全部投了赞成票。）

⑤ archaeological，形容词，表示"考古的、考古学的"，比如：These archaeological findings are part of the national patrimony.（这些考古发现属于国家文物。）

⑥ relic，名词，表示"遗物、遗迹"，比如：a cultural relic（文化遗迹）。

⑦ turn up，动词词组，表示"发现、找到"，比如：Investigations have never turned up any evidence.（调查从未发现过任何证据。）

⑧ on a regular basis，固定搭配，表示"经常地"，比如：I'm saving money on a regular basis.（我经常存钱。）

⑨ present，动词，表示"呈现、表示"，比如：a case that presents some difficulty（有些棘手的案子）。

第二步 注意断句

Lecce was once a critical crossroads /in the Mediterranean. /Severo Martini, /a member of the City Council, / said archaeological relics turn up /on a regular basis — /and can present a headache /for urban planning.

第三步 句型解析

① 第一句中，Lecce was once a critical crossroads 是主系表结构，in the Mediterranean 是地点状语，主语 Lecce 可能不太熟悉，所以翻译时可以用音译的方法，后面用括号把单词抄下来，其余部分直接翻译即可。

② 第二句中，Severo Martini 是主语，翻译方法和前面的人名相同，a member of the City Council 是前面名词的同位语，同位语的译法一般来说有两种：第一种是"并列译法"，用逗号隔开，翻译为"塞维洛·马尔蒂尼（Severo Martini），本市的一位市议会议员……"；第二种是"主谓译法"，翻译为"塞维洛·马尔蒂尼（Severo Martini）是本市的一位市议会议员，他……"。一般采用主谓译法，said 是本句的核心谓语，后面接宾语从句，archaeological relics 是主语，turn up 是第一组谓语，on a regular basis 是状语，表示程度，翻译为"经常"，之后的破折号可以保留，and 连接并列的谓语，can present 是第二组谓语，a headache for urban planning 是第二组宾语。这个宾语从句若直接翻译为"考古遗迹经常出现"，会很唐突，若在这里增对象词"这个城市"，整个句子就比较通顺了，翻译为"这个城市经常发现一些考古遗迹"。

第四步 翻译来了

莱切（Lecce）曾经是地中海地区一个重要的汇集地。塞维洛·马尔蒂尼（Severo Martini）是本市的一位市议会议员，他说这个城市经常发现一些考古遗迹——这一点也让城市的规划部门很烦心。

> ## 本句考点总结
>
> 第一，本句考查了英文同位语的译法。同位语是两个前后相互说明的名词或名词短语，比如 Beijing, the capital of China，有两种译法，第一种是"并列译法"，翻译为"中国的首都北京"；第二种是"主谓译法"，翻译为"北京是中国的首都"。具体用哪一种，可以根据句子具体情况而定，有时两种都是可以使用的。
>
> 第二，本句考查了英汉互译增减词的问题，一般来说英译汉增词，汉译英减词，常见增词的种类有：一、增加对象词（范围词），这是由上文缺少句子的某个部分造成的；二、增加范畴词，这是较难的一部分，常见的范畴词有"水平、方式、方法、问题、情况、途径和方面"，但是不仅仅有这些，还有很多其他的；三、增加评论性词，这些常常出现在文学翻译中；四、增加动词，会在动词的"分配译法"中说明这点。

5. A project to build a shopping mall had to be redesigned after the discovery of an ancient Roman temple beneath the site of a planned parking lot.

第一步 词汇解析

① redesign，动词，表示"重新设计"，比如：The hotel has recently been redesigned and redecorated.（该酒店最近刚进行了重新设计及装修。）

② temple，名词，表示"神殿、寺庙"，比如：We go to temple on Saturdays.（我们每个星期六去寺庙。）

③ beneath，介词，表示"在……之下"，比如：Four levels of parking beneath the theatre was not enough.（剧院底下的四层停车库还不够。）

④ site，名词，表示"地方、场所"，比如：I was working as a foreman on a building site.（我在一个建筑工地当工头。）

⑤ parking lot，名词词组，表示"停车场"，比如：The vehicles cluttered up the parking lot.（车辆停满了停车场。）

第二步 注意断句

A project to build a shopping mall had to be redesigned /after the discovery of an ancient Roman temple / beneath the site of a planned parking lot.

第三步 句型解析

① 本句的主语是 A project to build a shopping mall，注意其中有不定式短语 to do sth. 作定语，had to be redesigned 是本句的谓语，句子当中出现了被动语态，在翻译时可以使用"有被不用被"的译法，这样会比较通顺。

② after... 为时间状语，the discovery of an ancient Roman temple 中有抽象名词 discovery，该词有动词词根，可以翻译为动词"发现了"，beneath the site of a planned parking lot 是地点状语，这个时间状语原本是一个短语，出现动词后就可以翻译成一个句子。

第四步 翻译来了

因为原本规划的停车场下面发现了一座古罗马庙宇，在此之后，建设购物中心的规划就不得不重新设计了。

> **本句考点总结**
>
> 第一，本句出现了被动语态的译法。被动语态是英文常见的一种形式，而在中文里常常少用"被"或者不用"被"。那么我们一般有什么样的译法呢？第一种是被动变主动，第二种是寻找替代词（比如："让……给""为……所"等结构），第三种是在科技文献中用"可以"来替代"被"，第四种是有"被"不用"被"。以上四种怎么用，那就看句子怎么通顺怎么翻译了啊！
>
> 第二，本句当中考查了"抽象名词"的译法。抽象名词一般处于冠词之后，又在介词之前，以"the＋抽象名词＋of"的形式居多。一般来说，抽象名词有两种译法。第一种，若抽象名词有动词词根，则翻译为动词，比如 the suggestion of mine，翻译为"我建议"，而不是"我的建议"；第二种，若抽象名词没有动词词根，可以增动词翻译，比如 the spirit of our nation，翻译为"我们民族所具有的精神"，而不是"我们民族的精神"。

6 One week quickly passed, as father and sons discovered a tomb of the Messapians, who lived in the region centuries before the birth of Jesus. Soon, the family discovered a chamber used to store grain by the ancient Romans.

第一步 词汇解析

❶ a tomb of the Messapians，名词词组，表示"一个麦撒比人（Messapians）的墓"。
文化小常识：
　　麦撒比人（Messapians）是古意大利南部居民，公元前1世纪初移居古卡拉布里亚地区，一说由希腊的克里特岛迁来，一说为来自巴尔干的伊利里亚人。

❷ the birth of Jesus，名词词组，表示"耶稣诞生"。
文化小常识：
　　公历纪年以耶稣诞生之年作为纪年的开始。在儒略历与格里高利历中，将耶稣诞生之后的日期，称为 Anno Domini（A.D.），也就是"公元"。而将耶稣诞生之前的日期，称为 Before Christ（B.C.），也就是"公元前"。

❸ chamber，名词，表示"（作特殊用途的）房间"，比如：a burial chamber（墓室）。
❹ store，动词，表示"存放"，比如：Store the cookies in an airtight tin.（把曲奇饼干存放在一个密封罐中。）
❺ grain，名词，表示"谷物"，比如：a bag of grain（一袋谷物）。

第二步 注意断句

One week quickly passed, /as father and sons discovered a tomb of the Messapians, /who lived in the region centuries /before the birth of Jesus. /Soon, /the family discovered a chamber /used to store grain by the ancient Romans.

第三步 句型解析

① One week quickly passed 是主句，是主谓结构，直接翻译即可。

② as 是时间状语的引导词，其实在这里可以讨论一个小问题，as 引导的是什么状语？对于我来说，我觉得这一点并不是特别重要，因为中文是意合式语言，所以中文的句子之间甚至可以不用连词，看看参考译文是不是这么处理的呢？做人别那么轴！这是翻译，又不是阅读理解，翻译出来，只要别人能够看懂，逻辑正确，通过考试，就可以了。father and sons discovered a tomb of the Messapians 是时间状语从句中的主语、谓语和宾语，who 引导了非限定性定语从句，所以在这里可以采用后置译法，但是采用后置译法时需要翻译关系词 who，这个 who 指代的是"麦撒比人"。定语从句中，lived in the region centuries 是谓语和地点状语，before the birth of Jesus 又是一个时间状语，只要稍微调整整个句子的语序，那么整个句子就非常完整和通顺了。

③ 第二句中，Soon 是时间状语，表示"不久"，the family discovered a chamber 是本句的主语、谓语和宾语，used to store grain by the ancient Romans 是过去分词短语作定语，用来修饰前面的 a chamber，定语较短，所以可以采用前置译法。而且要注意 be used to do sth. 是被动语态的表达法，这里可以使用"有被不用被"的译法，直接翻译为"可以"即可。

第四步 翻译来了

　　一个星期很快过去了，父子三人发现了一个麦撒比人（Messapians）的墓，实际上，在耶稣降生前几百年，麦撒比人就已经生活在这个地区了。不久，他们一家人又发现了一个古罗马人用来储存粮食的仓库。

本句考点总结

　　第一，非限定性定语从句是用逗号隔开的定语从句，这样的句子一般都要采用后置译法，在翻译时需要翻译出关系代词 which，who 等词，指明这些词的指代关系，将这些代词翻译出来。

　　第二，本句出现了分词或分词短语位于名词后的译法。一般来说，分词或分词短语位于名词后相当于定语或定语从句，定语按照"短前长后"的译法来进行翻译。

　　第三，本句出现了被动语态的译法。被动语态是英文常见的一种形式，而在中文里常常少用"被"或者不用"被"。那么我们一般有什么样的译法呢？第一种是被动变主动，第二种是寻找替代词（比如："让……给""为……所"等结构），第三种是在科技文献中用"可以"来替代"被"，第四种是有"被"不用"被"。以上四种怎么用，那就看句子怎么通顺怎么翻译了啊！

If this history only later became clear, what was immediately obvious was that finding the pipe would be a much bigger project than Mr. Faggiano had anticipated.

第一步 词汇解析

① only later，副词词组，表示"直到后来"，比如：Only later did she realize her mistake.（直到后来，她才意识到自己的错误。）

② obvious，形容词，表示"明显的"，比如：There are obvious continuities between diet and health.（日常饮食与健康之间有着明显的逻辑关联。）

③ finding，名词，表示"调查结果、研究结论"，比如：One of the main findings of the survey was the confusion about the facilities already in place.（该调查的主要发现之一是对已安装到位的设备的混淆。）

④ anticipate，动词，表示"预料、预期、预见"，比如：We anticipate that sales will rise next year.（我们预期明年销售量将会增加。）

第二步 注意断句

If this history only later became clear, /what was immediately obvious was that /finding the pipe would be a much bigger project /than Mr. Faggiano had anticipated.

第三步 句型解析

① If 引导条件状语从句，this history only later became clear 是主系表结构，表示的含义是"这段历史直到后来变得特别清晰"，但这么理解显然是错误的，"这段历史"表示的是上一句话当中所提到的"麦撒比人的历史"，所以在这里可以把"无灵主语句"变成"有灵主语句"，也就是将"这段历史变得清晰"变成"法加诺一家知道这段历史"，这样整个句子就更加清晰了。

② 主语从句 what was immediately obvious 是主句的主语，表示的是"马上变得清晰的事情是"，但是这么翻译也不太通顺，同样可以使用"无灵主语句"变成"有灵主语句"，翻译为"他们马上就会明白"。

③ that 引导的是表语从句，finding the pipe 是表语从句的主语，would be a much bigger project 是系表结构，than Mr. Faggiano had anticipated 是比较状语，这里要注意的一点是，在从句当中已经使用了"法加诺一家"，因此这里的 Mr. Faggiano 翻译为"他们"会更好，这也是代词的译法，注意一定要灵活。

第四步 翻译来了

　　如果法加诺一家知道这段历史，那么，他们马上就会明白，寻找下水道的这项工程要比他们原本预计的大得多。

本句考点总结

　　本句考查了"有灵主语句"和"无灵主语句"的转换。一般来说，以有生命的物体作为主语的句子，称为"有灵主语句"，而以无生命的物体作为主语的句子，称为"无灵主语句"，中文常用有灵主语，而英文则常用无灵主语，注意两者之间的互换。但是这种互换是为了让句子更加通顺，不是每个句子都需要用这种方法翻译。

> He did not initially tell his wife about the extent of the work. He tied a rope around the chest of his youngest son, Davide, then 12, and lowered him to dig in small, darkened openings. "I made sure to tell him not to tell his mama," he said.

第一步 词汇解析

① initially，副词，表示"最初"，比如：Forecasters say the storms may not be as bad as they initially predicted. （预报员们说暴风雨不像他们最初预报的那样糟。）

② extent，名词，表示"宽度、广度、大小、分量"，比如：200 square kilometers in extent（方圆200平方公里）。

③ chest，名词，表示"胸部"，比如：He was shot in the chest. （他胸部中弹。）

④ lower，动词，表示"（缓慢地）放下、降下"，比如：Two reporters had to help lower the coffin into the grave. （两名记者不得不帮忙把棺材下放至墓穴中。）

⑤ darkened，形容词，表示"漆黑的"，比如：He drove past darkened houses. （他开过一座座漆黑的房子。）

⑥ opening，名词，表示"作为通道的口子、洞"，比如：A small opening is left at the top. （顶部留有一个小口。）

第二步 注意断句

He did not initially tell his wife about the extent of the work. /He tied a rope around the chest of his youngest son, /Davide, /then 12, /and lowered him to dig in small, /darkened openings. /"I made sure to tell him not to tell his mama," /he said.

第三步 句型解析

① 第一句 He did not initially tell his wife about the extent of the work 是主谓宾宾的结构，也就是双宾语结构，his wife 是间接宾语，the extent of the work 是直接宾语，句子结构比较简单，直接翻译即可，但是这里需要翻译代词 He，因为上一句当中已经有两个代词没有翻译了，所以这个代词可以指明要点，翻译为"法加诺"。

② 第二句 He tied a rope around the chest of his youngest son 是主谓宾状的结构，Davide 是同位语，then 12 为同位语，二者同时用来解释 his youngest son，所以在翻译时注意句子结构如何处理，前面已经说到了两种处理的方式，一种是"并列译法"，一种是"主谓译法"，怎么通顺就怎么翻译。

③ and 是并列连词，lowered him to dig in small, darkened openings 是第二组谓宾宾补结构，这里的两个形容词 small 和 darkened 是并列结构，直接翻译为"狭小昏暗的"即可。

④ 第三句是直接引语结构，说话人可以放在句首，也可以放在原位，直接引语中 I made sure 是主谓结构，to tell him not to tell his mama 是不定式短语作宾语，所表达的含义是"我要确保孩子不告诉他妈妈"，但这里似乎缺少对象词，所以可以增对象词"这件事"，这样一来整个句子就完整了。

第四步 翻译来了

法加诺一开始没有告诉妻子这项工程的工作量。当时，小儿子戴维德（Davide）只有12岁，法加诺在他的胸部系上绳索，把他放下去，在狭小昏暗的通道中挖掘。他说："我得让孩子知道，不能把这件事告诉他妈妈。"

> **本句考点总结**
>
> 第一,关于英文代词的译法。英文中需要翻译的代词主要指第三人称 he, she, it, they 及其相应宾格和指示代词 this 和 that。这些单词在翻译时一定要注意,主要采用"不抽象、不具体"的译法。不能翻译成具体的人或物,但是也不能翻译为"他""她""它""他们""这个""那个",要注意取中间的译法。
>
> 第二,本句考查了英文同位语的译法。同位语是两个前后相互说明的名词或名词短语,比如 Beijing, the capital of China, 有两种译法,第一种是"并列译法",翻译为"中国的首都北京";第二种是"主谓译法",翻译为"北京是中国的首都"。具体用哪一种,可以根据句子具体情况而定,有时两种都是可以使用的。
>
> 第三,本句考查了英汉互译增减词的问题,一般来说英译汉增词,汉译英减词,常见增词的种类有:一、增加对象词(范围词),这是由上文缺少句子的某个部分造成的;二、增加范畴词,这是较难的一部分,常见的范畴词有"水平、方式、方法、问题、情况、途径和方面",但是不仅仅有这些,还有很多其他的;三、增加评论性词,这些常常出现在文学翻译中;四、增加动词,会在动词的"分配译法"中说明这点。
>
> 第四,本句考查了英文直接引语的译法,最简单的译法就是保留冒号和双引号,说话人的位置和说话的内容都保持不变。即说话人在什么位置,就放在什么位置翻译,当然,说话人放在句首也是可以接受的。

9 His wife, soon became suspicious. "We had all these dirty clothes, every day," she said. "I didn't understand what was going on."

第一步 词汇解析

❶ suspicious,形容词,表示"感觉可疑的、怀疑的、令人怀疑的",比如:Two officers on patrol became suspicious of two men in a car.(两位巡警对一辆小汽车内的两名男子起了疑心。)

第二步 注意断句

His wife, /soon became suspicious. /"We had all these dirty clothes, /every day," / she said. /"I didn't understand / what was going on."

第三步 句型解析

❶ 第一句中,His wife 是主语,soon became suspicious 是系表结构,直接翻译即可。
❷ 第二句中的直接引语 We had all these dirty clothes 是主谓宾结构,every day 是时间状语,这里中间用了逗号,你不用太在意,因为这是一种口语的表达法,之后的说话人 she said 可以放在句中翻译,也可以放在句首翻译,后面的直接引语 I didn't understand 是主谓结构,what was going on 是宾语从句。有人说,这个从句可以翻译为"到底发生了什么",当然可以,但是如果注意到上下文的关系,上文说到

"父子有很多脏衣服"，后面自然而然就会翻译为"他们怎么了"。上下文的联系才是翻译需要研究的事，翻译不是一个字对一个字的工作。

第四步　翻译来了

但是，他的妻子不久就起了疑心。"我们每天都有脏衣服。"她说，"我都不知道他们怎么了。"

本句考点总结

本句考查了英文直接引语的译法，最简单的译法就是保留冒号和双引号，说话人的位置和说话的内容都保持不变。即说话人在什么位置，就放在什么位置翻译，当然，说话人放在句首也是可以接受的。

---

10 After watching the Faggiano men haul away debris in the back seat of the family car, neighbors also became suspicious and notified the authorities. Investigators arrived and shut down the excavations, warning Mr. Faggiano against operating an unapproved archaeological work site. Mr. Faggiano responded that he was just looking for a sewage pipe.

第一步　词汇解析

① haul away，动词词组，表示"拖走、搬运"，比如：The tractor hauled the fertilizer away.（拖拉机把肥料拉走了。）

② debris，名词，表示"碎片、散乱的垃圾"，比如：There was a lot of party debris in the garden.（花园里有许多聚会留下的垃圾。）

③ back seat，名词词组，表示"汽车的后座"，比如：I climbed over into the back seat.（我爬过去坐在了后座上。）

④ notify，动词，表示"通知"，比如：The skipper notified the coastguard of the tragedy.（船长通知了海岸警卫队这一灾难。）

⑤ authorities，名词，常用复数，表示"当局"，比如：local authorities（地方当局）。

⑥ investigator，名词，表示"调查者"，比如：an undercover investigator（一位秘密侦探）。

⑦ shut down，动词词组，表示"（使）关闭、停工"，比如：The factory was shut down for lack of funds.（这家工厂因缺乏资金而倒闭。）

⑧ excavation，名词，表示"挖掘、发掘"，比如：the excavation of a Mayan archaeological site（玛雅考古遗址的挖掘工作）。

⑨ unapproved，形容词，表示"未经批准的、未被允许的"，比如：an unapproved protein additive（一种未经批准的蛋白质添加剂）。

第二步 注意断句

After watching the Faggiano men haul away debris in the back seat of the family car, /neighbors also became suspicious and notified the authorities. /Investigators arrived /and shut down the excavations, /warning Mr. Faggiano /against operating an unapproved archaeological work site. /Mr. Faggiano responded /that he was just looking for a sewage pipe.

第三步 句型解析

① 句首的 After 引导时间状语，watching the Faggiano men haul away debris in the back seat of the family car 是现在分词位于句首，这个知识点需要了解的是"分词位于句首，先找主语，再进行翻译"。这个短语的逻辑主语是 neighbors，谓语是 watching，后面是宾语和宾语补足语，句子总体意思不是特别难，直接翻译即可。注意小的知识点：the Faggiano men 翻译为"法加诺家的男人们"不如"法加诺一家人"好。

② neighbors 是本句的主语，also became suspicious 是系表结构，and notified the authorities 是并列连词连接的第二组谓语和宾语。

③ 第二句中，Investigators arrived 是主谓结构，and shut down the excavations 是并列连词连接的第二组谓语和宾语，后面接现在分词短语 warning Mr. Faggiano against operating an unapproved archaeological work site 作伴随状语。这里要注意一个短语，warn sb. against doing sth. 表示"警告某人不要做某事"；而且还要注意一个小的知识点，an unapproved archaeological work site 并不是表示"一个未经允许的考古作业现场"，这么翻也不通顺，实际上表示的是"未经允许就进行考古作业"，这里实际上是将定语 archaeological 变成了状语。以上这种翻译现象不需要上升到理论高度，只要你读着觉得不通顺就可以改变词性，所以词性转换是为了让句子更加通顺。

④ 第三句中，Mr. Faggiano responded 是主谓结构，that 引导宾语从句，he was just looking for a sewage pipe 是主谓宾结构，句子结构比较简单，但是要注意不需要翻译成过去进行时，翻译为一般过去时即可。

第四步 翻译来了

邻居们看到法加诺一家人从家用轿车后座拖出残渣，他们也疑惑起来，于是向当局汇报。之后，调查人员就来了，关停了挖掘工作，并且警告法加诺不许未经批准就在考古工作现场作业。法加诺说，他只是在找下水管道。

> **本句考点总结**
>
> 本句出现了分词位于句首的现象，一般来说，分词位于句首都要先找到其逻辑主语，再进行翻译，这样整个句子的主谓宾就会非常完整。

11 A year passed. Finally, Mr. Faggiano was allowed to resume his pursuit of the sewage pipe on condition that heritage officials observed the work. An underground treasure house emerged, as the family uncovered ancient vases, Roman devotional bottles, an ancient ring with Christian symbols, medieval artifacts, hidden frescoes and more.

第一步 词汇解析

① resume，动词，表示"重新开始"，比如：After the war he resumed his duties at Wellesley College.（那场战争之后，他恢复了在韦尔斯利学院的任职。）

② on condition that，介词词组，表示"条件是"，比如：He agreed to speak to reporters on condition that he was not identified.（他同意在不暴露身份的条件下和记者谈话。）

③ heritage，名词，表示"遗产"，比如：The building is part of our national heritage.（这个建筑是我们民族遗产的一部分。）

④ observed，动词，单词原形为：observe，表示"监视"，比如：observe a suspected person（监视可疑的人）。

⑤ treasure house，名词词组，表示"宝库"，比如：The area is a treasure house of archaeological relics.（这个地区是古文物遗迹的宝库。）

⑥ uncover，动词，表示"移去（某物的）遮盖物"，比如：When the seedlings sprout, uncover the tray.（幼苗发芽后，揭开盘上的遮盖物。）

⑦ devotional，形容词，表示"与宗教崇拜有关的"，比如：devotional pictures（宗教图画）。

⑧ medieval，形容词，表示"中世纪的"，比如：a medieval castle（一座中世纪的城堡）。

⑨ artifacts，名词，表示"手工艺品"，比如：ancient Egyptian artifacts（古埃及手工艺品）。

⑩ fresco，名词，表示"湿壁画"，湿壁画就是在墙壁灰泥未干时所绘的画。

第二步 注意断句

A year passed. /Finally, /Mr. Faggiano was allowed to resume his pursuit of the sewage pipe /on condition that heritage officials observed the work. /An underground treasure house emerged, /as the family uncovered ancient vases, /Roman devotional bottles, /an ancient ring with Christian symbols, /medieval artifacts, /hidden frescoes /and more.

第三步 句型解析

① A year passed 是主谓结构，本句较短，根据上下文的意思可以和下句合译。

② Finally 是连接副词，表示"最终"，Mr. Faggiano 是主语，was allowed 是谓语，是被动语态，这里可以用"有被不用被"的译法，翻译为"允许（获准）"，之后是不定式短语 to resume his pursuit of the sewage pipe 作宾语，这里有一个翻译的现象，即抽象名词的译法。his pursuit of 中的 pursuit 是典型的抽象名词，有动词词根，可以翻译为"寻找"或是"找寻"，所以译文当中出现了三个动词"获准来继续找寻"，那么有一个小问题，汉译英时这三个谓语动词如何处理？谁是一谓语，谁是二谓语，谁是三谓语呢？句中的 on condition that 是条件状语从句的引导词，表示"条件是"，heritage officials observed the work 是条件状语从句，是主谓宾结构，但是注意这几个词的翻译，译为"遗产官员监督工作"。

③ 第三句中，An underground treasure house emerged 是主谓结构，as 是时间状语从句的引导词，这里是什么状语无所谓，你就是不翻译，也无所谓，想想如何连接两个句子即可。在时间状语从句中，the family 是主语，uncovered 是谓语，ancient vases, Roman devotional bottles, an ancient ring with Christian symbols, medieval artifacts, hidden frescoes and more 是宾语，宾语中名词较多，注意使用顿号，其余名词正常翻译即可。

第四步 翻译来了

一年过去了，最终，法加诺获准来继续找寻下水管道，条件是要有遗产官员监督工作。于是，一家人挖出了一座地下宝库，有古代花瓶、罗马宗教圣瓶、一个带有基督标志的古老戒指、中世纪手工艺品、暗藏的壁画等。

> **本句考点总结**
>
> 　　第一，本句出现了被动语态的译法。被动语态是英文常见的一种形式，而在中文里常常少用"被"或者不用"被"。那么我们一般有什么样的译法呢？第一种是被动变主动，第二种是寻找替代词（比如："让……给""为……所"等结构），第三种是在科技文献中用"可以"来替代"被"，第四种是有"被"不用"被"。以上四种怎么用，那就看句子怎么通顺怎么翻译了啊！
>
> 　　第二，本句当中考查了"抽象名词"的译法。抽象名词一般处于冠词之后，又在介词之前，以"the＋抽象名词＋of"的形式居多。一般来说，抽象名词有两种译法。第一种，若抽象名词有动词词根，则翻译为动词，比如the suggestion of mine，翻译为"我建议"，而不是"我的建议"；第二种，若抽象名词没有动词词根，可以增动词翻译，比如the spirit of our nation，翻译为"我们民族所具有的精神"，而不是"我们民族的精神"。

12　Today, the building is Museum Faggiano, an independent archaeological museum authorized by the Lecce government.

第一步　词汇解析

❶ Museum Faggiano，名词词组，表示"法加诺博物馆"，采用音译和直译相结合的方法。
❷ independent，形容词，表示"独立的"，比如：an independent television station（一家独立的电视台）。
❸ authorize，动词，表示"批准、授权"，比如：Only the president could authorize the use of the atomic bomb.（只有总统能授权原子弹的使用。）

第二步　注意断句

　　Today, /the building is Museum Faggiano, /an independent archaeological museum /authorized by the Lecce government.

第三步　句型解析

❶ Today 表示"如今"，the building is Museum Faggiano 是本句的主句，an independent archaeological museum authorized by the Lecce government 是同位语，同位语的译法不用我再强调了，两种译法最常见了，译文使用了主谓译法。
❷ 而且这个同位语中还有一个过去分词短语 authorized by the Lecce government 作定语，这个定语较短，可以采用前置译法，这样就可以把整个句子整理通顺了。

第四步　翻译来了

　　如今，这所建筑已经是法加诺博物馆了，这是由莱切政府批准的独立考古博物馆。

> ### 本句考点总结
>
> 第一，本句考查了英文同位语的译法。同位语是两个前后相互说明的名词或名词短语，比如 Beijing, the capital of China, 有两种译法，第一种是"并列译法"，翻译为"中国的首都北京"；第二种是"主谓译法"，翻译为"北京是中国的首都"。具体用哪一种，可以根据句子具体情况而定，有时两种都是可以使用的。
>
> 第二，本句出现了分词或分词短语位于名词后的译法。一般来说，分词或分词短语位于名词后相当于定语或定语从句，定语按照"短前长后"的译法来进行翻译。

13. Mr. Faggiano is now satisfied with his museum, but he has not forgotten about the restaurant. A few years into his excavation, he finally found his sewage pipe. It was, indeed, broken.

第一步 词汇解析

① excavation，名词，表示"挖掘"，比如：the excavation of an ancient tomb（古墓的挖掘）。

② indeed，副词，表示"（用于强调真实性）确实"，比如：Later, he admitted that the payments had indeed been made.（后来，他承认说的确是付过款了。）

第二步 注意断句

Mr. Faggiano is now satisfied with his museum, /but he has not forgotten about the restaurant. /A few years into his excavation, /he finally found his sewage pipe. /It was, /indeed, /broken.

第三步 句型解析

① 第一句中，Mr. Faggiano is now satisfied with his museum 是主系表结构，后面接 with 的固定搭配，这里表示"对……非常满意"，要注意 his 的译法，第二次提到的人称代词可以不翻译，直接省略即可。but 是表示转折的连词，he has not forgotten about the restaurant 是主谓宾结构，这里直接翻译即可，中文用"开餐馆"这个动词词组，显示比较口语，你要翻译为"饭馆、饭店"也是可以的。

② 第二句中，A few years into his excavation 是时间状语，这里没有必要深入探究 into 的用法，知道这里的介词翻译为动词即可，也就是"进行"的意思，he finally found his sewage pipe 是本句的主句，表示"他最终找到了下水管"，但要注意人称代词的译法，这点特别重要，不要翻译为"他最终找到了他的下水管"。

③ It was, indeed, broken 是第三句，第二句和第三句在意思上有一定联系，可以合译，这里的 It 是代词，所以可以指明要点，翻译为"那根下水管"，indeed 是插入语，放在什么位置通顺就放在什么位置，问题不大。

第四步 翻译来了

法加诺先生现在对这座博物馆非常满意，但是，他并没有忘记开餐馆这件事。在他挖了几年之后，最终找到了那根下水管，那根水管确实是坏了。

> **本句考点总结**
>
> 第一，关于英文代词的译法。英文中需要翻译的代词主要指第三人称 he，she，it，they 及其相应宾格和指示代词 this 和 that。这些单词在翻译时一定要注意，主要采用"不抽象、不具体"的译法。不能翻译成具体的人或物，但是也不能翻译为"他""她""它""他们""这个""那个"，要注意取中间的译法。
>
> 第二，关于"介改动"的译法。英文里的介词常常翻译为动词，比如 He went to Beijing by plane. 翻译为"他坐飞机去北京"，这里的 by 翻译为"坐"，这就是"介改动"的译法。

14

He has since bought another building and is again planning for a restaurant, assuming it does not need any renovations. "I still want it," he said of the restaurant. "I'm very stubborn."

第一步 词汇解析

1. assume，动词，表示"假设、假定"，比如：He assumed that report to be valid.（他猜那报告是有根据的。）
2. renovation，名词，表示"革新、翻修、修整"比如：The museum has been closed for renovation.（博物馆已闭馆整修。）
3. stubborn，形容词，表示"固执的"，比如：He is a stubborn character used to getting his own way.（他是一个固执的人，习惯于随心所欲。）

第二步 注意断句

He has since bought another building /and is again planning for a restaurant, /assuming it does not need any renovations. /"I still want it," /he said of the restaurant. /"I'm very stubborn."

第三步 句型解析

1. He has since bought another building 是第一句的第一个分句，是主谓宾结构，这里要特别注意 since 的含义，只是表示"现在完成时态"，真正的含义是"自从发现水管坏了之后"，但这个单词根本不需要翻译，译文没有翻译这个词，也很通顺！
2. and 之后是第二组谓语和宾语，is again planning for a restaurant 是现在进行时态，表示"又正在计划着（开）饭店了"，这两句的时态都不用翻译出来，译文使用"又开始"替代了 is again doing，这样不是很好吗？逗号之后的分词短语 assuming it does not need any renovations 是伴随状语，表示"他假设……"，it 指的是"他要买的新房子"，译文中使用了"前提是"，这样翻译很机智，但按照原文翻译也可以。
3. 第二句是直接引语，"I still want it"表示"我还是想要（它）"，这里的"它"表示"开餐馆这件事"，he said of the restaurant 是主谓宾结构，之后再接直接引语，"I'm very stubborn"是主系表结构，表示"我这个人比较固执"。

第四步 翻译来了

他买下了另外一处房子,又开始计划着开餐馆了,但前提是这处房子不需要重新装修。"我还是想开餐馆,"他提到餐馆时说,"我这个人比较固执。"

第一,关于英文代词的译法。英文中需要翻译的代词主要指第三人称 he,she,it,they 及其相应宾格和指示代词 this 和 that。这些单词在翻译时一定要注意,主要采用"不抽象、不具体"的译法。不能翻译成具体的人或物,但是也不能翻译为"他""她""它""他们""这个""那个",要注意取中间的译法。

第二,本句考查了英文直接引语的译法,最简单的译法就是保留冒号和双引号,说话人的位置和说话的内容都保持不变。即说话人在什么位置,就放在什么位置翻译,当然,说话人放在句首也是可以接受的。

译后总结

这篇文章是典型的外刊文体,以记述为主,其中包括人物的对话和行为,要特别注意直接引语的翻译方法,其余常见的代词的译法、被动语态的译法、定语从句的译法、抽象名词的译法等也是非常重要的,所以,请大家一定要熟记翻译方法,这样在考试中才能灵活运用。

第二节 2017年上半年三级笔译汉译英

本研究院成立于 1968 年 2 月 20 日。隶属中国航天科技集团公司。

经过 40 年的发展,已成为中国主要的空间技术及产品研制基地,是中国空间事业最具实力的骨干力量。

主要从事空间技术开发,航天器研制,空间领域对外技术交流和合作,航天技术应用等服务。

还参与制定国家空间技术发展规划,研究有关探索、开发、利用外层空间的技术途径,承接用户需求的各类航天器和地面应用设备的研制业务并提供相应的服务。

本研究院下设研究机构,卫星制造厂等,拥有一家上市公司和多家全资子公司,建立了多个国家重点实验室和一家以研究生培养,员工培训,客户培训为中心任务的学院。

形成了七个产业基地,拥有空间飞行器总体设计,分系统研制生产,卫星总装测试,环境试验,地面设备制造及卫星应用,服务保障等配套完整的研制生产体系。

本研究院拥有员工一万余人,其中包括 8 名两院院士,12 名国家级突出贡献专家和 1 700 多名高级专业技术人才。

本研究院已与 10 多个国家和地区的宇航公司及空间研究机构建立了广泛联系。

CATTI 三级笔译 2017 年上半年的这篇汉译英延续了前两年的出题"套路",还是资讯介绍类文章的翻译,这类文章的翻译我们已经有一定经验了,主要把握本专题的词汇,考试时若确实不熟悉的单词可以求助汉译英字典,语法方面的问题只要不出大错就可以。

 本研究院成立于 1968 年 2 月 20 日。隶属中国航天科技集团公司。

第一步 词汇解析

① 研究院,institute,名词,比如:the National Cancer Institute(国家癌症研究所)。
② 成立,found,动词,比如:The New York Free-Loan Society was founded in 1892.(纽约无息贷款协会成立于 1892 年。)这里也可以替换为 establish。
③ 隶属,be affiliated to,动词词组,比如:The group is not affiliated to any political party.(该团体不隶属任何政党。)
affiliate 在法律英语中,表示"判定",比如:affiliate a child to its father(判定孩子的父亲)。
④ 中国航天科技集团公司,China Aerospace Science and Technology Corporation,专有名词。比较长的专有名词短语该如何翻译?教大家一个最简单的方法:把这些名词短语逐个写出来,中间不需要用任何的虚词,比如"中国航天科技集团公司",写成 China Aerospace Science Technology Corporation 也是勉强可以的,science 和 technology 中间可以用 and 连接一下。
航空航天,aerospace,名词,比如:His father is a machinist in an aerospace plant.(他的父亲是一家航空工厂的机械师。)
文化小常识:
　　中国航天科技集团有限公司是在我国战略高技术领域拥有自主知识产权和著名品牌,创新能力突出、核心竞争力强的国有特大型高科技企业。成立于 1999 年 7 月 1 日。

第二步 动词定位

本研究院<u>成立于</u> 1968 年 2 月 20 日。<u>隶属</u>中国航天科技集团公司。

第三步 句型解析

① 本句的主语是"本研究院",谓语是"成立于",时间状语是"1968 年 2 月 20 日",这里的时间状语是典型的过去时间,所以可以使用一般过去时。
② "隶属"是第二句的动词,本句缺少主语,主语也是前面的"本研究院",可以将两个句子合译。"中国航天科技集团公司"是动词的宾语,这么一分析,马上就能看出这个句子有两个动词,两个动词该如何翻译不用我再说了!"并列""伴随""下沉"这三种形式应该烂熟于胸。

第四步 翻译来了

　　Founded on February 20th, 1968, the institute is affiliated to China Aerospace Science and Technology Corporation.

> **本句考点总结**
>
> 汉译英句子中并列、伴随、下沉的结构。中文常常会出现多个句子聚集的情况，那么我们在翻译时需要考虑将这些句子进行"分堆"。但是"分堆"之后，一个句子中也可能会出现两个动词或两组动词，那么有两个动词或两组动词的句子我们该如何进行翻译呢？比如："我坐在那里看书"，这里有两个动词，一个是"坐"，一个是"看"，我们翻译时便会有三种方法：
>
> 第一种并列（两个动词并列的译法，使用并列连词连接，两个动词之间不一定是"并列"关系）：I sat there and read a book.
>
> 第二种伴随（将第二个动词翻译为二谓语，分词、从句、状语等都可以）：I sat there reading a book.
>
> 第三种下沉（将第一个动词翻译为二谓语，分词、从句、状语等都可以）：Sitting there, I read a book.
>
> 需要说明的是，并列、伴随和下沉只是动词的形式问题，不代表动词之间的逻辑关系，用这三种形式翻译两个动词或两组动词都是可以的，大家可以根据句子上下文的关系来判断使用。

2 经过 40 年的发展，已成为中国主要的空间技术及产品研制基地，是中国空间事业最具实力的骨干力量。

第一步 词汇解析

❶ 中国主要的空间技术及产品研制基地，a major base of China's space technology and product development，名词词组。

空间技术，space technology，名词词组，比如：We lead the way in space technology.（我们在航天技术方面处于领先地位。）

产品研制，product development，名词词组，比如：This will help you find problems at earlier stages of product development.（这将帮助您在产品研制的早期找出问题。）

研制，意思是"研究制造"，产品或武器制造，常用 develop，比如：develop new weapons（研制新式武器）。

❷ 是，turn into，动词词组，比如：The fighting is threatening to turn into full-scale war.（这次冲突可能要演变成全面战争。）

❸ 中国空间事业，China's space industry，名词词组，比如：Over the past decades, China's space industry has created one miracle after another.（几十年来，中国空间事业创造了一个又一个奇迹。）

❹ 骨干力量，backbone，名词，比如：Such men are the backbone of the country.（这样的人是国家的栋梁。）backbone 也有"骨气、坚毅、毅力"的意思。

第二步 动词定位

经过 40 年的发展，已成为中国主要的空间技术及产品研制基地，是中国空间事业最具实力的骨干力量。

第三步 句型解析

❶ 本句第一部分"经过40年的发展"是时间状语,这里使用after最简单,不要搞得太复杂。这是翻译考试,不是翻译竞赛!

❷ "已成为"是本句中的第一个动词,用现在完成时或一般现在时都是可以的,"中国主要的空间技术及产品研制基地"是第一个宾语,这个名词短语的翻译和前文一样,因为其中有"的",所以可以用of结构,翻译为China's major base of space technology and product development 即可。

❸ "是"是本句的第二个动词,"中国空间事业最具实力的骨干力量"是第二个宾语,这里翻译为一般现在时比较好,后面的名词短语也不是非常难,直接翻译即可。

❹ 本句有两个动词,如何翻译,不用我再次强调了吧!

第四步 翻译来了

After 40 years' development, it has become a major base of China's space technology and product development, and turns into the most powerful backbone of China's space industry.

本句考点总结

汉译英句子中并列、伴随、下沉的结构。中文常常会出现多个句子聚集的情况,那么我们在翻译时需要考虑将这些句子进行"分堆"。但是"分堆"之后,一个句子中也可能会出现两个动词或两组动词,那么有两个动词或两组动词的句子我们该如何进行翻译呢?比如:"我坐在那里看书",这里有两个动词,一个是"坐",一个是"看",我们翻译时便会有三种方法:

第一种并列(两个动词并列的译法,使用并列连词连接,两个动词之间不一定是"并列"关系):I sat there and read a book.

第二种伴随(将第二个动词翻译为二谓语,分词、从句、状语等都可以):I sat there reading a book.

第三种下沉(将第一个动词翻译为二谓语,分词、从句、状语等都可以):Sitting there, I read a book.

需要说明的是,并列、伴随和下沉只是动词的形式问题,不代表动词之间的逻辑关系,用这三种形式翻译两个动词或两组动词都是可以的,大家可以根据句子上下文的关系来判断使用。

3 主要从事空间技术开发,航天器研制,空间领域对外技术交流和合作,航天技术应用等服务。

第一步 词汇解析

❶ 从事,be engaged in,动词词组,比如:He is engaged in scientific research.(他从事科研工作。)

❷ 航天器研制,spacecrafts research and development,名词词组。"研制"既可以翻译为 development,也可以翻译为 research and development,当然后者更好一些。

航天器，spacecrafts，名词，单词原形为：spacecraft，比如：the world's largest and most expensive unmanned spacecraft（世界上最大、最贵的无人航天器）。

❸ 对外技术交流和合作，international technology exchange and cooperation，名词词组。句中"对外"的意思是"国际"，所以翻译为 international。

❹ 航天技术应用，space technology application，名词词组。

应用，application，名词，比如：the application of atomic energy to manufacturing（原子能在制造业上的实际应用）。若表示"广泛应用"，则搭配形容词 general；若表示"大范围的应用"，则搭配形容词 wide。

第二步 动词定位

主要**从事**空间技术开发，航天器研制，空间领域对外技术交流和合作，航天技术应用等服务。

第三步 句型解析

❶ 本句中的"主要从事"是核心谓语，缺少主语，主语是上文的"研究院"，这里可以用代词"不抽象、不具体"的译法，既不翻译为完整的名词，也不用翻译为代词，翻译为 The institute 即可。

❷ "空间技术开发，航天器研制，空间领域对外技术交流和合作，航天技术应用等服务"则是核心的宾语，这里我们一个一个来看如何翻译的："空间技术开发"翻译为 space technology development；"航天器研制"翻译为 spacecrafts research and development；"空间领域对外技术交流和合作"翻译为 international technology exchange and cooperation in space industry；"航天技术应用"翻译为 space technology application。注意以上单词写对即可，其余无所谓，不要在单复数、名词的 of 或是冠词上较劲，考试时想不到那么多，只要写对就行！

第四步 翻译来了

The institute is mainly engaged in such services as space technology development, spacecrafts research and development, international technology exchange and cooperation in space industry, and space technology application.

还参与制定国家空间技术发展规划，研究有关探索、开发、利用外层空间的技术途径，承接用户需求的各类航天器和地面应用设备的研制业务并提供相应的服务。

第一步 词汇解析

❶ 参与……，participate in，动词词组，比如：They expected him to participate in the ceremony.（他们希望他参加这个典礼。）

【同义词辨析】

participate：正式用词，特指参加团体活动，暗示以一个积极的角色参加；

take part in：侧重参加某项群众性、集体性的事业、工作或活动；

join：普通用词，指加入党派、团体或游戏活动等；

attend：侧重参加或出席会议或学术活动等。

❷ 国家空间技术发展规划，the development plan of national space technology，名词词组。句中指的是"国家空间技术（的）发展规划"，有"的"有 of，无"的"无 of，翻译为 national space technology development plan 也凑合。

科技小常识：
空间技术，是探索、开发和利用太空以及地球以外天体的综合性工程技术，亦称航天技术。

❸ 探索、开发、利用外层空间，outer space exploration, development and exploitation，名词词组。

❹ 技术途径，technical approaches，名词词组。

途径、方法，approach，名词，比如：We will be exploring different approaches to gathering information.（我们将探索收集信息的不同方法。）英英释义便于我们理解这一单词：Your approach to a task, problem, or situation is the way you deal with it or think about it.

❺ 承接……，undertake，动词，比如：She undertook the task of monitoring the elections.（她承担了监督选举的任务。）名词形式为：undertaking，表示"事业、任务"。

❻ 各类航天器，various aircrafts，名词词组。

航空器、飞机、飞艇，aircrafts，名词，单词原形为：aircraft，比如：Several aircrafts were intercepted and brought down.（有几架飞机遭到拦截，被击落了。）

❼ 地面应用设备，ground application equipment，名词词组。

【同义词辨析】

equipment：多指成套的或重型的设备或装备，通常用作不可数名词；

appliance：侧重指家用机器或设备，尤指家用电器；

tool：一般指进行特种工作的手工工具，也可指人造使用动力的工具，还可作引申用。

第二步 动词定位

还<u>参与制定</u>国家空间技术发展规划，<u>研究</u>有关探索、开发、利用外层空间的技术途径，<u>承接</u>用户需求的各类航天器和地面应用设备的研制业务<u>并提供</u>相应的服务。

第三步 句型解析

❶ 本句中的"还"表示"进一步来说""除此以外"等意思，这里翻译为 Besides，Furthermore 等都可以。

❷ 本句的第一个核心谓语是"参与制定"，翻译"参与"就行，动词越少越好，"国家空间技术发展规划"是第一个宾语；第二个并列的核心谓语是"研究"，宾语是"有关探索、开发、利用外层空间的技术途径"，这里的宾语较长，而且"有关的"可以翻译为 relevant to 这样的短语，参考译文中还出现了 research on，这里的 on 用不用问题都不大，因为译文想表达的是"在哪一方面"的含义，第三个核心谓语是"承接"，宾语是"用户需求的各类航天器和地面应用设备的研制业务"，后面又出现了一个动词"并提供"，宾语是"相应的服务"，这个有点难理解，这里表示的是"从事研制业务（'业务'这里可以理解为范畴词，不翻译）和提供服务＋用户所需要的各类航天器和地面应用设备"，这样是否能理解呢？大家不理解的点是将"提供服务"放在宾语前翻译了，为什么会这样呢？因为有"相应的"，这个"相应的"指的就是"用户所需要的各类航天器和地面应用设备"，这样应该好理解了。翻译成两组谓语和宾语肯定是不对的。

第四步 翻译来了

Besides, it also participates in the development plan of national space technology, research on technical approaches relevant to outer space exploration, development and exploitation, and undertakes research and development and provides services as required on various aircrafts and ground application equipment.

> **本句考点总结**
>
> 本句考查了英汉互译增减词的问题，一般来说英译汉增词，汉译英减词，常见增词的种类有：一、增加对象词（范围词），这是由上文缺少句子的某个部分造成的；二、增加范畴词，这是较难的一部分，常见的范畴词有"水平、方式、方法、问题、情况、途径和方面"，但是不仅仅有这些，还有很多其他的；三、增加评论性词，这些常常出现在文学翻译中；四、增加动词，会在动词的"分配译法"中说明这点。

5 本研究院下设研究机构，卫星制造厂等，拥有一家上市公司和多家全资子公司，建立了多个国家重点实验室和一家以研究生培养，员工培训，客户培训为中心任务的学院。

第一步 词汇解析

① 下设……（附属机构），composed of subsidiary organs，分词词组。
附属的、附设的，subsidiary，形容词，比如：a subsidiary factory（附属工厂）。
机关、机构，organs，名词，单词原形为：organ，比如：Parliament is the chief organ of government.（议会是主要的政治机构。）organ 还有"新闻媒体"的意思，比如：The publication is the official organ of the American Association for Cancer Research.（该出版物是美国癌症研究协会的官方报刊。）

② 卫星制造厂，satellite manufacturer，名词词组。
制造厂，manufacturer，名词，比如：the manufacturer of furniture（家具制造厂）。"制造厂"一词，还可以翻译为 manufactory。manufacturer 一词特指用机器大量生产，成批制造。

③ 一家上市公司，a listed company，名词词组。
上市的，listed，形容词，比如：Some of Australia's largest listed companies are expected to announce huge interim earnings this week.（澳大利亚一些最大的上市公司预期会在本周公布高额中期盈利。）

④ 多家全资子公司，several wholly-owned subsidiaries，名词词组。

⑤ 多个国家重点实验室，multiple national key laboratories，名词词组。
"多个"和"多家"分别翻译为 several 和 multiple，体现词汇的多样性。"国家重点实验室"翻译为 national key laboratories，建议直接记忆，不要自己造词。

⑥ 以……为中心任务，as a core，介词词组。

⑦ 研究生培养，postgraduate education，名词词组，比如：Sun Yat-sen University adopts a two-year postgraduate education system.（中山大学的研究生教育是两年制。）

⑧ 员工培训，internal training，名词词组，比如：Companies already have their own extensive internal training programs.（公司本身已经有了大量的内部培训项目。）"员工培训"意思是"内部培训"，也可以翻译为 staff/employee training。

第二步 动词定位

本研究院<u>下设</u>研究机构，卫星制造厂等，<u>拥有</u>一家上市公司和多家全资子公司，<u>建立了</u>多个国家重点实验室和一家以研究生培养，员工培训，客户培训为中心任务的学院。

第三步 句型解析

① "本研究院"是本句的主语，"下设"是谓语，"研究机构，卫星制造厂等"是宾语，这里需要注意"等"的译法，其实聪明的译法在于如何理解"下设"，也就是"本研究院有很多下属机构，比如研究机构、卫星制造厂等"，这样总分结构就可以看出来了。

② 本句的第二个谓语是"拥有"，宾语是"一家上市公司和多家全资子公司"，这个谓语和宾语的结构相对简单；"建立了"是本句的第三个谓语，"多个国家重点实验室和一家以研究生培养，员工培训，客户培训为中心任务的学院"是第三组宾语，这组宾语较长，咱们来一一分析："多个国家重点实验室"是名词短语，直接翻译，不需要用 of 结构或 the，把名词写对才是最重要的事；"一家以研究生培养，员工培训，客户培训为中心任务的学院"是第二个名词短语，其中定语较多，所以可以先翻译"学院"，再翻译"以研究生培养，员工培训，客户培训为中心任务的"，这些词处理为 for postgraduate education, internal training as well as customers training as a core 最好，这里的"为中心任务的"非要翻译为 core task 也勉强可以，这里本来就是范畴词。

③ 本句三个动词"下设""拥有"和"建立"可以处理为"下沉""核心"和"伴随"的经典结构。

第四步 翻译来了

Composed of subsidiary organs like research institute and satellite manufacturer, the institute owns a listed company and several wholly-owned subsidiaries, establishing multiple national key laboratories and a college for postgraduate education, internal training as well as customers training as a core.

> **本句考点总结**
>
> 中英文的总分关系，中文一般是先分后总，而英文则是先总后分，比如中文会说"我喜欢吃香蕉、苹果、梨子等水果"，但是英文的表达是 I like fruits such as bananas, apples and pears. 注意总分关系是如何在两种语言中体现出来的。

6 形成了七个产业基地，拥有空间飞行器总体设计，分系统研制生产，卫星总装测试，环境试验，地面设备制造及卫星应用，服务保障等配套完整的研制生产体系。

第一步 词汇解析

① 产业基地，industrial bases，名词词组，比如：Shanghai is the most important industrial base of China.（上海是中国最重要的产业基地。）

② 拥有……，be qualified，动词词组，表示"符合资格"，比如：He is qualified to teach English.（他教英语是合格的。）be qualified 后面接 in，表示"在……方面有资格"。

③ 空间飞行器总体设计，overall design of spacecrafts，名词词组。

④ 分系统研制生产，subsystem development and production，名词词组。
分系统，subsystem，名词，比如：disk subsystem（磁盘子系统）。sub- 来源于拉丁文的介词 sub，意为 under/from 等，表示"在下面"。

⑤ 卫星总装测试，satellite assembly test，名词词组。句中"总装"的意思是"把零件和部件装配成总体"。组装，assembly，名词，比如：For the rest of the day, he worked on the assembly of an explosive device.（那天余下的时间里，他在进行一个爆炸装置的组装。）

⑥ 环境试验，environmental experiment，名词词组。

科技小常识：

环境试验一般指环境模拟试验，环境模拟试验，是为了在预期的使用、运输或贮存的所有环境下，保持功能可靠性而进行的活动。

⑦ 地面设备制造，ground equipment manufacturing，名词词组。"地面设备"翻译为 ground equipment，属于专业领域的术语。

⑧ 卫星应用，satellite application，名词词组，比如：a satellite ground application system（一个卫星地面应用系统）。

⑨ 服务保障，service assurance，名词词组，比如：This leads to the second challenge: service assurance.（这将导致第二个难题：服务保障。）
保障、保证，assurance，名词，比如：He gave me his assurance that he would help.（他向我保证他愿意帮忙。）

⑩ 配套完整的研制生产体系，a complete research and production system，名词词组。

第二步 动词定位

<u>形成了</u>七个产业基地，<u>拥有</u>空间飞行器总体设计，分系统研制生产，卫星总装测试，环境试验，地面设备制造及卫星应用，服务保障等配套完整的研制生产体系。

第三步 句型解析

① 本句实际上和上一句是一整句，中间是我人为"分堆"的，因为前面已经有三个动词，后面又是两个动词"形成了"和"拥有"，所以这里可以形成一堆。

② "形成了"是第一个动词，"七个产业基地"是第一组宾语，"拥有"是第二个动词，"空间飞行器总体设计，分系统研制生产，卫星总装测试，环境试验，地面设备制造及卫星应用，服务保障等配套完整的研制生产体系"是第二组宾语。出现两个动词应该怎么办呢？其实"并列""伴随""下沉"都是可以的，译文使用了下沉结构，句首出现了 With 结构，后面接主句，主语是 it，也就是前文的"研究院"，谓语是 forms，用并列就可以。宾语比较多，但是比较简单：空间飞行器总体设计，翻译为 overall design of spacecrafts；分系统研制生产，翻译为 subsystem development and production；卫星总装测试，翻译为 satellite assembly test；环境试验，翻译为 environmental experiment；地面设备制造及卫星应用，服务保障等，翻译为 ground equipment manufacturing, satellite application, and service assurance, etc.；"配套完整的研制生产体系"是真正的核心宾语，所以本句也是总分关系。翻译的时候应该先翻译核心宾语，翻译为 a complete research and production system。"配套完整的"如何解决呢？参考译文处理为 which is qualified...，把其中的"完整的"放在前面的名词短语中，翻译为 complete。

第四步 翻译来了

With seven industrial bases, it forms a complete research and production system which is qualified in overall design of spacecrafts, subsystem development and production, satellite assembly test, environmental experiment, ground equipment manufacturing, satellite application, and service assurance, etc.

> 💡 **本句考点总结**
>
> 　　第一，关于"动词分堆"的问题。中文里常常出现多个短句聚集的句型，我们一方面需要去考虑这些动词之间的关系，哪一个是最重要的，哪一个是其次重要的，哪一个又是最不重要的，这个过程称为分析"谓语动词的层次性"。除此之外，句子当中出现了大量的动词时，或者说大量的分句时，我们不可能将这些分句整体翻译为一个长句，那么，我们就需要考虑哪些动词放在一起翻译，这样的过程称为"动词分堆"。比如，一个句子当中有五个动词形成的五个分句，我们一般会考虑前三个动词翻译为一句，后两个动词翻译为一句，但是如何进行"分堆"要根据上下文的语境来判断，绝对不能形而上学，望文生义。
>
> 　　第二，汉译英句子中并列、伴随、下沉的结构。中文常常会出现多个句子聚集的情况，那么我们在翻译时需要考虑将这些句子进行"分堆"。但是"分堆"之后，一个句子中也可能会出现两个动词或两组动词，那么有两个动词或两组动词的句子我们该如何进行翻译呢？比如："我坐在那里看书"，这里有两个动词，一个是"坐"，一个是"看"，我们翻译时便会有三种方法：
>
> 　　第一种并列（两个动词并列的译法，使用并列连词连接，两个动词之间不一定是"并列"关系）：I sat there and read a book.
>
> 　　第二种伴随（将第二个动词翻译为二谓语，分词、从句、状语等都可以）：I sat there reading a book.
>
> 　　第三种下沉（将第一个动词翻译为二谓语，分词、从句、状语等都可以）：Sitting there, I read a book.
>
> 　　需要说明的是，并列、伴随和下沉只是动词的形式问题，不代表动词之间的逻辑关系，用这三种形式翻译两个动词或两组动词都是可以的，大家可以根据句子上下文的关系来判断使用。
>
> 　　第三，中英文的总分关系，中文一般是先分后总，而英文则是先总后分，比如中文会说"我喜欢吃香蕉、苹果、梨子等水果"，但是英文的表达是 I like fruits such as bananas, apples and pears. 注意总分关系是如何在两种语言中体现出来的。

7　本研究院拥有员工一万余人，其中包括 8 名两院院士，12 名国家级突出贡献专家和 1 700 多名高级专业技术人才。

第一步　词汇解析

① 员工，staff，名词，比如：The staff were very good.（员工们都很棒。）常见词组：full-time staff（全职职员）；part-time staff（兼职工作人员）；permanent staff（正式职员）；temporary staff（临时职员）。staff 还有动词词性，表示"为……配备"。

② 两院院士，Chinese Academicians，名词词组，这里大写首字母，"两院"翻译出来也是可以的。"两院院士"是"中国科学院院士"和"中国工程院院士"的统称。

　　院士，academician，名词，比如：the cradle for professors, academicians and university presidents（教

授、院士和大学校长的摇篮）。

中国科学院：Chinese Academy of Sciences (CAS)；中国工程院：Chinese Academy of Engineering (CAE)。

❸ 国家级突出贡献专家，national outstanding contribution experts，名词词组。

❹ 高级专业技术人才，senior professional，名词词组，比如：The company is now recruiting senior professionals globally.（该公司正面向全球招聘高级专业人才。）

第二步 动词定位

本研究院拥有员工一万余人，其中包括 8 名两院院士，12 名国家级突出贡献专家和 1 700 多名高级专业技术人才。

第三步 句型解析

❶ "本研究院"是本句的主语，"拥有"是谓语，"员工一万余人"是宾语，这句非常简单，译文使用了 there be 句型，这是最简单的译法。

❷ "其中包括"可以翻译为 including，这是常见的译法，"8 名两院院士，12 名国家级突出贡献专家和 1 700 多名高级专业技术人才"是三个名词短语，这里也比较简单，直接翻译即可。

第四步 翻译来了

There are more than 10,000 staff in the institute, including 8 Chinese Academicians, 12 national outstanding contribution experts and more than 1,700 senior professionals.

8 本研究院已与 10 多个国家和地区的宇航公司及空间研究机构建立了广泛联系。

第一步 词汇解析

❶ 与……建立了广泛联系，establish extensive ties with，动词词组。

建立联系，establish ties with，动词词组，比如：The key purpose of the visit is to establish ties with the Malaysian and Indonesian education sector.（本次走访最重要的目的是与马来西亚和印尼教育部门建立联系。）

❷ 宇航公司，aerospace corporation，名词词组。

❸ 空间研究机构，space research organization，名词词组。

第二步 动词定位

本研究院已与 10 多个国家和地区的宇航公司及空间研究机构建立了广泛联系。

第三步 句型解析

❶ "本研究院"是本句的主语，因为上文已经出现过，所以这里使用 it 比较好，"已建立"是核心谓语，"广泛联系"是宾语，主句这里可以使用一般现在时或现在完成时。

❷ "与 10 多个国家和地区的宇航公司及空间研究机构"是状语，其中"与 10 多个国家和地区"是地点状语，虽然这里有"的"，但是地点可以处理为状语。"宇航公司及空间研究机构"是核心名词词组，这里可以用复数形式，也可以是单数形式，一致即可。

It has established extensive ties with aerospace corporations and space research organizations in more than 10 countries and regions.

这篇文章是典型的资讯介绍类文章，文章的内容非常专业化，但是句式结构可以说是这些年考试中比较简单的。CATTI 重点考查的是学生的翻译能力，而不是专业术语的积累，大家在平时的学习中要学会积累，也一定要学会利用字典，把字典好好利用起来，在考试当中才能百战百胜！

第三节 2017 年下半年三级笔译英译汉

原文（请先通读全文）

It was just one word in one email, but it triggered huge financial losses for a multinational company.

The message, written in English, was sent by a native speaker to a colleague for whom English was a second language. Unsure of the word, the recipient found two contradictory meanings in his dictionary. He acted on the wrong one.

Months later, senior management investigated why the project had flopped, costing hundreds of thousands of dollars. "It all traced back to this one word," says Chia Suan Chong, a UK-based communications skills and intercultural trainer, who didn't reveal the tricky word because it is highly industry-specific and possibly identifiable. "Things spiraled out of control because both parties were thinking the opposite."

When such misunderstandings happen, it's usually the native speakers who are to blame. Ironically, they are worse at delivering their message than people who speak English as a second or third language, according to Chong.

The non-native speakers, it turns out, speak more purposefully and carefully, typical of someone speaking a second or third language. Anglophones, on the other hand, often talk too fast for others to follow, and use jokes, slang and references specific to their own culture, says Chong.

"The native English speaker is the only one who might not feel the need to accommodate or adapt to the others," she adds.

Non-native speakers generally use more limited vocabulary and simpler expressions, without flowery language or slang. And then there's cultural style, Zurich-based Michael Blattner says. When a Brit reacts to a proposal by saying "That's interesting", a fellow Brit might recognize this as understatement for, "That's rubbish." But other nationalities would take the word "interesting" at face value, he says.

In Berlin, Dale Coulter, head of English at one language course provider, saw German staff of a Fortune 500 company being briefed from their Californian HQ via video link. Despite being competent in English, the Germans gleaned only the gist of what their American project leader said. So among themselves they came up with an agreed version, which might or might not have been what was intended by the California staff.

It's the native speaker who often risks missing out on closing a deal, warns Frenchman Jean-Paul Nerriere, formerly a senior international marketing executive at IBM.

"Too many non-Anglophones, especially the Asians and the French, are too concerned about not 'losing face'

— and nod approvingly while not getting the message at all," he says.

"When trying to communicate in English with a group of people with varying levels of fluency, it's important to be receptive and adaptable, turning your ears into a whole range of different ways of using English", says Jenkins, professor of global Englishes at the UK's University of Southampton.

"People who've learned other languages are good at doing that, but native speakers of English generally are monolingual and not very good at tuning in to language variation," she says.

In meetings, anglophones tend to speed along at what they consider a normal pace, and also rush to fill gaps in conversation, according to Rob Steggles, senior marketing director for Europe at a telecommunications company. He recommends making the same point in a couple of different ways and asking for some acknowledgement, reaction or action.

2017 年下半年的 CATTI 英译汉是少见的文科类文章，多年以来 CATTI 英译汉都是理科类的文章，但是这篇文章谈到了有关语言对全球化的影响。文章总体难度不是很大，也比较容易理解，其中的翻译现象非常多，所以请大家一定要看懂文章，用好翻译方法，才能写出较好的译文。

 It was just one word in one email, but it triggered huge financial losses for a multinational company.

第一步 词汇解析

❶ trigger，动词，表示"引起、发动、促使"，比如：The current recession was triggered by a slump in consumer spending.（目前的经济衰退是由消费支出骤跌引起的。）

❷ loss，名词，表示"损失、亏损、丧失"，比如：The company made a whopping 75 million dollar loss.（公司遭受了 7 500 万美元的巨额损失。）

❸ multinational，形容词，表示"跨国的、涉及多国的"，比如：In the mass production era multinational firms tended to centralize their operations.（在大规模生产的时代，跨国公司往往实行集权化经营。）

第二步 注意断句

It was just one word /in one email, /but it triggered huge financial losses /for a multinational company.

第三步 句型解析

❶ It was just one word in one email 是主系表状结构，但是翻译的时候，若翻译为"仅仅是一封邮件里的一个单词"，感觉上下文不太搭，看看后面一个句子说的是什么再翻译。

❷ but 是转折连词，it 是主语，指代前文的"这个单词"，triggered huge financial losses 是谓语和宾语，for a multinational company 是状语。这样上下文联系起来翻译，你再看看参考译文是怎么解决的。这里可以把 financial losses 认为是抽象名词，由于没有动词词根，所以可以增动词"遭受"，当然你要认为不增词也通顺，那也是完全可以的。

第四步 翻译来了

区区一封电子邮件里的一个单词,却导致一家跨国公司遭受巨大经济损失。

> **本句考点总结**
>
> 本句当中考查了"抽象名词"的译法。抽象名词一般处于冠词之后,又在介词之前,以"the + 抽象名词 + of"的形式居多。一般来说,抽象名词有两种译法。第一种,若抽象名词有动词词根,则翻译为动词,比如 the suggestion of mine,翻译为"我建议",而不是"我的建议";第二种,若抽象名词没有动词词根,可以增加词翻译,比如 the spirit of our nation,翻译为"我们民族所具有的精神",而不是"我们民族的精神"。

2

The message, written in English, was sent by a native speaker to a colleague for whom English was a second language. Unsure of the word, the recipient found two contradictory meanings in his dictionary. He acted on the wrong one.

第一步 词汇解析

1. colleague,名词,表示"同事",比如:He was accused of plagiarizing his colleague's results.(他被指控剽窃同事的成果。)
2. second language,名词词组,表示"第二语言",比如:French remained her second language for the rest of her life.(在她的余生中,法语一直是她的第二语言。)
3. recipient,名词,表示"接受者",比如:A suppressed immune system puts a transplant recipient at risk of other infections.(接受器官移植的病人在免疫系统受到抑制后很可能会感染其他疾病。)
4. contradictory,形容词,表示"相互矛盾的、对立的、不一致的",比如:We are faced with two apparently contradictory statements.(我们面前这两种说法显然是矛盾的。)
5. act on,动词词组,表示"奉行、按照……行动",比如:Why didn't you act on her suggestion?(你为什么没有按照她的建议去做呢?)

第二步 注意断句

The message, /written in English, /was sent /by a native speaker /to a colleague /for whom English was a second language. /Unsure of the word, /the recipient found two contradictory meanings /in his dictionary. /He acted on the wrong one.

第三步 句型解析

1. The message 是本句的主语,written in English 是过去分词短语作定语,也可以认为是插入语,其实是什么语法成分并没有那么重要,知道这个成分是修饰前文的 massage 即可,有逗号隔开,相当于非限定性定语从句,所以采用后置译法较好。was sent by a native speaker to a colleague 是本句的谓语和宾语,而且是被动语态,这里可以使用"寻找替代词"的译法。for whom English was a second language 是定语从句，用来修饰 a colleague，从句较短，可以前置翻译。

❷ Unsure of the word 是形容词短语位于句首，相当于分词位于句首，先找主语，再进行翻译，the recipient found two contradictory meanings in his dictionary 是主谓宾状的结构，后面一句 He acted on the wrong one 是主谓宾结构，这两句意思相近，所以可以合译。

❸ 注意参考译文中这句的顺序，"收件人先收到邮件"，再"发现这个单词有两个截然不同的意思"，再"不能确定"，最后"理解错了"，这个时间顺序安排得非常好，所以翻译一定要联系上下文。

第四步　翻译来了

这封电子邮件是由一位以英语为母语的人士用英语所写，而邮件接收人是一位以英语为第二语言的同事。这个同事收到邮件后，发现该单词在字典里有两个截然相反的意思，他不能确定，并最终按照那个错误的意思理解了。

本句考点总结

第一，非限定性定语从句是用逗号隔开的定语从句，这样的句子一般都要采用后置译法，在翻译时需要翻译出关系代词 which，who 等词，指明这些词的指代关系，将这些代词翻译出来。

第二，本句出现了被动语态的译法。被动语态是英文常见的一种形式，而在中文里常常少用"被"或者不用"被"。那么我们一般有什么样的译法呢？第一种是被动变主动，第二种是寻找替代词（比如："让……给""为……所"等结构），第三种是在科技文献中用"可以"来替代"被"，第四种是有"被"不用"被"。以上四种怎么用，那就看句子怎么通顺怎么翻译了啊！

第三，本句出现了英文定语从句的译法。一般来说，定语从句按照"短前长后"的译法处理，较短的定语从句可以前置，较长的定语从句可以后置，这一切都取决于句子的通顺，并没有绝对的前置和后置译法。

第四，本句出现了分词或分词短语位于名词后的译法。一般来说，分词或分词短语位于名词后相当于定语或定语从句，定语按照"短前长后"的译法来进行翻译。

---

3 Months later, senior management investigated why the project had flopped, costing hundreds of thousands of dollars. "It all traced back to this one word," says Chia Suan Chong, a UK-based communications skills and intercultural trainer, who didn't reveal the tricky word because it is highly industry-specific and possibly identifiable. "Things spiraled out of control because both parties were thinking the opposite."

第一步　词汇解析

❶ senior management，名词词组，表示"高级管理层"，比如：In her current role she broke through the glass ceiling as the first woman to reach senior management level in the company.（她冲破了职场上那道无形的障碍升至现在的职位，成为公司里第一个升至高级管理层的女性。）

② flop，动词，表示"失败、不成功"，比如：The film flopped badly at the box office. （这部电影票房惨淡。）

③ trace back，动词词组，表示"查出、找到、发现、追踪、追溯"，比如：He could trace his ancestors back seven hundred years. （他的先祖可以上溯到七百年前。）

④ intercultural，形容词，表示"跨文化的"，比如：intercultural communication ability（跨文化交际能力）。

⑤ trainer，名词，表示"教员、教练"，比如：Her trainer decided she shouldn't run in the race. （她的教练决定她不应参加赛跑。）

⑥ reveal，动词，表示"透露、露出"，比如：The article revealed intimate details about his family life. （文章披露了他家庭生活中的隐私。）

⑦ tricky，形容词，表示"难办的、难对付的"，比如：It's a very tricky problem, but I think there are a number of things you can do. （那是个非常棘手的问题，但我想有几件事你是可以做到的。）

⑧ specific，形容词，表示"特有的、独特的、只与……有关的"，比如：Most studies of trade have been country-specific. （有关贸易的多数研究都是具体针对某个国家的。）

⑨ identifiable，形容词，表示"可识别的、可辨认的"，比如：The house is easily identifiable by the large tree outside. （这房子很容易从外面的这棵大树辨认出来。）

⑩ spiral，动词，表示"急剧增长"，比如：Prices are spiraling out of control. （物价飞涨，失去控制。）

⑪ opposite，名词，表示"对立的人（或物）、对立面、反面"，比如：I thought she would be small and blonde but she's the complete opposite . （我原以为她是一位身材娇小的金发女郎，但她恰恰相反。）

第二步 注意断句

Months later, /senior management investigated /why the project had flopped, /costing hundreds of thousands of dollars. / "It all traced back /to this one word," /says Chia Suan Chong, /a UK-based communications skills / and intercultural trainer, /who didn't reveal the tricky word /because it is highly industry-specific /and possibly identifiable. /"Things spiraled out of control /because both parties were thinking the opposite."

第三步 句型解析

❶ 第一句中，Months later 是时间状语，senior management 是主语，investigated 是谓语，why the project had flopped 是宾语从句，总体结构简单，可以直接翻译，costing hundreds of thousands of dollars 是现在分词短语作伴随状语，也就是"这个公司高层调查了项目失败并损失几十万的原因"，特别要注意这里的 why 不翻译为"为什么"，而是"……的原因"，这个译法非常好，要学会使用。

❷ 第二句中的 "It all traced back to this one word," 是典型的直接引语，says Chia Suan Chong 是动词和说话人，后面接同位语 a UK-based communications skills and intercultural trainer，同位语如何翻译，不需要我再提醒了，后面再接非限定性定语从句 who didn't reveal the tricky word，总体采用后置译法较好，because 引导原因状语从句 it is highly industry-specific and possibly identifiable，总体结构不是很难，但是要注意两个点，一个是直接引语的译法，一个是定语从句的译法。还有一个小知识点，这里的 Chia Suan Chong 是威妥玛式标音法，你要是不知道翻译为"庄家宣"，你就按照读音翻译一下，然后用括号把英文抄下来即可。

❸ "Things spiraled out of control because both parties were thinking the opposite." 又是一个直接引语，其实还是前面说话人的话，所以这里可以增加对象词"她还说"，直接引语当中的 Things spiraled out of control 是主句，是主谓状结构，后面 because 引导原因状语从句，both parties were thinking the opposite 是主谓宾结构。

第四步 翻译来了

　　数月过去了，该跨国公司的高管调查了这个项目失败并损失几十万美元的原因。庄家宣

（Chia Suan Chong）是一名交流技能和跨文化培训师，供职于一家英国的机构，她说："查到最后就是因为这个词。"她并没有透露这个让人难以捉摸的单词，因为这是某行业的专业词汇，且可能被人猜到。她还说："由于双方的理解截然相反，事件不断升级，最终失控。"

> **本句考点总结**
>
> 　　第一，本句考查了英文直接引语的译法，最简单的译法就是保留冒号和双引号，说话人的位置和说话的内容都保持不变。即说话人在什么位置，就放在什么位置翻译，当然，说话人放在句首也是可以接受的。
>
> 　　第二，本句考查了英文同位语的译法。同位语是两个前后相互说明的名词或名词短语，比如 Beijing, the capital of China，有两种译法，第一种是"并列译法"，翻译为"中国的首都北京"；第二种是"主谓译法"，翻译为"北京是中国的首都"。具体用哪一种，可以根据句子具体情况而定，有时两种都是可以使用的。
>
> 　　第三，非限定性定语从句是用逗号隔开的定语从句，这样的句子一般都要采用后置译法，在翻译时需要翻译出关系代词 which，who 等词，指明这些词的指代关系，将这些代词翻译出来。
>
> 　　第四，本句考查了英汉互译增减词的问题，一般来说英译汉增词，汉译英减词，常见增词的种类有：一、增加对象词（范围词），这是由上文缺少句子的某个部分造成的；二、增加范畴词，这是较难的一部分，常见的范畴词有"水平、方式、方法、问题、情况、途径和方面"，但是不仅仅有这些，还有很多其他的；三、增加评论性词，这些常常出现在文学翻译中；四、增加动词，会在动词的"分配译法"中说明这点。

4 When such misunderstandings happen, it's usually the native speakers who are to blame. Ironically, they are worse at delivering their message than people who speak English as a second or third language, according to Chong.

第一步　词汇解析

 misunderstanding，名词，表示"误解、误会"，比如：There is still a fundamental misunderstanding about the real purpose of this work.（对于这项工作的真实目的，仍然存在着严重的误解。）

❷ be to blame，动词词组，表示"（对坏事）负有责任"，比如：If anyone's to blame, it's me.（如果有人该承担责任，那就是我。）

❸ ironically，副词，表示"具有讽刺意味地"，比如：Ironically, the book she felt was her worst sold more copies than any of her others.（具有讽刺意味的是，那本书她觉得最糟糕，却比她的其他任何一本书卖得都好。）

第二步　注意断句

　　When such misunderstandings happen, /it's usually the native speakers /who are to blame. /Ironically, /they are worse /at delivering their message /than people /who speak English /as a second or third language, /according to Chong.

第三步 句型解析

❶ 第一句中，When such misunderstandings happen 是时间状语从句，是主谓结构，it's usually the native speakers who are to blame 是主句，是强调结构，这点可以看出来吧？所以总体翻译不是很难。

❷ 第二句中，Ironically 是长副词，位于句首，可以单独成句，放在句中翻译通顺的话也可以，这种是文学的翻译方法，在非文学中也可以适当使用，they are worse 是主系表结构，at delivering their message 是状语，than people who speak English as a second or third language 是比较状语。这里有两个重点，一个是 worse than，这是"事实与评论"的关系，另一个是 who 引导的定语从句，从句较短，可以采用前置译法。according to Chong 是本句的状语，翻译为"根据庄"不通顺，还是翻译为"她说"更好一些，这也是代词的译法，当然，放在句首翻译更加通顺一些。

第四步 翻译来了

出现此类误解，责任通常在以英语为母语的人士。她认为，以英语为母语的人士在传达信息方面比以英语为第二语言或第三语言的人士要糟糕，这点很耐人寻味。

本句考点总结

第一，本句出现了事实（Facts）和评论（Comments）的译法。中文一般先事实，后评论，而英文一般先评论，后事实。比如：It is important for her to go abroad. 翻译为"对于她来说，出国是很重要的"。英文中 It is important 是评论，for her to go abroad 是事实，从中英文的对比来看，可以知道中英文语序分别是怎么安排的。

第二，本句出现了英文定语从句的译法。一般来说，定语从句按照"短前长后"的译法处理，较短的定语从句可以前置，较长的定语从句可以后置，这一切都取决于句子的通顺，并没有绝对的前置和后置译法。

---

5 The non-native speakers, it turns out, speak more purposefully and carefully, typical of someone speaking a second or third language. Anglophones, on the other hand, often talk too fast for others to follow, and use jokes, slang and references specific to their own culture, says Chong.

第一步 词汇解析

❶ anglophone，名词，表示"（母语为英语或因所在国的官方语言为英语而）讲英语的人"，比如：It's felt there's no future for Anglophones in the province.（让人感觉在这个省讲英语的人是没有前途的。）

❷ slang，名词，表示"俚语"，比如：He tends to use a lot of slang expressions that I've never heard before.（他往往用许多我以前从未听说过的俚语。）

❸ reference，名词，表示"引语、引用的观点、引证"，比如：a reference from the Quran（《古兰经》的引文）。

第二步 注意断句

The non-native speakers, /it turns out, /speak more purposefully and carefully, /typical of someone speaking a second or third language. /Anglophones, /on the other hand, /often talk too fast /for others /to follow, /and use jokes, / slang /and references /specific to their own culture, /says Chong.

第三步 句型解析

❶ The non-native speakers 是第一句的主语，it turns out 是插入语，表示观点，可以放在句首翻译，speak 是谓语，more purposefully and carefully 是状语，typical of someone speaking a second or third language 这个结构很有意思，是形容词短语位于句末，这个短语是用来修饰 The non-native speakers 的，完整结构应该是 The non-native speakers are typical of someone speaking a second or third language，这么一拆分，这个句子就很好懂了。

❷ Anglophones 是第二句的主语，on the other hand 是插入语，表示观点，可以放在句首翻译，often talk too fast for others to follow 是谓语和状语，其中有 too...to 结构，表示"太……而不能"，and 是并列连词，use 是第二个并列的谓语，jokes, slang and references specific to their own culture 是三个并列的宾语，要注意 specific to their own culture 的结构，这也是典型的形容词位于名词后作定语的结构，相当于定语从句，从句较短，可以采用前置译法，says Chong 是动词和说话人，可以放在句首翻译。

第四步 翻译来了

事实证明，母语为非英语的人说英语时表达更有目的性，也更细心，这个特点在说第二语言或第三语言的人身上很常见。她说，恰恰相反，母语为英语者常常语速太快导致其他人听不懂，并且他们常常夹杂着他们自己文化中特有的笑话、俚语和引用词句。

🧑‍🏫 本句考点总结

第一，本句当中出现了插入语的成分，插入语不表示观点时，一般需要放在原位翻译，原始的标点符号保留；插入语表示观点时，可以放在句首翻译。

第二，本句出现了分词或分词短语位于名词后的译法。一般来说，分词或分词短语位于名词后相当于定语或定语从句，定语按照"短前长后"的译法来进行翻译。

"The native English speaker is the only one who might not feel the need to accommodate or adapt to the others," she adds.

第一步 词汇解析

❶ accommodate，动词，表示"顺应、适应（新情况）"，比如：I needed to accommodate to the new schedule. （我需要适应新的时间表。）

第二步 注意断句

"The native English speaker is the only one /who might not feel the need /to accommodate or adapt /to the others," /she adds.

第三步 句型解析

❶ 本句是直接引语，这点大家应该很熟悉了，但还是需要在"本句考点总结"中好好复习。

❷ 直接引语中，The native English speaker 是主语，is the only one 是系表结构，who 引导定语从句，从句较长，可以采用后置译法，究竟是前置还是后置还是要根据句子通顺程度的。might not feel 是谓语，the need to accommodate or adapt to the others 是宾语，这组宾语中 need 是典型的抽象名词，由于有动词词根，所以可以翻译为动词"需要"，后面两个动词还是很好处理的。

❸ she adds 是说话人和动词，这个结构既可以放在句首，也可以放在句末。

第四步 翻译来了

她又说："母语为英语者是唯一觉得可能不需要改变自己来让自己适应其他群体的人。"

本句考点总结

第一，本句考查了英文直接引语的译法，最简单的译法就是保留冒号和双引号，说话人的位置和说话的内容都保持不变。即说话人在什么位置，就放在什么位置翻译，当然，说话人放在句首也是可以接受的。

第二，本句出现了英文定语从句的译法。一般来说，定语从句按照"短前长后"的译法处理，较短的定语从句可以前置，较长的定语从句可以后置，这一切都取决于句子的通顺，并没有绝对的前置和后置译法。

第三，本句当中考查了"抽象名词"的译法。抽象名词一般处于冠词之后，又在介词之前，以"the + 抽象名词 + of"的形式居多。一般来说，抽象名词有两种译法。第一种，若抽象名词有动词词根，则翻译为动词，比如 the suggestion of mine，翻译为"我建议"，而不是"我的建议"；第二种，若抽象名词没有动词词根，可以增动词翻译，比如 the spirit of our nation，翻译为"我们民族所具有的精神"，而不是"我们民族的精神"。

7 Non-native speakers generally use more limited vocabulary and simpler expressions, without flowery language or slang. And then there's cultural style, Zurich-based Michael Blattner says. When a Brit reacts to a proposal by saying "That's interesting", a fellow Brit might recognize this as understatement for, "That's rubbish." But other nationalities would take the word "interesting" at face value, he says.

第一步 词汇解析

❶ expression，名词，表示"表达、表达方式"，比如：an old-fashioned expression（过时的表达方式）。

❷ flowery，形容词，表示"过分复杂费解的、华而不实的"，比如：They were using uncommonly flowery language.（他们使用了极其华丽的辞藻。）

❸ Zurich，苏黎世，地名，相对知名的地名大家还是多记忆，多了解，多背诵。

地理小常识：

　　苏黎世，位于瑞士联邦中北部，是瑞士联邦最大的城市、苏黎世州的首府，全国政治、经济、文化和交通中心，也是全欧洲最富有的城市。该市已连续多年被联合国人居署评为全球最宜居的城市之一。

❹ Michael Blattner，迈克尔·布拉特纳，人名，这里采用的是音译法，注意名和姓之间要加·，翻译英文人名不确定时，可以使用音译法，然后把英文人名抄下来，放在括号里，这样保险一些。

❺ Brit，名词，表示"英国人"，比如：Holiday mad Brits are packing their buckets and spades and heading for the sun.（酷爱假日的英国人正收拾小桶和锹铲前往阳光充足的地方。）

❻ react，动词，表示"（对……）做出反应、回应"，比如：Local residents have reacted angrily to the news.（当地居民对这一消息表示愤怒。）

❼ fellow，名词，表示"同事、同辈"，比如：She has a very good reputation among her fellows.（她在同事中的口碑甚佳。）

❽ understatement，名词，表示"轻描淡写、重事轻说、淡化"，比如：He informed us with massive understatement that he was feeling disappointed.（他极力轻描淡写地跟我们说他感到失望。）

❾ take sth. at face value，动词词组，表示"按照表面意思"，比如：You shouldn't take anything she says at face value.（她的话你绝对不能只看表面。）

第二步 注意断句

　　Non-native speakers generally use more limited vocabulary /and simpler expressions, /without flowery language or slang. /And then /there's cultural style, /Zurich-based Michael Blattner says. /When a Brit reacts to a proposal /by saying "That's interesting", /a fellow Brit might recognize this /as understatement for, /"That's rubbish." /But other nationalities would take the word "interesting" /at face value, / he says.

第三步 句型解析

❶ 第一句中，Non-native speakers generally use more limited vocabulary and simpler expressions 是主谓宾结构，without flowery language or slang 是状语，表示"而不是用……"，句式结构简单，直接翻译即可。

❷ 第二句中，And then 是并列连词和副词，这里表示"除了以上这些"，因为是承接上文的关系，所以翻译时需要注意上下文连接的问题，there's cultural style 是典型的 there be 句型，Zurich-based Michael Blattner says 是主谓结构，这里要注意 Zurich-based 的含义，表示"在苏黎世工作的"，而不是"以苏黎世为基地的"。

❸ 第三句中，When a Brit reacts to a proposal by saying "That's interesting" 是时间状语从句，by 引导方式状语，这个结构不难，但是翻译倒是值得研究，还记得我在《十二天突破英汉翻译》里说的吗？这里的"That's interesting" 是"中间语言"，所谓"中间语言"指的是用来解释的语言或是除了原文和译文的第三种语言，这里的 "That's interesting" 就是第一种情况，你要翻译为"蛮有趣"，只会让读者感到莫名其妙，所以先把原文抄下来，再进行翻译会更好。第三句的主句是 a fellow Brit might recognize this as understatement for, "That's rubbish." 这个句子是主谓宾状的结构，其中有 recognize...as 的结构，也就是"把……认为……"。

❹ 第四句中，But 是转折连词，other nationalities would take the word "interesting" at face value 是主谓宾状

结构，he says 是主谓结构，你可以把说话人和动词放在句首，放在句末也是可以的。

第四步 翻译来了

母语为非英语的人士在讲英语时，通常使用数量有限的词汇和简单的表达方式，不花哨，也不夹带俚语。在苏黎世工作的迈克尔·布拉特纳（Michael Blattner）说，除此之外，还有文化风格的问题。比如，一个英国人在评价一项提议时说"That's interesting"（蛮有趣），此时，另一个英国人会把这句话理解为"太垃圾"的含蓄说法。他说，而其他国家的人则只会取"interesting"（有趣）的字面意思进行理解。

In Berlin, Dale Coulter, head of English at one language course provider, saw German staff of a Fortune 500 company being briefed from their Californian HQ via video link. Despite being competent in English, the Germans gleaned only the gist of what their American project leader said. So among themselves they came up with an agreed version, which might or might not have been what was intended by the California staff.

第一步 词汇解析

① Berlin，柏林，地名，相对知名的地名大家还是多记忆，多了解，多背诵。

地理小常识：

柏林（Berlin），位于德国东北部，是德国的首都和最大的城市，也是德国的政治、文化、交通及经济中心。

② Dale Coulter，达勒·库尔特，人名，这里采用的是音译法，注意名和姓之间要加·，翻译英文人名不确定时，可以使用音译法，然后把英文人名抄下来，放在括号里，这样保险一些。

③ Fortune 500，专有名词，表示"世界 500 强"。

经济小常识：

"世界 500 强"，是中国人对美国财富杂志每年评选的"全球最大五百家公司"排行榜的一种约定俗成的叫法。《财富》世界 500 强排行榜一直是衡量全球大型公司的最著名、最权威的榜单。由《财富》杂志每年发布一次。

④ brief，动词，表示"（就某项工作或某一重大事件）向……简要介绍情况"，比如：A Defense Department spokesman briefed reporters.（一位国防部发言人向记者们简要介绍了情况。）

⑤ HQ，名词缩略语，即 headquarter，表示"总部"，比如：the European Commission's luxurious HQ（奢华的欧盟委员会总部）。

⑥ competent，形容词，表示"足以胜任的、有能力的、称职的"，比如：Make sure the firm is competent to carry out the work.（要确保这家公司有能力完成这项工作。）

⑦ glean，动词，表示"四处搜集（信息、知识等）"，比如：At present we're gleaning information from all sources.（目前，我们正从各种渠道收集信息。）

⑧ gist，名词，表示"要点、主旨、大意"，比如：I missed the beginning of the lecture — can you give me the gist of what he said?（我没听到讲座的开头——给我讲讲他说话的要点好吗？）

⑨ come up with，动词词组，表示"想出、提出（计划、想法等）"，比如：Several of the members have come up with suggestions of their own.（有几位成员提出了自己的建议。）

第二步 注意断句

In Berlin, /Dale Coulter, /head of English at one language course provider, /saw German staff of a Fortune 500 company /being briefed from their Californian HQ /via video link. /Despite being competent in English, /the Germans gleaned only the gist of what their American project leader said. /So /among themselves /they came up with an agreed version, /which might or might not have been what was intended /by the California staff.

第三步 句型解析

❶ 第一句中，In Berlin 是地点状语，Dale Coulter 是主语，head of English at one language course provider 是主语的同位语，同位语可以采用"并列译法"，也可以采用"主谓译法"，怎么通顺怎么翻译，saw 是核心谓语，German staff of a Fortune 500 company 是宾语，后面的 being briefed from their Californian HQ via video link 是宾语补足语，这里要注意 being briefed 是典型的被动语态，因为没有 by sb.，所以可以使用"被动变主动"的译法。

❷ 第二句中，Despite being competent in English 是让步状语，the Germans gleaned only the gist of what their American project leader said 是主句，也是主谓宾结构，要注意 what 的译法，和 the gist 有一定关系，就是"讲话的大意"。

❸ 第三句中，So 是并列连词，among themselves 是状语，they came up with an agreed version 是主谓宾结构，表示"他们达成了一致"，which 引导非限定性定语从句，might or might not have been 是系动词，what was intended by the California staff 是表语从句，非限定性定语从句需要采用后置译法，还要注意 what was intended 的含义，表示"……的本意"，其实这也是名词性从句变成名词的译法。

第四步 翻译来了

在柏林，达勒·库尔特（Dale Coulter）是某语言课程供应商英语部主任，他曾见过某世界500强公司的加州总部通过视频给该公司的德国员工开会。尽管这些德国人英语还不错，但是，他们只记住了美方项目领导讲话的大概意思。所以，对于该情况通报，德国员工内部达成一致意见，而他们的版本与加州总部相关人员的本意可能一致，也可能不一致。

本句考点总结

第一，本句考查了英文同位语的译法。同位语是两个前后相互说明的名词或名词短语，比如 Beijing, the capital of China，有两种译法，第一种是"并列译法"，翻译为"中国的首都北京"；第二种是"主谓译法"，翻译为"北京是中国的首都"。具体用哪一种，可以根据句子具体情况而定，有时两种都是可以使用的。

第二，本句出现了被动语态的译法。被动语态是英文常见的一种形式，而在中文里常常少用"被"或者不用"被"。那么我们一般有什么样的译法呢？第一种是被动变主动，第二种是寻找替代词（比如："让……给""为……所"等结构），第三种是在科技文献中用"可以"来替代"被"，第四种是有"被"不用"被"。以上四种怎么用，那就看句子怎么通顺怎么翻译了啊！

9. It's the native speaker who often risks missing out on closing a deal, warns Frenchman Jean-Paul Nerriere, formerly a senior international marketing executive at IBM.

第一步 词汇解析

1. risk，动词，表示"冒……的风险（或危险）"，比如：They knew they risked being arrested.（他们知道自己冒着被捕的危险。）
2. miss out on，动词词组，表示"错过、错失、错过机会"，比如：Of course I'm coming — I don't want to miss out on all the fun!（我当然要来——我可不想错失好玩的机会。）
3. close a deal，动词词组，表示"成交、做成一笔交易"，比如：close a deal with a solvent service company（与一个有偿付能力的服务公司谈成生意）。
4. Jean-Paul Nerriere，让·保罗·奈易耶，人名，这里采用的是音译法，注意名和姓之间要加·，翻译英文人名不确定时，可以使用音译法，然后把英文人名抄下来，放在括号里，这样保险一些。
5. a senior international marketing executive，名词词组，表示"国际营销部高级执行总裁"。

第二步 注意断句

It's the native speaker /who often risks missing out on closing a deal, /warns Frenchman Jean-Paul Nerriere, /formerly a senior international marketing executive /at IBM.

第三步 句型解析

1. 本句是强调句，the native speaker 是被强调的部分，后面的 who 引导其余部分，often risks missing out on closing a deal 是谓宾结构，warns Frenchman Jean-Paul Nerriere 是动词和说话人，这个部分放在句首或是句末都是可以的，formerly a senior international marketing executive at IBM 是前面人名的同位语，翻译的方法都很清楚吧！

第四步 翻译来了

正是母语为英语者常常导致交易可能无法达成，法国人让·保罗·奈易耶（Jean-Paul Nerriere）说道。他曾担任 IBM 国际营销部高级执行总裁。

本句考点总结

本句考查了英文同位语的译法。同位语是两个前后相互说明的名词或名词短语，比如 Beijing, the capital of China，有两种译法，第一种是"并列译法"，翻译为"中国的首都北京"；第二种是"主谓译法"，翻译为"北京是中国的首都"。具体用哪一种，可以根据句子具体情况而定，有时两种都是可以使用的。

"Too many non-Anglophones, especially the Asians and the French, are too concerned about not 'losing face' — and nod approvingly while not getting the message at all," he says.

第一步 词汇解析

① nod，动词，表示"点头"，比如：I asked him if he would help me and he nodded.（我问他能不能帮我一下，他点了点头。）

② approvingly，副词，表示"赞许地、满意地"，比如：Eve nodded, almost approvingly.（伊芙几乎赞同地点了点头。）

第二步 注意断句

"Too many non-Anglophones, /especially the Asians and the French, /are too concerned /about not 'losing face' — /and nod approvingly /while not getting the message at all," /he says.

第三步 句型解析

① 本句考查的是直接引语的译法，这个方法我们在前面的真题解析中已经解释得非常清晰，请大家参考"本句考点总结"。

② 直接引语中，Too many non-Anglophones 是主语，especially the Asians and the French 解释前面的名词，are too concerned about not 'losing face' 是系表结构，后面的破折号可以保留，也可以变成逗号，and 是并列连词，nod 是第二个谓语动词，approvingly 是副词作状语，while 引导时间状语，not getting the message at all 这个动作和前面的 nod 是同时进行的。

第四步 翻译来了

他说："太多的母语为非英语者，特别是亚洲人和法国人，把'不丢脸'看得太重，所以，即使不懂，也要点头装懂。"

本句考点总结

本句考查了英文直接引语的译法，最简单的译法就是保留冒号和双引号，说话人的位置和说话的内容都保持不变。即说话人在什么位置，就放在什么位置翻译，当然，说话人放在句首也是可以接受的。

"When trying to communicate in English with a group of people with varying levels of fluency, it's important to be receptive and adaptable, turning your ears into a whole range of different ways of using English", says Jenkins, professor of global Englishes at the UK's University of Southampton.

第一步 词汇解析

❶ varying，形容词，表示"不同的"，比如：New techniques were introduced with varying degrees of success.（引进新技术的成功程度不尽相同。）

❷ fluency，名词，表示"流利、流畅"，比如：The research investigates how foreign speakers gain fluency.（这项研究旨在调查讲外语的人如何增加流利程度。）

❸ receptive，形容词，表示"（对新观点、建议等）愿意倾听的、乐于接受的"，比如：She was always receptive to new ideas.（她总是愿意接受新观点。）

❹ Jenkins，詹金斯，人名，这里采用的是音译法，翻译英文人名不确定时，可以使用音译法，然后把英文人名抄下来，放在括号里，这样保险一些。

❺ University of Southampton，专有名词，表示"南安普顿大学"。

教育小常识：

  南安普顿大学，勋衔 Soton，世界百强名校，英国顶尖学府。英国皇家勋授大学，英国罗素大学集团创始成员，世界大学联盟、科学与工程南联盟、国际大学气候联盟、世界港口城市大学联盟、RENKEI 成员。

第二步 注意断句

"When trying to communicate /in English /with a group of people /with varying levels of fluency, /it's important /to be receptive and adaptable, /turning your ears /into a whole range of different ways of using English", / says Jenkins, /professor of global Englishes /at the UK's University of Southampton.

第三步 句型解析

❶ 本句考查的是直接引语的译法，这个方法我们在前面的真题解析中已经解释得非常清晰，请大家参考"本句考点总结"。

❷ 直接引语中的 When trying to communicate in English with a group of people with varying levels of fluency 是时间状语，分词 trying 前缺少主语，需要增主语，根据上下文，增"你"更加合适。it's important 后面的不定式短语 to be receptive and adaptable 是真正的主语，这里是"事实与评论"的关系，先翻译不定式短语，注意后面的 turning your ears into a whole range of different ways of using English 也要一同翻译出来，因为这个动作是前面动作的伴随状态，最后再翻译"评论"important。

❸ says Jenkins 是动词和说话人，放在句首翻译或是句末翻译都是可以的，professor of global Englishes at the UK's University of Southampton 是同位语，用来解释说明前面的说话人，同位语的译法已经强调过很多遍，注意看"本句考点总结"。

第四步 翻译来了

  "和英语水平参差不齐的一群人用英语交流时，你要善于倾听和适应，多听听其他人是如何用不同方式使用英语的，这一点很重要。"英国南安普顿大学国际英语教授詹金斯（Jenkins）这样说道。

259

本句考点总结

第一,本句考查了英文直接引语的译法,最简单的译法就是保留冒号和双引号,说话人的位置和说话的内容都保持不变。即说话人在什么位置,就放在什么位置翻译,当然,说话人放在句首也是可以接受的。

第二,本句出现了事实(Facts)和评论(Comments)的译法。中文一般先事实,后评论,而英文一般先评论,后事实。比如:It is important for her to go abroad. 翻译为"对于她来说,出国是很重要的"。 英文中 It is important 是评论,for her to go abroad 是事实,从中英文的对比来看,可以知道中英文语序分别是怎么安排的。

第三,本句考查了英文同位语的译法。同位语是两个前后相互说明的名词或名词短语,比如 Beijing, the capital of China,有两种译法,第一种是"并列译法",翻译为"中国的首都北京";第二种是"主谓译法",翻译为"北京是中国的首都"。具体用哪一种,可以根据句子具体情况而定,有时两种都是可以使用的。

12

"People who've learned other languages are good at doing that, but native speakers of English generally are monolingual and not very good at tuning in to language variation," she says.

第一步 词汇解析

❶ monolingual,形容词,表示"单语的、只用一种语言的",比如:a native monolingual speaker of English(母语为英语的单语说话者)。

❷ tune in to,动词词组,表示"适应、收听、收看",比如:Budding linguists can tune in to the activity cassettes in French, German, Spanish and Italian.(崭露头角的语言学家们可以收听法语、德语、西班牙语和意大利语的活动磁带。)本句中表示的是"转向、适应"。

❸ variation,名词,表示"变化、变异、变更",比如:The survey found a wide variation in the prices charged for canteen food.(调查发现食堂饭菜的价格相差很大。)

第二步 注意断句

"People /who've learned other languages are good at doing that, /but native speakers of English generally are monolingual /and not very good at tuning in to language variation," /she says.

第三步 句型解析

❶ 本句考查的是直接引语的译法,这个方法我们在前面的真题解析中已经解释得非常清晰,请大家参考"本句考点总结"。

❷ 直接引语中,People who've learned other languages are good at doing that 是主系表结构,who 引导定语从句,从句较短,可以采用前置译法,特别要注意表语中的 that,这里指代的是上文教授说的话,可以译为"这点"。

❸ but 是转折连词，native speakers of English generally are monolingual 是主系表结构，and 是并列连词，not very good at tuning in to language variation 是第二组系表结构，句式结构简单，直接翻译即可，注意 tune in to 此处表示"适应、转向"。

❹ she says 是说话人和动词，放在句首翻译或是句末翻译都是可以的。

第四步 翻译来了

她说："学习了其他语言的人士在这点上就做得很好，而英语为母语的人士通常只会英语这个单一语言，他们不大适应语言的其他变化。"

本句考点总结

第一，本句考查了英文直接引语的译法，最简单的译法就是保留冒号和双引号，说话人的位置和说话的内容都保持不变。即说话人在什么位置，就放在什么位置翻译，当然，说话人放在句首也是可以接受的。

第二，本句出现了英文定语从句的译法。一般来说，定语从句按照"短前长后"的译法处理，较短的定语从句可以前置，较长的定语从句可以后置，这一切都取决于句子的通顺，并没有绝对的前置和后置译法。

---

13 In meetings, anglophones tend to speed along at what they consider a normal pace, and also rush to fill gaps in conversation, according to Rob Steggles, senior marketing director for Europe at a telecommunications company. He recommends making the same point in a couple of different ways and asking for some acknowledgement, reaction or action.

第一步 词汇解析

❶ rush to，动词词组，表示"急于、着急做"，比如：Before you rush to book a table, bear in mind that lunch for two would cost ￡150.（在你抢着订桌之前，记住两个人在那里吃一顿午饭得花 150 英镑。）

❷ Rob Steggles，罗伯·斯特格勒斯，人名，这里采用的是音译法，注意名和姓之间要加·，翻译英文人名不确定时，可以使用音译法，然后把英文人名抄下来，放在括号里，这样保险一些。

❸ acknowledgement，名词，表示"（对事实、现实、存在的）承认"，比如：This report is an acknowledgement of the size of the problem.（这个报告承认了问题的严重性。）

❹ reaction，名词，表示"反应、回应"，比如：People's reaction to the film has varied greatly.（人们对这部影片的反应大不一样。）

第二步 注意断句

In meetings, /anglophones tend to speed along /at what they consider a normal pace, /and also rush to fill gaps /in conversation, /according to Rob Steggles, /senior marketing director /for Europe /at a telecommunications company. /He recommends making the same point /in a couple of different ways /and asking for some acknowledgement, /reaction or action.

第三步　句型解析

❶ 第一句中，In meetings 是地点状语，anglophones tend to speed along 是主谓状结构，后面再接状语 at what they consider a normal pace，注意这里的 at...pace 表示"以……的速度"。

❷ and 是并列连词，also rush to fill gaps in conversation 是第二组谓语和宾语，according to Rob Steggles 是状语，前文就是这个人说的话。senior marketing director for Europe at a telecommunications company 是同位语，用来解释说明前面的名词，同位语的译法讲解了很多遍，请大家仔细查阅"本句考点总结"。

❸ 第二句中，He recommends making the same point 是主谓宾结构，后面接状语 in a couple of different ways，and 是并列连词，asking for some acknowledgement, reaction or action 是和 making the same point 并列，直接翻译似乎不是很完整，可以增词"母语为英语者说话时"，与其说这是增词，不如说是增句子，这样是为了让句子更加通顺。

第四步　翻译来了

在开会的时候，母语为英语者常常语速飞快，而他们自己则认为这是正常的语速，并且在对话的空隙，他们会见缝插针讲上几句，某电信企业欧洲市场营销部门高级主任罗伯·斯特格勒斯（Rob Steggles）这样说。他建议，母语为英语者说话时，用多种不同方式来表达同一要点，并且让听者给些认可、反应或行动。

本句考点总结

第一，本句考查了英文同位语的译法。同位语是两个前后相互说明的名词或名词短语，比如 Beijing, the capital of China，有两种译法，第一种是"并列译法"，翻译为"中国的首都北京"；第二种是"主谓译法"，翻译为"北京是中国的首都"。具体用哪一种，可以根据句子具体情况而定，有时两种都是可以使用的。

第二，本句考查了英汉互译增减词的问题，一般来说英译汉增词，汉译英减词，常见增词的种类有：一、增加对象词（范围词），这是由上文缺少句子的某个部分造成的；二、增加范畴词，这是较难的一部分，常见的范畴词有"水平、方式、方法、问题、情况、途径和方面"，但是不仅仅有这些，还有很多其他的；三、增加评论性词，这些常常出现在文学翻译中；四、增加动词，会在动词的"分配译法"中说明这点。

译后总结

这篇文章也是典型的外刊文体，但是文章罕见地谈到了语言的问题，文章整体难度不大，还是没有绕开有关直接引语的译法。但是不知道大家发现没有，其实文科的文章比理科的文章更加"绕"一些，语言上也要更加通俗一些，如何把直接引语内的话翻译得更加口语，这也是翻译中很重要的问题，请大家继续好好训练！

第四节　2017年下半年三级笔译汉译英

气候变化已不是单纯的环境保护问题，而成为人类生存与发展问题。中国需要改变以煤为主的能源结构和高污染、高能耗的产业结构，以治理环境和应对全球气候变化。

同时，积极应对气候变化也是中国参与全球治理的责任，也是实现可持续发展的迫切需要。中国作为世界最大的发展中国家，需要积极推动经济与能源的转型，以推动全球可持续发展。

长期以来，中国高度重视气候变化问题，把积极应对气候变化作为国家经济社会发展的重大战略，把绿色低碳发展作为生态文明建设的重要内容，采取了一系列行动，为应对全球气候变化做出了重要贡献。

到2020年单位国内生产总值二氧化碳排放比2005年下降40%~45%，非化石能源占一次能源消费总量的比重达到15%，森林面积比2005年增加4 000万公顷，森林蓄积量比2005年增加13亿立方米。

中国还将在农业、林业、水资源等重点领域和城市、沿海、生态脆弱地区形成有效抵御气候变化风险的机制，提高抵抗能力。

CATTI三级笔译2017年下半年的这篇汉译英又回到了《政府工作报告》和政府白皮书的类型，这种类型的文章内容不是特别难，而且这篇文章是大家熟悉的环保问题，需要注意的是有关词汇的积累和简单句式结构的运用，保证单词不错，句型不错，这些才是汉译英的王道！

气候变化已不是单纯的环境保护问题，而成为人类生存与发展问题。中国需要改变以煤为主的能源结构和高污染、高能耗的产业结构，以治理环境和应对全球气候变化。

第一步　词汇解析

❶ 气候变化，climate change，名词词组，比如：Climate change is still very much a subject for debate.（气候变化很大程度上仍是一个争论的话题。）

❷ 环境保护问题，an environmental protection issue，名词词组，比如：The attention to environmental protection issue has become an irreversible historical trend.（对环境问题的关注已经成为一种不可逆转的历史潮流。）

【同义词辨析】

problem：指客观上存在的、难以处理或难以理解的问题；

question：通常指口头或书面提出来要求回答或有待讨论解决的问题；

issue：多指意见能达到一致的问题，着重指争论或讨论中的问题；

matter：含义不是很具体，暗示人们考虑和关心的事和话题。

❸ 人类生存与发展（问题），human existence and development，名词词组。

❹ 以煤为主的能源结构，coal-centered energy mix，名词词组。
以……为主的，centered，形容词，用以构成复合词，比如：a dark-centered coneflower（黑色花心的金光菊花）。

❺ 高污染、高能耗的产业结构，industrial structure that leads to high pollution and high energy consumption，名词词组。
产业结构，industrial structure，名词词组，比如：We will adjust and optimize the industrial structure.（我们要调整并优化产业结构。）
能耗，意思是"能源消耗"，energy consumption，名词词组，比如：Energy consumption rises as countries industrialize.（能源消耗随着各国工业化而增加。）

❻ 治理，clean up，动词词组，比如：Under pressure from the public, many regional governments cleaned up their beaches.（迫于公众的压力，许多地区政府治理了海滩污染。）

第二步 动词定位

气候变化已不是单纯的环境保护问题，而成为人类生存与发展问题。中国需要改变以煤为主的能源结构和高污染、高能耗的产业结构，以治理环境和应对全球气候变化。

第三步 句型解析

❶ 第一句中，"气候变化"是主语，"已不是"是谓语，这里用一般现在时比较好，"单纯的环境保护问题"是宾语，谓语翻译为 is not 是完全可以的，参考译文使用 more than 是为了强调，其实没必要翻译得这么复杂，还要注意一个小问题，这里的"单纯的"只是强调，可以不翻译，"环境保护问题"可以翻译为 an environmental protection issue。

❷ 本句的第二个谓语是"而成为"，注意句子之间的连接，这两句之间没有太大关系，可以用 and 连接，"人类生存与发展问题"是宾语，这里的"问题"是典型的范畴词，可以不翻译，直接翻译为 human existence and development 即可。

❸ 第二句中，"中国"是主语，"需要改变"是谓语，"以煤为主的能源结构和高污染、高能耗的产业结构"是宾语，但是要注意理解"改变"，这里的"改变"是指"产业的升级和改造"，所以使用 upgrade 更好一些，翻译为 change 肯定是不对的，宾语中"能源结构和产业结构"是核心宾语，两个宾语前分别有两组定语，一组是"以煤为主的"，翻译为 coal-centered，一组是"高污染、高能耗的"，这组定语较长，可以采用后置译法，翻译为定语从句 that leads to high pollution and high energy consumption。

❹ 句子后面的"以治理……和应对……"是本句的第二组动词，这里表示目的，"环境"和"全球气候变化"分别是两个动词的宾语，直接翻译即可，都是常见的单词和词组，请大家一定要熟记！本句考查的重点是两个（组）动词的翻译方法，应该如何处理呢？请大家仔细看看"本句考点总结"。

第四步 翻译来了

Climate change is more than an environmental protection issue and also affects human existence and development. To clean up the environment and cope with global climate change, China needs to upgrade its coal-centered energy mix and industrial structure that leads to high pollution and high energy consumption.

> **本句考点总结**
>
> 汉译英句子中并列、伴随、下沉的结构。中文常常会出现多个句子聚集的情况,那么我们在翻译时需要考虑将这些句子进行"分堆"。但是"分堆"之后,一个句子中也可能会出现两个动词或两组动词,那么有两个动词或两组动词的句子我们该如何进行翻译呢?比如:"我坐在那里看书",这里有两个动词,一个是"坐",一个是"看",我们翻译时便会有三种方法:
>
> 第一种并列(两个动词并列的译法,使用并列连词连接,两个动词之间不一定是"并列"关系):I sat there and read a book.
>
> 第二种伴随(将第二个动词翻译为二谓语,分词、从句、状语等都可以):I sat there reading a book.
>
> 第三种下沉(将第一个动词翻译为二谓语,分词、从句、状语等都可以):Sitting there, I read a book.
>
> 需要说明的是,并列、伴随和下沉只是动词的形式问题,不代表动词之间的逻辑关系,用这三种形式翻译两个动词或两组动词都是可以的,大家可以根据句子上下文的关系来判断使用。

2 同时,积极应对气候变化也是中国参与全球治理的责任,也是实现可持续发展的迫切需要。中国作为世界最大的发展中国家,需要积极推动经济与能源的转型,以推动全球可持续发展。

第一步 词汇解析

❶ 应对,cope with,动词词组,比如:Fit people are better able to cope with stress.(健康的人能更好地应对压力。)

❷ 全球治理,global governance,名词词组,比如:an equitable global governance structure(一个公平的全球治理架构)。

治理,governance,比如:He will meet with officials from several countries to discuss ways to promote good governance.(他将与诸国官员会面,讨论如何促进对国家的良性管理。)本文中"治理"一词出现了两次,但词义是不同的。"治理环境"的意思是"清洁环境",翻译为动词词组 clean up。"全球治理"的意思是"(国家的)统治方式、管理方式",翻译为名词 governance。

❸ 可持续发展,sustainable development,名词词组,比如:How to maintain sustainable development is a matter of significant importance facing all countries.(如何保持可持续发展是所有国家面临的一个重大问题。)

❹ 迫切需要,an urgent requirement for,名词词组。

❺ 发展中国家,(a) developing country,名词词组,比如:As a developing country, South Africa has also made great efforts in environmental protection.(作为发展中国家,南非在环保方面也做出了巨大努力。)"发达国家"翻译为 (a) developed country。

❻ 经济与能源的转型,the transformation of economy and the upgrading of energy mix,名词词组。这个词组的意思是"经济转型和能源结构的升级"。

转型，transformation，名词，意思是"变革"，比如：The transformation of American sea power began in 1940.（美国海军力量的改革始于1940年。）

升级，upgrading，名词，比如：Upgrading is harder than expanding.（升级比扩张要困难得多。）

第二步 动词定位

同时，积极应对气候变化也是中国参与全球治理的责任，也是实现可持续发展的迫切需要。中国作为世界最大的发展中国家，需要积极推动经济与能源的转型，以推动全球可持续发展。

第三步 句型解析

❶ 第一句中，句首的"同时"是时间状语，翻译为 At the same time，Meanwhile 等词都是可以的。

❷ 第一句中，"积极应对气候变化"是本句的主语，动词作主语时的主要翻译方法是使用动名词或不定式结构，选择哪一种都是可以的，"也是"是本句的谓语，英文中是系动词结构，这里使用一般现在时比较好，所以翻译为 is 最合适，"中国参与全球治理的责任"是本句的宾语，核心名词是"责任"，前面"中国参与全球治理的"是定语，定语较长，可以采用后置译法，注意这里的"治理"是四谓语，不需要翻译，参考译文中给出了 China's responsibility in global governance 的结构，把 in 理解为动词"参与"也可以，这个知识点确实很难。本句的第二组宾语是"迫切需要"，前面的定语是"实现可持续发展的"，动词"实现"和上一句是同样的译法，也翻译为三谓语介词 for 或者四谓语不译。以上处理动词的方法，大家一定要仔细理解，这就是常说的"谓语动词的层次性"，请大家仔细看看"本句考点总结"。

❸ 第二句中，"中国"是本句的主语，"作为世界最大的发展中国家"是第一组谓语和宾语，"需要积极推动"是第二组谓语，"经济与能源的转型"是宾语，"以推动"是第三组谓语，"全球可持续发展"是宾语，本句有三组动词，如何处理更好呢？本质上是两个动词的问题，第一个动词处理为下沉结构 as，第二个动词处理为核心结构，第三个动词处理为目的状语 to do，这样的结构相信谁看到都会觉得很漂亮，那么，本句就是"下沉"+"核心"+"伴随"的结构，这样大家就很清楚了。

第四步 翻译来了

At the same time, actively addressing climate change is also China's responsibility in global governance and an urgent requirement for sustainable development. As the world's largest developing country, China needs to actively promote the transformation of economy and the upgrading of energy mix to enhance global sustainable development.

本句考点总结

第一，关于谓语动词的层次性。汉译英的核心问题是厘清句子当中多个动词之间的关系，我们要学会在多个动词当中找到最核心的动词，翻译为核心谓语（也称为一谓语），找到其次核心的动词，翻译为分词、从句、其他状语或定语的形式（也称为二谓语）；再找到不重要的动词，翻译为介词（也称为三谓语）；最后最不重要的动词，可以不译（也称为四谓语）。这些动词在句子当中如何划分层次，需要大家在长期不断的实践中摸索，而且每个句子的翻译也不是固定的。有些句子当中的"一谓语"（核心谓语），在别的译本当中可能就是"二谓语"或者是"三谓语"。只要句子整体结构正确，逻辑清晰，那这就是一个好的译本。

> 第二，汉译英句子中并列、伴随、下沉的结构。中文常常会出现多个句子聚集的情况，那么我们在翻译时需要考虑将这些句子进行"分堆"。但是"分堆"之后，一个句子中也可能会出现两个动词或两组动词，那么有两个动词或两组动词的句子我们该如何进行翻译呢？比如："我坐在那里看书"，这里有两个动词，一个是"坐"，一个是"看"，我们翻译时便会有三种方法：
> 　　第一种并列（两个动词并列的译法，使用并列连词连接，两个动词之间不一定是"并列"关系）：I sat there and read a book.
> 　　第二种伴随（将第二个动词翻译为二谓语，分词、从句、状语等都可以）：I sat there reading a book.
> 　　第三种下沉（将第一个动词翻译为二谓语，分词、从句、状语等都可以）：Sitting there, I read a book.
> 　　需要说明的是，并列、伴随和下沉只是动词的形式问题，不代表动词之间的逻辑关系，用这三种形式翻译两个动词或两组动词都是可以的，大家可以根据句子上下文的关系来判断使用。

3

长期以来，中国高度重视气候变化问题，把积极应对气候变化作为国家经济社会发展的重大战略，把绿色低碳发展作为生态文明建设的重要内容，采取了一系列行动，为应对全球气候变化做出了重要贡献。

第一步 词汇解析

❶ 长期以来，in the long run，介词词组，比如：This measure inevitably means higher taxes in the long run.（从长远来看这项举措的结果就是要多纳税。）

❷ 高度重视，attach great importance to，动词词组，比如：They attach great importance to the project.（他们高度重视这个项目。）"高度重视"也可以翻译为 pay high attention to 或 put a high value on。

❸ 把……作为……，意思是"融入"，integrated...into...，动词词组，比如：Many young people successfully integrated themselves into their new surroundings.（许多年轻人成功地融入了新的环境。）

❹ 国家经济社会发展的重大战略，national great strategies for economic and social development，名词词组。"经济社会发展"是并列词组，意思是"经济（发展）和社会发展"。

❺ 绿色低碳发展，green and low-carbon development，名词词组。
低碳（的），low-carbon，形容词，比如：low-carbon technologies（低碳技术）。

❻ 生态文明（建设），ecological civilization，名词词组。
生态（的），ecological，形容词，比如：We risk upsetting the ecological balance of the area.（我们有可能破坏这个地区的生态平衡。）
【同义词辨析】
civilization：指广义的文化，标志人类发展开化的进程，强调物质方面的文明；
culture：指精神方面，即多由科技、文化等所体现的人类智力开发的程度。

❼ 为……做出了重要贡献，make significant contributions to...，动词词组，比如：They make significant contributions to their communities.（他们对所在的社区做出了重要贡献。）

第二步 动词定位

长期以来，中国高度重视气候变化问题，把积极应对气候变化作为国家经济社会发展的重大战略，把绿色低碳发展作为生态文明建设的重要内容，采取了一系列行动，为应对全球气候变化做出了重要贡献。

第三步 句型解析

❶ "长期以来"是本句的时间状语，"中国"是主语，"高度重视"是第一个谓语动词，"气候变化问题"是宾语，但是注意这个宾语中的"问题"是典型的范畴词，可以不翻译，这就是我们常说的汉译英减词。

❷ "把……作为"是第二个谓语动词，"应对气候变化"是宾语，这里的动词"应对"可以是四谓语不翻译，非要翻译为 cope/deal with 等词也可以，"国家经济社会发展的重大战略"是状语，注意这个名词短语的翻译，其中出现了"的"，可以用 of/for 等结构，那么"中文的英文语序"就是"国家（的）重大战略 of/for 经济（的）和社会（的）发展"。

❸ "把……作为"是第三个谓语动词，"绿色低碳发展"是宾语，"生态文明建设的重要内容"是状语，这里的"生态文明建设"中的"建设"是典型的范畴词，可以不翻译，这个短语中有"的"，所以也可以使用 of 结构。

❹ "采取了"是第四个谓语动词，"一系列行动"是宾语，"做出了"是第五个谓语动词，"重要贡献"是宾语，"为应对全球气候变化"是状语，其中动词"应对"又是四谓语，可以不翻译，这点一定要好好体会。

❺ 本句共出现了五个谓语动词，该怎么办呢？当然是"先分堆，再分层"，前三个动词说的是一件事，所以形成"一堆"，后面两个动词"一堆"，第一"堆"中可以是三个并列的动词，第二"堆"中可以形成并列、伴随或下沉，这就是各自的选择了，看看参考译文是怎么做的，总体还是不错的，还要注意句子之间的连接，这点真的特别重要！

第四步 翻译来了

Attaching great importance to climate change in the long run, China has integrated climate change measures into national great strategies for economic and social development, and taken green and low-carbon development as the important content of ecological civilization. Moreover, China has made significant contributions to global efforts against climate change by adopting a series of measures.

本句考点总结

第一，本句考查了英汉互译增减词的问题，一般来说英译汉增词，汉译英减词，常见增词的种类有：一、增加对象词（范围词），这是由上文缺少句子的某个部分造成的；二、增加范畴词，这是较难的一部分，常见的范畴词有"水平、方式、方法、问题、情况、途径和方面"，但是不仅仅有这些，还有很多其他的；三、增加评论性词，这些常常出现在文学翻译中；四、增加动词，会在动词的"分配译法"中说明这点。

第二，关于谓语动词的层次性。汉译英的核心问题是厘清句子当中多个动词之间的关系，我们要学会在多个动词当中找到最核心的动词，翻译为核心谓语（也称为一谓语），找到其次核心的动词，翻译为分词、从句、其他状语或定语的形式（也称为二谓语）；再找到不重要的动词，翻译为介词（也称为三谓语）；最后最不重要的动词，可以不译（也称为四谓语）。这些动词在句子当中如何划分层次，需要大家在长期不断的实践中摸索，而且每个句子的翻译也不是固定的。有些句子当中的"一谓语"（核心谓语），在别的译本当中可能就是"二谓语"或者是"三谓语"。只要句子整体结构正确，逻辑清晰，那这就是一个好的译本。

第三，关于"动词分堆"的问题。中文里常常出现多个短句聚集的句型，我们一方面需要去考虑这些动词之间的关系，哪一个是最重要的，哪一个是其次重要的，哪一个又是最不重要的，这个过程称为分析"谓语动词的层次性"。除此之外，句子当中出现了大量的动词时，或者说大量的分句时，我们不可能将这些分句整体翻译为一个长句，那么，我们就需要考虑哪些动词放在一起翻译，这样的过程称为"动词分堆"。比如，一个句子当中有五个动词形成的五个分句，我们一般会考虑前三个动词翻译为一句，后两个动词翻译为一句，但是如何进行"分堆"要根据上下文的语境来判断，绝对不能形而上学，望文生义。

到 2020 年单位国内生产总值二氧化碳排放比 2005 年下降 40%~45%，非化石能源占一次能源消费总量的比重达到 15%，森林面积比 2005 年增加 4 000 万公顷，森林蓄积量比 2005 年增加 13 亿立方米。

第一步 词汇解析

❶ 单位国内生产总值，per unit of GDP，名词词组，这类常用词组建议直接记忆。

❷ 二氧化碳排放，carbon dioxide emissions，名词词组，比如：Industrialized countries must reduce carbon dioxide emissions.（工业化国家必须减少二氧化碳的排放。）

排放，emissions，名词，单词原形为：emission，比如：The emission of gases such as carbon dioxide should be stabilized at their present level.（二氧化碳之类气体的排放应该被控制在目前的水平。）

❸ 比……，意思是"根据……"，翻译为 on the basis of 更加合适，介词词组，比如：We do not try to fine-tune the economy on the basis of short-term predictions.（我们不会根据短期预测试图对经济作微调。）

❹ 非化石能源，non-fossil fuels，名词词组，比如：raise the share of non-fossil fuels（提高非化石能源的比重）。non- 为否定前缀，"化石能源"翻译为 fossil fuels。

❺ 一次能源消费总量，primary energy consumption，名词词组，比如：the primary energy consumption of Henan province from 1978 to 2009（1978 年至 2009 年河南省一次能源消费总量）。

科技小常识：
一次能源是指自然界中以原有形式存在的、未经加工转换的能量资源，又称天然能源，如煤炭、石油、天然气、水能等。

❻ 公顷，hectare，名词，比如：The farms there are quite large, typically around 800 hectares.（那里的农场都很大，最具有代表性的在 800 公顷左右。）

❼ 森林蓄积量，forest stock volume，名词词组。

量，volume，名词，比如：This work has grown in volume recently.（这项工作的量最近增加了。）

科技小常识：

森林蓄积量是指一定森林面积上存在着的林木树干部分的总材积。

❽ 立方米，cubic meter，名词词组。

第二步 动词定位

到2020年单位国内生产总值二氧化碳排放比2005年下降40%~45%，非化石能源占一次能源消费总量的比重达到15%，森林面积比2005年增加4 000万公顷，森林蓄积量比2005年增加13亿立方米。

第三步 句型解析

❶ 本句的重点是数字翻译，其实说来也简单，数字翻译只需要按照原样抄写下来即可，比如2005年，翻译为 in 2005，再比如13亿翻译为1.3 billion，而不是1,300,000,000。

❷ "到2020年"是时间状语，翻译未来的时间时，用 By 比较好，后面谓语动词要使用将来完成时，"单位国内生产总值二氧化碳排放"是本句的主语，"比2005年"是时间状语，"下降"是谓语，"40%~45%"是宾语，"非化石能源占一次能源消费总量的比重"是第二个主语，"达到15%"是谓语和宾语，"森林面积"是第三个主语，"比2005年"是时间状语，"增加4 000万公顷"是谓语和宾语，"森林蓄积量"是主语，"比2005年"是时间状语，"增加13亿立方米"是谓语和宾语。以上这样分析好像正确，但是仔细看看便会发现，整个句子变得非常松散，而且由多个小句子构成，实际上这样的译法是不正确的，这句话应该要找到合适的或者说正确的主语。

❸ 本句的时间状语是"到2020年"，还有一个时间状语"比2005年"，重复的内容翻译一次即可。那么本句的主语是谁呢？当然是"中国"，这就是典型的"寻找隐藏主语"，这是非常非常难的一点。主语变成"中国"之后，谓语则谓语是"下降""达到""增加"和"增加"，后面分别接四个宾语。这样，本句就变成了一个主语和四个谓语动词的结构，而且第三个和第四个谓语动词都是"增加"，只翻译一次即可，译文处理为 reduce，increase 和 enlarge，再看看译文是不是就能明白了呢？

第四步 翻译来了

By 2020, China will have reduced its carbon dioxide emissions per unit of GDP by 40% to 45% on the basis of its 2005 level, increased the share of non-fossil fuels in primary energy consumption to 15%, and enlarged its forest area by 40 million hectares and forest stock volume by 1.3 billion cubic meters.

5 中国还将在农业、林业、水资源等重点领域和城市、沿海、生态脆弱地区形成有效抵御气候变化风险的机制，提高抵抗能力。

第一步 词汇解析

❶ 林业，forestry，名词，比如：commercial forestry（经济林业）。

❷ 重点领域，priority sectors，名词词组。

❸ 沿海（地区），coastal regions，名词词组，比如：People were evacuated from the coastal regions in advance of the hurricane.（飓风袭来之前，沿海地区的人已经撤离。）

❹ 生态脆弱地区，ecologically vulnerable regions，名词词组。

脆弱（的），vulnerable，形容词，比如：a vulnerable point（弱点）。

【同义词辨析】

district：多指由政府等机构出于行政管理等目的而明确划分的地区；

region：普通用词，常指地球上、大气中具有自然分界线的区域，特指按照气候、人体或其他特征自成一体的地区；

zone：科技用词，指圆形或弧形地带，尤指地图上按温度划分的五个地带，用作一般意义时，也可指具有某种特征的其他地区。

⑤ 抵御风险，counter the risks，动词词组。

⑥ 机制，mechanism，名词，比如：There's no mechanism for punishing arms exporters who break the rules.（对于违反规定的军火出口商还没有惩罚机制。）

⑦ 提高抵抗能力，strengthen resistance capacity，动词词组。

提高、加强，strengthen/enhance，比如：This appointment was an attempt to strengthen her hand in policy discussions.（这次任命旨在加强她在政策讨论中的作用。）

第二步 动词定位

中国还将在农业、林业、水资源等重点领域和城市、沿海、生态脆弱地区<u>形成</u>有效<u>抵御</u>气候变化风险的机制，<u>提高</u>抵抗能力。

第三步 句型解析

① "中国"是本句的主语，"在农业、林业、水资源等重点领域"是第一组状语，注意这里考查了总分关系，先翻译"重点领域"，再翻译"农业、林业、水资源"，"和"是连词，"城市、沿海、生态脆弱地区"是另外三个并列的短语。

② "形成"是第一个核心谓语，"有效抵御气候变化风险的机制"是宾语，这里有"的"，可以用 of/for 等词，参考译文使用的 mechanisms to 完全可以，这里的 to 也表示"的"，"提高"是第二个核心谓语，"抵抗能力"是宾语，所以这里有两个动词。两个动词有多种译法，但是并列是最简单的。

第四步 翻译来了

In priority sectors — including agriculture, forestry and water resources — and in cities, coastal regions and ecologically vulnerable regions, China will build mechanisms to effectively counter the risks of climate change and strengthen resistance capacity.

本句考点总结

第一，中英文的总分关系，中文一般是先分后总，而英文则是先总后分，比如中文会说"我喜欢吃香蕉、苹果、梨子等水果"，但是英文的表达是 I like fruits such as bananas, apples and pears. 注意总分关系是如何在两种语言中体现出来的。

第二，汉译英句子中并列、伴随、下沉的结构。中文常常会出现多个句子聚集的情况，那么我们在翻译时需要考虑将这些句子进行"分堆"。但是"分堆"之后，一个句子中也可能会出现两个动词或两组动词，那么有两个动词或两组动词的句子我们该如何进行翻译呢？比如："我

坐在那里看书",这里有两个动词,一个是"坐",一个是"看",我们翻译时便会有三种方法:

第一种并列(两个动词并列的译法,使用并列连词连接,两个动词之间不一定是"并列"关系):I sat there and read a book.

第二种伴随(将第二个动词翻译为二谓语,分词、从句、状语等都可以):I sat there reading a book.

第三种下沉(将第一个动词翻译为二谓语,分词、从句、状语等都可以):Sitting there, I read a book.

需要说明的是,并列、伴随和下沉只是动词的形式问题,不代表动词之间的逻辑关系,用这三种形式翻译两个动词或两组动词都是可以的,大家可以根据句子上下文的关系来判断使用。

这篇文章是典型的政府工作报告类的文体,原文中出现了大量的生词,但是环保问题确实是常考的类型,所以对这个话题一定要非常熟悉。关于句式结构,这篇文章不是很难,简单来说,有两个动词的句子最保险的译法还是并列结构,其余在考试中少用。

第六章 2016年实务真题解析与方法技巧

第一节 2016年上半年三级笔译英译汉

Old people in Thiengoly say they can remember when there were so many trees that you couldn't see the sky.

Now, miles of reddish-brown sand surround this village in northwestern Senegal, dotted with occasional bushes and trees.

Dried animal dung is scattered everywhere, but hardly any dried grass is.

Overgrazing and climate change are the major causes of the Sahara's advance, said Gilles Boetsch, an anthropologist who directs a team of French scientists working with Senegalese researchers in the region.

"The local Peul people are herders, often nomadic. But the pressure of the herds on the land has become too great," Mr. Boetsch said in an interview. "The vegetation can't regenerate itself."

Since 2008, however, Senegal has been fighting back against the encroaching desert.

Each year it has planted some two million seedling trees along a 545-kilometer, or 340-mile, ribbon of land that is the country's segment of a major pan-African regeneration project, the Great Green Wall.

First proposed in 2005, the program links Senegal and 10 other Saharan states in an alliance to plant a 15 kilometer-wide, 7,100-kilometer-long green belt to fend off the desert.

While many countries have still to start on their sections of the barrier, Senegal has taken the lead, with the creation of a National Agency for the Great Green Wall.

"This semi-arid region is becoming less and less habitable. We want to make it possible for people to continue to live here," Col. Pap Sarr, the agency's technical director, said in an interview here.

Colonel Sarr has forged working alliances between Senegalese researchers and the French team headed by Mr. Boetsch, in fields as varied as soil microbiology, ecology, medicine and anthropology.

"In Senegal we hope to experiment with different ways of doing things that will benefit the other countries as they become more active," the colonel said.

Each year since 2008, from May to June, about 400 people are employed in eight nurseries, choosing and overseeing germination of seeds and tending the seedlings until they are ready for planting.

In August, 1,000 people are mobilized to plant out rows of seedlings, about 2 million plants, allowing them a full two months of the rainy season to take root before the long, dry season sets in.

After their first dry season, the saplings look dead, brown twigs sticking out of holes in the ground, but 80 percent survive. Six years on, trees planted in 2008 are up to three meters, or 10 feet, tall.

So far, 30,000 hectares, or about 75,000 acres, have been planted, including 4,000 hectares this summer.

There are already discernible impacts on the microclimate, said Jean-Luc Peiry, a physical geography professor at the Université Blaise Pascal in Clermont-Ferrand, France, who has placed 30 sensors to record temperatures in some planted parcels.

"Preliminary results show that clumps of four to eight small trees can have an important impact on temperature," Professor Peiry said in an interview.

"The transpiration of the trees creates a microclimate that moderates daily temperature extremes."

"The trees also have an important role in slowing the soil erosion caused by the wind, reducing the dust, and acting like a large rough doormat, halting the sand-laden winds from the Sahara," he added.

Wildlife is responding to the changes. "Migratory birds are reappearing," Mr. Boetsch said.

The project uses eight groundwater pumping stations built in 1954, before Senegal achieved its independence from France in 1960.

The pumps fill giant basins that provide water for animals, tree nurseries and gardens where fruit and vegetables are grown.

2016 年上半年的 CATTI 英译汉真题仍然是外刊中的文章，主要阐述了非洲塞内加尔防风治沙的成就，在 2015 年的文章中我们已经学习了直接引语和间接引语的翻译，这篇文章仍然要巩固这种句型的翻译，而且大家要慢慢学会看出"考点"，非文学的考点是非常明确的，所以请大家一定要慢慢体会，慢慢学会识别！

1 Old people in Thiengoly say they can remember when there were so many trees that you couldn't see the sky.

第一步 词汇解析

 Thiengoly，司恩高利村，地名，这里采用的是音译法，翻译英文地名不确定时，可以使用音译法，然后把英文地名抄下来，放在括号里，这样保险一些。

第二步 注意断句

Old people in Thiengoly say /they can remember /when there were so many trees /that you couldn't see the sky.

第三步 句型解析

 Old people in Thiengoly 是本句的主语，say 是谓语，后面接宾语从句 they can remember，后面又接宾语从句 when there were so many trees，that you couldn't see the sky 是 that 引导的结果状语从句。

第四步 翻译来了

司恩高利村（Thiengoly）的老人们说，他们记得该村周边的树木曾经郁郁葱葱，遮天蔽日。

2 Now, miles of reddish-brown sand surround this village in northwestern Senegal, dotted with occasional bushes and trees.

第一步 词汇解析

① mile，名词，表示"英里"，比如：Who was the first person to run a mile in under four minutes?（是谁第一个不到四分钟就跑完了一英里？）

② reddish-brown，形容词，表示"红棕色的、红褐色的"，比如：Her hair is a reddish-brown colour.（她的头发是红棕色的。）

③ surround，动词，表示"围绕、包围"，比如：The general detached a large force to surround the airport.（将军派遣了一支大部队去包围机场。）

④ northwestern，形容词，表示"西北部的"，比如：Virtually every river in northwestern Oregon was near flood stage.（俄勒冈西北部差不多每条河都接近洪涝阶段了。）

⑤ Senegal，地名，表示"塞内加尔"。
文化小常识：
塞内加尔共和国（The Republic of Senegal），简称塞内加尔，位于非洲西部凸出部位的最西端，首都是达喀尔。

⑥ dot with，动词词组，表示"散布、点缀"，比如：The sky was dotted with stars.（繁星满天。）

⑦ occasional，形容词，表示"偶尔的、零星的"，比如：I have difficulty swallowing, pain and discomfort and occasional throwing up.（我有吞咽困难，疼痛和不适，还偶尔呕吐。）

⑧ bush，名词，表示"灌木"，比如：They walked through the dense Mozambican bush for thirty-six hours.（他们步行穿过茂密的莫桑比克灌木丛区，走了36个小时。）

第二步 注意断句

Now, /miles of reddish-brown sand surround this village /in northwestern Senegal, /dotted with occasional bushes and trees.

第三步 句型解析

① Now 是时间状语，miles of reddish-brown sand 是主语，surround 谓语，this village in northwestern Senegal 是宾语，翻译时可以直接翻译为"沙子包围了村庄"，参考译文采用了"主动变被动"的译法，其实没什么技巧，两者都可以，有点像"有灵主语句"和"无灵主语句"的特点，但不是特别明显。

② dotted with occasional bushes and trees 是过去分词短语位于名词后，相当于定语从句，而且有逗号隔开，就是非限定性定语从句，但是要知道它修饰谁，若是修饰 Senegal，则不应该有逗号，所以它是修饰 this village，远离了先行词，翻译时主要突出被修饰词的特点和被动语态的特点即可。

第四步 翻译来了

如今，这个塞内加尔（Senegal）西北部的小村已让绵延数英里的红棕色沙地给包围了，这个村庄零星散布着灌木丛和树木。

◆本句考点总结◆

第一，本句考查了"有灵主语句"和"无灵主语句"的转换。一般来说，以有生命的物体作为主语的句子，称为"有灵主语句"，而以无生命的物体作为主语的句子，称为"无灵主语句"，中文常用有灵主语，而英文则常用无灵主语，注意两者之间的互换。但是这种互换是为了让句子更加通顺，不是每个句子都需要用这种方法翻译。

第二，本句出现了分词或分词短语位于名词后的译法。一般来说，分词或分词短语位于名词后相当于定语或定语从句，定语按照"短前长后"的译法来进行翻译。

3 Dried animal dung is scattered everywhere, but hardly any dried grass is.

第一步 词汇解析

① dung，名词，表示"粪"，比如：A beetle was rolling a pellet of dried dung up the hill.（一只屎壳郎正在把一个干粪球往山上滚。）

② scatter，动词，表示"分散、散开"，比如：They've been scattering toys everywhere.（他们总是把玩具扔得到处都是。）

③ hardly any，副词词组，表示"几乎没有"，比如：Most of the others were so young that they had hardly any experience.（其他人大多都很年轻，几乎没什么经验。）

第二步 注意断句

Dried animal dung is scattered everywhere, /but hardly any dried grass is.

第三步 句型解析

① 逗号前 Dried animal dung 是主语，is scattered 是谓语，是被动语态，所以可以采用"有被不用被"的译法。当然你用"被"也没事，只是说尽量少用"被"，没说不让用，everywhere 是状语。

② 逗号后的句子是省略，实际上是 hardly any dried grass is scattered everywhere，因为谓语相同，所以省略了实意动词和状语，翻译时注意 hardly 的否定含义，然后处理一下被动语态即可。

第四步 翻译来了

干结的动物粪便到处都是，但干枯的草却几乎看不见。

本句考点总结

本句出现了被动语态的译法。被动语态是英文常见的一种形式，而在中文里常常少用"被"或者不用"被"。那么我们一般有什么样的译法呢？第一种是被动变主动，第二种是寻找替代词（比如："让……给""为……所"等结构），第三种是在科技文献中用"可以"来替代"被"，第四种是有"被"不用"被"译法。以上四种怎么用，那就看句子怎么通顺怎么翻译了啊！

> **Overgrazing and climate change are the major causes of the Sahara's advance, said Gilles Boetsch, an anthropologist who directs a team of French scientists working with Senegalese researchers in the region.**

第一步 词汇解析

① overgraze，动词，表示"过度放牧"，比如：Widespread overgrazing disturbs water cycles, reducing replenishment of above and below ground water resources.（大面积过度放牧扰乱了水循环，减少了地表和地下水资源的补充。）

② cause，名词，表示"原因"，比如：Unemployment is a major cause of poverty.（失业是贫困的主要原因。）

③ Sahara，即 the Sahara Desert，专有名词，表示"撒哈拉沙漠"，比如：The Sahara Desert is a natural barrier between North and Central Africa.（撒哈拉沙漠是北非与中非之间的天然屏障。）

地理小常识：

撒哈拉沙漠形成于约 250 万年前，是世界最大的沙质荒漠，面积约 932 万平方千米，位于非洲北部。该地区气候条件非常恶劣，是地球上最不适合生物生存的地方之一。

④ Gilles Boetsch，吉勒思·波特舍，人名，这里采用的是音译法，注意名和姓之间要加"·"，翻译英文人名不确定时，可以使用音译法，然后把英文人名抄下来，放在括号里，这样保险一些。

⑤ anthropologist，名词，表示"人类学家"，比如：Wade Davis is an anthropologist and plant expert.（韦德·戴维斯是一位人类学家和植物专家。）

⑥ direct，动词，表示"指挥"，比如：Christopher will direct day-to-day operations.（克里斯托弗将指挥日常工作。）

第二步 注意断句

Overgrazing and climate change are the major causes /of the Sahara's advance, /said Gilles Boetsch, /an anthropologist /who directs a team of French scientists /working with Senegalese researchers /in the region.

第三步 句型解析

① Overgrazing and climate change 是主语，are 是系动词，the major causes of the Sahara's advance 是表语，直接翻译即可，比较简单，也可以增词扩句，但增与不增不是必须的。

② said Gilles Boetsch 是一个完全倒装，Gilles Boetsch 是主语，said 是谓语，前面的句子是宾语从句，翻译时这个成分可以放在原位翻译，然后先翻译人名，再翻译谓语。

③ an anthropologist who directs a team of French scientists working with Senegalese researchers in the region 是 Gilles Boetsch 的同位语，同位语可以采用"主谓译法"，也可以用"并列译法"，如"他是一个人类学家……"是完全可以的。

④ who directs a team of French scientists working with Senegalese researchers in the region 是定语从句，从句较长，可以采用后置译法，working with Senegalese researchers in the region 是现在分词短语作定语，相当于定语从句，修饰 French scientists，较长，采用后置译法较好。

第四步 翻译来了

过度放牧和气候变化是导致撒哈拉沙漠扩张的主要原因，人类学家吉勒思·波特舍（Gilles

Boetsch）这样说道，他带领的一些法国科学家和塞内加尔研究员一起在这一地区开展研究工作。

> **本句考点总结**
>
> 　　第一，本句考查了英文同位语的译法。同位语是两个前后相互说明的名词或名词短语，比如 Beijing, the capital of China，有两种译法，第一种是"并列译法"，翻译为"中国的首都北京"，第二种是"主谓译法"，翻译为"北京是中国的首都"。具体用哪一种，可以根据句子具体情况而定，有时两种都是可以使用的。
>
> 　　第二，本句出现了英文定语从句的译法。一般来说，定语从句按照"短前长后"的译法处理，较短的定语从句可以前置，较长的定语从句可以后置，这一切都取决于句子的通顺，并没有绝对的前置和后置译法。
>
> 　　第三，本句出现了分词或分词短语位于名词后的译法。一般来说，分词或是分词短语位于名词后相当于定语或定语从句，定语按照"短前长后"的译法来进行翻译。

5 "The local Peul people are herders, often nomadic. But the pressure of the herds on the land has become too great," Mr. Boetsch said in an interview. "The vegetation can't regenerate itself."

第一步 词汇解析

① Peul，专有名词，表示"颇耳族"。

文化小常识：

　　根据中华人民共和国驻马里共和国大使馆经济商务参赞处官网的介绍：马里共有 23 个部族，颇耳族（Peul）是其中之一，约占总人口的 11%，多居住在巴马科至莫普提之间的尼日尔河盆地、尼日尔河中游河套和基达尔大区等地。

② herder，名词，表示"牧人"，比如：She was discovered by a reindeer herder on a river bank in northwestern Siberia.（一名驯鹿牧人在西伯利亚西北方的河岸找到了她。）

③ nomadic，形容词，表示"游牧的"，比如：The formation of ancient nomadic and agricultural nationalities is the inevitable result of natural choice and human choice.（古代游牧民族和农业民族的形成，是自然选择和人的选择的必然结果。）

④ herd，名词，表示"兽群、牧群"，比如：The males in the herd protect the females and the young.（牧群中的雄性动物保护雌性动物和幼崽。）

⑤ vegetation，名词，表示"植被"，比如：The lake is now extinct, but our ancestors would have depended on the water and vegetation that grew around it.（湖泊现在消失了，但是我们的祖先可能曾经依赖于湖水和湖周围生长的植被。）

⑥ regenerate，动词，表示"再生"，比如：Once destroyed, brain cells do not regenerate.（脑细胞一旦遭到破坏，就不能再生。）

第二步 注意断句

"The local Peul people are herders, /often nomadic. /But the pressure of the herds /on the land has become too great," /Mr. Boetsch said /in an interview. /"The vegetation can't regenerate itself."

第三步 句型解析

❶ 双引号中的句子是直接引语，翻译时仍然保留双引号。
❷ 第一个引号内 The local Peul people 是主语，are 是系动词，herders 是表语，often nomadic 是同位语，直接并列翻译即可；But 是表示转折的连词，the pressure of the herds on the land 是第二个主语，has become 是系动词，too great 是表语，pressure 是抽象名词，没有动词词根，可以增词。若不增词通顺，也可不增词。
❸ Mr. Boetsch said in an interview 是放在句子中间的插入语，有主语和谓语，这样放在句中的情况，翻译时把说话人放在句首、原位或句末都可以。
❹ 第二个引号内 The vegetation 是主语，can't regenerate 是谓语，itself 是宾语，直接翻译即可。

第四步 翻译来了

"当地的颇耳族人（Peul）是牧民，且常常是流动放牧。但是，牧畜群给草地带来的压力太大了，植被都无法复生。"波特舍（Boetsch）先生在一次采访中说道。

本句考点总结

第一，本句考查了英文直接引语的译法，最简单的译法就是保留冒号和双引号，说话人的位置和说话的内容都保持不变。即说话人在什么位置，就放在什么位置翻译，当然，说话人放在句首也是可以接受的。

第二，本句当中考查了"抽象名词"的译法。抽象名词一般处于冠词之后，又在介词之前，以"the + 抽象名词 + of"的形式居多，一般来说，抽象名词有两种译法。第一种，若抽象名词有动词词根，则翻译为动词，比如 the suggestion of mine，翻译为"我建议"，而不是"我的建议"；第二种，若抽象名词没有动词词根，可以增动词翻译，比如 the spirit of our nation，翻译为"我们民族所具有的精神"，而不是"我们民族的精神"。

 Since 2008, however, Senegal has been fighting back against the encroaching desert.

第一步 词汇解析

❶ fight back，动词词组，表示"对抗、反击"，比如：He feels a sense of injustice about the world and it's time for him to fight back.（他深切感受到世界的不公，而此刻正是他反击的时候了。）
❷ encroach，动词，表示"侵占"，比如：But the desert is encroaching on this metropolis.（但是，沙漠正侵蚀着这个大都市。）encroaching desert 中的 encroaching 是现在分词作形容词，表示"不断进犯的"。

第二步 注意断句

Since 2008, /however, /Senegal has been fighting back against the encroaching desert.

第三步 句型解析

① however 是插入语，表示观点，可以放在句首翻译。
② Since 2008 是时间状语，Senegal 是主语，has been fighting back against 是谓语，the encroaching desert 是宾语，可以把主语放在前面，再把时间状语放在后面，直接翻译即可。如果翻译成"抗击不断进犯的沙漠"肯定不好，这里显然是"偏正互换"的结构，翻译为"抗击沙漠的侵袭"更好！

第四步 翻译来了

然而，塞内加尔（Senegal）自从 2008 年起，就一直在抗击沙漠的侵袭。

本句考点总结

第一，本句当中出现了插入语的成分，插入语不表示观点时，一般需要放在原位翻译，原始的标点符号保留；插入语表示观点时，可以放在句首翻译。

第二，本句当中考查了英译汉"偏正互换"的译法。一般来说，A of B 翻译为"B 的 A"，但是若这样翻译不通顺，大家可以尝试换成"A 的 B"，这就是"偏正互换"的译法。

Each year it has planted some two million seedling trees along a 545-kilometer, or 340-mile, ribbon of land that is the country's segment of a major pan-African regeneration project, the Great Green Wall.

第一步 词汇解析

① some，限定词，表示"大约"，比如：I have kept birds for some 30 years.（我养鸟大约有 30 年了。）
② seedling，名词，表示"幼苗、树苗"，比如：Keep the soil moist. That way, the seedling will flourish.（保持土壤湿润，那幼苗就能茁壮成长。）
③ ribbon，名词，表示"带状物、狭长的东西、丝带"，比如：There was a white ribbon in her black hair.（她的黑发中扎了一根白色的缎带。）
④ segment，名词，表示"部分"，比如：She cleaned a small segment of the painting.（她擦干净了这幅画的一小部分。）
⑤ pan-African，形容词，表示"泛非的"，比如：In 1919, Du Bois sponsored and organized first pan-African Congress.（1919 年，杜波依斯发起并组织召开了第一届泛非大会。）

第二步 注意断句

Each year /it has planted some two million seedling trees /along a 545-kilometer, /or 340-mile, /

ribbon of land /that is the country's segment /of a major pan-African regeneration project, /the Great Green Wall.

第三步 句型解析

❶ Each year 是时间状语，it 是主语，指代前面的"塞内加尔"，在这里可以翻译成"该国"，当然用"塞内加尔"也行，用"它"是错误的，这才是要关注的焦点，而不是关注 each year 翻译为"每年"还是"每一年"。

❷ has planted 是谓语，some two million seedling trees 是宾语，along a 545-kilometer 是地点状语，or 340-mile 是对 545-kilometer 的解释，可以放在括号内翻译，当然放在原位翻译也是可以的。

❸ ribbon of land that is the country's segment of a major pan-African regeneration project, the Great Green Wall 是前者的同位语，译文采用了"主谓译法"，而且在同位语中出现了定语从句，称为"同位定语从句"，这种定语从句一定是后置翻译，而不是前置翻译。

❹ the Great Green Wall 又是前面 project 的同位语，在这里使用了"并列译法"，非要后置形成主谓结构也是可以的。

第四步 翻译来了

每年，该国在 545 千米（约 340 英里）长的地带上种植约两百万株树苗，这片狭长地带是"绿色长城"这一泛非植被再生工程在塞内加尔（Senegal）境内的部分。

> **本句考点总结**
>
> 第一，关于英文代词的译法。英文中需要翻译的代词主要指第三人称 he, she, it, they 及其相应宾格和指示代词 this 和 that。这些单词在翻译时一定要注意，主要采用"不抽象、不具体"的译法。不能翻译成具体的人或物，但是也不能翻译为"他""她""它""他们""这个""那个"，要注意取中间的译法。
>
> 第二，本句考查了英文同位语的译法。同位语是两个前后相互说明的名词或名词短语，比如 Beijing, the capital of China，有两种译法，第一种是"并列译法"，翻译为"中国的首都北京"，第二种是"主谓译法"，翻译为"北京是中国的首都"。具体用哪一种，可以根据句子具体情况而定，有时两种都是可以使用的。

First proposed in 2005, the program links Senegal and 10 other Saharan states in an alliance to plant a 15 kilometer-wide, 7,100-kilometer-long green belt to fend off the desert.

第一步 词汇解析

❶ propose，动词，表示"提出"，比如：He has proposed a resolution limiting the role of U.S. troops.（他提出了一项限制美军的决议。）

❷ state，名词，表示"国家"，比如：European Union member states（欧盟成员国）。

③ alliance，名词，表示"联盟、联合"，比如：The two parties were still too much apart to form an alliance.（这两个党派分歧大得还不能形成联盟。）

④ belt，名词，表示"带"，green belt 表示"绿化带"，比如：The new community can link the north and south green land together to form a complete city green belt.（新的小区可以将南北的绿地联系起来，形成一条完整的城市绿化带。）

⑤ fend off，动词词组，表示"避开、挡住"，比如：Somehow she managed to fend off the awkward questions.（她以某种方式避开了这个尴尬的问题。）

第二步 注意断句

First proposed /in 2005, /the program links Senegal and 10 other Saharan states /in an alliance / to plant a 15 kilometer-wide, /7,100-kilometer-long green belt /to fend off the desert.

第三步 句型解析

① First proposed in 2005 是过去分词短语位于句首，先找逻辑主语 the program，再进行翻译。

② the program 是主语，links 是谓语，Senegal and 10 other Saharan states 是宾语，in an alliance 是状语，to plant a 15 kilometer-wide, 7,100-kilometer-long green belt 是状语，to fend off the desert 是目的状语。

③ in an alliance 是一个状语，表示"形成了联盟"，在这里处理为"合作"更加贴切，翻译为"形成了联盟"也是可以的，只是不太通顺。

第四步 翻译来了

这个工程在 2005 年第一次被提出，塞内加尔（Senegal）和其他 10 个地处撒哈拉的国家合作，通过植树创建了一个 15 千米宽，7 100 千米长的绿化带，以此来阻挡沙漠的侵袭。

> **本句考点总结**
>
> 本句出现了分词或分词短语位于名词后的译法。一般来说，分词或分词短语位于名词后相当于定语或定语从句，定语按照"短前长后"的译法来进行翻译。

9 While many countries have still to start on their sections of the barrier, Senegal has taken the lead, with the creation of a National Agency for the Great Green Wall.

第一步 词汇解析

① start on，动词词组，表示"开始进行"，比如：Before you start on these chapters, clear your head.（在你开始这些章节之前，先理清思路。）

② barrier，名词，表示"围栏、屏障"，比如：The Yangtze river is a natural barrier to the north-east.（长江是东北方向的一道天然屏障。）

❸ take the lead，动词词组，表示"领先、带头"，比如：Now everybody sing! I'll take the lead.（现在大家唱歌！我起头。）

❹ National Agency，专有名词，表示"国家机构"，比如：The study was funded by the National Agency for Research, the Foundation for Medical Research, and other groups.（这项研究是由美国国家研究机构、医学研究基金会等团体赞助的。）

第二步 注意断句

While many countries have still to start on their sections of the barrier, /Senegal has taken the lead, /with the creation of a National Agency /for the Great Green Wall.

第三步 句型解析

❶ While 在英语当中一般都表示转折含义，翻译为"虽然、尽管"比较恰当。

❷ many countries 是主语，have still to start on 是谓语，直接翻译是"不得不仍然开始做某事"，但是根据上下文来看是不是可以简化一下？their sections of the barrier 是宾语，这里的 barrier 指的是上文的"绿化带"，这就是常说的"根据上下文来判断句意"，也就可以理解所谓的"词本无意，意由句生"了。

❸ Senegal 是主句主语，has taken the lead 是谓语和宾语，with the creation of a National Agency for the Great Green Wall 是伴随状语，其中的 creation 是典型的抽象名词，有动词词根 create，翻译为动词"成立"，译成"建造""创造"都不太妥当！

❹ 主句当中 with 在翻译时可以放在主语 Senegal 之前，creation 译为动词后，前面缺少主语，可以用 Senegal 作主语。

第四步 翻译来了

尽管许多国家甚至都还没有着手建设自己国家的绿化带，但是，随着塞内加尔（Senegal）成立了"绿色长城工程"的国家机关，它在植树治沙方面已经走在了前列。

本句考点总结

第一，本句当中考查了"抽象名词"的译法。抽象名词一般处于冠词之后，又在介词之前，以"the + 抽象名词 + of"的形式居多，一般来说，抽象名词有两种译法。第一种，若抽象名词有动词词根，则翻译为动词，比如 the suggestion of mine，翻译为"我建议"，而不是"我的建议"；第二种，若抽象名词没有动词词根，可以增动词翻译，比如 the spirit of our nation，翻译为"我们民族所具有的精神"，而不是"我们民族的精神"。

第二，本句考查了中英文语序的问题，一般来说，中文的语序是"主语 + 废话（定语、状语、补语、插入语，等等）+ 重要成分"，而英文的语序是"废话（定语、状语、补语、插入语，等等）+ 主语 + 重要成分 + 废话（定语、状语、补语、插入语，等等）"，翻译时需要注意调整语序。

> "This semi-arid region is becoming less and less habitable. We want to make it possible for people to continue to live here," Col. Pap Sarr, the agency's technical director, said in an interview here.

第一步 词汇解析

① semi-arid，形容词，表示"半干旱的"，比如：The report also points out that the rate of increase in food crop yields has slowed because of climate change in the past decades, particularly in semi-arid areas.（该报告还指出，由于过去几十年的气候变化，粮食作物产量的增加率已经减慢，特别是半干旱地区。）

② habitable，形容词，表示"可居住的、适于居住的"，比如：Some areas of the country are just too cold to be habitable.（这个国家的一些地方太冷了，因而不能居住。）

③ technical director，名词词组，表示"技术主管、技术总监"，比如：The technical director stopped her on the way to the company.（技术总监在她去公司的路上叫住了她。）

第二步 注意断句

"This semi-arid region is becoming less and less habitable. /We want to make it possible for people /to continue /to live here,"/ Col. Pap Sarr, /the agency's technical director, /said /in an interview here.

第三步 句型解析

① 双引号中的语句是直接引语，直接翻译即可，说话人在句末，可以放在句首翻译，也可以放在原位翻译。

② 引号中的第一句中，This semi-arid region 是主语，is becoming 是系动词，less and less habitable 是表语，直接翻译即可。

③ 第二句中，We 是主语，want to make 是谓语，it 是形式宾语，possible 是宾语补足语，for people to continue to live here 是真正的宾语，这些知识可以参见各种语法书，当然看第三版《十二天突破英语语法》也可以。

④ Col. 实际上是 Colonel 的缩写，不知道的同学要好好记住。

⑤ the agency's technical director 是 Col. Pap Sarr 的同位语，可以采用"并列译法"，也可以用"主谓译法"，参考译文中采用了"主谓译法"。

第四步 翻译来了

"这个半干旱地区正变得越来越不适合人类居住。我们想让人们还能够继续在此生活，"帕萨上校（Col. Pap Sarr）在一次采访中说道，他是这个部门的技术主任。

本句考点总结

第一，本句考查了英文直接引语的译法，最简单的译法就是保留冒号和双引号，说话人的位置和说话的内容都保持不变。即说话人在什么位置，就放在什么位置翻译，当然，说话人放在句首也是可以接受的。

第二，本句考查了英文同位语的译法。同位语是两个前后相互说明的名词或名词短语，比如 Beijing, the capital of China，有两种译法，第一种是"并列译法"，翻译为"中国的首都北京"，第二种是"主谓译法"，翻译为"北京是中国的首都"。具体用哪一种，可以根据句子具体情况而定，有时两种都是可以使用的。

Colonel Sarr has forged working alliances between Senegalese researchers and the French team headed by Mr. Boetsch, in fields as varied as soil microbiology, ecology, medicine and anthropology.

第一步 词汇解析

❶ forge，动词，表示"锻造、缔造"，比如：The prime minister is determined to forge a good relationship with the country's new leader.（该首相决意与该国的新领袖建立良好的关系。）

❷ varied，形容词，表示"各种各样的"，比如：It is essential that your diet is varied and balanced.（重要的是你的饮食应当是多样而平衡的。）

❸ soil microbiology，名词词组，表示"土壤微生物学"。

生物小常识：

土壤微生物学主要研究土壤中微生物的种类、数量、分布、生命活动规律及其与土壤中的物质和能量转化、土壤肥力、植物生长等的关系。土壤微生物学不仅是微生物学的分支学科，也是土壤学的一个组成部分，而且与生物化学、农业化学、植物生理学和植物病理学等学科相互渗透。

❹ ecology，名词，表示"生态学"，比如：Having gone through the earthquake, he cared for nature more than before. So he started to study ecology.（在经历了地震之后，他比以前更关注大自然了，因此开始学习起生态学来。）

❺ medicine，名词，表示"医学"，比如：traditional Chinese medicine（中医）。

❻ anthropology，名词，表示"人类学"，前面说到吉勒思·波特舍（Gilles Boetsch）是一位人类学家（anthropologist）。

第二步 注意断句

Colonel Sarr has forged working alliances /between Senegalese researchers and the French team /headed by Mr. Boetsch, /in fields /as varied as soil microbiology, /ecology, /medicine and anthropology.

第三步 句型解析

❶ 本句 Colonel Sarr 是主语，前文已经出现过，所以只需要翻译"上校"，has forged 是谓语，working alliances 是宾语，between Senegalese researchers and the French team 是状语，headed by Mr. Boetsch 是过去分词短语作定语，修饰前面的名词 team。

❷ headed by Mr. Boetsch 修饰名词，相当于定语从句，较短，所以采用前置译法，而且特别要注意这个词组修饰谁，到底是 Senegalese researchers and the French team，还是 the French team，这才是翻译需要研

究的问题。根据上下文会发现一定是修饰 the French team，为什么？因为这个科学家是法国人，他带了一队科学家嘛！

❸ in fields as varied as soil microbiology, ecology, medicine and anthropology 是另一个状语，要注意这句话的翻译现象，一定是"总分关系"，中文先分后总，英文先总后分，所以在翻译时需要先翻译 soil microbiology, ecology, medicine and anthropology，再翻译 fields，这也是翻译需要注意的问题，应该学习的问题！不要只关心如何理解 as varied as，它就是"很多"的意思，想太多只会影响学习进度！

第四步 翻译来了

上校已促成塞内加尔（Senegal）的研究人员和波特舍（Boetsch）领导的法国科学家团队在土壤微生物学、生态学、医学和人类学方面进行共同研究。

> **本句考点总结**
>
> 第一，本句出现了分词或分词短语位于名词后的译法。一般来说，分词或分词短语位于名词后相当于定语或定语从句，定语按照"短前长后"的译法来进行翻译。
>
> 第二，中英文的总分关系，中文一般是先分后总，而英文则是先总后分，比如中文会说"我喜欢吃香蕉、苹果、梨子等水果"，但是英文的表达是 I like fruits such as bananas, apples and pears. 注意总分关系是如何在两种语言中体现出来的。

12

"In Senegal we hope to experiment with different ways of doing things that will benefit the other countries as they become more active," the colonel said.

第一步 词汇解析

❶ experiment with，动词词组，表示"尝试、试用"，比如：People experiment with different roles at work.（人们在工作中尝试着不同的角色。）

第二步 注意断句

"In Senegal /we hope /to experiment with different ways of doing things /that will benefit the other countries / as they become more active," /the colonel said.

第三步 句型解析

❶ 这句也是典型的直接引语，句末出现说话人，说话人可以放在句首翻译，也可以放在句末翻译；可以指代明确，也可以直接翻译为"上校说"。

❷ 直接引语中，In Senegal 是地点状语，we 是主语，hope 是谓语，后面的不定式 to experiment with different ways of doing things 是宾语，that will benefit the other countries 是 that 引导的定语从句，从句较短，可以采取前置译法，但是参考译文采用了后置译法，不管是前置还是后置，通顺就行。

❸ as they become more active 这里的 as 含义比较模糊，但可以肯定是状语从句，译文中也理解为伴随状

语，且要注意句中的 they 是代词，需要指明要点，这也是"翻译的知识点"，不要纠结那些没有用的东西。

第四步 翻译来了

帕萨上校（Col. Pap Sarr）说："随着其他国家变得更加积极，我们希望，我国尝试的不同治沙方式能让这些国家也受益。"

> **本句考点总结**
>
> 第一，本句考查了英文直接引语的译法，最简单的译法就是保留冒号和双引号，说话人的位置和说话的内容都保持不变。即说话人在什么位置，就放在什么位置翻译，当然，说话人放在句首也是可以接受的。
>
> 第二，本句出现了英文定语从句的译法。一般来说，定语从句按照"短前长后"的译法处理，较短的定语从句可以前置，较长的定语从句可以后置，这一切都取决于句子的通顺，并没有绝对的前置和后置译法。
>
> 第三，关于英文代词的译法。英文中需要翻译的代词主要指第三人称 he, she, it, they 及其相应宾格和指示代词 this 和 that。这些单词在翻译时一定要注意，主要采用"不抽象、不具体"的译法。不能翻译成具体的人或物，但是也不能翻译为"他""她""它""他们""这个""那个"，要注意取中间的译法。

13

Each year since 2008, from May to June, about 400 people are employed in eight nurseries, choosing and overseeing germination of seeds and tending the seedlings until they are ready for planting.

第一步 词汇解析

❶ nursery，名词，表示"苗圃"，比如：I saw lots of peonies in a private nursery.（我在一家私人苗圃看到了许多牡丹花。）

❷ oversee，动词，表示"监督、审查、看管"，比如：Soldiers oversee the food handouts.（士兵们看管着救济食品。）

❸ germination，名词，表示"发芽"，动词形式是 germinate，比如：Seeds germinate in the spring.（种子在春天发芽。）

❹ tend，动词，表示"照料、照顾"，比如：Doctors and nurses tended the injured.（医生和护士照料受伤者。）

第二步 注意断句

Each year since 2008, /from May to June, /about 400 people are employed /in eight nurseries, /choosing and overseeing germination of seeds /and tending the seedlings /until they are ready for planting.

第三步 句型解析

❶ Each year since 2008 是时间状语，from May to June 也是时间状语，about 400 people 是主语，are employed 是被动语态，这里可以用"寻找替代词"的译法，翻译为"受雇于"。我的意见是少用"被"，但不是不用"被"。

❷ in eight nurseries 是状语，choosing and overseeing germination of seeds and tending the seedlings 是伴随状语，逻辑主语是 about 400 people，可以省略主语，也可以用"他们"作主语。

❸ choosing and overseeing germination of seeds 翻译为"挑选和照看种子的发芽"似乎不妥，germination of seeds 是不是"偏正互换"会更好呢？实话实说，如果非要翻译为"种子的发芽"，这真的错了啊！

❹ until they are ready for planting 是时间状语从句，until 翻译成"直到"似乎不好，应该处理为"最后"，这样的处理是不是特别好呢？所以，翻译不是字对字，而是要真正理解上下文。

❺ 注意 they are ready 中的 they，代词需要指明要点，指代"幼苗"，如果不指明代词指代谁，那就错了，"他们"确实不太妥当。

第四步 翻译来了

自 2008 年起，每年五月到六月，约 400 名工人会受雇于八个苗圃室，挑选和照看发芽的种子，然后照料幼苗，最后这些幼苗就能用于栽种了。

本句考点总结

第一，本句出现了被动语态的译法。被动语态是英文常见的一种形式，而在中文里常常少用"被"或者不用"被"。那么我们一般有什么样的译法呢？第一种是被动变主动，第二种是寻找替代词（比如："让……给""为……所"等结构），第三种是在科技文献中用"可以"来替代"被"，第四种是有"被"不用"被"。以上四种怎么用，那就看句子怎么通顺怎么翻译了啊！

第二，本句当中考查了"偏正互换"的译法。一般来说，A of B 翻译为"B 的 A"，但是若这样翻译不通顺，大家可以尝试换成"A 的 B"，这就是"偏正互换"的译法。

第三，关于英文代词的译法。英文中需要翻译的代词主要指第三人称 he, she, it, they 及其相应宾格和指示代词 this 和 that。这些单词在翻译时一定要注意，主要采用"不抽象、不具体"的译法。不能翻译成具体的人或物，但是也不能翻译为"他""她""它""他们""这个""那个"，要注意取中间的译法。

---

14 In August, 1,000 people are mobilized to plant out rows of seedlings, about 2 million plants, allowing them a full two months of the rainy season to take root before the long, dry season sets in.

第一步 词汇解析

❶ mobilize，动词，表示"调动、动员"，比如：He helped energize and mobilize millions of people around the nation. (他帮助激励和动员了全国数百万人。)

② plant out，动词词组，表示"移植"，比如：Plant out the spring cabbage whenever opportunities arise. （一有机会就把春季卷心菜移种到地里。）

③ row，名词，表示"一排、一列、一行"，比如：These two rows of trees are planted too close together. （这两行树栽得太密了。）

④ take root，动词词组，表示"生根、扎根"，比如：The seedlings of bushes and trees might take root there. （灌木和树的幼苗也许可以在那里扎根生长。）

⑤ set in，动词词组，表示"开始、到来"，比如：Winter is setting in and the population is facing food and fuel shortages. （冬天来了，人们正面临着食物和燃料的短缺。）

第二步 注意断句

In August, /1,000 people are mobilized /to plant out rows of seedlings, /about 2 million plants, / allowing them a full two months of the rainy season /to take root /before the long, /dry season sets in.

第三步 句型解析

① In August 是时间状语，1,000 people 是主语，are mobilized 是谓语，而且是被动语态，这里采用了"被动变主动"的译法。

② to plant out rows of seedlings 是不定式作宾语，about 2 million plants 是前面 seedlings 的同位语，直接用并列结构翻译，当然放在 seedlings 前面作定语也是可以的。

③ allowing them a full two months of the rainy season 是伴随结构，实际上它的主语是前面那件事。大家在翻译时要有一个意识，看到动词要想到主语，这是翻译的基本套路，记得！记得！记得！其中的 them 是代词，需要指明要点，指的是"这些树苗"，翻译为"这就让它们"是不是有点不太妥当呢？

④ to take root 是 allow 后的不定式，注意 before the long, dry season sets in 这个时间状语，既然是状语，那就是"废话"，放在动词 allow 后面是不是更好呢？

第四步 翻译来了

到了八月，调 1 000 多人来栽种一排排的小树苗，约有 200 万株，这就让这些树苗在漫长而干燥的旱季到来前，有足足两个月的雨季来扎根了。

> **本句考点总结**
>
> 第一，本句出现了被动语态的译法。被动语态是英文常见的一种形式，而在中文里常常少用"被"或者不用"被"。那么我们一般有什么样的译法呢？第一种是被动变主动，第二种是寻找替代词（比如："让……给""为……所"等结构），第三种是在科技文献中用"可以"来替代"被"，第四种是有"被"不用"被"。以上四种怎么用，那就看句子怎么通顺怎么翻译了啊！
>
> 第二，本句考查了英文同位语的译法。同位语是两个前后相互说明的名词或名词短语，比如 Beijing, the capital of China，有两种译法，第一种是"并列译法"，翻译为"中国的首都北京"，第二种是"主谓译法"，翻译为"北京是中国的首都"。具体用哪一种，可以根据句子具体情况而定，有时两种都是可以使用的。

第三，关于英文代词的译法。英文中需要翻译的代词主要指第三人称 he, she, it, they 及其相应宾格和指示代词 this 和 that。这些单词在翻译时一定要注意，主要采用"不抽象、不具体"的译法。不能翻译成具体的人或物，但是也不能翻译为"他""她""它""他们""这个""那个"，要注意取中间的译法。

After their first dry season, the saplings look dead, brown twigs sticking out of holes in the ground, but 80 percent survive. Six years on, trees planted in 2008 are up to three meters, or 10 feet, tall.

第一步 词汇解析

① sapling，名词，表示"树苗"，比如：A sapling needs pruning, a child discipline.（小树要砍，小孩要管。）
② twig，名词，表示"小树枝、细枝"，比如：The child touched the worm with a twig.（这个孩子用小树枝碰了碰这条虫子。）
③ stick，动词，表示"伸、伸出"，比如：Don't stick your fingers into the cage.（不要把手指伸进笼子里。）
④ foot，名词，表示"英尺"，复数形式为 feet，比如：The oil well extended several hundreds of feet in depth.（油井向下延伸了数百英尺。）

第二步 注意断句

After their first dry season, /the saplings look dead, /brown twigs /sticking out of holes /in the ground, /but 80 percent survive. /Six years on, /trees planted /in 2008 are up to three meters, /or 10 feet, /tall.

第三步 句型解析

① After their first dry season 是时间状语，其中的 their 可用模糊翻译法，指代明确也是可以的。
② the saplings 是主语，look dead 是系表结构，brown twigs sticking out of holes in the ground 是分词的独立主格结构。独立主格结构按照主谓结构翻译即可，不要想太多。
③ but 是转折连词，80 percent survive 是主谓结构，直接翻译即可。
④ Six years on 是时间状语，on 表示"时间的继续"。
⑤ trees planted in 2008 是主语，其中 planted in 2008 是过去分词短语作定语，相当于定语从句，较短，采用前置译法。
⑥ are up to three meters 是系表结构，or 10 feet, tall 是同位语，直接翻译，用不用括号都行。

第四步 翻译来了

在经历了第一个旱季之后，这些小树苗看上去都死了，只剩下棕色的小树枝从地上的洞穴里钻出来，但是八成的树苗都会存活。六年之后，这些 2008 年栽下的树苗已经长到三米高了（大约 10 英尺）。

> **本句考点总结**
>
> 本句出现了分词或分词短语位于名词后的译法。一般来说,分词或分词短语位于名词后相当于定语或定语从句,定语按照"短前长后"的译法来进行翻译。

16 So far, 30,000 hectares, or about 75,000 acres, have been planted, including 4,000 hectares this summer.

第一步 词汇解析

1. So far,副词词组,表示"迄今、到目前为止",比如:So far we haven't been able to find anything, but we're still researching.(目前,我们还没有任何发现,但是我们仍在研究。)
2. hectare,名词,表示"公顷";acre,名词,表示"英亩"。均为土地丈量单位,1 公顷等于 1 万平方米或约 2.5 英亩。

第二步 注意断句

So far, /30,000 hectares, /or about 75,000 acres, /have been planted, /including 4,000 hectares this summer.

第三步 句型解析

1. So far 为时间状语,30,000 hectares, or about 75,000 acres 是主语,后者是前者的同位语,可以用"并列译法",简单翻译即可。
2. have been planted 是谓语,且是被动语态,可以用"有被不用被"的译法。
3. including 4,000 hectares this summer 是状语,为了让句子更加完整和通顺,翻译时可以增词。总不能翻译为"其中 4 000 公顷在今年夏天"吧!

第四步 翻译来了

迄今已有 3 万公顷,大约 7.5 万英亩的地区已经种上树苗,其中 4 000 公顷是今年夏天栽种的。

> **本句考点总结**
>
> 第一,本句出现了被动语态的译法。被动语态是英文常见的一种形式,而在中文里常常少用"被"或者不用"被"。那么我们一般有什么样的译法呢?第一种是被动变主动,第二种是寻找替代词(比如:"让……给""为……所"等结构),第三种是在科技文献中用"可以"来替代"被",第四种是有"被"不用"被"。以上四种怎么用,那就看句子怎么通顺怎么翻译了啊!

第二，本句考查了英文同位语的译法。同位语是两个前后相互说明的名词或名词短语，比如 Beijing, the capital of China, 有两种译法，第一种是"并列译法"，翻译为"中国的首都北京"，第二种是"主谓译法"，翻译为"北京是中国的首都"。具体用哪一种，可以根据句子具体情况而定，有时两种都是可以使用的。

17 There are already discernible impacts on the microclimate, said Jean-Luc Peiry, a physical geography professor at the Université Blaise Pascal in Clermont-Ferrand, France, who has placed 30 sensors to record temperatures in some planted parcels.

第一步 词汇解析

❶ discernible，形容词，表示"可辨别的、看得见的"，比如：These pills had no discernible effect on mortality.（这些药对死亡率没有明显影响。）

❷ microclimate，名词，表示"微气候"，词根 micro- 表示"微"，比如：microwave（微波）。

❸ Jean-Luc Peiry，让－吕克·派瑞，人名；Blaise Pascal，布莱斯·帕斯卡，人名，这里采用的是音译法，注意名和姓之间要加"·"，翻译英文人名不确定时，可以使用音译法，然后把英文人名抄下来，放在括号里，这样保险一些。

❹ physical geography，名词词组，表示"自然地理学"，比如：As a comprehensive discipline, physical geography has the face of environmental science.（作为一门综合学科的自然地理学具有环境科学的面貌。）

❺ université，法语，名词，表示"大学"。

❻ Clermont-Ferrand，克莱蒙费朗市，地名，这里采用的是音译法，翻译英文地名不确定时，可以使用音译法，然后把英文地名抄下来，放在括号里，这样保险一些。

地理小常识：

克莱蒙费朗，法国中南部城市，原奥弗涅大区的首府和多姆山省的省会，是该地区政治、经济、文化、教育中心和最大的城市。

❼ sensor，名词，表示"传感器"，比如：The latest Japanese vacuum cleaners contain sensors that detect the amount of dust and type of floor.（日本最新款吸尘器装有传感器，能测出灰尘量和地板类型。）

❽ parcel，名词，表示"一块地、一片地"，比如：These small parcels of land were purchased for the most part by local people.（这些小块土地大多数是当地人买下的。）

第二步 注意断句

There are already discernible impacts on the microclimate, /said Jean-Luc Peiry, /a physical geography professor /at the Université Blaise Pascal /in Clermont-Ferrand, /France, /who has placed 30 sensors /to record temperatures /in some planted parcels.

第三步 句型解析

❶ There are already discernible impacts on the microclimate 是 there be 句型，翻译时用"有"会比较好，那

什么对微气候有影响呢？当然是前一句的内容了，因为"有"是动词，所以需要安排主语，主语用"植物""植被"都可以，这里是典型的根据上下文增词。

❷ said Jean-Luc Peiry 是完全倒装，这样的写作手法是为了后面的同位语能顺利出现，而翻译时，可以按照正常语序翻译，也可放在句首翻译，实话实说，考试时没有时间想那么多，原位翻译多好啊，别没事找事。

❸ a physical geography professor at the Université Blaise Pascal in Clermont-Ferrand, France 和前面的 Jean-Luc Peiry 形成了同位语关系，这里可以用前置定语的翻译方法，也可以放在原位使用"主谓译法"。不知道大家发现没有，其实考试中这种情况挺多的，这也是西方自然科学文章的写作方法。除此之外，还要注意其中的地点大小关系，中文地点从大到小，英文地点从小到大，赶紧记下来！

❹ who has placed 30 sensors to record temperatures in some planted parcels 是 who 引导的非限定性定语从句，后置较好，要弄清楚 who 指代谁，翻译为"他"更好。

❺ 定语从句中，who 是主语，has placed 30 sensors 是谓语和宾语，to record temperatures 是状语，in some planted parcels 是状语，注意翻译时的顺序。

第四步 翻译来了

植树对微气候的影响已经十分明显，法国克莱蒙费朗市（Clermont-Ferrand）布莱斯·帕斯卡（Blaise Pascal）大学的自然地理学教授让－吕克·派瑞（Jean-Luc Peiry）说道，他在一些已经栽种了树木的地区放置了30个传感器来记录温度（的变化）。

本句考点总结

第一，本句考查了英汉互译增减词的问题。一般来说英译汉增词，汉译英减词，常见增词的种类有：一、增加对象词（范围词），这是由上文缺少句子的某个部分造成的；二、增加范畴词，这是较难的一部分，常见的范畴词有"水平、方式、方法、问题、情况、途径和方面"，但是不仅仅有这些，还有其他很多；三、增加评论性词，这些常常出现在文学翻译中；四、增加动词，会在动词的"分配译法"中说明这点。

第二，本句考查了英文同位语的译法。同位语是两个前后相互说明的名词或名词短语，比如 Beijing, the capital of China，有两种译法，第一种是"并列译法"，翻译为"中国的首都北京"，第二种是"主谓译法"，翻译为"北京是中国的首都"。具体用哪一种，可以根据句子具体情况而定，有时两种都是可以使用的。

第三，本句出现了英文定语从句的译法。一般来说，定语从句按照"短前长后"的译法处理，较短的定语从句可以前置，较长的定语从句可以后置，这一切都取决于句子的通顺，并没有绝对的前置和后置译法。

18 "Preliminary results show that clumps of four to eight small trees can have an important impact on temperature," Professor Peiry said in an interview.

第一步 词汇解析

1. preliminary，形容词，表示"初步的"，比如：The team hopes to have some preliminary data models this summer.（研究小组希望在今年夏天建立一些初步的数据模型。）
2. clump，名词，表示"（树或植物的）丛"，比如：A stream meanders gently through a clump of trees.（一条小溪从树丛中蜿蜒流过。）
3. have an impact on，动词词组，表示"对……产生影响"，比如：Society begins to have an impact on the developing child.（社会开始对成长中的孩子产生影响。）

第二步 注意断句

"Preliminary results show /that clumps of four to eight small trees can have an important impact on temperature," /Professor Peiry said /in an interview.

第三步 句型解析

1. 双引号中的句子是直接引语，前面已经出现过多次，放在原位翻译即可。
2. Preliminary results show 是主语和谓语，这个用法可以记住，口译中经常使用。
3. clumps of four to eight small trees 是 that 引导的宾语从句的主语，can have 是谓语，an important impact on temperature 是宾语，Professor Peiry said in an interview 是主句的主语和谓语，按照原语序翻译即可。

第四步 翻译来了

"初步结果显示，四到八棵树组成的树丛能对温度产生重要的影响，"他在一次采访中说道。

本句考点总结

本句考查了英文直接引语的译法，最简单的译法就是保留冒号和双引号，说话人的位置和说话的内容都保持不变。即说话人在什么位置，就放在什么位置翻译，当然，说话人放在句首也是可以接受的。

---

19 "The transpiration of the trees creates a microclimate that moderates daily temperature extremes."

第一步 词汇解析

1. transpiration，名词，表示"蒸发、蒸腾"，比如：Plants release water through their leaves by transpiration.（植物通过蒸腾作用从叶片中释放水分。）
2. moderate，动词，表示"缓和、调节、节制"，比如：She should moderate her language when children are present.（在孩子面前，她说话应该节制。）
3. extreme，名词，表示"极端"，比如：He used to be very shy, but now he's gone to the opposite extreme.（他以前很腼腆，现在却走向了另一个极端。）

第二步 注意断句

"The transpiration /of the trees creates a microclimate /that moderates daily temperature extremes."

第三步 句型解析

❶ 这个句子接着上文那个句子，这样的双引号就好理解了，翻译时需要保留双引号。
❷ The transpiration of the trees 是主语，翻译时可增加"体表"或者"表面"，只要通顺，也可以不增词。
❸ creates a microclimate 是谓语和宾语，that moderates daily temperature extremes 是定语从句，从句较短，可以采用前置译法，这样句子更加通顺。

第四步 翻译来了

"树木体表的水分蒸发，能创造一个可以调节日常极端温度的微气候。"

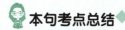 **本句考点总结**

本句出现了英文定语从句的译法。一般来说，定语从句按照"短前长后"的译法处理，较短的定语从句可以前置，较长的定语从句可以后置，这一切都取决于句子的通顺，并没有绝对的前置和后置译法。

---

20 "The trees also have an important role in slowing the soil erosion caused by the wind, reducing the dust, and acting like a large rough doormat, halting the sand-laden winds from the Sahara," he added.

第一步 词汇解析

❶ soil erosion，名词词组，表示"水土流失"，比如：Soil erosion, as a global problem, can be caused and impacted by many factors.（水土流失是一个全球性环境问题，引发和影响水土流失的因素是多方面的。）
❷ dust，名词，表示"灰尘、沙尘"，比如：Dust floats in the air.（灰尘飘浮在空中。）
❸ rough，形容词，表示"粗糙的"，比如：He nipped Billy's cheek with two rough fingers.（他用两根粗糙的手指捏了捏比利的脸蛋。）
❹ doormat，名词，表示"门垫"，比如：If you slide your feet across this doormat, it will open your door!（如果你在门垫上用脚向右滑一下，门就会开！）
❺ halt，动词，表示"使停住、停住"，比如：She walked towards him and then halted.（她向他走去，然后停下。）
❻ sand-laden，形容词，表示"含沙的"，其中后缀 -laden（用于构成形容词）表示"充满……的、装载……的"，比如：calorie-laden cream cakes（高热量的奶油蛋糕）。

第二步 注意断句

"The trees also have an important role /in slowing the soil erosion /caused by the wind, /reducing the dust, /and acting like a large rough doormat, /halting the sand-laden winds from the Sahara," /he added.

第三步 句型解析

① 双引号中的内容是直接引语，说话人在后面，所以是倒装。有人开始疑惑起来，这里的代词需要指明要点吗？想想前一句是怎么翻译的？如果是全称，那么这里可以用代词，"先全称，后代词"这样会比较好，琢磨一下这个问题，千万不要形而上学。有人又说，老师，我翻译为全称可以吗？可以！是不是啰唆？没有！

② The trees also have an important role 是主谓宾结构，in slowing the soil erosion 是状语，caused by the wind 是过去分词短语，相当于定语从句，从句较短，采用前置译法。

③ reducing, acting, halting 是和 slowing 并列的状语，有人问，为什么这个 and 放在第二个和第三个动词的中间啊？简单解释，这就是作者想表达一、二动词和三、四动词并列，一和二关系密切，三和四关系密切，从翻译上很难体现这一点。更简单地说，and 在哪里你就在哪里翻译。

④ 本句还有一个要点，an important role 是评论，而后面的 in slowing 是事实，是不是想到"事实与评论"的关系了呢？

第四步 翻译来了

"同时，这些树木在减轻大风造成的土壤侵蚀、减少沙尘，并且起到粗糙的地垫作用，阻挡从撒哈拉刮来的风沙方面功不可没。"他补充道。

> **本句考点总结**
>
> 第一，本句出现了分词或分词短语位于名词后的译法。一般来说，分词或分词短语位于名词后相当于定语或定语从句，定语按照"短前长后"的译法来进行翻译。
>
> 第二，本句出现了事实 (Facts) 和评论 (Comments) 的译法。中文一般先事实，后评论，而英文一般先评论，后事实。比如：It is important for her to go abroad. 翻译为"对于她来说，出国是很重要的"。英文中 It is important 是评论，for her to go abroad 是事实。从中英文的对比来看，可以知道中英文语序分别是怎么安排的。

Wildlife is responding to the changes. "Migratory birds are reappearing," Mr. Boetsch said.

第一步 词汇解析

① wildlife，名词，表示"野生动物"，比如：People were concerned that pets or wildlife could be affected by the pesticides.（人们担心宠物或野生生物会受到杀虫剂的影响。）

② respond to，动词词组，表示"响应、顺从、对……做出反应"，比如：We must respond to well-founded criticism with a willingness to change.（对于有根有据的批评，我们必须乐意做出改变。）

③ migratory，形容词，表示"迁徙的、迁移的"，比如：Migratory birds fly long distances between a winter home and a summer home.（候鸟要在冬巢和夏巢之间飞很远的距离。）

❹ reappear,动词,表示"重现",比如:Thirty seconds later she reappeared and beckoned them forward.(30秒后她又出现了,示意他们往前来。)

第二步 注意断句

Wildlife is responding to the changes. /"Migratory birds are reappearing," /Mr. Boetsch said.

第三步 句型解析

❶ Wildlife 是主语,is responding to 是谓语,the changes 是宾语,句式简单工整,可以直接翻译。直译就是"野生动物对这些变化做出了反应",感觉和上一句不是很搭,再想想怎么说更合适呢?这个知识点也印证了翻译是需要联系上下文的,而不只是翻译句子,所以一定要多读几遍才可以。
❷ 第二句是典型的直接引语,后面的说话人和动词可以置于句首或者句末,只要通顺就行;直接引语中,Migratory birds 是主语,are reappearing 是谓语。

第四步 翻译来了

野生动物也因此改变了行为,波特舍(Boestch)先生说:"迁徙的鸟类在这一地区重现。"

本句考点总结

本句考查了英文直接引语的译法,最简单的译法就是保留冒号和双引号,说话人的位置和说话的内容都保持不变。即说话人在什么位置,就放在什么位置翻译,当然,说话人放在句首也是可以接受的。

The project uses eight groundwater pumping stations built in 1954, before Senegal achieved its independence from France in 1960.

第一步 词汇解析

❶ groundwater,名词,表示"地下水",比如:Residents have complained of groundwater pollution and contaminated air.(当地居民抱怨地下水和空气遭到污染。)
❷ pumping station,名词词组,表示"水泵站",比如:There is a pumping station on the edge of the lake.(湖边有座水泵站。)
❸ independence,名词,表示"独立",比如:In 1816, Argentina declared its independence from Spain.(1816年,阿根廷脱离西班牙,宣布独立。)

第二步 注意断句

The project uses eight groundwater pumping stations /built in 1954, /before Senegal achieved its independence /from France /in 1960.

第三步 句型解析

① The project 是主语，uses 是谓语，eight groundwater pumping stations 是宾语，built in 1954 是过去分词短语位于名词后，相当于定语从句，从句较短，采用前置译法，翻译为"八个建于 1954 年的"和"建于 1954 年的八个"都可以。一般来说，在没有歧义的情况下，中文将数词放在修饰语的最前面。

② before Senegal achieved its independence from France in 1960 是时间状语，要知道它的作用是什么，它其实是 1954 的同位语，也就是解释说明"塞内加尔在 1954 年到底是什么情况"。

③ before 引导时间状语从句，从句中 Senegal 是主语，achieved 是谓语，its independence 是宾语，from France in 1960 是两个状语，直接翻译即可，但是最后要带上"之前修建的"。

第四步 翻译来了

该工程用了八个建于 1954 年的地下水泵站，都是在塞内加尔（Senegal）1960 年脱离法国统治取得独立之前修建的。

本句出现了分词或分词短语位于名词后的译法。一般来说，分词或分词短语位于名词后相当于定语或定语从句，定语按照"短前长后"的译法来进行翻译。

The pumps fill giant basins that provide water for animals, tree nurseries and gardens where fruit and vegetables are grown.

第一步 词汇解析

① fill，动词，表示"装满"，比如：She went to the bathroom, filled a glass with water, and returned to the bed.（她去了盥洗室，灌满了一杯水，然后回到床前。）

② giant，形容词，表示"巨大的"，比如：giant panda（大熊猫）。

③ basin，名词，表示"盆、水池"，比如：Water dripped into a basin at the back of the room.（水滴入房间后面的一个盆里。）

第二步 注意断句

The pumps fill giant basins /that provide water for animals, /tree nurseries and gardens /where fruit and vegetables are grown.

第三步 句型解析

① The pumps 是主语，fill 是谓语，giant basins 是宾语，that provide water for animals, tree nurseries and gardens where fruit and vegetables are grown 是定语从句，从句较长，所以采用后置译法。

② that provide water for animals, tree nurseries and gardens 这个定语从句修饰的是 giant basins，where fruit and vegetables are grown 这个定语从句修饰的是 gardens，按照原理来说，这是一个"循环套用"的定语从句，在《十二天突破英汉翻译》中讲过这点，但如果生硬地套技巧那就错了。本句要考虑第二个定语从句修饰 gardens，句子较短，所以采用前置译法。

❸ where fruit and vegetables are grown 这个定语从句中还有被动语态的翻译，可以使用"被动变主动"的译法，也可以使用别的译法，重要的是通顺。

第四步 翻译来了

这些水泵抽出水来灌满巨型的蓄水盆，而这些蓄水盆为动物、苗圃室和种有水果和蔬菜的花园供水。

本句考点总结

第一，本句出现了英文定语从句的译法。一般来说，定语从句按照"短前长后"的译法处理，较短的定语从句可以前置，较长的定语从句可以后置，这一切都取决于句子的通顺，并没有绝对的前置和后置译法。

第二，本句出现了被动语态的译法。被动语态是英文常见的一种形式，而在中文里常常少用"被"或者不用"被"。那么我们一般有什么样的译法呢？第一种是被动变主动，第二种是寻找替代词（比如："让……给""为……所"等结构），第三种是在科技文献中用"可以"来替代"被"，第四种是有"被"不用"被"。以上四种怎么用，那就看句子怎么通顺怎么翻译了啊！

译后总结

这篇英译汉总体符合 CATTI 历年考试的难度，选材也和大多数年份的考试很相似，句中多次出现了直接引语、定语从句、被动语态、总分关系，等等，这些都需要大家认真学习，认真思考，每篇文章的句子和段落可能不同，但是句式结构永远是相似的，翻译方法更是相同的。

第二节 2016 年上半年三级笔译汉译英

原文（请先通读全文）

健康是促进人的全面发展的必然要求。提高人民健康水平，实现病有所医的理想，是人类社会的共同追求。

在中国这个有着 13 亿多人口的发展中大国，医疗卫生关系亿万人民健康，是一个重大民生问题。

中国高度重视保护和增进人民健康。宪法规定，国家发展医疗卫生事业，发展现代医药和传统医药，保护人民健康。

多年来，中国坚持"以农村为重点，预防为主，中西医并重，依靠科技与教育，动员全社会参与，为人民健康服务，为社会主义现代化建设服务"的卫生工作方针，努力发展具有中国特色的医疗卫生事业。

经过不懈努力，覆盖城乡的医疗卫生服务体系基本形成，疾病防治能力不断增强，医疗保障覆盖人口逐步扩大，卫生科技水平日益提高，居民健康水平明显改善。

随着中国工业化、城市化进程和人口老龄化趋势的加快，居民健康面临着传染病和慢性病的双重威胁，公众对医疗卫生服务的需求日益提高。

与此同时，中国卫生资源特别是优质资源短缺、分布不均衡的矛盾依然存在，医疗卫生事业改革与发展的任务十分艰巨。

 译前指导

本篇 CATTI 三级笔译汉译英还是政府白皮书的内容，2016 年上半年考题的主要内容是关于中国的卫生事业发展问题，总体来说，难度不大，和以往的考试难度一致，句式结构工整，词汇短语丰富，请大家务必要学会各种医疗卫生的常见词汇。

1. 健康是促进人的全面发展的必然要求。提高人民健康水平，实现病有所医的理想，是人类社会的共同追求。

第一步　词汇解析

① 健康，good health，名词词组，比如：As I said last time, I am in good health.（正如我上次所说，我现在身体很健康。）

② 促进，promote，动词，比如：Swimming promotes health.（游泳增进健康。）若表示"旨在促进"，则用词组 designed to promote，比如：measures designed to promote economic growth（旨在促进经济增长的措施）。

③ 全面发展，all-round development，名词词组，比如：The theory of the all-round development of human beings is the important part of Marxism.（人的全面发展理论是马克思主义理论的重要组成部分。）

④ 必然要求，prerequisite，名词，比如：Good self-esteem is a prerequisite for a happy life.（良好的自尊心是幸福生活的先决条件。）
先决条件、前提、必备条件，prerequisite，名词，常与 for 或 to 连用，比如：two usual prerequisites to a peaceful settlement（和平解决的两个常见前提）。

⑤ 提高，improve，动词，比如：Their French has improved enormously.（他们的法语水平提高了很多。）若表示"明显改进、显著提高"，则用副词 markedly/noticeably。若表示"略有提高、稍有改进"，则用副词 marginally/slightly。

⑥ 病有所医，ensure (their) rights to medical care，动词词组，指的是医疗制度方面的改革，必须让相应的医疗能够惠及各个阶层的民众，也就是让大家都有就医的权利。

⑦ 共同追求，common pursuit，名词词组，比如：Harmony is the common pursuit of people all over the world.（和谐是世界各国人民的共同追求。）

第二步　动词定位

健康**是**促进人的全面发展的必然要求。**提高**人民健康水平，**实现**病有所医的理想，**是**人类社会的共同追求。

第三步 句型解析

❶ 第一句中,"健康"是主语,"是"是谓语,"必然要求"是宾语,"促进人的全面发展的"是定语,这里你可以用 to promote 或 for promoting,问题都不大,甚至用定语从句都可以,汉译英千万别死板!这里有很多"的",用 the person's all-round development 也不能算错!教你一个小技巧,一般有"的"可以用 of 结构,但也不是绝对的,要灵活哦!

❷ "提高人民健康水平,实现病有所医的理想"是第二句的原始主语,这里第一组动词是"提高",宾语是"人民健康水平","水平"是典型的范畴词,翻译时要省略。"实现病有所医的理想"简单分析就是"实现"是动词,"理想"是宾语,"病有所医"的意思是"让所有人都有看病的权利",建议大家记一下。本句原始的谓语是"是",宾语是"人类社会的共同追求",这里的"的"可以用 of,这样相对简单一点。把前面的动词翻译为动名词,谓语和宾语一搭,这个句子就出来了,绝对没有问题。但是参考译文使用了形式主语和真正主语的译法,大家也可以尝试使用。

第四步 翻译来了

Good health is a prerequisite for promoting all-round development of the person. And it is the common pursuit of human society to improve people's health and ensure their rights to medical care.

> **本句考点总结**
>
> 本句考查了英汉互译增减词的问题,一般来说英译汉增词,汉译英减词,常见增词的种类有:一、增加对象词(范围词),这是由上文缺少句子的某个部分造成的;二、增加范畴词,这是较难的一部分,常见的范畴词有"水平、方式、方法、问题、情况、途径和方面",但是不仅仅有这些,还有其他很多;三、增加评论性词,这些常常出现在文学翻译中;四、增加动词,会在动词的"分配译法"中说明这点。

在中国这个有着 13 亿多人口的发展中大国,医疗卫生关系亿万人民健康,是一个重大民生问题。

第一步 词汇解析

❶ 13 亿多人口,population of over 1.3 billion,名词词组。

❷ 发展中大国,a large developing country,名词词组,比如:China is a large developing country with a strong sense of responsibility.(中国是一个发展中国家,也是一个负责任的国家。)
发展中国家为 developing countries,发达国家为 developed countries。

❸ 医疗卫生,medical and healthcare,名词词组,注意"医疗"与"卫生"是并列的,比如:For the first time the country clarifies and implements universal medical and healthcare coverage.(该国第一次明确提出并落实医保全面覆盖。)

❹ 关系,be of vital importance to,动词词组,注意"关系"在汉语中的词性为动词,意思是"关系重大、对……很重要",比如:Undoubtedly, practical courses can be used to the reality, which is of vital importance to their development in the future.（毫无疑问，实用性课程可以用于实际中，这对他们未来的发展非常重要。）

❺ 重大民生问题，a major issue concerning its people's well-being，名词词组。
康乐、安康，well-being，名词，比如：contribute to the well-being of mankind（为人类造福）。

第二步 动词定位

在中国这个有着13亿多人口的发展中大国，医疗卫生关系亿万人民健康，是一个重大民生问题。

第三步 句型解析

❶ 本句的第一个分句中，"在中国"是状语，翻译为 In China 和 For China 问题都不大，"这个有着"是典型的同位语结构，所以 in/for China 后面接逗号，再接"13亿多人口"，这样句前的状语就完整了。

❷ 本句的第二个分句中出现主语，主语是"医疗卫生"，谓语是"关系"，也就是"对……很重要"，宾语是"亿万人民健康"，有没有发现这个"亿万人民"和前面的"13亿多人口"是重复的呢？把前面的数字放在后面翻译其实更好，当然翻译成"亿万人民"也可以，但是有点重复，考试时可能会失分。

❸ 第三个分句要用 and 连接，因为英文是形合语言，句子之间要有连接词，"是"是第二个谓语动词，"一个重大民生问题"是固定搭配，需要大家记忆一下。

第四步 翻译来了

For China, a large developing country, medical and healthcare is of vital importance to its population of over 1.3 billion, and is a major issue concerning its people's well-being.

中国高度重视保护和增进人民健康。宪法规定，国家发展医疗卫生事业，发展现代医药和传统医药，保护人民健康。

第一步 词汇解析

❶ 高度重视，pays great attention to，动词词组，词组原形为：pay great attention to，比如：Japan pays great attention to the development of forestry.（日本非常重视林业的发展。）

❷ 宪法，Constitution，名词，比如：The king was forced to adopt a new Constitution which reduced his powers.（国王被迫通过了削减其权力的新宪法。）大写首字母表示某个国家的宪法，小写表示一般的宪法，不指具体的宪法。

❸ 规定，stipulate，动词，比如：The document stipulated three criteria as the basis for any reform.（文件中规定了三项准则作为所有改革的基础。）

❹ 国家，state，名词，比如：Many heads of state are here.（许多国家元首都在这里。）
【同义词辨析】
特别要注意表示"国家"的三个单词，第一个是 state，一般指的是"代表政府的，代表政权的"；第二个是 nation，一般指的是"人民，民族相关的"；第三个是 country，一般指的是和"国家客观条件相关的"，比如：一个国家的地理环境，一个国家的领土领空等。但是这三个单词也没有绝对的界限，有的时候也可以通用。

❺ 发展，develops, promotes 等词，动词，单词原形为：develop, promote，比如：develop the national economy

（发展国民经济）或 promote mutual understanding between the two countries（增进两国的相互了解）。

❻ 医疗卫生事业，medical and health services，名词词组，比如：Everyone will have access to basic medical and health services.（人人都将享有基本医疗卫生服务。）这里的"事业"勉强可以认为是范畴词，不翻译也可以。

❼ 现代医药，modern medicine，名词词组，比如：Attitudes to hygiene in the West have evolved not only with modern medicine and microbiology.（西方对保健学的态度不仅与现代医学有关，还和微生物学的演变有关。）

❽ 传统医药，traditional Chinese medicine，名词词组，简称 TCM，比如：Electronic technology has also been introduced into traditional Chinese medicine.（中医也采用了电子技术。）

❾ 保护，protection，名词，比如：It is clear that the primary duty of parents is to provide protection for our children.（很明显，父母的首要职责就是为孩子提供保护。）

第二步 动词定位

中国高度重视保护和增进人民健康。宪法规定，国家发展医疗卫生事业，发展现代医药和传统医药，保护人民健康。

第三步 句型解析

❶ 第一句中，"中国"是主语，"高度重视"是谓语，特别要注意的是 pay attention to 后面需要接 doing sth. 或是 sth.，所以后面的"保护和增进"要用 ing 的形式，这点必须要牢记啊！"人民健康"是动词的宾语，必须强调一下代词的译法，这里要翻译为 protecting and improving its people's health，其中的 its 代指"中国"，中文常常省略名词或是使用名词，但英文需要用代词，特别是名词前必须要有代词，这点一定要牢记于心。

❷ 第二句中，"宪法"是主语，"规定"是谓语，后面直接接宾语从句比较合适，当然按照参考译文的方法，用 As 来引导也是可以的，逗号后面的内容是宪法的内容，所以用双引号更好一些。双引号中的"国家"是主语，"发展"是谓语，"医疗卫生事业"是宾语，句式工整，直接翻译即可。第二组谓语动词是"发展"，宾语是"现代医药和传统医药"，也许大家认为这里的"发展"可以只翻译一次，不过也可以翻译两次，但是一定要翻译为两个不同的单词，如果相同单词写两次，这肯定是错的，这点要牢记！那就是动词分配的反向用法。"保护人民健康"是本句的第三个动词和宾语，从整个句子的意思来看，"保护"是目的状语，所以翻译为不定式是可以的，翻译为"for + 抽象名词"也是可以的，其实再仔细想想，这里的 for the protection of 就是"抽象名词"，且抽象名词有动词词根，可以翻译为动词"保护"。

第四步 翻译来了

China pays great attention to protecting and improving its people's health. As the Constitution stipulates, "The state develops medical and health services, promotes modern medicine and traditional Chinese medicine for the protection of the people's health."

本句考点总结

第一，本句考查了形容词的"分配"译法和动词或名词的"分配"译法。形容词分配的译法是两个或多个形容词位于名词之前，"翻译公式"是 (A+B)*C=AC+BC，比如 international and strategic questions 翻译为"国际问题和战略问题";动词或名词分配的译法是一个动词位于多个名词宾语之前,或者一个名词位于多个名词前,"翻译公式"是 A*(B+C)=AB+AC,比如 wear a hat and a scarf 翻译为"戴着帽子,系着围巾"。而汉译英时,以上这些方法全部要反过来使用。

第二,本句当中考查了"抽象名词"的反向译法(汉译英)。抽象名词在英文里一般处于冠词之后,又在介词之前,以"the + 抽象名词 + of"的形式居多。一般来说,抽象名词有两种译法。第一种,若抽象名词有动词词根,则翻译为动词,比如 the suggestion of mine,翻译为"我建议",而不是"我的建议";第二种,若抽象名词没有动词词根,可以增动词翻译,比如 the spirit of our nation,翻译为"我们民族所具有的精神",而不是"我们民族的精神"。但是在汉译英时,需要能想到哪些动词是抽象名词,将动词变为名词,把句子变得更加"静态"才是我们需要的。

多年来,中国坚持"以农村为重点,预防为主,中西医并重,依靠科技与教育,动员全社会参与,为人民健康服务,为社会主义现代化建设服务"的卫生工作方针,努力发展具有中国特色的医疗卫生事业。

第一步 词汇解析

① 多年来,over the years,介词词组,比如:Over the years we have had our differences, but I always love you.(这些年来,虽然我们常有意见不合的地方,但我一直敬爱着您。)over 强调时间过程。当然也可以用其他介词,比如 for,注意这个词组后面要接完成时,其他时态不要考虑。

② 以……为(工作的)重点,making...the focus of our work,动词词组,词组原形为:make...the focus of our work,翻译为 focus on 也是可以的,这里用 make 属于"谓语动词的过渡"。

③ 农村,rural areas,名词词组,比如:The city personnel of hospitals rotate in teams in the rural areas.(城市医院的医务工作人员分小队轮流在农村地区服务。)

④ 预防,prevention,名词,比如:It's a thing there's no prevention for.(那是件无法预防的事。)

⑤ ……为主,putting...first,动词词组,词组原形为:put...first,比如:Career women put work first.(职业女性把工作放在第一位。)

⑥ 中西医,both traditional Chinese medicine and Western medicine,名词词组。"中医"指的是"中国传统医学",所以要翻译为 traditional Chinese medicine,简称 TCM,不要翻译为 Chinese medicine。

⑦ 并重,supporting both...and...,动词词组,词组原形为:support both... and...,比如:Do the services support both authentication and authorization?(服务同时支持身份验证和授权吗?)"并重"指的是"不分主次,同等看待",一般是两者。

⑧ 科技,science, technology,这里的"科技"并没有用 and 连接,因为后面还说了教育,如果只提及"科技",二者之间可以加 and。

⑨ 动员,mobilize,动词,比如:The best hope is that we will mobilize international support and get down to action.(最大的希望就是我们将动员国际社会的支持,开始行动。)若表示"鼓动……反对……",则用介词 against,比如:They successfully mobilized public opinion against him.(他们成功地发动起舆论

反对他。)

⑩ 为……服务，improve 或 serve，译文中使用了两个动词。"为人民健康服务"，也就是"改善人民健康"，所以第一处使用了 improve，第二处使用了 serve。比如：It is unfair to soldiers who have served their country well for many years.（对忠心效力国家多年的士兵们来说，这是不公平的。）

⑪ 社会主义现代化（建设），socialist modernization，名词词组，比如：shift the focus of work to socialist modernization（把工作重点转移到社会主义现代化建设上来）。

⑫ ……的方针，the policy of，名词词组，比如：advocate the policy of administration（赞成政府的政策）。"方针"指的是"指导工作或事业前进的纲领"，也就是 policy（政策）。

⑬ 具有中国特色的，with Chinese characteristics，介词词组，比如：create a new situation in building socialism with Chinese characteristics（开创具有中国特色的社会主义建设新局面）。这类具有中国特色的词汇，建议记忆和背诵，没有任何其他方法。

⑭ 医疗卫生事业，medical and health services，名词词组，比如：To provide both urban and rural residents with safe, effective, convenient and affordable medical and health services.（为城乡居民提供安全、有效、方便、廉价的医疗卫生服务。）

第二步 动词定位

多年来，中国坚持"以农村为重点，预防为主，中西医并重，依靠科技与教育，动员全社会参与，为人民健康服务，为社会主义现代化建设服务"的卫生工作方针，努力发展具有中国特色的医疗卫生事业。

第三步 句型解析

① 本句是长句，先看看动词是如何进行"分层"的，多个动词一定要搞清楚动词之间的层次性。

② "多年来"是时间状语，这里使用了 Over the years，所以可以用现在完成时。

③ "中国"是本句的核心主语，"坚持……"是第一个动词，后面双引号可以保留，"努力发展……"是第二个动词，这样整个句子就是两组动词，那么两组动词是并列、伴随还是下沉呢？本句重点在于这两个动词之间的关系，"努力发展"是"坚持……政策"而来的，所以先翻译"努力发展"，再翻译"坚持……政策"。这句话不需要"分堆"，而是直接翻译为主句加从句（或者介词短语的句型）。

④ 本句的核心谓语是"努力发展"，翻译为 work hard to develop，这是典型的"谓语动词的过渡"，你把这些词组背下来就会了。本句的宾语是"具有中国特色的医疗卫生事业"，这里"具有中国特色的"也是常见词汇，需要好好记忆。

⑤ 谓语和宾语解决了，接下来需要解决的是"坚持……方针"的问题，这里的"坚持"翻译为三谓语（介词短语 in accordance with），即使翻译为 sticking 之类的词，也是分词短语（二谓语），其实分词短语和介词短语没什么区别，都不是核心谓语，这也是"谓语动词的层次性"。"坚持……方针"变成了介词短语 in accordance with the policy of，后面接什么动词都很简单了。

⑥ 引号当中的内容处理："以农村为重点"翻译为 make...the focus of...；"预防为主"理解为"把疾病预防放在首位"，翻译为 putting disease prevention first；"中西医并重"理解为"同时支持中医还有西医"，翻译为 supporting both traditional Chinese medicine and Western medicine；"依靠科技与教育"翻译为 relying on...science, technology and education，注意这里是"科学""技术"和"教育"；"动员全社会参与"理解为"动员全社会来参与"，这里的两个动词之间是目的关系，翻译为 mobilizing the whole of society to join；"为人民健康服务，为社会主义现代化建设服务"是以上这些事情的目的，所以这里

就不是动名词的并列结构了,而是不定式作目的状语的结构,所以翻译为 to improve the people's health and serve socialist modernization,这里的两个"服务"都进行了翻译,当然你翻译一次成 serve 也是可以的。还要分析一个问题,"社会主义现代化建设"中的"建设"是典型的范畴词,你可以不翻译,要翻译也是 socialist modernization drive,记住这个短语!

第四步 翻译来了

Over the years, China has worked hard to develop its medical and health services with Chinese characteristics in accordance with the policy of "making rural areas the focus of our work, putting disease prevention first, supporting both traditional Chinese medicine and Western medicine, relying on science, technology and education, and mobilizing the whole of society to join to improve the people's health and serve socialist modernization."

本句考点总结

第一,句中出现了谓语动词过渡的译法,这是英汉互译当中非常难的知识点。中文是动态性语言,常用动词,用强势动词,英文是静态性语言,常用名词,用弱势动词,这点要牢记在心。比如 I give you my support. 不要翻译为"我给你我的支持",直接翻译为"我支持你"即可。give 是弱势动词,support 是强势动词,因为中英文的差异,只要翻译强势动词,不须翻译弱势动词。这点常常在英译汉当中使用,汉译英中用得比较少!

第二,关于谓语动词的层次性。汉译英的核心问题是厘清句子当中多个动词之间的关系,我们要学会在多个动词当中找到最核心的动词,翻译为核心谓语(也称为一谓语);找到其次核心的动词,翻译为分词、从句、其他状语或定语的形式(也称为二谓语);再找到不重要的动词,翻译为介词(也称为三谓语);最后最不重要的动词,可以不译(也称为四谓语)。这些动词在句子当中如何划分层次,需要大家在长期不断的实践中摸索,而且每个句子的翻译也不是固定的。有些句子当中的"一谓语"(核心谓语),在别的译本当中可能就是"二谓语"或者是"三谓语"。只要句子整体结构正确,逻辑清晰,那这就是一个好的译本。

第三,汉译英句子中并列、伴随、下沉的结构。中文常常会出现多个句子聚集的情况,那么我们在翻译时需要考虑将这些句子进行"分堆"。但是"分堆"之后,一个句子中也可能会出现两个动词或两组动词,那么有两个动词或两组动词的句子我们该如何进行翻译呢?比如:"我坐在那里看书",这里有两个动词,一个是"坐",一个是"看",我们翻译时便会有三种方法:

第一种并列(两个动词并列的译法,使用并列连词连接,两个动词之间不一定是"并列"关系):I sat there and read a book.

第二种伴随(将第二个动词翻译为二谓语,分词、从句、状语等都可以):I sat there reading a book.

第三种下沉(将第一个动词翻译为二谓语,分词、从句、状语等都可以):Sitting there, I read a book.

需要说明的是,并列、伴随和下沉只是动词的形式问题,不代表动词之间的逻辑关系,用这三种形式翻译两个动词或两组动词都是可以的,大家可以根据句子上下文的关系来判断使用。

> 第四，本句考查了英汉互译增减词的问题，一般来说英译汉增词，汉译英减词，常见增词的种类有：一、增加对象词（范围词），这是由上文缺少句子的某个部分造成的；二、增加范畴词，这是较难的一部分，常见的范畴词有"水平、方式、方法、问题、情况、途径和方面"，但是不仅仅有这些，还有其他很多；三、增加评论性词，这些常常出现在文学翻译中；四、增加动词，会在动词的"分配译法"中说明这点。

经过不懈努力，覆盖城乡的医疗卫生服务体系基本形成，疾病防治能力不断增强，医疗保障覆盖人口逐步扩大，卫生科技水平日益提高，居民健康水平明显改善。

第一步 词汇解析

① 经过……，意思是"由于、因为……"，thanks to，介词词组，比如：Thanks to his stupidity, this work is going to be delayed a great deal.（由于他的愚蠢，这项工作要大大延误了。）

② 不懈努力，unremitting efforts，名词词组，比如：We always keep unremitting efforts to pursue the excellent quality.（我们始终保持不懈的努力，以追求卓越品质。）

③ 覆盖，cover，动词，比如：a course covering business law（一门涵盖商业法的课程）。

④ 城乡的（居民），both urban and rural (residents)，句中指的是"城市和乡村地区的居民"，因为是二者，所以使用了 both...and... 的结构。比如：The income of both urban and rural residents is continuously growing.（城乡居民收入水平不断提高。）

⑤ 医疗卫生服务体系，medical and healthcare systems，名词词组，这里的"医疗"和"卫生"是并列关系。

⑥ （基本）形成，have been shaped，现在完成时的被动语态，单词原形为：shape，比如：Geography played a big part in shaping those opposite ways of thinking.（地理环境在形成那些对立的思维方式上起了重要作用。）

⑦ 疾病防治能力，the capabilities of disease prevention and control，名词词组。"防治"指的是"预防和治疗（疾病、病虫害等）"。

⑧ （不断）增强，have been enhanced，现在完成时的被动语态，单词原形为：enhance，比如：enhance one's confidence（增强信心）。

⑨ 医疗保障，medical insurance，名词词组，比如：You should balance the benefits against the costs of medical insurance.（你应该权衡医疗保险的好处和它的花费。）

⑩ 覆盖（人口），the coverage of，名词词组，比如：The coverage of HIV interventions for children remains alarmingly low.（儿童艾滋病毒干预措施的覆盖率仍然非常低。）

⑪ （逐步）扩大，has been expanded，现在完成时的被动语态，单词原形为：expand，比如：We have to expand the size of the image.（我们不得不扩大图像的尺寸。）

⑫ 卫生科技（水平），medical science and technology，名词词组，首先，要注意本文中的"卫生"指的是医疗方面，而不是是否干净。其次，这里二者并不是并列关系，而是"卫生的科技水平"。

⑬ （日益）提高、（明显）改善，has been improved，现在完成时的被动语态，单词原形为：improve，比如：Their French has improved enormously.（他们的法语水平提高了很多。）

⑭ 居民健康（水平），the people's health，名词词组，比如：The polluted air in the city seriously endangers the people's health.（城市中的空气污染严重危及人民的健康。）参考译文中除了被动语态这一特点外，还有一个特点就是将动词转化为名词词组，这也体现了英文偏静态，而中文偏动态的特点。

第二步 动词定位

经过不懈努力，<u>覆盖</u>城乡的医疗卫生服务体系基本<u>形成</u>，疾病防治能力不断<u>增强</u>，医疗保障覆盖人口逐步<u>扩大</u>，卫生科技水平日益<u>提高</u>，居民健康水平明显<u>改善</u>。

第三步 句型解析

❶ 句首"经过不懈努力"理解为状语，翻译为 by+doing 是完全可以的，但是参考译文处理为 thanks to，类似词组 Due to、Because of 等都是可以的，这样一来，"不懈努力"就变成了名词短语，译者后面还增补了 that have been made，也可以不增，这里只是补充强调一下而已。

❷ "经过不懈努力"之后跟了五个句子，主要是说明中国医疗有大幅度进步，所以后面的句子都可以形成并列结构，或者翻译成六个单独的句子也是可以的。

❸ 第一个句子"覆盖城乡的医疗卫生服务体系基本形成"的主语是"覆盖城乡的医疗卫生服务体系"，其中"覆盖城乡的"是定语，翻译为定语从句或分词结构都是可以的，这里的"城乡"，可以是"城乡地区"，也可以是"城乡居民"，这些不是关键。关键是这里的"隐藏被动语态"，也就是说"医疗卫生服务体系（被）形成了"，而且后面的五个句子全部使用了现在完成时，这是前面"不懈的努力"的结果，所以完成时最合适。

❹ 第二句"疾病防治能力不断增强"的主语是"能力"，前面的"疾病预防"是定语，"不断增强"是谓语，这里也是"隐藏被动语态"。这里的"能力"大家可能会理解为范畴词，直接翻译"疾病预防"，但是这样不对，因为"能力才能（被）提高"，"疾病预防不能"被"提高"！

❺ 第三句"医疗保障覆盖人口逐步扩大"的主语是"医疗保障覆盖人口"，这里的真正主语应该是"覆盖率"而不是"人口"，所以译文为 coverage，而不是 population。而且这里的"医疗保障"指的是"医疗保险"，而不是所谓的"保障"之类的词，切记这一点！本句的谓语是"逐步扩大"，这里翻译为 has been expanded，少了一个"逐步"，原因很简单，因为这里的参考译文是口译的句子，口译员在翻译时一般不会关注副词、形容词等内容，名词更加重要。而且大家会发现，这里的五个句子都是并列结构，那更加证明这是口译的句子，因为口译员赶紧把话说明白才是最重要的。实话实说，这种方法挺好，也挺实用，别总是纠结一两个单词，因为你一张嘴就忘了，希望把我这段话分享给所有人！

❻ 第四句"卫生科技水平日益提高"中的"卫生科技水平"是主语，其中的"水平"是典型的范畴词，可以不翻译，直接翻译"卫生和科技"，谓语是"日益提高"，这里的策略依旧和前文一致，没有翻译"日益"，这是口译的策略，但是要体现出是现在完成时。

❼ 第五句"居民健康水平明显改善"中的"居民健康水平"是主语，其中的"水平"还是范畴词，可以不翻译，直接翻译"居民健康"，谓语是"明显改善"，依旧没有翻译"明显"，现在知道是怎么回事了吧？

第四步 翻译来了

Thanks to unremitting efforts that have been made, medical and healthcare service systems covering both urban and rural residents have been shaped, the capabilities of disease prevention and control have been enhanced, the coverage of medical insurance has been expanded, medical science and technology has been improved, and the people's health has been improved.

本句考点总结

第一，本句出现了中文里隐藏被动语态的译法。被动语态是英文常见的一种形式，而在中文里常常少用"被"或者不用"被"。那么中文当中一般如何隐藏被动语态呢？第一种是被动变主动，第二种是寻找替代词（比如："让……给""为……所"等结构），第三种是在科技文献中用"可以"来替代"被"，第四种是有"被"不用"被"。在中文里识别出来以上四种隐藏的被动语态不是一件容易的事，需要大家仔细认真地识别这种现象，在汉译英时体现出来。

第二，本句考查了汉英互译增减词的问题，一般来说英译汉增词，汉译英减词，常见增词的种类有：一、增加对象词（范围词），这是由上文缺少句子的某个部分造成的；二、增加范畴词，这是较难的一部分，常见的范畴词有"水平、方式、方法、问题、情况、途径和方面"，但是不仅仅有这些，还有其他很多；三、增加评论性词，这些常常出现在文学翻译中；四、增加动词，会在动词的"分配译法"中说明这点。

---

6 随着中国工业化、城市化进程和人口老龄化趋势的加快，居民健康面临着传染病和慢性病的双重威胁，公众对医疗卫生服务的需求日益提高。

第一步 词汇解析

① 随着……（节奏）的加快，with the quickened pace of，介词词组。
加快的，quickened，形容词，单词来源于动词 quicken，比如：quicken one's pace（加快步子）。
节奏、速度，pace，名词，比如：slow down the pace of new-product development（放慢开放新产品的速度）。

② 工业化（进程），industrialization，名词，比如：blaze new roads in industrialization（在工业化方面开辟新路）。

③ 城市化（进程），urbanization，名词，比如：the increasing drift toward urbanization（日益增长的城市化趋势）。

④ 人口老龄化（趋势），aging population，名词词组，这里可以理解为"主谓结构变偏正结构"的译法，翻译为"老龄化的人口"，比如：The best way to compensate for an aging population is higher productivity.（弥补人口老龄化的最佳办法是提高生产率。）

⑤ 居民，the Chinese people，名词词组。注意"中国人"，要用三个词，the Chinese people。中华民族，也要用三个词，the Chinese nation。

⑥ 面临着，face，动词，比如：face bankruptcy（面临破产）。

⑦ 传染病，infectious diseases，名词词组，比如：Leprosy is an indolent infectious disease.（麻风是一种进展缓慢的传染病。）

⑧ 慢性病，chronic diseases，名词词组，比如：suffer from a chronic disease（患慢性疾病）。（疾病）慢性的、（人）久病的，chronic，形容词，比如：chronic indigestion（慢性消化不良）。

⑨ 双重威胁，dual health threats，名词词组，即"双重健康威胁"。

⑩ 公众，the public，"the + 形容词"表示一类人，比如：a collection of books recently made accessible to the public.（近来才向公众开放的一批藏书）。
⑪ 需求，need，动词，比如：Plants needs sun in order to grow.（植物生长需要阳光。）
⑫ 日益提高，better，形容词，句中指的是"需求日益提高"，也就是"需要更好的医疗卫生服务"。

第二步 动词定位

随着中国工业化、城市化进程和人口老龄化趋势的加快，居民健康<u>面临着</u>传染病和慢性病的双重威胁，公众对医疗卫生服务的需求日益<u>提高</u>。

第三步 句型解析

❶ "随着中国工业化、城市化进程和人口老龄化趋势的加快"是介词短语位于句首，特别是这里出现了"随着"，常用的结构是With...，而且这里"……的加快"可以用各种单词，比如 acceleration。参考译文使用了 the quickened pace of，大家可以记住，这样就能丰富自己的词汇量了。"中国工业化、城市化进程和人口老龄化趋势"是三个并列的定语结构，可以处理为三个名词结构，这里要重点关注范畴词的问题，"城市化进程"当中的"进程"是典型的范畴词，"人口老龄化趋势"中的"趋势"也是范畴词，翻译为"人口老龄化"即可。

❷ 接着本句的主语出现，"居民健康"是主语，但是如果仔细分析句子的结构，就会发现"面临威胁"的主语应当是"居民"，也就是"中国人民"，而不是"健康"，这里有点难理解，但尝试去理解吧！这里说一句：汉译英尽量用原始主语去翻译，不要换主语。

❸ 本句的主语是"居民"，谓语是"面临着"，宾语是"传染病和慢性病的双重威胁"，这里要注意的是怎么翻译"传染病和慢性病"，参考译文翻译为 infectious and chronic diseases，这里出现了定语的分配。而且参考译文中出现了 the dual health threats，这里 health 很写意，因为主语当中的"健康"在这里出现了。

❹ 主句当中的第二句和前面一句没有必然联系，所以用 and 连接是最好的，"公众"是主语，"对医疗卫生服务的需求日益提高"就是"需要更好的医疗卫生服务"。翻译啊！简单一点，千万不要弄得太复杂。

第四步 翻译来了

With the quickened pace of China's industrialization and urbanization, as well as its aging population, the Chinese people are facing the dual health threats of infectious and chronic diseases, and the public needs better medical and health services.

> **本句考点总结**
>
> 第一，本句中使用了"主谓结构变偏正结构"的译法，这是什么意思呢？也就是说主谓结构 Eyes are gleaming.（眼睛炯炯有神。）可以翻译为偏正结构 gleaming eyes（炯炯有神的眼睛），这种译法是为了让句子更加通顺，当然有时候也可以用"偏正结构变成主谓结构"的译法。"主谓变偏正"或"偏正变主谓"在英汉互译当中都可能出现，须灵活使用。

第二，本句考查了英汉互译增减词的问题，一般来说英译汉增词，汉译英减词，常见增词的种类有：一、增加对象词（范围词），这是由上文缺少句子的某个部分造成的；二、增加范畴词，这是较难的一部分，常见的范畴词有"水平、方式、方法、问题、情况、途径和方面"，但是不仅仅有这些，还有其他很多；三、增加评论性词，这些常常出现在文学翻译中；四、增加动词，会在动词的"分配译法"中说明这点。

第三，本句考查了形容词的"分配"译法和动词或名词的"分配"译法。形容词分配的译法是两个或多个形容词位于名词之前，"翻译公式"是 (A+B)*C=AC+BC，比如 international and strategic questions 翻译为"国际问题和战略问题"；动词或名词分配的译法是一个动词位于多个名词宾语之前，或者一个名词位于多个名词前，"翻译公式"是 A*(B+C)=AB+AC，比如 wear a hat and a scarf 翻译为"戴着帽子，系着围巾"。而汉译英时，以上这些方法全部要反过来使用。

7 与此同时，中国卫生资源特别是优质资源短缺、分布不均衡的矛盾依然存在，医疗卫生事业改革与发展的任务十分艰巨。

第一步 词汇解析

① 与此同时，in the meantime，介词词组，比如：I didn't see her for another five years, and in the meantime she had got married and had a couple of kids.（我又有五年没见过她，与此同时，她结了婚还生了几个孩子。）若要使用 at the same time, meanwhile, furthermore, moreover 表示"与此同时"，也是可以的。

② 卫生资源，health resources，名词词组，比如：the need to ration health resources（控制卫生资源分配的必要性）。注意这里的 resources 要使用复数，指的是"众多卫生资源"。

③ 特别是，especially，副词，比如：We go skiing a lot, especially in February.（我们常去滑雪，尤其是在二月份。）especially 侧重程度上的"格外或尤其是"，往往用来修饰作为状语的介词短语、从句以及句中的名词成分。

④ 优质资源短缺，the shortage of high-quality resources，名词词组。
优质的，high-quality，复合形容词，由形容词＋名词构成，比如：We will take high-quality service and products to satisfy you.（我们将提供优质的服务和高质量的产品来满足您。）

⑤ （资源）分布不均衡，unbalanced distribution (of those resources)，这里使用了 those，代指前面的"卫生资源"。

⑥ 矛盾，problem，名词，句中的"矛盾"指的是"疑难问题"，比如：the unemployment problem（失业问题）。用 issue 也是可以的，但是这里的"矛盾"不能使用 contradiction，因为这个单词指的是"相互排斥的两个概念"，也就是"两个判断不能同时真，也不能同时假"。

⑦ 存在，exist，动词，比如：Research opportunities exist in a wide range of areas.（研究机会存在于广泛的领域中。）

⑧ 改革，reform，动词，比如：He spent years trying to reform the world.（他花了多年时间，力图改造世界。）

⑨ 发展，develop，动词，比如：develop the national economy（发展国民经济）。

❿ 任务十分艰巨，意思是"未来艰巨的任务"，arduous tasks ahead，名词词组，增词"将来、未来"。艰巨的、费力的，arduous，形容词，比如：arduous training（艰苦的训练）。

第二步 动词定位

与此同时，中国卫生资源特别是优质资源短缺、分布不均衡的矛盾依然存在，医疗卫生事业改革与发展的任务十分艰巨。

第三步 句型解析

❶ "与此同时"是时间状语，翻译时放在句首更好，这里使用了 In the meantime，记住这个短语后面要用逗号。

❷ "中国卫生资源特别是优质资源短缺、分布不均衡的矛盾"是本句的主语，但是主语过长，该如何处理呢？选择"取偏"作主语是可以的，但是主语好像仍然很长。换种思路，直接拿"矛盾"作主语，"依然存在"作谓语，这里没有宾语，而且本句使用一般现在时会更好。但是，还要解决"中国卫生资源特别是优质资源短缺、分布不均衡的"这个定语的问题，仔细想想还是比较简单的，因为"特别是"肯定是 especially，那么后面就是状语结构，"优质资源短缺"和"（优质资源）分布不均衡"是两个主谓结构，翻译为状语可以采用"主谓结构的偏正译法"。也就是把"优质资源短缺"和"（优质资源）分布不均衡"翻译为"优质资源的短缺"和"（优质资源）不均衡的分布"。注意：第一个短语也可以翻译为"短缺的优质资源"，只要翻译成偏正结构就可以了，其余问题不大。那么这里的定语还剩下"中国卫生资源（的矛盾）"，可以用 of 结构，这样比较简单，译文当中使用了 regarding，相当于状语结构，把这个结构翻译在谓语的后面，整个句子就平衡了，其实这也是处理汉语主语较长的一种方法，非常实用，但是较难。

❸ 因为后面一句"医疗卫生事业改革与发展的任务十分艰巨"和前一句整体意思差别不小，所以可以单独成句。本句的"医疗卫生事业改革与发展的任务"是主语，谓语是"十分艰巨"，稍微用点心就知道，这句是"事实与评论"的关系，"十分艰巨"显然是评论性词，本句需要"寻找隐藏主语"，这里主语应当是"中国"，谓语是"拥有了"，宾语是"十分艰巨的医疗卫生事业改革与发展的任务"，这样能理解吧？当然有人说看不出来，要把"医疗卫生事业改革与发展""取偏"作为主语，然后谓语是"拥有"，宾语是"十分艰巨的任务"，这么处理也是可以的，只是主语还是很长。所以这句还真是有点难，译文里的主语是"中国"，谓语是"拥有"，宾语是"艰巨的任务"，"医疗卫生事业改革与发展的"变成了状语，这样是不是更好呢？这里的状语可以用 to do，也可以用 for doing，这里是把主谓结构"医疗卫生事业改革与发展"变成了偏正结构"改革与发展医疗卫生事业（的任务）"。

第四步 翻译来了

In the meantime, problems still exist regarding China's health resources, especially the shortage of high-quality resources and the unbalanced distribution of those resources. China has arduous tasks ahead for reforming and developing its medical and health services.

> 🧑‍🏫 **本句考点总结**
>
> 第一，本句中使用了"主谓结构变偏正结构"的译法，这是什么意思呢？也就是说主谓结构 Eyes are gleaming.（眼睛炯炯有神。）可以翻译为偏正结构 gleaming eyes（炯炯有神的眼睛），

这种译法是为了让句子更加通顺，当然有时候也可以用"偏正结构变主谓结构"的译法。"主谓变偏正"或"偏正变主谓"在英汉互译当中都可能出现，须灵活使用。

第二，本句出现了事实 (Facts) 和评论 (Comments) 的译法。中文一般先事实，后评论，而英文一般先评论，后事实。比如：It is important for her to go abroad. 翻译为"对于她来说，出国是很重要的"。 英文中 It is important 是评论，for her to go abroad 是事实。从中英文的对比来看，可以知道中英文语序分别是怎么安排的。

这篇政府白皮书的内容是 CATTI 汉译英考试当中的重点内容，这几年卫生问题出现的比较多，也是重点话题之一。这类文章的句式结构有一定难度，而且也要注意常见的医疗方面的词汇，这些内容都是大家复习时需要关注的重点。

第三节　2016 年下半年三级笔译英译汉

Harper Lee was an ordinary woman as stunned as anybody by the extraordinary success of *To Kill a Mockingbird*.

"It was like being hit over the head and knocked cold," Lee, who died at age 89, said during a 1964 interview. "I didn't expect the book to sell in the first place. I was hoping for a quick and merciful death at the hands of reviewers but at the same time I sort of hoped that maybe someone would like it enough to give me encouragement."

To Kill a Mockingbird may not be the Great American Novel.

But it's likely the most universally known work of fiction by an American author over the past 70 years. Lee was cited for her subtle, graceful style and gift for explaining the world through a child's eye, but the secret to the novel's ongoing appeal was also in how many books this single book contained.

To Kill a Mockingbird was a coming of age story; a courtroom thriller; a Southern novel; a period piece; a drama about class; and, of course, a drama of race. "All I want to be is the Jane Austen of South Alabama," she once observed.

The story of Lee is essentially the story of her book, and how she responded to it.

She was a warm, vibrant and witty woman who played golf, fished, ate at McDonald's, fed ducks by tossing seed corn, read voraciously and got about to plays and concerts. She just didn't want to talk about it before an audience.

To Kill a Mockingbird was an instant and ongoing hit, published in 1960, as the civil rights movement was accelerating.

It's the story of a girl nicknamed Scout growing up in a Depression-era Southern town.

A black man has been wrongly accused of raping a white woman, and Scout's father, the resolute lawyer, defends him despite threats and the scorn of many.

Praised by *The New Yorker* as "skilled, unpretentious, and totally ingenious," the book won the Pulitzer Prize and was made into a memorable movie in 1962.

"Mockingbird" inspired a generation of young lawyers and social workers, was assigned in high schools all over the country and was a popular choice for citywide, or nationwide, reading programs, although it was also occasionally removed from shelves for its racial content and references to rape.

By 2015, sales topped 40 million copies. When the Library of Congress did a survey in 1991 on books that have affected people's lives, *To Kill a Mockingbird* was second only to the Bible.

Lee herself became more elusive to the public as her book became more famous. At first, she dutifully promoted her work. She spoke frequently to the press, wrote about herself and gave speeches, once to a class of cadets at West Point.

But she began declining interviews in the mid-1960s and, until late in her life, firmly avoided making any public comment about her novel or her career. Her novel, while hugely popular, was not ranked many scholars in the same category as the work of other Southern authors.

Decades after its publication, little was written about it in scholarly journals. Some critics has called the book naive and sentimental, whether dismissing the Ku Klux Klan as a minor nuisance or advocating change through personal persuasion rather than collective action.

2016 年下半年的 CATTI 英译汉真题和前些年的文章有很大区别，之前的文章大都是外刊上的文章，而且题材以自然科学为主，但是这篇文章则是介绍了一部伟大的文学作品《杀死一只知更鸟》，所以大家在翻译的时候要对文学翻译有一定的认识和了解，但是这种文体在 CATTI 考试中不常见，所以不用太担心！

> **1** Harper Lee was an ordinary woman as stunned as anybody by the extraordinary success of *To Kill a Mockingbird.*

 第一步 词汇解析

❶ Harper Lee，哈泊·李，人名，这里采用的是音译法，注意名和姓之间要加·，翻译英文人名不确定时，可以使用音译法，然后把英文人名抄下来，放在括号里，这样保险一些。
文学小常识：
哈珀·李，1926 年出生于美国南方亚拉巴马州的一个小镇，1960 年发表她一生中唯一的长篇小说《杀死一只知更鸟》，使她获得巨大的声誉，这部小说获得当年的普利策小说奖，至今已经被翻译成 40 多种语言，全球销量超过 3 000 万册。

❷ ordinary，形容词，表示"普通的、一般的、平凡的"，比如：The manager of the company is a person of ordinary common sense.（该公司的经理是一个见识平凡的人。）

❸ stunned，形容词，表示"目瞪口呆的"，比如：He looked completely stunned.（他看上去完全惊呆了。）

❹ extraordinary，形容词，表示"非凡的、惊人的"，比如：The task requires extraordinary patience and endurance.（那项任务需要非凡的耐心和毅力。）

❺ *To Kill a Mockingbird*，专有名词，书名，翻译为《杀死一只知更鸟》。

文学小常识：

《杀死一只知更鸟》讲述了一个名叫汤姆·鲁滨逊的年轻人被人诬告犯了强奸罪的故事。因为汤姆是一个黑人，因此尽管辩护律师阿迪克斯·芬奇握有汤姆不是强奸犯的证据，都无法阻止陪审团给出汤姆有罪的结论。该妄加之罪，导致汤姆死于乱枪之下。

第二步 注意断句

Harper Lee was an ordinary woman /as stunned as anybody /by the extraordinary success of *To Kill a Mockingbird*.

第三步 句型解析

❶ Harper Lee 是本句的主语，was an ordinary woman 是系表结构，as stunned as anybody 是方式状语，或者认为是比较状语也是可以的，by 在这里理解为原因，也就是"由于"的意思，the extraordinary success of *To Kill a Mockingbird* 是名词短语，其中的 extraordinary success 可以认为是抽象名词，没有动词词根，翻译时可以增词"取得"，所以翻译为"取得了如此巨大的成功"。

❷ by the extraordinary success of *To Kill a Mockingbird* 是本句的事实，as stunned as anybody 是本句的评论，中文先事实后评论，英文先评论后事实，所以先翻译事实 by the extraordinary success of *To Kill a Mockingbird*。

❸ 重点要注意 *To Kill a Mockingbird* 是一本书的名字，翻译成中文要用书名号，英文并没有这个标点符号，需要注意，现在考试都是机考，所以标点符号一定要规范。

第四步 翻译来了

哈泊·李（Harper Lee）是一个普通的女人，《杀死一只知更鸟》取得了如此巨大的成功，这让她和所有人一样大吃一惊。

本句考点总结

第一，本句当中考查了"抽象名词"的译法。抽象名词一般处于冠词之后，又在介词之前，以"the + 抽象名词 + of"的形式居多。一般来说，抽象名词有两种译法。第一种，若抽象名词有动词词根，则翻译为动词，比如 the suggestion of mine，翻译为"我建议"，而不是"我的建议"；第二种，若抽象名词没有动词词根，可以增动词翻译，比如 the spirit of our nation，翻译为"我们民族所具有的精神"，而不是"我们民族的精神"。

第二，本句出现了事实（Facts）和评论（Comments）的译法。中文一般先事实，后评论，而英文一般先评论，后事实。比如：It is important for her to go abroad. 翻译为"对于她来说，出国是很重要的"。英文中 It is important 是评论，for her to go abroad 是事实，从中英文的对比来看，可以知道中英文语序分别是怎么安排的。

2

"It was like being hit over the head and knocked cold," Lee, who died at age 89, said during a 1964 interview. "I didn't expect the book to sell in the first place. I was hoping for a quick and merciful death at the hands of reviewers but at the same time I sort of hoped that maybe someone would like it enough to give me encouragement."

第一步 词汇解析

① be hit over the head，动词词组，表示"被打中头"，比如：He was hit over the head with a broken bottle. （他被一只破瓶子击中了头部。）

② be knocked cold，动词词组，表示"击倒、击昏"，比如：He ran into the wall and was knocked cold. （他撞在墙上，昏了过去。）

③ in the first place，副词词组，表示"首先、起初"，比如：In the first place you must warm the engine. （首先，你必须让发动机热起来。）

④ merciful，形容词，表示"仁慈的、宽厚的"，比如：We can only hope the court is merciful. （我们只能寄希望于法庭的宽大处理了。）

⑤ at the hands of，介词词组，表示"出自……之手"，比如：He suffered ill usage at the hands of his captors. （他受到了俘获他的那些人的虐待。）

⑥ reviewer，名词，表示"评论家"，比如：The reviewer padded out his review with a lengthy biography of the author. （评论者在他的评论中添加了冗长的作者生平以拉长篇幅。）

⑦ sort of，固定搭配，表示"有几分、有那么点儿"，比如：Vern laughed sort of. （弗恩微微一笑。）

第二步 注意断句

"It was like being hit over the head and /knocked cold," /Lee, /who died at age 89, /said during a 1964 interview. /"I didn't expect the book to sell in the first place. /I was hoping for a quick and merciful death /at the hands of reviewers /but at the same time /I sort of hoped that /maybe someone would like it enough/ to give me encouragement."

第三步 句型解析

① 本句是典型的直接引语，翻译时一定要保留原来的标点符号，然后直接翻译即可，说话人的位置也是一样，翻译时基本放在原始位置。

② 第一个引号当中的内容 It was like being hit over the head 是主系表结构，这里的 It 是代词，代词需要指明要点，这里看看上文就知道它指的是什么了，而且这里的 being hit 还是被动语态，可以用"让……给"的结构来翻译，之后的 and 是并列连词，knocked cold 是第二个被动语态，这里使用了"有被不用被"的译法。大家要注意，这里是人物平常的对话，翻译要"生活化"，也要有人物的感觉。

③ Lee 是说话人，后面接非限定性定语从句 who died at age 89，可以采用后置译法，而不是前置译法，said during a 1964 interview 是说话人后面接的谓语和状语，之后本句再接直接引语，注意保留原始的标点符号。

④ 第二个引号之后的内容 I didn't expect the book to sell 是主谓宾结构，要注意 in the first place 这个状语的含义，表示"在一开始"。

⑤ 第二句 I was hoping for a quick and merciful death 是主谓宾结构，这里要注意 was doing 结构，是过去进

行时态，表示"原本以为……"，at the hands of reviewers 是状语结构，but 是转折连词，at the same time 是时间状语，I 是主语，sort of 是口语中的插入语，没有什么实际的意思，可以不用翻译，hoped 是谓语，that 是宾语从句引导词，maybe someone would like it enough 是宾语从句中的主谓宾结构，to give me encouragement 是不定式短语作结果状语。

第四步 翻译来了

"成功的感觉就像是脑袋让人给打了，然后蒙圈了，"李在89岁那年去世，她在1964年的一次采访中这样说道，"一开始啊，我都没指望这本书能卖出去。当时，我只盼着书评家们给我来个痛快的、仁慈的了断，但是，与此同时，我也抱着一线希望，希望也许有人会喜欢这本书，也能给我一点儿鼓励。"

本句考点总结

第一，本句考查了英文直接引语的译法，最简单的译法就是保留冒号和双引号，说话人的位置和说话的内容都保持不变。即说话人在什么位置，就放在什么位置翻译，当然，说话人放在句首也是可以接受的。

第二，关于英文代词的译法。英文中需要翻译的代词主要指第三人称 he，she，it，they 及其相应宾格和指示代词 this 和 that。这些单词在翻译时一定要注意，主要采用"不抽象、不具体"的译法。不能翻译成具体的人或物，但是也不能翻译为"他""她""它""他们""这个""那个"，要注意取中间的译法。

第三，本句出现了被动语态的译法。被动语态是英文常见的一种形式，而在中文里常常少用"被"或者不用"被"。那么我们一般有什么样的译法呢？第一种是被动变主动，第二种是寻找替代词（比如："让……给""为……所"等结构），第三种是在科技文献中用"可以"来替代"被"，第四种是有"被"不用"被"。以上四种怎么用，那就看句子怎么通顺怎么翻译了啊！

第四，非限定性定语从句是用逗号隔开的定语从句，这样的句子一般都要采用后置译法，在翻译时需要翻译出关系代词 which，who 等词，指明这些词的指代关系，将这些代词翻译出来。

---

3 *To Kill a Mockingbird* may not be the Great American Novel.

第一步 词汇解析

 the Great American Novel，名词词组，表示"一部伟大的美国小说"，这里大写首字母，表示强调。

第二步 注意断句

To Kill a Mockingbird may not be /the Great American Novel.

第三步 句型解析

 本句是主系表结构，这里不需要断句，只是断句会更加清晰一些。

第四步 翻译来了

《杀死一只知更鸟》可能不是一部伟大的美国小说。

But it's likely the most universally known work of fiction by an American author over the past 70 years. Lee was cited for her subtle, graceful style and gift for explaining the world through a child's eye, but the secret to the novel's ongoing appeal was also in how many books this single book contained.

第一步 词汇解析

❶ fiction,名词,表示"小说、虚构的事",比如:His new novel is a must for all lovers of crime fiction.(他的新作是所有犯罪小说爱好者的必读书。)

❷ cite,动词,表示"表彰、表扬",比如:He was cited for bravery.(他因表现勇敢而得到嘉奖。)

❸ subtle,形容词,表示"奥妙的、巧妙的",比如:His film, over two hours in length, is a subtle study of family life.(他这部片长逾两个小时的电影对家庭生活进行了巧妙的剖析。)

❹ gift,名词,表示"天赋、才能",比如:a gift for languages(语言天赋)。

❺ ongoing,形容词,表示"继续存在的、不间断的",比如:There is an ongoing debate on the issue.(关于这个问题的争论还在继续。)

❻ appeal,名词,表示"吸引力、感染力",比如:Its new title was meant to give the party greater public appeal.(新的名字意在给予该党更大的公众吸引力。)

第二步 注意断句

But /it's likely the most universally known work of fiction /by an American author /over the past 70 years. /Lee was cited for her subtle, /graceful style /and gift for explaining the world /through a child's eye, /but /the secret to the novel's ongoing appeal was also in how many books /this single book contained.

第三步 句型解析

❶ But 是转折连词,表示"但是",it 是本句的主语,这里需要指明要点,表示"这本书",也就是"《杀死一只知更鸟》"。is likely the most universally known work of fiction 是本句的系表结构,by an American author over the past 70 years 是两个状语,by 引导的是方式状语,表示"由……创作的",后面的 over... 是时间状语,表示"在过去 70 年当中"。在整个句子的翻译中,可以将废话(两个状语)放在主语之后翻译,中文当然是先说主语,再说废话。

❷ 第二句中,Lee 是本句的主语,was cited for her subtle, graceful style 是被动语态,要注意这里 be cited for 的用法,表示"受到赞誉",采用了被动语态"寻找替代词"的译法。for 后面接了两组短语,一组是 her subtle, graceful style,表示"巧妙、优雅的(写作)风格",这里的"写作"是增词,是通过对本句的理解增的对象词;另一组是 gift for explaining the world through a child's eye,这里的 gift 理解为"天赋、才能",那么又是什么样的"天赋"或是"才能"呢?后面的 for doing 进行了解释,就是"通过孩子的视角来阐释世界的才能",这里也要注意状语 through a child's eye,因为是废话,所以要放在句子内部翻译,而不是放在句首或是句末。

❸ but 表示转折的含义，the secret to the novel's ongoing appeal 是本句的主语，特别要注意主语中 appeal 的理解，这里表示"吸引力"，即"这本书一直有吸引力的秘密"。was 是系词，后面是表语，这里的 also in 表示"在于"，不要总想着每个词都翻译，这里的 also 只是表示语气的程度，前面谈到了作者的写作很厉害，后面"又"如何如何，没必要生硬地翻译出这个单词。"在于"后面跟 how many books，表示"在于很多书"，this single book contained 是定语从句，从句较短，可以采用前置译法，翻译为"这本书涵盖了许多书"，再看看译文是怎么处理的，是不是更加简单呢？

第四步　翻译来了

但是，这本书可能是过去 70 年当中美国作家所创作的最为人所知的虚构小说。作者因其巧妙、优雅的写作风格和通过孩子的视角来阐释世界的天赋而被大加赞誉，但是，这本书一直受到青睐的秘诀是它集多本书于一体。

本句考点总结

第一，关于英文代词的译法。英文中需要翻译的代词主要指第三人称 he，she，it，they 及其相应宾格和指示代词 this 和 that。这些单词在翻译时一定要注意，主要采用"不抽象、不具体"的译法。不能翻译成具体的人或物，但是也不能翻译为"他""她""它""他们""这个""那个"，要注意取中间的译法。

第二，本句考查了中英文语序的问题，一般来说，中文的语序是"主语＋废话（定语、状语、补语、插入语，等等）＋重要成分"，而英文的语序则是"废话（定语、状语、补语、插入语，等等）＋主语＋重要成分＋废话（定语、状语、补语、插入语，等等）"，翻译时需要注意调整语序。

第三，本句出现了被动语态的译法。被动语态是英文常见的一种形式，而在中文里常常少用"被"或者不用"被"。那么我们一般有什么样的译法呢？第一种是被动变主动，第二种是寻找替代词（比如："让……给""为……所"等结构），第三种是在科技文献中用"可以"来替代"被"，第四种是有"被"不用"被"。以上四种怎么用，那就看句子怎么通顺怎么翻译了啊！

第四，本句考查了英汉互译增减词的问题，一般来说英译汉增词，汉译英减词，常见增词的种类有：一、增加对象词（范围词），这是由上文缺少句子的某个部分造成的；二、增加范畴词，这是较难的一部分，常见的范畴词有"水平、方式、方法、问题、情况、途径和方面"，但是不仅仅有这些，还有很多其他的；三、增加评论性词，这些常常出现在文学翻译中；四、增加动词，会在动词的"分配译法"中说明这点。

第五，本句出现了英文定语从句的译法。一般来说，定语从句按照"短前长后"的译法处理，较短的定语从句可以前置，较长的定语从句可以后置，这一切都取决于句子的通顺，并没有绝对的前置和后置译法。

5 *To Kill a Mockingbird* was a coming of age story; a courtroom thriller; a Southern novel; a period piece; a drama about class; and, of course, a drama of race. "All I want to be is the Jane Austen of South Alabama," she once observed.

第一步 词汇解析

① thriller，名词，表示"（尤指关于罪案或间谍的）惊险小说（或戏剧、电影）"，比如：Fact and fiction merge together in his latest thriller.（在他最近的惊险小说中，真实和虚构交织在一起。）

② piece，名词，表示"（文章、艺术品、音乐作品等的）一件、一篇、一首、一支"，比如：They performed pieces by Bach and Handel.（他们演奏了巴赫和亨德尔的几支曲子。）

③ class，名词，表示"阶级"，比如：the relationship between social classes（社会阶级间的关系）。

④ Jane Austen，简·奥斯汀，人名，这里采用的是音译法，注意名和姓之间要加·，翻译英文人名不确定时，可以使用音译法，然后把英文人名抄下来，放在括号里，这样保险一些。

文学小常识：
简·奥斯汀（Jane Austen，1775年12月16日—1817年7月18日），英国女小说家，主要作品有《傲慢与偏见》《理智与情感》等。

⑤ South Alabama，地名，表示"南亚拉巴马州"。

⑥ observe，动词，表示"说、评论、评述"，比如：I have little to observe on what has been said.（对于所说的这些，我没有什么意见要说。）

第二步 注意断句

To Kill a Mockingbird was a coming of age story; /a courtroom thriller; /a Southern novel; /a period piece; /a drama about class; /and, /of course, /a drama of race. /"All I want to be is the Jane Austen of South Alabama," /she once observed.

第三步 句型解析

① *To Kill a Mockingbird* 是本句的主语，可以翻译为"《杀死一只知更鸟》"，也可以翻译为"这本书"，代词和名词混搭，was a coming of age story 是句子的系动词和表语。本句后面的分号可以保留，也可以变成逗号，实际上就是连续性的表语结构，搞清楚每一个结构表示的含义即可。a courtroom thriller 表示"一部法庭的惊悚片"；a Southern novel 表示"一部南方的小说"；a period piece 表示"一部年代小说"；a drama about class 表示"一部关于阶级的剧本"；a drama of race 表示"一部关于种族的剧本"。这里只有一个点要注意，was 是动词，需要分配翻译，所以在每个表语前增加动词"是"，其余正常翻译就可以。

② "All I want to be is the Jane Austen of South Alabama," she once observed 本句出现了直接引语，翻译时需要保留双引号，说话人的位置也不要发生变化。All 后面是定语从句 I want to be，这种较为口语和文学化的东西不要直译，要不没法读，你翻译为"我所想要的一切就是"，这不是翻译腔吗？翻译为"我想要成为……"更好。这句话中还有一个知识点，即 observe，在文学作品中，这个单词常常表示"说"，当然还有许多其他意思，自己可以去查字典！

第四步 翻译来了

这本书是一本成长的故事集，是一部法庭的惊悚片，是一部南方的小说，是一部年代小说，是一部关于阶级的剧本，当然也是一部关于种族的剧本。"我想成为南亚拉巴马州的简·奥斯汀（Jane Austen）。"这位作家曾经说道。

> **本句考点总结**
>
> 　　第一，本句考查了英汉互译增减词的问题，一般来说英译汉增词，汉译英减词，常见增词的种类有：一、增加对象词（范围词），这是由上文缺少句子的某个部分造成的；二、增加范畴词，这是较难的一部分，常见的范畴词有"水平、方式、方法、问题、情况、途径和方面"，但是不仅仅有这些，还有很多其他的；三、增加评论性词，这些常常出现在文学翻译中；四、增加动词，会在动词的"分配译法"中说明这点。
>
> 　　第二，本句考查了英文直接引语的译法，最简单的译法就是保留冒号和双引号，说话人的位置和说话的内容都保持不变。即说话人在什么位置，就放在什么位置翻译，当然，说话人放在句首也是可以接受的。

6　The story of Lee is essentially the story of her book, and how she responded to it.

第一步　词汇解析

❶ essentially，副词，表示"基本上、本质上"，比如：Suicide rates have remained essentially unchanged.（自杀率基本上没什么变化。）

第二步　注意断句

The story of Lee is essentially the story of her book, /and how she responded to it.

第三步　句型解析

❶ The story of Lee is essentially the story of her book 是主系表结构，其中要特别注意 essentially 这个单词的用法，长的形容词和副词可以单独成句，这里翻译为"从本质上来说"，放在句首翻译也是非常合适的。还要注意一个知识点，这句话是"同指结构"，the story is the story，作者是为了强调才写出这样的结构，但是你不能翻译为"故事是故事"，所以，译文使用了"李的故事也就在这本书中"，后面的 story 并没有直接翻译，这些小的知识点都要细致地分析。

❷ and 是并列连词，后面是 how 引导的表语从句 how she responded to it，这里的 it 一定要注意，因为是代词，代词需要指明要点，这里表示"对这个事件的看法"，这点也要细致一些。

第四步　翻译来了

从本质上来说，李的故事就在她的书中，以及她对整个故事的看法中。

> **本句考点总结**
>
> 关于英文代词的译法。英文中需要翻译的代词主要指第三人称 he，she，it，they 及其相应宾格和指示代词 this 和 that。这些单词在翻译时一定要注意，主要采用"不抽象、不具体"的译法。不能翻译成具体的人或物，但是也不能翻译为"他""她""它""他们""这个""那个"，要注意取中间的译法。

7

She was a warm, vibrant and witty woman who played golf, fished, ate at McDonald's, fed ducks by tossing seed corn, read voraciously and got about to plays and concerts. She just didn't want to talk about it before an audience.

第一步 词汇解析

① vibrant，形容词，表示"充满生机的、生气勃勃的、精力充沛的"，比如：Tom felt himself being drawn towards her vibrant personality.（汤姆感觉自己被她充满朝气的个性所吸引。）

② witty，形容词，表示"言辞诙谐的、巧妙的、妙趣横生的、机智的"，比如：He was witty, amusing and gifted with a sharp business brain.（他机智诙谐，具有敏锐的商业头脑。）

③ toss，动词，表示"扔、投、掷"，比如：Just toss it in the rubbish.（把它扔进垃圾桶就可以了。）

④ voraciously，副词，voracious 是形容词形式，表示"狼吞虎咽的、（对信息、知识）渴求的、求知欲强的"，比如：Joseph Smith was a voracious book collector.（约瑟夫·史密斯是个如饥似渴的藏书家。）

第二步 注意断句

She was a warm, /vibrant /and witty woman /who played golf, /fished, /ate at McDonald's, /fed ducks by tossing seed corn, /read voraciously /and got about to plays and concerts. /She just didn't want to talk about it / before an audience.

第三步 句型解析

① She was a warm, vibrant and witty woman 是主系表结构，这里注意三个形容词的译法，有人说，武哥这里是同指现象吧？你这么认为完全可以，翻译为"她是……女人"或者是"她……"都是可以的。

② who 引导定语从句，从句中并列动词较多，你只要看懂了就可以直接翻译，但是需要注意的是，定语从句较长，需要采用后置译法，played golf 表示"打高尔夫"；fished 表示"钓鱼"；ate at McDonald's 表示"吃麦当劳"，不要说"在麦当劳里吃饭"；fed ducks by tossing seed corn 表示"扔玉米粒喂鸭子"，这里的 by 表示方式；read voraciously 表示"如饥似渴地读书"；and got about to plays and concerts 表示"到处去看戏和听音乐会"，注意这里的 to，应采用介词变为动词的译法，翻译为"看"和"听"更好。

③ She just didn't want to talk about it 是主谓宾结构，before an audience 是地点状语，注意这是"废话"，所以翻译的时候要放在句中，而不是句首或是句末。

第四步 翻译来了

她是一个热心肠、活泼和机智的女人,她打高尔夫、钓鱼、吃麦当劳、扔玉米粒喂鸭子、如饥似渴地读书、到处去看戏和听音乐会。她只是不想在观众面前讨论这些故事。

> **本句考点总结**
>
> 第一,本句出现了英文定语从句的译法。一般来说,定语从句按照"短前长后"的译法处理,较短的定语从句可以前置,较长的定语从句可以后置,这一切都取决于句子的通顺,并没有绝对的前置和后置译法。
>
> 第二,本句考查了中英文语序的问题,一般来说,中文的语序是"主语+废话(定语、状语、补语、插入语,等等)+重要成分",而英文的语序则是"废话(定语、状语、补语、插入语,等等)+主语+重要成分+废话(定语、状语、补语、插入语,等等)",翻译时需要注意调整语序。

8. *To Kill a Mockingbird* was an instant and ongoing hit, published in 1960, as the civil rights movement was accelerating.

第一步 词汇解析

① hit,名词,表示"很受欢迎的人(或事物)、风行一时的流行歌曲(或唱片)",比如:Her new series is a smash hit.(她的新系列节目极为成功,引起轰动。)

② civil rights movement,名词词组,表示"民权运动"。
文化小常识:
美国黑人民权运动,美国民权运动的一部分,于1950年兴起,直至1970年,是通过非暴力的抗议行动来争取非裔美国人民权的群众斗争。

第二步 注意断句

To Kill a Mockingbird was an instant and ongoing hit, /published in 1960, /as the civil rights movement was accelerating.

第三步 句型解析

① *To Kill a Mockingbird* was an instant and ongoing hit 是主系表结构,注意这里的两个形容词 instant 和 ongoing 分别是什么含义。

② published in 1960 是过去分词短语,修饰前面的 *To Kill a Mockingbird*,相当于定语从句,有逗号,当然是非限定性定语从句,这里可以用后置译法,但是你看看参考译文是怎么处理的?参考译文有点文学的感觉,把这里的 published 作为谓语,前面的 instant 和 ongoing 放在后面翻译,这就是"事实与评论"的译法,中文先事实后评论。当然这个知识点你要是想不到也没关系,直接按照原文翻译,中规中矩也是一件好事!

❸ as 引导时间状语从句，the civil rights movement was accelerating 是主谓结构，参考译文使用了"方兴未艾"这样的词汇，非常好，可以好好学起来。

第四步 翻译来了

《杀死一只知更鸟》于 1960 年出版，随后热销，一直畅销，那时正值民权运动方兴未艾之时。

本句考点总结

第一，非限定性定语从句是用逗号隔开的定语从句，这样的句子一般都要采用后置译法，在翻译时需要翻译出关系代词 which，who 等词，指明这些词的指代关系，将这些代词翻译出来。

第二，本句出现了事实（Facts）和评论（Comments）的译法。中文一般先事实，后评论，而英文一般先评论，后事实。比如：It is important for her to go abroad. 翻译为"对于她来说，出国是很重要的"。英文中 It is important 是评论，for her to go abroad 是事实，从中英文的对比来看，可以知道中英文语序分别是怎么安排的。

9 It's the story of a girl nicknamed Scout growing up in a Depression-era Southern town.

第一步 词汇解析

❶ nickname，动词，表示"给……起绰号"，比如：When he got older, I nicknamed him Little Alf.（他长大些后，我给他起了绰号"小阿尔夫"。）

❷ Scout，"童子军"，人名，这里采用了直译的方法。很多版本的译文中也采用了音译的方法，翻译为"斯各特"。

文化小常识：

Scout 是《杀死一只知更鸟》故事的叙述者和主人公。她和父亲阿迪克斯、哥哥杰姆，还有黑人厨师卡尔普尼亚一起住在梅岗镇。她很聪明，如果按照她所生活的时代和地方的标准来衡量，她也是个顽皮的小姑娘。她性格中虽然有好斗的一面，但她内心相信，小镇的居民是善良的。

❸ a Depression-era，名词词组，表示"大萧条时代"。Depression 大写首字母，等同于 Great Depression。

经济小常识：

大萧条，1929 年至 1933 年之间发源于美国，后来波及整个资本主义世界。这一危机具有持续时间长、范围广、破坏力强的特点，其根源在于资本主义制度的基本矛盾，也就是生产社会化和资本主义生产资料私有制之间的矛盾。

第二步 注意断句

It's the story of a girl /nicknamed Scout /growing up /in a Depression-era Southern town.

第三步 句型解析

❶ It's the story of a girl 是主系表结构，nicknamed Scout 是过去分词短语作定语，定语较短，可以采用前置译法。

❷ growing up in a Depression-era Southern town 是现在分词短语作定语，修饰 Scout，定语较长，可以采用后置译法，怎么通顺怎么来就可以。

第四步 翻译来了

这是一个成长在大萧条时代，在南方某镇绰号叫"童子军"的女孩的故事。

 本句考点总结

本句出现了分词或分词短语位于名词后的译法。一般来说，分词或分词短语位于名词后相当于定语或定语从句，定语按照"短前长后"的译法来进行翻译。

10 A black man has been wrongly accused of raping a white woman, and Scout's father, the resolute lawyer, defends him despite threats and the scorn of many.

第一步 词汇解析

❶ be accused of，动词词组，表示"被指控、被控告"，比如：Her assistant was accused of theft and fraud by the police. （她的助手被警方指控偷窃和诈骗。）

❷ rape，动词，表示"强奸"，比如：A young woman was brutally raped in her own home. （一个年轻妇女在自己家中被粗暴地强奸了。）

❸ resolute，形容词，表示"坚决的、坚定的"，比如：Voters perceive him as a decisive and resolute international leader. （选民认为他是一位果断、坚定的国际领袖。）

❹ defend，动词，表示"为……辩护"，比如：He has hired a lawyer to defend him against the allegation. （他已聘请一位律师为他所受的指控辩护。）

❺ scorn，名词，表示"轻蔑、鄙视"，比如：Researchers greeted the proposal with scorn. （研究者们对这个提议报以轻蔑的态度。）

第二步 注意断句

A black man has been wrongly accused of raping a white woman, /and Scout's father, /the resolute lawyer, / defends him /despite threats and the scorn of many.

第三步 句型解析

❶ A black man has been wrongly accused of raping a white woman 是主谓宾结构，这里要注意 wrongly 这个副词的作用，到底是修饰 accuse 还是 rape，这点不用我再提醒大家了吧？句中还出现了被动语态，想

想该如何翻译？

❷ and 是并列连词，连接两个句子，可以不用翻译，Scout's father 和 the resolute lawyer 是同位语关系，也是本句的主语，注意同位语的翻译，可以用两种，第一种是并列关系"'童子军'的父亲，一名立场坚定的律师"，第二种是主谓关系"'童子军'的父亲是一名立场坚定的律师"，这两种翻译方法都是可以的，这两种译法也都得掌握。

❸ defends him 是本句的谓语和宾语，但是前面的同位语形成主谓关系后缺少了主语，这里增主语"他"，翻译为"他为他辩护"不太好，这里的 him 要指明要点，指的是"这名黑人男性"，这里也是代词的译法。

❹ despite 引导让步状语，threats and the scorn of many 指的是"众人的威胁和蔑视"，这里特别注意 many 的含义，表示"大多数人"。

第四步 翻译来了

一名黑人男性被诬告强奸了一名白人女性，"童子军"的父亲是一名立场坚定的律师，他不顾众人的威胁和蔑视为这名黑人男性辩护。

> **本句考点总结**
>
> 　　第一，本句出现了被动语态的译法。被动语态是英文常见的一种形式，而在中文里常常少用"被"或者不用"被"。那么我们一般有什么样的译法呢？第一种是被动变主动，第二种是寻找替代词（比如："让……给""为……所"等结构），第三种是在科技文献中用"可以"来替代"被"，第四种是有"被"不用"被"。以上四种怎么用，那就看句子怎么通顺怎么翻译了啊！
>
> 　　第二，本句考查了英文同位语的译法。同位语是两个前后相互说明的名词或名词短语，比如 Beijing, the capital of China，有两种译法，第一种是"并列译法"，翻译为"中国的首都北京"；第二种是"主谓译法"，翻译为"北京是中国的首都"。具体用哪一种，可以根据句子具体情况而定，有时两种都是可以使用的。
>
> 　　第三，关于英文代词的译法。英文中需要翻译的代词主要指第三人称 he, she, it, they 及其相应宾格和指示代词 this 和 that。这些单词在翻译时一定要注意，主要采用"不抽象、不具体"的译法。不能翻译成具体的人或物，但是也不能翻译为"他""她""它""他们""这个""那个"，要注意取中间的译法。

Praised by *The New Yorker* as "skilled, unpretentious, and totally ingenious," the book won the Pulitzer Prize and was made into a memorable movie in 1962.

第一步 词汇解析

❶ *The New Yorker*，专有名词，表示《纽约客》。
   文化小常识：
   　　《纽约客》也译作《纽约人》，是一份美国知识、文艺类的综合杂志，以非虚构作品为主，包括对政治、国际事务、大众文化和艺术、科技以及商业的报道和评论，另外也会刊发一些文学作品，主要是短篇小说和诗歌，以及幽默小品和漫画作品。

❷ unpretentious，形容词，表示"不矫饰的、朴实无华的"，比如：She managed to impart great elegance to the unpretentious dress she was wearing.（她使自己朴素的衣着看起来也十分优雅。）

❸ ingenious，形容词，表示"精巧的、新颖独特的"，比如：Gautier's solution to the puzzle is ingenious.（戈蒂埃破解这道难题的方法很巧妙。）

❹ the Pulitzer Prize，专有名词，表示"普利策奖"。

文化小常识：

普利策奖也称为"普利策新闻奖"。1917年根据美国报业巨头约瑟夫·普利策（Joseph Pulitzer）的遗愿设立，到二十世纪七八十年代时已经发展成为美国新闻界的一项最高荣誉奖。现在，不断完善的评选制度已使普利策奖成为全球性的一个奖项，被称为"新闻界的诺贝尔奖"。

❺ memorable，形容词，表示"令人难忘的"，比如：Her speech was memorable for its polemic rather than its substance.（她的演说之所以令人难忘，不是因其内容而是因其辩论方法。）

第二步 注意断句

Praised by *The New Yorker* /as "skilled, unpretentious, and totally ingenious," /the book won the Pulitzer Prize /and was made into a memorable movie /in 1962.

第三步 句型解析

❶ Praised by *The New Yorker* 是分词短语位于句首，先找主语，再进行翻译，本句的主语是 the book，所以翻译时需要先有主语。as "skilled, unpretentious, and totally ingenious" 是 praise 的内容，表示"技巧娴熟、朴实无华、情真意切"，参考译文这几个词用得挺好的，你非要用自己的词也没问题，考试不会扣分。

❷ the book won the Pulitzer Prize 是主谓宾结构，这里和前面的 praise 有一定关系，所以翻译时增加"又"，而且不用增主语，直接翻译为"又获得"，两句之间连接得非常紧密，非常合适。

❸ and 是并列连词，was made into a memorable movie in 1962 是被动语态的结构，这里的主语是前文的 the book，所以这里可以不翻译，直接处理为被动语态即可，被动语态的四种译法大家要烂熟于胸。

第四步 翻译来了

这本书曾受到《纽约客》的褒奖，被称赞"技巧娴熟、朴实无华、情真意切"，又获得普利策奖，在 1962 年翻拍为一部令人难忘的电影。

> **本句考点总结**
>
> 第一，本句出现了分词位于句首的现象，一般来说，分词位于句首都要先找到其逻辑主语，再进行翻译，这样整个句子的主谓宾就会非常完整。
>
> 第二，本句出现了被动语态的译法。被动语态是英文常见的一种形式，而在中文里常常少用"被"或者不用"被"。那么我们一般有什么样的译法呢？第一种是被动变主动，第二种是寻找替代词（比如："让……给""为……所"等结构），第三种是在科技文献中用"可以"来替代"被"，第四种是有"被"不用"被"。以上四种怎么用，那就看句子怎么通顺怎么翻译了啊！

12

"Mockingbird" inspired a generation of young lawyers and social workers, was assigned in high schools all over the country and was a popular choice for citywide, or nationwide, reading programs, although it was also occasionally removed from shelves for its racial content and references to rape.

第一步 词汇解析

❶ assign，动词，表示"指定"，比如：They've assigned their best man to the job.（他们指派了最优秀的人负责这项工作。）

❷ citywide，形容词，表示"全市的"，比如：a citywide campaign（全市范围的活动）。

❸ reference，名词，表示"提及"，比如：The book is full of references to growing up in India.（这本书谈到许多在印度怎样长大成人的事。）

第二步 注意断句

"Mockingbird" inspired a generation of young lawyers and social workers, /was assigned in high schools /all over the country /and was a popular choice for citywide, /or nationwide, /reading programs, /although it was also occasionally removed from shelves /for its racial content and references to rape.

第三步 句型解析

❶ "Mockingbird" inspired a generation of young lawyers and social workers 是主句的第一组主谓宾结构，注意这里的一般过去时，翻译为"曾"，可以体现出其中的含义，其余部分正常翻译。

❷ was assigned in high schools all over the country 是主句的第二组谓语和宾语，这里涉及被动语态，你想想用什么方法？选择"有被不用被"是不是很好呢？翻译为"成了"，此处意为"被分配到"，all over the country 是后置定语，修饰 high schools。

❸ and 是并列连词，was a popular choice for citywide, or nationwide, reading programs 是主句的第三组系表结构，popular choice 表示"大家选择最多的，最普遍的"，也就是"热门选择"，for citywide, or nationwide, reading programs 是后置定语，修饰 a popular choice，可以作为前置定语翻译。

❹ although 引导让步状语从句，it 是本句的主语，可以指明要点，也可以采用"不抽象、不具体"的译法，was also occasionally removed from shelves 是典型的被动语态的译法，想想怎么用才好呢？for 表示"原因"，是原因状语的引导词，its 是代词，代词多次出现，想想怎么翻译呢？用"其"是不是特别好？racial content and references to rape 是两个并列的名词短语，可以直接翻译。

第四步 翻译来了

尽管这本书因为其种族方面的内容和涉及强奸而被偶尔下架，但是它曾激励了一代年轻的律师和社会工作者，成了全美中学的指定读物，是全市乃至全国阅读计划的热门选择。

> **本句考点总结**
>
> 第一，本句出现了被动语态的译法。被动语态是英文常见的一种形式，而在中文里常常少用"被"或者不用"被"。那么我们一般有什么样的译法呢？第一种是被动变主动，第二种是寻找替代词（比如："让……给""为……所"等结构），第三种是在科技文献中用"可以"来替代"被"，第四种是有"被"不用"被"。以上四种怎么用，那就看句子怎么通顺怎么翻译了啊！
>
> 第二，关于英文代词的译法。英文中需要翻译的代词主要指第三人称 he，she，it，they 及其相应宾格和指示代词 this 和 that。这些单词在翻译时一定要注意，主要采用"不抽象、不具体"的译法。不能翻译成具体的人或物，但是也不能翻译为"他""她""它""他们""这个""那个"，要注意取中间的译法。

13

By 2015, sales topped 40 million copies. When the Library of Congress did a survey in 1991 on books that have affected people's lives, *To Kill a Mockingbird* was second only to the Bible.

第一步　词汇解析

❶ top，动词，表示"高过、超过"，比如：Unemployment has already topped the 25,000 mark.（失业人数已超过 2.5 万大关。）

❷ copy，名词，表示"书或报的一本、一份"，比如：5,000 copies of the new dictionary（5 000 本新字典）。

❸ the Library of Congress，专有名词，表示"国会图书馆"。

文化小常识：

美国国会图书馆建于 1800 年，1800 年 4 月正式开放，它设立在华盛顿国会山上，是世界上最大的图书馆，也是全球最重要的图书馆之一。

❹ the Bible，专有名词，表示《圣经》。

文化小常识：

《圣经》是犹太教与基督教的共同经典，源于希伯来文 kethubhim，意为"文章"；希腊文作 graphai；拉丁文作 Scripturoe；而后汉语译作"圣经"。

第二步　注意断句

By 2015, /sales topped 40 million copies. /When the Library of Congress did a survey in 1991 / on books /that have affected people's lives, /*To Kill a Mockingbird* was second /only to the Bible.

第三步　句型解析

❶ By 2015 是第一句的时间状语，主句中 sales 是主语，topped 是谓语，40 million copies 是宾语，sales 前面可以增对象词"这本书"，如果不增，读起来不太通顺。

❷ 第二句中，When 引导时间状语从句，the Library of Congress 是主语，did 是谓语，a survey 是宾语，

in 1991 是时间状语，on books 也是状语，that 引导定语从句，从句较短，可以采用前置译法，have affected people's lives 翻译为"影响人们生活的""对人们生活有影响的""对人生有影响的"都可以。
③ *To Kill a Mockingbird* was second only to the Bible 是主系表结构，这里的 only to 表示"除了"，而且这里还有一个小知识点，可以把这句理解为"事实与评论"之间的关系，"除了《圣经》"是事实，"第二"是评论，这么一想，这个语序该怎么排列呢？可以看看参考译文的译法。

第四步 翻译来了

到 2015 年，这本书的销量达到 4 000 万册。国会图书馆于 1991 年做了一份对人生有影响图书的问卷调查，《杀死一只知更鸟》仅次于《圣经》，名列第二。

本句考点总结

第一，本句出现了英文定语从句的译法。一般来说，定语从句按照"短前长后"的译法处理，较短的定语从句可以前置，较长的定语从句可以后置，这一切都取决于句子的通顺，并没有绝对的前置和后置译法。

第二，本句出现了事实（Facts）和评论（Comments）的译法。中文一般先事实，后评论，而英文一般先评论，后事实。比如：It is important for her to go abroad. 翻译为"对于她来说，出国是很重要的"。英文中 It is important 是评论，for her to go abroad 是事实，从中英文的对比来看，可以知道中英文语序分别是怎么安排的。

---

14 Lee herself became more elusive to the public as her book became more famous. At first, she dutifully promoted her work. She spoke frequently to the press, wrote about herself and gave speeches, once to a class of cadets at West Point.

第一步 词汇解析

① elusive，形容词，表示"难找的、难以解释的、难以达到的"，比如：Eric, as elusive as ever, was nowhere to be found.（埃里克总是这样神出鬼没，哪儿都找不着他。）
② dutifully，副词，表示"尽责地、忠诚地"，比如：I dutifully wrote down every word.（我尽责地写下了每一个字。）
③ frequently，副词，表示"经常地、频繁地"，比如：She speaks French frequently.（她常常讲法语。）
④ the press，名词词组，表示"报刊、新闻业、记者们"，通常表示总称。比如：A government spokesperson made a statement to the press.（政府发言人向新闻界发表了一份声明。）
⑤ cadet，名词，表示"（军校或警校的）学员"，比如：army cadets（陆军军校学员们）。
⑥ West Point，专有名词，表示"西点军校"。
文化小常识：
西点军校是美国第一所军事学校，西点军校的校训是"责任、荣誉、国家"，该校是美国历史最悠久的军事学院之一，与弗吉尼亚军事学院齐名。

第二步 注意断句

　　Lee herself became more elusive to the public /as her book became more famous. /At first, /she dutifully promoted her work. /She spoke frequently to the press, /wrote about herself /and gave speeches, /once to a class of cadets at West Point.

第三步 句型解析

❶ Lee herself became more elusive 是主系表结构，to the public 是状语，表示"对公众来说"，as 引导时间状语从句，her book became more famous 也是主系表结构。可能很多人不懂这里的 as 引导的为什么是"时间"，而不是"让步"，不是"伴随"，不是"原因"，不是"目的"，我的答案是"都可以"，参考译文没有翻译这个 as，直接处理为"不译"，为什么呢？因为中文是意合语言，英文是形合语言，中文不用连词也是可以的。

❷ At first 是第二句的时间状语，she dutifully promoted her work 是主谓宾结构，这里的 promote 指的是"推广"，为什么这么说，你看看后文的内容就知道了。

❸ She 是第三句的主语，spoke frequently to the press 是第一组谓语和宾语，wrote about herself 是第二组谓语和宾语，gave speeches 是第三组谓语和宾语，once to a class of cadets at West Point 是状语，表示"做演讲的一次特殊经历"。

❹ 这里涉及一个小问题，第二句和第三句的合译，因为两句内容关系密切，都是说一开始 Lee 做了哪些事，前面是抽象的，后面是具体的，所以放在一起翻译比较好。当然，非要一句一句翻译，那也可以。

第四步 翻译来了

　　李的这本书名声越来越大，她自己却让公众越来越难以捉摸。一开始，她尽心尽力地推广自己的作品，经常和媒体对话，写写自己的故事，发表演讲，还曾经在西点军校给学员们做过演讲。

But she began declining interviews in the mid-1960s and, until late in her life, firmly avoided making any public comment about her novel or her career. Her novel, while hugely popular, was not ranked many scholars in the same category as the work of other Southern authors.

第一步 词汇解析

❶ decline，动词，表示"拒绝"，比如：I offered to give them a lift but they declined.（我主动邀请他们搭车，但他们婉言谢绝了。）

❷ scholar，名词，表示"学者"，比如：a famous Latin scholar（著名的拉丁语学者）。

❸ category，名词，表示"（人或事物的）类别"，比如：This book falls into the category of reference books.（这本书属参考书类。）

第二步 注意断句

　　But /she began declining interviews /in the mid-1960s and, /until late in her life, /firmly avoided making any public comment about her novel or her career. /Her novel, /while hugely popular, /was not ranked /many scholars in the same category /as the work of other Southern authors.

第三步 句型解析

1. 第一句中，But 是转折连词，表示"但是"，she began declining interviews in the mid-1960s 是主谓宾结构，后面接时间状语，注意时间状语后 and 的用法，为什么 and 后面用逗号呢？因为后面的 until late in her life 是时间的插入语，其实翻译不用管这么多，没什么太大用处，直接放在原位翻译即可。

2. firmly 是副词，作状语，avoided making any public comment 是第一句的第二组谓语和宾语，about her novel or her career 是状语，注意句子内部各个成分的排序问题。特别要注意这个状语中代词的译法，her 在这里可以翻译为"她的"，但是翻译为"自己的"更好，因为代词出现多次之后（在本句是第三次，第一次是 she，第二次是 her life）需要指明要点，也可以采用"不抽象、不具体"的译法。

3. Her novel 是第二句的主语，while hugely popular 是 while 引导的让步状语，相当于 in spite of，hugely popular 表示"广为流传"，不用想那么多结构，直接放在原位翻译即可。

4. was not ranked (by) many scholars in the same category as the work of other Southern authors 是本句的谓语和宾语，这里的 was not ranked 是被动语态，译文采用了"寻找替代词"的译法，其实这里的原始句型是 many scholars in the same category ranked her novel as the work of other Southern authors，这里变成被动语态之后直接省略了 by，在美式英语当中这样是可以的，翻译时注意一下这个知识点。

第四步 翻译来了

但是，在 20 世纪 60 年代中期，她开始拒绝采访，一直到晚年，她都坚决不再对自己的小说和事业公开发表评论。尽管她的小说广为人知，但是，这本书并没有让很多同行的学者把它归在南方作家的作品之中。

> **本句考点总结**
>
> 第一，关于英文代词的译法。英文中需要翻译的代词主要指第三人称 he，she，it，they 及其相应宾格和指示代词 this 和 that。这些单词在翻译时一定要注意，主要采用"不抽象、不具体"的译法。不能翻译成具体的人或物，但是也不能翻译为"他""她""它""他们""这个""那个"，要注意取中间的译法。
>
> 第二，本句出现了被动语态的译法。被动语态是英文常见的一种形式，而在中文里常常少用"被"或者不用"被"。那么我们一般有什么样的译法呢？第一种是被动变主动，第二种是寻找替代词（比如："让……给""为……所"等结构），第三种是在科技文献中用"可以"来替代"被"，第四种是有"被"不用"被"。以上四种怎么用，那就看句子怎么通顺怎么翻译了啊！

Decades after its publication, little was written about it in scholarly journals. Some critics has called the book naive and sentimental, whether dismissing the Ku Klux Klan as a minor nuisance or advocating change through personal persuasion rather than collective action.

第一步 词汇解析

❶ scholarly journals,名词词组,表示"学术期刊",比如:Exploration is an index for judging the quality of top scholarly journals.(探索性是顶级学术期刊质量的评价指标之一。)

❷ critic,名词,表示"批评家、评论家",比如:The critic's review of the play was just a paragraph of bile.(那位批评家对这部戏剧的评论不过是在发泄怒气。)

❸ naive,形容词,也可写作 naïve,表示"幼稚的、天真的",比如:a naive young girl(天真的小女孩)。

❹ sentimental,形容词,表示"多愁善感的、感情化的",比如:I'm trying not to be sentimental about the past.(我尽力不为过去的事情而多愁善感。)

❺ dismiss...as...,动词词组,表示"不予考虑、摒弃、对……不屑一顾",比如:The police dismissed the incident as a "misunderstanding".(警方把这件事作为"误会"草草了事。)

❻ the Ku Klux Klan,专有名词,表示"三 K 党"。
   文化小常识:
   三 K 党是美国历史上和如今的一个奉行白人至上和歧视有色族裔主义运动的党派,也是美国种族主义的代表性组织。三 K 党是美国最悠久、最庞大的种族主义组织。Ku Klux 二字源于希腊文 Ku Kloo,意为"集会"。Klan 是种族。因三个单词的首字母都是 K,故称三 K 党。

❼ nuisance,名词,表示"讨厌的东西、恼人的事情",比如:He could be a bit of a nuisance when he was drunk.(他喝醉时会是一个有点令人讨厌的人。)

❽ persuasion,名词,表示"劝说、规劝",比如:She agreed to come, after a little gentle persuasion.(经过一阵细心劝说,她表示愿意来。)

第二步 注意断句

Decades after its publication, /little was written about it in scholarly journals. /Some critics has called the book naive and sentimental, /whether dismissing the Ku Klux Klan as a minor nuisance /or advocating change /through personal persuasion /rather than collective action.

第三步 句型解析

❶ Decades after its publication 是第一句的时间状语,其中代词 its 可以采用"不抽象、不具体"的译法,哪怕是翻译为"它",你也要知道,这里指代的是什么。little was written about it in scholarly journals 是第一句的主句,是典型的被动语态,译文使用了"有被不用被"的译法,而且把地点状语提前了,注意这里不是地点状语作主语。

❷ 第二句 Some critics has called the book naive and sentimental 是主谓宾宾补的结构,之后 whether...or... 引导状语,这个状语和主句之间是什么关系呢?能读出什么关系就是什么状语,千万不要自己在那里"想当然创造"关系,如果读不出来,就翻译为"要么……要么……"。

❸ whether dismissing the Ku Klux Klan as a minor nuisance 是第一组状语,dismissing 是动词,前面缺少逻辑主语,增主语"这本书",动词表示"把……轻描淡写为",a minor nuisance 则表示"小麻烦"。or 连接第二组状语,advocating change 表示"提倡改变(社会)",这里可以增加宾语"社会",也可以不增加,没看出来也没事,through personal persuasion 是第一个状语,rather than collective action 是第二个状语,状语相当于"废话",所以可以放在句中翻译。

第四步 翻译来了

在本书出版几十年之后，学术期刊中很少有关于这本书的文章。一些评论家认为这本书幼稚且感情化，因为这本书要么把三K党轻描淡写为小麻烦，要么提倡通过个人规劝而非集体行动来改变社会。

本句考点总结

第一，关于英文代词的译法。英文中需要翻译的代词主要指第三人称 he，she，it，they 及其相应宾格和指示代词 this 和 that。这些单词在翻译时一定要注意，主要采用"不抽象、不具体"的译法。不能翻译成具体的人或物，但是也不能翻译为"他""她""它""他们""这个""那个"，要注意取中间的译法。

第二，本句出现了被动语态的译法。被动语态是英文常见的一种形式，而在中文里常常少用"被"或者不用"被"。那么我们一般有什么样的译法呢？第一种是被动变主动，第二种是寻找替代词（比如："让……给""为……所"等结构），第三种是在科技文献中用"可以"来替代"被"，第四种是有"被"不用"被"。以上四种怎么用，那就看句子怎么通顺怎么翻译了啊！

第三，本句考查了英汉互译增减词的问题，一般来说英译汉增词，汉译英减词，常见增词的种类有：一、增加对象词（范围词），这是由上文缺少句子的某个部分造成的；二、增加范畴词，这是较难的一部分，常见的范畴词有"水平、方式、方法、问题、情况、途径和方面"，但是不仅仅有这些，还有很多其他的；三、增加评论性词，这些常常出现在文学翻译中；四、增加动词，会在动词的"分配译法"中说明这点。

第四，本句考查了中英文语序的问题，一般来说，中文的语序是"主语+废话（定语、状语、补语、插入语，等等）+重要成分"，而英文的语序则是"废话（定语、状语、补语、插入语，等等）+主语+重要成分+废话（定语、状语、补语、插入语，等等）"，翻译时需要注意调整语序。

这篇英译汉是少见的介绍文学著作的文章，本文的特点主要是美国社会与文化的内容特别多，这点大家一定要仔细学习，文化常识的学习是翻译学习中的重要内容，因为语言的背后是文化，不了解文化背景，想要做两种语言之间的转换工作肯定是不可能的。

第四节　2016年下半年三级笔译汉译英

本公司是一家大型国有房地产上市公司，国家一级房地产开发资质企业，连续五年荣获中国房地产行

业领导品牌。

2006年7月，本公司股票在上海证券交易所上市。截至2015年底，本公司总资产突破3 600亿元，实现签约金额1 366.76亿元。

本公司成立于1992年，经过十年扎实发展，2002年成功完成股份制改造，遂开始实施全国化战略，加强专业化运作。持续实现跨越式发展。

目前，本公司已完成广州，北京，上海为中心，覆盖57个城市的全国化战略布局，拥有292家控股子公司，业务拓展到房地产开发、建筑设计、工程施工、物业管理、销售代理、商业会展、酒店经营等相关行业，本公司坚持以商品住宅开发为主，适度持有经营性物业。

在住宅开发方面，本公司逐渐形成了四大产品系列以及多元化优质住宅物业的先进创新格局。经营中高端住宅，公寓，别墅多种物业形态。

商业化物业囊括商业写字楼，高端休闲地产，星级酒店，商贸会展，购物中心，城市综合体等，具备多品类物业综合开发的实力。

CATTI三级笔译汉译英2016年下半年的考题和2015年上半年的考题在一定程度上相似，都是资讯介绍类文章，特别有趣的一点是，本篇文章是某大型房地产公司的官网介绍。这篇文章的考点主要还是在专有名词和句型结构上，大家要学会快速在字典中找到这些单词，并且也能快速识别这些句子的结构，这样才能提高翻译的速度和准确性。

 本公司是一家大型国有房地产上市公司，国家一级房地产开发资质企业，连续五年荣获中国房地产行业领导品牌。

第一步 词汇解析

❶ 大型国有房地产上市公司，a large-scale state-owned listed real estate one，名词词组。因为此句主语为"公司"，所以这里处理为one。

大型，意思是"规模大的"，large-scale，形容词，比如：large-scale operations（大规模的军事行动）。

国有，state-owned，形容词，比如：state-owned shares（国有股）。

私有，privately-owned，形容词，比如：privately-owned companies（私有企业）。

房地产，real estate，名词词组，比如：By investing in real estate, he was one of the richest men in the United States.（通过投资房地产，他成了美国最富的人之一。）

上市（的），listed，形容词，比如：a basket of blue chip stocks listed on the American Exchange（在美国证券交易所上市的一组绩优股）。

❷ 国家一级房地产开发资质企业，a national First-Class Real Estate Qualification Enterprise，名词词组，这里大写表示强调。

一级，first-class，形容词，比如：a first-class writer（一流作家）。

资质，qualification，名词，比如：The author's experience gave him the qualifications to write this book.（作者的经历让他有资格写这本书。）

企业，enterprise，比如：There are plenty of small industrial enterprises.（有很多小型的工业企业。）这里不建议翻译为 Co. Ltd，因为这个单词的意思是"有限责任公司"。

③ 连续五年，continuous five years，名词词组。
连续的、持续的，continuous，形容词，比如：Residents report that they heard continuous gunfire.（居民们说他们听到了持续的枪声。）

④ 荣获，句中指的是"名列"，ranks，动词，单词原形为：rank，比如：The report ranks the U.S. 20th out of 22 advanced nations.（这份报告把美国排在 22 个发达国家中的第 20 位。）

⑤ 行业，industry，名词，比如：the motor vehicle and textile industries（机动车与纺织行业），field 也是可以的。

⑥ 领导品牌，Leading Company Brand，名词词组，这里大写表示强调，不大写也是可以的，问题不大。

第二步 动词定位

本公司<u>是</u>一家大型国有房地产上市公司，国家一级房地产开发资质企业，连续五年<u>荣获</u>中国房地产行业领导品牌。

第三步 句型解析

① "本公司"是本句的主语，可以使用 The company，译文当中使用的 Our company 也是可以的，"是"是系动词，"上市公司"是第一个表语，"国家一级房地产开发资质企业"是第二个表语，两个表语之间可以用 and 连接，这样就形成了第一个句子。

② "连续五年"是时间状语，"荣获"是动词谓语，这里缺少主语，主语是"本公司"，因为第一句的主语使用了 Our company，那么第二句的主语就可以使用代词 It 了，"中国房地产行业领导品牌"是宾语，句子结构还是比较简单的。

③ 很多人会问关于汉译英时态的问题，就说明性文章而言，或者说就资讯介绍类文章而言，我们大多使用一般现在时，句子当中有明确的时间状语时，也要考虑使用现在、过去还是将来时。

④ 但是本句的参考译文和上面的句子结构分析不太一样，这句话中有三个动词，第一个动词和第二个动词是"是"，第三个动词是"荣获"，从句子结构的角度来说，最简单的译法是将三个动词译成并列结构，中间不用断句。即使断句的话，也可以将第一个动词和第二个动词放在一起翻译，第三个动词单独翻译。译文却将第一个动词单独翻译，第二个动词和第三个动词放在一起翻译，这样的译法可能是考虑到第一个句子是"介绍本企业的总体概况"，第二个句子和第三个句子是对"本企业进行分述"，所以将第一句话单独翻译，第二句话和第三句话放在一起翻译，这种译法大家不要学习，个人建议还是简单翻译比较好。

⑤ 还有两个小问题需要说明：第一，名词前有多个形容词出现时，直接按序翻译即可，不要考虑调换顺序，更不要用所谓的 of 结构，这样只会让非常简单的翻译变得更加复杂，简单问题简单处理是翻译的核心要素。第二，第二句中的"一级房地产开发资质企业"采用了首字母大写，这里是起到了强调作用，个人建议在考试当中用小写即可，没有必要这么复杂。

第四步 翻译来了

Our company is a large-scale state-owned listed real estate one. It is a national First-Class Real Estate Qualification Enterprise and ranks Leading Company Brand in China's real estate industry for continuous five years.

> **本句考点总结**
>
> 关于"动词分堆"的问题。中文里常常出现多个短句聚集的句型，我们一方面需要去考虑这些动词之间的关系，哪一个是最重要的，哪一个是其次重要的，哪一个又是最不重要的，这个过程称为分析"谓语动词的层次性"。除此之外，句子当中出现了大量的动词时，或者说大量的分句时，我们不可能将这些分句整体翻译为一个长句，那么，我们就需要考虑哪些动词放在一起翻译，这样的过程称为"动词分堆"。比如，一个句子当中有五个动词形成的五个分句，我们一般会考虑前三个动词翻译为一句，后两个动词翻译为一句，但是如何进行"分堆"要根据上下文的语境来判断，绝对不能形而上学，望文生义。

2 2006年7月，本公司股票在上海证券交易所上市。截至2015年底，本公司总资产突破3 600亿元，实现签约金额1 366.76亿元。

第一步 词汇解析

① 上海证券交易所，Shanghai Stock Exchange，专有名词。
   经济小常识：
   　1990年12月19日上海证券交易所开始正式营业。截至2019年底，上证所拥有1 572家沪市上市公司，股票市价总值35.6万亿元。

② 上市，list，动词，比如：a basket of blue chip stocks listed on the American Exchange（在美国证券交易所上市的一组绩优股）。

③ 总资产，total assets，名词词组，比如：Despite total assets of 3 million, the takeover bid valued at only 2.5 million was successful.（尽管总资产为300万，但出价仅250万就收购成功了。）

④ 突破，exceed，动词，比如：Its research budget exceeds $700 million a year.（其研究预算每年超过7亿美元。）此处因为有"by the end of + 过去时间"，所以使用了过去完成时，这个语法知识点一定要知道。

⑤ 签约金额，sales offer，名词词组。
   （商业领域）报价、开价，offer，名词，比如：renew an offer（重新报价）。

第二步 动词定位

　2006年7月，本公司股票在上海证券交易所<u>上市</u>。截至2015年底，本公司总资产<u>突破</u>3 600亿元，<u>实现</u>签约金额1 366.76亿元。

第三步 句型解析

① 第一句中，"2006年7月"是时间状语，出现具体的时间状语时需要考虑时态的问题，这里可以用一般过去时，注意月份前用in，不是on，"本公司"是本句的主语，"在上海证券交易所"是地点状语，"股票上市"是一个动作，所以是核心谓语，而且这里是"隐藏的被动语态"，股票是"被上市"。在这里简单吐个槽：有的时候大家会认为汉译英特别难，我就在想"难点"在什么地方，如果是三级笔译的

话，考试的难度也就是以上这样的句子，说一句极具讽刺含义的话，这样的句子，成绩好一点的高中生都能写出来！再回到原始的问题上，汉译英究竟难在哪里？无非就是单词不会写，语法容易错，那么我们从第一个问题开始解决，遇到了不会的单词就查出来、记下来，再学会使用，语法的问题尽量不要错，或者说少错，至于什么翻译方法、翻译技巧都是忽悠！希望我这段话能让更多的人看见，不要总想着搞技巧、搞方法，还是要踏踏实实背单词、学语法！

❷ 第二句"截至2015年底"是时间状语，若要用 by the end of，就要注意后面句子的时态。"本公司总资产"是本句的主语，"突破"是谓语，"3 600亿元"是宾语，注意和第二句之间需要连接，这里用 and 即可，第二句要理解"实现"这个单词，并不是"本公司实现签约"，而是"签约金额实现（达到）1 366.76亿元"。

❸ 说一下笔译当中数字的译法（注意不是口译），比如3 600亿元，最好不要写成 360 000 000 000 Yuan，写成 360 billion Yuan 最好，当然其他的译法也可以，千万别抬杠！

第四步 翻译来了

　　In July 2006, it was listed in Shanghai Stock Exchange. By the end of 2015, its total assets had exceeded 360 billion Yuan, and the sales offer had reached 136.676 billion Yuan.

　　本句出现了中文里隐藏被动语态的译法。被动语态是英文常见的一种形式，而在中文里常常少用"被"或者不用"被"。那么中文当中一般如何隐藏被动语态呢？第一种是被动变主动，第二种是寻找替代词的译法（比如："让……给""为……所"等结构），第三种是在科技文献中用"可以"来替代"被"，第四种是有"被"不用"被"。在中文里识别出来以上四种隐藏的被动语态不是一件容易的事，需要大家仔细认真地识别这种现象，在汉译英时体现出来。

本公司成立于1992年，经过十年扎实发展，2002年成功完成股份制改造，遂开始实施全国化战略，加强专业化运作。持续实现跨越式发展。

第一步 词汇解析

❶ 成立，found，动词，比如：His father founded the American Socialist Party.（他的父亲创建了美国社会党。）这里翻译为 establish 等词也可以。

❷ 扎实发展，solid development，名词词组，比如：Only about 20% of the world's people have attained solid development.（只有约20%的世界人民已经取得了稳固的发展。）

❸ 成功完成，completion，名词，比如：Completion of this bridge is expected in a year or so.（这座桥一年半载可望竣工。）对于句中的"成功"，加上 successfully 完全可以。

【同义词辨析】
complete：侧重指完成预定的任务或使某事完善，补足缺少的部分等；
end：普通用词，着重事情的完成，也指某种活动因达到目的而自然结束或由于某种原因而突然中止；

conclude：正式用词，多指以某事或活动达到预期目的而告终。

❹ 股份制改造，the transformation of joint-stock system，名词词组。

改造、改革，transformation，名词，比如：the social and political transformation of a country（一个国家的社会和政治改革）。

合资的、合股的，joint-stock，形容词，比如：a joint-stock company（合股公司）。

经济小常识：
　　设立股份有限公司的第一件事情是要确定发起人，由发起人签订设立公司的协议，承担设立公司的责任。发起人在达成设立公司的协议后，可以委托一个发起人办理设立公司的申请手续。

❺ 实施，implement，动词，比如：The government promised to implement a new system to control financial loan institutions.（政府许诺要实施新的制度来控制金融贷款机构。）

❻ 全国化战略，national strategy，名词词组，比如：As we confront these crises, our national strategy must take a longer view.（由于我们面临着这些危机，我们的国家战略必须要有一个长远的打算。）这个词组在《政府工作报告》中出现过，用的是 state's strategy，个人认为这个更好，因为 national 指的是"全体国民"，而 state's 侧重于"国家和政府层面"。

❼ 加强，strengthen，动词，比如：Giving the president the authority to go to war would strengthen his hand for peace.（给予总统发动战争的权力会加强他对于和平的掌控权。）

❽ 专业化运作，professional operation，名词词组，比如：The professional operation is our greatest advantage.（专业运营是我们最大的优势。）

❾ （持续的）跨越式发展，continuous leap-forward development，名词词组。跨越式（的），leap-forward，形容词，比如：10 years' leap-forward development（10 年以来跨越式的发展历程）。

第二步　动词定位

本公司成立于 1992 年，经过十年扎实发展，2002 年成功完成股份制改造，遂开始实施全国化战略，加强专业化运作。持续实现跨越式发展。

第三步　句型解析

❶ 本句的主语是"本公司"，谓语动词有很多，我们要逐个进行分析。

❷ 第一个动词是"成立于"，时间状语是"1992 年"，这里显然要用一般过去时。

❸ "经过十年扎实发展"是典型的状语结构，这里的"经过"可以用动词变成介词的译法，翻译为 after 或是 through 等词都可以。

❹ 第三个动词是"成功完成"，若翻译为动词形式，就是 complete successfully，宾语是"股份制改造"，"2002 年"是时间状语，这里显然也需要使用一般过去时。

❺ 第四个动词是"开始实施"，宾语是"全国化战略"，第五个动词是"加强"，特别要注意句号之后的句子，因为这是短句，并且和本句有着紧密的联系，所以这里可以用合译的方法，那么"持续实现"就变成了第六个动词，"跨越式发展"是它的宾语。

❻ 本句从结构上看出现了六个动词，那么我们翻译的基本方法就是进行"分堆"，根据句子上下文的关系，可以将第一个动词、第二个动词和第三个动词放在一起翻译，形成一个句子；后面三个动词形成另一个句子，这样断句是因为句中有"遂"。

❼ 但是参考译文给出的答案则不是这样，译文将第一个动词、第二个动词和第三个动词放在句首，形成"下沉结构"，"建立"翻译为过去分词，"成功完成"翻译为抽象名词，全部位于句首。接下来"本公司"作为主语，"开始实施""加强"和"持续实现"形成三个并列的谓语，前面三个动词形成的"下沉结构"和后面三个动词形成的"并列结构"让整个句子变得较为平衡，这种译法大家可以尝试使用。

简单说，也就是将本句的六个动词变成了两组动词，然后按照两个动词的原则来进行翻译。

第四步 翻译来了

Founded in 1992, after 10 year's solid development, and the successful completion of the transformation of joint-stock system in 2002, the company began to implement the national strategy, strengthen the professional operation, and thus realized the continuous leap-forward development.

本句考点总结

第一，关于"动改介"的译法。英文里的介词常常翻译为动词，比如 He went to Beijing by plane. 翻译为"他坐飞机去北京"，这里的 by 翻译为"坐"，这就是"介改动"的译法，但是汉译英时则恰好相反，你需要把"坐"翻译为介词 by，这就是"动改介"的译法，英汉互译是相通的！

第二，关于"动词分堆"的问题。中文里常常出现多个短句聚集的句型，我们一方面需要去考虑这些动词之间的关系，哪一个是最重要的，哪一个是其次重要的，哪一个又是最不重要的，这个过程称为分析"谓语动词的层次性"。除此之外，句子当中出现了大量的动词时，或者说大量的分句时，我们不可能将这些分句整体翻译为一个长句，那么，我们就需要考虑哪些动词放在一起翻译，这样的过程称为"动词分堆"。比如，一个句子当中有五个动词形成的五个分句，我们一般会考虑前三个动词翻译为一句，后两个动词翻译为一句，但是如何进行"分堆"要根据上下文的语境来判断，绝对不能形而上学，望文生义。

第三，汉译英句子中并列、伴随、下沉的结构。中文常常会出现多个句子聚集的情况，那么我们在翻译时需要考虑将这些句子进行"分堆"。但是"分堆"之后，一个句子中也可能会出现两个动词或两组动词，那么有两个动词或两组动词的句子我们该如何进行翻译呢？比如："我坐在那里看书"，这里有两个动词，一个是"坐"，一个是"看"，我们翻译时便会有三种方法：

第一种并列（两个动词并列的译法，使用并列连词连接，两个动词之间不一定是"并列"关系）：I sat there and read a book.

第二种伴随（将第二个动词翻译为二谓语，分词、从句、状语等都可以）：I sat there reading a book.

第三种下沉（将第一个动词翻译为二谓语，分词、从句、状语等都可以）：Sitting there, I read a book.

需要说明的是，并列、伴随和下沉只是动词的形式问题，不代表动词之间的逻辑关系，用这三种形式翻译两个动词或两组动词都是可以的，大家可以根据句子上下文的关系来判断使用。

目前，本公司已完成广州，北京，上海为中心，覆盖 57 个城市的全国化战略布局，拥有 292 家控股子公司，业务拓展到房地产开发、建筑设计、工程施工、物业管理、销售代理、商业会展、酒店经营等相关行业，本公司坚持以商品住宅开发为主，适度持有经营性物业。

第一步 词汇解析

❶ 全国化战略布局，nationwide strategic layout，名词词组。
全国化，nationwide，形容词，比如：The rising number of car crimes is a nationwide problem.（汽车犯罪不断增加是个全国性的问题。）

❷ 控股子公司，holding subsidiary corporations，名词词组。
控制，holding，名词。
隶属的、附设的，subsidiary，形容词，比如：a subsidiary factory（附属工厂）。
经济小常识：
　　控股子公司是指其公司出资或股份的 50% 以上被另一家公司所控制，但未达到 100%。

❸ 拓展，expands，动词，单词原形为：expand，比如：a totally revised and expanded edition（经彻底修订和扩充的版本）。

❹ 房地产开发，real estate development，比如：high-level real estate development model（高层次的房地产开发模式）。

❺ 工程施工，engineering construction，名词词组，比如：The supervision system is widely applied in the area of engineering construction.（监理制是工程建设领域广泛使用的一项制度。）
【同义词辨析】
construct：较正式用词，强调根据一定计划进行的规模较大、结构较复杂、技术要求较高的建造；
erect：侧重指高而垂直的物体的建造；
set up：作"建立"用时，侧重于"开始"，可指具体或抽象的建立。

❻ 物业管理，property management，名词词组。
❼ 商业会展，句中指的是"商业的会议和展览"，commercial conference and exhibition，名词词组。
❽ 坚持以……为主，persists in taking...as its core，动词词组，词组原形为：persist in taking...as its core。
坚持、执意，persist in，动词词组，比如：Why do people persist in begging for money in the street?（为什么人们非要在街上讨钱呢？）

❾ 商品住宅开发，commercial residential building，名词词组。
住宅的，residential，形容词，比如：a posh residential area 20 minutes from the White House（距离白宫 20 分钟路程的一个豪华住宅区）。

❿ 经营性物业，operation property，名词词组。
房地产小常识：
　　经营性物业是指完成竣工验收并投入商业运营，经营性现金流量较为充裕、综合收益较好、还款来源稳定的商业营业用房和办公用房。

第二步 动词定位

　　目前，本公司已完成广州，北京，上海为中心，覆盖 57 个城市的全国化战略布局，拥有 292 家控股子公司，业务拓展到房地产开发、建筑设计、工程施工、物业管理、销售代理、商业会展、酒店经营等相关行业，本公司坚持以商品住宅开发为主，适度持有经营性物业。

第三步 句型解析

❶ "目前"是本句的时间状语，可以使用 So far，By now 这类词组，注意主句需要使用现在完成时。
❷ 本句的主语是"本公司"，谓语是"已完成"，宾语是"全国化战略布局"，这个宾语前面出现了两组定语，一组是"广州、北京、上海为中心"，也就是"以广州、北京、上海为中心的"，另一组是"覆盖

57个城市的"，这两组定语都可以后置，译文当中使用了"by + doing something"的译法，形成方式状语，这样也完全可以接受。

❸ 本句的第二个谓语是"拥有"，宾语是"292家控股子公司"，第三个谓语是"拓展到"，"房地产开发、建筑设计、工程施工、物业管理、销售代理、商业会展、酒店经营等相关行业"是宾语。本句到这里可以认为是一个大句子，因为后面又出现了一个主语"本公司"，所以前面三个动词可以"分成一堆"，后面另起一句。

❹ 先来分析前面三个动词，将第一个动词"已完成"和第二个动词"拥有"分成一堆比较好，第三个动词"拓展到"再形成一个新句子，因为这样两个句子之间比较平衡。但是参考译文却没有这么做，我们"试图"来理解一下，因为第一个动词使用了现在完成时，而第二个动词和第三个动词需要用一般现在时，所以形成了两个不同的句子，其实这些都不是关键，关键在于这些并列的名词短语你是否会写！

❺ 最后一句的主语是"本公司"，第一组谓语是"坚持以……为主"，宾语是"商品住宅开发"，第二组谓语是"适度持有"，宾语是"经营性物业"，第一组谓语和第二组谓语之间需要用连词连接，这里表示并列关系，可以用and。

第四步　翻译来了

By now, the company has formed the nationwide strategic layout by taking Guangzhou, Beijing and Shanghai as centers and covering 57 cities. Now it owns 292 holding subsidiary corporations and its business expands to many related industries such as real estate development, building design, engineering construction, property management, sale agency, commercial conference and exhibition, hotel management, etc. Our company persists in taking the commercial residential building as its core and properly holds the operation property.

本句考点总结

关于"动词分堆"的问题。中文里常常出现多个短句聚集的句型，我们一方面需要去考虑这些动词之间的关系，哪一个是最重要的，哪一个是其次重要的，哪一个又是最不重要的，这个过程称为分析"谓语动词的层次性"。除此之外，句子当中出现了大量的动词时，或者说大量的分句时，我们不可能将这些分句整体翻译为一个长句，那么，我们就需要考虑哪些动词放在一起翻译，这样的过程称为"动词分堆"。比如，一个句子当中有五个动词形成的五个分句，我们一般会考虑前三个动词翻译为一句，后两个动词翻译为一句，但是如何进行"分堆"要根据上下文的语境来判断，绝对不能形而上学，望文生义。

5

在住宅开发方面，本公司逐渐形成了四大产品系列以及多元化优质住宅物业的先进创新格局。经营中高端住宅，公寓，别墅多种物业形态。

第一步　词汇解析

❶ 逐渐，gradually，副词，比如：Electricity lines to 30,000 homes were gradually being restored yesterday. （通向3万户人家的电线昨日被逐步修复。）

❷ 四大产品（系列），句中指的是"四个主要产品（系列）"，four major products，名词词组。
❸ 多元化优质住宅物业，diversified high-quality residential buildings，名词词组。
多元化（的），diversified，形容词，比如：a diversified program ranging from classical to modern（包括从古典到现代的多样化的音乐节目）。
优质的，high-quality，形容词，比如：The high-quality mineral water has passed the state-level test.（优质矿泉水已通过国家级鉴定）。
❹ 先进创新格局，advanced and innovative layout，名词词组。
❺ 中高端住宅，medium and high-end residential buildings，名词词组。中高端，指的是"中端和高端的"，medium and high-end 是个好词，要学会使用。
❻ 别墅，villa，名词，比如：He lives in a secluded five-bedroom luxury villa.（他住在一幢僻静的、有五间卧室的豪华别墅里。）
❼ 多种物业（形态），various properties，名词词组。这里的"形态"可以理解为范畴词，不翻译。

第二步 动词定位

在住宅开发方面，本公司逐渐<u>形成</u>了四大产品系列以及多元化优质住宅物业的先进创新格局。<u>经营</u>中高端住宅，公寓，别墅多种物业形态。

第三步 句型解析

❶ "在住宅开发方面"是典型的状语，译文中使用了 In terms of，换其他类似的词也可以，"住宅开发"在上一句中已经提过。
❷ "本公司"是本句的主语，"逐渐"是状语，"形成"是谓语动词，这里的时态可以是一般现在时，也可以是一般过去时，"四大产品系列"是第一个宾语，"以及"是连词，可以用 and，"多元化优质住宅物业的先进创新格局"是第二个宾语，核心词是"先进的和创新的格局"，前面出现修饰词"多元化优质住宅物业的"。所以本句是"主语+谓语+两个宾语"的结构，请大家尽量使用简单的句型结构，不要搞从句，不要搞特殊结构，让句子变得越简单越好。
❸ 第二句"经营"是核心谓语，"中高端住宅，公寓，别墅多种物业形态"是宾语，但要注意本句没有主语，所以翻译时需要增主语，这里的主语是"本公司"，最简单的译法就是直接使用 it，另起一句。
❹ 参考译文中使用了比较难的译法，把这一句和上一句进行合译，那么这句话就有两个动词，一个是"形成"，一个是"经营"，第一个动词译为核心动词，第二个动词译为伴随结构，当然第二个动词你要翻译为并列谓语结构也是可以的。特别要注意第二句宾语中的"中高端住宅，公寓，别墅多种物业形态"，这是典型的总分结构，"多种物业形态"是总，"中高端住宅，公寓，别墅"是分，中文先分后总，英文先总后分，在翻译上注意排序。

第四步 翻译来了

In terms of the residential building development, the company gradually formed four major products, and advanced and innovative layout of diversified high-quality residential buildings, covering various properties such as medium and high-end residential buildings, apartments and villas.

本句考点总结

第一，汉译英句子中并列、伴随、下沉的结构。中文常常会出现多个句子聚集的情况，那么我们在翻译时需要考虑将这些句子进行"分堆"。但是"分堆"之后，一个句子中也可能会出现两个动词或两组动词，那么有两个动词或两组动词的句子我们该如何进行翻译呢？比如："我坐在那里看书"，这里有两个动词，一个是"坐"，一个是"看"，我们翻译时便会有三种方法：

第一种并列（两个动词并列的译法，使用并列连词连接，两个动词之间不一定是"并列"关系）：I sat there and read a book.

第二种伴随（将第二个动词翻译为二谓语，分词、从句、状语等都可以）：I sat there reading a book.

第三种下沉（将第一个动词翻译为二谓语，分词、从句、状语等都可以）：Sitting there, I read a book.

需要说明的是，并列、伴随和下沉只是动词的形式问题，不代表动词之间的逻辑关系，用这三种形式翻译两个动词或两组动词都是可以的，大家可以根据句子上下文的关系来判断使用。

第二，中英文的总分关系，中文一般是先分后总，而英文则是先总后分，比如中文会说"我喜欢吃香蕉、苹果、梨子等水果"，但是英文的表达是 I like fruits such as bananas, apples and pears. 注意总分关系是如何在两种语言中体现出来的。

6 商业化物业囊括商业写字楼，高端休闲地产，星级酒店，商贸会展，购物中心，城市综合体等，具备多品类物业综合开发的实力。

第一步 词汇解析

① 商业写字楼，commercial office building，名词词组，比如：Commercial office buildings represent a large building segment.（商业办公建筑是一个庞大的建筑分类。）

② 高端休闲地产，high-end leisure real estate，名词词组。高档的、高端的，high-end，形容词，一般用于名词前。

③ 商贸会展（中心），commercial convention and exhibition center，名词词组。会展，指的是"会议和展览"，所以翻译为 convention and exhibition。

④ 购物中心，shopping mall，名词词组，比如：A new shopping mall is being constructed.（一座新的购物商场正在建设中）。

⑤ 城市综合体，urban complex，名词词组。
综合体，complex，名词，比如：a complex of new buildings（新建筑群）。

⑥ ……的实力，句中指的是"……的能力"，the capability of...，比如：They both have the capability of winning.（他们都具备获胜的能力。）

⑦ 多品类物业，various forms of property，名词词组。这里使用 various, different kinds of 等都是可以的。品类，指的是"类别"，翻译为 form。

第二步 动词定位

商业化物业囊括商业写字楼，高端休闲地产，星级酒店，商贸会展，购物中心，城市综合体等，具备多品类物业综合开发的实力。

第三步 句型解析

❶ 本句的主语是"商业化物业"，在这个词组前面可以加上物主代词 Its，当然也可以用冠词 The，这里需要理解一下"物业"，既可以翻成 real estate，也可以翻译成 property，本句中这两个单词的含义是一样的。

❷ 本句的谓语是"囊括"，这里可以用一般现在时，"写字楼，高端休闲地产，星级酒店，商贸会展，购物中心，城市综合体"是宾语，注意每个词组的写法，这里要注意：若所有的名词词组都不用复数形式，那就全部用单数；若所有的名词词组都需要用复数形式，请注意可数名词词组的形式变化，不可数名词和集体名词一般来说形式都不发生变化。这里还需要注意"等"的译法，用 and so on 是可以接受的，这个相对来说比较口语化，不是特别官方，参考译文中使用了 etc.，这就比较专业，也经常出现在正式的文体当中。

❸ "具备多品类物业综合开发的实力"虽然是用逗号隔开，好像和本句有非常紧密的联系，但是你仔细思考就会发现，这句话的主语不再是"商业化物业"，而是"本公司"，所以这里需要分译而不是合译。分译与合译是根据上下文的语境来判断的，没有固定的方法。本句要形成一个单独的句子，增主语"本公司"，译文当中使用了主语"我们"，这点完全可以接受，谓语是"具有……能力"，宾语是"多品类物业综合开发"，这里也需要注意宾语的翻译，"多品类物业综合开发"也就是"多种多样的物业形式"。按照汉译英的翻译标准来看，"综合开发"实际上属于范畴词，在这里可以不翻译，当然你要是翻译，也没有问题，但是需要选择合适的词汇。

第四步 翻译来了

Its commercial real estate includes commercial office building, high-end leisure real estate, star hotel, commercial convention and exhibition center, shopping mall, urban complex, etc. We now have the capability of developing various forms of property.

> 🧑‍🏫 **本句考点总结**
>
> 第一，在翻译中，无论是英译汉，还是汉译英，我们常常将长句断成短句，然后一句一句翻译，短的句子由于上下文的联系，也可以放在一起翻译。非文学翻译中，分译与合译出现得比较少，一般按照正常句子翻译即可，但是在文学翻译中出现得特别多，特别要读懂上下文内在的关系，分译与合译没有固定的翻译规则，而且每个译者的尺度也是不同的，重要的前提就是句意正确和句意通顺。
>
> 第二，本句考查了英汉互译增减词的问题，一般来说英译汉增词，汉译英减词，常见增词的种类有：一、增加对象词（范围词），这是由上文缺少句子的某个部分造成的；二、增加范畴词，这是较难的一部分，常见的范畴词有"水平、方式、方法、问题、情况、途径和方面"，但是不仅仅有这些，还有很多其他的；三、增加评论性词，这些常常出现在文学翻译中；四、增加动词，会在动词的"分配译法"中说明这点。

资讯介绍类文章在这几年的考试中出现得越来越多,这类文章的时态比较简单,但是难点有两个:第一,不同种类的名词或名词短语多次出现;第二,句式结构虽然简单,但动词之间的关系至关重要,如何判断动词之间的关系是非常核心的问题,所以希望大家把握好这两点。